PROVERBS

IN A

HAYSTACK

Finding

That

Hidden

Truth

In

God's

Word

PROVERBS IN A HAYSTACK

I dedicate this book to the people of Shepherd of the Hills Church (www.theshepherd.org) in Porter Ranch, California. It has been one of the great privileges of my life to serve and minister in this remarkable church. Your prayers and faithfulness have been so uplifting. Your commitment to the Lordship of Jesus Christ is what motivates me to lead. Your diversity is a picture of what Heaven will be like. Thank you for allowing me the honor of serving as your pastor.

Contents

AN APPRECIATION

First I want to thank Virginia Bentley who initially encouraged me to write this book.

I want to express my appreciation to Henry Jackson, Jeremy Hoff and Jeremy Czarnecki who helped me develop the software needed to produce the book.

My gratitude as well to Jane Kasel for her attention to detail and to Murry Whiteman for his cover design.

I want to thank my executive assistant Kari Macer without whose help this book would never have become a reality.

I have a deep sense of appreciation for my executive pastor Tim Winters who spends his life freeing me up, enabling me the time to study, write and preach.

I want to acknowledge Coach John Wooden who reminds me that all wisdom ultimately comes from above.

Finally, I want to thank my family for their love and support through this project

PREFACE

The book of Proverbs is far more than just a collection of pithy truisms. Every verse is to be considered divine wisdom. From God to Solomon to us, this book speaks to the heart of mankind throughout the ages. The 31 chapters that convey heavenly wisdom contain 915 verses. Each of these 915 verses is a sermon in and of itself. The wealth of knowledge found in these sentence-long sermons is truly worth more than "silver or gold."

One helpful practice when studying Proverbs is to read a chapter a day and to allow God to speak to your heart. As with all of the Holy Scriptures each Proverb is powerful to save and can be a source of strength to anyone who will simply listen and obey.

For the new Christian, or the person who has been a life-long believer, the book of Proverbs always proves to be mesmerizing in its depth of knowledge. It is readily available for those who open their minds and hearts to these heavenly insights.

To read, understand and apply these multiple passages of Scripture has never been a problem. However, on occasion, it can be difficult to find that one rare jewel of truth when you need to locate it. Whether it's for a time of personal reflection, or if you are in need of finding that perfect verse to put the finishing touch on a sermon or lesson, many times it's like finding a needle in a haystack. Thus the title of this book, Proverbs in a Haystack.

This book was arranged for the purpose of expediting research when preparing to speak to any audience. It is also useful for personal exploration and illumination of Godly wisdom on virtually any topic imaginable.

May you find useful the 3,185 different topics that are available at your fingertips.

Simply thumb through the alphabetized topics and locate the one verse that you need. Your life, as well as any lesson, speech or sermon, will be blessed by the use of this pertinent verse.

May the Lord use this reference book to help you communicate God's word.

Dudley C. Rutherford

A

abandonment
Wealth brings many friends, but a poor man's friend deserts him.

19 : 4

abhors
The Lord abhors dishonest scales, but accurate weights are his delight.

11 : 1

abominations
Though his speech is charming, do not believe him, for seven abominations fill his heart.

26 : 25

above all else
Above all else, guard your heart, for it is the wellspring of life.

4 : 23

absent
When words are many, sin is not absent, but he who holds his tongue is wise.

10 : 19

abundance
Gold there is, and rubies in abundance, but lips that speak knowledge are a rare jewel.

20 : 15

abundant
He who works his land will have abundant food, but he who chases fantasies lacks judgment.

12 : 11

abundant food
A poor man's field may produce abundant food, but injustice sweeps it away.

13 : 23

Where there are no oxen, the manger is empty, but from the strength of an ox comes an abundant harvest.

14 : 4

He who works his land will have abundant food, but the one who chases fantasies will have his fill of poverty.

28 : 19

abundant harvest
Where there are no oxen, the manger is empty, but from the strength of an ox comes an abundant harvest.

14 : 4

abundant life
The wages of the righteous bring them life, but the income of the wicked brings them punishment.

10 : 16

He who heeds discipline shows the way to life, but whoever ignores correction leads others astray.

10 : 17

The blessing of the Lord brings wealth, and he adds no trouble to it.

10 : 22

The fear of the Lord adds length to life, but the years of the wicked are cut short.

10 : 27

The truly righteous man attains life, but he who pursues evil goes to his death.

11 : 19

A generous man will prosper; he who refreshes others will himself be refreshed.

11 : 25

The fruit of the righteous is a tree of life, and he who wins souls is wise.

11 : 30

The teaching of the wise is a fountain of life, turning a man from the snares of death.

13 : 14

The fear of the Lord is a fountain of life, turning a man from the snares of death.

14 : 27

Understanding is a fountain of life to those who have it, but folly brings punishment to fools.

16 : 22

The fear of the Lord leads to life: Then one rests content, untouched by trouble.

19 : 23

He who pursues righteousness and love finds life, prosperity and honor.

21 : 21

Humility and the fear of the Lord bring wealth and honor and life.

22 : 4

abuse

Whoever corrects a mocker invites insult; whoever rebukes a wicked man incurs abuse.

9 : 7

"There are those who curse their fathers and do not bless their mothers;

30 : 11

those whose teeth are swords and whose jaws are set with knives to devour the poor from the earth, the needy from among mankind.

30 : 14

accept

since they would not accept my advice and spurned my rebuke,

1 : 30

My son, if you accept my words and store up my commands within you,

2 · 1

Listen, my son, accept what I say, and the years of your life will be many.

4 : 10

He will not accept any compensation; he will refuse the bribe, however great it is.

6 : 35

Say to wisdom, "You are my sister," and call understanding your kinsman;

7 : 4

accept instruction

The wise in heart accept commands, but a chattering fool comes to ruin.

10 : 8

Listen to advice and accept instruction, and in the end you will be wise.

19 : 20

acceptable

To do what is right and just is more acceptable to the Lord than sacrifice.

21 : 3

accepting a bribe

A wicked man accepts a bribe in secret to pervert the course of justice.

17 : 23

accepting advice

The wise in heart accept commands, but a chattering fool comes to ruin.

10 : 8

accomplice

The accomplice of a thief is his own enemy; he is put under oath and dare not testify.

29 : 24

accountability
Righteousness guards the man of
integrity, but wickedness overthrows
the sinner.

13 : 6

As iron sharpens iron, so one man
sharpens another.

27 : 17

accurate
The Lord abhors dishonest scales, but
accurate weights are his delight.

11 : 1

accurate weights
The Lord abhors dishonest scales, but
accurate weights are his delight.

11 : 1

accusation
Do not accuse a man for no reason --
when he has done you no harm.

3 : 30

accuse
Do not accuse a man for no reason --
when he has done you no harm.

3 : 30

ache
Even in laughter the heart may ache,
and joy may end in grief.

14 : 13

acknowledge
in all your ways acknowledge him, and
he will make your paths straight.

3 : 6

acquaintance
Seldom set foot in your neighbor's
house -- too much of you, and he will
hate you.

25 : 17

acquire
Buy the truth and do not sell it; get
wisdom, discipline and understanding.

23 : 23

acquires
The heart of the discerning acquires
knowledge; the ears of the wise seek it
out.

18 : 15

acquires knowledge
The heart of the discerning acquires
knowledge; the ears of the wise seek it
out.

18 : 15

acquiring a disciplined life
for acquiring a disciplined and prudent
life, doing what is right and just and
fair;

1 : 3

acquiring a prudent life
for acquiring a disciplined and prudent
life, doing what is right and just and
fair;

1 : 3

acquitting
Acquitting the guilty and condemning
the innocent -- the Lord detests them
both.

17 : 15

act
Do not withhold good from those who
deserve it, when it is in your power to
act.

3 : 27

actions
Even a child is known by his actions, by
whether his conduct is pure and right.

20 : 11

acts
A righteous man cares for the needs of
his animal, but the kindest acts of the
wicked are cruel.

12 : 10

Every prudent man acts out of
knowledge, but a fool exposes his folly.

13 : 16

add
let the wise listen and add to their
learning, and let the discerning get
guidance --

1 : 5

Instruct a wise man and he will be wiser
still; teach a righteous man and he will
add to his learning.

9 : 9

Do not add to his words, or he will
rebuke you and prove you a liar.

30 : 6

added
For through me your days will be many,
and years will be added to your life.

9 : 11

addicted
and put a knife to your throat if you are
given to gluttony.

23 : 2

"They hit me," you will say, "but I'm
not hurt! They beat me, but I don't feel
it! When will I wake up so I can find
another drink?"

23 : 35

addictions
The righteousness of the upright
delivers them, but the unfaithful are
trapped by evil desires.

11 : 6

He who loves pleasure will become
poor; whoever loves wine and oil will
never be rich.

21 : 17

adds
The blessing of the Lord brings wealth,
and he adds no trouble to it.

10 : 22

The fear of the Lord adds length to life,
but the years of the wicked are cut
short.

10 : 27

admiration
Her children arise and call her blessed;
her husband also, and he praises her:

31 : 28

admire
Her children arise and call her blessed;
her husband also, and he praises her:

31 : 28

adorn
They will be a garland to grace your
head and a chain to adorn your neck.

1 : 9

adulteress
It will save you also from the
adulteress, from the wayward wife with
her seductive words,

2 : 16

For the lips of an adulteress drip honey,
and her speech is smoother than oil;

5 : 3

She gives no thought to the way of life;
her paths are crooked, but she knows it
not.

5 : 6

Why be captivated, my son, by an
adulteress? Why embrace the bosom of
another man's wife?

5 : 20

for the prostitute reduces you to a loaf
of bread, and the adulteress preys upon
your very life.

6 : 26

they will keep you from the adulteress,
from the wayward wife with her
seductive words.

7 : 5

Then out came a woman to meet him, dressed like a prostitute and with crafty intent.

7 : 10

She is loud and defiant, her feet never stay at home;

7 : 11

I have covered my bed with colored linens from Egypt.

7 : 16

Many are the victims she has brought down; her slain are a mighty throng.

7 : 26

Her house is a highway to the grave, leading down to the chambers of death.

7 : 27

The mouth of an adulteress is a deep pit; he who is under the Lord's wrath will fall into it.

22 : 14

"This is the way of an adulteress: She eats and wipes her mouth and says, 'I've done nothing wrong.'

30 : 20

adultery

It will save you also from the adulteress, from the wayward wife with her seductive words,

2 : 16

who has left the partner of her youth and ignored the covenant she made before God.

2 : 17

For her house leads down to death and her paths to the spirits of the dead.

2 : 18

For the lips of an adulteress drip honey, and her speech is smoother than oil;

5 : 3

Keep to a path far from her, do not go near the door of her house,

5 : 8

keeping you from the immoral woman, from the smooth tongue of the wayward wife.

6 : 24

Can a man scoop fire into his lap without his clothes being burned?

6 : 27

Can a man walk on hot coals without his feet being scorched?

6 : 28

So is he who sleeps with another man's wife; no one who touches her will go unpunished.

6 : 29

But a man who commits adultery lacks judgment; whoever does so destroys himself.

6 : 32

My husband is not at home; he has gone on a long journey.

7 : 19

for a prostitute is a deep pit and a wayward wife is a narrow well.

23 : 27

Like a bandit she lies in wait, and multiplies the unfaithful among men.

23 : 28

Like a bird that strays from its nest is a man who strays from his home.

27 : 8

A man who loves wisdom brings joy to his father, but a companion of prostitutes squanders his wealth.

29 : 3

advance

locusts have no king, yet they advance together in ranks;

30 : 27

adversity

A friend loves at all times, and a brother is born for adversity.

17 : 17

advice

my son, do not go along with them, do not set foot on their paths;

1 : 15

since you ignored all my advice and would not accept my rebuke,

1 : 25

since they would not accept my advice and spurned my rebuke,

1 : 30

My son, if you accept my words and store up my commands within you,

2 : 1

My son, do not forget my teaching, but keep my commands in your heart,

3 : 1

My son, preserve sound judgment and discernment, do not let them out of your sight;

3 : 21

Listen, my sons, to a father's instruction; pay attention and gain understanding.

4 : 1

I give you sound learning, so do not forsake my teaching.

4 : 2

he taught me and said, "Lay hold of my words with all your heart; keep my commands and you will live.

4 : 4

Get wisdom, get understanding; do not forget my words or swerve from them.

4 : 5

When you walk, your steps will not be hampered; when you run, you will not stumble.

4 : 12

Do not set foot on the path of the wicked or walk in the way of evil men.

4 : 14

Avoid it, do not travel on it; turn from it and go on your way.

4 : 15

My son, pay attention to what I say; listen closely to my words.

4 : 20

Do not let them out of your sight, keep them within your heart;

4 : 21

Now then, my sons, listen to me; do not turn aside from what I say.

5 : 7

My son, keep my words and store up my commands within you.

7 : 1

Listen to my instruction and be wise; do not ignore it.

8 : 33

Do not rebuke a mocker or he will hate you; rebuke a wise man and he will love you.

9 : 8

The wise in heart accept commands, but a chattering fool comes to ruin.

10 : 8

The plans of the righteous are just, but the advice of the wicked is deceitful.

12 : 5

The way of a fool seems right to him, but a wise man listens to advice.

12 : 15

Pride only breeds quarrels, but wisdom is found in those who take advice.

13 : 10

He who scorns instruction will pay for it, but he who respects a command is rewarded.

13 : 13

A man finds joy in giving an apt reply-- and how good is a timely word!

15 : 23

Listen to advice and accept instruction, and in the end you will be wise.

19 : 20

Stop listening to instruction, my son, and you will stray from the words of knowledge.

19 : 27

Make plans by seeking advice; if you wage war, obtain guidance.

20 : 18

advise

My son, if sinners entice you, do not give in to them.

1 : 10

advisers

For lack of guidance a nation falls, but many advisers make victory sure.

11 : 14

Plans fail for lack of counsel, but with many advisers they succeed.

15 : 22

for waging war you need guidance, and for victory many advisers.

24 : 6

advocate

for their Defender is strong; he will take up their case against you.

23 : 11

"Speak up for those who cannot speak for themselves, for the rights of all who are destitute.

31 : 8

afar

She is like the merchant ships, bringing her food from afar.

31 : 14

affairs

She watches over the affairs of her household and does not eat the bread of idleness.

31 : 27

afraid

when you lie down, you will not be afraid; when you lie down, your sleep will be sweet.

3 : 24

against

An evil man is bent only on rebellion; a merciless official will be sent against him.

17 : 11

A man's own folly ruins his life, yet his heart rages against the Lord.

19 : 3

aged

Children's children are a crown to the aged, and parents are the pride of their children.

17 : 6

agony

The prudent see danger and take refuge, but the simple keep going and suffer for it.

27 : 12

agreeing
A man lacking in judgment strikes hands in pledge and puts up security for his neighbor.

17 : 18

agreement
My son, if you have put up security for your neighbor, if you have struck hands in pledge for another,

6 : 1

Do not be a man who strikes hands in pledge or puts up security for debts;

22 : 26

agricultural
A sluggard does not plow in season; so at harvest time he looks but finds nothing.

20 : 4

agriculture
A poor man's field may produce abundant food, but injustice sweeps it away.

13 : 23

Where there are no oxen, the manger is empty, but from the strength of an ox comes an abundant harvest.

14 : 4

She considers a field and buys it; out of her earnings she plants a vineyard.

31 : 16

airing
A fool finds no pleasure in understanding but delights in airing his own opinions.

18 : 2

alcohol
Those who linger over wine, who go to sample bowls of mixed wine,

23 : 30

Do not gaze at wine when it is red, when it sparkles in the cup, when it goes down smoothly!

23 : 31

Your eyes will see strange sights and your mind imagine confusing things.

23 : 33

You will be like one sleeping on the high seas, lying on top of the rigging.

23 : 34

"They hit me," you will say, "but I'm not hurt! They beat me, but I don't feel it! When will I wake up so I can find another drink?"

23 : 35

Give beer to those who are perishing, wine to those who are in anguish;

31 : 6

let them drink and forget their poverty and remember their misery no more.

31 : 7

alcoholic
Wine is a mocker and beer a brawler; whoever is led astray by them is not wise.

20 : 1

Do not join those who drink too much wine or gorge themselves on meat,

23 : 20

for drunkards and gluttons become poor, and drowsiness clothes them in rags.

23 : 21

Who has woe? Who has sorrow? Who has strife? Who has complaints? Who has needless bruises? Who has bloodshot eyes?

23 : 29

"They hit me," you will say, "but I'm not hurt! They beat me, but I don't feel it! When will I wake up so I can find another drink?"

23 : 35

alive

let's swallow them alive, like the grave, and whole, like those who go down to the pit;

1 : 12

all

Such is the end of all who go after ill-gotten gain; it takes away the life of those who get it.

1 : 19

Trust in the Lord with all your heart and lean not on your own understanding;

3 : 5

in all your ways acknowledge him, and he will make your paths straight.

3 : 6

Honor the Lord with your wealth, with the firstfruits of all your crops;

3 : 9

Her ways are pleasant ways, and all her paths are peace.

3 : 17

he taught me and said, "Lay hold of my words with all your heart; keep my commands and you will live.

4 : 4

Wisdom is supreme; therefore get wisdom. Though it cost all you have, get understanding.

4 : 7

Above all else, guard your heart, for it is the wellspring of life.

4 : 23

For a man's ways are in full view of the Lord, and he examines all his paths.

5 : 21

Yet if he is caught, he must pay sevenfold, though it costs him all the wealth of his house.

6 : 31

All the words of my mouth are just; none of them is crooked or perverse.

8 : 8

To the discerning all of them are right; they are faultless to those who have knowledge.

8 : 9

by me princes govern, and all nobles who rule on earth.

8 : 16

But whoever fails to find me harms himself; all who hate me love death.

8 : 36

"Let all who are simple come in here!" she says to those who lack judgment.

9 : 4

"Let all who are simple come in here!" she says to those who lack judgment.

9 : 16

Hatred stirs up dissension, but love covers over all wrongs.

10 : 12

When a wicked man dies, his hope perishes; all he expected from his power comes to nothing.

11 : 7

All hard work brings a profit, but mere talk leads only to poverty.

14 : 23

All the days of the oppressed are wretched, but the cheerful heart has a continual feast.

15 : 15

All a man's ways seem innocent to him, but motives are weighed by the Lord.

16 : 2

The Lord detests all the proud of heart. Be sure of this: They will not go unpunished.

16 : 5

A friend loves at all times, and a brother is born for adversity.

17 : 17

An unfriendly man pursues selfish ends; he defies all sound judgment.

18 : 1

A poor man is shunned by all his relatives -- how much more do his friends avoid him! Though he pursues them with pleading, they are nowhere to be found.

19 : 7

When a king sits on his throne to judge, he winnows out all evil with his eyes.

20 : 8

All a man's ways seem right to him, but the Lord weighs the heart.

21 : 2

In the house of the wise are stores of choice food and oil, but a foolish man devours all he has.

21 : 20

All day long he craves for more, but the righteous give without sparing.

21 : 26

Rich and poor have this in common: The Lord is the Maker of them all.

22 : 2

for it is pleasing when you keep them in your heart and have all of them ready on your lips.

22 : 18

for riches do not endure forever, and a crown is not secure for all generations.

27 : 24

If a ruler listens to lies, all his officials become wicked.

29 : 12

"Speak up for those who cannot speak for themselves, for the rights of all who are destitute.

31 : 8

She brings him good, not harm, all the days of her life.

31 : 12

When it snows, she has no fear for her household; for all of them are clothed in scarlet.

31 : 21

Many women do noble things, but you surpass them all."

31 : 29

all your ways
in all your ways acknowledge him, and he will make your paths straight.

3 : 6

all-knowing
For a man's ways are in full view of the Lord, and he examines all his paths.

5 : 21

In his heart a man plans his course, but the Lord determines his steps.

16 : 9

The lamp of the Lord searches the spirit of a man; it searches out his inmost being.

20 : 27

allow
Allow no sleep to your eyes, no slumber to your eyelids.

6 : 4

aloes
I have perfumed my bed with myrrh, aloes and cinnamon.

7 : 17

alone
Let them be yours alone, never to be shared with strangers.
5 : 17

If you are wise, your wisdom will reward you; if you are a mocker, you alone will suffer."
9 : 12

always
A loving doe, a graceful deer -- may her breasts satisfy you always, may you ever be captivated by her love.
5 : 19

who plots evil with deceit in his heart -- he always stirs up dissension.
6 : 14

Then I was the craftsman at his side. I was filled with delight day after day, rejoicing always in his presence,
8 : 30

for he is the kind of man who is always thinking about the cost. "Eat and drink," he says to you, but his heart is not with you.
23 : 7

Do not let your heart envy sinners, but always be zealous for the fear of the Lord.
23 : 17

Blessed is the man who always fears the Lord, but he who hardens his heart falls into trouble.
28 : 14

If a king judges the poor with fairness, his throne will always be secure.
29 : 14

amasses
He who increases his wealth by exorbitant interest amasses it for another, who will be kind to the poor.
28 : 8

amazing
There are three things that are too amazing for me, four that I do not understand:
30 : 18

ambush
If they say, "Come along with us; let's lie in wait for someone's blood, let's waylay some harmless soul;
1 : 11

amends
Fools mock at making amends for sin, but goodwill is found among the upright.
14 : 9

among
I saw among the simple, I noticed among the young men, a youth who lacked judgment.
7 : 7

ancestors
Do not move an ancient boundary stone set up by your forefathers.
22 : 28

ancient
Do not move an ancient boundary stone set up by your forefathers.
22 : 28

Do not move an ancient boundary stone or encroach on the fields of the fatherless,
23 : 10

ancient boundary stone
Do not move an ancient boundary stone set up by your forefathers.
22 : 28

Do not move an ancient boundary stone or encroach on the fields of the fatherless,
23 : 10

anger

A fool shows his annoyance at once, but a prudent man overlooks an insult.

12 . 16

A quick-tempered man does foolish things, and a crafty man is hated.

14 : 17

A patient man has great understanding, but a quick-tempered man displays folly.

14 : 29

A gentle answer turns away wrath, but a harsh word stirs up anger.

15 : 1

A hot-tempered man stirs up dissension, but a patient man calms a quarrel.

15 : 18

A king's wrath is a messenger of death, but a wise man will appease it.

16 : 14

A man of knowledge uses words with restraint, and a man of understanding is even-tempered.

17 : 27

A king's rage is like the roar of a lion, but his favor is like dew on the grass.

19 : 12

A hot-tempered man must pay the penalty; if you rescue him, you will have to do it again.

19 : 19

A king's wrath is like the roar of a lion; he who angers him forfeits his life.

20 : 2

A gift given in secret soothes anger, and a bribe concealed in the cloak pacifies great wrath.

21 : 14

Better to live in a desert than with a quarrelsome and ill-tempered wife.

21 : 19

Do not make friends with a hot-tempered man, do not associate with one easily angered,

22 : 24

or you may learn his ways and get yourself ensnared.

22 : 25

Anger is cruel and fury overwhelming, but who can stand before jealousy?

27 : 4

Like a roaring lion or a charging bear is a wicked man ruling over a helpless people.

28 : 15

Mockers stir up a city, but wise men turn away anger.

29 : 8

If a wise man goes to court with a fool, the fool rages and scoffs, and there is no peace.

29 : 9

A fool gives full vent to his anger, but a wise man keeps himself under control.

29 : 11

An angry man stirs up dissension, and a hot-tempered one commits many sins.

29 : 22

For as churning the milk produces butter, and as twisting the nose produces blood, so stirring up anger produces strife."

30 : 33

anger management

Better a patient man than a warrior, a man who controls his temper than one who takes a city.

16 : 32

angry looks
As a north wind brings rain, so a sly tongue brings angry looks.

25 : 23

angry man
An angry man stirs up dissension, and a hot-tempered one commits many sins.

29 : 22

anguish
Give beer to those who are perishing, wine to those who are in anguish;

31 : 6

animal
A righteous man cares for the needs of his animal, but the kindest acts of the wicked are cruel.

12 : 10

animals
How useless to spread a net in full view of all the birds!

1 : 17

A loving doe, a graceful deer -- may her breasts satisfy you always, may you ever be captivated by her love.

5 : 19

Free yourself, like a gazelle from the hand of the hunter, like a bird from the snare of the fowler.

6 : 5

Go to the ant, you sluggard; consider its ways and be wise!

6 : 6

till an arrow pierces his liver, like a bird darting into a snare, little knowing it will cost him his life.

7 : 23

Where there are no oxen, the manger is empty, but from the strength of an ox comes an abundant harvest.

14 : 4

Better to meet a bear robbed of her cubs than a fool in his folly.

17 : 12

A king's rage is like the roar of a lion, but his favor is like dew on the grass.

19 : 12

A king's wrath is like the roar of a lion; he who angers him forfeits his life.

20 : 2

The horse is made ready for the day of battle, but victory rests with the Lord.

21 : 31

The sluggard says, "There is a lion outside!" or "I will be murdered in the streets!"

22 : 13

Cast but a glance at riches, and they are gone, for they will surely sprout wings and fly off to the sky like an eagle.

23 : 5

In the end it bites like a snake and poisons like a viper.

23 : 32

Like a fluttering sparrow or a darting swallow, an undeserved curse does not come to rest.

26 : 2

A whip for the horse, a halter for the donkey, and a rod for the backs of fools!

26 : 3

As a dog returns to its vomit, so a fool repeats his folly.

26 : 11

The sluggard says, "There is a lion in the road, a fierce lion roaming the streets!"

26 : 13

Like one who seizes a dog by the ears is a passer-by who meddles in a quarrel not his own.

26 : 17

Like a bird that strays from its nest is a man who strays from his home.

27 : 8

the lambs will provide you with clothing, and the goats with the price of a field.

27 : 26

The wicked man flees though no one pursues, but the righteous are as bold as a lion.

28 : 1

Like a roaring lion or a charging bear is a wicked man ruling over a helpless people.

28 : 15

"The leech has two daughters. 'Give! Give!' they cry. "There are three things that are never satisfied, four that never say, 'Enough!':

30 : 15

The eye that mocks a father, that scorns obedience to a mother, will be pecked out by the ravens of the valley, will be eaten by the vultures.

30 : 17

the way of an eagle in the sky, the way of a snake on a rock, the way of a ship on the high seas, and the way of a man with a maiden.

30 : 19

Ants are creatures of little strength, yet they store up their food in the summer;

30 : 25

coneys are creatures of little power, yet they make their home in the crags;

30 : 26

locusts have no king, yet they advance together in ranks;

30 : 27

a lizard can be caught with the hand, yet it is found in kings' palaces.

30 : 28

a lion, mighty among beasts, who retreats before nothing;

30 : 30

a strutting rooster, a he-goat, and a king with his army around him.

30 : 31

annoyance
A fool shows his annoyance at once, but a prudent man overlooks an insult.

12 : 16

another man's wife
Why be captivated, my son, by an adulteress? Why embrace the bosom of another man's wife?

5 : 20

So is he who sleeps with another man's wife; no one who touches her will go unpunished.

6 : 29

answer
"Then they will call to me but I will not answer; they will look for me but will not find me.

1 : 28

A gentle answer turns away wrath, but a harsh word stirs up anger.

15 : 1

A man finds joy in giving an apt reply-- and how good is a timely word!

15 : 23

If a man shuts his ears to the cry of the poor, he too will cry out and not be answered.

21 : 13

An honest answer is like a kiss on the lips.

24 : 26

Do not answer a fool according to his folly, or you will be like him yourself

26 : 4

Answer a fool according to his folly, or he will be wise in his own eyes.

26 : 5

The sluggard is wiser in his own eyes than seven men who answer discreetly.

26 : 16

Be wise, my son, and bring joy to my heart; then I can answer anyone who treats me with contempt.

27 : 11

answered prayer
The Lord is far from the wicked but he hears the prayer of the righteous.

15 : 29

answers
The heart of the righteous weighs its answers, but the mouth of the wicked gushes evil.

15 : 28

He who answers before listening -- that is his folly and his shame.

18 : 13

A poor man pleads for mercy, but a rich man answers harshly.

18 : 23

teaching you true and reliable words, so that you can give sound answers to him who sent you?

22 : 21

ant
Go to the ant, you sluggard; consider its ways and be wise!

6 : 6

ants
Ants are creatures of little strength, yet they store up their food in the summer;

30 : 25

anxious heart
An anxious heart weighs a man down, but a kind word cheers him up.

12 : 25

apologizing
Fools mock at making amends for sin, but goodwill is found among the upright.

14 : 9

appease
A king's wrath is a messenger of death, but a wise man will appease it.

16 : 14

appetite
The laborer's appetite works for him; his hunger drives him on.

16 : 26

apple of your eye
Keep my commands and you will live; guard my teachings as the apple of your eye.

7 : 2

apples of gold
A word aptly spoken is like apples of gold in settings of silver.

25 : 11

application
turning your ear to wisdom and applying your heart to understanding,

2 : 2

Pay attention and listen to the sayings of the wise; apply your heart to what I teach,

22 : 17

Apply your heart to instruction and your ears to words of knowledge.

23 : 12

I applied my heart to what I observed
and learned a lesson from what I saw:

24 : 32

apply

Bind them upon your heart forever;
fasten them around your neck.

6 : 21

Pay attention and listen to the sayings
of the wise; apply your heart to what I
teach,

22 : 17

Apply your heart to instruction and your
ears to words of knowledge.

23 : 12

applying

turning your ear to wisdom and
applying your heart to understanding,

2 : 2

appointed

I was appointed from eternity, from the
beginning, before the world began,

8 : 23

appreciative

Do not rebuke a mocker or he will hate
you; rebuke a wise man and he will love
you.

9 : 8

appropriate

It is not fitting for a fool to live in
luxury -- how much worse for a slave to
rule over princes!

19 : 10

approval

A king delights in a wise servant, but a
shameful servant incurs his wrath.

14 : 35

apt reply

A man finds joy in giving an apt reply--
and how good is a timely word!

15 : 23

aptly spoken

A word aptly spoken is like apples of
gold in settings of silver.

25 : 11

arbitration

If you argue your case with a neighbor,
do not betray another man's confidence,

25 : 9

archer

Like an archer who wounds at random
is he who hires a fool or any passer-by.

26 : 10

argue

Pride only breeds quarrels, but wisdom
is found in those who take advice.

13 : 10

A foolish son is his father's ruin, and a
quarrelsome wife is like a constant
dripping.

19 : 13

It is to a man's honor to avoid strife, but
every fool is quick to quarrel.

20 : 3

Better to live on a corner of the roof
than share a house with a quarrelsome
wife.

21 : 9

Better to live in a desert than with a
quarrelsome and ill-tempered wife.

21 : 19

Drive out the mocker, and out goes
strife; quarrels and insults are ended.

22 : 10

If you argue your case with a neighbor,
do not betray another man's confidence,

25 : 9

arguing

A quarrelsome wife is like a constant
dripping on a rainy day;

27 : 15

argument
Stone is heavy and sand a burden, but
provocation by a fool is heavier than
both.

27 : 3

arguments
Pride only breeds quarrels, but wisdom
is found in those who take advice.

13 : 10

A foolish son is his father's ruin, and a
quarrelsome wife is like a constant
dripping.

19 : 13

Better to live on a corner of the roof
than share a house with a quarrelsome
wife.

21 : 9

Better to live in a desert than with a
quarrelsome and ill-tempered wife.

21 : 19

Better to live on a corner of the roof
than share a house with a quarrelsome
wife.

25 : 24

Like one who seizes a dog by the ears is
a passer-by who meddles in a quarrel
not his own.

26 : 17

As charcoal to embers and as wood to
fire, so is a quarrelsome man for
kindling strife.

26 : 21

A quarrelsome wife is like a constant
dripping on a rainy day;

27 : 15

arise
Her children arise and call her blessed;
her husband also, and he praises her:

31 : 28

armed
and poverty will come on you like a
bandit and scarcity like an armed man.

6 : 11

and poverty will come on you like a
bandit and scarcity like an armed man.

24 : 34

armed man
and poverty will come on you like a
bandit and scarcity like an armed man.

6 : 11

and poverty will come on you like a
bandit and scarcity like an armed man.

24 : 34

arms
She sets about her work vigorously; her
arms are strong for her tasks.

31 : 17

She opens her arms to the poor and
extends her hands to the needy.

31 : 20

army
a strutting rooster, a he-goat, and a king
with his army around him.

30 : 31

arouses
for jealousy arouses a husband's fury,
and he will show no mercy when he
takes revenge.

6 : 34

arrogance
To fear the Lord is to hate evil; I hate
pride and arrogance, evil behavior and
perverse speech.

8 : 13

Pride only breeds quarrels, but wisdom
is found in those who take advice.

13 : 10

arrogant
Arrogant lips are unsuited to a fool --
how much worse lying lips to a ruler!
17 : 7

arrogant man
The proud and arrogant man --
"Mocker" is his name; he behaves with
overweening pride.
21 : 24

arrow
till an arrow pierces his liver, like a bird
darting into a snare, little knowing it
will cost him his life.
7 : 23

arrows
Like a madman shooting firebrands or
deadly arrows
26 : 18

art of the deal
"It's no good, it's no good!" says the
buyer; then off he goes and boasts about
his purchase.
20 : 14

ask
then do this, my son, to free yourself,
since you have fallen into your
neighbor's hands: Go and humble
yourself; press your plea with your
neighbor!
6 : 3

assembly
I have come to the brink of utter ruin in
the midst of the whole assembly.
5 : 14

Wisdom is too high for a fool; in the
assembly at the gate he has nothing to
say.
24 : 7

His malice may be concealed by
deception, but his wickedness will be
exposed in the assembly.
26 : 26

assist
"Speak up for those who cannot speak
for themselves, for the rights of all who
are destitute.
31 : 8

associate
Do not make friends with a hot-
tempered man, do not associate with
one easily angered,
22 : 24

assured victory
For lack of guidance a nation falls, but
many advisers make victory sure.
11 : 14

astray
He will die for lack of discipline, led
astray by his own great folly.
5 : 23

With persuasive words she led him
astray; she seduced him with her
smooth talk.
7 : 21

He who heeds discipline shows the way
to life, but whoever ignores correction
leads others astray.
10 : 17

A righteous man is cautious in
friendship, but the way of the wicked
leads them astray.
12 : 26

Do not those who plot evil go astray?
But those who plan what is good find
love and faithfulness.
14 : 22

Wine is a mocker and beer a brawler;
whoever is led astray by them is not
wise.
20 : 1

atonement
Through love and faithfulness sin is atoned for; through the fear of the Lord a man avoids evil.

16 : 6

attack
If they say, "Come along with us; let's lie in wait for someone's blood, let's waylay some harmless soul;

1 : 11

let's swallow them alive, like the grave, and whole, like those who go down to the pit;

1 : 12

A wise man attacks the city of the mighty and pulls down the stronghold in which they trust.

21 : 22

attain
for attaining wisdom and discipline; for understanding words of insight;

1 : 2

Then you will understand what is right and just and fair -- every good path.

2 : 9

None who go to her return or attain the paths of life.

2 : 19

The truly righteous man attains life, but he who pursues evil goes to his death.

11 : 19

Gray hair is a crown of splendor; it is attained by a righteous life.

16 : 31

attaining life
The truly righteous man attains life, but he who pursues evil goes to his death.

11 : 19

attaining wisdom
for attaining wisdom and discipline; for understanding words of insight;

1 : 2

attention
Listen, my sons, to a father's instruction; pay attention and gain understanding.

4 : 1

My son, pay attention to what I say; listen closely to my words.

4 : 20

My son, pay attention to my wisdom, listen well to my words of insight,

5 : 1

A wicked man listens to evil lips; a liar pays attention to a malicious tongue.

17 : 4

Pay attention and listen to the sayings of the wise; apply your heart to what I teach,

22 : 17

Be sure you know the condition of your flocks, give careful attention to your herds;

27 : 23

attentive
My son, give me your heart and let your eyes keep to my ways,

23 : 26

audience
Many seek an audience with a ruler, but it is from the Lord that man gets justice.

29 : 26

avoid
Avoid it, do not travel on it; turn from it and go on your way.

4 : 15

Through love and faithfulness sin is atoned for; through the fear of the Lord a man avoids evil.

16 : 6

The highway of the upright avoids evil; he who guards his way guards his life.

16 : 17

A poor man is shunned by all his relatives -- how much more do his friends avoid him! Though he pursues them with pleading, they are nowhere to be found.

19 : 7

It is to a man's honor to avoid strife, but every fool is quick to quarrel.

20 : 3

A gossip betrays a confidence; so avoid a man who talks too much.

20 : 19

avoid sexual sins
Keep to a path far from her, do not go near the door of her house,

5 : 8

avoid strife
It is to a man's honor to avoid strife, but every fool is quick to quarrel.

20 : 3

avoid temptation
Do not let your heart turn to her ways or stray into her paths.

7 : 25

avoiding evil
Through love and faithfulness sin is atoned for; through the fear of the Lord a man avoids evil.

16 : 6

The highway of the upright avoids evil; he who guards his way guards his life.

16 : 17

avoiding immorality
they will keep you from the adulteress, from the wayward wife with her seductive words.

7 : 5

avoiding temptation
keeping you from the immoral woman, from the smooth tongue of the wayward wife.

6 : 24

Do not lust in your heart after her beauty or let her captivate you with her eyes,

6 : 25

awake
When you walk, they will guide you; when you sleep, they will watch over you; when you awake, they will speak to you.

6 : 22

Do not love sleep or you will grow poor; stay awake and you will have food to spare.

20 : 13

aware
Pay attention and listen to the sayings of the wise; apply your heart to what I teach,

22 : 17

awareness
When you sit to dine with a ruler, note well what is before you,

23 : 1

it is better for him to say to you, "Come up here," than for him to humiliate you before a nobleman. What you have seen with your eyes

25 : 7

27

away
Such is the end of all who go after ill-gotten gain; it takes away the life of those who get it.

1 : 19

or the Lord will see and disapprove and turn his wrath away from him.

24 : 18

B

back

Do not say to your neighbor, "Come back later; I'll give it tomorrow" -- when you now have it with you.

3 : 28

Wisdom is found on the lips of the discerning, but a rod is for the back of him who lacks judgment.

10 : 13

A fool's talk brings a rod to his back, but the lips of the wise protect them.

14 : 3

The sluggard buries his hand in the dish; he will not even bring it back to his mouth!

19 : 24

Penalties are prepared for mockers, and beatings for the backs of fools.

19 : 29

Do not say, "I'll pay you back for this wrong!" Wait for the Lord, and he will deliver you.

20 : 22

Rescue those being led away to death; hold back those staggering toward slaughter.

24 : 11

Do not say, "I'll do to him as he has done to me; I'll pay that man back for what he did."

24 : 29

The sluggard buries his hand in the dish; he is too lazy to bring it back to his mouth.

26 : 15

If a man digs a pit, he will fall into it; if a man rolls a stone, it will roll back on him.

26 : 27

backs of fools

A whip for the horse, a halter for the donkey, and a rod for the backs of fools!

26 : 3

bad

It is not good to have zeal without knowledge, nor to be hasty and miss the way.

19 : 2

"It's no good, it's no good!" says the buyer; then off he goes and boasts about his purchase.

20 : 14

or he who hears it may shame you and you will never lose your bad reputation.

25 : 10

bad company

throw in your lot with us, and we will share a common purse" --

1 : 14

my son, do not go along with them, do not set foot on their paths;

1 : 15

A wicked man listens to evil lips; a liar pays attention to a malicious tongue.

17 : 4

Do not envy wicked men, do not desire their company;

24 : 1

for their hearts plot violence, and their lips talk about making trouble.

24 : 2

Fear the Lord and the king, my son, and do not join with the rebellious,

24 : 21

Like a bad tooth or a lame foot is reliance on the unfaithful in times of trouble.

25 : 19

Those who forsake the law praise the wicked, but those who keep the law resist them.

28 : 4

The accomplice of a thief is his own enemy; he is put under oath and dare not testify.

29 : 24

bad example
Do not envy a violent man or choose any of his ways,

3 : 31

Do not set foot on the path of the wicked or walk in the way of evil men.

4 : 14

For they cannot sleep till they do evil; they are robbed of slumber till they make someone fall.

4 : 16

bad language
A scoundrel and villain, who goes about with a corrupt mouth,

6 : 12

bad luck
Misfortune pursues the sinner, but prosperity is the reward of the righteous.

13 : 21

bad reputation
or he who hears it may shame you and you will never lose your bad reputation.

25 : 10

bad temper
Anger is cruel and fury overwhelming, but who can stand before jealousy?

27 : 4

bad tooth
Like a bad tooth or a lame foot is reliance on the unfaithful in times of trouble.

25 : 19

bad weather
As a north wind brings rain, so a sly tongue brings angry looks.

25 : 23

badgers
coneys are creatures of little power, yet they make their home in the crags;

30 : 26

bag
Honest scales and balances are from the Lord; all the weights in the bag are of his making.

16 : 11

balance
The first to present his case seems right, till another comes forward and questions him.

18 : 17

balances
Honest scales and balances are from the Lord; all the weights in the bag are of his making.

16 : 11

bandit
and poverty will come on you like a bandit and scarcity like an armed man.

6 : 11

Like a bandit she lies in wait, and
multiplies the unfaithful among men.

23 : 28

and poverty will come on you like a
bandit and scarcity like an armed man.

24 : 34

barns
then your barns will be filled to
overflowing, and your vats will brim
over with new wine.

3 : 10

barred
An offended brother is more unyielding
than a fortified city, and disputes are
like the barred gates of a citadel.

18 : 19

barred gates
An offended brother is more unyielding
than a fortified city, and disputes are
like the barred gates of a citadel.

18 : 19

barren
the grave, the barren womb, land, which
is never satisfied with water, and fire,
which never says, 'Enough!'

30 : 16

barren womb
the grave, the barren womb, land, which
is never satisfied with water, and fire,
which never says, 'Enough!'

30 : 16

battle
Casting the lot settles disputes and
keeps strong opponents apart.

18 : 18

A man's own folly ruins his life, yet his
heart rages against the Lord.

19 : 3

The horse is made ready for the day of
battle, but victory rests with the Lord.

21 : 31

for waging war you need guidance, and
for victory many advisers.

24 : 6

be aware
Allow no sleep to your eyes, no slumber
to your eyelids.

6 : 4

be careful how you live
Do not swerve to the right or the left;
keep your foot from evil.

4 : 27

be careful where you walk
Make level paths for your feet and take
only ways that are firm.

4 : 26

be faithful to your wife
Drink water from your own cistern,
running water from your own well.

5 : 15

be open and teachable
Listen to advice and accept instruction,
and in the end you will be wise.

19 : 20

be sure of this
Be sure of this: The wicked will not go
unpunished, but those who are righteous
will go free.

11 : 21

The Lord detests all the proud of heart.
Be sure of this: They will not go
unpunished.

16 : 5

be watchful
Be sure you know the condition of your
flocks, give careful attention to your
herds;

27 : 23

be wise
Go to the ant, you sluggard; consider its
ways and be wise!

6 : 6

bear
Better to meet a bear robbed of her cubs
than a fool in his folly.

17 : 12

A man's spirit sustains him in sickness,
but a crushed spirit who can bear?

18 : 14

Like a roaring lion or a charging bear is
a wicked man ruling over a helpless
people.

28 : 15

"Under three things the earth trembles,
under four it cannot bear up:

30 : 21

bearing
"There are three things that are stately
in their stride, four that move with
stately bearing:

30 : 29

beasts
a lion, mighty among beasts, who
retreats before nothing;

30 : 30

beat
"They hit me," you will say, "but I'm
not hurt! They beat me, but I don't feel
it! When will I wake up so I can find
another drink?"

23 : 35

beating
A fool's lips bring him strife, and his
mouth invites a beating.

18 : 6

Penalties are prepared for mockers, and
beatings for the backs of fools.

19 : 29

beatings
Blows and wounds cleanse away evil,
and beatings purge the inmost being.

20 : 30

beautiful
Like a gold ring in a pig's snout is a
beautiful woman who shows no
discretion.

11 : 22

through knowledge its rooms are filled
with rare and beautiful treasures.

24 : 4

beautiful woman
Like a gold ring in a pig's snout is a
beautiful woman who shows no
discretion.

11 : 22

beauty
They will be a garland to grace your
head and a chain to adorn your neck.

1 : 9

Do not lust in your heart after her
beauty or let her captivate you with her
eyes,

6 : 25

A wife of noble character is her
husband's crown, but a disgraceful wife
is like decay in his bones.

12 : 4

Charm is deceptive, and beauty is
fleeting; but a woman who fears the
Lord is to be praised.

31 : 30

beauty is fleeting
Charm is deceptive, and beauty is
fleeting; but a woman who fears the
Lord is to be praised.

31 : 30

become
If a ruler listens to lies, all his officials
become wicked.

29 : 12

bed
I have covered my bed with colored linens from Egypt.
7 : 16

I have perfumed my bed with myrrh, aloes and cinnamon.
7 : 17

if you lack the means to pay, your very bed will be snatched from under you.
22 : 27

A little sleep, a little slumber, a little folding of the hands to rest --
24 : 33

As a door turns on its hinges, so a sluggard turns on his bed.
26 : 14

She makes coverings for her bed; she is clothed in fine linen and purple.
31 : 22

bee
Eat honey, my son, for it is good; honey from the comb is sweet to your taste.
24 : 13

beer
Wine is a mocker and beer a brawler; whoever is led astray by them is not wise.
20 : 1

"It is not for kings, O Lemuel -- not for kings to drink wine, not for rulers to crave beer,
31 : 4

Give beer to those who are perishing, wine to those who are in anguish;
31 : 6

before
He who answers before listening -- that is his folly and his shame.
18 : 13

begging
A poor man pleads for mercy, but a rich man answers harshly.
18 : 23

If a man shuts his ears to the cry of the poor, he too will cry out and not be answered.
21 : 13

beginning
The fear of the Lord is the beginning of knowledge, but fools despise wisdom and discipline.
1 : 7

"The Lord brought me forth as the first of his works, before his deeds of old;
8 : 22

I was appointed from eternity, from the beginning, before the world began,
8 : 23

before the mountains were settled in place, before the hills, I was given birth,
8 : 25

"The fear of the Lord is the beginning of wisdom, and knowledge of the Holy One is understanding.
9 : 10

An inheritance quickly gained at the beginning will not be blessed at the end.
20 : 21

beginning of knowledge
The fear of the Lord is the beginning of knowledge, but fools despise wisdom and discipline.
1 : 7

beginning of wisdom
"The fear of the Lord is the beginning of wisdom, and knowledge of the Holy One is understanding.
9 : 10

behaves
The proud and arrogant man --
"Mocker" is his name; he behaves with
overweening pride.

21 : 24

behavior
Even a child is known by his actions, by
whether his conduct is pure and right.

20 : 11

The way of the guilty is devious, but the
conduct of the innocent is upright.

21 : 8

being
for the Lord will be your confidence
and will keep your foot from being
snared.

3 : 26

Can a man scoop fire into his lap
without his clothes being burned?

6 : 27

The lamp of the Lord searches the spirit
of a man; it searches out his inmost
being.

20 : 27

Blows and wounds cleanse away evil,
and beatings purge the inmost being.

20 : 30

my inmost being will rejoice when your
lips speak what is right.

23 : 16

Rescue those being led away to death;
hold back those staggering toward
slaughter.

24 : 11

being burned
Can a man scoop fire into his lap
without his clothes being burned?

6 : 27

being mean
He who walks maliciously causes grief,
and a chattering fool comes to ruin.

10 : 10

being scorched
Can a man walk on hot coals without
his feet being scorched?

6 : 28

believe
A simple man believes anything, but a
prudent man gives thought to his steps.

14 : 15

Though his speech is charming, do not
believe him, for seven abominations fill
his heart.

26 : 25

bending the knee
Evil men will bow down in the presence
of the good, and the wicked at the gates
of the righteous.

14 : 19

benefit
A greedy man stirs up dissension, but
he who trusts in the Lord will prosper.

28 : 25

If a king judges the poor with fairness,
his throne will always be secure.

29 : 14

benefiting
bestowing wealth on those who love me
and making their treasuries full.

8 : 21

benefits
For through me your days will be many,
and years will be added to your life.

9 : 11

A kind man benefits himself, but a cruel
man brings trouble on himself.

11 : 17

He who conceals his sins does not prosper, but whoever confesses and renounces them finds mercy.

28 : 13

bent

He who winks with his eye is plotting perversity; he who purses his lips is bent on evil.

16 : 30

An evil man is bent only on rebellion; a merciless official will be sent against him.

17 : 11

best

lest you give your best strength to others and your years to one who is cruel,

5 : 9

All hard work brings a profit, but mere talk leads only to poverty.

14 : 23

Do you see a man skilled in his work? He will serve before kings, he will not serve before obscure men.

22 : 29

it is better for him to say to you, "Come up here," than for him to humiliate you before a nobleman. What you have seen with your eyes

25 : 7

She sets about her work vigorously; her arms are strong for her tasks.

31 : 17

betray

The lips of the king speak as an oracle, and his mouth should not betray justice.

16 : 10

If you argue your case with a neighbor, do not betray another man's confidence,

25 : 9

betrays

A gossip betrays a confidence, but a trustworthy man keeps a secret

11 : 13

A gossip betrays a confidence; so avoid a man who talks too much.

20 : 19

better

for she is more profitable than silver and yields better returns than gold.

3 : 14

My fruit is better than fine gold; what I yield surpasses choice silver.

8 : 19

Better to be a nobody and yet have a servant than pretend to be somebody and have no food.

12 : 9

Better a little with the fear of the Lord than great wealth with turmoil.

15 : 16

Better a little with righteousness than much gain with injustice.

16 : 8

How much better to get wisdom than gold, to choose understanding rather than silver!

16 : 16

Better to be lowly in spirit and among the oppressed than to share plunder with the proud.

16 : 19

Better a patient man than a warrior, a man who controls his temper than one who takes a city.

16 : 32

Better a dry crust with peace and quiet than a house full of feasting with strife.

17 : 1

Better to meet a bear robbed of her cubs
than a fool in his folly.

17 : 12

Better a poor man whose walk is
blameless than a fool whose lips are
perverse.

19 : 1

What a man desires is unfailing love;
better to be poor than a liar.

19 : 22

Better to live on a corner of the roof
than share a house with a quarrelsome
wife.

21 : 9

Better to live in a desert than with a
quarrelsome and ill-tempered wife.

21 : 19

A good name is more desirable than
great riches; to be esteemed is better
than silver or gold.

22 : 1

it is better for him to say to you, "Come
up here," than for him to humiliate you
before a nobleman. What you have seen
with your eyes

25 : 7

Better to live on a corner of the roof
than share a house with a quarrelsome
wife.

25 : 24

Better is open rebuke than hidden love.

27 : 5

Better a poor man whose walk is
blameless than a rich man whose ways
are perverse.

28 : 6

beyond remedy
A man who remains stiff-necked after
many rebukes will suddenly be
destroyed -- without remedy.

29 : 1

Bible
Every word of God is flawless; he is a
shield to those who take refuge in him.

30 : 5

Do not add to his words, or he will
rebuke you and prove you a liar.

30 : 6

bicker
If you argue your case with a neighbor,
do not betray another man's confidence,

25 : 9

big city
A large population is a king's glory, but
without subjects a prince is ruined.

14 : 28

bind
Let love and faithfulness never leave
you; bind them around your neck, write
them on the tablet of your heart.

3 : 3

Bind them upon your heart forever;
fasten them around your neck.

6 : 21

Bind them on your fingers; write them
on the tablet of your heart.

7 : 3

bird
Free yourself, like a gazelle from the
hand of the hunter, like a bird from the
snare of the fowler.

6 : 5

till an arrow pierces his liver, like a bird
darting into a snare, little knowing it
will cost him his life.

7 : 23

Like a bird that strays from its nest is a
man who strays from his home.

27 : 8

birds

How useless to spread a net in full view of all the birds!

1 : 17

Like a fluttering sparrow or a darting swallow, an undeserved curse does not come to rest.

26 : 2

birth

When there were no oceans, I was given birth, when there were no springs abounding with water;

8 : 24

before the mountains were settled in place, before the hills, I was given birth,

8 : 25

May your father and mother be glad; may she who gave you birth rejoice!

23 : 25

bites

In the end it bites like a snake and poisons like a viper.

23 : 32

bitter

but in the end she is bitter as gall, sharp as a double-edged sword.

5 : 4

He who is full loathes honey, but to the hungry even what is bitter tastes sweet.

27 : 7

bitterness

He who conceals his hatred has lying lips, and whoever spreads slander is a fool.

10 : 18

Each heart knows its own bitterness, and no one else can share its joy.

14 : 10

A heart at peace gives life to the body, but envy rots the bones.

14 : 30

A foolish son brings grief to his father and bitterness to the one who bore him.

17 : 25

Do not say, "I'll pay you back for this wrong!" Wait for the Lord, and he will deliver you.

20 : 22

Do not gloat when your enemy falls; when he stumbles, do not let your heart rejoice,

24 : 17

Do not say, "I'll do to him as he has done to me; I'll pay that man back for what he did."

24 : 29

Like one who takes away a garment on a cold day, or like vinegar poured on soda, is one who sings songs to a heavy heart.

25 : 20

blameless

He holds victory in store for the upright, he is a shield to those whose walk is blameless,

2 : 7

For the upright will live in the land, and the blameless will remain in it;

2 : 21

The righteousness of the blameless makes a straight way for them, but the wicked are brought down by their own wickedness.

11 : 5

The Lord detests men of perverse heart but he delights in those whose ways are blameless.

11 : 20

Better a poor man whose walk is blameless than a fool whose lips are perverse.

19 : 1

The righteous man leads a blameless life; blessed are his children after him.

20 : 7

Better a poor man whose walk is blameless than a rich man whose ways are perverse.

28 : 6

He who leads the upright along an evil path will fall into his own trap, but the blameless will receive a good inheritance.

28 : 10

He whose walk is blameless is kept safe, but he whose ways are perverse will suddenly fall.

28 : 18

When the righteous thrive, the people rejoice; when the wicked rule, the people groan.

29 : 2

bless
"There are those who curse their fathers and do not bless their mothers;

30 : 11

bless others
Do not say to your neighbor, "Come back later; I'll give it tomorrow" -- when you now have it with you.

3 : 28

blessed
Blessed is the man who finds wisdom, the man who gains understanding,

3 : 13

She is a tree of life to those who embrace her; those who lay hold of her will be blessed.

3 : 18

May your fountain be blessed, and may you rejoice in the wife of your youth.

5 : 18

Now then, my sons, listen to me; blessed are those who keep my ways.

8 : 32

Blessed is the man who listens to me, watching daily at my doors, waiting at my doorway.

8 : 34

He who despises his neighbor sins, but blessed is he who is kind to the needy.

14 : 21

Whoever gives heed to instruction prospers, and blessed is he who trusts in the Lord.

16 : 20

The righteous man leads a blameless life; blessed are his children after him.

20 : 7

An inheritance quickly gained at the beginning will not be blessed at the end.

20 : 21

A generous man will himself be blessed, for he shares his food with the poor.

22 : 9

Blessed is the man who always fears the Lord, but he who hardens his heart falls into trouble.

28 : 14

A faithful man will be richly blessed, but one eager to get rich will not go unpunished.

28 : 20

Where there is no revelation, the people cast off restraint; but blessed is he who keeps the law.

29 : 18

Her children arise and call her blessed; her husband also, and he praises her:

31 : 28

blessed life

For through me your days will be many,
and years will be added to your life.

9 : 11

blesses

The Lord's curse is on the house of the
wicked, but he blesses the home of the
righteous.

3 : 33

If a man loudly blesses his neighbor
early in the morning, it will be taken as
a curse.

27 : 14

blessing

They will be a garland to grace your
head and a chain to adorn your neck.

1 : 9

The path of the righteous is like the first
gleam of dawn, shining ever brighter till
the full light of day.

4 : 18

The memory of the righteous will be a
blessing, but the name of the wicked
will rot.

10 : 7

The blessing of the Lord brings wealth,
and he adds no trouble to it.

10 : 22

The righteous will never be uprooted,
but the wicked will not remain in the
land.

10 : 30

Through the blessing of the upright a
city is exalted, but by the mouth of the
wicked it is destroyed.

11 : 11

People curse the man who hoards grain,
but blessing crowns him who is willing
to sell.

11 : 26

Good understanding wins favor, but the
way of the unfaithful is hard.

13 : 15

The house of the wicked will be
destroyed, but the tent of the upright
will flourish.

14 : 11

The way of the sluggard is blocked with
thorns, but the path of the upright is a
highway.

15 : 19

Children's children are a crown to the
aged, and parents are the pride of their
children.

17 : 6

The tongue has the power of life and
death, and those who love it will eat its
fruit.

18 : 21

He who finds a wife finds what is good
and receives favor from the Lord.

18 : 22

Do not love sleep or you will grow
poor; stay awake and you will have
food to spare.

20 : 13

There is surely a future hope for you,
and your hope will not be cut off.

23 : 18

But it will go well with those who
convict the guilty, and rich blessing will
come upon them.

24 : 25

Like cold water to a weary soul is good
news from a distant land.

25 : 25

He who tends a fig tree will eat its fruit,
and he who looks after his master will
be honored.

27 : 18

When a country is rebellious, it has many rulers, but a man of understanding and knowledge maintains order.

28 : 2

A faithful man will be richly blessed, but one eager to get rich will not go unpunished.

28 : 20

A greedy man stirs up dissension, but he who trusts in the Lord will prosper.

28 : 25

He who trusts in himself is a fool, but he who walks in wisdom is kept safe.

28 : 26

When the wicked rise to power, people go into hiding; but when the wicked perish, the righteous thrive.

28 : 28

blessing of God
Commit to the Lord whatever you do, and your plans will succeed.

16 : 3

blessings
If you had responded to my rebuke, I would have poured out my heart to you and made my thoughts known to you.

1 : 23

but whoever listens to me will live in safety and be at ease, without fear of harm."

1 : 33

For the Lord gives wisdom, and from his mouth come knowledge and understanding.

2 : 6

He holds victory in store for the upright, he is a shield to those whose walk is blameless,

2 : 7

for he guards the course of the just and protects the way of his faithful ones.

2 : 8

For wisdom will enter your heart, and knowledge will be pleasant to your soul.

2 : 10

For the upright will live in the land, and the blameless will remain in it;

2 : 21

for they will prolong your life many years and bring you prosperity.

3 : 2

Then you will win favor and a good name in the sight of God and man.

3 : 4

This will bring health to your body and nourishment to your bones.

3 : 8

Honor the Lord with your wealth, with the firstfruits of all your crops;

3 : 9

then your barns will be filled to overflowing, and your vats will brim over with new wine.

3 : 10

Then you will go on your way in safety, and your foot will not stumble;

3 : 23

for the Lord will be your confidence and will keep your foot from being snared.

3 : 26

The Lord's curse is on the house of the wicked, but he blesses the home of the righteous.

3 : 33

He mocks proud mockers but gives grace to the humble.

3 : 34

The wise inherit honor, but fools he holds up to shame.

3 : 35

She will set a garland of grace on your head and present you with a crown of splendor.

4 : 9

Listen, my son, accept what I say, and the years of your life will be many.

4 : 10

that you may maintain discretion and your lips may preserve knowledge.

5 : 2

Keep my commands and you will live; guard my teachings as the apple of your eye.

7 : 2

With me are the riches and honor, enduring wealth and prosperity.

8 : 18

My fruit is better than fine gold; what I yield surpasses choice silver.

8 : 19

bestowing wealth on those who love me and making their treasuries full.

8 : 21

For whoever finds me finds life and receives favor from the Lord.

8 : 35

For through me your days will be many, and years will be added to your life.

9 : 11

The Lord does not let the righteous go hungry but he thwarts the craving of the wicked.

10 : 3

Lazy hands make a man poor, but diligent hands bring wealth.

10 : 4

Blessings crown the head of the righteous, but violence overwhelms the mouth of the wicked.

10 : 6

The mouth of the righteous is a fountain of life, but violence overwhelms the mouth of the wicked.

10 : 11

The fear of the Lord adds length to life, but the years of the wicked are cut short.

10 : 27

The prospect of the righteous is joy, but the hopes of the wicked come to nothing.

10 : 28

When the righteous prosper, the city rejoices; when the wicked perish, there are shouts of joy.

11 : 10

The wicked man earns deceptive wages, but he who sows righteousness reaps a sure reward.

11 : 18

The Lord detests men of perverse heart but he delights in those whose ways are blameless.

11 : 20

He who seeks good finds goodwill, but evil comes to him who searches for it.

11 : 27

If the righteous receive their due on earth, how much more the ungodly and the sinner!

11 : 31

A good man obtains favor from the Lord, but the Lord condemns a crafty man.

12 : 2

He who works his land will have abundant food, but he who chases fantasies lacks judgment.

12 : 11

In the way of righteousness there is life; along that path is immortality.

12 : 28

A wicked messenger falls into trouble, but a trustworthy envoy brings healing.

13 : 17

Misfortune pursues the sinner, but prosperity is the reward of the righteous.

13 : 21

The righteous eat to their hearts' content, but the stomach of the wicked goes hungry.

13 : 25

Where there are no oxen, the manger is empty, but from the strength of an ox comes an abundant harvest.

14 : 4

The faithless will be fully repaid for their ways, and the good man rewarded for his.

14 : 14

The simple inherit folly, but the prudent are crowned with knowledge.

14 : 18

Righteousness exalts a nation, but sin is a disgrace to any people.

14 : 34

Whoever gives heed to instruction prospers, and blessed is he who trusts in the Lord.

16 : 20

A wise servant will rule over a disgraceful son, and will share the inheritance as one of the brothers.

17 : 2

He who gets wisdom loves his own soul; he who cherishes understanding prospers.

19 : 8

In doing this, you will heap burning coals on his head, and the Lord will reward you.

25 : 22

blocked

The way of the sluggard is blocked with thorns, but the path of the upright is a highway.

15 : 19

blood

If they say, "Come along with us; let's lie in wait for someone's blood, let's waylay some harmless soul;

1 : 11

for their feet rush into sin, they are swift to shed blood.

1 : 16

These men lie in wait for their own blood; they waylay only themselves!

1 : 18

haughty eyes, a lying tongue, hands that shed innocent blood,

6 : 17

The words of the wicked lie in wait for blood, but the speech of the upright rescues them.

12 : 6

For as churning the milk produces butter, and as twisting the nose produces blood, so stirring up anger produces strife."

30 : 33

bloodshot eyes

Who has woe? Who has sorrow? Who has strife? Who has complaints? Who has needless bruises? Who has bloodshot eyes?

23 : 29

bloodthirsty men

Bloodthirsty men hate a man of integrity and seek to kill the upright.

29 : 10

blows

Blows and disgrace are his lot, and his shame will never be wiped away;

6 : 33

Blows and wounds cleanse away evil, and beatings purge the inmost being.

20 : 30

blueprints

By wisdom a house is built, and through understanding it is established;

24 : 3

boast

Do not boast about tomorrow, for you do not know what a day may bring forth.

27 : 1

boasting

"It's no good, it's no good!" says the buyer; then off he goes and boasts about his purchase.

20 : 14

Like clouds and wind without rain is a man who boasts of gifts he does not give.

25 : 14

A lying tongue hates those it hurts, and a flattering mouth works ruin.

26 : 28

Let another praise you, and not your own mouth; someone else, and not your own lips.

27 : 2

boasts

Like clouds and wind without rain is a man who boasts of gifts he does not give.

25 : 14

body

This will bring health to your body and nourishment to your bones.

3 : 8

for they are life to those who find them and health to a man's whole body.

4 : 22

At the end of your life you will groan, when your flesh and body are spent.

5 : 11

A heart at peace gives life to the body, but envy rots the bones.

14 : 30

body parts

my son, do not go along with them, do not set foot on their paths;

1 : 15

If you had responded to my rebuke, I would have poured out my heart to you and made my thoughts known to you.

1 : 23

But since you rejected me when I called and no one gave heed when I stretched out my hand,

1 : 24

My son, do not forget my teaching, but keep my commands in your heart,

3 : 1

Let love and faithfulness never leave you; bind them around your neck, write them on the tablet of your heart.

3 : 3

This will bring health to your body and nourishment to your bones.

3 : 8

Then you will go on your way in safety, and your foot will not stumble;

3 : 23

he taught me and said, "Lay hold of my words with all your heart; keep my commands and you will live.

4 : 4

Do not set foot on the path of the wicked or walk in the way of evil men.

4 : 14

Do not let them out of your sight, keep them within your heart;

4 : 21

Put away perversity from your mouth; keep corrupt talk far from your lips.

4 : 24

For the lips of an adulteress drip honey, and her speech is smoother than oil;

5 : 3

Her feet go down to death; her steps lead straight to the grave.

5 : 5

Why be captivated, my son, by an adulteress? Why embrace the bosom of another man's wife?

5 : 20

if you have been trapped by what you said, ensnared by the words of your mouth,

6 : 2

A scoundrel and villain, who goes about with a corrupt mouth,

6 : 12

haughty eyes, a lying tongue, hands that shed innocent blood,

6 : 17

keeping you from the immoral woman, from the smooth tongue of the wayward wife.

6 : 24

Bind them on your fingers; write them on the tablet of your heart.

7 : 3

till an arrow pierces his liver, like a bird darting into a snare, little knowing it will cost him his life.

7 : 23

Listen, for I have worthy things to say; I open my lips to speak what is right.

8 : 6

All the words of my mouth are just; none of them is crooked or perverse.

8 : 8

Lazy hands make a man poor, but diligent hands bring wealth.

10 : 4

Blessings crown the head of the righteous, but violence overwhelms the mouth of the wicked.

10 : 6

The wise in heart accept commands, but a chattering fool comes to ruin.

10 : 8

He who walks maliciously causes grief, and a chattering fool comes to ruin.

10 : 10

Wise men store up knowledge, but the mouth of a fool invites ruin.

10 : 14

He who conceals his hatred has lying lips, and whoever spreads slander is a fool.

10 : 18

When words are many, sin is not absent, but he who holds his tongue is wise.

10 : 19

The tongue of the righteous is choice silver, but the heart of the wicked is of little value.

10 : 20

The lips of the righteous nourish many, but fools die for lack of judgment.

10 : 21

The lips of the righteous know what is fitting, but the mouth of the wicked only what is perverse.

10 : 32

A man who lacks judgment derides his neighbor, but a man of understanding holds his tongue.

11 : 12

The Lord detests men of perverse heart but he delights in those whose ways are blameless.

11 : 20

A wife of noble character is her husband's crown, but a disgraceful wife is like decay in his bones.

12 : 4

From the fruit of his lips a man is filled with good things as surely as the work of his hands rewards him.

12 : 14

A truthful witness gives honest testimony, but a false witness tells lies.

12 : 17

Truthful lips endure forever, but a lying tongue lasts only a moment.

12 : 19

The Lord detests lying lips, but he delights in men who are truthful.

12 : 22

A prudent man keeps his knowledge to himself, but the heart of fools blurts out folly.

12 : 23

An anxious heart weighs a man down, but a kind word cheers him up.

12 : 25

From the fruit of his lips a man enjoys good things, but the unfaithful have a craving for violence.

13 : 2

He who guards his lips guards his life, but he who speaks rashly will come to ruin.

13 : 3

The righteous eat to their hearts' content, but the stomach of the wicked goes hungry.

13 : 25

The wise woman builds her house, but with her own hands the foolish one tears hers down.

14 : 1

A fool's talk brings a rod to his back, but the lips of the wise protect them.

14 : 3

Stay away from a foolish man, for you will not find knowledge on his lips.

14 : 7

Each heart knows its own bitterness, and no one else can share its joy.

14 : 10

A heart at peace gives life to the body, but envy rots the bones.

14 : 30

The eyes of the Lord are everywhere, keeping watch on the wicked and the good.

15 : 3

45

The tongue that brings healing is a tree of life, but a deceitful tongue crushes the spirit.

15 : 4

The lips of the wise spread knowledge; not so the hearts of fools.

15 : 7

Death and Destruction lie open before the Lord -- how much more the hearts of men!

15 : 11

A happy heart makes the face cheerful, but heartache crushes the spirit.

15 : 13

All the days of the oppressed are wretched, but the cheerful heart has a continual feast.

15 : 15

A cheerful look brings joy to the heart, and good news gives health to the bones.

15 : 30

To man belong the plans of the heart, but from the Lord comes the reply of the tongue.

16 : 1

The lips of the king speak as an oracle, and his mouth should not betray justice.

16 : 10

Kings take pleasure in honest lips; they value a man who speaks the truth.

16 : 13

A wise man's heart guides his mouth, and his lips promote instruction.

16 : 23

Pleasant words are a honeycomb, sweet to the soul and healing to the bones.

16 : 24

He who winks with his eye is plotting perversity; he who purses his lips is bent on evil.

16 : 30

The crucible for silver and the furnace for gold, but the Lord tests the heart.

17 : 3

Arrogant lips are unsuited to a fool -- how much worse lying lips to a ruler!

17 : 7

A cheerful heart is good medicine, but a crushed spirit dries up the bones.

17 : 22

Even a fool is thought wise if he keeps silent, and discerning if he holds his tongue.

17 : 28

A fool's lips bring him strife, and his mouth invites a beating.

18 : 6

A fool's mouth is his undoing, and his lips are a snare to his soul.

18 : 7

The heart of the discerning acquires knowledge; the ears of the wise seek it out.

18 : 15

The tongue has the power of life and death, and those who love it will eat its fruit.

18 : 21

Better a poor man whose walk is blameless than a fool whose lips are perverse.

19 : 1

Many are the plans in the man's heart, but it is the Lord's purpose that prevails.

19 : 21

46

A corrupt witness mocks at justice, and the mouth of the wicked gulps down evil.

19 : 28

Who can say, "I have kept my heart pure; I am clean and without sin"?

20 : 9

Ears that hear and eyes that see -- the Lord has made them both.

20 : 12

Gold there is, and rubies in abundance, but lips that speak knowledge are a rare jewel.

20 : 15

Food gained by fraud tastes sweet to a man, but he ends up with a mouth full of gravel.

20 : 17

All a man's ways seem right to him, but the Lord weighs the heart.

21 : 2

Haughty eyes and a proud heart, the lamp of the wicked, are sin!

21 : 4

A fortune made by a lying tongue is a fleeting vapor and a deadly snare.

21 : 6

He who loves a pure heart and whose speech is gracious will have the king for his friend.

22 : 11

Folly is bound up in the heart of a child, but the rod of discipline will drive it far from him.

22 : 15

Pay attention and listen to the sayings of the wise; apply your heart to what I teach,

22 : 17

Apply your heart to instruction and your ears to words of knowledge.

23 : 12

my inmost being will rejoice when your lips speak what is right.

23 : 16

My son, give me your heart and let your eyes keep to my ways,

23 : 26

Your eyes will see strange sights and your mind imagine confusing things.

23 : 33

for their hearts plot violence, and their lips talk about making trouble.

24 : 2

If you say, "But we knew nothing about this," does not he who weighs the heart perceive it? Does not he who guards your life know it? Will he not repay each person according to what he has done?

24 : 12

Do not gloat when your enemy falls; when he stumbles, do not let your heart rejoice,

24 : 17

As the heavens are high and the earth is deep, so the hearts of kings are unsearchable.

25 : 3

Through patience a ruler can be persuaded, and a gentle tongue can break a bone.

25 : 15

Seldom set foot in your neighbor's house -- too much of you, and he will hate you.

25 . 17

Like a bad tooth or a lame foot is reliance on the unfaithful in times of trouble.

25 : 19

As a north wind brings rain, so a sly tongue brings angry looks.

25 : 23

Answer a fool according to his folly, or he will be wise in his own eyes.

26 : 5

Like cutting off one's feet or drinking violence is the sending of a message by the hand of a fool.

26 : 6

Like a lame man's legs that hang limp is a proverb in the mouth of a fool.

26 : 7

Like a thornbush in a drunkard's hand is a proverb in the mouth of a fool.

26 : 9

The sluggard buries his hand in the dish; he is too lazy to bring it back to his mouth.

26 : 15

Like a coating of glaze over earthenware are fervent lips with an evil heart.

26 : 23

A malicious man disguises himself with his lips, but in his heart he harbors deceit.

26 : 24

Though his speech is charming, do not believe him, for seven abominations fill his heart.

26 : 25

A lying tongue hates those it hurts, and a flattering mouth works ruin.

26 : 28

Let another praise you, and not your own mouth; someone else, and not your own lips.

27 : 2

Perfume and incense bring joy to the heart, and the pleasantness of one's friend springs from his earnest counsel.

27 : 9

Be wise, my son, and bring joy to my heart; then I can answer anyone who treats me with contempt.

27 : 11

As water reflects a face, so a man's heart reflects the man.

27 : 19

Blessed is the man who always fears the Lord, but he who hardens his heart falls into trouble.

28 : 14

He who rebukes a man will in the end gain more favor than he who has a flattering tongue.

28 : 23

Whoever flatters his neighbor is spreading a net for his feet.

29 : 5

The poor man and the oppressor have this in common: The Lord gives sight to the eyes of both.

29 : 13

Who has gone up to heaven and come down? Who has gathered up the wind in the hollow of his hands? Who has wrapped up the waters in his cloak? Who has established all the ends of the earth? What is his name, and the name of his son? Tell me if you know!

30 : 4

those who are pure in their own eyes and yet are not cleansed of their filth;

30 : 12

The eye that mocks a father, that scorns obedience to a mother, will be pecked out by the ravens of the valley, will be eaten by the vultures.

30 : 17

"This is the way of an adulteress: She eats and wipes her mouth and says, 'I've done nothing wrong.'

30 : 20

"If you have played the fool and exalted yourself, or if you have planned evil, clap your hand over your mouth!

30 : 32

In her hand she holds the distaff and grasps the spindle with her fingers.

31 : 19

She opens her arms to the poor and extends her hands to the needy.

31 : 20

She speaks with wisdom, and faithful instruction is on her tongue.

31 : 26

bold

A wicked man puts up a bold front, but an upright man gives thought to his ways.

21 : 29

The wicked man flees though no one pursues, but the righteous are as bold as a lion.

28 : 1

bold front

A wicked man puts up a bold front, but an upright man gives thought to his ways.

21 : 29

boldness

He who rebukes a man will in the end gain more favor than he who has a flattering tongue.

28 : 23

bone

Through patience a ruler can be persuaded, and a gentle tongue can break a bone.

25 : 15

bones

This will bring health to your body and nourishment to your bones.

3 : 8

A wife of noble character is her husband's crown, but a disgraceful wife is like decay in his bones.

12 : 4

A heart at peace gives life to the body, but envy rots the bones.

14 : 30

A cheerful look brings joy to the heart, and good news gives health to the bones.

15 : 30

Pleasant words are a honeycomb, sweet to the soul and healing to the bones.

16 : 24

A cheerful heart is good medicine, but a crushed spirit dries up the bones.

17 : 22

bore

A foolish son brings grief to his father and bitterness to the one who bore him.

17 : 25

born

A friend loves at all times, and a brother is born for adversity.

17 : 17

borrow

The rich rule over the poor, and the borrower is servant to the lender.

22 . 7

Do not be a man who strikes hands in pledge or puts up security for debts;

22 : 26

if you lack the means to pay, your very
bed will be snatched from under you.

22 : 27

borrower
The rich rule over the poor, and the
borrower is servant to the lender.

22 : 7

bosom
Why be captivated, my son, by an
adulteress? Why embrace the bosom of
another man's wife?

5 : 20

both
Acquitting the guilty and condemning
the innocent -- the Lord detests them
both.

17 : 15

bound
Folly is bound up in the heart of a child,
but the rod of discipline will drive it far
from him.

22 : 15

bound up
Folly is bound up in the heart of a child,
but the rod of discipline will drive it far
from him.

22 : 15

boundaries
The Lord tears down the proud man's
house, but he keeps the widow's
boundaries intact.

15 : 25

boundary
when he gave the sea its boundary so
the waters would not overstep his
command, and when he marked out the
foundations of the earth.

8 : 29

Do not move an ancient boundary stone
set up by your forefathers.

22 : 28

Do not move an ancient boundary stone
or encroach on the fields of the
fatherless,

23 : 10

boundary stone
Do not move an ancient boundary stone
set up by your forefathers.

22 : 28

Do not move an ancient boundary stone
or encroach on the fields of the
fatherless,

23 : 10

bow down
Evil men will bow down in the presence
of the good, and the wicked at the gates
of the righteous.

14 : 19

bowls
Those who linger over wine, who go to
sample bowls of mixed wine,

23 : 30

boy
When I was a boy in my father's house,
still tender, and an only child of my
mother,

4 : 3

bragging
A prudent man keeps his knowledge to
himself, but the heart of fools blurts out
folly.

12 : 23

A fool's talk brings a rod to his back,
but the lips of the wise protect them.

14 : 3

A fool finds no pleasure in
understanding but delights in airing his
own opinions.

18 : 2

"It's no good, it's no good!" says the buyer; then off he goes and boasts about his purchase.

20 : 14

Do not exalt yourself in the king's presence, and do not claim a place among great men;

25 : 6

Like clouds and wind without rain is a man who boasts of gifts he does not give.

25 : 14

It is not good to eat too much honey, not is it honorable to seek one's own honor.

25 : 27

A lying tongue hates those it hurts, and a flattering mouth works ruin.

26 : 28

Do not boast about tomorrow, for you do not know what a day may bring forth.

27 : 1

Let another praise you, and not your own mouth; someone else, and not your own lips.

27 : 2

brawler
Wine is a mocker and beer a brawler; whoever is led astray by them is not wise.

20 : 1

brazen
She took hold of him and kissed him and with a brazen face she said:

7 : 13

brazen face
She took hold of him and kissed him and with a brazen face she said:

7 : 13

breaching a dam
Starting a quarrel is like breaching a dam; so drop the matter before a dispute breaks out.

17 : 14

bread
They eat the bread of wickedness and drink the wine of violence.

4 : 17

for the prostitute reduces you to a loaf of bread, and the adulteress preys upon your very life.

6 : 26

To show partiality is not good -- yet a man will do wrong for a piece of bread.

28 : 21

Keep falsehood and lies far from me; give me neither poverty nor riches, but give me only my daily bread.

30 : 8

She watches over the affairs of her household and does not eat the bread of idleness.

31 : 27

break
Through patience a ruler can be persuaded, and a gentle tongue can break a bone.

25 : 15

break the law
If anyone turns a deaf ear to the law, even his prayers are detestable.

28 : 9

breaking a promise
A gossip betrays a confidence, but a trustworthy man keeps a secret.

11 : 13

breaks out
Starting a quarrel is like breaching a
dam; so drop the matter before a dispute
breaks out.

17 : 14

breasts
A loving doe, a graceful deer -- may her
breasts satisfy you always, may you
ever be captivated by her love.

5 : 19

Why be captivated, my son, by an
adulteress? Why embrace the bosom of
another man's wife?

5 : 20

breeds
Pride only breeds quarrels, but wisdom
is found in those who take advice.

13 : 10

bribe
He will not accept any compensation;
he will refuse the bribe, however great
it is.

6 : 35

A bribe is a charm to the one who gives
it; wherever he turns, he succeeds.

17 : 8

A wicked man accepts a bribe in secret
to pervert the course of justice.

17 : 23

A gift given in secret soothes anger, and
a bribe concealed in the cloak pacifies
great wrath.

21 : 14

bribes
A greedy man brings trouble to his
family, but he who hates bribes will
live.

15 : 27

By justice a king gives a country
stability, but one who is greedy for
bribes tears it down.

29 : 4

brighter
The path of the righteous is like the first
gleam of dawn, shining ever brighter till
the full light of day.

4 : 18

brim
then your barns will be filled to
overflowing, and your vats will brim
over with new wine.

3 : 10

bring
for they will prolong your life many
years and bring you prosperity.

3 : 2

This will bring health to your body and
nourishment to your bones.

3 : 8

Lazy hands make a man poor, but
diligent hands bring wealth.

10 : 4

The wages of the righteous bring them
life, but the income of the wicked
brings them punishment.

10 : 16

A fool's lips bring him strife, and his
mouth invites a beating.

18 : 6

The sluggard buries his hand in the
dish; he will not even bring it back to
his mouth!

19 : 24

Humility and the fear of the Lord bring
wealth and honor and life.

22 : 4

for those two will send sudden destruction upon them, and who knows what calamities they can bring?

24 : 22

do not bring hastily to court, for what will you do in the end if your neighbor puts you to shame?

25 : 8

The sluggard buries his hand in the dish; he is too lazy to bring it back to his mouth.

26 : 15

Do not boast about tomorrow, for you do not know what a day may bring forth.

27 : 1

Perfume and incense bring joy to the heart, and the pleasantness of one's friend springs from his earnest counsel.

27 : 9

Be wise, my son, and bring joy to my heart; then I can answer anyone who treats me with contempt.

27 : 11

If a man pampers his servant from youth, he will bring grief in the end.

29 : 21

Give her the reward she has earned, and let her works bring her praise at the city gate.

31 : 31

bring health
This will bring health to your body and nourishment to your bones.

3 : 8

brings
The proverbs of Solomon: A wise son brings joy to his father, but a foolish son grief to his mother.

10 : 1

A wise son brings joy to his father, but a foolish man despises his mother.

15 : 20

A cheerful look brings joy to the heart, and good news gives health to the bones.

15 : 30

To have a fool for a son brings grief; there is no joy for the father of a fool.

17 : 21

A man who loves wisdom brings joy to his father, but a companion of prostitutes squanders his wealth.

29 : 3

She brings him good, not harm, all the days of her life.

31 : 12

brings forth
The mouth of the righteous brings forth wisdom, but a perverse tongue will be cut out.

10 : 31

brings healing
A wicked messenger falls into trouble, but a trustworthy envoy brings healing.

13 : 17

brings joy
The proverbs of Solomon: A wise son brings joy to his father, but a foolish son grief to his mother.

10 : 1

A wise son brings joy to his father, but a foolish man despises his mother.

15 : 20

A cheerful look brings joy to the heart, and good news gives health to the bones.

15 : 30

A man who loves wisdom brings joy to his father, but a companion of prostitutes squanders his wealth.

29 : 3

brings shame
He who robs his father and drives out his mother is a son who brings shame and disgrace.

19 : 26

brink
I have come to the brink of utter ruin in the midst of the whole assembly.

5 : 14

broke
and poverty will come on you like a bandit and scarcity like an armed man.

6 : 11

broken down
Like a city whose walls are broken down is a man who lacks self-control.

25 : 28

brokenness
He who ignores discipline comes to poverty and shame, but whoever heeds correction is honored.

13 : 18

brook
The words of a man's mouth are deep waters, but the fountain of wisdom is a bubbling brook.

18 : 4

brother
Say to wisdom, "You are my sister," and call understanding your kinsman;

7 : 4

A friend loves at all times, and a brother is born for adversity.

17 : 17

One who is slack in his work is brother to one who destroys.

18 : 9

An offended brother is more unyielding than a fortified city, and disputes are like the barred gates of a citadel.

18 : 19

A man of many companions may come to ruin, but there is a friend who sticks closer than a brother.

18 : 24

Do not forsake your friend and the friend of your father, and do not go to your brother's house when disaster strikes you -- better a neighbor nearby than a brother far away.

27 : 10

brothers
a false witness who pours out lies and a man who stirs up dissension among brothers.

6 : 19

A wise servant will rule over a disgraceful son, and will share the inheritance as one of the brothers.

17 : 2

brother's
Do not forsake your friend and the friend of your father, and do not go to your brother's house when disaster strikes you -- better a neighbor nearby than a brother far away.

27 : 10

brought
Many are the victims she has brought down; her slain are a mighty throng.

7 : 26

The righteousness of the blameless makes a straight way for them, but the wicked are brought down by their own wickedness.

11 : 5

When calamity comes, the wicked are brought down, but even in death the righteous have a refuge.

14 : 32

The sacrifice of the wicked is detestable -- how much more so when brought with evil intent!

21 : 27

for though a righteous man falls seven times, he rises again, but the wicked are brought down by calamity.

24 : 16

brought down

Many are the victims she has brought down; her slain are a mighty throng.

7 : 26

The righteousness of the blameless makes a straight way for them, but the wicked are brought down by their own wickedness.

11 : 5

When calamity comes, the wicked are brought down, but even in death the righteous have a refuge.

14 : 32

for though a righteous man falls seven times, he rises again, but the wicked are brought down by calamity.

24 : 16

bruises

Who has woe? Who has sorrow? Who has strife? Who has complaints? Who has needless bruises? Who has bloodshot eyes?

23 : 29

brutal

those whose teeth are swords and whose jaws are set with knives to devour the poor from the earth, the needy from among mankind.

30 : 14

bubbling brook

The words of a man's mouth are deep waters, but the fountain of wisdom is a bubbling brook.

18 : 4

build

Finish your outdoor work and get your fields ready; after that, build your house.

24 : 27

building

By wisdom a house is built, and through understanding it is established;

24 : 3

builds

The wise woman builds her house, but with her own hands the foolish one tears hers down.

14 : 1

He who loves a quarrel loves sin; he who builds a high gate invites destruction.

17 : 19

built

Wisdom has built her house; she has hewn out its seven pillars.

9 : 1

By wisdom a house is built, and through understanding it is established;

24 : 3

burden

Stone is heavy and sand a burden, but provocation by a fool is heavier than both.

27 : 3

"The leech has two daughters. 'Give! Give!' they cry. "There are three things that are never satisfied, four that never say, 'Enough!':

30 : 15

buries
The sluggard buries his hand in the dish; he will not even bring it back to his mouth!

19 : 24

The sluggard buries his hand in the dish; he is too lazy to bring it back to his mouth.

26 : 15

burned
Can a man scoop fire into his lap without his clothes being burned?

6 : 27

burning coals
In doing this, you will heap burning coals on his head, and the Lord will reward you.

25 : 22

burning the midnight oil
She sees that her trading is profitable, and her lamp does not go out at night.

31 : 18

business
People curse the man who hoards grain, but blessing crowns him who is willing to sell.

11 : 26

The laborer's appetite works for him; his hunger drives him on.

16 : 26

"It's no good, it's no good!" says the buyer; then off he goes and boasts about his purchase.

20 : 14

It is a trap for a man to dedicate something rashly and only later to consider his vows.

20 : 25

A fortune made by a lying tongue is a fleeting vapor and a deadly snare.

21 : 6

Like an archer who wounds at random is he who hires a fool or any passer-by.

26 : 10

When the righteous triumph, there is great elation; but when the wicked rise to power, men go into hiding.

28 : 12

Like a roaring lion or a charging bear is a wicked man ruling over a helpless people.

28 : 15

A tyrannical ruler lacks judgment, but he who hates ill-gotten gain will enjoy a long life.

28 : 16

He who works his land will have abundant food, but the one who chases fantasies will have his fill of poverty.

28 : 19

business practices
Better a little with righteousness than much gain with injustice.

16 : 8

business woman
She sees that her trading is profitable, and her lamp does not go out at night.

31 : 18

She makes linen garments and sells them, and supplies the merchants with sashes.

31 : 24

busy
She selects wool and flax and works with eager hands.

31 : 13

She watches over the affairs of her household and does not eat the bread of idleness.

31 : 27

butter
For as churning the milk produces
butter, and as twisting the nose
produces blood, so stirring up anger
produces strife."

30 : 33

buy
Buy the truth and do not sell it; get
wisdom, discipline and understanding.

23 : 23

buyer
"It's no good, it's no good!" says the
buyer; then off he goes and boasts about
his purchase.

20 : 14

buys
She considers a field and buys it; out of
her earnings she plants a vineyard

31 : 16

by-product
From the fruit of his mouth a man's
stomach is filled; with the harvest from
his lips he is satisfied.

18 : 20

C

calamities
for those two will send sudden
destruction upon them, and who knows
what calamities they can bring?

24 : 22

calamity
I in turn will laugh at your disaster; I
will mock when calamity overtakes you

1 : 26

when calamity overtakes you like a
storm, when disaster sweeps over you
like a whirlwind, when distress and
trouble overwhelm you.

1 : 27

Have no fear of sudden disaster or of
the ruin that overtakes the wicked,

3 : 25

A poor man's field may produce
abundant food, but injustice sweeps it
away.

13 : 23

When calamity comes, the wicked are
brought down, but even in death the
righteous have a refuge.

14 : 32

He who guards his mouth and his
tongue keeps himself from calamity.

21 : 23

for though a righteous man falls seven
times, he rises again, but the wicked are
brought down by calamity.

24 : 16

calf
Better a meal of vegetables where there
is love than a fattened calf with hatred.

15 : 17

call
"Then they will call to me but I will not
answer; they will look for me but will
not find me.

1 : 28

and if you call out for insight and cry
aloud for understanding,

2 : 3

Say to wisdom, "You are my sister,"
and call understanding your kinsman;

7 : 4

Does not wisdom call out? Does not
understanding raise her voice?

8 : 1

"To you, O men, I call out; I raise my
voice to all mankind.

8 : 4

Her children arise and call her blessed;
her husband also, and he praises her:

31 : 28

called
But since you rejected me when I called
and no one gave heed when I stretched
out my hand,

1 : 24

calling
calling out to those who pass by, who
go straight on their way.

9 : 15

callousness
Blessed is the man who always fears the
Lord, but he who hardens his heart falls
into trouble.

28 : 14

calls
Wisdom calls aloud in the street, she raises her voice in the public squares;

1 : 20

She has sent out her maids, and she calls from the highest point of the city.

9 : 3

calms a quarrel
A hot-tempered man stirs up dissension, but a patient man calms a quarrel.

15 : 18

camaraderie
throw in your lot with us, and we will share a common purse" --

1 : 14

A man of many companions may come to ruin, but there is a friend who sticks closer than a brother.

18 : 24

cannot
For they cannot sleep till they do evil; they are robbed of slumber till they make someone fall.

4 : 16

A man cannot be established through wickedness, but the righteous cannot be uprooted.

12 : 3

A servant cannot be corrected by mere words; though he understands, he will not respond.

29 : 19

"Under three things the earth trembles, under four it cannot bear up:

30 : 21

"Speak up for those who cannot speak for themselves, for the rights of all who are destitute.

31 : 8

captivate
Do not lust in your heart after her beauty or let her captivate you with her eyes,

6 : 25

captivated
A loving doe, a graceful deer -- may her breasts satisfy you always, may you ever be captivated by her love.

5 : 19

Why be captivated, my son, by an adulteress? Why embrace the bosom of another man's wife?

5 : 20

capture
The evil deeds of a wicked man ensnare him; the cords of his sin hold him fast.

5 : 22

captured
An evil man is trapped by his sinful talk, but a righteous man escapes trouble.

12 : 13

care free
The blessing of the Lord brings wealth, and he adds no trouble to it.

10 : 22

careful
Make level paths for your feet and take only ways that are firm.

4 : 26

He who spares the rod hates his son, but he who loves him is careful to discipline him.

13 : 24

A simple man believes anything, but a prudent man gives thought to his steps.

14 : 15

A wise man's heart guides his mouth, and his lips promote instruction.

16 : 23

A man of knowledge uses words with restraint, and a man of understanding is even-tempered.

17 : 27

Be sure you know the condition of your flocks, give careful attention to your herds;

27 : 23

cares

A righteous man cares for the needs of his animal, but the kindest acts of the wicked are cruel.

12 : 10

caring

Do not say to your neighbor, "Come back later; I'll give it tomorrow" -- when you now have it with you.

3 : 28

case

The first to present his case seems right, till another comes forward and questions him.

18 : 17

for the Lord will take up their case and will plunder those who plunder them.

22 : 23

for their Defender is strong; he will take up their case against you.

23 : 11

If you argue your case with a neighbor, do not betray another man's confidence,

25 : 9

cast

The lot is cast into the lap, but its every decision is from the Lord.

16 : 33

Cast but a glance at riches, and they are gone, for they will surely sprout wings and fly off to the sky like an eagle.

23 : 5

cast aside

The poor are shunned even by their neighbors, but the rich have many friends.

14 : 20

A poor man is shunned by all his relatives -- how much more do his friends avoid him! Though he pursues them with pleading, they are nowhere to be found.

19 : 7

cast off

Where there is no revelation, the people cast off restraint; but blessed is he who keeps the law.

29 : 18

casting lots

The lot is cast into the lap, but its every decision is from the Lord.

16 : 33

Casting the lot settles disputes and keeps strong opponents apart.

18 : 18

catastrophe

when calamity overtakes you like a storm, when disaster sweeps over you like a whirlwind, when distress and trouble overwhelm you.

1 : 27

caught

Yet if he is caught, he must pay sevenfold, though it costs him all the wealth of his house.

6 : 31

All at once he followed her like an ox going to the slaughter, like a deer stepping into a noose

7 : 22

till an arrow pierces his liver, like a bird darting into a snare, little knowing it will cost him his life.

7 : 23

The righteousness of the upright delivers them, but the unfaithful are trapped by evil desires.

11 . 6

a lizard can be caught with the hand, yet it is found in kings' palaces.

30 : 28

cause
Do not testify against your neighbor without cause, or use your lips to deceive.

24 : 28

causes
He who walks maliciously causes grief, and a chattering fool comes to ruin.

10 : 10

causing one to sin
He who leads the upright along an evil path will fall into his own trap, but the blameless will receive a good inheritance.

28 : 10

cautious
A righteous man is cautious in friendship, but the way of the wicked leads them astray.

12 : 26

celebration
When the righteous prosper, the city rejoices; when the wicked perish, there are shouts of joy.

11 : 10

chain
They will be a garland to grace your head and a chain to adorn your neck.

1 : 9

chambers
Her house is a highway to the grave, leading down to the chambers of death.

7 : 27

change
Though you grind a fool in a mortar, grinding him like grain with a pestle, you will not remove his folly from him.

27 : 22

changing perspective
The poor man and the oppressor have this in common: The Lord gives sight to the eyes of both.

29 : 13

character
The integrity of the upright guides them, but the unfaithful are destroyed by their duplicity.

11 : 3

A gossip betrays a confidence, but a trustworthy man keeps a secret.

11 : 13

A wife of noble character is her husband's crown, but a disgraceful wife is like decay in his bones.

12 : 4

The righteous hate what is false, but the wicked bring shame and disgrace.

13 : 5

Righteousness guards the man of integrity, but wickedness overthrows the sinner.

13 : 6

It is not good to punish an innocent man, or to flog officials for their integrity.

17 : 26

Before his downfall a man's heart is proud, but humility comes before honor.

18 : 12

What a man desires is unfailing love; better to be poor than a liar.

19 : 22

Who can say, "I have kept my heart pure; I am clean and without sin"?

20 : 9

Even a child is known by his actions, by whether his conduct is pure and right.

20 : 11

A good name is more desirable than great riches; to be esteemed is better than silver or gold.

22 : 1

An honest answer is like a kiss on the lips.

24 : 26

remove the wicked from the king's presence, and his throne will be established through righteousness.

25 : 5

or he who hears it may shame you and you will never lose your bad reputation.

25 : 10

Like the coolness of snow at harvest time is a trustworthy messenger to those who send him; he refreshes the spirit of his masters.

25 : 13

A malicious man disguises himself with his lips, but in his heart he harbors deceit.

26 : 24

Though his speech is charming, do not believe him, for seven abominations fill his heart.

26 : 25

His malice may be concealed by deception, but his wickedness will be exposed in the assembly.

26 : 26

As water reflects a face, so a man's heart reflects the man.

27 : 19

A rich man may be wise in his own eyes, but a poor man who has discernment sees through him.

28 : 11

He who robs his father or mother and says, "It's not wrong" -- he is partner to him who destroys.

28 : 24

Bloodthirsty men hate a man of integrity and seek to kill the upright.

29 : 10

The righteous detest the dishonest; the wicked detest the upright.

29 : 27

A wife of noble character who can find? She is worth far more than rubies.

31 : 10

characteristics
The glory of young men is their strength, gray hair the splendor of the old.

20 : 29

charcoal
As charcoal to embers and as wood to fire, so is a quarrelsome man for kindling strife.

26 : 21

charging bear
Like a roaring lion or a charging bear is a wicked man ruling over a helpless people.

28 : 15

charm
A bribe is a charm to the one who gives it; wherever he turns, he succeeds.

17 : 8

Charm is deceptive, and beauty is fleeting; but a woman who fears the Lord is to be praised.

31 : 30

charming
Though his speech is charming, do not believe him, for seven abominations fill his heart.
26 : 25

chases
He who works his land will have abundant food, but he who chases fantasies lacks judgment.
12 : 11

He who works his land will have abundant food, but the one who chases fantasies will have his fill of poverty.
28 : 19

chases fantasies
He who works his land will have abundant food, but he who chases fantasies lacks judgment.
12 : 11

He who works his land will have abundant food, but the one who chases fantasies will have his fill of poverty.
28 : 19

chastisement
My son, do not despise the Lord's discipline and do not resent his rebuke,
3 : 11

chattering
The wise in heart accept commands, but a chattering fool comes to ruin.
10 : 8

chattering fool
He who walks maliciously causes grief, and a chattering fool comes to ruin.
10 : 10

cheat
A bribe is a charm to the one who gives it; wherever he turns, he succeeds.
17 : 8

cheating
The Lord abhors dishonest scales, but accurate weights are his delight.
11 : 1

Better a little with righteousness than much gain with injustice.
16 : 8

A wicked man accepts a bribe in secret to pervert the course of justice.
17 : 23

cheerful
A happy heart makes the face cheerful, but heartache crushes the spirit.
15 : 13

All the days of the oppressed are wretched, but the cheerful heart has a continual feast.
15 : 15

A cheerful look brings joy to the heart, and good news gives health to the bones.
15 : 30

A cheerful heart is good medicine, but a crushed spirit dries up the bones.
17 : 22

cheerful heart
A cheerful heart is good medicine, but a crushed spirit dries up the bones.
17 : 22

cheers
An anxious heart weighs a man down, but a kind word cheers him up.
12 : 25

cherishes
He who gets wisdom loves his own soul; he who cherishes understanding prospers.
19 : 8

child
When I was a boy in my father's house,
still tender, and an only child of my
mother,

4 : 3

The proverbs of Solomon: A wise son
brings joy to his father, but a foolish
son grief to his mother.

10 : 1

Even a child is known by his actions, by
whether his conduct is pure and right.

20 : 11

Train a child in the way he should go,
and when he is old he will not turn from
it.

22 : 6

Folly is bound up in the heart of a child,
but the rod of discipline will drive it far
from him.

22 : 15

Do not withhold discipline from a child;
if you punish him with the rod, he will
not die.

23 : 13

The rod of correction imparts wisdom,
but a child left to himself disgraces his
mother.

29 : 15

"O my son, O son of my womb, O son
of my vows,

31 : 2

childhood
When I was a boy in my father's house,
still tender, and an only child of my
mother,

4 : 3

children
My son, keep your father's commands
and do not forsake your mother's
teaching.

6 : 20

I saw among the simple, I noticed
among the young men, a youth who
lacked judgment.

7 : 7

Now then, my sons, listen to me; pay
attention to what I say.

7 : 24

The proverbs of Solomon: A wise son
brings joy to his father, but a foolish
son grief to his mother.

10 : 1

He who gathers crops in summer is a
wise son, but he who sleeps during
harvest is a disgraceful son.

10 : 5

A wise son heeds his father's
instruction, but a mocker does not listen
to rebuke.

13 : 1

A good man leaves an inheritance for
his children's children, but a sinner's
wealth is stored up for the righteous.

13 : 22

He who spares the rod hates his son, but
he who loves him is careful to
discipline him.

13 : 24

He who fears the Lord has a secure
fortress, and for his children it will be a
refuge.

14 : 26

A fool spurns the father's discipline, but
whoever heeds correction shows
prudence.

15 : 5

A wise son brings joy to his father, but
a foolish man despises his mother.

15 : 20

He who ignores discipline despises himself, but whoever heeds correction gains understanding.

15 : 32

Children's children are a crown to the aged, and parents are the pride of their children.

17 : 6

To have a fool for a son brings grief; there is no joy for the father of a fool.

17 : 21

A foolish son brings grief to his father and bitterness to the one who bore him.

17 : 25

Discipline your son, for in that there is hope; do not be a willing party to his death.

19 : 18

He who robs his father and drives out his mother is a son who brings shame and disgrace.

19 : 26

The righteous man leads a blameless life; blessed are his children after him.

20 : 7

Even a child is known by his actions, by whether his conduct is pure and right.

20 : 11

If a man curses his father or mother, his lamp will be snuffed out in pitch darkness.

20 : 20

Punish him with the rod and save his soul from death.

23 : 14

The father of a righteous man has great joy; he who has a wise son delights in him.

23 : 24

Be wise, my son, and bring joy to my heart; then I can answer anyone who treats me with contempt.

27 : 11

He who robs his father or mother and says, "It's not wrong" -- he is partner to him who destroys.

28 : 24

Discipline your son, and he will give you peace; he will bring delight to your soul.

29 : 17

"There are those who curse their fathers and do not bless their mothers;

30 : 11

The eye that mocks a father, that scorns obedience to a mother, will be pecked out by the ravens of the valley, will be eaten by the vultures.

30 : 17

"O my son, O son of my womb, O son of my vows,

31 : 2

Her children arise and call her blessed; her husband also, and he praises her:

31 : 28

choice

Choose my instruction instead of silver, knowledge rather than choice gold,

8 : 10

My fruit is better than fine gold; what I yield surpasses choice silver.

8 : 19

The tongue of the righteous is choice silver, but the heart of the wicked is of little value.

10 : 20

The words of gossip are like choice morsels; they go down to a man's inmost parts.

18 : 8

In the house of the wise are stores of choice food and oil, but a foolish man devours all he has.

21 : 20

The words of a gossip are like choice morsels; they go down to a man's inmost parts.

26 : 22

choice food

In the house of the wise are stores of choice food and oil, but a foolish man devours all he has.

21 : 20

choice morsels

The words of gossip are like choice morsels; they go down to a man's inmost parts.

18 : 8

The words of a gossip are like choice morsels; they go down to a man's inmost parts.

26 : 22

choice words

Like an earring of gold or an ornament of fine gold is a wise man's rebuke to a listening ear.

25 : 12

choices

Choose my instruction instead of silver, knowledge rather than choice gold,

8 : 10

Good understanding wins favor, but the way of the unfaithful is hard.

13 : 15

The lot is cast into the lap, but its every decision is from the Lord.

16 : 33

choose

Since they hated knowledge and did not choose to fear the Lord,

1 : 29

Do not envy a violent man or choose any of his ways,

3 : 31

Choose my instruction instead of silver, knowledge rather than choice gold,

8 : 10

How much better to get wisdom than gold, to choose understanding rather than silver!

16 : 16

chooses

In his heart a man plans his course, but the Lord determines his steps.

16 : 9

choosing

The lot is cast into the lap, but its every decision is from the Lord.

16 : 33

churning

For as churning the milk produces butter, and as twisting the nose produces blood, so stirring up anger produces strife."

30 : 33

cinnamon

I have perfumed my bed with myrrh, aloes and cinnamon.

7 : 17

cistern

Drink water from your own cistern, running water from your own well.

5 : 15

citadel

An offended brother is more unyielding than a fortified city, and disputes are like the barred gates of a citadel.

18 : 19

city
at the head of the noisy streets she cries out, in the gateways of the city she makes her speech:

1 : 21

beside the gates leading into the city, at the entrances, she cries aloud:

8 : 3

She has sent out her maids, and she calls from the highest point of the city.

9 : 3

She sits at the door of her house, on a seat at the highest point of the city,

9 : 14

The wealth of the rich is their fortified city, but poverty is the ruin of the poor.

10 : 15

When the righteous prosper, the city rejoices; when the wicked perish, there are shouts of joy.

11 : 10

Through the blessing of the upright a city is exalted, but by the mouth of the wicked it is destroyed.

11 : 11

Better a patient man than a warrior, a man who controls his temper than one who takes a city.

16 : 32

The wealth of the rich is their fortified city; they imagine it an unscalable wall.

18 : 11

An offended brother is more unyielding than a fortified city, and disputes are like the barred gates of a citadel.

18 : 19

A wise man attacks the city of the mighty and pulls down the stronghold in which they trust.

21 : 22

Like a city whose walls are broken down is a man who lacks self-control.

25 · 28

Mockers stir up a city, but wise men turn away anger.

29 : 8

Her husband is respected at the city gate, where he takes his seat among the elders of the land.

31 : 23

Give her the reward she has earned, and let her works bring her praise at the city gate.

31 : 31

city gate
Her husband is respected at the city gate, where he takes his seat among the elders of the land.

31 : 23

Give her the reward she has earned, and let her works bring her praise at the city gate.

31 : 31

civil obedience
Evil men do not understand justice, but those who seek the Lord understand it fully.

28 : 5

He who keeps the law is a discerning son, but a companion of gluttons disgraces his father.

28 : 7

If anyone turns a deaf ear to the law, even his prayers are detestable.

28 : 9

Where there is no revelation, the people cast off restraint; but blessed is he who keeps the law.

29 : 18

claim
Do not exalt yourself in the king's
presence, and do not claim a place
among great men;
25 : 6

claims
Many a man claims to have unfailing
love, but a faithful man who can find?
20 : 6

clap
"If you have played the fool and exalted
yourself, or if you have planned evil,
clap your hand over your mouth!
30 : 32

clean
Who can say, "I have kept my heart
pure; I am clean and without sin"?
20 : 9

Remove the dross from the silver, and
out comes material for the silversmith;
25 : 4

cleanse
Blows and wounds cleanse away evil,
and beatings purge the inmost being.
20 : 30

cleansed
those who are pure in their own eyes
and yet are not cleansed of their filth;
30 : 12

cliffs
coneys are creatures of little power, yet
they make their home in the crags;
30 : 26

cloak
A gift given in secret soothes anger, and
a bribe concealed in the cloak pacifies
great wrath.
21 : 14

Who has gone up to heaven and come
down? Who has gathered up the wind
in the hollow of his hands? Who has
wrapped up the waters in his cloak?
Who has established all the ends of the
earth? What is his name, and the name
of his son? Tell me if you know!
30 : 4

close
A perverse man stirs up dissension, and
a gossip separates close friends.
16 : 28

He who covers over an offense
promotes love, but whoever repeats the
matter separates close friends.
17 : 9

close friends
He who covers over an offense
promotes love, but whoever repeats the
matter separates close friends.
17 : 9

closely
My son, pay attention to what I say;
listen closely to my words.
4 : 20

closeness
Like a bird that strays from its nest is a
man who strays from his home.
27 : 8

closer
A man of many companions may come
to ruin, but there is a friend who sticks
closer than a brother.
18 : 24

closes his eyes
He who gives to the poor will lack
nothing, but he who closes his eyes to
them receives many curses.
28 : 27

clothed

When it snows, she has no fear for her household; for all of them are clothed in scarlet.

31 : 21

She makes coverings for her bed; she is clothed in fine linen and purple.

31 : 22

She is clothed with strength and dignity; she can laugh at the days to come.

31 : 25

clothes

Can a man scoop fire into his lap without his clothes being burned?

6 : 27

Then out came a woman to meet him, dressed like a prostitute and with crafty intent.

7 : 10

Take the garment of one who puts up security for a stranger; hold it in pledge if he does it for a wayward woman.

20 : 16

for drunkards and gluttons become poor, and drowsiness clothes them in rags.

23 : 21

Take a garment of one who puts up security for a stranger; hold it in pledge if he does it for a wayward woman.

27 : 13

clothing

the lambs will provide you with clothing, and the goats with the price of a field.

27 : 26

cloud

When a king's face brightens, it means life; his favor is like a rain cloud in spring

16 : 15

clouds

by his knowledge the deeps were divided, and the clouds let drop the dew.

3 : 20

when he established the clouds above and fixed securely the fountains of the deep,

8 : 28

Like clouds and wind without rain is a man who boasts of gifts he does not give.

25 : 14

coaching

Better is open rebuke than hidden love.

27 : 5

coals

Can a man walk on hot coals without his feet being scorched?

6 : 28

In doing this, you will heap burning coals on his head, and the Lord will reward you.

25 : 22

cold day

Like one who takes away a garment on a cold day, or like vinegar poured on soda, is one who sings songs to a heavy heart.

25 : 20

cold water

Like cold water to a weary soul is good news from a distant land.

25 : 25

collateral
My son, if you have put up security for your neighbor, if you have struck hands in pledge for another,

6 : 1

Take a garment of one who puts up security for a stranger; hold it in pledge if he does it for a wayward woman.

27 : 13

color
Do not gaze at wine when it is red, when it sparkles in the cup, when it goes down smoothly!

23 : 31

colored linens
I have covered my bed with colored linens from Egypt.

7 : 16

come
If they say, "Come along with us; let's lie in wait for someone's blood, let's waylay some harmless soul;

1 : 11

For the Lord gives wisdom, and from his mouth come knowledge and understanding.

2 : 6

Do not say to your neighbor, "Come back later; I'll give it tomorrow" -- when you now have it with you.

3 : 28

I have come to the brink of utter ruin in the midst of the whole assembly.

5 : 14

and poverty will come on you like a bandit and scarcity like an armed man.

6 : 11

Come, let's drink deep of love till morning; let's enjoy ourselves with love!

7 : 18

"Let all who are simple come in here!" she says to those who lack judgment.

9 : 4

"Come, eat my food and drink the wine I have mixed.

9 : 5

"Let all who are simple come in here!" she says to those who lack judgment.

9 : 16

The prospect of the righteous is joy, but the hopes of the wicked come to nothing.

10 : 28

He who guards his lips guards his life, but he who speaks rashly will come to ruin.

13 : 3

A man of many companions may come to ruin, but there is a friend who sticks closer than a brother.

18 : 24

He who oppresses the poor to increase his wealth and he who gives gifts to the rich -- both come to poverty.

22 : 16

But it will go well with those who convict the guilty, and rich blessing will come upon them.

24 : 25

thorns had come up everywhere, the ground was covered with weeds, and the stone wall was in ruins.

24 : 31

and poverty will come on you like a bandit and scarcity like an armed man.

24 : 34

it is better for him to say to you, "Come up here," than for him to humiliate you before a nobleman. What you have seen with your eyes

25 : 7

70

Like a fluttering sparrow or a darting swallow, an undeserved curse does not come to rest.

26 : 2

Who has gone up to heaven and come down? Who has gathered up the wind in the hollow of his hands? Who has wrapped up the waters in his cloak? Who has established all the ends of the earth? What is his name, and the name of his son? Tell me if you know!

30 : 4

She is clothed with strength and dignity; she can laugh at the days to come.

31 : 25

come in

"Let all who are simple come in here!" she says to those who lack judgment.

9 : 4

"Let all who are simple come in here!" she says to those who lack judgment.

9 : 16

come up here

it is better for him to say to you, "Come up here," than for him to humiliate you before a nobleman. What you have seen with your eyes

25 : 7

comes

The righteous man is rescued from trouble, and it comes on the wicked instead.

11 : 8

When wickedness comes, so does contempt, and with shame comes disgrace.

18 : 3

comfort

when you lie down, you will not be afraid; when you lie down, your sleep will be sweet.

3 : 24

command

when he gave the sea its boundary so the waters would not overstep his command, and when he marked out the foundations of the earth.

8 : 29

He who scorns instruction will pay for it, but he who respects a command is rewarded.

13 : 13

commander

It has no commander, no overseer or ruler,

6 : 7

commands

My son, if you accept my words and store up my commands within you,

2 : 1

My son, do not forget my teaching, but keep my commands in your heart,

3 : 1

he taught me and said, "Lay hold of my words with all your heart; keep my commands and you will live.

4 : 4

My son, keep your father's commands and do not forsake your mother's teaching.

6 : 20

For these commands are a lamp, this teaching is a light, and the corrections of discipline are the way to life,

6 : 23

My son, keep my words and store up my commands within you.

7 : 1

Keep my commands and you will live;
guard my teachings as the apple of your
eye.

7 : 2

Bind them on your fingers; write them
on the tablet of your heart.

7 : 3

The wise in heart accept commands, but
a chattering fool comes to ruin.

10 : 8

commit to the Lord
Commit to the Lord whatever you do,
and your plans will succeed.

16 : 3

commitment
Trust in the Lord with all your heart and
lean not on your own understanding;

3 : 5

It is a trap for a man to dedicate
something rashly and only later to
consider his vows.

20 : 25

commits
But a man who commits adultery lacks
judgment; whoever does so destroys
himself.

6 : 32

An angry man stirs up dissension, and a
hot-tempered one commits many sins.

29 : 22

commits adultery
But a man who commits adultery lacks
judgment; whoever does so destroys
himself.

6 : 32

common
Rich and poor have this in common:
The Lord is the Maker of them all.

22 : 2

The poor man and the oppressor have
this in common: The Lord gives sight to
the eyes of both.

29 : 13

common purse
throw in your lot with us, and we will
share a common purse" --

1 : 14

common sense
Does not wisdom call out? Does not
understanding raise her voice?

8 : 1

A man who lacks judgment derides his
neighbor, but a man of understanding
holds his tongue.

11 : 12

The wisdom of the prudent is to give
thought to their ways, but the folly of
fools is deception.

14 : 8

It is a trap for a man to dedicate
something rashly and only later to
consider his vows.

20 : 25

companion
He who walks with the wise grows
wise, but a companion of fools suffers
harm.

13 : 20

A man of many companions may come
to ruin, but there is a friend who sticks
closer than a brother.

18 : 24

He who keeps the law is a discerning
son, but a companion of gluttons
disgraces his father.

28 : 7

companion of prostitutes
A man who loves wisdom brings joy to his father, but a companion of prostitutes squanders his wealth.

29 : 3

companions
The accomplice of a thief is his own enemy; he is put under oath and dare not testify.

29 : 24

company
A man who strays from the path of understanding comes to rest in the company of the dead.

21 : 16

Do not envy wicked men, do not desire their company;

24 : 1

company one keeps
He who walks with the wise grows wise, but a companion of fools suffers harm.

13 : 20

compare
She is more precious than rubies; nothing you desire can compare with her.

3 : 15

for wisdom is more precious than rubies, and nothing you desire can compare with her.

8 : 11

comparison
She is more precious than rubies; nothing you desire can compare with her.

3 : 15

compassion
A fool shows his annoyance at once, but a prudent man overlooks an insult.

12 : 16

He who despises his neighbor sins, but blessed is he who is kind to the needy.

14 : 21

He who oppresses the poor shows contempt for their Maker, but whoever is kind to the needy honors God.

14 : 31

A friend loves at all times, and a brother is born for adversity.

17 : 17

He who is kind to the poor lends to the Lord, and he will reward him for what he has done.

19 : 17

If a man shuts his ears to the cry of the poor, he too will cry out and not be answered.

21 : 13

The righteous care about justice for the poor, but the wicked have no such concern.

29 : 7

She opens her arms to the poor and extends her hands to the needy.

31 : 20

compensation
He will not accept any compensation; he will refuse the bribe, however great it is.

6 : 35

complacency
For the waywardness of the simple will kill them, and the complacency of fools will destroy them;

1 : 32

complaints
Who has woe? Who has sorrow? Who has strife? Who has complaints? Who has needless bruises? Who has bloodshot eyes?

23 : 29

completeness

for they are life to those who find them
and health to a man's whole body.

4 : 22

compliments

You will vomit up the little you have
eaten and will have wasted your
compliments.

23 : 8

Whoever flatters his neighbor is
spreading a net for his feet.

29 : 5

comprehend

There are three things that are too
amazing for me, four that I do not
understand:

30 : 18

the way of an eagle in the sky, the way
of a snake on a rock, the way of a ship
on the high seas, and the way of a man
with a maiden.

30 : 19

a servant who becomes a king, a fool
who is full of food,

30 : 22

conceal

It is the glory of God to conceal a
matter; to search out a matter is the
glory of kings.

25 : 2

concealed

His malice may be concealed by
deception, but his wickedness will be
exposed in the assembly.

26 : 26

concealing sin

He who conceals his sins does not
prosper, but whoever confesses and
renounces them finds mercy.

28 : 13

conceals

He who conceals his hatred has lying
lips, and whoever spreads slander is a
fool.

10 : 18

He who conceals his sins does not
prosper, but whoever confesses and
renounces them finds mercy.

28 : 13

concern

The righteous care about justice for the
poor, but the wicked have no such
concern.

29 : 7

condemn

People curse the man who hoards grain,
but blessing crowns him who is willing
to sell.

11 : 26

condemning

Acquitting the guilty and condemning
the innocent -- the Lord detests them
both.

17 : 15

condemns

A good man obtains favor from the
Lord, but the Lord condemns a crafty
man.

12 : 2

condition

Be sure you know the condition of your
flocks, give careful attention to your
herds;

27 : 23

conduct

A fool finds pleasure in evil conduct,
but a man of understanding delights in
wisdom.

10 : 23

Even a child is known by his actions, by
whether his conduct is pure and right.

20 : 11

The way of the guilty is devious, but the conduct of the innocent is upright.

21 : 8

coneys
coneys are creatures of little power, yet they make their home in the crags;

30 : 26

confesses
He who conceals his sins does not prosper, but whoever confesses and renounces them finds mercy.

28 : 13

confidence
for the Lord will be your confidence and will keep your foot from being snared.

3 : 26

for the Lord detests a perverse man but takes the upright into his confidence.

3 : 32

A gossip betrays a confidence, but a trustworthy man keeps a secret.

11 : 13

A gossip betrays a confidence; so avoid a man who talks too much.

20 : 19

If you argue your case with a neighbor, do not betray another man's confidence,

25 : 9

Her husband has full confidence in her and lacks nothing of value.

31 : 11

confidently
The man of integrity walks securely, but he who takes crooked paths will be found out.

10 : 9

confront
He who rebukes a man will in the end gain more favor than he who has a flattering tongue.

28 : 23

confusing
Your eyes will see strange sights and your mind imagine confusing things.

23 : 33

conqueror
Better a patient man than a warrior, a man who controls his temper than one who takes a city.

16 : 32

conscience
"This is the way of an adulteress: She eats and wipes her mouth and says, 'I've done nothing wrong.'

30 : 20

consequence
From the fruit of his lips a man is filled with good things as surely as the work of his hands rewards him.

12 : 14

A fool's talk brings a rod to his back, but the lips of the wise protect them.

14 : 3

A heart at peace gives life to the body, but envy rots the bones.

14 : 30

A ruler who oppresses the poor is like a driving rain that leaves no crops.

28 : 3

He who leads the upright along an evil path will fall into his own trap, but the blameless will receive a good inheritance.

28 : 10

A man tomented by the guilt of murder will be a fugitive till death; let no one support him.

28 : 17

He who robs his father or mother and says, "It's not wrong" -- he is partner to him who destroys.

28 : 24

An evil man is snared by his own sin, but a righteous one can sing and be glad.

29 : 6

Do not slander a servant to his master, or he will curse you, and you will pay for it.

30 : 10

consequences

But since you rejected me when I called and no one gave heed when I stretched out my hand,

1 : 24

since you ignored all my advice and would not accept my rebuke,

1 : 25

I in turn will laugh at your disaster; I will mock when calamity overtakes you

1 : 26

they will eat the fruit of their ways and be filled with the fruit of their schemes.

1 : 31

None who go to her return or attain the paths of life.

2 : 19

but the wicked will be cut off from the land, and the unfaithful will be torn from it.

2 : 22

then your barns will be filled to overflowing, and your vats will brim over with new wine.

3 : 10

The Lord's curse is on the house of the wicked, but he blesses the home of the righteous.

3 : 33

The wise inherit honor, but fools he holds up to shame.

3 : 35

She will set a garland of grace on your head and present you with a crown of splendor.

4 : 9

Listen, my son, accept what I say, and the years of your life will be many.

4 : 10

But the way of the wicked is like deep darkness; they do not know what makes them stumble.

4 : 19

but in the end she is bitter as gall, sharp as a double-edged sword.

5 : 4

Her feet go down to death; her steps lead straight to the grave.

5 : 5

lest you give your best strength to others and your years to one who is cruel,

5 : 9

lest strangers feast on your wealth and your toil enrich another man's house.

5 : 10

At the end of your life you will groan, when your flesh and body are spent.

5 : 11

You will say, "How I hated discipline! How my heart spurned correction!

5 : 12

I have come to the brink of utter ruin in the midst of the whole assembly.

5 : 14

The evil deeds of a wicked man ensnare him; the cords of his sin hold him fast.

5 : 22

Therefore disaster will overtake him in an instant; he will suddenly be destroyed -- without remedy.

6 : 15

for the prostitute reduces you to a loaf of bread, and the adulteress preys upon your very life.

6 : 26

Can a man scoop fire into his lap without his clothes being burned?

6 : 27

Can a man walk on hot coals without his feet being scorched?

6 : 28

So is he who sleeps with another man's wife; no one who touches her will go unpunished.

6 : 29

Yet if he is caught, he must pay sevenfold, though it costs him all the wealth of his house.

6 : 31

But a man who commits adultery lacks judgment; whoever does so destroys himself.

6 : 32

Blows and disgrace are his lot, and his shame will never be wiped away;

6 : 33

for jealousy arouses a husband's fury, and he will show no mercy when he takes revenge.

6 : 34

Keep my commands and you will live; guard my teachings as the apple of your eye.

7 : 2

All at once he followed her like an ox going to the slaughter, like a deer stepping into a noose

7 : 22

till an arrow pierces his liver, like a bird darting into a snare, little knowing it will cost him his life.

7 : 23

Her house is a highway to the grave, leading down to the chambers of death.

7 : 27

bestowing wealth on those who love me and making their treasuries full.

8 : 21

For whoever finds me finds life and receives favor from the Lord.

8 : 35

But whoever fails to find me harms himself; all who hate me love death.

8 : 36

If you are wise, your wisdom will reward you; if you are a mocker, you alone will suffer."

9 : 12

But little do they know that the dead are there, that her guests are in the depths of the grave.

9 : 18

The Lord does not let the righteous go hungry but he thwarts the craving of the wicked.

10 : 3

Blessings crown the head of the righteous, but violence overwhelms the mouth of the wicked.

10 : 6

The man of integrity walks securely, but he who takes crooked paths will be found out.

10 : 9

The mouth of the righteous is a fountain of life, but violence overwhelms the mouth of the wicked.

10 : 11

The wages of the righteous bring them life, but the income of the wicked brings them punishment.

10 : 16

The fear of the Lord adds length to life, but the years of the wicked are cut short.

10 : 27

The way of the Lord is a refuge for the righteous, but it is the ruin of those who do evil.

10 : 29

The righteous will never be uprooted, but the wicked will not remain in the land.

10 : 30

When pride comes, then comes disgrace, but with humility comes wisdom.

11 : 2

Wealth is worthless in the day of wrath, but righteousness delivers from death.

11 : 4

The righteousness of the blameless makes a straight way for them, but the wicked are brought down by their own wickedness.

11 : 5

The righteousness of the upright delivers them, but the unfaithful are trapped by evil desires.

11 : 6

A kindhearted woman gains respect, but ruthless men gain only wealth.

11 : 16

A kind man benefits himself, but a cruel man brings trouble on himself.

11 : 17

The truly righteous man attains life, but he who pursues evil goes to his death.

11 : 19

Be sure of this: The wicked will not go unpunished, but those who are righteous will go free.

11 : 21

One man gives freely, yet gains even more; another withholds unduly, but comes to poverty.

11 : 24

He who seeks good finds goodwill, but evil comes to him who searches for it.

11 : 27

Whoever trusts in his riches will fall, but the righteous will thrive like a green leaf.

11 : 28

He who brings trouble on his family will inherit only wind, and the fool will be servant to the wise.

11 : 29

If the righteous receive their due on earth, how much more the ungodly and the sinner!

11 : 31

A good man obtains favor from the Lord, but the Lord condemns a crafty man.

12 : 2

No harm befalls the righteous, but the wicked have their fill of trouble.

12 : 21

Diligent hands will rule, but laziness ends in slave labor.

12 : 24

In the way of righteousness there is life; along that path is immortality.

12 : 28

The light of the righteous shines brightly, but the lamp of the wicked is snuffed out.

13 : 9

He who walks with the wise grows wise, but a companion of fools suffers harm.

13 : 20

A poor man's field may produce abundant food, but injustice sweeps it away.

13 : 23

The righteous eat to their hearts' content, but the stomach of the wicked goes hungry.

13 : 25

The house of the wicked will be destroyed, but the tent of the upright will flourish.

14 : 11

There is a way that seems right to a man, but in the end it leads to death.

14 : 12

The faithless will be fully repaid for their ways, and the good man rewarded for his.

14 : 14

Do not those who plot evil go astray? But those who plan what is good find love and faithfulness.

14 : 22

All hard work brings a profit, but mere talk leads only to poverty.

14 : 23

He who fears the Lord has a secure fortress, and for his children it will be a refuge.

14 : 26

Righteousness exalts a nation, but sin is a disgrace to any people.

14 : 34

The Lord detests all the proud of heart. Be sure of this: They will not go unpunished.

16 : 5

The highway of the upright avoids evil; he who guards his way guards his life.

16 : 17

Pride goes before destruction, a haughty spirit before a fall.

16 : 18

Understanding is a fountain of life to those who have it, but folly brings punishment to fools.

16 : 22

He who mocks the poor shows contempt for their Maker; whoever gloats over disaster will not go unpunished.

17 : 5

If a man pays back evil for good, evil will never leave his house.

17 : 13

A man of perverse heart does not prosper; he whose tongue is deceitful falls into trouble.

17 : 20

A false witness will not go unpunished, and he who pours out lies will not go free.

19 : 5

He who gets wisdom loves his own soul; he who cherishes understanding prospers.

19 : 8

Discipline your son, for in that there is hope; do not be a willing party to his death.

19 : 18

A hot-tempered man must pay the penalty; if you rescue him, you will have to do it again.

19 : 19

The righteous man leads a blameless life; blessed are his children after him.

20 : 7

Food gained by fraud tastes sweet to a man, but he ends up with a mouth full of gravel.

20 : 17

If a man curses his father or mother, his lamp will be snuffed out in pitch darkness.

20 : 20

The violence of the wicked will drag them away, for they refuse to do what is right.

21 : 7

A man who strays from the path of understanding comes to rest in the company of the dead.

21 : 16

A false witness will perish, and whoever listens to him will be destroyed forever.

21 : 28

A prudent man sees danger and takes refuge, but the simple keep going and suffer for it.

22 : 3

He who sows wickedness reaps trouble, and the rod of his fury will be destroyed.

22 : 8

In the end it bites like a snake and poisons like a viper.

23 : 32

If you say, "But we knew nothing about this," does not he who weighs the heart perceive it? Does not he who guards your life know it? Will he not repay each person according to what he has done?

24 : 12

for though a righteous man falls seven times, he rises again, but the wicked are brought down by calamity.

24 : 16

for those two will send sudden destruction upon them, and who knows what calamities they can bring?

24 : 22

As a north wind brings rain, so a sly tongue brings angry looks.

25 : 23

His malice may be concealed by deception, but his wickedness will be exposed in the assembly.

26 : 26

If a man digs a pit, he will fall into it; if a man rolls a stone, it will roll back on him.

26 : 27

The prudent see danger and take refuge, but the simple keep going and suffer for it.

27 : 12

He who conceals his sins does not prosper, but whoever confesses and renounces them finds mercy.

28 : 13

He whose walk is blameless is kept safe, but he whose ways are perverse will suddenly fall.

28 : 18

A faithful man will be richly blessed, but one eager to get rich will not go unpunished.

28 . 20

A stingy man is eager to get rich and is unaware that poverty awaits him.

28 : 22

He who gives to the poor will lack nothing, but he who closes his eyes to them receives many curses.

28 : 27

A man who remains stiff-necked after many rebukes will suddenly be destroyed -- without remedy.

29 : 1

When the righteous thrive, the people rejoice; when the wicked rule, the people groan.

29 : 2

By justice a king gives a country stability, but one who is greedy for bribes tears it down.

29 : 4

If a ruler listens to lies, all his officials become wicked.

29 : 12

If a man pampers his servant from youth, he will bring grief in the end.

29 : 21

consider
Go to the ant, you sluggard; consider its ways and be wise!

6 : 6

It is a trap for a man to dedicate something rashly and only later to consider his vows.

20 : 25

consistency
Let love and faithfulness never leave you; bind them around your neck, write them on the tablet of your heart.

3 : 3

conspiracy
who winks with his eye, signals with his feet and motions with his fingers,

6 : 13

constant dripping
A foolish son is his father's ruin, and a quarrelsome wife is like a constant dripping.

19 : 13

A quarrelsome wife is like a constant dripping on a rainy day;

27 : 15

construction
Wisdom has built her house; she has hewn out its seven pillars.

9 : 1

If a man digs a pit, he will fall into it; if a man rolls a stone, it will roll back on him.

26 : 27

consult
A mocker resents correction; he will not consult the wise.

15 : 12

contempt
He who oppresses the poor shows contempt for their Maker, but whoever is kind to the needy honors God.

14 : 31

He who mocks the poor shows contempt for their Maker; whoever gloats over disaster will not go unpunished.

17 : 5

When wickedness comes, so does contempt, and with shame comes disgrace.

18 : 3

Be wise, my son, and bring joy to my heart; then I can answer anyone who treats me with contempt.

27 : 11

those whose eyes are ever so haughty, whose glances are so disdainful;

30 : 13

contemptuous

He who obeys instructions guards his life, but he who is contemptuous of his ways will die.

19 : 16

content

The righteous eat to their hearts' content, but the stomach of the wicked goes hungry.

13 : 25

The fear of the Lord leads to life: Then one rests content, untouched by trouble.

19 : 23

Do not eat the food of a stingy man, do not crave his delicacies.

23 : 6

contentment

when you lie down, you will not be afraid; when you lie down, your sleep will be sweet.

3 : 24

A loving doe, a graceful deer -- may her breasts satisfy you always, may you ever be captivated by her love.

5 : 19

For whoever finds me finds life and receives favor from the Lord.

8 : 35

The prospect of the righteous is joy, but the hopes of the wicked come to nothing.

10 : 28

A man's riches may ransom his life, but a poor man hears no threat.

13 : 8

Better a dry crust with peace and quiet than a house full of feasting with strife.

17 : 1

He who loves pleasure will become poor; whoever loves wine and oil will never be rich.

21 : 17

Death and Destruction are never satisfied, and neither are the eyes of man.

27 : 20

continual

All the days of the oppressed are wretched, but the cheerful heart has a continual feast.

15 : 15

contract

A man lacking in judgment strikes hands in pledge and puts up security for his neighbor.

17 : 18

control

A man of knowledge uses words with restraint, and a man of understanding is even-tempered.

17 : 27

Even a fool is thought wise if he keeps silent, and discerning if he holds his tongue.

17 : 28

A fool gives full vent to his anger, but a wise man keeps himself under control.

29 : 11

controlled speech
A man who lacks judgment derides his
neighbor, but a man of understanding
holds his tongue.
11 : 12

controlling anger
A wise man fears the Lord and shuns
evil, but a fool is hotheaded and
reckless.
14 : 16

A patient man has great understanding,
but a quick-tempered man displays
folly.
14 : 29

A hot-tempered man must pay the
penalty; if you rescue him, you will
have to do it again.
19 : 19

A king's wrath is like the roar of a lion;
he who angers him forfeits his life.
20 : 2

controlling your temper
A quick-tempered man does foolish
things, and a crafty man is hated.
14 : 17

Better a patient man than a warrior, a
man who controls his temper than one
who takes a city.
16 : 32

Do not make friends with a hot-
tempered man, do not associate with
one easily angered,
22 : 24

convict
But it will go well with those who
convict the guilty, and rich blessing will
come upon them.
24 : 25

coolness of snow
Like the coolness of snow at harvest
time is a trustworthy messenger to those
who send him; he refreshes the spirit of
his masters.
25 : 13

copied
These are more proverbs of Solomon,
copied by the men of Hezekiah king of
Judah:
25 : 1

cords
The evil deeds of a wicked man ensnare
him; the cords of his sin hold him fast.
5 : 22

core
Above all else, guard your heart, for it
is the wellspring of life.
4 : 23

corner
He was going down the street near her
corner, walking along in the direction of
her house
7 : 8

now in the street, now in the squares, at
every corner she lurks.
7 : 12

Better to live on a corner of the roof
than share a house with a quarrelsome
wife.
21 : 9

Better to live on a corner of the roof
than share a house with a quarrelsome
wife.
25 : 24

corner of the roof
Better to live on a corner of the roof
than share a house with a quarrelsome
wife.
21 : 9

Better to live on a corner of the roof than share a house with a quarrelsome wife.

25 : 24

corrected
A servant cannot be corrected by mere words; though he understands, he will not respond.

29 : 19

correction
You will say, "How I hated discipline! How my heart spurned correction!

5 : 12

Wisdom is found on the lips of the discerning, but a rod is for the back of him who lacks judgment.

10 : 13

He who heeds discipline shows the way to life, but whoever ignores correction leads others astray.

10 : 17

Whoever loves discipline loves knowledge, but he who hates correction is stupid.

12 : 1

A wise son heeds his father's instruction, but a mocker does not listen to rebuke.

13 : 1

He who ignores discipline comes to poverty and shame, but whoever heeds correction is honored.

13 : 18

He who spares the rod hates his son, but he who loves him is careful to discipline him.

13 : 24

A fool spurns the father's discipline, but whoever heeds correction shows prudence.

15 : 5

Stern discipline awaits him who leaves the path; he who hates correction will die.

15 : 10

A mocker resents correction; he will not consult the wise.

15 : 12

He who listens to a life-giving rebuke will be at home among the wise.

15 : 31

He who ignores discipline despises himself, but whoever heeds correction gains understanding.

15 : 32

A rebuke impresses a man of discernment more than a hundred lashes a fool.

17 : 10

Like an earring of gold or an ornament of fine gold is a wise man's rebuke to a listening ear.

25 : 12

Better is open rebuke than hidden love.

27 : 5

The rod of correction imparts wisdom, but a child left to himself disgraces his mother.

29 : 15

Discipline your son, and he will give you peace; he will bring delight to your soul.

29 : 17

corrections of discipline
For these commands are a lamp, this teaching is a light, and the corrections of discipline are the way to life,

6 : 23

84

corrects
Whoever corrects a mocker invites
insult; whoever rebukes a wicked man
incurs abuse.
9 : 7

corrupt
Put away perversity from your mouth;
keep corrupt talk far from your lips.
4 : 24

A scoundrel and villain, who goes about
with a corrupt mouth,
6 : 12

A corrupt witness mocks at justice, and
the mouth of the wicked gulps down
evil.
19 : 28

corrupt mouth
A scoundrel and villain, who goes about
with a corrupt mouth,
6 : 12

corrupt witness
A corrupt witness mocks at justice, and
the mouth of the wicked gulps down
evil.
19 : 28

co-signing
My son, if you have put up security for
your neighbor, if you have struck hands
in pledge for another,
6 : 1

He who puts up security for another
will surely suffer, but whoever refuses
to strike hands in pledge is safe.
11 : 15

A man lacking in judgment strikes
hands in pledge and puts up security for
his neighbor.
17 : 18

cost
Wisdom is supreme; therefore get
wisdom. Though it cost all you have,
get understanding.
4 : 7

till an arrow pierces his liver, like a bird
darting into a snare, little knowing it
will cost him his life.
7 : 23

for he is the kind of man who is always
thinking about the cost. "Eat and
drink," he says to you, but his heart is
not with you.
23 : 7

costs
Yet if he is caught, he must pay
sevenfold, though it costs him all the
wealth of his house.
6 : 31

counsel
since you ignored all my advice and
would not accept my rebuke,
1 : 25

I give you sound learning, so do not
forsake my teaching.
4 : 2

Get wisdom, get understanding; do not
forget my words or swerve from them.
4 : 5

When you walk, your steps will not be
hampered; when you run, you will not
stumble.
4 : 12

My son, pay attention to what I say;
listen closely to my words.
4 : 20

My son, pay attention to my wisdom,
listen well to my words of insight,
5 : 1

Now then, my sons, listen to me; do not turn aside from what I say.

5 : 7

When you walk, they will guide you; when you sleep, they will watch over you; when you awake, they will speak to you.

6 : 22

Counsel and sound judgment are mine; I have understanding and power.

8 : 14

Listen to my instruction and be wise; do not ignore it.

8 : 33

For lack of guidance a nation falls, but many advisers make victory sure.

11 : 14

The plans of the righteous are just, but the advice of the wicked is deceitful.

12 : 5

The way of a fool seems right to him, but a wise man listens to advice.

12 : 15

Pride only breeds quarrels, but wisdom is found in those who take advice.

13 : 10

He who walks with the wise grows wise, but a companion of fools suffers harm.

13 : 20

Plans fail for lack of counsel, but with many advisers they succeed.

15 : 22

He who listens to a life-giving rebuke will be at home among the wise.

15 : 31

Have I not written thirty sayings for you, sayings of counsel and knowledge,

22 : 20

for waging war you need guidance, and for victory many advisers.

24 : 6

Perfume and incense bring joy to the heart, and the pleasantness of one's friend springs from his earnest counsel.

27 : 9

Do not forsake your friend and the friend of your father, and do not go to your brother's house when disaster strikes you -- better a neighbor nearby than a brother far away.

27 : 10

country

When a country is rebellious, it has many rulers, but a man of understanding and knowledge maintains order.

28 : 2

By justice a king gives a country stability, but one who is greedy for bribes tears it down.

29 : 4

course

for he guards the course of the just and protects the way of his faithful ones.

2 : 8

Folly delights a man who lacks judgment, but a man of understanding keeps a straight course.

15 : 21

In his heart a man plans his course, but the Lord determines his steps.

16 : 9

A wicked man accepts a bribe in secret to pervert the course of justice.

17 : 23

court

A truthful witness does not deceive, but a false witness pours out lies.

14 : 5

A truthful witness saves lives, but a false witness is deceitful.

14 : 25

Acquitting the guilty and condemning the innocent -- the Lord detests them both.

17 : 15

The first to present his case seems right, till another comes forward and questions him.

18 : 17

Do not exploit the poor because they are poor and do not crush the needy in court,

22 : 22

Whoever says to the guilty, "You are innocent" -- peoples will curse him and nations denounce him.

24 : 24

But it will go well with those who convict the guilty, and rich blessing will come upon them.

24 : 25

do not bring hastily to court, for what will you do in the end if your neighbor puts you to shame?

25 : 8

If a wise man goes to court with a fool, the fool rages and scoffs, and there is no peace.

29 : 9

covenant
who has left the partner of her youth and ignored the covenant she made before God.

2 : 17

covered
I have covered my bed with colored linens from Egypt.

7 : 16

thorns had come up everywhere, the ground was covered with weeds, and the stone wall was in ruins.

24 : 31

covering up
He who conceals his sins does not prosper, but whoever confesses and renounces them finds mercy.

28 : 13

coverings
She makes coverings for her bed; she is clothed in fine linen and purple.

31 : 22

covers
Hatred stirs up dissension, but love covers over all wrongs.

10 : 12

He who covers over an offense promotes love, but whoever repeats the matter separates close friends.

17 : 9

craftsman
Then I was the craftsman at his side. I was filled with delight day after day, rejoicing always in his presence,

8 : 30

crafty
Then out came a woman to meet him, dressed like a prostitute and with crafty intent.

7 : 10

A good man obtains favor from the Lord, but the Lord condemns a crafty man.

12 : 2

A quick-tempered man does foolish things, and a crafty man is hated.

14 : 17

crafty intent
Then out came a woman to meet him,
dressed like a prostitute and with crafty
intent.

7 : 10

crafty man
A good man obtains favor from the
Lord, but the Lord condemns a crafty
man.

12 : 2

crags
coneys are creatures of little power, yet
they make their home in the crags;

30 : 26

crave
Do not crave his delicacies, for that
food is deceptive.

23 : 3

Do not eat the food of a stingy man, do
not crave his delicacies.

23 : 6

"It is not for kings, O Lemuel -- not for
kings to drink wine, not for rulers to
crave beer,

31 : 4

craves
The wicked man craves evil; his
neighbor gets no mercy from him.

21 : 10

All day long he craves for more, but the
righteous give without sparing.

21 : 26

craving
The Lord does not let the righteous go
hungry but he thwarts the craving of the
wicked.

10 : 3

From the fruit of his lips a man enjoys
good things, but the unfaithful have a
craving for violence.

13 : 2

The sluggard's craving will be the death
of him, because his hands refuse to
work.

21 : 25

cravings
The sluggard craves and gets nothing,
but the desires of the diligent are fully
satisfied.

13 : 4

cream rises to the top
Do you see a man skilled in his work?
He will serve before kings, he will not
serve before obscure men.

22 : 29

creation
By wisdom the Lord laid the earth's
foundations, by understanding he set the
heavens in place;

3 : 19

"The Lord brought me forth as the first
of his works, before his deeds of old;

8 : 22

When there were no oceans, I was given
birth, when there were no springs
abounding with water;

8 : 24

before he made the earth or its fields or
any of the dust of the world.

8 : 26

I was there when he set the heavens in
place, when he marked out the horizon
on the face of the deep,

8 : 27

when he established the clouds above
and fixed securely the fountains of the
deep,

8 : 28

Ears that hear and eyes that see -- the
Lord has made them both.

20 : 12

Creator
Who has gone up to heaven and come down? Who has gathered up the wind in the hollow of his hands? Who has wrapped up the waters in his cloak? Who has established all the ends of the earth? What is his name, and the name of his son? Tell me if you know!

30 : 4

creatures
Ants are creatures of little strength, yet they store up their food in the summer;

30 : 25

coneys are creatures of little power, yet they make their home in the crags;

30 : 26

credit
Take the garment of one who puts up security for a stranger; hold it in pledge if he does it for a wayward woman.

20 : 16

cries
at the head of the noisy streets she cries out, in the gateways of the city she makes her speech:

1 : 21

beside the gates leading into the city, at the entrances, she cries aloud:

8 : 3

crime
A man tomented by the guilt of murder will be a fugitive till death; let no one support him.

28 : 17

criminal
A scoundrel and villain, who goes about with a corrupt mouth,

6 : 12

Do not lie in wait like an outlaw against a righteous man's house, do not raid his dwelling place;

24 : 15

crippled
Like a lame man's legs that hang limp is a proverb in the mouth of a fool.

26 : 7

criticism
With his mouth the godless destroys his neighbor, but through knowledge the righteous escape.

11 : 9

A fool shows his annoyance at once, but a prudent man overlooks an insult.

12 : 16

The tongue that brings healing is a tree of life, but a deceitful tongue crushes the spirit.

15 : 4

He who guards his mouth and his tongue keeps himself from calamity.

21 : 23

criticize
Do not slander a servant to his master, or he will curse you, and you will pay for it.

30 : 10

crooked
whose paths are crooked and who are devious in their ways.

2 : 15

She gives no thought to the way of life; her paths are crooked, but she knows it not.

5 : 6

All the words of my mouth are just; none of them is crooked or perverse.

8 : 8

The man of integrity walks securely, but he who takes crooked paths will be found out.

10 : 9

crooked paths

whose paths are crooked and who are devious in their ways.

2 : 15

She gives no thought to the way of life; her paths are crooked, but she knows it not.

5 : 6

The man of integrity walks securely, but he who takes crooked paths will be found out.

10 : 9

crops

Honor the Lord with your wealth, with the firstfruits of all your crops;

3 : 9

He who gathers crops in summer is a wise son, but he who sleeps during harvest is a disgraceful son.

10 : 5

A ruler who oppresses the poor is like a driving rain that leaves no crops.

28 : 3

crown

She will set a garland of grace on your head and present you with a crown of splendor.

4 : 9

Blessings crown the head of the righteous, but violence overwhelms the mouth of the wicked.

10 : 6

People curse the man who hoards grain, but blessing crowns him who is willing to sell.

11 : 26

A wife of noble character is her husband's crown, but a disgraceful wife is like decay in his bones.

12 : 4

The simple inherit folly, but the prudent are crowned with knowledge.

14 : 18

The wealth of the wise is their crown, but the folly of fools yields folly.

14 : 24

Gray hair is a crown of splendor; it is attained by a righteous life.

16 : 31

Children's children are a crown to the aged, and parents are the pride of their children.

17 : 6

for riches do not endure forever, and a crown is not secure for all generations.

27 : 24

crown of splendor

Gray hair is a crown of splendor; it is attained by a righteous life.

16 : 31

crowned

The simple inherit folly, but the prudent are crowned with knowledge.

14 : 18

crucible

The crucible for silver and the furnace for gold, but the Lord tests the heart.

17 : 3

The crucible for silver and the furnace for gold, but man is tested by the praise he receives.

27 : 21

cruel

lest you give your best strength to others and your years to one who is cruel,

5 : 9

A kind man benefits himself, but a cruel man brings trouble on himself.

11 : 17

A righteous man cares for the needs of his animal, but the kindest acts of the wicked are cruel.

12 : 10

Anger is cruel and fury overwhelming, but who can stand before jealousy?

27 : 4

crush

Do not exploit the poor because they are poor and do not crush the needy in court,

22 : 22

crushed spirit

A cheerful heart is good medicine, but a crushed spirit dries up the bones.

17 : 22

A man's spirit sustains him in sickness, but a crushed spirit who can bear?

18 : 14

crushes

The tongue that brings healing is a tree of life, but a deceitful tongue crushes the spirit.

15 : 4

A happy heart makes the face cheerful, but heartache crushes the spirit.

15 : 13

crust

Better a dry crust with peace and quiet than a house full of feasting with strife.

17 : 1

cry

and if you call out for insight and cry aloud for understanding,

2 : 3

If a man shuts his ears to the cry of the poor, he too will cry out and not be answered.

21 : 13

"The leech has two daughters. 'Give! Give!' they cry. "There are three things that are never satisfied, four that never say, 'Enough!':

30 : 15

cry aloud

and if you call out for insight and cry aloud for understanding,

2 : 3

cry of the poor

If a man shuts his ears to the cry of the poor, he too will cry out and not be answered.

21 : 13

cubs

Better to meet a bear robbed of her cubs than a fool in his folly.

17 : 12

cup

Do not gaze at wine when it is red, when it sparkles in the cup, when it goes down smoothly!

23 : 31

curry

Many curry favor with a ruler, and everyone is the friend of a man who gives gifts.

19 : 6

curse

The Lord's curse is on the house of the wicked, but he blesses the home of the righteous.

3 : 33

People curse the man who hoards grain, but blessing crowns him who is willing to sell.

11 : 26

Whoever says to the guilty, "You are innocent"　peoples will curse him and nations denounce him.

24 : 24

Like a fluttering sparrow or a darting swallow, an undeserved curse does not come to rest.

26 : 2

If a man loudly blesses his neighbor early in the morning, it will be taken as a curse.

27 : 14

A ruler who oppresses the poor is like a driving rain that leaves no crops.

28 : 3

Do not slander a servant to his master, or he will curse you, and you will pay for it.

30 : 10

"There are those who curse their fathers and do not bless their mothers;

30 : 11

cursed
but the wicked will be cut off from the land, and the unfaithful will be torn from it.

2 : 22

curses
If a man curses his father or mother, his lamp will be snuffed out in pitch darkness.

20 : 20

thorns had come up everywhere, the ground was covered with weeds, and the stone wall was in ruins.

24 : 31

He who gives to the poor will lack nothing, but he who closes his eyes to them receives many curses.

28 : 27

cursing
Put away perversity from your mouth; keep corrupt talk far from your lips.

4 : 24

The lips of the righteous know what is fitting, but the mouth of the wicked only what is perverse.

10 : 32

The heart of the righteous weighs its answers, but the mouth of the wicked gushes evil.

15 : 28

cut
There is surely a future hope for you, and your hope will not be cut off.

23 : 18

Know also that wisdom is sweet to your soul; if you find it, there is a future hope for you, and your hope will not be cut off.

24 : 14

cut off
but the wicked will be cut off from the land, and the unfaithful will be torn from it.

2 : 22

There is surely a future hope for you, and your hope will not be cut off.

23 : 18

Know also that wisdom is sweet to your soul; if you find it, there is a future hope for you, and your hope will not be cut off.

24 : 14

cut out
The mouth of the righteous brings forth wisdom, but a perverse tongue will be cut out.

10 : 31

cut short
The fear of the Lord adds length to life, but the years of the wicked are cut short.

10 : 27

cutting

Like cutting off one's feet or drinking
violence is the sending of a message by
the hand of a fool.

26 : 6

D

daily

Blessed is the man who listens to me, watching daily at my doors, waiting at my doorway.

8 : 34

Keep falsehood and lies far from me; give me neither poverty nor riches, but give me only my daily bread.

30 : 8

daily bread

Keep falsehood and lies far from me; give me neither poverty nor riches, but give me only my daily bread.

30 : 8

dam

Starting a quarrel is like breaching a dam; so drop the matter before a dispute breaks out.

17 : 14

danger

A prudent man sees danger and takes refuge, but the simple keep going and suffer for it.

22 : 3

Like a bird that strays from its nest is a man who strays from his home.

27 : 8

The prudent see danger and take refuge, but the simple keep going and suffer for it.

27 : 12

dare

The accomplice of a thief is his own enemy; he is put under oath and dare not testify.

29 : 24

dark

who leave the straight paths to walk in dark ways,

2 : 13

at twilight, as the day was fading, as the dark of night set in.

7 : 9

She gets up while it is still dark; she provides food for her family and portions for her servant girls.

31 : 15

darkness

But the way of the wicked is like deep darkness; they do not know what makes them stumble.

4 : 19

If a man curses his father or mother, his lamp will be snuffed out in pitch darkness.

20 : 20

David

The proverbs of Solomon son of David, king of Israel:

1 : 1

dawn

The path of the righteous is like the first gleam of dawn, shining ever brighter till the full light of day.

4 : 18

day

The path of the righteous is like the first gleam of dawn, shining ever brighter till the full light of day.

4 : 18

at twilight, as the day was fading, as the
dark of night set in.

7 : 9

Then I was the craftsman at his side. I
was filled with delight day after day,
rejoicing always in his presence,

8 : 30

Wealth is worthless in the day of wrath,
but righteousness delivers from death.

11 : 4

The Lord works out everything for his
own ends -- even the wicked for a day
of disaster.

16 : 4

All day long he craves for more, but the
righteous give without sparing.

21 : 26

The horse is made ready for the day of
battle, but victory rests with the Lord.

21 : 31

Do not boast about tomorrow, for you
do not know what a day may bring
forth.

27 : 1

day of battle
The horse is made ready for the day of
battle, but victory rests with the Lord.

21 : 31

day of wrath
Wealth is worthless in the day of wrath,
but righteousness delivers from death.

11 : 4

days
For through me your days will be many,
and years will be added to your life.

9 : 11

All the days of the oppressed are
wretched, but the cheerful heart has a
continual feast.

15 : 15

She brings him good, not harm, all the
days of her life.

31 . 12

She is clothed with strength and
dignity; she can laugh at the days to
come.

31 : 25

dead
For her house leads down to death and
her paths to the spirits of the dead.

2 : 18

But little do they know that the dead are
there, that her guests are in the depths
of the grave.

9 : 18

A man who strays from the path of
understanding comes to rest in the
company of the dead.

21 : 16

deadly
A fortune made by a lying tongue is a
fleeting vapor and a deadly snare.

21 : 6

Like a madman shooting firebrands or
deadly arrows

26 : 18

deadly sins
There are six things the Lord hates,
seven that are detestable to him:

6 : 16

deaf ear
If a man shuts his ears to the cry of the
poor, he too will cry out and not be
answered.

21 : 13

If anyone turns a deaf ear to the law,
even his prayers are detestable.

28 : 9

death

let's swallow them alive, like the grave, and whole, like those who go down to the pit;

1 : 12

For her house leads down to death and her paths to the spirits of the dead.

2 : 18

Her feet go down to death; her steps lead straight to the grave.

5 : 5

Her house is a highway to the grave, leading down to the chambers of death.

7 : 27

But whoever fails to find me harms himself; all who hate me love death.

8 : 36

Ill-gotten treasures are of no value, but righteousness delivers from death.

10 : 2

The fear of the Lord adds length to life, but the years of the wicked are cut short.

10 : 27

Wealth is worthless in the day of wrath, but righteousness delivers from death.

11 : 4

When a wicked man dies, his hope perishes; all he expected from his power comes to nothing.

11 : 7

When the righteous prosper, the city rejoices; when the wicked perish, there are shouts of joy.

11 : 10

The truly righteous man attains life, but he who pursues evil goes to his death.

11 : 19

The teaching of the wise is a fountain of life, turning a man from the snares of death.

13 : 14

There is a way that seems right to a man, but in the end it leads to death.

14 : 12

The fear of the Lord is a fountain of life, turning a man from the snares of death.

14 : 27

When calamity comes, the wicked are brought down, but even in death the righteous have a refuge.

14 : 32

Stern discipline awaits him who leaves the path; he who hates correction will die.

15 : 10

Death and Destruction lie open before the Lord -- how much more the hearts of men!

15 : 11

The path of life leads upward for the wise to keep him from going down to the grave.

15 : 24

A king's wrath is a messenger of death, but a wise man will appease it.

16 : 14

There is a way that seems right to a man, but in the end it leads to death.

16 : 25

The tongue has the power of life and death, and those who love it will eat its fruit.

18 : 21

He who obeys instructions guards his life, but he who is contemptuous of his ways will die.

19 : 16

Discipline your son, for in that there is hope; do not be a willing party to his death.

19 : 18

The sluggard's craving will be the death of him, because his hands refuse to work.

21 : 25

Do not withhold discipline from a child; if you punish him with the rod, he will not die.

23 : 13

Punish him with the rod and save his soul from death.

23 : 14

Rescue those being led away to death; hold back those staggering toward slaughter.

24 : 11

Death and Destruction are never satisfied, and neither are the eyes of man.

27 : 20

A man tomented by the guilt of murder will be a fugitive till death; let no one support him.

28 : 17

When the wicked rise to power, people go into hiding; but when the wicked perish, the righteous thrive.

28 : 28

A man who remains stiff-necked after many rebukes will suddenly be destroyed -- without remedy.

29 : 1

"Two things I ask of you, O Lord; do not refuse me before I die:

30 : 7

"The leech has two daughters. 'Give! Give!' they cry. "There are three things that are never satisfied, four that never say, 'Enough!':

30 : 15

the grave, the barren womb, land, which is never satisfied with water, and fire, which never says, 'Enough!'

30 : 16

debt
The rich rule over the poor, and the borrower is servant to the lender.

22 : 7

if you lack the means to pay, your very bed will be snatched from under you.

22 : 27

debts
Do not be a man who strikes hands in pledge or puts up security for debts;

22 : 26

decay
A wife of noble character is her husband's crown, but a disgraceful wife is like decay in his bones.

12 : 4

deceit
who plots evil with deceit in his heart -- he always stirs up dissension.

6 : 14

There is deceit in the hearts of those who plot evil, but joy for those who promote peace.

12 : 20

A malicious man disguises himself with his lips, but in his heart he harbors deceit.

26 : 24

deceitful
The plans of the righteous are just, but the advice of the wicked is deceitful.

12 : 5

A truthful witness saves lives, but a false witness is deceitful.

14 : 25

A man of perverse heart does not prosper; he whose tongue is deceitful falls into trouble.

17 : 20

deceitful heart
who plots evil with deceit in his heart -- he always stirs up dissension.

6 : 14

deceitful tongue
The tongue that brings healing is a tree of life, but a deceitful tongue crushes the spirit.

15 : 4

deceive
A truthful witness does not deceive, but a false witness pours out lies.

14 : 5

The wisdom of the prudent is to give thought to their ways, but the folly of fools is deception.

14 : 8

Do not testify against your neighbor without cause, or use your lips to deceive.

24 : 28

deceives
is a man who deceives his neighbor and says, "I was only joking!"

26 : 19

deception
The wicked man earns deceptive wages, but he who sows righteousness reaps a sure reward.

11 : 18

The way of a fool seems right to him, but a wise man listens to advice.

12 : 15

There is deceit in the hearts of those who plot evil, but joy for those who promote peace.

12 : 20

A truthful witness does not deceive, but a false witness pours out lies.

14 : 5

The wisdom of the prudent is to give thought to their ways, but the folly of fools is deception.

14 : 8

A fortune made by a lying tongue is a fleeting vapor and a deadly snare.

21 : 6

His malice may be concealed by deception, but his wickedness will be exposed in the assembly.

26 : 26

deceptive
Do not crave his delicacies, for that food is deceptive.

23 : 3

Charm is deceptive, and beauty is fleeting; but a woman who fears the Lord is to be praised.

31 : 30

deceptive wages
The wicked man earns deceptive wages, but he who sows righteousness reaps a sure reward.

11 : 18

decision making
The lot is cast into the lap, but its every decision is from the Lord.

16 : 33

dedicate
It is a trap for a man to dedicate something rashly and only later to consider his vows.

20 : 25

deeds

The evil deeds of a wicked man ensnare him; the cords of his sin hold him fast.
5 : 22

"The Lord brought me forth as the first of his works, before his deeds of old;
8 : 22

If you say, "But we knew nothing about this," does not he who weighs the heart perceive it? Does not he who guards your life know it? Will he not repay each person according to what he has done?
24 : 12

deep

But the way of the wicked is like deep darkness; they do not know what makes them stumble.
4 : 19

Come, let's drink deep of love till morning; let's enjoy ourselves with love!
7 : 18

I was there when he set the heavens in place, when he marked out the horizon on the face of the deep,
8 : 27

when he established the clouds above and fixed securely the fountains of the deep,
8 : 28

The words of a man's mouth are deep waters, but the fountain of wisdom is a bubbling brook.
18 : 4

Laziness brings on deep sleep, and the shiftless man goes hungry.
19 : 15

The purposes of a man's heart are deep waters, but a man of understanding draws them out.
20 : 5

The mouth of an adulteress is a deep pit; he who is under the Lord's wrath will fall into it.
22 : 14

for a prostitute is a deep pit and a wayward wife is a narrow well.
23 : 27

As the heavens are high and the earth is deep, so the hearts of kings are unsearchable.
25 : 3

deep pit

The mouth of an adulteress is a deep pit; he who is under the Lord's wrath will fall into it.
22 : 14

for a prostitute is a deep pit and a wayward wife is a narrow well.
23 : 27

deep sleep

Laziness brings on deep sleep, and the shiftless man goes hungry.
19 : 15

deep waters

The words of a man's mouth are deep waters, but the fountain of wisdom is a bubbling brook.
18 : 4

The purposes of a man's heart are deep waters, but a man of understanding draws them out.
20 : 5

deeps

by his knowledge the deeps were divided, and the clouds let drop the dew.
3 : 20

deer
A loving doe, a graceful deer -- may her
breasts satisfy you always, may you
ever be captivated by her love.
                                        5 : 19

All at once he followed her like an ox
going to the slaughter, like a deer
stepping into a noose
                                        7 : 22

defeat
Wicked men are overthrown and are no
more, but the house of the righteous
stands firm.
                                        12 : 7

Anger is cruel and fury overwhelming,
but who can stand before jealousy?
                                        27 : 4

defend
for the Lord will take up their case and
will plunder those who plunder them.
                                        22 : 23

Speak up and judge fairly; defend the
rights of the poor and needy."
                                        31 : 9

Defender
for their Defender is strong; he will take
up their case against you.
                                        23 : 11

defense
for their Defender is strong; he will take
up their case against you.
                                        23 : 11

deferred
Hope deferred makes the heart sick, but
a longing fulfilled is a tree of life.
                                        13 : 12

defiant
She is loud and defiant, her feet never
stay at home;
                                        7 : 11

defies
An unfriendly man pursues selfish ends;
he defies all sound judgment.
                                        18 : 1

defuse
A king's wrath is a messenger of death,
but a wise man will appease it.
                                        16 : 14

delicacies
Do not crave his delicacies, for that
food is deceptive.
                                        23 : 3

Do not eat the food of a stingy man, do
not crave his delicacies.
                                        23 : 6

delicious
Stolen water is sweet; food eaten in
secret is delicious!"
                                        9 : 17

delight
"How long will you simple ones love
your simple ways? How long will
mockers delight in mockery and fools
hate knowledge?
                                        1 : 22

who delight in doing wrong and rejoice
in the perverseness of evil,
                                        2 : 14

Then I was the craftsman at his side. I
was filled with delight day after day,
rejoicing always in his presence,
                                        8 : 30

rejoicing in his whole world and
delighting in mankind.
                                        8 : 31

The Lord abhors dishonest scales, but
accurate weights are his delight.
                                        11 : 1

Discipline your son, and he will give you peace; he will bring delight to your soul.

29 : 17

delights

because the Lord disciplines those he loves, as a father the son he delights in.

3 : 12

A fool finds pleasure in evil conduct, but a man of understanding delights in wisdom.

10 : 23

The Lord detests men of perverse heart but he delights in those whose ways are blameless.

11 : 20

The Lord detests lying lips, but he delights in men who are truthful.

12 : 22

A king delights in a wise servant, but a shameful servant incurs his wrath.

14 : 35

Folly delights a man who lacks judgment, but a man of understanding keeps a straight course.

15 : 21

A fool finds no pleasure in understanding but delights in airing his own opinions.

18 : 2

The father of a righteous man has great joy; he who has a wise son delights in him.

23 : 24

delirious

Your eyes will see strange sights and your mind imagine confusing things.

23 : 33

deliver

The words of the wicked lie in wait for blood, but the speech of the upright rescues them.

12 : 6

Do not say, "I'll pay you back for this wrong!" Wait for the Lord, and he will deliver you.

20 : 22

deliverance

Do not say, "I'll pay you back for this wrong!" Wait for the Lord, and he will deliver you.

20 : 22

deliverer

A wicked messenger falls into trouble, but a trustworthy envoy brings healing.

13 : 17

delivers

Ill-gotten treasures are of no value, but righteousness delivers from death.

10 : 2

Wealth is worthless in the day of wrath, but righteousness delivers from death.

11 : 4

The righteousness of the upright delivers them, but the unfaithful are trapped by evil desires.

11 : 6

demeanor

A cheerful look brings joy to the heart, and good news gives health to the bones.

15 : 30

He who winks with his eye is plotting perversity; he who purses his lips is bent on evil.

16 : 30

denounce
Whoever says to the guilty, "You are innocent" -- peoples will curse him and nations denounce him.
24 : 24

dependence
Like a bad tooth or a lame foot is reliance on the unfaithful in times of trouble.
25 : 19

deprive
It is not good to be partial to the wicked or to deprive the innocent of justice.
18 : 5

depths
by his knowledge the deeps were divided, and the clouds let drop the dew.
3 : 20

But little do they know that the dead are there, that her guests are in the depths of the grave.
9 : 18

derides
A man who lacks judgment derides his neighbor, but a man of understanding holds his tongue.
11 : 12

desert
Better to live in a desert than with a quarrelsome and ill-tempered wife.
21 : 19

deserts
Wealth brings many friends, but a poor man's friend deserts him.
19 : 4

deserve
Do not withhold good from those who deserve it, when it is in your power to act.
3 : 27

deserving
It is not good to be partial to the wicked or to deprive the innocent of justice.
18 : 5

design
Wisdom has built her house; she has hewn out its seven pillars.
9 : 1

The plans of the righteous are just, but the advice of the wicked is deceitful.
12 : 5

desirable
A good name is more desirable than great riches; to be esteemed is better than silver or gold.
22 : 1

desire
She is more precious than rubies; nothing you desire can compare with her.
3 : 15

for wisdom is more precious than rubies, and nothing you desire can compare with her.
8 : 11

What the wicked dreads will overtake him; what the righteous desire will be granted.
10 : 24

The desire of the righteous ends only in good, but the hope of the wicked only in wrath.
11 : 23

The wicked desire the plunder of evil men, but the root of the righteous flourishes.
12 : 12

From the fruit of his lips a man enjoys good things, but the unfaithful have a craving for violence.
13 : 2

A longing fulfilled is sweet to the soul, but fools detest turning from evil.

13 : 19

Of what use is money in the hand of a fool, since he has no desire to get wisdom?

17 : 16

What a man desires is unfailing love; better to be poor than a liar.

19 : 22

All day long he craves for more, but the righteous give without sparing.

21 : 26

Do not crave his delicacies, for that food is deceptive.

23 : 3

Do not eat the food of a stingy man, do not crave his delicacies.

23 : 6

Do not envy wicked men, do not desire their company;

24 : 1

desires
The sluggard craves and gets nothing, but the desires of the diligent are fully satisfied.

13 : 4

The wicked man craves evil; his neighbor gets no mercy from him.

21 : 10

Death and Destruction are never satisfied, and neither are the eyes of man.

27 : 20

despair
Stone is heavy and sand a burden, but provocation by a fool is heavier than both.

27 : 3

desperate
Men do not despise a thief if he steals to satisfy his hunger when he is starving.

6 : 30

despise
The fear of the Lord is the beginning of knowledge, but fools despise wisdom and discipline.

1 : 7

My son, do not despise the Lord's discipline and do not resent his rebuke,

3 : 11

Men do not despise a thief if he steals to satisfy his hunger when he is starving.

6 : 30

Do not rebuke a mocker or he will hate you; rebuke a wise man and he will love you.

9 : 8

Listen to your father, who gave you life, and do not despise your mother when she is old.

23 : 22

despised
A man is praised according to his wisdom, but men with warped minds are despised.

12 : 8

A quick-tempered man does foolish things, and a crafty man is hated.

14 : 17

despises
He whose walk is upright fears the Lord, but he whose ways are devious despises him.

14 : 2

He who despises his neighbor sins, but blessed is he who is kind to the needy.

14 : 21

A wise son brings joy to his father, but a foolish man despises his mother.

15 : 20

He who ignores discipline despises himself, but whoever heeds correction gains understanding.

15 : 32

destitute

"Speak up for those who cannot speak for themselves, for the rights of all who are destitute.

31 : 8

destroy

For the waywardness of the simple will kill them, and the complacency of fools will destroy them;

1 : 32

destroyed

Therefore disaster will overtake him in an instant; he will suddenly be destroyed -- without remedy.

6 : 15

The integrity of the upright guides them, but the unfaithful are destroyed by their duplicity.

11 : 3

Through the blessing of the upright a city is exalted, but by the mouth of the wicked it is destroyed.

11 : 11

The house of the wicked will be destroyed, but the tent of the upright will flourish.

14 : 11

A large population is a king's glory, but without subjects a prince is ruined.

14 : 28

A false witness will perish, and whoever listens to him will be destroyed forever.

21 : 28

He who sows wickedness reaps trouble, and the rod of his fury will be destroyed.

22 : 8

A man who remains stiff-necked after many rebukes will suddenly be destroyed -- without remedy.

29 : 1

destroys

But a man who commits adultery lacks judgment; whoever does so destroys himself.

6 : 32

With his mouth the godless destroys his neighbor, but through knowledge the righteous escape.

11 : 9

He who robs his father or mother and says, "It's not wrong" -- he is partner to him who destroys.

28 : 24

destruction

These men lie in wait for their own blood; they waylay only themselves!

1 : 18

For the waywardness of the simple will kill them, and the complacency of fools will destroy them;

1 : 32

For her house leads down to death and her paths to the spirits of the dead.

2 : 18

I have come to the brink of utter ruin in the midst of the whole assembly.

5 : 14

Therefore disaster will overtake him in an instant; he will suddenly be destroyed -- without remedy.

6 : 15

But a man who commits adultery lacks judgment; whoever does so destroys himself.

6 : 32

But little do they know that the dead are there, that her guests are in the depths of the grave.

9 : 18

The wise in heart accept commands, but a chattering fool comes to ruin.

10 : 8

He who walks maliciously causes grief, and a chattering fool comes to ruin.

10 : 10

Wise men store up knowledge, but the mouth of a fool invites ruin.

10 : 14

The way of the Lord is a refuge for the righteous, but it is the ruin of those who do evil.

10 : 29

The righteousness of the blameless makes a straight way for them, but the wicked are brought down by their own wickedness.

11 : 5

Through the blessing of the upright a city is exalted, but by the mouth of the wicked it is destroyed.

11 : 11

For lack of guidance a nation falls, but many advisers make victory sure.

11 : 14

The teaching of the wise is a fountain of life, turning a man from the snares of death.

13 : 14

The house of the wicked will be destroyed, but the tent of the upright will flourish.

14 : 11

There is a way that seems right to a man, but in the end it leads to death.

14 : 12

The fear of the Lord is a fountain of life, turning a man from the snares of death.

14 : 27

A heart at peace gives life to the body, but envy rots the bones.

14 : 30

When calamity comes, the wicked are brought down, but even in death the righteous have a refuge.

14 : 32

Righteousness exalts a nation, but sin is a disgrace to any people.

14 : 34

Stern discipline awaits him who leaves the path; he who hates correction will die.

15 : 10

Death and Destruction lie open before the Lord -- how much more the hearts of men!

15 : 11

The path of life leads upward for the wise to keep him from going down to the grave.

15 : 24

A king's wrath is a messenger of death, but a wise man will appease it.

16 : 14

Pride goes before destruction, a haughty spirit before a fall.

16 : 18

There is a way that seems right to a man, but in the end it leads to death.

16 : 25

A scoundrel plots evil, and his speech is like a scorching fire.

16 : 27

He who covers over an offense promotes love, but whoever repeats the matter separates close friends.

17 : 9

He who loves a quarrel loves sin; he who builds a high gate invites destruction.

17 : 19

A fool's lips bring him strife, and his mouth invites a beating.

18 : 6

A fool's mouth is his undoing, and his lips are a snare to his soul.

18 : 7

One who is slack in his work is brother to one who destroys.

18 : 9

Before his downfall a man's heart is proud, but humility comes before honor.

18 : 12

The tongue has the power of life and death, and those who love it will eat its fruit.

18 : 21

A man of many companions may come to ruin, but there is a friend who sticks closer than a brother.

18 : 24

A man's own folly ruins his life, yet his heart rages against the Lord.

19 : 3

A false witness will not go unpunished, and he who pours out lies will perish.

19 : 9

A foolish son is his father's ruin, and a quarrelsome wife is like a constant dripping.

19 : 13

He who obeys instructions guards his life, but he who is contemptuous of his ways will die.

19 : 16

Discipline your son, for in that there is hope; do not be a willing party to his death.

19 : 18

A king's wrath is like the roar of a lion; he who angers him forfeits his life.

20 : 2

A fortune made by a lying tongue is a fleeting vapor and a deadly snare.

21 : 6

The Righteous One takes note of the house of the wicked and brings the wicked to ruin.

21 : 12

A false witness will perish, and whoever listens to him will be destroyed forever.

21 : 28

He who sows wickedness reaps trouble, and the rod of his fury will be destroyed.

22 : 8

The mouth of an adulteress is a deep pit; he who is under the Lord's wrath will fall into it.

22 : 14

for drunkards and gluttons become poor, and drowsiness clothes them in rags.

23 : 21

for a prostitute is a deep pit and a wayward wife is a narrow well.

23 : 27

for those two will send sudden destruction upon them, and who knows what calamities they can bring?

24 : 22

I ike a city whose walls are broken down is a man who lacks self-control.

25 : 28

Death and Destruction are never satisfied, and neither are the eyes of man.

27 : 20

A ruler who oppresses the poor is like a driving rain that leaves no crops.

28 : 3

Blessed is the man who always fears the Lord, but he who hardens his heart falls into trouble.

28 : 14

He who robs his father or mother and says, "It's not wrong" -- he is partner to him who destroys.

28 : 24

When the wicked rise to power, people go into hiding; but when the wicked perish, the righteous thrive.

28 : 28

A man who loves wisdom brings joy to his father, but a companion of prostitutes squanders his wealth.

29 : 3

By justice a king gives a country stability, but one who is greedy for bribes tears it down.

29 : 4

When the wicked thrive, so does sin, but the righteous will see their downfall.

29 : 16

Do you see a man who speaks in haste? There is more hope for a fool than for him.

29 : 20

A man's pride brings him low, but a man of lowly spirit gains honor.

29 : 23

deteriorate
The memory of the righteous will be a blessing, but the name of the wicked will rot.

10 : 7

determines
In his heart a man plans his course, but the Lord determines his steps.

16 : 9

detest
My mouth speaks what is true, for my lips detest wickedness.

8 : 7

A longing fulfilled is sweet to the soul, but fools detest turning from evil.

13 : 19

Kings detest wrongdoing, for a throne is established through righteousness.

16 : 12

The schemes of folly are sin, and men detest a mocker.

24 : 9

The righteous detest the dishonest; the wicked detest the upright.

29 : 27

detestable
There are six things the Lord hates, seven that are detestable to him:

6 : 16

The sacrifice of the wicked is detestable -- how much more so when brought with evil intent!

21 : 27

If anyone turns a deaf ear to the law,
even his prayers are detestable.

28 : 9

detests

for the Lord detests a perverse man but
takes the upright into his confidence.

3 : 32

The Lord detests men of perverse heart
but he delights in those whose ways are
blameless.

11 : 20

The Lord detests lying lips, but he
delights in men who are truthful.

12 : 22

The Lord detests the sacrifice of the
wicked, but the prayer of the upright
pleases him.

15 : 8

The Lord detests the way of the wicked
but he loves those who pursue
righteousness.

15 : 9

The Lord detests the thoughts of the
wicked, but those of the pure are
pleasing to him.

15 : 26

The Lord detests all the proud of heart.
Be sure of this: They will not go
unpunished.

16 : 5

Acquitting the guilty and condemning
the innocent -- the Lord detests them
both.

17 : 15

Differing weights and differing
measures -- the Lord detests them both.

20 : 10

The Lord detests differing weights, and
dishonest scales do not please him.

20 : 23

devious

whose paths are crooked and who are
devious in their ways.

2 : 15

He whose walk is upright fears the
Lord, but he whose ways are devious
despises him.

14 : 2

The way of the guilty is devious, but the
conduct of the innocent is upright.

21 : 8

devour

In the house of the wise are stores of
choice food and oil, but a foolish man
devours all he has.

21 : 20

those whose teeth are swords and whose
jaws are set with knives to devour the
poor from the earth, the needy from
among mankind.

30 : 14

dew

by his knowledge the deeps were
divided, and the clouds let drop the
dew.

3 : 20

dew on the grass

A king's rage is like the roar of a lion,
but his favor is like dew on the grass.

19 : 12

dictatorship

Like a roaring lion or a charging bear is
a wicked man ruling over a helpless
people.

28 : 15

die

He will die for lack of discipline, led
astray by his own great folly.

5 : 23

The lips of the righteous nourish many, but fools die for lack of judgment.

10 : 21

Stern discipline awaits him who leaves the path; he who hates correction will die.

15 : 10

He who obeys instructions guards his life, but he who is contemptuous of his ways will die.

19 : 16

A man who strays from the path of understanding comes to rest in the company of the dead.

21 : 16

Do not withhold discipline from a child; if you punish him with the rod, he will not die.

23 : 13

Punish him with the rod and save his soul from death.

23 : 14

"Two things I ask of you, O Lord; do not refuse me before I die:

30 : 7

dies
When a wicked man dies, his hope perishes; all he expected from his power comes to nothing.

11 : 7

Without wood a fire goes out; without gossip a quarrel dies down.

26 : 20

diet
Eat honey, my son, for it is good; honey from the comb is sweet to your taste.

24 : 13

If you find honey, just eat enough -- too much of it, and you will vomit.

25 : 16

He who is full loathes honey, but to the hungry even what is bitter tastes sweet.

27 . 7

different
Differing weights and differing measures -- the Lord detests them both.

20 : 10

differing measures
Differing weights and differing measures -- the Lord detests them both.

20 : 10

differing weights
Differing weights and differing measures -- the Lord detests them both.

20 : 10

The Lord detests differing weights, and dishonest scales do not please him.

20 : 23

difficulties
When the storm has swept by, the wicked are gone, but the righteous stand firm forever.

10 : 25

Better to live on a corner of the roof than share a house with a quarrelsome wife.

21 : 9

difficulty
Good understanding wins favor, but the way of the unfaithful is hard.

13 : 15

dignified
"There are three things that are stately in their stride, four that move with stately bearing:

30 : 29

dignity
She is clothed with strength and dignity; she can laugh at the days to come.

31 : 25

digs

If a man digs a pit, he will fall into it; if a man rolls a stone, it will roll back on him.

26 : 27

dilemma

The lot is cast into the lap, but its every decision is from the Lord.

16 : 33

diligent

Lazy hands make a man poor, but diligent hands bring wealth.

10 : 4

Diligent hands will rule, but laziness ends in slave labor.

12 : 24

The lazy man does not roast his game, but the diligent man prizes his possessions.

12 : 27

The sluggard craves and gets nothing, but the desires of the diligent are fully satisfied.

13 : 4

The plans of the diligent lead to profit as surely as haste leads to poverty.

21 : 5

She is like the merchant ships, bringing her food from afar.

31 : 14

She sets about her work vigorously; her arms are strong for her tasks.

31 : 17

She sees that her trading is profitable, and her lamp does not go out at night.

31 : 18

She watches over the affairs of her household and does not eat the bread of idleness.

31 : 27

diligent man

The lazy man does not roast his game, but the diligent man prizes his possessions.

12 : 27

dine

When you sit to dine with a ruler, note well what is before you,

23 : 1

directed by the Lord

A man's steps are directed by the Lord. How then can anyone understand his own way?

20 : 24

directing

For these commands are a lamp, this teaching is a light, and the corrections of discipline are the way to life,

6 : 23

direction

in all your ways acknowledge him, and he will make your paths straight.

3 : 6

Do not swerve to the right or the left; keep your foot from evil.

4 : 27

He was going down the street near her corner, walking along in the direction of her house

7 : 8

The desire of the righteous ends only in good, but the hope of the wicked only in wrath.

11 : 23

Commit to the Lord whatever you do, and your plans will succeed.

16 : 3

Many are the plans in the man's heart, but it is the Lord's purpose that prevails.

19 : 21

directly
Let your eyes look straight ahead, fix
your gaze directly before you.

4 : 25

directs
The integrity of the upright guides
them, but the unfaithful are destroyed
by their duplicity.

11 : 3

The king's heart is in the hand of the
Lord; he directs it like a watercourse
wherever he pleases.

21 : 1

dirty jokes
Put away perversity from your mouth;
keep corrupt talk far from your lips.

4 : 24

disagreement
A quarrelsome wife is like a constant
dripping on a rainy day;

27 : 15

disappear
Wicked men are overthrown and are no
more, but the house of the righteous
stands firm.

12 : 7

disapprove
or the Lord will see and disapprove and
turn his wrath away from him.

24 : 18

disaster
I in turn will laugh at your disaster; I
will mock when calamity overtakes you

1 : 26

when calamity overtakes you like a
storm, when disaster sweeps over you
like a whirlwind, when distress and
trouble overwhelm you.

1 : 27

Have no fear of sudden disaster or of
the ruin that overtakes the wicked,

3 : 25

Therefore disaster will overtake him in
an instant; he will suddenly be
destroyed -- without remedy.

6 : 15

The Lord works out everything for his
own ends -- even the wicked for a day
of disaster.

16 : 4

He who mocks the poor shows
contempt for their Maker; whoever
gloats over disaster will not go
unpunished.

17 : 5

Do not forsake your friend and the
friend of your father, and do not go to
your brother's house when disaster
strikes you -- better a neighbor nearby
than a brother far away.

27 : 10

discerning
let the wise listen and add to their
learning, and let the discerning get
guidance --

1 : 5

To the discerning all of them are right;
they are faultless to those who have
knowledge.

8 : 9

Wisdom is found on the lips of the
discerning, but a rod is for the back of
him who lacks judgment.

10 : 13

The mocker seeks wisdom and finds
none, but knowledge comes easily to
the discerning.

14 : 6

Wisdom reposes in the heart of the discerning and even among fools she lets herself be known.

14 : 33

The discerning heart seeks knowledge, but the mouth of a fool feeds on folly.

15 : 14

The wise in heart are called discerning, and pleasant words promote instruction.

16 : 21

A discerning man keeps wisdom in view, but a fool's eyes wander to the ends of the earth.

17 : 24

Even a fool is thought wise if he keeps silent, and discerning if he holds his tongue.

17 : 28

The heart of the discerning acquires knowledge; the ears of the wise seek it out.

18 : 15

Flog a mocker, and the simple will learn prudence; rebuke a discerning man, and he will gain knowledge.

19 : 25

discerning heart
The discerning heart seeks knowledge, but the mouth of a fool feeds on folly.

15 : 14

discerning man
A discerning man keeps wisdom in view, but a fool's eyes wander to the ends of the earth.

17 : 24

Flog a mocker, and the simple will learn prudence; rebuke a discerning man, and he will gain knowledge.

19 : 25

discerning son
He who keeps the law is a discerning son, but a companion of gluttons disgraces his father.

28 : 7

discernment
My son, preserve sound judgment and discernment, do not let them out of your sight;

3 : 21

He who works his land will have abundant food, but he who chases fantasies lacks judgment.

12 : 11

A rebuke impresses a man of discernment more than a hundred lashes a fool.

17 : 10

When a king sits on his throne to judge, he winnows out all evil with his eyes.

20 : 8

A rich man may be wise in his own eyes, but a poor man who has discernment sees through him.

28 : 11

discipline
for attaining wisdom and discipline; for understanding words of insight;

1 : 2

for acquiring a disciplined and prudent life, doing what is right and just and fair;

1 : 3

The fear of the Lord is the beginning of knowledge, but fools despise wisdom and discipline.

1 : 7

My son, do not despise the Lord's discipline and do not resent his rebuke,

3 : 11

Avoid it, do not travel on it; turn from it and go on your way.

4 : 15

You will say, "How I hated discipline! How my heart spurned correction!

5 : 12

He will die for lack of discipline, led astray by his own great folly.

5 : 23

For these commands are a lamp, this teaching is a light, and the corrections of discipline are the way to life,

6 : 23

Do not let your heart turn to her ways or stray into her paths.

7 : 25

The woman Folly is loud; she is undisciplined and without knowledge.

9 : 13

Wisdom is found on the lips of the discerning, but a rod is for the back of him who lacks judgment.

10 : 13

He who heeds discipline shows the way to life, but whoever ignores correction leads others astray.

10 : 17

When words are many, sin is not absent, but he who holds his tongue is wise.

10 : 19

Whoever loves discipline loves knowledge, but he who hates correction is stupid.

12 : 1

He who guards his lips guards his life, but he who speaks rashly will come to ruin.

13 : 3

He who ignores discipline comes to poverty and shame, but whoever heeds correction is honored.

13 : 18

He who spares the rod hates his son, but he who loves him is careful to discipline him.

13 : 24

A fool spurns the father's discipline, but whoever heeds correction shows prudence.

15 : 5

Stern discipline awaits him who leaves the path; he who hates correction will die.

15 : 10

A mocker resents correction; he will not consult the wise.

15 : 12

He who listens to a life-giving rebuke will be at home among the wise.

15 : 31

He who ignores discipline despises himself, but whoever heeds correction gains understanding.

15 : 32

Discipline your son, for in that there is hope; do not be a willing party to his death.

19 : 18

Penalties are prepared for mockers, and beatings for the backs of fools.

19 : 29

Blows and wounds cleanse away evil, and beatings purge the inmost being.

20 : 30

Folly is bound up in the heart of a child, but the rod of discipline will drive it far from him.

22 : 15

Do not wear yourself out to get rich;
have the wisdom to show restraint.

23 : 4

Do not withhold discipline from a child;
if you punish him with the rod, he will
not die.

23 : 13

Punish him with the rod and save his
soul from death.

23 : 14

Do not join those who drink too much
wine or gorge themselves on meat,

23 : 20

Buy the truth and do not sell it; get
wisdom, discipline and understanding.

23 : 23

A whip for the horse, a halter for the
donkey, and a rod for the backs of
fools!

26 : 3

Better is open rebuke than hidden love.

27 : 5

The rod of correction imparts wisdom,
but a child left to himself disgraces his
mother.

29 : 15

Discipline your son, and he will give
you peace; he will bring delight to your
soul.

29 : 17

A servant cannot be corrected by mere
words; though he understands, he will
not respond.

29 : 19

disciplined
A man of knowledge uses words with
restraint, and a man of understanding is
even-tempered.

17 : 27

disciplined life
for acquiring a disciplined and prudent
life, doing what is right and just and
fair;

1 : 3

disciplines
because the Lord disciplines those he
loves, as a father the son he delights in.

3 : 12

discontent
the grave, the barren womb, land, which
is never satisfied with water, and fire,
which never says, 'Enough!'

30 : 16

discourage
Like one who takes away a garment on
a cold day, or like vinegar poured on
soda, is one who sings songs to a heavy
heart.

25 : 20

discreet
A gift given in secret soothes anger, and
a bribe concealed in the cloak pacifies
great wrath.

21 : 14

discreetly
The sluggard is wiser in his own eyes
than seven men who answer discreetly.

26 : 16

discretion
for giving prudence to the simple,
knowledge and discretion to the young -
-

1 : 4

Discretion will protect you, and
understanding will guard you.

2 : 11

that you may maintain discretion and
your lips may preserve knowledge.

5 : 2

I, wisdom, dwell together with prudence; I possess knowledge and discretion.

8 . 12

When words are many, sin is not absent, but he who holds his tongue is wise.

10 : 19

Like a gold ring in a pig's snout is a beautiful woman who shows no discretion.

11 : 22

disdainful
those whose eyes are ever so haughty, whose glances are so disdainful;

30 : 13

disgrace
I have come to the brink of utter ruin in the midst of the whole assembly.

5 : 14

Blows and disgrace are his lot, and his shame will never be wiped away;

6 : 33

When pride comes, then comes disgrace, but with humility comes wisdom.

11 : 2

The righteous hate what is false, but the wicked bring shame and disgrace.

13 : 5

Righteousness exalts a nation, but sin is a disgrace to any people.

14 : 34

When wickedness comes, so does contempt, and with shame comes disgrace.

18 : 3

He who robs his father and drives out his mother is a son who brings shame and disgrace.

19 : 26

disgraceful
A wife of noble character is her husband's crown, but a disgraceful wife is like decay in his bones.

12 : 4

disgraceful son
He who gathers crops in summer is a wise son, but he who sleeps during harvest is a disgraceful son.

10 : 5

A wise servant will rule over a disgraceful son, and will share the inheritance as one of the brothers.

17 : 2

disgraceful wife
A wife of noble character is her husband's crown, but a disgraceful wife is like decay in his bones.

12 : 4

disgraces
He who keeps the law is a discerning son, but a companion of gluttons disgraces his father.

28 : 7

The rod of correction imparts wisdom, but a child left to himself disgraces his mother.

29 : 15

disguises
A malicious man disguises himself with his lips, but in his heart he harbors deceit.

26 : 24

dish
The sluggard buries his hand in the dish; he will not even bring it back to his mouth!

19 : 24

The sluggard buries his hand in the dish; he is too lazy to bring it back to his mouth.

26 : 15

dishonest
who winks with his eye, signals with
his feet and motions with his fingers,
6 : 13

The Lord abhors dishonest scales, but
accurate weights are his delight.
11 : 1

The plans of the righteous are just, but
the advice of the wicked is deceitful.
12 : 5

The Lord detests differing weights, and
dishonest scales do not please him.
20 : 23

The righteous detest the dishonest; the
wicked detest the upright.
29 : 27

dishonest scales
The Lord abhors dishonest scales, but
accurate weights are his delight.
11 : 1

The Lord detests differing weights, and
dishonest scales do not please him.
20 : 23

dishonesty
Dishonest money dwindles away, but he
who gathers money little by little makes
it grow.
13 : 11

Food gained by fraud tastes sweet to a
man, but he ends up with a mouth full
of gravel.
20 : 17

By justice a king gives a country
stability, but one who is greedy for
bribes tears it down.
29 : 4

dishonor
Like tying a stone in a sling is the
giving of honor to a fool.
26 : 8

Otherwise, I may have too much and
disown you and say, 'Who is the Lord?'
Or I may become poor and steal, and so
dishonor the name of my God.
30 : 9

"There are those who curse their fathers
and do not bless their mothers;
30 : 11

The eye that mocks a father, that scorns
obedience to a mother, will be pecked
out by the ravens of the valley, will be
eaten by the vultures.
30 : 17

dislike
Seldom set foot in your neighbor's
house -- too much of you, and he will
hate you.
25 : 17

disobedience
for their feet rush into sin, they are swift
to shed blood.
1 : 16

I would not obey my teachers or listen
to my instructors.
5 : 13

An evil man is bent only on rebellion; a
merciless official will be sent against
him.
17 : 11

The violence of the wicked will drag
them away, for they refuse to do what is
right.
21 : 7

If anyone turns a deaf ear to the law,
even his prayers are detestable.
28 : 9

"There are those who curse their fathers
and do not bless their mothers;
30 : 11

disobedient
The Lord's curse is on the house of the wicked, but he blesses the home of the righteous.

3 : 33

disobey
I would not obey my teachers or listen to my instructors.

5 : 13

disown
Otherwise, I may have too much and disown you and say, 'Who is the Lord?' Or I may become poor and steal, and so dishonor the name of my God.

30 : 9

dispute
Starting a quarrel is like breaching a dam; so drop the matter before a dispute breaks out.

17 : 14

disputes
Casting the lot settles disputes and keeps strong opponents apart.

18 : 18

An offended brother is more unyielding than a fortified city, and disputes are like the barred gates of a citadel.

18 : 19

disrespect
He who mocks the poor shows contempt for their Maker; whoever gloats over disaster will not go unpunished.

17 : 5

Arrogant lips are unsuited to a fool -- how much worse lying lips to a ruler!

17 : 7

dissension
who plots evil with deceit in his heart -- he always stirs up dissension.

6 : 14

a false witness who pours out lies and a man who stirs up dissension among brothers.

6 : 19

Hatred stirs up dissension, but love covers over all wrongs.

10 : 12

A hot-tempered man stirs up dissension, but a patient man calms a quarrel.

15 : 18

A perverse man stirs up dissension, and a gossip separates close friends.

16 : 28

A greedy man stirs up dissension, but he who trusts in the Lord will prosper.

28 : 25

An angry man stirs up dissension, and a hot-tempered one commits many sins.

29 : 22

distaff
In her hand she holds the distaff and grasps the spindle with her fingers.

31 : 19

distant
Like cold water to a weary soul is good news from a distant land.

25 : 25

distant land
Like cold water to a weary soul is good news from a distant land.

25 : 25

distress
when calamity overtakes you like a storm, when disaster sweeps over you like a whirlwind, when distress and trouble overwhelm you.

1 : 27

distrustful
who winks with his eye, signals with his feet and motions with his fingers,

6 : 13

disturb

If a man loudly blesses his neighbor early in the morning, it will be taken as a curse.

27 : 14

disunity

a false witness who pours out lies and a man who stirs up dissension among brothers.

6 : 19

Hatred stirs up dissension, but love covers over all wrongs.

10 : 12

A perverse man stirs up dissension, and a gossip separates close friends.

16 : 28

Starting a quarrel is like breaching a dam; so drop the matter before a dispute breaks out.

17 : 14

He who loves a quarrel loves sin; he who builds a high gate invites destruction.

17 : 19

A greedy man stirs up dissension, but he who trusts in the Lord will prosper.

28 : 25

An angry man stirs up dissension, and a hot-tempered one commits many sins.

29 : 22

division

He who loves a quarrel loves sin; he who builds a high gate invites destruction.

17 : 19

Casting the lot settles disputes and keeps strong opponents apart.

18 : 18

An offended brother is more unyielding than a fortified city, and disputes are like the barred gates of a citadel.

18 : 19

divorce

an unloved woman who is married, and a maidservant who displaces her mistress.

30 : 23

do

But the way of the wicked is like deep darkness; they do not know what makes them stumble.

4 : 19

then do this, my son, to free yourself, since you have fallen into your neighbor's hands: Go and humble yourself; press your plea with your neighbor!

6 : 3

But little do they know that the dead are there, that her guests are in the depths of the grave.

9 : 18

The way of the Lord is a refuge for the righteous, but it is the ruin of those who do evil.

10 : 29

Commit to the Lord whatever you do, and your plans will succeed.

16 : 3

A poor man is shunned by all his relatives -- how much more do his friends avoid him! Though he pursues them with pleading, they are nowhere to be found.

19 : 7

A hot-tempered man must pay the penalty; if you rescue him, you will have to do it again.

19 : 19

To do what is right and just is more acceptable to the Lord than sacrifice.

21 : 3

The violence of the wicked will drag them away, for they refuse to do what is right.

21 : 7

Do not say, "I'll do to him as he has done to me; I'll pay that man back for what he did."

24 : 29

do not bring hastily to court, for what will you do in the end if your neighbor puts you to shame?

25 : 8

Do you see a man wise in his own eyes? There is more hope for a fool than for him.

26 : 12

Do you see a man who speaks in haste? There is more hope for a fool than for him.

29 : 20

Many women do noble things, but you surpass them all."

31 : 29

do evil
The way of the Lord is a refuge for the righteous, but it is the ruin of those who do evil.

10 : 29

do not
Listen, my son, to your father's instruction and do not forsake your mother's teaching.

1 : 8

My son, if sinners entice you, do not give in to them.

1 : 10

my son, do not go along with them, do not set foot on their paths;

1 : 15

My son, do not forget my teaching, but keep my commands in your heart,

3 : 1

Do not be wise in your own eyes; fear the Lord and shun evil.

3 : 7

My son, do not despise the Lord's discipline and do not resent his rebuke,

3 : 11

My son, preserve sound judgment and discernment, do not let them out of your sight;

3 : 21

Do not withhold good from those who deserve it, when it is in your power to act.

3 : 27

Do not say to your neighbor, "Come back later; I'll give it tomorrow" -- when you now have it with you.

3 : 28

Do not plot harm against your neighbor, who lives trustfully near you.

3 : 29

Do not accuse a man for no reason -- when he has done you no harm.

3 : 30

Do not envy a violent man or choose any of his ways,

3 : 31

I give you sound learning, so do not forsake my teaching.

4 : 2

Get wisdom, get understanding; do not forget my words or swerve from them.

4 : 5

Do not forsake wisdom, and she will protect you; love her, and she will watch over you.

4 : 6

Hold on to instruction, do not let it go; guard it well, for it is your life.

4 : 13

Do not set foot on the path of the wicked or walk in the way of evil men.

4 : 14

Avoid it, do not travel on it; turn from it and go on your way.

4 : 15

But the way of the wicked is like deep darkness; they do not know what makes them stumble.

4 : 19

Do not let them out of your sight, keep them within your heart;

4 : 21

Do not swerve to the right or the left; keep your foot from evil.

4 : 27

Now then, my sons, listen to me; do not turn aside from what I say.

5 : 7

Keep to a path far from her, do not go near the door of her house,

5 : 8

My son, keep your father's commands and do not forsake your mother's teaching.

6 : 20

Do not lust in your heart after her beauty or let her captivate you with her eyes,

6 : 25

Men do not despise a thief if he steals to satisfy his hunger when he is starving.

6 : 30

Do not let your heart turn to her ways or stray into her paths.

7 : 25

Listen to my instruction and be wise; do not ignore it.

8 : 33

Do not rebuke a mocker or he will hate you; rebuke a wise man and he will love you.

9 : 8

Do not those who plot evil go astray? But those who plan what is good find love and faithfulness.

14 : 22

Discipline your son, for in that there is hope; do not be a willing party to his death.

19 : 18

Do not love sleep or you will grow poor; stay awake and you will have food to spare.

20 : 13

Do not say, "I'll pay you back for this wrong!" Wait for the Lord, and he will deliver you.

20 : 22

The Lord detests differing weights, and dishonest scales do not please him.

20 : 23

Do not exploit the poor because they are poor and do not crush the needy in court,

22 : 22

Do not make friends with a hot-tempered man, do not associate with one easily angered,

22 : 24

Do not be a man who strikes hands in pledge or puts up security for debts;

22 : 26

120

Do not move an ancient boundary stone
set up by your forefathers.

22 : 28

Do not crave his delicacies, for that
food is deceptive.

23 : 3

Do not wear yourself out to get rich;
have the wisdom to show restraint.

23 : 4

Do not eat the food of a stingy man, do
not crave his delicacies.

23 : 6

Do not speak to a fool, for he will scorn
the wisdom of your words.

23 : 9

Do not move an ancient boundary stone
or encroach on the fields of the
fatherless,

23 : 10

Do not withhold discipline from a child;
if you punish him with the rod, he will
not die.

23 : 13

Do not let your heart envy sinners, but
always be zealous for the fear of the
Lord.

23 : 17

Do not join those who drink too much
wine or gorge themselves on meat,

23 : 20

Listen to your father, who gave you life,
and do not despise your mother when
she is old.

23 : 22

Buy the truth and do not sell it; get
wisdom, discipline and understanding.

23 : 23

Do not gaze at wine when it is red,
when it sparkles in the cup, when it
goes down smoothly!

23 : 31

Do not envy wicked men, do not desire
their company;

24 : 1

Do not lie in wait like an outlaw against
a righteous man's house, do not raid his
dwelling place;

24 : 15

Do not gloat when your enemy falls;
when he stumbles, do not let your heart
rejoice,

24 : 17

Do not fret because of evil men or be
envious of the wicked,

24 : 19

Fear the Lord and the king, my son, and
do not join with the rebellious,

24 : 21

Do not testify against your neighbor
without cause, or use your lips to
deceive.

24 : 28

Do not say, "I'll do to him as he has
done to me; I'll pay that man back for
what he did."

24 : 29

Do not exalt yourself in the king's
presence, and do not claim a place
among great men;

25 : 6

do not bring hastily to court, for what
will you do in the end if your neighbor
puts you to shame?

25 : 8

If you argue your case with a neighbor,
do not betray another man's confidence,

25 : 9

Do not answer a fool according to his folly, or you will be like him yourself.

27 : 4

Though his speech is charming, do not believe him, for seven abominations fill his heart.

26 : 25

Do not boast about tomorrow, for you do not know what a day may bring forth.

27 : 1

Do not forsake your friend and the friend of your father, and do not go to your brother's house when disaster strikes you -- better a neighbor nearby than a brother far away.

27 : 10

for riches do not endure forever, and a crown is not secure for all generations.

27 : 24

Evil men do not understand justice, but those who seek the Lord understand it fully.

28 : 5

Do not add to his words, or he will rebuke you and prove you a liar.

30 : 6

"Two things I ask of you, O Lord; do not refuse me before I die:

30 : 7

Do not slander a servant to his master, or he will curse you, and you will pay for it.

30 : 10

"There are those who curse their fathers and do not bless their mothers;

30 : 11

do not spend your strength on women, your vigor on those who ruin kings.

31 : 3

do what is right
To do what is right and just is more acceptable to the Lord than sacrifice.

21 : 3

The violence of the wicked will drag them away, for they refuse to do what is right.

21 : 7

do wrong
To show partiality is not good -- yet a man will do wrong for a piece of bread.

28 : 21

doe
A loving doe, a graceful deer -- may her breasts satisfy you always, may you ever be captivated by her love.

5 : 19

does not
The Lord does not let the righteous go hungry but he thwarts the craving of the wicked.

10 : 3

She watches over the affairs of her household and does not eat the bread of idleness.

31 : 27

dog
As a dog returns to its vomit, so a fool repeats his folly.

26 : 11

Like one who seizes a dog by the ears is a passer-by who meddles in a quarrel not his own.

26 : 17

doing
who delight in doing wrong and rejoice in the perverseness of evil,

2 : 14

doing what is right
for acquiring a disciplined and prudent life, doing what is right and just and fair;

1 : 3

doing your best
All hard work brings a profit, but mere talk leads only to poverty.

14 : 23

done
He who is kind to the poor lends to the Lord, and he will reward him for what he has done.

19 : 17

donkey
A whip for the horse, a halter for the donkey, and a rod for the backs of fools!

26 : 3

don't commit adultery
Drink water from your own cistern, running water from your own well.

5 : 15

door
Keep to a path far from her, do not go near the door of her house,

5 : 8

She sits at the door of her house, on a seat at the highest point of the city,

9 : 14

As a door turns on its hinges, so a sluggard turns on his bed.

26 : 14

doors
Blessed is the man who listens to me, watching daily at my doors, waiting at my doorway.

8 : 34

doorway
Blessed is the man who listens to me, watching daily at my doors, waiting at my doorway.

8 : 34

double-edged sword
but in the end she is bitter as gall, sharp as a double-edged sword.

5 : 4

down
let's swallow them alive, like the grave, and whole, like those who go down to the pit;

1 : 12

For her house leads down to death and her paths to the spirits of the dead.

2 : 18

when you lie down, you will not be afraid; when you lie down, your sleep will be sweet.

3 : 24

Her feet go down to death; her steps lead straight to the grave.

5 : 5

He was going down the street near her corner, walking along in the direction of her house

7 : 8

Many are the victims she has brought down; her slain are a mighty throng.

7 : 26

Her house is a highway to the grave, leading down to the chambers of death.

7 : 27

The righteousness of the blameless makes a straight way for them, but the wicked are brought down by their own wickedness.

11 : 5

An anxious heart weighs a man down, but a kind word cheers him up.

12 : 25

The wise woman builds her house, but with her own hands the foolish one tears hers down.

14 : 1

Evil men will bow down in the presence of the good, and the wicked at the gates of the righteous.

14 : 19

When calamity comes, the wicked are brought down, but even in death the righteous have a refuge.

14 : 32

The path of life leads upward for the wise to keep him from going down to the grave.

15 : 24

The Lord tears down the proud man's house, but he keeps the widow's boundaries intact.

15 : 25

A violent man entices his neighbor and leads him down a path that is not good.

16 : 29

The words of gossip are like choice morsels; they go down to a man's inmost parts.

18 : 8

A corrupt witness mocks at justice, and the mouth of the wicked gulps down evil.

19 : 28

A wise man attacks the city of the mighty and pulls down the stronghold in which they trust.

21 : 22

Do not gaze at wine when it is red, when it sparkles in the cup, when it goes down smoothly!

23 : 31

for though a righteous man falls seven times, he rises again, but the wicked are brought down by calamity.

24 : 16

Like a city whose walls are broken down is a man who lacks self-control.

25 : 28

Without wood a fire goes out; without gossip a quarrel dies down.

26 : 20

The words of a gossip are like choice morsels; they go down to a man's inmost parts.

26 : 22

By justice a king gives a country stability, but one who is greedy for bribes tears it down.

29 : 4

Who has gone up to heaven and come down? Who has gathered up the wind in the hollow of his hands? Who has wrapped up the waters in his cloak? Who has established all the ends of the earth? What is his name, and the name of his son? Tell me if you know!

30 : 4

down to the grave
The path of life leads upward for the wise to keep him from going down to the grave.

15 : 24

downfall
Many are the victims she has brought down; her slain are a mighty throng.

7 : 26

Before his downfall a man's heart is proud, but humility comes before honor.

18 : 12

When the wicked thrive, so does sin, but the righteous will see their downfall.

29 : 16

drag
The violence of the wicked will drag them away, for they refuse to do what is right.

21 : 7

draws
The purposes of a man's heart are deep waters, but a man of understanding draws them out.

20 : 5

dreads
What the wicked dreads will overtake him; what the righteous desire will be granted.

10 : 24

dreams
A longing fulfilled is sweet to the soul, but fools detest turning from evil.

13 : 19

Plans fail for lack of counsel, but with many advisers they succeed.

15 : 22

Commit to the Lord whatever you do, and your plans will succeed.

16 : 3

Many are the plans in the man's heart, but it is the Lord's purpose that prevails.

19 : 21

dressed
Then out came a woman to meet him, dressed like a prostitute and with crafty intent.

7 : 10

dries up
A cheerful heart is good medicine, but a crushed spirit dries up the bones.

17 : 22

drink
They eat the bread of wickedness and drink the wine of violence.

4 : 17

Drink water from your own cistern, running water from your own well.

5 : 15

Come, let's drink deep of love till morning; let's enjoy ourselves with love!

7 : 18

"Come, eat my food and drink the wine I have mixed.

9 : 5

for he is the kind of man who is always thinking about the cost. "Eat and drink," he says to you, but his heart is not with you.

23 : 7

Do not join those who drink too much wine or gorge themselves on meat,

23 : 20

Those who linger over wine, who go to sample bowls of mixed wine,

23 : 30

"They hit me," you will say, "but I'm not hurt! They beat me, but I don't feel it! When will I wake up so I can find another drink?"

23 : 35

If your enemy is hungry, give him food to eat; if he is thirsty, give him water to drink.

25 . 21

"It is not for kings, O Lemuel -- not for kings to drink wine, not for rulers to crave beer,

31 : 4

lest they drink and forget what the law decrees, and deprive all the oppressed of the rights.

31 : 5

Give beer to those who are perishing, wine to those who are in anguish;

31 : 6

let them drink and forget their poverty and remember their misery no more.

31 : 7

drink deep of love
Come, let's drink deep of love till morning; let's enjoy ourselves with love!

7 : 18

drinking
Who has woe? Who has sorrow? Who has strife? Who has complaints? Who has needless bruises? Who has bloodshot eyes?

23 : 29

Do not gaze at wine when it is red, when it sparkles in the cup, when it goes down smoothly!

23 : 31

In the end it bites like a snake and poisons like a viper.

23 : 32

Your eyes will see strange sights and your mind imagine confusing things.

23 : 33

You will be like one sleeping on the high seas, lying on top of the rigging.

23 : 34

Like cutting off one's feet or drinking violence is the sending of a message by the hand of a fool.

26 : 6

Give beer to those who are perishing, wine to those who are in anguish;

31 : 6

let them drink and forget their poverty and remember their misery no more.

31 : 7

drip
For the lips of an adulteress drip honey, and her speech is smoother than oil;

5 : 3

dripping
A foolish son is his father's ruin, and a quarrelsome wife is like a constant dripping.

19 : 13

A quarrelsome wife is like a constant dripping on a rainy day;

27 : 15

drive
The laborer's appetite works for him; his hunger drives him on.

16 : 26

drive out
He who robs his father and drives out his mother is a son who brings shame and disgrace.

19 : 26

Drive out the mocker, and out goes strife; quarrels and insults are ended.

22 : 10

driven from the land
The righteous will never be uprooted, but the wicked will not remain in the land.

10 : 30

drives
A wise king winnows out the wicked;
he drives the threshing wheel over
them.

20 : 26

driving rain
A ruler who oppresses the poor is like a
driving rain that leaves no crops.

28 : 3

drop
Starting a quarrel is like breaching a
dam; so drop the matter before a dispute
breaks out.

17 : 14

dross
Remove the dross from the silver, and
out comes material for the silversmith;

25 : 4

drowsiness
for drunkards and gluttons become
poor, and drowsiness clothes them in
rags.

23 : 21

drunk
Who has woe? Who has sorrow? Who
has strife? Who has complaints? Who
has needless bruises? Who has
bloodshot eyes?

23 : 29

Your eyes will see strange sights and
your mind imagine confusing things.

23 : 33

You will be like one sleeping on the
high seas, lying on top of the rigging.

23 : 34

"They hit me," you will say, "but I'm
not hurt! They beat me, but I don't feel
it! When will I wake up so I can find
another drink?"

23 : 35

Give beer to those who are perishing,
wine to those who are in anguish;

31 : 6

let them drink and forget their poverty
and remember their misery no more.

31 : 7

drunkard
Do not gaze at wine when it is red,
when it sparkles in the cup, when it
goes down smoothly!

23 : 31

Like a thornbush in a drunkard's hand is
a proverb in the mouth of a fool.

26 : 9

drunkards
for drunkards and gluttons become
poor, and drowsiness clothes them in
rags.

23 : 21

drunkenness
Wine is a mocker and beer a brawler;
whoever is led astray by them is not
wise.

20 : 1

Do not join those who drink too much
wine or gorge themselves on meat,

23 : 20

dry crust
Better a dry crust with peace and quiet
than a house full of feasting with strife.

17 : 1

dry land
"The leech has two daughters. 'Give!
Give!' they cry. "There are three things
that are never satisfied, four that never
say, 'Enough!':

30 : 15

due
If the righteous receive their due on earth, how much more the ungodly and the sinner!

11 : 31

dumb
I am the most ignorant of men; I do not have a man's understanding.

30 : 2

duplicity
The integrity of the upright guides them, but the unfaithful are destroyed by their duplicity.

11 : 3

dust
before he made the earth or its fields or any of the dust of the world.

8 : 26

dwell
For the upright will live in the land, and the blameless will remain in it;

2 : 21

I, wisdom, dwell together with prudence; I possess knowledge and discretion.

8 : 12

dwelling place
Do not lie in wait like an outlaw against a righteous man's house, do not raid his dwelling place;

24 : 15

dwindles
Dishonest money dwindles away, but he who gathers money little by little makes it grow.

13 : 11

E

eager
A stingy man is eager to get rich and is unaware that poverty awaits him.

28 : 22

eager hands
She selects wool and flax and works with eager hands.

31 : 13

eager to get rich
A faithful man will be richly blessed, but one eager to get rich will not go unpunished.

28 : 20

eagle
Cast but a glance at riches, and they are gone, for they will surely sprout wings and fly off to the sky like an eagle.

23 : 5

the way of an eagle in the sky, the way of a snake on a rock, the way of a ship on the high seas, and the way of a man with a maiden.

30 : 19

ear
turning your ear to wisdom and applying your heart to understanding,

2 : 2

If a man shuts his ears to the cry of the poor, he too will cry out and not be answered.

21 : 13

Like an earring of gold or an ornament of fine gold is a wise man's rebuke to a listening ear.

25 : 12

If anyone turns a deaf ear to the law, even his prayers are detestable.

28 : 9

earned
Give her the reward she has earned, and let her works bring her praise at the city gate.

31 : 31

earnest
Perfume and incense bring joy to the heart, and the pleasantness of one's friend springs from his earnest counsel.

27 : 9

earnings
She considers a field and buys it; out of her earnings she plants a vineyard.

31 : 16

earns
The wicked man earns deceptive wages, but he who sows righteousness reaps a sure reward.

11 : 18

earring
Like an earring of gold or an ornament of fine gold is a wise man's rebuke to a listening ear.

25 : 12

ears
The heart of the discerning acquires knowledge; the ears of the wise seek it out.

18 : 15

Ears that hear and eyes that see -- the Lord has made them both.

20 : 12

129

Apply your heart to instruction and your
ears to words of knowledge.

23 : 12

Like one who seizes a dog by the ears is
a passer-by who meddles in a quarrel
not his own.

26 : 17

earth

By wisdom the Lord laid the earth's
foundations, by understanding he set the
heavens in place;

3 : 19

by me princes govern, and all nobles
who rule on earth.

8 : 16

I was appointed from eternity, from the
beginning, before the world began,

8 : 23

before he made the earth or its fields or
any of the dust of the world.

8 : 26

when he gave the sea its boundary so
the waters would not overstep his
command, and when he marked out the
foundations of the earth.

8 : 29

rejoicing in his whole world and
delighting in mankind.

8 : 31

If the righteous receive their due on
earth, how much more the ungodly and
the sinner!

11 : 31

A discerning man keeps wisdom in
view, but a fool's eyes wander to the
ends of the earth.

17 : 24

As the heavens are high and the earth is
deep, so the hearts of kings are
unsearchable.

25 : 3

Who has gone up to heaven and come
down? Who has gathered up the wind
in the hollow of his hands? Who has
wrapped up the waters in his cloak?
Who has established all the ends of the
earth? What is his name, and the name
of his son? Tell me if you know!

30 : 4

those whose teeth are swords and whose
jaws are set with knives to devour the
poor from the earth, the needy from
among mankind.

30 : 14

"Under three things the earth trembles,
under four it cannot bear up:

30 : 21

"Four things on earth are small, yet they
are extremely wise:

30 : 24

ease

but whoever listens to me will live in
safety and be at ease, without fear of
harm."

1 : 33

The mocker seeks wisdom and finds
none, but knowledge comes easily to
the discerning.

14 : 6

easily

The mocker seeks wisdom and finds
none, but knowledge comes easily to
the discerning.

14 : 6

Do not make friends with a hot-
tempered man, do not associate with
one easily angered,

22 : 24

easy prey

"Let all who are simple come in here!"
she says to those who lack judgment.

9 : 16

eat

they will eat the fruit of their ways and be filled with the fruit of their schemes.

1 : 31

They eat the bread of wickedness and drink the wine of violence.

4 : 17

"Come, eat my food and drink the wine I have mixed.

9 : 5

Stolen water is sweet; food eaten in secret is delicious!"

9 : 17

The righteous eat to their hearts' content, but the stomach of the wicked goes hungry.

13 : 25

The tongue has the power of life and death, and those who love it will eat its fruit.

18 : 21

When you sit to dine with a ruler, note well what is before you,

23 : 1

Do not crave his delicacies, for that food is deceptive.

23 : 3

Do not eat the food of a stingy man, do not crave his delicacies.

23 : 6

for he is the kind of man who is always thinking about the cost. "Eat and drink," he says to you, but his heart is not with you.

23 : 7

Eat honey, my son, for it is good; honey from the comb is sweet to your taste.

24 : 13

If you find honey, just eat enough -- too much of it, and you will vomit.

25 : 16

If your enemy is hungry, give him food to eat; if he is thirsty, give him water to drink.

25 : 21

It is not good to eat too much honey, not is it honorable to seek one's own honor.

25 : 27

He who tends a fig tree will eat its fruit, and he who looks after his master will be honored.

27 : 18

She watches over the affairs of her household and does not eat the bread of idleness.

31 : 27

eaten

You will vomit up the little you have eaten and will have wasted your compliments.

23 : 8

The eye that mocks a father, that scorns obedience to a mother, will be pecked out by the ravens of the valley, will be eaten by the vultures.

30 : 17

eats

"This is the way of an adulteress: She eats and wipes her mouth and says, 'I've done nothing wrong.'

30 : 20

edge

I have come to the brink of utter ruin in the midst of the whole assembly.

5 ; 14

edify

The lips of the righteous nourish many, but fools die for lack of judgment.

10 : 21

education

Instruct a wise man and he will be wiser still; teach a righteous man and he will add to his learning.

9 : 9

Pride only breeds quarrels, but wisdom is found in those who take advice.

13 : 10

The teaching of the wise is a fountain of life, turning a man from the snares of death.

13 : 14

The heart of the discerning acquires knowledge; the ears of the wise seek it out.

18 : 15

ego

Before his downfall a man's heart is proud, but humility comes before honor.

18 : 12

Do not exalt yourself in the king's presence, and do not claim a place among great men;

25 : 6

A lying tongue hates those it hurts, and a flattering mouth works ruin.

26 : 28

Let another praise you, and not your own mouth; someone else, and not your own lips.

27 : 2

Anger is cruel and fury overwhelming, but who can stand before jealousy?

27 : 4

Egypt

I have covered my bed with colored linens from Egypt.

7 : 16

elation

When the righteous triumph, there is great elation; but when the wicked rise to power, men go into hiding.

28 : 12

elderly

Gray hair is a crown of splendor; it is attained by a righteous life.

16 : 31

Children's children are a crown to the aged, and parents are the pride of their children.

17 : 6

The glory of young men is their strength, gray hair the splendor of the old.

20 : 29

Listen to your father, who gave you life, and do not despise your mother when she is old.

23 : 22

elders

Her husband is respected at the city gate, where he takes his seat among the elders of the land.

31 : 23

embarrass

Righteousness exalts a nation, but sin is a disgrace to any people.

14 : 34

do not bring hastily to court, for what will you do in the end if your neighbor puts you to shame?

25 : 8

or he who hears it may shame you and you will never lose your bad reputation.

25 : 10

embarrassment

I have come to the brink of utter ruin in the midst of the whole assembly.

5 : 14

When pride comes, then comes disgrace, but with humility comes wisdom.

11 : 2

When wickedness comes, so does contempt, and with shame comes disgrace.

18 : 3

He who answers before listening -- that is his folly and his shame.

18 : 13

He who robs his father and drives out his mother is a son who brings shame and disgrace.

19 : 26

embrace

She is a tree of life to those who embrace her; those who lay hold of her will be blessed.

3 : 18

Esteem her, and she will exalt you; embrace her, and she will honor you.

4 : 8

Why be captivated, my son, by an adulteress? Why embrace the bosom of another man's wife?

5 : 20

embraced

She took hold of him and kissed him and with a brazen face she said:

7 : 13

embracing wisdom

Say to wisdom, "You are my sister," and call understanding your kinsman;

7 : 4

emotional stability

Better a patient man than a warrior, a man who controls his temper than one who takes a city.

16 : 32

emotions

Even in laughter the heart may ache, and joy may end in grief.

14 : 13

employee

The laborer's appetite works for him; his hunger drives him on.

16 : 26

employment

Lazy hands make a man poor, but diligent hands bring wealth.

10 : 4

One who is slack in his work is brother to one who destroys.

18 : 9

emptiness

But the way of the wicked is like deep darkness; they do not know what makes them stumble.

4 : 19

The prospect of the righteous is joy, but the hopes of the wicked come to nothing.

10 : 28

Better to be a nobody and yet have a servant than pretend to be somebody and have no food.

12 : 9

Where there are no oxen, the manger is empty, but from the strength of an ox comes an abundant harvest.

14 : 4

for the evil man has no future hope, and the lamp of the wicked will be snuffed out.

24 : 20

emptiness of life

A kindhearted woman gains respect, but ruthless men gain only wealth.

11 : 16

empty

Where there are no oxen, the manger is empty, but from the strength of an ox comes an abundant harvest.

14 : 4

encourage

Let another praise you, and not your own mouth; someone else, and not your own lips.

27 : 2

encouragement

The lips of the righteous nourish many, but fools die for lack of judgment.

10 : 21

An anxious heart weighs a man down, but a kind word cheers him up.

12 : 25

The wise woman builds her house, but with her own hands the foolish one tears hers down.

14 : 1

The tongue that brings healing is a tree of life, but a deceitful tongue crushes the spirit.

15 : 4

A man finds joy in giving an apt reply-- and how good is a timely word!

15 : 23

A cheerful look brings joy to the heart, and good news gives health to the bones.

15 : 30

The wise in heart are called discerning, and pleasant words promote instruction.

16 : 21

A wise man's heart guides his mouth, and his lips promote instruction.

16 : 23

Pleasant words are a honeycomb, sweet to the soul and healing to the bones

16 : 24

A friend loves at all times, and a brother is born for adversity.

17 : 17

The tongue has the power of life and death, and those who love it will eat its fruit.

18 : 21

He who loves a pure heart and whose speech is gracious will have the king for his friend.

22 : 11

A word aptly spoken is like apples of gold in settings of silver.

25 : 11

Like the coolness of snow at harvest time is a trustworthy messenger to those who send him; he refreshes the spirit of his masters.

25 : 13

Like cold water to a weary soul is good news from a distant land.

25 : 25

Do not forsake your friend and the friend of your father, and do not go to your brother's house when disaster strikes you -- better a neighbor nearby than a brother far away.

27 : 10

encourager

A generous man will prosper; he who refreshes others will himself be refreshed.

11 : 25

encroach

Do not move an ancient boundary stone or encroach on the fields of the fatherless,

23 : 10

end

Such is the end of all who go after ill-gotten gain; it takes away the life of those who get it.

1 : 19

but in the end she is bitter as gall, sharp as a double-edged sword.

5 : 4

At the end of your life you will groan, when your flesh and body are spent.

5 : 11

There is a way that seems right to a man, but in the end it leads to death.

14 : 12

Even in laughter the heart may ache, and joy may end in grief.

14 : 13

There is a way that seems right to a man, but in the end it leads to death.

16 : 25

Listen to advice and accept instruction, and in the end you will be wise.

19 : 20

An inheritance quickly gained at the beginning will not be blessed at the end.

20 : 21

In the end it bites like a snake and poisons like a viper.

23 : 32

do not bring hastily to court, for what will you do in the end if your neighbor puts you to shame?

25 : 8

He who rebukes a man will in the end gain more favor than he who has a flattering tongue

28 : 23

If a man pampers his servant from youth, he will bring grief in the end.

29 : 21

end of the day

at twilight, as the day was fading, as the dark of night set in.

7 : 9

end result

But little do they know that the dead are there, that her guests are in the depths of the grave.

9 : 18

The desire of the righteous ends only in good, but the hope of the wicked only in wrath.

11 : 23

There is surely a future hope for you, and your hope will not be cut off.

23 : 18

ended

Drive out the mocker, and out goes strife; quarrels and insults are ended.

22 : 10

ends

The desire of the righteous ends only in good, but the hope of the wicked only in wrath.

11 : 23

Diligent hands will rule, but laziness ends in slave labor.

12 : 24

The Lord works out everything for his own ends -- even the wicked for a day of disaster.

16 : 4

A discerning man keeps wisdom in view, but a fool's eyes wander to the ends of the earth.

17 : 24

An unfriendly man pursues selfish ends; he defies all sound judgment.

18 : 1

Food gained by fraud tastes sweet to a man, but he ends up with a mouth full of gravel.

20 : 17

Who has gone up to heaven and come down? Who has gathered up the wind in the hollow of his hands? Who has wrapped up the waters in his cloak? Who has established all the ends of the earth? What is his name, and the name of his son? Tell me if you know!

30 : 4

ends of the earth

A discerning man keeps wisdom in view, but a fool's eyes wander to the ends of the earth.

17 : 24

endure

Truthful lips endure forever, but a lying tongue lasts only a moment.

12 : 19

for riches do not endure forever, and a crown is not secure for all generations.

27 : 24

"Under three things the earth trembles, under four it cannot bear up:

30 : 21

enduring

With me are the riches and honor, enduring wealth and prosperity.

8 : 18

enemies

When a man's ways are pleasing to the Lord, he makes even his enemies live at peace with him.

16 : 7

enemy

Do not gloat when your enemy falls; when he stumbles, do not let your heart rejoice,

24 : 17

Seldom set foot in your neighbor's house -- too much of you, and he will hate you.

25 : 17

If your enemy is hungry, give him food to eat; if he is thirsty, give him water to drink.

25 : 21

Wounds from a friend can be trusted, but an enemy multiplies kisses.

27 : 6

The accomplice of a thief is his own enemy; he is put under oath and dare not testify.

29 : 24

enjoy

May your fountain be blessed, and may you rejoice in the wife of your youth.

5 : 18

Come, let's drink deep of love till morning; let's enjoy ourselves with love!

7 : 18

A tyrannical ruler lacks judgment, but he who hates ill-gotten gain will enjoy a long life.

28 : 16

enjoys

From the fruit of his lips a man enjoys good things, but the unfaithful have a craving for violence.

13 : 2

enough

If you find honey, just eat enough -- too much of it, and you will vomit.

25 : 16

"The leech has two daughters. 'Give! Give!' they cry. "There are three things that are never satisfied, four that never say, 'Enough!':

30 : 15

the grave, the barren womb, land, which is never satisfied with water, and fire, which never says, 'Enough!'

30 : 16

enrich

lest strangers feast on your wealth and your toil enrich another man's house.

5 : 10

ensnare

The evil deeds of a wicked man ensnare him; the cords of his sin hold him fast.

5 : 22

ensnared

if you have been trapped by what you said, ensnared by the words of your mouth,

6 : 2

or you may learn his ways and get yourself ensnared.

22 : 25

enter

For wisdom will enter your heart, and knowledge will be pleasant to your soul.

2 : 10

enthusiasm

It is not good to have zeal without knowledge, nor to be hasty and miss the way.

19 : 2

entice

My son, if sinners entice you, do not give in to them.

1 : 10

A violent man entices his neighbor and leads him down a path that is not good.

16 : 29

entire

rejoicing in his whole world and delighting in mankind.

8 : 31

entrance

beside the gates leading into the city, at the entrances, she cries aloud:

8 : 3

entrap

If they say, "Come along with us; let's lie in wait for someone's blood, let's waylay some harmless soul;

1 : 11

envious

Do not fret because of evil men or be envious of the wicked,

24 : 19

envoy

A wicked messenger falls into trouble, but a trustworthy envoy brings healing.

13 : 17

envy

Do not envy a violent man or choose any of his ways,

3 : 31

A heart at peace gives life to the body, but envy rots the bones.

14 : 30

Do not let your heart envy sinners, but always be zealous for the fear of the Lord.

23 : 17

Do not envy wicked men, do not desire their company;

24 : 1

escape

With his mouth the godless destroys his neighbor, but through knowledge the righteous escape.

11 : 9

escapes

An evil man is trapped by his sinful talk, but a righteous man escapes trouble.

12 : 13

essence

The wicked desire the plunder of evil men, but the root of the righteous flourishes.

12 : 12

establish

Kings detest wrongdoing, for a throne is established through righteousness.

16 : 12

established

when he established the clouds above and fixed securely the fountains of the deep,

8 : 28

A man cannot be established through wickedness, but the righteous cannot be uprooted.

12 : 3

By wisdom a house is built, and through understanding it is established;

24 : 3

Who has gone up to heaven and come down? Who has gathered up the wind in the hollow of his hands? Who has wrapped up the waters in his cloak? Who has established all the ends of the earth? What is his name, and the name of his son? Tell me if you know!

30 : 4

esteem

Esteem her, and she will exalt you; embrace her, and she will honor you.

4 : 8

esteemed

A good name is more desirable than great riches; to be esteemed is better than silver or gold.

22 : 1

eternal

When the storm has swept by, the wicked are gone, but the righteous stand firm forever.

10 : 25

Truthful lips endure forever, but a lying tongue lasts only a moment.

12 : 19

eternal reward

He who is kind to the poor lends to the Lord, and he will reward him for what he has done.

19 : 17

eternity

I was appointed from eternity, from the beginning, before the world began,

8 : 23

When the storm has swept by, the wicked are gone, but the righteous stand firm forever.

10 : 25

Do not boast about tomorrow, for you do not know what a day may bring forth.

27 : 1

for riches do not endure forever, and a crown is not secure for all generations.

27 : 24

evangelism

The fruit of the righteous is a tree of life, and he who wins souls is wise.

11 : 30

The lips of the wise spread knowledge; not so the hearts of fools.

15 : 7

evening

at twilight, as the day was fading, as the dark of night set in.

7 : 9

even-tempered

A man of knowledge uses words with restraint, and a man of understanding is even-tempered.

17 : 27

everlasting life

In the way of righteousness there is life; along that path is immortality.

12 : 28

everlasting love

A loving doe, a graceful deer -- may her breasts satisfy you always, may you ever be captivated by her love.

5 : 19

every

Every prudent man acts out of knowledge, but a fool exposes his folly.

13 : 16

everyone

Many curry favor with a ruler, and everyone is the friend of a man who gives gifts.

19 : 6

everywhere

The eyes of the Lord are everywhere, keeping watch on the wicked and the good.

15 : 3

evil

These men lie in wait for their own blood; they waylay only themselves!

1 : 18

who delight in doing wrong and rejoice in the perverseness of evil,

2 : 14

Do not be wise in your own eyes; fear the Lord and shun evil.

3 : 7

Do not plot harm against your neighbor, who lives trustfully near you.

3 : 29

for the Lord detests a perverse man but takes the upright into his confidence.

3 : 32

For they cannot sleep till they do evil; they are robbed of slumber till they make someone fall.

4 : 16

They eat the bread of wickedness and drink the wine of violence.

4 : 17

But the way of the wicked is like deep darkness; they do not know what makes them stumble.

4 : 19

Do not swerve to the right or the left; keep your foot from evil.

4 : 27

She gives no thought to the way of life; her paths are crooked, but she knows it not.

5 : 6

The evil deeds of a wicked man ensnare him; the cords of his sin hold him fast.
5 : 22

who winks with his eye, signals with his feet and motions with his fingers,
6 : 13

who plots evil with deceit in his heart -- he always stirs up dissension.
6 : 14

a heart that devises wicked schemes, feet that are quick to rush into evil,
6 : 18

now in the street, now in the squares, at every corner she lurks.
7 : 12

The way of the Lord is a refuge for the righteous, but it is the ruin of those who do evil.
10 : 29

A kindhearted woman gains respect, but ruthless men gain only wealth.
11 : 16

The truly righteous man attains life, but he who pursues evil goes to his death.
11 : 19

He who seeks good finds goodwill, but evil comes to him who searches for it.
11 : 27

A man cannot be established through wickedness, but the righteous cannot be uprooted.
12 : 3

The wicked desire the plunder of evil men, but the root of the righteous flourishes.
12 : 12

There is deceit in the hearts of those who plot evil, but joy for those who promote peace.
12 : 20

Righteousness guards the man of integrity, but wickedness overthrows the sinner.
13 : 6

A longing fulfilled is sweet to the soul, but fools detest turning from evil.
13 : 19

The house of the wicked will be destroyed, but the tent of the upright will flourish.
14 : 11

A wise man fears the Lord and shuns evil, but a fool is hotheaded and reckless.
14 : 16

A quick-tempered man does foolish things, and a crafty man is hated.
14 : 17

Do not those who plot evil go astray? But those who plan what is good find love and faithfulness.
14 : 22

The eyes of the Lord are everywhere, keeping watch on the wicked and the good.
15 : 3

The Lord detests the way of the wicked but he loves those who pursue righteousness.
15 : 9

All the days of the oppressed are wretched, but the cheerful heart has a continual feast.
15 : 15

The heart of the righteous weighs its answers, but the mouth of the wicked gushes evil.
15 : 28

The Lord is far from the wicked but he hears the prayer of the righteous.
15 : 29

Through love and faithfulness sin is atoned for; through the fear of the Lord a man avoids evil.

16 : 6

A scoundrel plots evil, and his speech is like a scorching fire.

16 : 27

He who winks with his eye is plotting perversity; he who purses his lips is bent on evil.

16 : 30

If a man pays back evil for good, evil will never leave his house.

17 : 13

A man of perverse heart does not prosper; he whose tongue is deceitful falls into trouble.

17 : 20

A wicked man accepts a bribe in secret to pervert the course of justice.

17 : 23

It is not good to be partial to the wicked or to deprive the innocent of justice.

18 : 5

A corrupt witness mocks at justice, and the mouth of the wicked gulps down evil.

19 : 28

When a king sits on his throne to judge, he winnows out all evil with his eyes.

20 : 8

Blows and wounds cleanse away evil, and beatings purge the inmost being.

20 : 30

Haughty eyes and a proud heart, the lamp of the wicked, are sin!

21 : 4

The violence of the wicked will drag them away, for they refuse to do what is right.

21 : 7

The wicked man craves evil; his neighbor gets no mercy from him.

21 : 10

The Righteous One takes note of the house of the wicked and brings the wicked to ruin.

21 : 12

The wicked become a ransom for the righteous, and the unfaithful for the upright.

21 : 18

Do not envy wicked men, do not desire their company;

24 : 1

for their hearts plot violence, and their lips talk about making trouble.

24 : 2

He who plots evil will be known as a schemer,

24 : 8

Do not fret because of evil men or be envious of the wicked,

24 : 19

for the evil man has no future hope, and the lamp of the wicked will be snuffed out.

24 : 20

Like a coating of glaze over earthenware are fervent lips with an evil heart.

26 : 23

His malice may be concealed by deception, but his wickedness will be exposed in the assembly.

26 : 26

Those who forsake the law praise the wicked, but those who keep the law resist them.

28 · 4

"If you have played the fool and exalted yourself, or if you have planned evil, clap your hand over your mouth!

30 : 32

evil behavior

To fear the Lord is to hate evil; I hate pride and arrogance, evil behavior and perverse speech.

8 : 13

evil conduct

A fool finds pleasure in evil conduct, but a man of understanding delights in wisdom.

10 : 23

evil desires

The righteousness of the upright delivers them, but the unfaithful are trapped by evil desires.

11 : 6

evil heart

Like a coating of glaze over earthenware are fervent lips with an evil heart.

26 : 23

evil intent

The sacrifice of the wicked is detestable -- how much more so when brought with evil intent!

21 : 27

Like a coating of glaze over earthenware are fervent lips with an evil heart.

26 : 23

evil lips

A wicked man listens to evil lips; a liar pays attention to a malicious tongue.

17 : 4

evil man

Whoever corrects a mocker invites insult; whoever rebukes a wicked man incurs abuse.

9 : 7

An evil man is trapped by his sinful talk, but a righteous man escapes trouble.

12 : 13

An evil man is bent only on rebellion; a merciless official will be sent against him.

17 : 11

for the evil man has no future hope, and the lamp of the wicked will be snuffed out.

24 : 20

An evil man is snared by his own sin, but a righteous one can sing and be glad.

29 : 6

evil men

Do not set foot on the path of the wicked or walk in the way of evil men.

4 : 14

The wicked desire the plunder of evil men, but the root of the righteous flourishes.

12 : 12

Evil men will bow down in the presence of the good, and the wicked at the gates of the righteous.

14 : 19

Do not fret because of evil men or be envious of the wicked,

24 : 19

Evil men do not understand justice, but those who seek the Lord understand it fully.

28 : 5

evil path

He who leads the upright along an evil path will fall into his own trap, but the blameless will receive a good inheritance.

28 : 10

evil plans

for their hearts plot violence, and their lips talk about making trouble.

24 : 2

He who plots evil will be known as a schemer,

24 : 8

evil thoughts

The Lord detests the thoughts of the wicked, but those of the pure are pleasing to him.

15 : 26

evil words

The lips of the righteous know what is fitting, but the mouth of the wicked only what is perverse.

10 : 32

evildoers

When justice is done, it brings joy to the righteous but terror to evildoers.

21 : 15

exalt

Esteem her, and she will exalt you; embrace her, and she will honor you.

4 : 8

Righteousness exalts a nation, but sin is a disgrace to any people.

14 : 34

Do not exalt yourself in the king's presence, and do not claim a place among great men;

25 : 6

exalted

Through the blessing of the upright a city is exalted, but by the mouth of the wicked it is destroyed.

11 : 11

it is better for him to say to you, "Come up here," than for him to humiliate you before a nobleman. What you have seen with your eyes

25 : 7

"If you have played the fool and exalted yourself, or if you have planned evil, clap your hand over your mouth!

30 : 32

examines

For a man's ways are in full view of the Lord, and he examines all his paths.

5 : 21

example

I guide you in the way of wisdom and lead you along straight paths.

4 : 11

The lips of the king speak as an oracle, and his mouth should not betray justice.

16 : 10

A violent man entices his neighbor and leads him down a path that is not good.

16 : 29

or you may learn his ways and get yourself ensnared.

22 : 25

I applied my heart to what I observed and learned a lesson from what I saw:

24 : 32

excuses

The sluggard says, "There is a lion outside!" or "I will be murdered in the streets!"

22 : 13

exhortation
The way of a fool seems right to him,
but a wise man listens to advice.

15 : 12

The tongue that brings healing is a tree
of life, but a deceitful tongue crushes
the spirit.

15 : 4

A man finds joy in giving an apt reply--
and how good is a timely word!

15 : 23

A wise man's heart guides his mouth,
and his lips promote instruction.

16 : 23

existence
before the mountains were settled in
place, before the hills, I was given birth,

8 : 25

exoneration
An evil man is trapped by his sinful
talk, but a righteous man escapes
trouble.

12 : 13

exorbitant
He who increases his wealth by
exorbitant interest amasses it for
another, who will be kind to the poor.

28 : 8

expensive clothes
She makes coverings for her bed; she is
clothed in fine linen and purple.

31 : 22

exploit
He who oppresses the poor to increase
his wealth and he who gives gifts to the
rich -- both come to poverty.

22 : 16

Do not exploit the poor because they
are poor and do not crush the needy in
court,

22 : 22

exposed
His malice may be concealed by
deception, but his wickedness will be
exposed in the assembly.

26 : 26

exposes
Every prudent man acts out of
knowledge, but a fool exposes his folly.

13 : 16

extends
She opens her arms to the poor and
extends her hands to the needy.

31 : 20

extremely
"Four things on earth are small, yet they
are extremely wise:

30 : 24

eye
who winks with his eye, signals with
his feet and motions with his fingers,

6 : 13

Keep my commands and you will live;
guard my teachings as the apple of your
eye.

7 : 2

He who winks with his eye is plotting
perversity; he who purses his lips is
bent on evil.

16 : 30

A discerning man keeps wisdom in
view, but a fool's eyes wander to the
ends of the earth.

17 : 24

The eye that mocks a father, that scorns
obedience to a mother, will be pecked
out by the ravens of the valley, will be
eaten by the vultures.

30 : 17

eyelids
Allow no sleep to your eyes, no slumber
to your eyelids.

6 : 4

eyes
Do not be wise in your own eyes; fear
the Lord and shun evil.

3 : 7

Let your eyes look straight ahead, fix
your gaze directly before you.

4 : 25

Allow no sleep to your eyes, no slumber
to your eyelids.

6 : 4

haughty eyes, a lying tongue, hands that
shed innocent blood,

6 : 17

Do not lust in your heart after her
beauty or let her captivate you with her
eyes,

6 : 25

As vinegar to the teeth and smoke to the
eyes, so is a sluggard to those who send
him.

10 : 26

The eyes of the Lord are everywhere,
keeping watch on the wicked and the
good.

15 : 3

When a king sits on his throne to judge,
he winnows out all evil with his eyes.

20 : 8

Ears that hear and eyes that see -- the
Lord has made them both.

20 : 12

Haughty eyes and a proud heart, the
lamp of the wicked, are sin!

21 : 4

The eyes of the Lord keep watch over
knowledge, but he frustrates the words
of the unfaithful,

22 : 12

My son, give me your heart and let your
eyes keep to my ways,

23 : 26

Who has woe? Who has sorrow? Who
has strife? Who has complaints? Who
has needless bruises? Who has
bloodshot eyes?

23 : 29

Your eyes will see strange sights and
your mind imagine confusing things.

23 : 33

it is better for him to say to you, "Come
up here," than for him to humiliate you
before a nobleman. What you have seen
with your eyes

25 : 7

Answer a fool according to his folly, or
he will be wise in his own eyes.

26 : 5

Do you see a man wise in his own eyes?
There is more hope for a fool than for
him.

26 : 12

The sluggard is wiser in his own eyes
than seven men who answer discreetly.

26 : 16

Death and Destruction are never
satisfied, and neither are the eyes of
man.

27 : 20

A rich man may be wise in his own
eyes, but a poor man who has
discernment sees through him.

28 : 11

The poor man and the oppressor have this in common: The Lord gives sight to the eyes of both.

29 : 13

those who are pure in their own eyes and yet are not cleansed of their filth;

30 : 12

those whose eyes are ever so haughty, whose glances are so disdainful;

30 : 13

eyes of the Lord
The eyes of the Lord are everywhere, keeping watch on the wicked and the good.

15 : 3

The eyes of the Lord keep watch over knowledge, but he frustrates the words of the unfaithful.

22 : 12

F

façade
The wealth of the rich is their fortified
city; they imagine it an unscalable wall.

18 : 11

face
She took hold of him and kissed him
and with a brazen face she said:

7 : 13

I was there when he set the heavens in
place, when he marked out the horizon
on the face of the deep,

8 : 27

A happy heart makes the face cheerful,
but heartache crushes the spirit.

15 : 13

When a king's face brightens, it means
life; his favor is like a rain cloud in
spring.

16 : 15

Ears that hear and eyes that see -- the
Lord has made them both.

20 : 12

As water reflects a face, so a man's
heart reflects the man.

27 : 19

facial expressions
He who winks with his eye is plotting
perversity; he who purses his lips is
bent on evil.

16 : 30

fact
Be sure of this: The wicked will not go
unpunished, but those who are righteous
will go free.

11 : 21

faction
A greedy man stirs up dissension, but
he who trusts in the Lord will prosper.

28 : 25

factual
Be sure of this: The wicked will not go
unpunished, but those who are righteous
will go free.

11 : 21

fading
at twilight, as the day was fading, as the
dark of night set in.

7 : 9

fail
Whoever trusts in his riches will fall,
but the righteous will thrive like a green
leaf.

11 : 28

failing plans
Plans fail for lack of counsel, but with
many advisers they succeed.

15 : 22

fails
But whoever fails to find me harms
himself; all who hate me love death.

8 : 36

failure to listen
I would not obey my teachers or listen
to my instructors.

5 : 13

fair
for acquiring a disciplined and prudent
life, doing what is right and just and
fair;

1 : 3

Then you will understand what is right and just and fair -- every good path.

2 : 9

Do not withhold good from those who deserve it, when it is in your power to act.

3 : 27

By me kings reign and rulers make laws that are just;

8 : 15

It is not good to be partial to the wicked or to deprive the innocent of justice.

18 : 5

These also are sayings to the wise: To show partiality in judging is not good:

24 : 23

Speak up and judge fairly; defend the rights of the poor and needy."

31 : 9

fairly

Speak up and judge fairly; defend the rights of the poor and needy."

31 : 9

fairness

for acquiring a disciplined and prudent life, doing what is right and just and fair;

1 : 3

I walk in the way of righteousness, along the paths of justice,

8 : 20

The Lord abhors dishonest scales, but accurate weights are his delight.

11 : 1

Better a little with righteousness than much gain with injustice.

16 : 8

Honest scales and balances are from the Lord; all the weights in the bag are of his making.

16 : 11

Kings detest wrongdoing, for a throne is established through righteousness.

16 : 12

Acquitting the guilty and condemning the innocent -- the Lord detests them both.

17 : 15

A wicked man accepts a bribe in secret to pervert the course of justice.

17 : 23

It is not good to punish an innocent man, or to flog officials for their integrity.

17 : 26

The first to present his case seems right, till another comes forward and questions him.

18 : 17

Differing weights and differing measures -- the Lord detests them both.

20 : 10

The Lord detests differing weights, and dishonest scales do not please him.

20 : 23

When justice is done, it brings joy to the righteous but terror to evildoers.

21 : 15

Do not exploit the poor because they are poor and do not crush the needy in court,

22 : 22

Do not move an ancient boundary stone or encroach on the fields of the fatherless,

23 : 10

These also are sayings to the wise: To show partiality in judging is not good:

24 : 23

But it will go well with those who convict the guilty, and rich blessing will come upon them.

24 : 25

To show partiality is not good -- yet a man will do wrong for a piece of bread.

28 : 21

The righteous care about justice for the poor, but the wicked have no such concern.

29 : 7

If a king judges the poor with fairness, his throne will always be secure.

29 : 14

Many seek an audience with a ruler, but it is from the Lord that man gets justice.

29 : 26

Speak up and judge fairly; defend the rights of the poor and needy."

31 : 9

faith
A wise man attacks the city of the mighty and pulls down the stronghold in which they trust.

21 : 22

So that your trust may be in the Lord, I teach you today, even you.

22 : 19

faithful
for he guards the course of the just and protects the way of his faithful ones.

2 : 8

Many a man claims to have unfailing love, but a faithful man who can find?

20 : 6

She speaks with wisdom, and faithful instruction is on her tongue.

31 : 26

faithful man
Many a man claims to have unfailing love, but a faithful man who can find?

20 : 6

A faithful man will be richly blessed, but one eager to get rich will not go unpunished.

28 : 20

faithfulness
My son, if sinners entice you, do not give in to them.

1 : 10

Let love and faithfulness never leave you; bind them around your neck, write them on the tablet of your heart.

3 : 3

Drink water from your own cistern, running water from your own well.

5 : 15

Should your springs overflow in the streets, your streams of water in the public squares?

5 : 16

Let them be yours alone, never to be shared with strangers.

5 : 17

May your fountain be blessed, and may you rejoice in the wife of your youth.

5 : 18

for jealousy arouses a husband's fury, and he will show no mercy when he takes revenge.

6 : 34

they will keep you from the adulteress, from the wayward wife with her seductive words.

7 : 5

Do not those who plot evil go astray?
But those who plan what is good find
love and faithfulness.

14 : 22

Through love and faithfulness sin is
atoned for; through the fear of the Lord
a man avoids evil.

16 : 6

Love and faithfulness keep a king safe;
through love his throne is made secure.

20 : 28

Like the coolness of snow at harvest
time is a trustworthy messenger to those
who send him; he refreshes the spirit of
his masters.

25 : 13

Like a bird that strays from its nest is a
man who strays from his home.

27 : 8

faithless
The faithless will be fully repaid for
their ways, and the good man rewarded
for his.

14 : 14

fall
For they cannot sleep till they do evil;
they are robbed of slumber till they
make someone fall.

4 : 16

Whoever trusts in his riches will fall,
but the righteous will thrive like a green
leaf.

11 : 28

Pride goes before destruction, a haughty
spirit before a fall.

16 : 18

A man of perverse heart does not
prosper; he whose tongue is deceitful
falls into trouble.

17 : 20

The mouth of an adulteress is a deep
pit; he who is under the Lord's wrath
will fall into it.

22 : 14

If a man digs a pit, he will fall into it; if
a man rolls a stone, it will roll back on
him.

26 : 27

He who leads the upright along an evil
path will fall into his own trap, but the
blameless will receive a good
inheritance.

28 : 10

He whose walk is blameless is kept
safe, but he whose ways are perverse
will suddenly fall.

28 : 18

fallen
then do this, my son, to free yourself,
since you have fallen into your
neighbor's hands: Go and humble
yourself; press your plea with your
neighbor!

6 : 3

Many are the victims she has brought
down; her slain are a mighty throng.

7 : 26

When pride comes, then comes
disgrace, but with humility comes
wisdom.

11 : 2

falls
For lack of guidance a nation falls, but
many advisers make victory sure.

11 : 14

A wicked messenger falls into trouble,
but a trustworthy envoy brings healing.

13 : 17

Do not gloat when your enemy falls;
when he stumbles, do not let your heart
rejoice,

24 : 17

Blessed is the man who always fears the
Lord, but he who hardens his heart falls
into trouble.

28 : 14

false

Do not accuse a man for no reason --
when he has done you no harm.

3 : 30

The righteous hate what is false, but the
wicked bring shame and disgrace.

13 : 5

false accusation

Do not accuse a man for no reason --
when he has done you no harm.

3 : 30

false testimony

Like a club or a sword or a sharp arrow
is the man who gives false testimony
against his neighbor.

25 : 18

false witness

Do not accuse a man for no reason --
when he has done you no harm.

3 : 30

a false witness who pours out lies and a
man who stirs up dissension among
brothers.

6 : 19

A truthful witness gives honest
testimony, but a false witness tells lies.

12 : 17

A truthful witness does not deceive, but
a false witness pours out lies.

14 : 5

A truthful witness saves lives, but a
false witness is deceitful.

14 : 25

A false witness will not go unpunished,
and he who pours out lies will not go
free.

19 : 5

A false witness will not go unpunished,
and he who pours out lies will perish.

19 : 9

A false witness will perish, and
whoever listens to him will be
destroyed forever.

21 : 28

Like a club or a sword or a sharp arrow
is the man who gives false testimony
against his neighbor.

25 : 18

falsehood

Keep falsehood and lies far from me;
give me neither poverty nor riches, but
give me only my daily bread.

30 : 8

falter

If you falter in times of trouble, how
small is your strength!

24 : 10

fame

The memory of the righteous will be a
blessing, but the name of the wicked
will rot.

10 : 7

family

He who brings trouble on his family
will inherit only wind, and the fool will
be servant to the wise.

11 : 29

He who fears the Lord has a secure
fortress, and for his children it will be a
refuge.

14 : 26

The house of the righteous contains great treasure, but the income of the wicked brings them trouble.

15 : 6

Better a meal of vegetables where there is love than a fattened calf with hatred.

15 : 17

A greedy man brings trouble to his family, but he who hates bribes will live.

15 : 27

Better a dry crust with peace and quiet than a house full of feasting with strife.

17 : 1

Children's children are a crown to the aged, and parents are the pride of their children.

17 : 6

Starting a quarrel is like breaching a dam; so drop the matter before a dispute breaks out.

17 : 14

To have a fool for a son brings grief; there is no joy for the father of a fool.

17 : 21

A foolish son brings grief to his father and bitterness to the one who bore him.

17 : 25

He who robs his father and drives out his mother is a son who brings shame and disgrace.

19 : 26

Many a man claims to have unfailing love, but a faithful man who can find?

20 : 6

The righteous man leads a blameless life; blessed are his children after him.

20 : 7

Even a child is known by his actions, by whether his conduct is pure and right.

20 : 11

If a man curses his father or mother, his lamp will be snuffed out in pitch darkness.

20 : 20

May your father and mother be glad; may she who gave you birth rejoice!

23 : 25

By wisdom a house is built, and through understanding it is established;

24 : 3

through knowledge its rooms are filled with rare and beautiful treasures.

24 : 4

Finish your outdoor work and get your fields ready; after that, build your house.

24 : 27

You will have plenty of goat's milk to feed you and your family and to nourish your servant girls.

27 : 27

She gets up while it is still dark; she provides food for her family and portions for her servant girls.

31 : 15

family matters
He who loves a quarrel loves sin; he who builds a high gate invites destruction.

17 : 19

famine
He who is full loathes honey, but to the hungry even what is bitter tastes sweet.

27 : 7

fantasies

He who works his land will have
abundant food, but he who chases
fantasies lacks judgment.

12 : 11

He who works his land will have
abundant food, but the one who chases
fantasies will have his fill of poverty.

28 : 19

far

Put away perversity from your mouth;
keep corrupt talk far from your lips.

4 : 24

The Lord is far from the wicked but he
hears the prayer of the righteous.

15 : 29

In the paths of the wicked lie thorns and
snares, but he who guards his soul stays
far from them.

22 : 5

Folly is bound up in the heart of a child,
but the rod of discipline will drive it far
from him.

22 : 15

farmer

A poor man's field may produce
abundant food, but injustice sweeps it
away.

13 : 23

farming

yet it stores its provisions in summer
and gathers its food at harvest.

6 : 8

He who gathers crops in summer is a
wise son, but he who sleeps during
harvest is a disgraceful son.

10 : 5

He who works his land will have
abundant food, but he who chases
fantasies lacks judgment.

12 : 11

Where there are no oxen, the manger is
empty, but from the strength of an ox
comes an abundant harvest.

14 : 4

A sluggard does not plow in season; so
at harvest time he looks but finds
nothing.

20 : 4

Finish your outdoor work and get your
fields ready; after that, build your
house.

24 : 27

When the hay is removed and new
growth appears and the grass from the
hills is gathered in,

27 : 25

He who works his land will have
abundant food, but the one who chases
fantasies will have his fill of poverty.

28 : 19

She considers a field and buys it; out of
her earnings she plants a vineyard.

31 : 16

fasten

Bind them upon your heart forever;
fasten them around your neck.

6 : 21

fatal

Her house is a highway to the grave,
leading down to the chambers of death.

7 : 27

father

Listen, my son, to your father's
instruction and do not forsake your
mother's teaching.

1 : 8

My son, do not forget my teaching, but
keep my commands in your heart,

3 : 1

because the Lord disciplines those he loves, as a father the son he delights in.

3 : 12

When I was a boy in my father's house, still tender, and an only child of my mother,

4 : 3

I guide you in the way of wisdom and lead you along straight paths.

4 : 11

My son, keep your father's commands and do not forsake your mother's teaching.

6 : 20

The proverbs of Solomon: A wise son brings joy to his father, but a foolish son grief to his mother.

10 : 1

A wise son heeds his father's instruction, but a mocker does not listen to rebuke.

13 : 1

A fool spurns the father's discipline, but whoever heeds correction shows prudence.

15 : 5

A wise son brings joy to his father, but a foolish man despises his mother.

15 : 20

To have a fool for a son brings grief; there is no joy for the father of a fool.

17 : 21

A foolish son brings grief to his father and bitterness to the one who bore him.

17 : 25

A foolish son is his father's ruin, and a quarrelsome wife is like a constant dripping.

19 : 13

Discipline your son, for in that there is hope; do not be a willing party to his death.

19 : 18

He who robs his father and drives out his mother is a son who brings shame and disgrace.

19 : 26

If a man curses his father or mother, his lamp will be snuffed out in pitch darkness.

20 : 20

Train a child in the way he should go, and when he is old he will not turn from it.

22 : 6

Listen to your father, who gave you life, and do not despise your mother when she is old.

23 : 22

The father of a righteous man has great joy; he who has a wise son delights in him.

23 : 24

May your father and mother be glad; may she who gave you birth rejoice!

23 : 25

Do not forsake your friend and the friend of your father, and do not go to your brother's house when disaster strikes you -- better a neighbor nearby than a brother far away.

27 : 10

He who keeps the law is a discerning son, but a companion of gluttons disgraces his father.

28 : 7

He who robs his father or mother and says, "It's not wrong" -- he is partner to him who destroys.

28 : 24

A man who loves wisdom brings joy to his father, but a companion of prostitutes squanders his wealth.

29 : 3

The eye that mocks a father, that scorns obedience to a mother, will be pecked out by the ravens of the valley, will be eaten by the vultures.

30 : 17

fatherhood

Be wise, my son, and bring joy to my heart; then I can answer anyone who treats me with contempt.

27 : 11

fatherless

Do not move an ancient boundary stone or encroach on the fields of the fatherless,

23 : 10

fatherly advice

Listen, my sons, to a father's instruction; pay attention and gain understanding.

4 : 1

My son, pay attention to what I say; listen closely to my words.

4 : 20

My son, pay attention to my wisdom, listen well to my words of insight,

5 : 1

Now then, my sons, listen to me; do not turn aside from what I say.

5 : 7

Now then, my sons, listen to me; pay attention to what I say.

7 : 24

fathers

"There are those who curse their fathers and do not bless their mothers;

30 : 11

father's advice

A wise son heeds his father's instruction, but a mocker does not listen to rebuke.

13 : 1

father's discipline

A fool spurns the father's discipline, but whoever heeds correction shows prudence.

15 : 5

father's house

When I was a boy in my father's house, still tender, and an only child of my mother,

4 : 3

father's instruction

Listen, my son, to your father's instruction and do not forsake your mother's teaching.

1 : 8

Listen, my sons, to a father's instruction; pay attention and gain understanding.

4 : 1

fattened calf

Better a meal of vegetables where there is love than a fattened calf with hatred.

15 : 17

faultless

To the discerning all of them are right; they are faultless to those who have knowledge.

8 : 9

The righteous man leads a blameless life; blessed are his children after him.

20 : 7

favor

Then you will win favor and a good name in the sight of God and man.

3 : 4

For whoever finds me finds life and receives favor from the Lord.

8 : 35

A good man obtains favor from the Lord, but the Lord condemns a crafty man.

12 : 2

Good understanding wins favor, but the way of the unfaithful is hard.

13 : 15

Fools mock at making amends for sin, but goodwill is found among the upright.

14 : 9

When a king's face brightens, it means life; his favor is like a rain cloud in spring.

16 : 15

It is not good to be partial to the wicked or to deprive the innocent of justice.

18 : 5

He who finds a wife finds what is good and receives favor from the Lord.

18 : 22

Many curry favor with a ruler, and everyone is the friend of a man who gives gifts.

19 : 6

A king's rage is like the roar of a lion, but his favor is like dew on the grass.

19 : 12

He who rebukes a man will in the end gain more favor than he who has a flattering tongue.

28 : 23

favoritism
He who oppresses the poor to increase his wealth and he who gives gifts to the rich -- both come to poverty.

22 : 16

These also are sayings to the wise: To show partiality in judging is not good:

24 : 23

fear
The fear of the Lord is the beginning of knowledge, but fools despise wisdom and discipline.

1 : 7

but whoever listens to me will live in safety and be at ease, without fear of harm."

1 : 33

then you will understand the fear of the Lord and find the knowledge of God.

2 : 5

when you lie down, you will not be afraid; when you lie down, your sleep will be sweet.

3 : 24

When justice is done, it brings joy to the righteous but terror to evildoers.

21 : 15

Fear of man will prove to be a snare, but whoever trusts in the Lord is kept safe.

29 : 25

When it snows, she has no fear for her household; for all of them are clothed in scarlet.

31 : 21

fear of the Lord
The fear of the Lord is the beginning of knowledge, but fools despise wisdom and discipline.

1 : 7

then you will understand the fear of the Lord and find the knowledge of God.

2 : 5

"The fear of the Lord is the beginning of wisdom, and knowledge of the Holy One is understanding.

9 : 10

The fear of the Lord adds length to life, but the years of the wicked are cut short.

10 : 27

The fear of the Lord is a fountain of life, turning a man from the snares of death.

14 : 27

Better a little with the fear of the Lord than great wealth with turmoil.

15 : 16

The fear of the Lord teaches a man wisdom, and humility comes before honor.

15 : 33

Through love and faithfulness sin is atoned for; through the fear of the Lord a man avoids evil.

16 : 6

The fear of the Lord leads to life: Then one rests content, untouched by trouble.

19 : 23

Humility and the fear of the Lord bring wealth and honor and life.

22 : 4

Do not let your heart envy sinners, but always be zealous for the fear of the Lord.

23 : 17

fear the Lord
Since they hated knowledge and did not choose to fear the Lord,

1 : 29

Do not be wise in your own eyes; fear the Lord and shun evil.

3 : 7

To fear the Lord is to hate evil; I hate pride and arrogance, evil behavior and perverse speech.

8 : 13

He whose walk is upright fears the Lord, but he whose ways are devious despises him.

14 : 2

A wise man fears the Lord and shuns evil, but a fool is hotheaded and reckless.

14 : 16

He who fears the Lord has a secure fortress, and for his children it will be a refuge.

14 : 26

Fear the Lord and the king, my son, and do not join with the rebellious,

24 : 21

Blessed is the man who always fears the Lord, but he who hardens his heart falls into trouble.

28 : 14

Charm is deceptive, and beauty is fleeting; but a woman who fears the Lord is to be praised.

31 : 30

fears
What the wicked dreads will overtake him; what the righteous desire will be granted.

10 : 24

feast
lest strangers feast on your wealth and your toil enrich another man's house.

5 : 10

All the days of the oppressed are wretched, but the cheerful heart has a continual feast.

15 : 15

feasting
Better a dry crust with peace and quiet than a house full of feasting with strife.

17 : 1

feed
You will have plenty of goat's milk to feed you and your family and to nourish your servant girls.

27 : 27

feeding the poor
He who despises his neighbor sins, but blessed is he who is kind to the needy.

14 : 21

He who oppresses the poor shows contempt for their Maker, but whoever is kind to the needy honors God.

14 : 31

feeds
The discerning heart seeks knowledge, but the mouth of a fool feeds on folly.

15 : 14

feel
"They hit me," you will say, "but I'm not hurt! They beat me, but I don't feel it! When will I wake up so I can find another drink?"

23 : 35

feelings
Do not gloat when your enemy falls; when he stumbles, do not let your heart rejoice,

24 : 17

feet
for their feet rush into sin, they are swift to shed blood.

1 : 16

Make level paths for your feet and take only ways that are firm.

4 : 26

Her feet go down to death; her steps lead straight to the grave.

5 : 5

who winks with his eye, signals with his feet and motions with his fingers,

6 : 13

a heart that devises wicked schemes, feet that are quick to rush into evil,

6 : 18

Can a man walk on hot coals without his feet being scorched?

6 : 28

She is loud and defiant, her feet never stay at home;

7 : 11

Like cutting off one's feet or drinking violence is the sending of a message by the hand of a fool.

26 : 6

Whoever flatters his neighbor is spreading a net for his feet.

29 : 5

fellowship
"I have fellowship offerings at home; today I fulfilled my vows.

7 : 14

fervent
Like a coating of glaze over earthenware are fervent lips with an evil heart.

26 : 23

field
A poor man's field may produce abundant food, but injustice sweeps it away.

13 : 23

I went past the field of the sluggard, past the vineyard of the man who lacks judgment;

24 : 30

the lambs will provide you with clothing, and the goats with the price of a field.

27 : 26

She considers a field and buys it; out of her earnings she plants a vineyard.

31 : 16

fields

before he made the earth or its fields or any of the dust of the world.

8 : 26

Do not move an ancient boundary stone or encroach on the fields of the fatherless,

23 : 10

Finish your outdoor work and get your fields ready; after that, build your house.

24 : 27

fields of the fatherless

Do not move an ancient boundary stone or encroach on the fields of the fatherless,

23 : 10

fig tree

He who tends a fig tree will eat its fruit, and he who looks after his master will be honored.

27 : 18

fight

It is to a man's honor to avoid strife, but every fool is quick to quarrel.

20 : 3

If you argue your case with a neighbor, do not betray another man's confidence,

25 : 9

fighting

Hatred stirs up dissension, but love covers over all wrongs

10 : 12

Starting a quarrel is like breaching a dam; so drop the matter before a dispute breaks out.

17 : 14

He who loves a quarrel loves sin; he who builds a high gate invites destruction.

17 : 19

A foolish son is his father's ruin, and a quarrelsome wife is like a constant dripping.

19 : 13

Better to live on a corner of the roof than share a house with a quarrelsome wife.

21 : 9

Better to live in a desert than with a quarrelsome and ill-tempered wife.

21 : 19

Drive out the mocker, and out goes strife; quarrels and insults are ended.

22 : 10

Like one who seizes a dog by the ears is a passer-by who meddles in a quarrel not his own.

26 : 17

Without wood a fire goes out; without gossip a quarrel dies down.

26 : 20

As charcoal to embers and as wood to fire, so is a quarrelsome man for kindling strife.

26 : 21

Stone is heavy and sand a burden, but provocation by a fool is heavier than both.

27 : 3

A quarrelsome wife is like a constant dripping on a rainy day;

27 : 15

fill

we will get all sorts of valuable things and fill our houses with plunder;

1 : 13

No harm befalls the righteous, but the wicked have their fill of trouble.

12 : 21

Though his speech is charming, do not believe him, for seven abominations fill his heart.

26 : 25

He who works his land will have abundant food, but the one who chases fantasies will have his fill of poverty.

28 : 19

filled

they will eat the fruit of their ways and be filled with the fruit of their schemes.

1 : 31

then your barns will be filled to overflowing, and your vats will brim over with new wine.

3 : 10

He took his purse filled with money and will not be home till full moon."

7 : 20

Then I was the craftsman at his side. I was filled with delight day after day, rejoicing always in his presence,

8 : 30

From the fruit of his lips a man is filled with good things as surely as the work of his hands rewards him.

12 : 14

From the fruit of his mouth a man's stomach is filled; with the harvest from his lips he is satisfied.

18 : 20

through knowledge its rooms are filled with rare and beautiful treasures.

24 : 4

filth

Put away perversity from your mouth; keep corrupt talk far from your lips.

4 : 24

those who are pure in their own eyes and yet are not cleansed of their filth;

30 : 12

filthy mouth

The mouth of the righteous brings forth wisdom, but a perverse tongue will be cut out.

10 : 31

The lips of the righteous know what is fitting, but the mouth of the wicked only what is perverse.

10 : 32

final judgment

There is a way that seems right to a man, but in the end it leads to death.

16 : 25

finances

Such is the end of all who go after ill-gotten gain; it takes away the life of those who get it.

1 : 19

for they will prolong your life many years and bring you prosperity.

3 : 2

Honor the Lord with your wealth, with the firstfruits of all your crops;

3 : 9

and poverty will come on you like a bandit and scarcity like an armed man.

6 : 11

Lazy hands make a man poor, but diligent hands bring wealth.

10 : 4

The wealth of the rich is their fortified city, but poverty is the ruin of the poor.

10 : 15

When the righteous prosper, the city rejoices; when the wicked perish, there are shouts of joy.

11 : 10

One man gives freely, yet gains even more; another withholds unduly, but comes to poverty.

11 : 24

A generous man will prosper; he who refreshes others will himself be refreshed.

11 : 25

One man pretends to be rich, yet has nothing; another pretends to be poor, yet has great wealth.

13 : 7

Dishonest money dwindles away, but he who gathers money little by little makes it grow.

13 : 11

He who ignores discipline comes to poverty and shame, but whoever heeds correction is honored.

13 : 18

A good man leaves an inheritance for his children's children, but a sinner's wealth is stored up for the righteous.

13 : 22

All hard work brings a profit, but mere talk leads only to poverty.

14 : 23

Better a little with the fear of the Lord than great wealth with turmoil.

15 : 16

How much better to get wisdom than gold, to choose understanding rather than silver!

16 : 16

A man of perverse heart does not prosper; he whose tongue is deceitful falls into trouble.

17 : 20

The wealth of the rich is their fortified city; they imagine it an unscalable wall.

18 : 11

He who is kind to the poor lends to the Lord, and he will reward him for what he has done.

19 : 17

Do not love sleep or you will grow poor; stay awake and you will have food to spare.

20 : 13

The plans of the diligent lead to profit as surely as haste leads to poverty.

21 : 5

He who loves pleasure will become poor; whoever loves wine and oil will never be rich.

21 : 17

He who pursues righteousness and love finds life, prosperity and honor.

21 : 21

The rich rule over the poor, and the borrower is servant to the lender.

22 : 7

He who oppresses the poor to increase his wealth and he who gives gifts to the rich -- both come to poverty.

22 : 16

Do not be a man who strikes hands in pledge or puts up security for debts;

22 : 26

Do not wear yourself out to get rich; have the wisdom to show restraint.

23 : 4

Cast but a glance at riches, and they are gone, for they will surely sprout wings and fly off to the sky like an eagle.

23 : 5

and poverty will come on you like a bandit and scarcity like an armed man.

24 : 34

He who conceals his sins does not prosper, but whoever confesses and renounces them finds mercy.

28 : 13

A tyrannical ruler lacks judgment, but he who hates ill-gotten gain will enjoy a long life.

28 : 16

He who works his land will have abundant food, but the one who chases fantasies will have his fill of poverty.

28 : 19

A stingy man is eager to get rich and is unaware that poverty awaits him.

28 : 22

A greedy man stirs up dissension, but he who trusts in the Lord will prosper.

28 : 25

He who gives to the poor will lack nothing, but he who closes his eyes to them receives many curses.

28 : 27

financial planning

A good man leaves an inheritance for his children's children, but a sinner's wealth is stored up for the righteous.

13 : 22

An inheritance quickly gained at the beginning will not be blessed at the end.

20 : 21

He who leads the upright along an evil path will fall into his own trap, but the blameless will receive a good inheritance.

28 : 10

financial stability

Dishonest money dwindles away, but he who gathers money little by little makes it grow.

13 : 11

find

"Then they will call to me but I will not answer; they will look for me but will not find me.

1 : 28

then you will understand the fear of the Lord and find the knowledge of God.

2 : 5

for they are life to those who find them and health to a man's whole body.

4 : 22

I love those who love me, and those who seek me find me.

8 : 17

But whoever fails to find me harms himself; all who hate me love death.

8 : 36

Stay away from a foolish man, for you will not find knowledge on his lips.

14 : 7

Do not those who plot evil go astray? But those who plan what is good find love and faithfulness.

14 : 22

A poor man is shunned by all his relatives -- how much more do his friends avoid him! Though he pursues them with pleading, they are nowhere to be found.

19 : 7

162

Many a man claims to have unfailing love, but a faithful man who can find?

20 : 6

"They hit me," you will say, "but I'm not hurt! They beat me, but I don't feel it! When will I wake up so I can find another drink?"

23 : 35

Know also that wisdom is sweet to your soul; if you find it, there is a future hope for you, and your hope will not be cut off.

24 : 14

If you find honey, just eat enough -- too much of it, and you will vomit.

25 : 16

A wife of noble character who can find? She is worth far more than rubies.

31 : 10

finding joy
A man finds joy in giving an apt reply-- and how good is a timely word!

15 : 23

finding love
Do not those who plot evil go astray? But those who plan what is good find love and faithfulness.

14 : 22

finding wisdom
Listen to advice and accept instruction, and in the end you will be wise.

19 : 20

finds
Blessed is the man who finds wisdom, the man who gains understanding,

3 : 13

For whoever finds me finds life and receives favor from the Lord.

8 : 35

A fool finds pleasure in evil conduct, but a man of understanding delights in wisdom.

10 : 23

He who seeks good finds goodwill, but evil comes to him who searches for it.

11 : 27

The mocker seeks wisdom and finds none, but knowledge comes easily to the discerning.

14 : 6

A man finds joy in giving an apt reply-- and how good is a timely word!

15 : 23

A fool finds no pleasure in understanding but delights in airing his own opinions.

18 : 2

He who finds a wife finds what is good and receives favor from the Lord.

18 : 22

A sluggard does not plow in season; so at harvest time he looks but finds nothing.

20 : 4

He who pursues righteousness and love finds life, prosperity and honor.

21 : 21

He who conceals his sins does not prosper, but whoever confesses and renounces them finds mercy.

28 : 13

fine linen
She makes coverings for her bed; she is clothed in fine linen and purple.

31 : 22

fingers
who winks with his eye, signals with his feet and motions with his fingers,

6 : 13

Bind them on your fingers; write them on the tablet of your heart.

7 : 3

In her hand she holds the distaff and grasps the spindle with her fingers.

31 : 19

finish

Finish your outdoor work and get your fields ready; after that, build your house.

24 : 27

finished

When justice is done, it brings joy to the righteous but terror to evildoers.

21 : 15

fire

Can a man scoop fire into his lap without his clothes being burned?

6 : 27

A scoundrel plots evil, and his speech is like a scorching fire.

16 : 27

Without wood a fire goes out; without gossip a quarrel dies down.

26 : 20

As charcoal to embers and as wood to fire, so is a quarrelsome man for kindling strife.

26 : 21

the grave, the barren womb, land, which is never satisfied with water, and fire, which never says, 'Enough!'

30 : 16

firebrands

Like a madman shooting firebrands or deadly arrows

26 : 18

firm

Make level paths for your feet and take only ways that are firm.

4 : 26

When the storm has swept by, the wicked are gone, but the righteous stand firm forever.

10 : 25

Wicked men are overthrown and are no more, but the house of the righteous stands firm.

12 : 7

first

"The Lord brought me forth as the first of his works, before his deeds of old;

8 : 22

The first to present his case seems right, till another comes forward and questions him.

18 : 17

firstfruits

Honor the Lord with your wealth, with the firstfruits of all your crops;

3 : 9

fitting

The lips of the righteous know what is fitting, but the mouth of the wicked only what is perverse.

10 : 32

It is not fitting for a fool to live in luxury -- how much worse for a slave to rule over princes!

19 : 10

Like snow in summer or rain in harvest, honor is not fitting for a fool.

26 : 1

fix your gaze

Let your eyes look straight ahead, fix your gaze directly before you.

4 : 25

fixed

when he established the clouds above and fixed securely the fountains of the deep,

8 : 28

flatter
Whoever flatters his neighbor is
spreading a net for his feet.

29 : 5

flattering
A lying tongue hates those it hurts, and
a flattering mouth works ruin.

26 : 28

He who rebukes a man will in the end
gain more favor than he who has a
flattering tongue.

28 : 23

flattering tongue
He who rebukes a man will in the end
gain more favor than he who has a
flattering tongue.

28 : 23

flatters
Whoever flatters his neighbor is
spreading a net for his feet.

29 : 5

flawless
To the discerning all of them are right;
they are faultless to those who have
knowledge.

8 : 9

The words of the wicked lie in wait for
blood, but the speech of the upright
rescues them.

12 : 6

Every word of God is flawless; he is a
shield to those who take refuge in him.

30 : 5

flax
She selects wool and flax and works
with eager hands.

31 : 13

flees
The wicked man flees though no one
pursues, but the righteous are as bold as
a lion.

28 : 1

fleeting
A fortune made by a lying tongue is a
fleeting vapor and a deadly snare.

21 : 6

Charm is deceptive, and beauty is
fleeting; but a woman who fears the
Lord is to be praised.

31 : 30

flesh
At the end of your life you will groan,
when your flesh and body are spent.

5 : 11

flirting with sin
He was going down the street near her
corner, walking along in the direction of
her house

7 : 8

flocks
Be sure you know the condition of your
flocks, give careful attention to your
herds;

27 : 23

flog
It is not good to punish an innocent
man, or to flog officials for their
integrity.

17 : 26

Flog a mocker, and the simple will learn
prudence; rebuke a discerning man, and
he will gain knowledge.

19 : 25

flourish
Whoever trusts in his riches will fall,
but the righteous will thrive like a green
leaf.

11 : 28

The house of the wicked will be destroyed, but the tent of the upright will flourish.

14 : 11

flourishes

The wicked desire the plunder of evil men, but the root of the righteous flourishes.

12 : 12

fly

Cast but a glance at riches, and they are gone, for they will surely sprout wings and fly off to the sky like an eagle.

23 : 5

focus

Let your eyes look straight ahead, fix your gaze directly before you.

4 : 25

Do not swerve to the right or the left; keep your foot from evil.

4 : 27

My son, give me your heart and let your eyes keep to my ways,

23 : 26

focused

A discerning man keeps wisdom in view, but a fool's eyes wander to the ends of the earth.

17 : 24

folding

A little sleep, a little slumber, a little folding of the hands to rest--

6 : 10

A little sleep, a little slumber, a little folding of the hands to rest --

24 : 33

foliage

Whoever trusts in his riches will fall, but the righteous will thrive like a green leaf.

11 : 28

follow

Do not envy a violent man or choose any of his ways,

3 : 31

Get wisdom, get understanding; do not forget my words or swerve from them.

4 : 5

Esteem her, and she will exalt you; embrace her, and she will honor you.

4 : 8

Leave your simple ways and you will live; walk in the way of understanding.

9 : 6

followed

All at once he followed her like an ox going to the slaughter, like a deer stepping into a noose

7 : 22

folly

He will die for lack of discipline, led astray by his own great folly.

5 : 23

The woman Folly is loud; she is undisciplined and without knowledge.

9 : 13

A prudent man keeps his knowledge to himself, but the heart of fools blurts out folly.

12 : 23

Every prudent man acts out of knowledge, but a fool exposes his folly.

13 : 16

The wisdom of the prudent is to give thought to their ways, but the folly of fools is deception.

14 : 8

The simple inherit folly, but the prudent are crowned with knowledge.

14 : 18

The wealth of the wise is their crown, but the folly of fools yields folly.

14 : 24

A patient man has great understanding, but a quick-tempered man displays folly.

14 : 29

The tongue of the wise commends knowledge, but the mouth of the fool gushes folly.

15 : 2

The discerning heart seeks knowledge, but the mouth of a fool feeds on folly.

15 : 14

Folly delights a man who lacks judgment, but a man of understanding keeps a straight course.

15 : 21

Understanding is a fountain of life to those who have it, but folly brings punishment to fools.

16 : 22

Better to meet a bear robbed of her cubs than a fool in his folly.

· 17 : 12

He who answers before listening -- that is his folly and his shame.

18 : 13

A man's own folly ruins his life, yet his heart rages against the Lord.

19 : 3

Folly is bound up in the heart of a child, but the rod of discipline will drive it far from him.

22 : 15

The schemes of folly are sin, and men detest a mocker.

24 : 9

Do not answer a fool according to his folly, or you will be like him yourself.

26 : 4

Answer a fool according to his folly, or he will be wise in his own eyes.

26 : 5

As a dog returns to its vomit, so a fool repeats his folly.

26 : 11

Though you grind a fool in a mortar, grinding him like grain with a pestle, you will not remove his folly from him.

27 : 22

food

yet it stores its provisions in summer and gathers its food at harvest.

6 : 8

She has prepared her meat and mixed her wine; she has also set her table.

9 : 2

"Come, eat my food and drink the wine I have mixed.

9 : 5

Stolen water is sweet; food eaten in secret is delicious!"

9 : 17

The Lord does not let the righteous go hungry but he thwarts the craving of the wicked.

10 : 3

People curse the man who hoards grain, but blessing crowns him who is willing to sell.

11 : 26

Better to be a nobody and yet have a servant than pretend to be somebody and have no food.

12 : 9

167

He who works his land will have abundant food, but he who chases fantasies lacks judgment.

12 : 11

A poor man's field may produce abundant food, but injustice sweeps it away.

13 : 23

The righteous eat to their hearts' content, but the stomach of the wicked goes hungry.

13 : 25

Better a meal of vegetables where there is love than a fattened calf with hatred.

15 : 17

The words of gossip are like choice morsels; they go down to a man's inmost parts.

18 : 8

Laziness brings on deep sleep, and the shiftless man goes hungry.

19 : 15

Food gained by fraud tastes sweet to a man, but he ends up with a mouth full of gravel.

20 : 17

In the house of the wise are stores of choice food and oil, but a foolish man devours all he has.

21 : 20

A generous man will himself be blessed, for he shares his food with the poor.

22 : 9

and put a knife to your throat if you are given to gluttony.

23 : 2

Do not crave his delicacies, for that food is deceptive.

23 : 3

Do not eat the food of a stingy man, do not crave his delicacies.

23 : 6

Eat honey, my son, for it is good; honey from the comb is sweet to your taste.

24 : 13

If you find honey, just eat enough -- too much of it, and you will vomit.

25 : 16

If your enemy is hungry, give him food to eat; if he is thirsty, give him water to drink.

25 : 21

It is not good to eat too much honey, not is it honorable to seek one's own honor.

25 : 27

He who is full loathes honey, but to the hungry even what is bitter tastes sweet.

27 : 7

He who tends a fig tree will eat its fruit, and he who looks after his master will be honored.

27 : 18

He who works his land will have abundant food, but the one who chases fantasies will have his fill of poverty.

28 : 19

To show partiality is not good -- yet a man will do wrong for a piece of bread.

28 : 21

Keep falsehood and lies far from me; give me neither poverty nor riches, but give me only my daily bread.

30 : 8

a servant who becomes a king, a fool who is full of food,

30 : 22

Ants are creatures of little strength, yet they store up their food in the summer;

30 : 25

She is like the merchant ships, bringing her food from afar.

31 : 14

She gets up while it is still dark; she provides food for her family and portions for her servant girls.

31 : 15

food to spare

Do not love sleep or you will grow poor; stay awake and you will have food to spare.

20 : 13

fool

The woman Folly is loud; she is undisciplined and without knowledge.

9 : 13

The wise in heart accept commands, but a chattering fool comes to ruin.

10 : 8

He who walks maliciously causes grief, and a chattering fool comes to ruin.

10 : 10

Wise men store up knowledge, but the mouth of a fool invites ruin.

10 : 14

He who conceals his hatred has lying lips, and whoever spreads slander is a fool.

10 : 18

A fool finds pleasure in evil conduct, but a man of understanding delights in wisdom.

10 : 23

He who brings trouble on his family will inherit only wind, and the fool will be servant to the wise.

11 : 29

The way of a fool seems right to him, but a wise man listens to advice.

12 : 15

A fool shows his annoyance at once, but a prudent man overlooks an insult.

12 : 16

Every prudent man acts out of knowledge, but a fool exposes his folly.

13 : 16

A fool's talk brings a rod to his back, but the lips of the wise protect them.

14 : 3

The mocker seeks wisdom and finds none, but knowledge comes easily to the discerning.

14 : 6

Stay away from a foolish man, for you will not find knowledge on his lips.

14 : 7

A wise man fears the Lord and shuns evil, but a fool is hotheaded and reckless.

14 : 16

The tongue of the wise commends knowledge, but the mouth of the fool gushes folly.

15 : 2

A fool spurns the father's discipline, but whoever heeds correction shows prudence.

15 : 5

The discerning heart seeks knowledge, but the mouth of a fool feeds on folly.

15 : 14

Arrogant lips are unsuited to a fool -- how much worse lying lips to a ruler!

17 · 7

A rebuke impresses a man of discernment more than a hundred lashes a fool.

17 : 10

Better to meet a bear robbed of her cubs than a fool in his folly.

17 : 12

Of what use is money in the hand of a fool, since he has no desire to get wisdom?

17 : 16

To have a fool for a son brings grief; there is no joy for the father of a fool.

17 : 21

Even a fool is thought wise if he keeps silent, and discerning if he holds his tongue.

17 : 28

A fool finds no pleasure in understanding but delights in airing his own opinions.

18 : 2

Better a poor man whose walk is blameless than a fool whose lips are perverse.

19 : 1

It is not fitting for a fool to live in luxury -- how much worse for a slave to rule over princes!

19 : 10

It is to a man's honor to avoid strife, but every fool is quick to quarrel.

20 : 3

Do not speak to a fool, for he will scorn the wisdom of your words.

23 : 9

Wisdom is too high for a fool; in the assembly at the gate he has nothing to say.

24 : 7

Like snow in summer or rain in harvest, honor is not fitting for a fool.

26 : 1

Do not answer a fool according to his folly, or you will be like him yourself.

26 : 4

Answer a fool according to his folly, or he will be wise in his own eyes.

26 : 5

Like cutting off one's feet or drinking violence is the sending of a message by the hand of a fool.

26 : 6

Like a lame man's legs that hang limp is a proverb in the mouth of a fool.

26 : 7

Like tying a stone in a sling is the giving of honor to a fool.

26 : 8

Like a thornbush in a drunkard's hand is a proverb in the mouth of a fool.

26 : 9

Like an archer who wounds at random is he who hires a fool or any passer-by.

26 : 10

As a dog returns to its vomit, so a fool repeats his folly.

26 : 11

Do you see a man wise in his own eyes? There is more hope for a fool than for him.

26 : 12

Stone is heavy and sand a burden, but provocation by a fool is heavier than both.

27 : 3

Though you grind a fool in a mortar, grinding him like grain with a pestle, you will not remove his folly from him.

27 : 22

170

He who trusts in himself is a fool, but he who walks in wisdom is kept safe.
28 : 26

If a wise man goes to court with a fool, the fool rages and scoffs, and there is no peace.
29 : 9

A fool gives full vent to his anger, but a wise man keeps himself under control.
29 : 11

Do you see a man who speaks in haste? There is more hope for a fool than for him.
29 : 20

a servant who becomes a king, a fool who is full of food,
30 : 22

"If you have played the fool and exalted yourself, or if you have planned evil, clap your hand over your mouth!
30 : 32

fooled

A simple man believes anything, but a prudent man gives thought to his steps.
14 : 15

foolish

How useless to spread a net in full view of all the birds!
1 : 17

You who are simple, gain prudence; you who are foolish, gain understanding.
8 : 5

Stolen water is sweet; food eaten in secret is delicious!"
9 : 17

The proverbs of Solomon: A wise son brings joy to his father, but a foolish son grief to his mother.
10 : 1

The wise woman builds her house, but with her own hands the foolish one tears hers down.
14 : 1

A quick-tempered man does foolish things, and a crafty man is hated.
14 : 17

A wise son brings joy to his father, but a foolish man despises his mother.
15 : 20

A foolish son brings grief to his father and bitterness to the one who bore him.
17 : 25

A foolish son is his father's ruin, and a quarrelsome wife is like a constant dripping.
19 : 13

Wine is a mocker and beer a brawler; whoever is led astray by them is not wise.
20 : 1

foolish heart

A prudent man keeps his knowledge to himself, but the heart of fools blurts out folly.
12 : 23

foolish man

A wise son brings joy to his father, but a foolish man despises his mother.
15 : 20

In the house of the wise are stores of choice food and oil, but a foolish man devours all he has.
21 : 20

foolish schemes

A faithful man will be richly blessed, but one eager to get rich will not go unpunished.
28 : 20

foolish son

A foolish son is his father's ruin, and a quarrelsome wife is like a constant dripping.

19 : 13

foolishness

How useless to spread a net in full view of all the birds!

1 : 17

"How long will you simple ones love your simple ways? How long will mockers delight in mockery and fools hate knowledge?

1 : 22

He will die for lack of discipline, led astray by his own great folly.

5 : 23

Like a gold ring in a pig's snout is a beautiful woman who shows no discretion.

11 : 22

Whoever loves discipline loves knowledge, but he who hates correction is stupid.

12 : 1

Every prudent man acts out of knowledge, but a fool exposes his folly.

13 : 16

A fool's talk brings a rod to his back, but the lips of the wise protect them.

14 : 3

Stay away from a foolish man, for you will not find knowledge on his lips.

14 : 7

The simple inherit folly, but the prudent are crowned with knowledge.

14 : 18

A patient man has great understanding, but a quick-tempered man displays folly.

14 : 29

The tongue of the wise commends knowledge, but the mouth of the fool gushes folly.

15 : 2

The discerning heart seeks knowledge, but the mouth of a fool feeds on folly.

15 : 14

Understanding is a fountain of life to those who have it, but folly brings punishment to fools.

16 : 22

Better to meet a bear robbed of her cubs than a fool in his folly.

17 : 12

He who answers before listening -- that is his folly and his shame.

18 : 13

A man's own folly ruins his life, yet his heart rages against the Lord.

19 : 3

Folly is bound up in the heart of a child, but the rod of discipline will drive it far from him.

22 : 15

The schemes of folly are sin, and men detest a mocker.

24 : 9

Do not answer a fool according to his folly, or you will be like him yourself.

26 : 4

is a man who deceives his neighbor and says, "I was only joking!"

26 : 19

The prudent see danger and take refuge, but the simple keep going and suffer for it.

27 : 12

Though you grind a fool in a mortar,
grinding him like grain with a pestle,
you will not remove his folly from him.

27 . 22

fools
The fear of the Lord is the beginning of
knowledge, but fools despise wisdom
and discipline.

1 : 7

"How long will you simple ones love
your simple ways? How long will
mockers delight in mockery and fools
hate knowledge?

1 : 22

For the waywardness of the simple will
kill them, and the complacency of fools
will destroy them;

1 : 32

The wise inherit honor, but fools he
holds up to shame.

3 : 35

The lips of the righteous nourish many,
but fools die for lack of judgment.

10 : 21

A prudent man keeps his knowledge to
himself, but the heart of fools blurts out
folly.

12 : 23

A longing fulfilled is sweet to the soul,
but fools detest turning from evil.

13 : 19

He who walks with the wise grows
wise, but a companion of fools suffers
harm.

13 : 20

The wisdom of the prudent is to give
thought to their ways, but the folly of
fools is deception.

14 : 8

Fools mock at making amends for sin,
but goodwill is found among the
upright.

14 : 9

The wealth of the wise is their crown,
but the folly of fools yields folly.

14 : 24

Wisdom reposes in the heart of the
discerning and even among fools she
lets herself be known.

14 : 33

The lips of the wise spread knowledge;
not so the hearts of fools.

15 : 7

Understanding is a fountain of life to
those who have it, but folly brings
punishment to fools.

16 : 22

Penalties are prepared for mockers, and
beatings for the backs of fools.

19 : 29

A whip for the horse, a halter for the
donkey, and a rod for the backs of
fools!

26 : 3

fools despise discipline
The fear of the Lord is the beginning of
knowledge, but fools despise wisdom
and discipline.

1 : 7

fools despise wisdom
The fear of the Lord is the beginning of
knowledge, but fools despise wisdom
and discipline.

1 : 7

fool's eye
A discerning man keeps wisdom in
view, but a fool's eyes wander to the
ends of the earth.

17 : 24

173

fool's lips
A fool's lips bring him strife, and his mouth invites a beating.

18 : 6

fool's mouth
A fool's mouth is his undoing, and his lips are a snare to his soul.

18 : 7

fool's talk
A fool's talk brings a rod to his back, but the lips of the wise protect them.

14 : 3

foot
my son, do not go along with them, do not set foot on their paths;

1 : 15

Then you will go on your way in safety, and your foot will not stumble;

3 : 23

for the Lord will be your confidence and will keep your foot from being snared.

3 : 26

Do not set foot on the path of the wicked or walk in the way of evil men.

4 : 14

Do not swerve to the right or the left; keep your foot from evil.

4 : 27

Seldom set foot in your neighbor's house -- too much of you, and he will hate you.

25 : 17

Like a bad tooth or a lame foot is reliance on the unfaithful in times of trouble.

25 : 19

forefathers
Do not move an ancient boundary stone set up by your forefathers.

22 : 28

forever
Bind them upon your heart forever; fasten them around your neck.

6 : 21

When the storm has swept by, the wicked are gone, but the righteous stand firm forever.

10 : 25

Truthful lips endure forever, but a lying tongue lasts only a moment.

12 : 19

A false witness will perish, and whoever listens to him will be destroyed forever.

21 : 28

for riches do not endure forever, and a crown is not secure for all generations.

27 : 24

forfeits
A king's wrath is like the roar of a lion; he who angers him forfeits his life.

20 : 2

forget
My son, do not forget my teaching, but keep my commands in your heart,

3 : 1

Get wisdom, get understanding; do not forget my words or swerve from them.

4 : 5

lest they drink and forget what the law decrees, and deprive all the oppressed of the rights.

31 : 5

let them drink and forget their poverty and remember their misery no more.

31 : 7

forgiveness
Hatred stirs up dissension, but love covers over all wrongs.

10 : 12

He who covers over an offense promotes love, but whoever repeats the matter separates close friends.

17 : 9

Do not say, "I'll pay you back for this wrong!" Wait for the Lord, and he will deliver you.

20 : 22

Do not say, "I'll do to him as he has done to me; I'll pay that man back for what he did."

24 : 29

In doing this, you will heap burning coals on his head, and the Lord will reward you.

25 : 22

fork in the road
The way of a fool seems right to him, but a wise man listens to advice.

12 : 15

Good understanding wins favor, but the way of the unfaithful is hard.

13 : 15

forsake
Listen, my son, to your father's instruction and do not forsake your mother's teaching.

1 : 8

I give you sound learning, so do not forsake my teaching.

4 : 2

Do not forsake wisdom, and she will protect you; love her, and she will watch over you.

4 : 6

My son, keep your father's commands and do not forsake your mother's teaching.

6 : 20

Do not forsake your friend and the friend of your father, and do not go to your brother's house when disaster strikes you -- better a neighbor nearby than a brother far away.

27 : 10

Those who forsake the law praise the wicked, but those who keep the law resist them.

28 : 4

forsake the law
Those who forsake the law praise the wicked, but those who keep the law resist them.

28 : 4

forsaken
Wealth brings many friends, but a poor man's friend deserts him.

19 : 4

forth
Do not boast about tomorrow, for you do not know what a day may bring forth.

27 : 1

fortified
The wealth of the rich is their fortified city, but poverty is the ruin of the poor.

10 : 15

The wealth of the rich is their fortified city; they imagine it an unscalable wall.

18 : 11

An offended brother is more unyielding than a fortified city, and disputes are like the barred gates of a citadel.

18 : 19

fortified city
The wealth of the rich is their fortified city; they imagine it an unscalable wall.

18 : 11

An offended brother is more unyielding than a fortified city, and disputes are like the barred gates of a citadel.

18 : 19

fortress

He who fears the Lord has a secure fortress, and for his children it will be a refuge.

14 : 26

fortune

A fortune made by a lying tongue is a fleeting vapor and a deadly snare.

21 : 6

forward

The first to present his case seems right, till another comes forward and questions him.

18 : 17

found

So I came out to meet you; I looked for you and have found you!

7 : 15

The man of integrity walks securely, but he who takes crooked paths will be found out.

10 : 9

Wisdom is found on the lips of the discerning, but a rod is for the back of him who lacks judgment.

10 : 13

Pride only breeds quarrels, but wisdom is found in those who take advice.

13 : 10

Fools mock at making amends for sin, but goodwill is found among the upright.

14 : 9

A poor man is shunned by all his relatives -- how much more do his friends avoid him! Though he pursues them with pleading, they are nowhere to be found.

19 : 7

a lizard can be caught with the hand, yet it is found in kings' palaces.

30 : 28

foundation

By wisdom the Lord laid the earth's foundations, by understanding he set the heavens in place;

3 : 19

Wisdom has built her house; she has hewn out its seven pillars.

9 : 1

A man cannot be established through wickedness, but the righteous cannot be uprooted.

12 : 3

By wisdom a house is built, and through understanding it is established;

24 : 3

foundations

By wisdom the Lord laid the earth's foundations, by understanding he set the heavens in place;

3 : 19

when he gave the sea its boundary so the waters would not overstep his command, and when he marked out the foundations of the earth.

8 : 29

fountain

Above all else, guard your heart, for it is the wellspring of life.

4 : 23

May your fountain be blessed, and may you rejoice in the wife of your youth.

5 : 18

The mouth of the righteous is a fountain of life, but violence overwhelms the mouth of the wicked.

10 : 11

The teaching of the wise is a fountain of life, turning a man from the snares of death.

13 : 14

The fear of the Lord is a fountain of life, turning a man from the snares of death.

14 : 27

Understanding is a fountain of life to those who have it, but folly brings punishment to fools.

16 : 22

The words of a man's mouth are deep waters, but the fountain of wisdom is a bubbling brook.

18 : 4

fountain of life
The fear of the Lord is a fountain of life, turning a man from the snares of death.

14 : 27

Understanding is a fountain of life to those who have it, but folly brings punishment to fools.

16 : 22

fountain of wisdom
The words of a man's mouth are deep waters, but the fountain of wisdom is a bubbling brook.

18 : 4

fountains
when he established the clouds above and fixed securely the fountains of the deep,

8 : 28

four
"The leech has two daughters. 'Give! Give!' they cry, "There are three things that are never satisfied, four that never say, 'Enough!':

30 : 15

There are three things that are too amazing for me, four that I do not understand:

30 : 18

"Under three things the earth trembles, under four it cannot bear up:

30 : 21

"Four things on earth are small, yet they are extremely wise:

30 : 24

"There are three things that are stately in their stride, four that move with stately bearing:

30 : 29

fowler
Free yourself, like a gazelle from the hand of the hunter, like a bird from the snare of the fowler.

6 : 5

fragrance
I have perfumed my bed with myrrh, aloes and cinnamon.

7 : 17

fraud
Food gained by fraud tastes sweet to a man, but he ends up with a mouth full of gravel.

20 : 17

Like clouds and wind without rain is a man who boasts of gifts he does not give.

25 : 14

free

then do this, my son, to free yourself, since you have fallen into your neighbor's hands: Go and humble yourself; press your plea with your neighbor!

6 : 3

Free yourself, like a gazelle from the hand of the hunter, like a bird from the snare of the fowler.

6 : 5

Be sure of this: The wicked will not go unpunished, but those who are righteous will go free.

11 : 21

A false witness will not go unpunished, and he who pours out lies will not go free.

19 : 5

free from sin

Through love and faithfulness sin is atoned for; through the fear of the Lord a man avoids evil.

16 : 6

free yourself

then do this, my son, to free yourself, since you have fallen into your neighbor's hands: Go and humble yourself; press your plea with your neighbor!

6 : 3

Free yourself, like a gazelle from the hand of the hunter, like a bird from the snare of the fowler.

6 : 5

freedom

Free yourself, like a gazelle from the hand of the hunter, like a bird from the snare of the fowler.

6 : 5

The righteousness of the upright delivers them, but the unfaithful are trapped by evil desires.

11 : 6

fret

Do not fret because of evil men or be envious of the wicked,

24 : 19

friend

A friend loves at all times, and a brother is born for adversity.

17 : 17

A man of many companions may come to ruin, but there is a friend who sticks closer than a brother.

18 : 24

Wealth brings many friends, but a poor man's friend deserts him.

19 : 4

Many curry favor with a ruler, and everyone is the friend of a man who gives gifts.

19 : 6

He who loves a pure heart and whose speech is gracious will have the king for his friend.

22 : 11

Wounds from a friend can be trusted, but an enemy multiplies kisses.

27 : 6

Perfume and incense bring joy to the heart, and the pleasantness of one's friend springs from his earnest counsel.

27 : 9

Do not forsake your friend and the friend of your father, and do not go to your brother's house when disaster strikes you -- better a neighbor nearby than a brother far away.

27 : 10

friends

The poor are shunned even by their neighbors, but the rich have many friends.

14 : 20

A perverse man stirs up dissension, and a gossip separates close friends.

16 : 28

He who covers over an offense promotes love, but whoever repeats the matter separates close friends.

17 : 9

Wealth brings many friends, but a poor man's friend deserts him.

19 : 4

A poor man is shunned by all his relatives -- how much more do his friends avoid him! Though he pursues them with pleading, they are nowhere to be found.

19 : 7

Do not make friends with a hot-tempered man, do not associate with one easily angered,

22 : 24

friendship

A righteous man is cautious in friendship, but the way of the wicked leads them astray.

12 : 26

A perverse man stirs up dissension, and a gossip separates close friends.

16 : 28

He who covers over an offense promotes love, but whoever repeats the matter separates close friends.

17 : 9

A man of many companions may come to ruin, but there is a friend who sticks closer than a brother.

18 : 24

Do not envy wicked men, do not desire their company;

24 : 1

Like a club or a sword or a sharp arrow is the man who gives false testimony against his neighbor.

25 : 18

Without wood a fire goes out; without gossip a quarrel dies down.

26 : 20

As iron sharpens iron, so one man sharpens another.

27 : 17

friendship with the enemy

Those who forsake the law praise the wicked, but those who keep the law resist them.

28 : 4

front

A wicked man puts up a bold front, but an upright man gives thought to his ways.

21 : 29

fruit

they will eat the fruit of their ways and be filled with the fruit of their schemes.

1 : 31

My fruit is better than fine gold; what I yield surpasses choice silver.

8 : 19

The fruit of the righteous is a tree of life, and he who wins souls is wise.

11 : 30

The wicked desire the plunder of evil men, but the root of the righteous flourishes.

12 : 12

From the fruit of his lips a man is filled with good things as surely as the work of his hands rewards him.

12 : 14

From the fruit of his lips a man enjoys good things, but the unfaithful have a craving for violence.

13 : 2

From the fruit of his mouth a man's stomach is filled; with the harvest from his lips he is satisfied.

18 : 20

The tongue has the power of life and death, and those who love it will eat its fruit.

18 : 21

He who tends a fig tree will eat its fruit, and he who looks after his master will be honored.

27 : 18

fruit of his lips
From the fruit of his lips a man enjoys good things, but the unfaithful have a craving for violence.

13 : 2

fruit of their ways
they will eat the fruit of their ways and be filled with the fruit of their schemes.

1 : 31

frustrates
The eyes of the Lord keep watch over knowledge, but he frustrates the words of the unfaithful.

22 : 12

fuel
Without wood a fire goes out; without gossip a quarrel dies down.

26 : 20

fugitive
A man tomented by the guilt of murder will be a fugitive till death; let no one support him.

28 : 17

fulfilled
"I have fellowship offerings at home; today I fulfilled my vows.

7 : 14

Hope deferred makes the heart sick, but a longing fulfilled is a tree of life.

13 : 12

A longing fulfilled is sweet to the soul, but fools detest turning from evil.

13 : 19

fulfillment
The righteous eat to their hearts' content, but the stomach of the wicked goes hungry.

13 : 25

full
How useless to spread a net in full view of all the birds!

1 : 17

The path of the righteous is like the first gleam of dawn, shining ever brighter till the full light of day.

4 : 18

For a man's ways are in full view of the Lord, and he examines all his paths.

5 : 21

bestowing wealth on those who love me and making their treasuries full.

8 : 21

Better a dry crust with peace and quiet than a house full of feasting with strife.

17 : 1

Food gained by fraud tastes sweet to a man, but he ends up with a mouth full of gravel.

20 : 17

He who is full loathes honey, but to the hungry even what is bitter tastes sweet.

27 : 7

180

A fool gives full vent to his anger, but a wise man keeps himself under control.

29 : 11

a servant who becomes a king, a fool who is full of food,

30 : 22

Her husband has full confidence in her and lacks nothing of value.

31 : 11

full moon

He took his purse filled with money and will not be home till full moon."

7 : 20

full of food

a servant who becomes a king, a fool who is full of food,

30 : 22

full vent

A fool gives full vent to his anger, but a wise man keeps himself under control.

29 : 11

full view

How useless to spread a net in full view of all the birds!

1 : 17

fully

The sluggard craves and gets nothing, but the desires of the diligent are fully satisfied.

13 : 4

The faithless will be fully repaid for their ways, and the good man rewarded for his.

14 : 14

Evil men do not understand justice, but those who seek the Lord understand it fully.

28 : 5

furnace

The crucible for silver and the furnace for gold, but the Lord tests the heart.

17 : 3

The crucible for silver and the furnace for gold, but man is tested by the praise he receives.

27 : 21

fury

for jealousy arouses a husband's fury, and he will show no mercy when he takes revenge.

6 : 34

A king's rage is like the roar of a lion, but his favor is like dew on the grass.

19 : 12

He who sows wickedness reaps trouble, and the rod of his fury will be destroyed.

22 : 8

Anger is cruel and fury overwhelming, but who can stand before jealousy?

27 : 4

future

There is surely a future hope for you, and your hope will not be cut off.

23 : 18

Know also that wisdom is sweet to your soul; if you find it, there is a future hope for you, and your hope will not be cut off.

24 : 14

for the evil man has no future hope, and the lamp of the wicked will be snuffed out.

24 : 20

Do not boast about tomorrow, for you do not know what a day may bring forth.

27 : 1

future hope

There is surely a future hope for you,
and your hope will not be cut off.

23 : 18

for the evil man has no future hope, and
the lamp of the wicked will be snuffed
out.

24 : 20

G

gain
Such is the end of all who go after ill-gotten gain; it takes away the life of those who get it.

1 : 19

Listen, my sons, to a father's instruction; pay attention and gain understanding.

4 : 1

You who are simple, gain prudence; you who are foolish, gain understanding.

8 : 5

Better a little with righteousness than much gain with injustice.

16 : 8

Flog a mocker, and the simple will learn prudence; rebuke a discerning man, and he will gain knowledge.

19 : 25

Food gained by fraud tastes sweet to a man, but he ends up with a mouth full of gravel.

20 : 17

When a mocker is punished, the simple gain wisdom; when a wise man is instructed, he gets knowledge.

21 : 11

A tyrannical ruler lacks judgment, but he who hates ill-gotten gain will enjoy a long life.

28 : 16

He who rebukes a man will in the end gain more favor than he who has a flattering tongue.

28 : 23

gain knowledge
Flog a mocker, and the simple will learn prudence; rebuke a discerning man, and he will gain knowledge.

19 : 25

gained
Food gained by fraud tastes sweet to a man, but he ends up with a mouth full of gravel.

20 : 17

An inheritance quickly gained at the beginning will not be blessed at the end.

20 : 21

gaining respect
A kindhearted woman gains respect, but ruthless men gain only wealth.

11 : 16

gaining understanding
He who ignores discipline despises himself, but whoever heeds correction gains understanding.

15 : 32

gaining wealth
A faithful man will be richly blessed, but one eager to get rich will not go unpunished.

28 : 20

gaining wisdom
Listen to advice and accept instruction, and in the end you will be wise.

19 : 20

gains
Blessed is the man who finds wisdom, the man who gains understanding,

3 : 13

A kindhearted woman gains respect, but ruthless men gain only wealth.

11 : 16

One man gives freely, yet gains even more; another withholds unduly, but comes to poverty.

11 : 24

He who ignores discipline despises himself, but whoever heeds correction gains understanding.

15 : 32

A man's pride brings him low, but a man of lowly spirit gains honor.

29 : 23

gall
but in the end she is bitter as gall, sharp as a double-edged sword.

5 : 4

game
The lazy man does not roast his game, but the diligent man prizes his possessions.

12 : 27

garland
They will be a garland to grace your head and a chain to adorn your neck.

1 : 9

She will set a garland of grace on your head and present you with a crown of splendor.

4 : 9

garment
Take the garment of one who puts up security for a stranger; hold it in pledge if he does it for a wayward woman.

20 : 16

Like one who takes away a garment on a cold day, or like vinegar poured on soda, is one who sings songs to a heavy heart.

25 : 20

Take a garment of one who puts up security for a stranger; hold it in pledge if he does it for a wayward woman.

27 : 13

garments
She makes linen garments and sells them, and supplies the merchants with sashes.

31 : 24

gate
He who loves a quarrel loves sin; he who builds a high gate invites destruction.

17 : 19

Wisdom is too high for a fool; in the assembly at the gate he has nothing to say.

24 : 7

Her husband is respected at the city gate, where he takes his seat among the elders of the land.

31 : 23

Give her the reward she has earned, and let her works bring her praise at the city gate.

31 : 31

gates
beside the gates leading into the city, at the entrances, she cries aloud:

8 : 3

Evil men will bow down in the presence of the good, and the wicked at the gates of the righteous.

14 : 19

An offended brother is more unyielding than a fortified city, and disputes are like the barred gates of a citadel.

18 : 19

gateways
at the head of the noisy streets she cries
out, in the gateways of the city she
makes her speech·
1 : 21

gathered
When the hay is removed and new
growth appears and the grass from the
hills is gathered in,
27 : 25

Who has gone up to heaven and come
down? Who has gathered up the wind
in the hollow of his hands? Who has
wrapped up the waters in his cloak?
Who has established all the ends of the
earth? What is his name, and the name
of his son? Tell me if you know!
30 : 4

gathered up
Who has gone up to heaven and come
down? Who has gathered up the wind
in the hollow of his hands? Who has
wrapped up the waters in his cloak?
Who has established all the ends of the
earth? What is his name, and the name
of his son? Tell me if you know!
30 : 4

gathers
yet it stores its provisions in summer
and gathers its food at harvest.
6 : 8

He who gathers crops in summer is a
wise son, but he who sleeps during
harvest is a disgraceful son.
10 : 5

Dishonest money dwindles away, but he
who gathers money little by little makes
it grow.
13 : 11

gave
Listen to your father, who gave you life,
and do not despise your mother when
she is old.
23 : 22

May your father and mother be glad;
may she who gave you birth rejoice!
23 : 25

gazelle
Free yourself, like a gazelle from the
hand of the hunter, like a bird from the
snare of the fowler.
6 : 5

generations
for riches do not endure forever, and a
crown is not secure for all generations.
27 : 24

generosity
One man gives freely, yet gains even
more; another withholds unduly, but
comes to poverty.
11 : 24

A generous man will prosper; he who
refreshes others will himself be
refreshed.
11 : 25

Many curry favor with a ruler, and
everyone is the friend of a man who
gives gifts.
19 : 6

A generous man will himself be
blessed, for he shares his food with the
poor.
22 : 9

generous
Do not say to your neighbor, "Come
back later; I'll give it tomorrow" --
when you now have it with you.
3 : 28

A generous man will prosper; he who refreshes others will himself be refreshed.

11 : 25

A generous man will himself be blessed, for he shares his food with the poor.

22 : 9

generous man
A generous man will prosper; he who refreshes others will himself be refreshed.

11 : 25

A generous man will himself be blessed, for he shares his food with the poor.

22 : 9

gentle
A gentle answer turns away wrath, but a harsh word stirs up anger.

15 : 1

Through patience a ruler can be persuaded, and a gentle tongue can break a bone.

25 : 15

Mockers stir up a city, but wise men turn away anger.

29 : 8

gentle answer
A gentle answer turns away wrath, but a harsh word stirs up anger.

15 : 1

gentleness
Through patience a ruler can be persuaded, and a gentle tongue can break a bone.

25 : 15

A fool gives full vent to his anger, but a wise man keeps himself under control.

29 : 11

get
Such is the end of all who go after ill-gotten gain; it takes away the life of those who get it.

1 : 19

Get wisdom, get understanding; do not forget my words or swerve from them.

4 : 5

Wisdom is supreme; therefore get wisdom. Though it cost all you have, get understanding.

4 : 7

How much better to get wisdom than gold, to choose understanding rather than silver!

16 : 16

Of what use is money in the hand of a fool, since he has no desire to get wisdom?

17 : 16

get rich
Do not wear yourself out to get rich; have the wisdom to show restraint.

23 : 4

A stingy man is eager to get rich and is unaware that poverty awaits him.

28 : 22

get to work
How long will you lie there, you sluggard? When will you get up from your sleep?

6 : 9

get up
How long will you lie there, you sluggard? When will you get up from your sleep?

6 : 9

get wisdom
Buy the truth and do not sell it; get wisdom, discipline and understanding.

23 : 23

gift

A gift opens the way for the giver and ushers him into the presence of the great.

18 : 16

A gift given in secret soothes anger, and a bribe concealed in the cloak pacifies great wrath.

21 : 14

giftedness

Do you see a man skilled in his work? He will serve before kings, he will not serve before obscure men.

22 : 29

gifts

Many curry favor with a ruler, and everyone is the friend of a man who gives gifts.

19 : 6

He who oppresses the poor to increase his wealth and he who gives gifts to the rich -- both come to poverty.

22 : 16

Like clouds and wind without rain is a man who boasts of gifts he does not give.

25 : 14

girls

You will have plenty of goat's milk to feed you and your family and to nourish your servant girls.

27 : 27

She gets up while it is still dark; she provides food for her family and portions for her servant girls.

31 : 15

give

My son, if sinners entice you, do not give in to them.

1 : 10

Do not withhold good from those who deserve it, when it is in your power to act.

3 : 27

Do not say to your neighbor, "Come back later; I'll give it tomorrow" -- when you now have it with you.

3 : 28

I give you sound learning, so do not forsake my teaching.

4 : 2

lest you give your best strength to others and your years to one who is cruel,

5 : 9

The wisdom of the prudent is to give thought to their ways, but the folly of fools is deception.

14 : 8

All day long he craves for more, but the righteous give without sparing.

21 : 26

teaching you true and reliable words, so that you can give sound answers to him who sent you?

22 : 21

My son, give me your heart and let your eyes keep to my ways,

23 : 26

Like clouds and wind without rain is a man who boasts of gifts he does not give.

25 : 14

If your enemy is hungry, give him food to eat; if he is thirsty, give him water to drink.

25 : 21

Keep falsehood and lies far from me; give me neither poverty nor riches, but give me only my daily bread.

30 : 8

"The leech has two daughters. 'Give! Give!' they cry. "There are three things that are never satisfied, four that never say, 'Enough!':

30 : 15

Give beer to those who are perishing, wine to those who are in anguish;

31 : 6

Give her the reward she has earned, and let her works bring her praise at the city gate.

31 : 31

give in
My son, if sinners entice you, do not give in to them.

1 : 10

giver
A gift opens the way for the giver and ushers him into the presence of the great.

18 : 16

gives
For the Lord gives wisdom, and from his mouth come knowledge and understanding.

2 : 6

He mocks proud mockers but gives grace to the humble.

3 : 34

She gives no thought to the way of life; her paths are crooked, but she knows it not.

5 : 6

A truthful witness gives honest testimony, but a false witness tells lies.

12 : 17

A simple man believes anything, but a prudent man gives thought to his steps.

14 : 15

A heart at peace gives life to the body, but envy rots the bones.

14 : 30

A cheerful look brings joy to the heart, and good news gives health to the bones.

15 : 30

Whoever gives heed to instruction prospers, and blessed is he who trusts in the Lord.

16 : 20

A bribe is a charm to the one who gives it; wherever he turns, he succeeds.

17 : 8

Many curry favor with a ruler, and everyone is the friend of a man who gives gifts.

19 : 6

A man's wisdom gives him patience; it is to his glory to overlook an offense.

19 : 11

A wicked man puts up a bold front, but an upright man gives thought to his ways.

21 : 29

He who oppresses the poor to increase his wealth and he who gives gifts to the rich -- both come to poverty.

22 : 16

Like a club or a sword or a sharp arrow is the man who gives false testimony against his neighbor.

25 : 18

Like a muddied spring or a polluted well is a righteous man who gives way to the wicked.

25 : 26

He who gives to the poor will lack nothing, but he who closes his eyes to them receives many curses.

28 : 27

By justice a king gives a country stability, but one who is greedy for bribes tears it down

29 : 4

A fool gives full vent to his anger, but a wise man keeps himself under control.

29 : 11

The poor man and the oppressor have this in common: The Lord gives sight to the eyes of both.

29 : 13

gives to the poor
He who gives to the poor will lack nothing, but he who closes his eyes to them receives many curses.

28 : 27

gives way
Like a muddied spring or a polluted well is a righteous man who gives way to the wicked.

25 : 26

giving
for giving prudence to the simple, knowledge and discretion to the young -

1 : 4

One man gives freely, yet gains even more; another withholds unduly, but comes to poverty.

11 : 24

A man finds joy in giving an apt reply-- and how good is a timely word!

15 : 23

He who listens to a life-giving rebuke will be at home among the wise.

15 : 31

A gift opens the way for the giver and ushers him into the presence of the great.

18 : 16

A gift given in secret soothes anger, and a bribe concealed in the cloak pacifies great wrath.

21 : 14

A generous man will himself be blessed, for he shares his food with the poor.

22 : 9

Like tying a stone in a sling is the giving of honor to a fool.

26 : 8

A stingy man is eager to get rich and is unaware that poverty awaits him.

28 : 22

giving knowledge to the young
for giving prudence to the simple, knowledge and discretion to the young -

1 : 4

giving prudence to the simple
for giving prudence to the simple, knowledge and discretion to the young -

1 : 4

giving to the poor
He who increases his wealth by exorbitant interest amasses it for another, who will be kind to the poor.

28 : 8

glad
My son, if your heart is wise, then my heart will be glad;

23 : 15

my inmost being will rejoice when your lips speak what is right.

23 : 16

May your father and mother be glad; may she who gave you birth rejoice!

23 : 25

An evil man is snared by his own sin, but a righteous one can sing and be glad.

29 : 6

glances
those whose eyes are ever so haughty, whose glances are so disdainful;

30 : 13

gleam
The path of the righteous is like the first gleam of dawn, shining ever brighter till the full light of day.

4 : 18

gloat
Do not gloat when your enemy falls; when he stumbles, do not let your heart rejoice,

24 : 17

gloats
He who mocks the poor shows contempt for their Maker; whoever gloats over disaster will not go unpunished.

17 : 5

glorifying
When a man's ways are pleasing to the Lord, he makes even his enemies live at peace with him.

16 : 7

glory
A large population is a king's glory, but without subjects a prince is ruined.

14 : 28

A man's wisdom gives him patience; it is to his glory to overlook an offense.

19 : 11

The righteous man leads a blameless life; blessed are his children after him.

20 : 7

The glory of young men is their strength, gray hair the splendor of the old.

20 : 29

It is the glory of God to conceal a matter; to search out a matter is the glory of kings.

25 : 2

glory of God
It is the glory of God to conceal a matter; to search out a matter is the glory of kings.

25 : 2

glory of kings
It is the glory of God to conceal a matter; to search out a matter is the glory of kings.

25 : 2

gluttons
for drunkards and gluttons become poor, and drowsiness clothes them in rags.

23 : 21

He who keeps the law is a discerning son, but a companion of gluttons disgraces his father.

28 : 7

gluttony
and put a knife to your throat if you are given to gluttony.

23 : 2

Do not join those who drink too much wine or gorge themselves on meat,

23 : 20

go
let's swallow them alive, like the grave, and whole, like those who go down to the pit;

1 : 12

190

my son, do not go along with them, do not set foot on their paths;

1 : 15

None who go to her return or attain the paths of life.

2 : 19

Then you will go on your way in safety, and your foot will not stumble;

3 : 23

Hold on to instruction, do not let it go; guard it well, for it is your life.

4 : 13

Avoid it, do not travel on it; turn from it and go on your way.

4 : 15

Keep to a path far from her, do not go near the door of her house,

5 : 8

then do this, my son, to free yourself, since you have fallen into your neighbor's hands: Go and humble yourself; press your plea with your neighbor!

6 : 3

Go to the ant, you sluggard; consider its ways and be wise!

6 : 6

So is he who sleeps with another man's wife; no one who touches her will go unpunished.

6 : 29

calling out to those who pass by, who go straight on their way.

9 : 15

The Lord does not let the righteous go hungry but he thwarts the craving of the wicked.

10 : 3

Be sure of this: The wicked will not go unpunished, but those who are righteous will go free.

11 : 21

Do not those who plot evil go astray? But those who plan what is good find love and faithfulness.

14 : 22

The Lord detests all the proud of heart. Be sure of this: They will not go unpunished.

16 : 5

He who mocks the poor shows contempt for their Maker; whoever gloats over disaster will not go unpunished.

17 : 5

The words of gossip are like choice morsels; they go down to a man's inmost parts.

18 : 8

A false witness will not go unpunished, and he who pours out lies will not go free.

19 : 5

A false witness will not go unpunished, and he who pours out lies will perish.

19 : 9

Train a child in the way he should go, and when he is old he will not turn from it.

22 : 6

Those who linger over wine, who go to sample bowls of mixed wine,

23 : 30

The words of a gossip are like choice morsels; they go down to a man's inmost parts.

26 : 22

Do not forsake your friend and the friend of your father, and do not go to your brother's house when disaster strikes you - better a neighbor nearby than a brother far away.

27 : 10

When the righteous triumph, there is great elation; but when the wicked rise to power, men go into hiding.

28 : 12

A faithful man will be richly blessed, but one eager to get rich will not go unpunished.

28 : 20

When the wicked rise to power, people go into hiding; but when the wicked perish, the righteous thrive.

28 : 28

She sees that her trading is profitable, and her lamp does not go out at night.

31 : 18

go well
But it will go well with those who convict the guilty, and rich blessing will come upon them.

24 : 25

goal
A discerning man keeps wisdom in view, but a fool's eyes wander to the ends of the earth.

17 : 24

goals
Let your eyes look straight ahead, fix your gaze directly before you.

4 : 25

The desire of the righteous ends only in good, but the hope of the wicked only in wrath.

11 : 23

Commit to the Lord whatever you do, and your plans will succeed.

16 : 3

Many are the plans in the man's heart, but it is the Lord's purpose that prevails.

19 : 21

goat
a strutting rooster, a he-goat, and a king with his army around him.

30 : 31

goats
the lambs will provide you with clothing, and the goats with the price of a field.

27 : 26

goat's milk
You will have plenty of goat's milk to feed you and your family and to nourish your servant girls.

27 : 27

God
"Then they will call to me but I will not answer; they will look for me but will not find me.

1 : 28

then you will understand the fear of the Lord and find the knowledge of God.

2 : 5

who has left the partner of her youth and ignored the covenant she made before God.

2 : 17

Then you will win favor and a good name in the sight of God and man.

3 : 4

He who oppresses the poor shows contempt for their Maker, but whoever is kind to the needy honors God.

14 : 31

It is the glory of God to conceal a matter; to search out a matter is the glory of kings.

25 : 2

I have not learned the wisdom, nor have I knowledge of the Holy One.

30 : 3

Every word of God is flawless; he is a shield to those who take refuge in him.

30 : 5

Otherwise, I may have too much and disown you and say, 'Who is the Lord?' Or I may become poor and steal, and so dishonor the name of my God.

30 : 9

God laughing
I in turn will laugh at your disaster; I will mock when calamity overtakes you

1 : 26

God mocking
I in turn will laugh at your disaster; I will mock when calamity overtakes you

1 : 26

God sees all
For a man's ways are in full view of the Lord, and he examines all his paths.

5 : 21

godless
With his mouth the godless destroys his neighbor, but through knowledge the righteous escape.

11 : 9

godliness
A man cannot be established through wickedness, but the righteous cannot be uprooted.

12 : 3

The Lord detests the way of the wicked but he loves those who pursue righteousness.

15 : 9

Better a little with righteousness than much gain with injustice.

16 : 8

In the paths of the wicked lie thorns and snares, but he who guards his soul stays far from them.

22 : 5

godly
Wicked men are overthrown and are no more, but the house of the righteous stands firm.

12 : 7

The way of the guilty is devious, but the conduct of the innocent is upright.

21 : 8

godly people
Righteousness exalts a nation, but sin is a disgrace to any people.

14 : 34

godly wife
She opens her arms to the poor and extends her hands to the needy.

31 : 20

God's blessings
then your barns will be filled to overflowing, and your vats will brim over with new wine.

3 : 10

God's judgment
"Then they will call to me but I will not answer; they will look for me but will not find me.

1 : 28

God's leading
in all your ways acknowledge him, and he will make your paths straight.

3 : 6

God's protection
Then you will go on your way in safety, and your foot will not stumble;

3 : 23

going

A prudent man sees danger and takes
refuge, but the simple keep going and
suffer for it.

22 : 3

gold

for she is more profitable than silver
and yields better returns than gold.

3 : 14

Choose my instruction instead of silver,
knowledge rather than choice gold,

8 : 10

My fruit is better than fine gold; what I
yield surpasses choice silver.

8 : 19

Like a gold ring in a pig's snout is a
beautiful woman who shows no
discretion.

11 : 22

How much better to get wisdom than
gold, to choose understanding rather
than silver!

16 : 16

The crucible for silver and the furnace
for gold, but the Lord tests the heart.

17 : 3

Gold there is, and rubies in abundance,
but lips that speak knowledge are a rare
jewel.

20 : 15

A good name is more desirable than
great riches; to be esteemed is better
than silver or gold.

22 : 1

A word aptly spoken is like apples of
gold in settings of silver.

25 : 11

Like an earring of gold or an ornament
of fine gold is a wise man's rebuke to a
listening ear.

25 : 12

The crucible for silver and the furnace
for gold, but man is tested by the praise
he receives.

27 : 21

gold ring

Like a gold ring in a pig's snout is a
beautiful woman who shows no
discretion.

11 : 22

gone

My husband is not at home; he has gone
on a long journey.

7 : 19

gone up

Who has gone up to heaven and come
down? Who has gathered up the wind
in the hollow of his hands? Who has
wrapped up the waters in his cloak?
Who has established all the ends of the
earth? What is his name, and the name
of his son? Tell me if you know!

30 : 4

good

Then you will understand what is right
and just and fair -- every good path.

2 : 9

Thus you will walk in the ways of good
men and keep to the paths of the
righteous.

2 : 20

Then you will win favor and a good
name in the sight of God and man.

3 : 4

Do not withhold good from those who
deserve it, when it is in your power to
act.

3 : 27

The desire of the righteous ends only in
good, but the hope of the wicked only
in wrath.

11 : 23

He who seeks good finds goodwill, but evil comes to him who searches for it.

11 : 27

A good man obtains favor from the Lord, but the Lord condemns a crafty man.

12 : 2

From the fruit of his lips a man is filled with good things as surely as the work of his hands rewards him.

12 : 14

From the fruit of his lips a man enjoys good things, but the unfaithful have a craving for violence.

13 : 2

Good understanding wins favor, but the way of the unfaithful is hard.

13 : 15

A good man leaves an inheritance for his children's children, but a sinner's wealth is stored up for the righteous.

13 : 22

The faithless will be fully repaid for their ways, and the good man rewarded for his.

14 : 14

Evil men will bow down in the presence of the good, and the wicked at the gates of the righteous.

14 : 19

Do not those who plot evil go astray? But those who plan what is good find love and faithfulness.

14 : 22

The eyes of the Lord are everywhere, keeping watch on the wicked and the good.

15 : 3

A man finds joy in giving an apt reply-- and how good is a timely word!

15 : 23

A violent man entices his neighbor and leads him down a path that is not good.

16 : 29

If a man pays back evil for good, evil will never leave his house.

17 : 13

A cheerful heart is good medicine, but a crushed spirit dries up the bones.

17 : 22

It is not good to punish an innocent man, or to flog officials for their integrity.

17 : 26

He who finds a wife finds what is good and receives favor from the Lord.

18 : 22

"It's no good, it's no good!" says the buyer; then off he goes and boasts about his purchase.

20 : 14

A good name is more desirable than great riches; to be esteemed is better than silver or gold.

22 : 1

Eat honey, my son, for it is good; honey from the comb is sweet to your taste.

24 : 13

These also are sayings to the wise: To show partiality in judging is not good:

24 : 23

Like cold water to a weary soul is good news from a distant land.

25 : 25

He who leads the upright along an evil path will fall into his own trap, but the blameless will receive a good inheritance.

28 : 10

To show partiality is not good -- yet a man will do wrong for a piece of bread.

28 : 21

She brings him good, not harm, all the days of her life.

31 : 12

good health
This will bring health to your body and nourishment to your bones.

3 : 8

good life
Long life is in her right hand; in her left hand are riches and honor.

3 : 16

For through me your days will be many, and years will be added to your life.

9 : 11

good man
A good man obtains favor from the Lord, but the Lord condemns a crafty man.

12 : 2

The faithless will be fully repaid for their ways, and the good man rewarded for his.

14 : 14

good name
Then you will win favor and a good name in the sight of God and man.

3 : 4

A good name is more desirable than great riches; to be esteemed is better than silver or gold.

22 : 1

good news
A cheerful look brings joy to the heart, and good news gives health to the bones.

15 : 30

Like cold water to a weary soul is good news from a distant land.

25 : 25

good things
From the fruit of his lips a man is filled with good things as surely as the work of his hands rewards him.

12 : 14

From the fruit of his lips a man enjoys good things, but the unfaithful have a craving for violence.

13 : 2

good vs. evil
Those who forsake the law praise the wicked, but those who keep the law resist them.

28 : 4

Better a poor man whose walk is blameless than a rich man whose ways are perverse.

28 : 6

goodwill
He who seeks good finds goodwill, but evil comes to him who searches for it.

11 : 27

Fools mock at making amends for sin, but goodwill is found among the upright.

14 : 9

gorge
Do not join those who drink too much wine or gorge themselves on meat,

23 : 20

If you find honey, just eat enough -- too much of it, and you will vomit.

25 : 16

gossip
He who conceals his hatred has lying lips, and whoever spreads slander is a fool.

10 : 18

When words are many, sin is not absent, but he who holds his tongue is wise.

10 : 19

With his mouth the godless destroys his neighbor, but through knowledge the righteous escape.

11 : 9

A gossip betrays a confidence, but a trustworthy man keeps a secret.

11 : 13

A perverse man stirs up dissension, and a gossip separates close friends.

16 : 28

The words of gossip are like choice morsels; they go down to a man's inmost parts.

18 : 8

A gossip betrays a confidence; so avoid a man who talks too much.

20 : 19

Without wood a fire goes out; without gossip a quarrel dies down.

26 : 20

The words of a gossip are like choice morsels; they go down to a man's inmost parts.

26 : 22

A lying tongue hates those it hurts, and a flattering mouth works ruin.

26 : 28

govern
by me princes govern, and all nobles who rule on earth.

8 : 16

government
By me kings reign and rulers make laws that are just;

8 : 15

If a ruler listens to lies, all his officials become wicked.

29 : 12

If a king judges the poor with fairness, his throne will always be secure.

29 : 14

grace
They will be a garland to grace your head and a chain to adorn your neck.

1 : 9

they will be life for you, an ornament to grace your neck.

3 : 22

He mocks proud mockers but gives grace to the humble.

3 : 34

She will set a garland of grace on your head and present you with a crown of splendor.

4 : 9

When a king's face brightens, it means life; his favor is like a rain cloud in spring.

16 : 15

A poor man pleads for mercy, but a rich man answers harshly.

18 : 23

A man's wisdom gives him patience; it is to his glory to overlook an offense.

19 : 11

A king's rage is like the roar of a lion, but his favor is like dew on the grass.

19 : 12

The wicked man craves evil; his neighbor gets no mercy from him.

21 : 10

If your enemy is hungry, give him food to eat; if he is thirsty, give him water to drink.

25 : 21

He who conceals his sins does not prosper, but whoever confesses and renounces them finds mercy.

28 : 13

graceful deer

A loving doe, a graceful deer -- may her breasts satisfy you always, may you ever be captivated by her love.

5 : 19

gracious

He who loves a pure heart and whose speech is gracious will have the king for his friend.

22 : 11

grain

People curse the man who hoards grain, but blessing crowns him who is willing to sell.

11 : 26

Though you grind a fool in a mortar, grinding him like grain with a pestle, you will not remove his folly from him.

27 : 22

grandchildren

A good man leaves an inheritance for his children's children, but a sinner's wealth is stored up for the righteous.

13 : 22

Children's children are a crown to the aged, and parents are the pride of their children.

17 : 6

granted

What the wicked dreads will overtake him; what the righteous desire will be granted.

10 : 24

grasps

In her hand she holds the distaff and grasps the spindle with her fingers.

31 : 19

grass

A king's rage is like the roar of a lion, but his favor is like dew on the grass.

19 : 12

When the hay is removed and new growth appears and the grass from the hills is gathered in,

27 : 25

grave

let's swallow them alive, like the grave, and whole, like those who go down to the pit;

1 : 12

Her feet go down to death; her steps lead straight to the grave.

5 : 5

Her house is a highway to the grave, leading down to the chambers of death.

7 : 27

But little do they know that the dead are there, that her guests are in the depths of the grave.

9 : 18

The path of life leads upward for the wise to keep him from going down to the grave.

15 : 24

A man who strays from the path of understanding comes to rest in the company of the dead.

21 : 16

the grave, the barren womb, land, which is never satisfied with water, and fire, which never says, 'Enough!'

30 : 16

gravel

Food gained by fraud tastes sweet to a man, but he ends up with a mouth full of gravel.

20 : 17

gray hair
Gray hair is a crown of splendor; it is attained by a righteous life.

16 : 31

The glory of young men is their strength, gray hair the splendor of the old.

20 : 29

great
He will die for lack of discipline, led astray by his own great folly.

5 : 23

He will not accept any compensation; he will refuse the bribe, however great it is.

6 : 35

One man pretends to be rich, yet has nothing; another pretends to be poor, yet has great wealth.

13 : 7

A patient man has great understanding, but a quick-tempered man displays folly.

14 : 29

The house of the righteous contains great treasure, but the income of the wicked brings them trouble.

15 : 6

Better a little with the fear of the Lord than great wealth with turmoil.

15 : 16

A gift opens the way for the giver and ushers him into the presence of the great.

18 : 16

A gift given in secret soothes anger, and a bribe concealed in the cloak pacifies great wrath.

21 : 14

A good name is more desirable than great riches; to be esteemed is better than silver or gold.

22 : 1

The father of a righteous man has great joy; he who has a wise son delights in him.

23 : 24

A wise man has great power, and a man of knowledge increases strength;

24 : 5

When the righteous triumph, there is great elation; but when the wicked rise to power, men go into hiding.

28 : 12

great joy
The father of a righteous man has great joy; he who has a wise son delights in him.

23 : 24

great men
Do not exalt yourself in the king's presence, and do not claim a place among great men;

25 : 6

great power
A wise man has great power, and a man of knowledge increases strength;

24 : 5

great riches
A good name is more desirable than great riches; to be esteemed is better than silver or gold.

22 : 1

great wealth
She is more precious than rubies; nothing you desire can compare with her.

3 : 15

Better a little with the fear of the Lord than great wealth with turmoil.

15 : 16

greatness
It is the glory of God to conceal a matter; to search out a matter is the glory of kings.

25 : 2

greed
A greedy man brings trouble to his family, but he who hates bribes will live.

15 : 27

He who robs his father or mother and says, "It's not wrong" -- he is partner to him who destroys.

28 : 24

greedy
By justice a king gives a country stability, but one who is greedy for bribes tears it down.

29 : 4

greedy man
A greedy man brings trouble to his family, but he who hates bribes will live.

15 : 27

A greedy man stirs up dissension, but he who trusts in the Lord will prosper.

28 : 25

green leaf
Whoever trusts in his riches will fall, but the righteous will thrive like a green leaf.

11 : 28

grief
The proverbs of Solomon: A wise son brings joy to his father, but a foolish son grief to his mother.

10 : 1

He who walks maliciously causes grief, and a chattering fool comes to ruin.

10 : 10

Even in laughter the heart may ache, and joy may end in grief.

14 : 13

A happy heart makes the face cheerful, but heartache crushes the spirit.

15 : 13

To have a fool for a son brings grief; there is no joy for the father of a fool.

17 : 21

A foolish son brings grief to his father and bitterness to the one who bore him.

17 : 25

A man's spirit sustains him in sickness, but a crushed spirit who can bear?

18 : 14

If a man pampers his servant from youth, he will bring grief in the end.

29 : 21

grind
Though you grind a fool in a mortar, grinding him like grain with a pestle, you will not remove his folly from him.

27 : 22

groan
At the end of your life you will groan, when your flesh and body are spent.

5 : 11

When the righteous thrive, the people rejoice; when the wicked rule, the people groan.

29 : 2

gross
There are six things the Lord hates, seven that are detestable to him:

6 : 16

As a dog returns to its vomit, so a fool repeats his folly.

26 : 11

ground
thorns had come up everywhere, the ground was covered with weeds, and the stone wall was in ruins.

24 : 31

grow
Dishonest money dwindles away, but he who gathers money little by little makes it grow.

13 : 11

He who walks with the wise grows wise, but a companion of fools suffers harm.

13 : 20

Do not love sleep or you will grow poor; stay awake and you will have food to spare.

20 : 13

growing old
Gray hair is a crown of splendor; it is attained by a righteous life.

16 : 31

growth
He who walks with the wise grows wise, but a companion of fools suffers harm.

13 : 20

When the hay is removed and new growth appears and the grass from the hills is gathered in,

27 : 25

guard
Discretion will protect you, and understanding will guard you.

2 : 11

Hold on to instruction, do not let it go; guard it well, for it is your life.

4 : 13

Above all else, guard your heart, for it is the wellspring of life.

4 : 23

Keep my commands and you will live; guard my teachings as the apple of your eye.

7 : 2

guard your heart
Listen, my son, and be wise, and keep your heart on the right path.

23 : 19

guarding your heart
Do not let your heart envy sinners, but always be zealous for the fear of the Lord.

23 : 17

My son, give me your heart and let your eyes keep to my ways,

23 : 26

guards
for he guards the course of the just and protects the way of his faithful ones.

2 : 8

He who guards his lips guards his life, but he who speaks rashly will come to ruin.

13 : 3

Righteousness guards the man of integrity, but wickedness overthrows the sinner.

13 : 6

The highway of the upright avoids evil; he who guards his way guards his life.

16 : 17

He who obeys instructions guards his life, but he who is contemptuous of his ways will die.

19 : 16

He who guards his mouth and his tongue keeps himself from calamity.

21 : 23

In the paths of the wicked lie thorns and snares, but he who guards his soul stays far from them.

22 : 5

If you say, "But we knew nothing about this," does not he who weighs the heart perceive it? Does not he who guards your life know it? Will he not repay each person according to what he has done?

24 : 12

guests

But little do they know that the dead are there, that her guests are in the depths of the grave.

9 : 18

guidance

let the wise listen and add to their learning, and let the discerning get guidance --

1 : 5

For lack of guidance a nation falls, but many advisers make victory sure.

11 : 14

Whoever loves discipline loves knowledge, but he who hates correction is stupid.

12 : 1

The way of a fool seems right to him, but a wise man listens to advice.

12 : 15

Make plans by seeking advice; if you wage war, obtain guidance.

20 : 18

for waging war you need guidance, and for victory many advisers.

24 : 6

The sayings of King Lemuel -- an oracle his mother taught him:

31 : 1

guide

I guide you in the way of wisdom and lead you along straight paths.

4 : 11

When you walk, they will guide you; when you sleep, they will watch over you; when you awake, they will speak to you.

6 : 22

guides

The integrity of the upright guides them, but the unfaithful are destroyed by their duplicity.

11 : 3

A wise man's heart guides his mouth, and his lips promote instruction.

16 : 23

The king's heart is in the hand of the Lord; he directs it like a watercourse wherever he pleases.

21 : 1

guiding light

For these commands are a lamp, this teaching is a light, and the corrections of discipline are the way to life,

6 : 23

guilt

Evil men will bow down in the presence of the good, and the wicked at the gates of the righteous.

14 : 19

The wicked man flees though no one pursues, but the righteous are as bold as a lion.

28 : 1

A man tomented by the guilt of murder will be a fugitive till death; let no one support him.

28 : 17

When the wicked rise to power, people go into hiding; but when the wicked perish, the righteous thrive.

28 . 28

"This is the way of an adulteress: She eats and wipes her mouth and says, 'I've done nothing wrong.'

30 : 20

guilt-free

The wicked man flees though no one pursues, but the righteous are as bold as a lion.

28 : 1

guilty

Acquitting the guilty and condemning the innocent -- the Lord detests them both.

17 : 15

The way of the guilty is devious, but the conduct of the innocent is upright.

21 : 8

Whoever says to the guilty, "You are innocent" -- peoples will curse him and nations denounce him.

24 : 24

But it will go well with those who convict the guilty, and rich blessing will come upon them.

24 : 25

gullible

A simple man believes anything, but a prudent man gives thought to his steps.

14 : 15

gulps down evil

A corrupt witness mocks at justice, and the mouth of the wicked gulps down evil.

19 : 28

gushes

The heart of the righteous weighs its answers, but the mouth of the wicked gushes evil.

15 : 28

H

habits
When a man's ways are pleasing to the Lord, he makes even his enemies live at peace with him.

16 : 7

hair
Gray hair is a crown of splendor; it is attained by a righteous life.

16 : 31

The glory of young men is their strength, gray hair the splendor of the old.

20 : 29

hampered
When you walk, your steps will not be hampered; when you run, you will not stumble.

4 : 12

hand
But since you rejected me when I called and no one gave heed when I stretched out my hand,

1 : 24

Long life is in her right hand; in her left hand are riches and honor.

3 : 16

Free yourself, like a gazelle from the hand of the hunter, like a bird from the snare of the fowler.

6 : 5

hand of the Lord
The king's heart is in the hand of the Lord; he directs it like a watercourse wherever he pleases.

21 : 1

Of what use is money in the hand of a fool, since he has no desire to get wisdom?

17 : 16

The sluggard buries his hand in the dish; he will not even bring it back to his mouth!

19 : 24

Like cutting off one's feet or drinking violence is the sending of a message by the hand of a fool.

26 : 6

Like a thornbush in a drunkard's hand is a proverb in the mouth of a fool.

26 : 9

The sluggard buries his hand in the dish; he is too lazy to bring it back to his mouth.

26 : 15

restraining her is like restraining the wind or grasping oil with the hand.

27 : 16

a lizard can be caught with the hand, yet it is found in kings' palaces.

30 : 28

"If you have played the fool and exalted yourself, or if you have planned evil, clap your hand over your mouth!

30 : 32

In her hand she holds the distaff and grasps the spindle with her fingers.

31 : 19

hands
My son, if you have put up security for your neighbor, if you have struck hands in pledge for another,

6 : 1

then do this, my son, to free yourself, since you have fallen into your neighbor's hands: Go and humble yourself; press your plea with your neighbor!

6 : 3

A little sleep, a little slumber, a little folding of the hands to rest--

6 : 10

haughty eyes, a lying tongue, hands that shed innocent blood,

6 : 17

Lazy hands make a man poor, but diligent hands bring wealth.

10 : 4

He who puts up security for another will surely suffer, but whoever refuses to strike hands in pledge is safe.

11 : 15

From the fruit of his lips a man is filled with good things as surely as the work of his hands rewards him.

12 : 14

Diligent hands will rule, but laziness ends in slave labor.

12 : 24

The wise woman builds her house, but with her own hands the foolish one tears hers down.

14 : 1

A man lacking in judgment strikes hands in pledge and puts up security for his neighbor.

17 : 18

The sluggard's craving will be the death of him, because his hands refuse to work.

21 : 25

Do not be a man who strikes hands in pledge or puts up security for debts;

22 : 26

A little sleep, a little slumber, a little folding of the hands to rest --

24 : 33

Who has gone up to heaven and come down? Who has gathered up the wind in the hollow of his hands? Who has wrapped up the waters in his cloak? Who has established all the ends of the earth? What is his name, and the name of his son? Tell me if you know!

30 : 4

She selects wool and flax and works with eager hands.

31 : 13

She opens her arms to the poor and extends her hands to the needy.

31 : 20

hands that shed innocent blood
haughty eyes, a lying tongue, hands that shed innocent blood,

6 : 17

happiness
For through me your days will be many, and years will be added to your life.

9 : 11

The blessing of the Lord brings wealth, and he adds no trouble to it.

10 : 22

The prospect of the righteous is joy, but the hopes of the wicked come to nothing.

10 : 28

Each heart knows its own bitterness, and no one else can share its joy.

14 : 10

Even in laughter the heart may ache, and joy may end in grief.

14 : 13

A happy heart makes the face cheerful, but heartache crushes the spirit.

15 : 13

All the days of the oppressed are wretched, but the cheerful heart has a continual feast.

15 : 15

A cheerful look brings joy to the heart, and good news gives health to the bones.

15 : 30

A cheerful heart is good medicine, but a crushed spirit dries up the bones.

17 : 22

When justice is done, it brings joy to the righteous but terror to evildoers.

21 : 15

Better to live in a desert than with a quarrelsome and ill-tempered wife.

21 : 19

He who pursues righteousness and love finds life, prosperity and honor.

21 : 21

Perfume and incense bring joy to the heart, and the pleasantness of one's friend springs from his earnest counsel.

27 : 9

Be wise, my son, and bring joy to my heart; then I can answer anyone who treats me with contempt.

27 : 11

happy
A happy heart makes the face cheerful, but heartache crushes the spirit.

15 : 13

When a king's face brightens, it means life; his favor is like a rain cloud in spring.

16 : 15

My son, if your heart is wise, then my heart will be glad;

23 : 15

happy heart
A happy heart makes the face cheerful, but heartache crushes the spirit.

15 : 13

harbor
Fear of man will prove to be a snare, but whoever trusts in the Lord is kept safe.

29 : 25

harbors
A malicious man disguises himself with his lips, but in his heart he harbors deceit.

26 : 24

hard
Good understanding wins favor, but the way of the unfaithful is hard.

13 : 15

hard work
All hard work brings a profit, but mere talk leads only to poverty.

14 : 23

hard worker
She sees that her trading is profitable, and her lamp does not go out at night.

31 : 18

hardens his heart
Blessed is the man who always fears the Lord, but he who hardens his heart falls into trouble.

28 : 14

harm
but whoever listens to me will live in safety and be at ease, without fear of harm."

1 : 33

Do not plot harm against your neighbor, who lives trustfully near you.

3 : 29

Do not accuse a man for no reason --
when he has done you no harm.

3 : 30

No harm befalls the righteous, but the
wicked have their fill of trouble.

12 : 21

He who walks with the wise grows
wise, but a companion of fools suffers
harm.

13 : 20

She brings him good, not harm, all the
days of her life.

31 : 12

harmless
If they say, "Come along with us; let's
lie in wait for someone's blood, let's
waylay some harmless soul;

1 : 11

harms
But whoever fails to find me harms
himself; all who hate me love death.

8 : 36

harsh word
A gentle answer turns away wrath, but a
harsh word stirs up anger.

15 : 1

harshly
A poor man pleads for mercy, but a rich
man answers harshly.

18 : 23

harvest
yet it stores its provisions in summer
and gathers its food at harvest.

6 : 8

He who gathers crops in summer is a
wise son, but he who sleeps during
harvest is a disgraceful son.

10 : 5

Where there are no oxen, the manger is
empty, but from the strength of an ox
comes an abundant harvest.

14 : 4

From the fruit of his mouth a man's
stomach is filled; with the harvest from
his lips he is satisfied.

18 : 20

A sluggard does not plow in season; so
at harvest time he looks but finds
nothing.

20 : 4

Like the coolness of snow at harvest
time is a trustworthy messenger to those
who send him; he refreshes the spirit of
his masters.

25 : 13

Like snow in summer or rain in harvest,
honor is not fitting for a fool.

26 : 1

When the hay is removed and new
growth appears and the grass from the
hills is gathered in,

27 : 25

harvest time
A sluggard does not plow in season; so
at harvest time he looks but finds
nothing.

20 : 4

haste
The plans of the diligent lead to profit
as surely as haste leads to poverty.

21 : 5

Do you see a man who speaks in haste?
There is more hope for a fool than for
him.

29 : 20

hastily

do not bring hastily to court, for what will you do in the end if your neighbor puts you to shame?

25 : 8

hasty

It is not good to have zeal without knowledge, nor to be hasty and miss the way.

19 : 2

hate

"How long will you simple ones love your simple ways? How long will mockers delight in mockery and fools hate knowledge?

1 : 22

To fear the Lord is to hate evil; I hate pride and arrogance, evil behavior and perverse speech.

8 : 13

But whoever fails to find me harms himself; all who hate me love death.

8 : 36

Do not rebuke a mocker or he will hate you; rebuke a wise man and he will love you.

9 : 8

The Lord detests men of perverse heart but he delights in those whose ways are blameless.

11 : 20

The righteous hate what is false, but the wicked bring shame and disgrace.

13 : 5

A quick-tempered man does foolish things, and a crafty man is hated.

14 : 17

Kings detest wrongdoing, for a throne is established through righteousness.

16 : 12

Acquitting the guilty and condemning the innocent -- the Lord detests them both.

17 : 15

The schemes of folly are sin, and men detest a mocker.

24 : 9

Seldom set foot in your neighbor's house -- too much of you, and he will hate you.

25 : 17

Bloodthirsty men hate a man of integrity and seek to kill the upright.

29 : 10

hated

You will say, "How I hated discipline! How my heart spurned correction!

5 : 12

A quick-tempered man does foolish things, and a crafty man is hated.

14 : 17

hateful

If anyone turns a deaf ear to the law, even his prayers are detestable.

28 : 9

hates

for the Lord detests a perverse man but takes the upright into his confidence.

3 : 32

There are six things the Lord hates, seven that are detestable to him:

6 : 16

The Lord abhors dishonest scales, but accurate weights are his delight.

11 : 1

Whoever loves discipline loves knowledge, but he who hates correction is stupid.

12 : 1

The Lord detests lying lips, but he delights in men who are truthful.

12 : 22

He who spares the rod hates his son, but he who loves him is careful to discipline him.

13 : 24

Stern discipline awaits him who leaves the path; he who hates correction will die.

15 : 10

A greedy man brings trouble to his family, but he who hates bribes will live.

15 : 27

Differing weights and differing measures -- the Lord detests them both.

20 : 10

The Lord detests differing weights, and dishonest scales do not please him.

20 : 23

A lying tongue hates those it hurts, and a flattering mouth works ruin.

26 : 28

A tyrannical ruler lacks judgment, but he who hates ill-gotten gain will enjoy a long life.

28 : 16

hating knowledge
Since they hated knowledge and did not choose to fear the Lord,

1 : 29

hatred
Hatred stirs up dissension, but love covers over all wrongs.

10 : 12

He who conceals his hatred has lying lips, and whoever spreads slander is a fool.

10 : 18

He who spares the rod hates his son, but he who loves him is careful to discipline him.

13 : 24

A heart at peace gives life to the body, but envy rots the bones.

14 : 30

Better a meal of vegetables where there is love than a fattened calf with hatred.

15 : 17

An offended brother is more unyielding than a fortified city, and disputes are like the barred gates of a citadel.

18 : 19

Do not gloat when your enemy falls; when he stumbles, do not let your heart rejoice,

24 : 17

Do not say, "I'll do to him as he has done to me; I'll pay that man back for what he did."

24 : 29

those whose teeth are swords and whose jaws are set with knives to devour the poor from the earth, the needy from among mankind.

30 : 14

haughty
haughty eyes, a lying tongue, hands that shed innocent blood,

6 : 17

Pride goes before destruction, a haughty spirit before a fall.

16 : 18

Haughty eyes and a proud heart, the lamp of the wicked, are sin!

21 : 4

those whose eyes are ever so haughty, whose glances are so disdainful;

30 : 13

haughty eyes
haughty eyes, a lying tongue, hands that shed innocent blood,

6 : 17

Haughty eyes and a proud heart, the lamp of the wicked, are sin!

21 : 4

haughty spirit
Pride goes before destruction, a haughty spirit before a fall.

16 : 18

hay
When the hay is removed and new growth appears and the grass from the hills is gathered in,

27 : 25

head
They will be a garland to grace your head and a chain to adorn your neck.

1 : 9

at the head of the noisy streets she cries out, in the gateways of the city she makes her speech:

1 : 21

She will set a garland of grace on your head and present you with a crown of splendor.

4 : 9

Blessings crown the head of the righteous, but violence overwhelms the mouth of the wicked.

10 : 6

In doing this, you will heap burning coals on his head, and the Lord will reward you.

25 : 22

healing
Reckless words pierce like a sword, but the tongue of the wise brings healing.

12 : 18

A wicked messenger falls into trouble, but a trustworthy envoy brings healing.

13 : 17

The tongue that brings healing is a tree of life, but a deceitful tongue crushes the spirit.

15 : 4

A cheerful look brings joy to the heart, and good news gives health to the bones.

15 : 30

Pleasant words are a honeycomb, sweet to the soul and healing to the bones.

16 : 24

health
This will bring health to your body and nourishment to your bones.

3 : 8

for they are life to those who find them and health to a man's whole body.

4 : 22

A cheerful look brings joy to the heart, and good news gives health to the bones.

15 : 30

Pleasant words are a honeycomb, sweet to the soul and healing to the bones.

16 : 24

A cheerful heart is good medicine, but a crushed spirit dries up the bones.

17 : 22

A man's spirit sustains him in sickness, but a crushed spirit who can bear?

18 : 14

heap burning coals
In doing this, you will heap burning coals on his head, and the Lord will reward you.

25 : 22

hear

Ears that hear and eyes that see -- the Lord has made them both.

20 : 12

hears

A man's riches may ransom his life, but a poor man hears no threat.

13 : 8

The Lord is far from the wicked but he hears the prayer of the righteous.

15 : 29

or he who hears it may shame you and you will never lose your bad reputation.

25 : 10

heart

If you had responded to my rebuke, I would have poured out my heart to you and made my thoughts known to you.

1 : 23

turning your ear to wisdom and applying your heart to understanding,

2 : 2

For wisdom will enter your heart, and knowledge will be pleasant to your soul.

2 : 10

My son, do not forget my teaching, but keep my commands in your heart,

3 : 1

Let love and faithfulness never leave you; bind them around your neck, write them on the tablet of your heart.

3 : 3

Trust in the Lord with all your heart and lean not on your own understanding;

3 : 5

he taught me and said, "Lay hold of my words with all your heart; keep my commands and you will live.

4 : 4

Do not let them out of your sight, keep them within your heart;

4 : 21

Above all else, guard your heart, for it is the wellspring of life.

4 : 23

You will say, "How I hated discipline! How my heart spurned correction!

5 : 12

who plots evil with deceit in his heart -- he always stirs up dissension.

6 : 14

a heart that devises wicked schemes, feet that are quick to rush into evil,

6 : 18

Bind them upon your heart forever; fasten them around your neck.

6 : 21

Do not lust in your heart after her beauty or let her captivate you with her eyes,

6 : 25

Bind them on your fingers; write them on the tablet of your heart.

7 : 3

Do not let your heart turn to her ways or stray into her paths.

7 : 25

The wise in heart accept commands, but a chattering fool comes to ruin.

10 : 8

The tongue of the righteous is choice silver, but the heart of the wicked is of little value.

10 : 20

A kindhearted woman gains respect, but ruthless men gain only wealth.

11 : 16

211

The Lord detests men of perverse heart but he delights in those whose ways are blameless.

11 : 20

A prudent man keeps his knowledge to himself, but the heart of fools blurts out folly.

12 : 23

An anxious heart weighs a man down, but a kind word cheers him up.

12 : 25

Hope deferred makes the heart sick, but a longing fulfilled is a tree of life.

13 : 12

The righteous eat to their hearts' content, but the stomach of the wicked goes hungry.

13 : 25

Each heart knows its own bitterness, and no one else can share its joy.

14 : 10

Even in laughter the heart may ache, and joy may end in grief.

14 : 13

A heart at peace gives life to the body, but envy rots the bones.

14 : 30

Wisdom reposes in the heart of the discerning and even among fools she lets herself be known.

14 : 33

A happy heart makes the face cheerful, but heartache crushes the spirit.

15 : 13

The discerning heart seeks knowledge, but the mouth of a fool feeds on folly.

15 : 14

All the days of the oppressed are wretched, but the cheerful heart has a continual feast.

15 : 15

The heart of the righteous weighs its answers, but the mouth of the wicked gushes evil.

15 : 28

A cheerful look brings joy to the heart, and good news gives health to the bones.

15 : 30

To man belong the plans of the heart, but from the Lord comes the reply of the tongue.

16 : 1

All a man's ways seem innocent to him, but motives are weighed by the Lord.

16 : 2

The Lord detests all the proud of heart. Be sure of this: They will not go unpunished.

16 : 5

In his heart a man plans his course, but the Lord determines his steps.

16 : 9

The wise in heart are called discerning, and pleasant words promote instruction.

16 : 21

A wise man's heart guides his mouth, and his lips promote instruction.

16 : 23

The crucible for silver and the furnace for gold, but the Lord tests the heart.

17 : 3

A man of perverse heart does not prosper; he whose tongue is deceitful falls into trouble.

17 : 20

A cheerful heart is good medicine, but a crushed spirit dries up the bones.

17 : 22

Before his downfall a man's heart is proud, but humility comes before honor.

18 : 12

The heart of the discerning acquires knowledge; the ears of the wise seek it out.

18 : 15

A man's own folly ruins his life, yet his heart rages against the Lord.

19 : 3

Many are the plans in the man's heart, but it is the Lord's purpose that prevails.

19 : 21

The purposes of a man's heart are deep waters, but a man of understanding draws them out.

20 : 5

Who can say, "I have kept my heart pure; I am clean and without sin"?

20 : 9

The king's heart is in the hand of the Lord; he directs it like a watercourse wherever he pleases.

21 : 1

All a man's ways seem right to him, but the Lord weighs the heart.

21 : 2

Haughty eyes and a proud heart, the lamp of the wicked, are sin!

21 : 4

He who loves a pure heart and whose speech is gracious will have the king for his friend.

22 : 11

Folly is bound up in the heart of a child, but the rod of discipline will drive it far from him.

22 : 15

Pay attention and listen to the sayings of the wise; apply your heart to what I teach,

22 : 17

for it is pleasing when you keep them in your heart and have all of them ready on your lips.

22 : 18

for he is the kind of man who is always thinking about the cost. "Eat and drink," he says to you, but his heart is not with you.

23 : 7

Apply your heart to instruction and your ears to words of knowledge.

23 : 12

My son, if your heart is wise, then my heart will be glad;

23 : 15

Do not let your heart envy sinners, but always be zealous for the fear of the Lord.

23 : 17

Listen, my son, and be wise, and keep your heart on the right path.

23 : 19

My son, give me your heart and let your eyes keep to my ways,

23 : 26

If you say, "But we knew nothing about this," does not he who weighs the heart perceive it? Does not he who guards your life know it? Will he not repay each person according to what he has done?

24 : 12

Do not gloat when your enemy falls;
when he stumbles, do not let your heart
rejoice,

24 : 17

I applied my heart to what I observed
and learned a lesson from what I saw:

24 : 32

Like one who takes away a garment on
a cold day, or like vinegar poured on
soda, is one who sings songs to a heavy
heart.

25 : 20

Like a coating of glaze over
earthenware are fervent lips with an evil
heart.

26 : 23

A malicious man disguises himself with
his lips, but in his heart he harbors
deceit.

26 : 24

Though his speech is charming, do not
believe him, for seven abominations fill
his heart.

26 : 25

Perfume and incense bring joy to the
heart, and the pleasantness of one's
friend springs from his earnest counsel.

27 : 9

Be wise, my son, and bring joy to my
heart; then I can answer anyone who
treats me with contempt.

27 : 11

As water reflects a face, so a man's
heart reflects the man.

27 : 19

Blessed is the man who always fears the
Lord, but he who hardens his heart falls
into trouble.

28 : 14

heartache

Have no fear of sudden disaster or of
the ruin that overtakes the wicked,

3 : 25

Good understanding wins favor, but the
way of the unfaithful is hard.

13 : 15

Even in laughter the heart may ache,
and joy may end in grief.

14 : 13

A happy heart makes the face cheerful,
but heartache crushes the spirit.

15 : 13

A greedy man brings trouble to his
family, but he who hates bribes will
live.

15 : 27

To have a fool for a son brings grief;
there is no joy for the father of a fool.

17 : 21

A foolish son brings grief to his father
and bitterness to the one who bore him.

17 : 25

He who guards his mouth and his
tongue keeps himself from calamity.

21 : 23

hearts

There is deceit in the hearts of those
who plot evil, but joy for those who
promote peace.

12 : 20

The lips of the wise spread knowledge;
not so the hearts of fools.

15 : 7

Death and Destruction lie open before
the Lord -- how much more the hearts
of men!

15 : 11

for their hearts plot violence, and their lips talk about making trouble.

24 : 2

As the heavens are high and the earth is deep, so the hearts of kings are unsearchable.

25 : 3

hearts of men
Death and Destruction lie open before the Lord -- how much more the hearts of men!

15 : 11

heaven
There is surely a future hope for you, and your hope will not be cut off.

23 : 18

Who has gone up to heaven and come down? Who has gathered up the wind in the hollow of his hands? Who has wrapped up the waters in his cloak? Who has established all the ends of the earth? What is his name, and the name of his son? Tell me if you know!

30 : 4

heavens
By wisdom the Lord laid the earth's foundations, by understanding he set the heavens in place;

3 : 19

I was there when he set the heavens in place, when he marked out the horizon on the face of the deep,

8 : 27

As the heavens are high and the earth is deep, so the hearts of kings are unsearchable.

25 : 3

heavier
Stone is heavy and sand a burden, but provocation by a fool is heavier than both.

27 : 3

heavy
Stone is heavy and sand a burden, but provocation by a fool is heavier than both.

27 : 3

heavy heart
Like one who takes away a garment on a cold day, or like vinegar poured on soda, is one who sings songs to a heavy heart.

25 : 20

heavy hearted
A man's spirit sustains him in sickness, but a crushed spirit who can bear?

18 : 14

heed
But since you rejected me when I called and no one gave heed when I stretched out my hand,

1 : 24

Whoever gives heed to instruction prospers, and blessed is he who trusts in the Lord.

16 : 20

heeding
Pride only breeds quarrels, but wisdom is found in those who take advice.

13 : 10

heeding advice
He who scorns instruction will pay for it, but he who respects a command is rewarded.

13 : 13

He who listens to a life-giving rebuke will be at home among the wise.

15 : 31

heeding correction
A fool spurns the father's discipline, but whoever heeds correction shows prudence.

15 : 5

He who ignores discipline despises himself, but whoever heeds correction gains understanding.

15 : 32

heeds

He who heeds discipline shows the way to life, but whoever ignores correction leads others astray.

10 : 17

A wise son heeds his father's instruction, but a mocker does not listen to rebuke.

13 : 1

He who ignores discipline comes to poverty and shame, but whoever heeds correction is honored.

13 : 18

A fool spurns the father's discipline, but whoever heeds correction shows prudence.

15 : 5

He who ignores discipline despises himself, but whoever heeds correction gains understanding.

15 : 32

heights

On the heights along the way, where the paths meet, she takes her stand;

8 : 2

held in contempt

A man is praised according to his wisdom, but men with warped minds are despised.

12 : 8

hell

There is a way that seems right to a man, but in the end it leads to death.

14 : 12

The fear of the Lord is a fountain of life, turning a man from the snares of death.

14 : 27

help

A friend loves at all times, and a brother is born for adversity.

17 : 17

A man of many companions may come to ruin, but there is a friend who sticks closer than a brother.

18 : 24

A hot-tempered man must pay the penalty; if you rescue him, you will have to do it again.

19 : 19

Like a bad tooth or a lame foot is reliance on the unfaithful in times of trouble.

25 : 19

Do not forsake your friend and the friend of your father, and do not go to your brother's house when disaster strikes you -- better a neighbor nearby than a brother far away.

27 : 10

"Speak up for those who cannot speak for themselves, for the rights of all who are destitute.

31 : 8

helpful

He who despises his neighbor sins, but blessed is he who is kind to the needy.

14 : 21

She opens her arms to the poor and extends her hands to the needy.

31 : 20

216

helpless people
Like a roaring lion or a charging bear is
a wicked man ruling over a helpless
people.

28 : 15

her
It will save you also from the
adulteress, from the wayward wife with
her seductive words,

2 : 16

For her house leads down to death and
her paths to the spirits of the dead.

2 : 18

She is a tree of life to those who
embrace her; those who lay hold of her
will be blessed.

3 : 18

Esteem her, and she will exalt you;
embrace her, and she will honor you.

4 : 8

Do not lust in your heart after her
beauty or let her captivate you with her
eyes,

6 : 25

So is he who sleeps with another man's
wife; no one who touches her will go
unpunished.

6 : 29

She is loud and defiant, her feet never
stay at home;

7 : 11

for wisdom is more precious than
rubies, and nothing you desire can
compare with her.

8 : 11

Wisdom has built her house; she has
hewn out its seven pillars.

9 : 1

She has prepared her meat and mixed
her wine; she has also set her table.

9 : 2

her ways
Her ways are pleasant ways, and all her
paths are peace.

3 : 17

herds
Be sure you know the condition of your
flocks, give careful attention to your
herds;

27 : 23

hewn
Wisdom has built her house; she has
hewn out its seven pillars.

9 : 1

Hezekiah
These are more proverbs of Solomon,
copied by the men of Hezekiah king of
Judah:

25 : 1

hidden
and if you look for it as for silver and
search for it as for hidden treasure,

2 : 4

A gift given in secret soothes anger, and
a bribe concealed in the cloak pacifies
great wrath.

21 : 14

A malicious man disguises himself with
his lips, but in his heart he harbors
deceit.

26 : 24

Better is open rebuke than hidden love.

27 : 5

hidden treasure
and if you look for it as for silver and
search for it as for hidden treasure,

2 : 4

hide
A prudent man sees danger and takes
refuge, but the simple keep going and
suffer for it.

22 : 3

It is the glory of God to conceal a matter; to search out a matter is the glory of kings.

25 : 2

When the righteous triumph, there is great elation; but when the wicked rise to power, men go into hiding.

28 : 12

hiding

He who conceals his hatred has lying lips, and whoever spreads slander is a fool.

10 : 18

A malicious man disguises himself with his lips, but in his heart he harbors deceit.

26 : 24

The wicked man flees though no one pursues, but the righteous are as bold as a lion.

28 : 1

When the righteous triumph, there is great elation; but when the wicked rise to power, men go into hiding.

28 : 12

When the wicked rise to power, people go into hiding; but when the wicked perish, the righteous thrive.

28 : 28

high

He who loves a quarrel loves sin; he who builds a high gate invites destruction.

17 : 19

Wisdom is too high for a fool; in the assembly at the gate he has nothing to say.

24 : 7

As the heavens are high and the earth is deep, so the hearts of kings are unsearchable.

25 : 3

high gate

He who loves a quarrel loves sin; he who builds a high gate invites destruction.

17 : 19

high seas

You will be like one sleeping on the high seas, lying on top of the rigging.

23 : 34

the way of an eagle in the sky, the way of a snake on a rock, the way of a ship on the high seas, and the way of a man with a maiden.

30 : 19

highest

She has sent out her maids, and she calls from the highest point of the city.

9 : 3

She sits at the door of her house, on a seat at the highest point of the city,

9 : 14

highest point

She sits at the door of her house, on a seat at the highest point of the city,

9 : 14

highway

Her house is a highway to the grave, leading down to the chambers of death.

7 : 27

The way of the sluggard is blocked with thorns, but the path of the upright is a highway.

15 : 19

The highway of the upright avoids evil; he who guards his way guards his life.

16 : 17

218

hills
before the mountains were settled in place, before the hills, I was given birth,

8 : 25

When the hay is removed and new growth appears and the grass from the hills is gathered in,

27 : 25

hinges
As a door turns on its hinges, so a sluggard turns on his bed.

26 : 14

hires
Like an archer who wounds at random is he who hires a fool or any passer-by.

26 : 10

hit
"They hit me," you will say, "but I'm not hurt! They beat me, but I don't feel it! When will I wake up so I can find another drink?"

23 : 35

hoarding
One man gives freely, yet gains even more; another withholds unduly, but comes to poverty.

11 : 24

A stingy man is eager to get rich and is unaware that poverty awaits him.

28 : 22

hoards
People curse the man who hoards grain, but blessing crowns him who is willing to sell.

11 : 26

hold
She is a tree of life to those who embrace her; those who lay hold of her will be blessed.

3 : 18

he taught me and said, "Lay hold of my words with all your heart; keep my commands and you will live.

4 : 4

Hold on to instruction, do not let it go; guard it well, for it is your life.

4 : 13

The evil deeds of a wicked man ensnare him; the cords of his sin hold him fast.

5 : 22

She took hold of him and kissed him and with a brazen face she said:

7 : 13

Take the garment of one who puts up security for a stranger; hold it in pledge if he does it for a wayward woman.

20 : 16

Rescue those being led away to death; hold back those staggering toward slaughter.

24 : 11

Take a garment of one who puts up security for a stranger; hold it in pledge if he does it for a wayward woman.

27 : 13

hold back
Rescue those being led away to death; hold back those staggering toward slaughter.

24 : 11

hold down
lest they drink and forget what the law decrees, and deprive all the oppressed of the rights.

31 : 5

hold on
Hold on to instruction, do not let it go; guard it well, for it is your life.

4 : 13

Buy the truth and do not sell it; get wisdom, discipline and understanding.

23 : 23

holding your tongue
He who guards his mouth and his tongue keeps himself from calamity.

21 : 23

holds
He holds victory in store for the upright, he is a shield to those whose walk is blameless,

2 : 7

The wise inherit honor, but fools he holds up to shame.

3 : 35

When words are many, sin is not absent, but he who holds his tongue is wise.

10 : 19

A man who lacks judgment derides his neighbor, but a man of understanding holds his tongue.

11 : 12

In her hand she holds the distaff and grasps the spindle with her fingers.

31 : 19

holds his tongue
When words are many, sin is not absent, but he who holds his tongue is wise.

10 : 19

A man who lacks judgment derides his neighbor, but a man of understanding holds his tongue.

11 : 12

Even a fool is thought wise if he keeps silent, and discerning if he holds his tongue.

17 : 28

holds up
The wise inherit honor, but fools he holds up to shame.

3 : 35

holiness
The Lord detests the sacrifice of the wicked, but the prayer of the upright pleases him.

15 : 8

Who can say, "I have kept my heart pure; I am clean and without sin"?

20 : 9

those who are pure in their own eyes and yet are not cleansed of their filth;

30 : 12

hollow
Who has gone up to heaven and come down? Who has gathered up the wind in the hollow of his hands? Who has wrapped up the waters in his cloak? Who has established all the ends of the earth? What is his name, and the name of his son? Tell me if you know!

30 : 4

holy
"The fear of the Lord is the beginning of wisdom, and knowledge of the Holy One is understanding.

9 : 10

Even a child is known by his actions, by whether his conduct is pure and right.

20 : 11

I have not learned the wisdom, nor have I knowledge of the Holy One.

30 : 3

Holy One
"The fear of the Lord is the beginning of wisdom, and knowledge of the Holy One is understanding.

9 : 10

I have not learned the wisdom, nor have I knowledge of the Holy One.

30 : 3

home

The Lord's curse is on the house of the wicked, but he blesses the home of the righteous.

3 : 33

At the window of my house I looked out through the lattice.

7 : 6

She is loud and defiant, her feet never stay at home;

7 : 11

"I have fellowship offerings at home; today I fulfilled my vows.

7 : 14

My husband is not at home; he has gone on a long journey.

7 : 19

He took his purse filled with money and will not be home till full moon."

7 : 20

Wisdom has built her house; she has hewn out its seven pillars.

9 : 1

The wise woman builds her house, but with her own hands the foolish one tears hers down.

14 : 1

He who fears the Lord has a secure fortress, and for his children it will be a refuge.

14 : 26

Better a meal of vegetables where there is love than a fattened calf with hatred.

15 : 17

He who listens to a life-giving rebuke will be at home among the wise.

15 : 31

Better a dry crust with peace and quiet than a house full of feasting with strife.

17 : 1

To have a fool for a son brings grief; there is no joy for the father of a fool.

17 : 21

Train a child in the way he should go, and when he is old he will not turn from it.

22 : 6

By wisdom a house is built, and through understanding it is established;

24 : 3

through knowledge its rooms are filled with rare and beautiful treasures.

24 : 4

Finish your outdoor work and get your fields ready; after that, build your house.

24 : 27

Better to live on a corner of the roof than share a house with a quarrelsome wife.

25 : 24

Like a bird that strays from its nest is a man who strays from his home.

27 : 8

coneys are creatures of little power, yet they make their home in the crags;

30 : 26

homemaker

The wise woman builds her house, but with her own hands the foolish one tears hers down.

14 : 1

honest

A truthful witness gives honest testimony, but a false witness tells lies.

12 : 17

honest answer
An honest answer is like a kiss on the lips.

24 : 26

honest lips
Kings take pleasure in honest lips; they value a man who speaks the truth.

16 : 13

honest scales
Honest scales and balances are from the Lord; all the weights in the bag are of his making.

16 : 11

honesty
He who conceals his hatred has lying lips, and whoever spreads slander is a fool.

10 : 18

Honest scales and balances are from the Lord; all the weights in the bag are of his making.

16 : 11

Differing weights and differing measures -- the Lord detests them both.

20 : 10

The Lord detests differing weights, and dishonest scales do not please him.

20 : 23

Better is open rebuke than hidden love.

27 : 5

A tyrannical ruler lacks judgment, but he who hates ill-gotten gain will enjoy a long life.

28 : 16

He who rebukes a man will in the end gain more favor than he who has a flattering tongue.

28 : 23

honey
For the lips of an adulteress drip honey, and her speech is smoother than oil;

5 : 3

Eat honey, my son, for it is good, honey from the comb is sweet to your taste.

24 : 13

If you find honey, just eat enough -- too much of it, and you will vomit.

25 : 16

It is not good to eat too much honey, not is it honorable to seek one's own honor.

25 : 27

He who is full loathes honey, but to the hungry even what is bitter tastes sweet.

27 : 7

honeycomb
Pleasant words are a honeycomb, sweet to the soul and healing to the bones.

16 : 24

Eat honey, my son, for it is good; honey from the comb is sweet to your taste.

24 : 13

honor
Then you will win favor and a good name in the sight of God and man.

3 : 4

Honor the Lord with your wealth, with the firstfruits of all your crops;

3 : 9

Long life is in her right hand; in her left hand are riches and honor.

3 : 16

The wise inherit honor, but fools he holds up to shame.

3 : 35

Esteem her, and she will exalt you; embrace her, and she will honor you.

4 : 8

With me are the riches and honor,
enduring wealth and prosperity.

8 : 18

A kindhearted woman gains respect, but
ruthless men gain only wealth.

11 : 16

He whose walk is upright fears the
Lord, but he whose ways are devious
despises him.

14 : 2

A large population is a king's glory, but
without subjects a prince is ruined.

14 : 28

A wise son brings joy to his father, but
a foolish man despises his mother.

15 : 20

The fear of the Lord teaches a man
wisdom, and humility comes before
honor.

15 : 33

Arrogant lips are unsuited to a fool --
how much worse lying lips to a ruler!

17 : 7

To have a fool for a son brings grief;
there is no joy for the father of a fool.

17 : 21

Before his downfall a man's heart is
proud, but humility comes before
honor.

18 : 12

He who finds a wife finds what is good
and receives favor from the Lord.

18 : 22

A man's wisdom gives him patience; it
is to his glory to overlook an offense.

19 : 11

It is to a man's honor to avoid strife, but
every fool is quick to quarrel.

20 : 3

The righteous man leads a blameless
life; blessed are his children after him.

20 : 7

He who pursues righteousness and love
finds life, prosperity and honor.

21 : 21

Humility and the fear of the Lord bring
wealth and honor and life.

22 : 4

Listen to your father, who gave you life,
and do not despise your mother when
she is old.

23 : 22

The father of a righteous man has great
joy; he who has a wise son delights in
him.

23 : 24

May your father and mother be glad;
may she who gave you birth rejoice!

23 : 25

Fear the Lord and the king, my son, and
do not join with the rebellious,

24 : 21

It is not good to eat too much honey,
not is it honorable to seek one's own
honor.

25 : 27

Like snow in summer or rain in harvest,
honor is not fitting for a fool.

26 : 1

Like tying a stone in a sling is the
giving of honor to a fool.

26 : 8

A man's pride brings him low, but a
man of lowly spirit gains honor.

29 : 23

Fear of man will prove to be a snare,
but whoever trusts in the Lord is kept
safe.

29 : 25

Her husband is respected at the city gate, where he takes his seat among the elders of the land.

31 : 23

honor the Lord
Honor the Lord with your wealth, with the firstfruits of all your crops;

3 : 9

honorable
The words of the wicked lie in wait for blood, but the speech of the upright rescues them.

12 : 6

The way of the guilty is devious, but the conduct of the innocent is upright.

21 : 8

It is not good to eat too much honey, not is it honorable to seek one's own honor.

25 : 27

honored
He who ignores discipline comes to poverty and shame, but whoever heeds correction is honored.

13 : 18

He who tends a fig tree will eat its fruit, and he who looks after his master will be honored.

27 : 18

honoring God
He who oppresses the poor shows contempt for their Maker, but whoever is kind to the needy honors God.

14 : 31

hope
When a wicked man dies, his hope perishes; all he expected from his power comes to nothing.

11 : 7

The desire of the righteous ends only in good, but the hope of the wicked only in wrath.

11 : 23

Hope deferred makes the heart sick, but a longing fulfilled is a tree of life.

13 : 12

Discipline your son, for in that there is hope; do not be a willing party to his death.

19 : 18

There is surely a future hope for you, and your hope will not be cut off.

23 : 18

Know also that wisdom is sweet to your soul; if you find it, there is a future hope for you, and your hope will not be cut off.

24 : 14

for the evil man has no future hope, and the lamp of the wicked will be snuffed out.

24 : 20

Do you see a man wise in his own eyes? There is more hope for a fool than for him.

26 : 12

Do you see a man who speaks in haste? There is more hope for a fool than for him.

29 : 20

hopes
The prospect of the righteous is joy, but the hopes of the wicked come to nothing.

10 : 28

horse
The horse is made ready for the day of battle, but victory rests with the Lord.

21 : 31

A whip for the horse, a halter for the donkey, and a rod for the backs of fools!

26 : 3

hot coals

Can a man walk on hot coals without his feet being scorched?

6 : 28

hotheaded

A wise man fears the Lord and shuns evil, but a fool is hotheaded and reckless.

14 : 16

hot-tempered

A hot-tempered man stirs up dissension, but a patient man calms a quarrel.

15 : 18

A hot-tempered man must pay the penalty; if you rescue him, you will have to do it again.

19 : 19

or you may learn his ways and get yourself ensnared.

22 : 25

An angry man stirs up dissension, and a hot-tempered one commits many sins.

29 : 22

hot-tempered man

A hot-tempered man stirs up dissension, but a patient man calms a quarrel.

15 : 18

Do not make friends with a hot-tempered man, do not associate with one easily angered,

22 : 24

house

For her house leads down to death and her paths to the spirits of the dead.

2 : 18

When I was a boy in my father's house, still tender, and an only child of my mother,

4 : 3

Keep to a path far from her, do not go near the door of her house,

5 : 8

lest strangers feast on your wealth and your toil enrich another man's house.

5 : 10

Yet if he is caught, he must pay sevenfold, though it costs him all the wealth of his house.

6 : 31

At the window of my house I looked out through the lattice.

7 : 6

He was going down the street near her corner, walking along in the direction of her house

7 : 8

Her house is a highway to the grave, leading down to the chambers of death.

7 : 27

Wisdom has built her house; she has hewn out its seven pillars.

9 : 1

She sits at the door of her house, on a seat at the highest point of the city,

9 : 14

Wicked men are overthrown and are no more, but the house of the righteous stands firm.

12 : 7

The wise woman builds her house, but with her own hands the foolish one tears hers down.

14 : 1

The house of the wicked will be destroyed, but the tent of the upright will flourish.

14 : 11

The house of the righteous contains great treasure, but the income of the wicked brings them trouble.

15 : 6

The Lord tears down the proud man's house, but he keeps the widow's boundaries intact.

15 : 25

Better a dry crust with peace and quiet than a house full of feasting with strife.

17 : 1

If a man pays back evil for good, evil will never leave his house.

17 : 13

Better to live on a corner of the roof than share a house with a quarrelsome wife.

21 : 9

In the house of the wise are stores of choice food and oil, but a foolish man devours all he has.

21 : 20

By wisdom a house is built, and through understanding it is established;

24 : 3

through knowledge its rooms are filled with rare and beautiful treasures.

24 : 4

Do not lie in wait like an outlaw against a righteous man's house, do not raid his dwelling place;

24 : 15

Finish your outdoor work and get your fields ready; after that, build your house.

24 : 27

Seldom set foot in your neighbor's house -- too much of you, and he will hate you.

25 : 17

Better to live on a corner of the roof than share a house with a quarrelsome wife.

25 : 24

Do not forsake your friend and the friend of your father, and do not go to your brother's house when disaster strikes you -- better a neighbor nearby than a brother far away.

27 : 10

house of the wicked

The Lord's curse is on the house of the wicked, but he blesses the home of the righteous.

3 : 33

The Righteous One takes note of the house of the wicked and brings the wicked to ruin.

21 : 12

household

When it snows, she has no fear for her household; for all of them are clothed in scarlet.

31 : 21

She makes coverings for her bed; she is clothed in fine linen and purple.

31 : 22

She watches over the affairs of her household and does not eat the bread of idleness.

31 : 27

houses

we will get all sorts of valuable things and fill our houses with plunder;

1 : 13

Houses and wealth are inherited from parents, but a prudent wife is from the Lord.

19 : 14

human body
Ears that hear and eyes that see -- the Lord has made them both.

20 : 12

humanitarian
He who is kind to the poor lends to the Lord, and he will reward him for what he has done.

19 : 17

humble
He mocks proud mockers but gives grace to the humble.

3 : 34

then do this, my son, to free yourself, since you have fallen into your neighbor's hands: Go and humble yourself; press your plea with your neighbor!

6 : 3

Pride goes before destruction, a haughty spirit before a fall.

16 : 18

Better to be lowly in spirit and among the oppressed than to share plunder with the proud.

16 : 19

Before his downfall a man's heart is proud, but humility comes before honor.

18 : 12

humiliate
it is better for him to say to you, "Come up here," than for him to humiliate you before a nobleman. What you have seen with your eyes

25 : 7

humility
When pride comes, then comes disgrace, but with humility comes wisdom.

11 : 2

A prudent man keeps his knowledge to himself, but the heart of fools blurts out folly.

12 : 23

The fear of the Lord teaches a man wisdom, and humility comes before honor.

15 : 33

Pride goes before destruction, a haughty spirit before a fall.

16 : 18

Better to be lowly in spirit and among the oppressed than to share plunder with the proud.

16 : 19

Before his downfall a man's heart is proud, but humility comes before honor.

18 : 12

Humility and the fear of the Lord bring wealth and honor and life.

22 : 4

Do not exalt yourself in the king's presence, and do not claim a place among great men;

25 : 6

It is not good to eat too much honey, not is it honorable to seek one's own honor.

25 : 27

A man's pride brings him low, but a man of lowly spirit gains honor.

29 : 23

227

hundred
A rebuke impresses a man of discernment more than a hundred lashes a fool.

17 : 10

hunger
They eat the bread of wickedness and drink the wine of violence.

4 : 17

Men do not despise a thief if he steals to satisfy his hunger when he is starving.

6 : 30

The laborer's appetite works for him; his hunger drives him on.

16 : 26

To show partiality is not good -- yet a man will do wrong for a piece of bread.

28 : 21

hungry
The Lord does not let the righteous go hungry but he thwarts the craving of the wicked.

10 : 3

The righteous eat to their hearts' content, but the stomach of the wicked goes hungry.

13 : 25

Laziness brings on deep sleep, and the shiftless man goes hungry.

19 : 15

If your enemy is hungry, give him food to eat; if he is thirsty, give him water to drink.

25 : 21

He who is full loathes honey, but to the hungry even what is bitter tastes sweet.

27 : 7

hunter
Free yourself, like a gazelle from the hand of the hunter, like a bird from the snare of the fowler.

6 : 5

hurdles
The way of the sluggard is blocked with thorns, but the path of the upright is a highway.

15 : 19

hurry
It is not good to have zeal without knowledge, nor to be hasty and miss the way.

19 : 2

It is to a man's honor to avoid strife, but every fool is quick to quarrel.

20 : 3

hurt
let's swallow them alive, like the grave, and whole, like those who go down to the pit;

1 : 12

"They hit me," you will say, "but I'm not hurt! They beat me, but I don't feel it! When will I wake up so I can find another drink?"

23 : 35

husband
for jealousy arouses a husband's fury, and he will show no mercy when he takes revenge.

6 : 34

My husband is not at home; he has gone on a long journey.

7 : 19

A wife of noble character is her husband's crown, but a disgraceful wife is like decay in his bones.

12 : 4

Her husband has full confidence in her and lacks nothing of value.

31 : 11

IIer husband is respected at the city gate, where he takes his seat among the elders of the land.

31 : 23

Her children arise and call her blessed; her husband also, and he praises her:

31 : 28

husbands

He who finds a wife finds what is good and receives favor from the Lord.

18 : 22

Many a man claims to have unfailing love, but a faithful man who can find?

20 : 6

husband's

for jealousy arouses a husband's fury, and he will show no mercy when he takes revenge.

6 : 34

A wife of noble character is her husband's crown, but a disgraceful wife is like decay in his bones.

12 : 4

hypocrisy

The Lord detests the sacrifice of the wicked, but the prayer of the upright pleases him.

15 : 8

I

I

When I was a boy in my father's house, still tender, and an only child of my mother,

4 : 3

I guide you in the way of wisdom and lead you along straight paths.

4 : 11

My son, pay attention to what I say; listen closely to my words.

4 : 20

Now then, my sons, listen to me; do not turn aside from what I say.

5 : 7

I saw among the simple, I noticed among the young men, a youth who lacked judgment.

7 : 7

So I came out to meet you; I looked for you and have found you!

7 : 15

I have covered my bed with colored linens from Egypt.

7 : 16

I have perfumed my bed with myrrh, aloes and cinnamon.

7 : 17

I, wisdom, dwell together with prudence; I possess knowledge and discretion.

8 : 12

To fear the Lord is to hate evil; I hate pride and arrogance, evil behavior and perverse speech.

8 : 13

I was there when he set the heavens in place, when he marked out the horizon on the face of the deep,

8 : 27

Then I was the craftsman at his side. I was filled with delight day after day, rejoicing always in his presence,

8 : 30

I applied my heart to what I observed and learned a lesson from what I saw:

24 : 32

I noticed

I saw among the simple, I noticed among the young men, a youth who lacked judgment.

7 : 7

I saw

I saw among the simple, I noticed among the young men, a youth who lacked judgment.

7 : 7

I applied my heart to what I observed and learned a lesson from what I saw:

24 : 32

idleness

She watches over the affairs of her household and does not eat the bread of idleness.

31 : 27

idolatry

A wise man attacks the city of the mighty and pulls down the stronghold in which they trust.

21 : 22

if

My son, if sinners entice you, do not give in to them.

1 : 10

If they say, "Come along with us; let's lie in wait for someone's blood, let's waylay some harmless soul;

1 : 11

If you had responded to my rebuke, I would have poured out my heart to you and made my thoughts known to you.

1 : 23

My son, if you accept my words and store up my commands within you,

2 : 1

and if you call out for insight and cry aloud for understanding,

2 : 3

and if you look for it as for silver and search for it as for hidden treasure,

2 : 4

My son, if you have put up security for your neighbor, if you have struck hands in pledge for another,

6 : 1

if you have been trapped by what you said, ensnared by the words of your mouth,

6 : 2

Men do not despise a thief if he steals to satisfy his hunger when he is starving.

6 : 30

Yet if he is caught, he must pay sevenfold, though it costs him all the wealth of his house.

6 : 31

If you are wise, your wisdom will reward you; if you are a mocker, you alone will suffer."

9 : 12

If the righteous receive their due on earth, how much more the ungodly and the sinner!

11 : 31

If a man pays back evil for good, evil will never leave his house.

17 : 13

Even a fool is thought wise if he keeps silent, and discerning if he holds his tongue.

17 : 28

A hot-tempered man must pay the penalty; if you rescue him, you will have to do it again.

19 : 19

Take the garment of one who puts up security for a stranger; hold it in pledge if he does it for a wayward woman.

20 : 16

Make plans by seeking advice; if you wage war, obtain guidance.

20 : 18

If a man curses his father or mother, his lamp will be snuffed out in pitch darkness.

20 : 20

If a man shuts his ears to the cry of the poor, he too will cry out and not be answered.

21 : 13

if you lack the means to pay, your very bed will be snatched from under you.

22 : 27

and put a knife to your throat if you are given to gluttony.

23 : 2

Do not withhold discipline from a child, if you punish him with the rod, he will not die.

23 : 13

My son, if your heart is wise, then my heart will be glad;

23 : 15

If you falter in times of trouble, how small is your strength!

24 : 10

If you say, "But we knew nothing about this," does not he who weighs the heart perceive it? Does not he who guards your life know it? Will he not repay each person according to what he has done?

24 : 12

do not bring hastily to court, for what will you do in the end if your neighbor puts you to shame?

25 : 8

If you find honey, just eat enough -- too much of it, and you will vomit.

25 : 16

If your enemy is hungry, give him food to eat; if he is thirsty, give him water to drink.

25 : 21

If a man digs a pit, he will fall into it; if a man rolls a stone, it will roll back on him.

26 : 27

Take a garment of one who puts up security for a stranger; hold it in pledge if he does it for a wayward woman.

27 : 13

If a man loudly blesses his neighbor early in the morning, it will be taken as a curse.

27 : 14

If anyone turns a deaf ear to the law, even his prayers are detestable.

28 : 9

If a ruler listens to lies, all his officials become wicked.

29 : 12

If a king judges the poor with fairness, his throne will always be secure.

29 : 14

If a man pampers his servant from youth, he will bring grief in the end.

29 : 21

"If you have played the fool and exalted yourself, or if you have planned evil, clap your hand over your mouth!

30 : 32

ignorance
"Let all who are simple come in here!" she says to those who lack judgment.

9 : 16

The lips of the righteous nourish many, but fools die for lack of judgment.

10 : 21

ignorant
Do you see a man wise in his own eyes? There is more hope for a fool than for him.

26 : 12

Like one who seizes a dog by the ears is a passer-by who meddles in a quarrel not his own.

26 : 17

I am the most ignorant of men; I do not have a man's understanding.

30 : 2

ignore
But since you rejected me when I called and no one gave heed when I stretched out my hand,

1 : 24

since you ignored all my advice and would not accept my rebuke,

1 : 25

I would not obey my teachers or listen to my instructors.

5 : 13

Listen to my instruction and be wise; do not ignore it.

8 : 33

He who ignores discipline despises himself, but whoever heeds correction gains understanding.

15 : 32

If a man shuts his ears to the cry of the poor, he too will cry out and not be answered.

21 : 13

ignored

since you ignored all my advice and would not accept my rebuke,

1 : 25

who has left the partner of her youth and ignored the covenant she made before God.

2 : 17

ignores

He who heeds discipline shows the way to life, but whoever ignores correction leads others astray.

10 : 17

He who ignores discipline comes to poverty and shame, but whoever heeds correction is honored.

13 : 18

ill will

Be wise, my son, and bring joy to my heart; then I can answer anyone who treats me with contempt.

27 : 11

ill-gotten

Such is the end of all who go after ill-gotten gain; it takes away the life of those who get it.

1 : 19

Ill-gotten treasures are of no value, but righteousness delivers from death.

10 : 2

A tyrannical ruler lacks judgment, but he who hates ill-gotten gain will enjoy a long life.

28 : 16

ill-gotten gain

Such is the end of all who go after ill-gotten gain; it takes away the life of those who get it.

1 : 19

A tyrannical ruler lacks judgment, but he who hates ill-gotten gain will enjoy a long life.

28 : 16

ill-tempered wife

Better to live in a desert than with a quarrelsome and ill-tempered wife.

21 : 19

imagine

The wealth of the rich is their fortified city; they imagine it an unscalable wall.

18 : 11

Your eyes will see strange sights and your mind imagine confusing things.

23 : 33

imitate

Do not answer a fool according to his folly, or you will be like him yourself.

26 : 4

immoral woman

keeping you from the immoral woman, from the smooth tongue of the wayward wife.

6 : 24

immorality

for the Lord detests a perverse man but takes the upright into his confidence.

3 : 32

keeping you from the immoral woman, from the smooth tongue of the wayward wife.

6 : 24

Do not lust in your heart after her beauty or let her captivate you with her eyes,

6 : 25

Can a man walk on hot coals without his feet being scorched?

6 : 28

for jealousy arouses a husband's fury, and he will show no mercy when he takes revenge.

6 : 34

Then out came a woman to meet him, dressed like a prostitute and with crafty intent.

7 : 10

now in the street, now in the squares, at every corner she lurks.

7 : 12

Come, let's drink deep of love till morning; let's enjoy ourselves with love!

7 : 18

My husband is not at home; he has gone on a long journey.

7 : 19

All at once he followed her like an ox going to the slaughter, like a deer stepping into a noose

7 : 22

Her house is a highway to the grave, leading down to the chambers of death.

7 : 27

The integrity of the upright guides them, but the unfaithful are destroyed by their duplicity.

11 : 3

The righteousness of the upright delivers them, but the unfaithful are trapped by evil desires.

11 : 6

immortality
In the way of righteousness there is life; along that path is immortality.

12 : 28

importance
Above all else, guard your heart, for it is the wellspring of life.

4 : 23

Choose my instruction instead of silver, knowledge rather than choice gold,

8 : 10

for wisdom is more precious than rubies, and nothing you desire can compare with her.

8 : 11

Gold there is, and rubies in abundance, but lips that speak knowledge are a rare jewel.

20 : 15

important
Wisdom is supreme; therefore get wisdom. Though it cost all you have, get understanding.

4 : 7

impossible
restraining her is like restraining the wind or grasping oil with the hand.

27 : 16

impresses
A rebuke impresses a man of discernment more than a hundred lashes a fool.

17 : 10

impure

But a man who commits adultery lacks judgment; whoever does so destroys himself.

6 : 32

impure heart

a heart that devises wicked schemes, feet that are quick to rush into evil,

6 : 18

Do not lust in your heart after her beauty or let her captivate you with her eyes,

6 : 25

in shape

She sets about her work vigorously; her arms are strong for her tasks.

31 : 17

incense

Perfume and incense bring joy to the heart, and the pleasantness of one's friend springs from his earnest counsel.

27 : 9

income

The wages of the righteous bring them life, but the income of the wicked brings them punishment.

10 : 16

The house of the righteous contains great treasure, but the income of the wicked brings them trouble.

15 : 6

Better a little with righteousness than much gain with injustice.

16 : 8

increase

He who oppresses the poor to increase his wealth and he who gives gifts to the rich -- both come to poverty.

22 : 16

increases

A wise man has great power, and a man of knowledge increases strength;

24 : 5

He who increases his wealth by exorbitant interest amasses it for another, who will be kind to the poor.

28 : 8

incriminating

An evil man is trapped by his sinful talk, but a righteous man escapes trouble.

12 : 13

incurs

Whoever corrects a mocker invites insult; whoever rebukes a wicked man incurs abuse.

9 : 7

A king delights in a wise servant, but a shameful servant incurs his wrath.

14 : 35

individuality

Each heart knows its own bitterness, and no one else can share its joy.

14 : 10

indulge

If a man pampers his servant from youth, he will bring grief in the end.

29 : 21

industry

He who works his land will have abundant food, but he who chases fantasies lacks judgment.

12 : 11

inevitable

Death and Destruction are never satisfied, and neither are the eyes of man.

27 : 20

infidelity
It will save you also from the adulteress, from the wayward wife with her seductive words,

2 : 16

who has left the partner of her youth and ignored the covenant she made before God.

2 : 17

influence
My son, if sinners entice you, do not give in to them.

1 : 10

For they cannot sleep till they do evil; they are robbed of slumber till they make someone fall.

4 : 16

calling out to those who pass by, who go straight on their way.

9 : 15

The light of the righteous shines brightly, but the lamp of the wicked is snuffed out.

13 : 9

A gift opens the way for the giver and ushers him into the presence of the great.

18 : 16

Wealth brings many friends, but a poor man's friend deserts him.

19 : 4

Haughty eyes and a proud heart, the lamp of the wicked, are sin!

21 : 4

or you may learn his ways and get yourself ensnared.

22 : 25

Do not join those who drink too much wine or gorge themselves on meat,

23 : 20

for their hearts plot violence, and their lips talk about making trouble.

24 : 2

inherit
The wise inherit honor, but fools he holds up to shame.

3 : 35

He who brings trouble on his family will inherit only wind, and the fool will be servant to the wise.

11 : 29

The simple inherit folly, but the prudent are crowned with knowledge.

14 : 18

inheritance
A good man leaves an inheritance for his children's children, but a sinner's wealth is stored up for the righteous.

13 : 22

A wise servant will rule over a disgraceful son, and will share the inheritance as one of the brothers.

17 : 2

Houses and wealth are inherited from parents, but a prudent wife is from the Lord.

19 : 14

An inheritance quickly gained at the beginning will not be blessed at the end.

20 : 21

He who leads the upright along an evil path will fall into his own trap, but the blameless will receive a good inheritance.

28 : 10

inhumanity
A righteous man cares for the needs of his animal, but the kindest acts of the wicked are cruel.

12 : 10

initiating
Kings detest wrongdoing, for a throne is established through righteousness.
16 : 12

injury
Like an archer who wounds at random is he who hires a fool or any passer-by.
26 : 10

injustice
A poor man's field may produce abundant food, but injustice sweeps it away.
13 : 23

Better a little with righteousness than much gain with injustice.
16 : 8

A corrupt witness mocks at justice, and the mouth of the wicked gulps down evil.
19 : 28

inmost
The words of gossip are like choice morsels; they go down to a man's inmost parts.
18 : 8

The words of a gossip are like choice morsels; they go down to a man's inmost parts.
26 : 22

inmost being
The lamp of the Lord searches the spirit of a man; it searches out his inmost being.
20 : 27

Blows and wounds cleanse away evil, and beatings purge the inmost being.
20 : 30

my inmost being will rejoice when your lips speak what is right.
23 : 16

inmost parts
The words of gossip are like choice morsels; they go down to a man's inmost parts.
18 : 8

inner being
The words of gossip are like choice morsels; they go down to a man's inmost parts.
18 : 8

innocent
Do not accuse a man for no reason -- when he has done you no harm.
3 : 30

haughty eyes, a lying tongue, hands that shed innocent blood,
6 : 17

All a man's ways seem innocent to him, but motives are weighed by the Lord.
16 : 2

Acquitting the guilty and condemning the innocent -- the Lord detests them both.
17 : 15

It is not good to punish an innocent man, or to flog officials for their integrity.
17 : 26

It is not good to be partial to the wicked or to deprive the innocent of justice.
18 : 5

The way of the guilty is devious, but the conduct of the innocent is upright.
21 : 8

Whoever says to the guilty, "You are innocent" -- peoples will curse him and nations denounce him.
24 : 24

innocent man
It is not good to punish an innocent man, or to flog officials for their integrity.

17 : 26

insects
Go to the ant, you sluggard; consider its ways and be wise!

6 : 6

"The leech has two daughters. 'Give! Give!' they cry. "There are three things that are never satisfied, four that never say, 'Enough!':

30 : 15

Ants are creatures of little strength, yet they store up their food in the summer;

30 : 25

locusts have no king, yet they advance together in ranks;

30 : 27

insight
for attaining wisdom and discipline; for understanding words of insight;

1 : 2

and if you call out for insight and cry aloud for understanding,

2 : 3

My son, pay attention to my wisdom, listen well to my words of insight,

5 : 1

There is no wisdom, no insight, no plan that can succeed against the Lord.

21 : 30

insightful
A wicked man puts up a bold front, but an upright man gives thought to his ways.

21 : 29

instant
Therefore disaster will overtake him in an instant; he will suddenly be destroyed -- without remedy.

6 : 15

instruct
Instruct a wise man and he will be wiser still; teach a righteous man and he will add to his learning.

9 : 9

instructed
When a mocker is punished, the simple gain wisdom; when a wise man is instructed, he gets knowledge.

21 : 11

instruction
Listen, my son, to your father's instruction and do not forsake your mother's teaching.

1 : 8

Listen, my sons, to a father's instruction; pay attention and gain understanding.

4 : 1

Hold on to instruction, do not let it go; guard it well, for it is your life.

4 : 13

Do not let them out of your sight, keep them within your heart;

4 : 21

Choose my instruction instead of silver, knowledge rather than choice gold,

8 : 10

Listen to my instruction and be wise; do not ignore it.

8 : 33

A wise son heeds his father's instruction, but a mocker does not listen to rebuke.

13 : 1

He who scorns instruction will pay for it, but he who respects a command is rewarded.

13 : 13

Whoever gives heed to instruction prospers, and blessed is he who trusts in the Lord.

16 : 20

The wise in heart are called discerning, and pleasant words promote instruction.

16 : 21

A wise man's heart guides his mouth, and his lips promote instruction.

16 : 23

Listen to advice and accept instruction, and in the end you will be wise.

19 : 20

Stop listening to instruction, my son, and you will stray from the words of knowledge.

19 : 27

Apply your heart to instruction and your ears to words of knowledge.

23 : 12

The sayings of King Lemuel -- an oracle his mother taught him:

31 : 1

She speaks with wisdom, and faithful instruction is on her tongue.

31 : 26

instructions

my son, do not go along with them, do not set foot on their paths;

1 : 15

I would not obey my teachers or listen to my instructors.

5 : 13

He who obeys instructions guards his life, but he who is contemptuous of his ways will die.

19 : 16

instructors

I would not obey my teachers or listen to my instructors.

5 : 13

instrument

Through the blessing of the upright a city is exalted, but by the mouth of the wicked it is destroyed.

11 : 11

insult

Whoever corrects a mocker invites insult; whoever rebukes a wicked man incurs abuse.

9 : 7

A fool shows his annoyance at once, but a prudent man overlooks an insult.

12 : 16

insults

Drive out the mocker, and out goes strife; quarrels and insults are ended.

22 : 10

intact

The Lord tears down the proud man's house, but he keeps the widow's boundaries intact.

15 : 25

integrity

Avoid it, do not travel on it; turn from it and go on your way.

4 : 15

The man of integrity walks securely, but he who takes crooked paths will be found out.

10 : 9

The integrity of the upright guides them, but the unfaithful are destroyed by their duplicity.

11 : 3

A gossip betrays a confidence, but a trustworthy man keeps a secret.

11 : 13

A good man obtains favor from the Lord, but the Lord condemns a crafty man.

12 : 2

The wicked desire the plunder of evil men, but the root of the righteous flourishes.

12 : 12

The righteous hate what is false, but the wicked bring shame and disgrace.

13 : 5

Righteousness guards the man of integrity, but wickedness overthrows the sinner.

13 : 6

The lips of the king speak as an oracle, and his mouth should not betray justice.

16 : 10

It is not good to punish an innocent man, or to flog officials for their integrity.

17 : 26

A false witness will not go unpunished, and he who pours out lies will not go free.

19 : 5

What a man desires is unfailing love; better to be poor than a liar.

19 : 22

Who can say, "I have kept my heart pure; I am clean and without sin"?

20 : 9

A good name is more desirable than great riches; to be esteemed is better than silver or gold.

22 : 1

An honest answer is like a kiss on the lips.

24 : 26

remove the wicked from the king's presence, and his throne will be established through righteousness.

25 : 5

or he who hears it may shame you and you will never lose your bad reputation.

25 : 10

Like clouds and wind without rain is a man who boasts of gifts he does not give.

25 : 14

A malicious man disguises himself with his lips, but in his heart he harbors deceit.

26 : 24

Though his speech is charming, do not believe him, for seven abominations fill his heart.

26 : 25

His malice may be concealed by deception, but his wickedness will be exposed in the assembly.

26 : 26

As water reflects a face, so a man's heart reflects the man.

27 : 19

Bloodthirsty men hate a man of integrity and seek to kill the upright.

29 : 10

The righteous detest the dishonest; the wicked detest the upright.

29 : 27

intent
Then out came a woman to meet him, dressed like a prostitute and with crafty intent.

7 : 10

The sacrifice of the wicked is detestable -- how much more so when brought with evil intent!

21 : 27

Like a coating of glaze over earthenware are fervent lips with an evil heart.

26 : 23

interest
Dishonest money dwindles away, but he who gathers money little by little makes it grow.

13 : 11

internal
The words of gossip are like choice morsels; they go down to a man's inmost parts.

18 : 8

investing
Dishonest money dwindles away, but he who gathers money little by little makes it grow.

13 : 11

investment
People curse the man who hoards grain, but blessing crowns him who is willing to sell.

11 : 26

investments
for she is more profitable than silver and yields better returns than gold.

3 : 14

invitation
"Let all who are simple come in here!" she says to those who lack judgment.

9 : 4

"Come, eat my food and drink the wine I have mixed.

9 : 5

it is better for him to say to you, "Come up here," than for him to humiliate you before a nobleman. What you have seen with your eyes

25 : 7

invites
Whoever corrects a mocker invites insult; whoever rebukes a wicked man incurs abuse.

9 : 7

Wise men store up knowledge, but the mouth of a fool invites ruin.

10 : 14

He who loves a quarrel loves sin; he who builds a high gate invites destruction.

17 : 19

A fool's lips bring him strife, and his mouth invites a beating.

18 : 6

inviting
calling out to those who pass by, who go straight on their way.

9 : 15

IRA'S
The wealth of the rich is their fortified city, but poverty is the ruin of the poor.

10 : 15

iron
As iron sharpens iron, so one man sharpens another.

27 : 17

irony
Wounds from a friend can be trusted, but an enemy multiplies kisses.

27 : 6

irritating

As vinegar to the teeth and smoke to the eyes, so is a sluggard to those who send him.

10 : 26

irritation

A foolish son is his father's ruin, and a quarrelsome wife is like a constant dripping.

19 : 13

Israel

The proverbs of Solomon son of David, king of Israel:

1 : 1

J

jaws
those whose teeth are swords and whose jaws are set with knives to devour the poor from the earth, the needy from among mankind.

30 : 14

jealous
Do not fret because of evil men or be envious of the wicked,

24 : 19

jealousy
for jealousy arouses a husband's fury, and he will show no mercy when he takes revenge.

6 : 34

Anger is cruel and fury overwhelming, but who can stand before jealousy?

27 : 4

Jesus
A man of many companions may come to ruin, but there is a friend who sticks closer than a brother.

18 : 24

jewel
Gold there is, and rubies in abundance, but lips that speak knowledge are a rare jewel.

20 : 15

job
All hard work brings a profit, but mere talk leads only to poverty.

14 : 23

One who is slack in his work is brother to one who destroys.

18 : 9

The sluggard's craving will be the death of him, because his hands refuse to work.

21 : 25

join
Do not join those who drink too much wine or gorge themselves on meat,

23 : 20

Fear the Lord and the king, my son, and do not join with the rebellious,

24 : 21

join together
Say to wisdom, "You are my sister," and call understanding your kinsman;

7 : 4

joined
One who is slack in his work is brother to one who destroys.

18 : 9

joking
is a man who deceives his neighbor and says, "I was only joking!"

26 : 19

journey
My husband is not at home; he has gone on a long journey.

7 : 19

joy
The path of the righteous is like the first gleam of dawn, shining ever brighter till the full light of day.

4 : 18

For whoever finds me finds life and receives favor from the Lord.

8 : 35

The proverbs of Solomon: A wise son brings joy to his father, but a foolish son grief to his mother.

10 : 1

The prospect of the righteous is joy, but the hopes of the wicked come to nothing.

10 : 28

When the righteous prosper, the city rejoices; when the wicked perish, there are shouts of joy.

11 : 10

There is deceit in the hearts of those who plot evil, but joy for those who promote peace.

12 : 20

A man's riches may ransom his life, but a poor man hears no threat.

13 : 8

Each heart knows its own bitterness, and no one else can share its joy.

14 : 10

Even in laughter the heart may ache, and joy may end in grief.

14 : 13

A heart at peace gives life to the body, but envy rots the bones.

14 : 30

A happy heart makes the face cheerful, but heartache crushes the spirit.

15 : 13

All the days of the oppressed are wretched, but the cheerful heart has a continual feast.

15 : 15

A wise son brings joy to his father, but a foolish man despises his mother.

15 : 20

Folly delights a man who lacks judgment, but a man of understanding keeps a straight course.

15 : 21

A man finds joy in giving an apt reply-- and how good is a timely word!

15 : 23

A cheerful look brings joy to the heart, and good news gives health to the bones.

15 : 30

Kings take pleasure in honest lips; they value a man who speaks the truth.

16 : 13

Understanding is a fountain of life to those who have it, but folly brings punishment to fools.

16 : 22

Children's children are a crown to the aged, and parents are the pride of their children.

17 : 6

To have a fool for a son brings grief; there is no joy for the father of a fool.

17 : 21

A cheerful heart is good medicine, but a crushed spirit dries up the bones.

17 : 22

The fear of the Lord leads to life: Then one rests content, untouched by trouble.

19 : 23

When justice is done, it brings joy to the righteous but terror to evildoers.

21 : 15

The father of a righteous man has great joy; he who has a wise son delights in him.

23 : 24

Perfume and incense bring joy to the heart, and the pleasantness of one's friend springs from his earnest counsel.

27 . 9

Be wise, my son, and bring joy to my heart; then I can answer anyone who treats me with contempt.

27 : 11

When the righteous triumph, there is great elation; but when the wicked rise to power, men go into hiding.

28 : 12

When the righteous thrive, the people rejoice; when the wicked rule, the people groan.

29 : 2

A man who loves wisdom brings joy to his father, but a companion of prostitutes squanders his wealth.

29 : 3

An evil man is snared by his own sin, but a righteous one can sing and be glad.

29 : 6

Discipline your son, and he will give you peace; he will bring delight to your soul.

29 : 17

judge

For a man's ways are in full view of the Lord, and he examines all his paths.

5 : 21

The eyes of the Lord are everywhere, keeping watch on the wicked and the good.

15 : 3

When a king sits on his throne to judge, he winnows out all evil with his eyes.

20 . 8

Speak up and judge fairly; defend the rights of the poor and needy."

31 : 9

judges

All a man's ways seem right to him, but the Lord weighs the heart.

21 : 2

Whoever says to the guilty, "You are innocent" -- peoples will curse him and nations denounce him.

24 : 24

If a king judges the poor with fairness, his throne will always be secure.

29 : 14

judging

These also are sayings to the wise: To show partiality in judging is not good:

24 : 23

But it will go well with those who convict the guilty, and rich blessing will come upon them.

24 : 25

judgment

I in turn will laugh at your disaster; I will mock when calamity overtakes you

1 : 26

"Then they will call to me but I will not answer; they will look for me but will not find me.

1 : 28

they will eat the fruit of their ways and be filled with the fruit of their schemes.

1 : 31

For the waywardness of the simple will kill them, and the complacency of fools will destroy them;

1 : 32

but the wicked will be cut off from the land, and the unfaithful will be torn from it.

2 : 22

My son, preserve sound judgment and discernment, do not let them out of your sight;

3 : 21

He mocks proud mockers but gives grace to the humble.

3 : 34

The wise inherit honor, but fools he holds up to shame.

3 : 35

Therefore disaster will overtake him in an instant; he will suddenly be destroyed -- without remedy.

6 : 15

So is he who sleeps with another man's wife; no one who touches her will go unpunished.

6 : 29

But a man who commits adultery lacks judgment; whoever does so destroys himself.

6 : 32

I saw among the simple, I noticed among the young men, a youth who lacked judgment.

7 : 7

Counsel and sound judgment are mine; I have understanding and power.

8 : 14

"Let all who are simple come in here!" she says to those who lack judgment.

9 : 4

"Let all who are simple come in here!" she says to those who lack judgment.

9 : 16

Wisdom is found on the lips of the discerning, but a rod is for the back of him who lacks judgment.

10 : 13

The lips of the righteous nourish many, but fools die for lack of judgment.

10 : 21

Wealth is worthless in the day of wrath, but righteousness delivers from death.

11 : 4

When a wicked man dies, his hope perishes; all he expected from his power comes to nothing.

11 : 7

A man who lacks judgment derides his neighbor, but a man of understanding holds his tongue.

11 : 12

The Lord detests men of perverse heart but he delights in those whose ways are blameless.

11 : 20

Be sure of this: The wicked will not go unpunished, but those who are righteous will go free.

11 : 21

He who works his land will have abundant food, but he who chases fantasies lacks judgment.

12 : 11

The house of the wicked will be destroyed, but the tent of the upright will flourish.

14 : 11

There is a way that seems right to a man, but in the end it leads to death.

14 : 12

The faithless will be fully repaid for their ways, and the good man rewarded for his.

14 : 14

When calamity comes, the wicked are brought down, but even in death the righteous have a refuge.

14 : 32

A king delights in a wise servant, but a shameful servant incurs his wrath.

14 : 35

A gentle answer turns away wrath, but a harsh word stirs up anger.

15 : 1

Death and Destruction lie open before the Lord -- how much more the hearts of men!

15 : 11

Folly delights a man who lacks judgment, but a man of understanding keeps a straight course.

15 : 21

The Lord tears down the proud man's house, but he keeps the widow's boundaries intact.

15 : 25

All a man's ways seem innocent to him, but motives are weighed by the Lord.

16 : 2

The Lord works out everything for his own ends -- even the wicked for a day of disaster.

16 : 4

The Lord detests all the proud of heart. Be sure of this: They will not go unpunished.

16 : 5

When a king's face brightens, it means life; his favor is like a rain cloud in spring.

16 : 15

Understanding is a fountain of life to those who have it, but folly brings punishment to fools.

16 : 22

There is a way that seems right to a man, but in the end it leads to death.

16 : 25

The crucible for silver and the furnace for gold, but the Lord tests the heart.

17 : 3

He who mocks the poor shows contempt for their Maker; whoever gloats over disaster will not go unpunished.

17 : 5

An evil man is bent only on rebellion; a merciless official will be sent against him.

17 : 11

Acquitting the guilty and condemning the innocent -- the Lord detests them both.

17 : 15

A man lacking in judgment strikes hands in pledge and puts up security for his neighbor.

17 : 18

It is not good to punish an innocent man, or to flog officials for their integrity.

17 : 26

An unfriendly man pursues selfish ends; he defies all sound judgment.

18 : 1

The first to present his case seems right, till another comes forward and questions him.

18 : 17

Casting the lot settles disputes and keeps strong opponents apart.

18 : 18

A false witness will not go unpunished, and he who pours out lies will perish.

19 : 9

A king's rage is like the roar of a lion, but his favor is like dew on the grass.

19 : 12

Penalties are prepared for mockers, and beatings for the backs of fools.

19 : 29

A king's wrath is like the roar of a lion; he who angers him forfeits his life.

20 : 2

When a king sits on his throne to judge, he winnows out all evil with his eyes.

20 : 8

Differing weights and differing measures -- the Lord detests them both.

20 : 10

A wise king winnows out the wicked; he drives the threshing wheel over them.

20 : 26

The lamp of the Lord searches the spirit of a man; it searches out his inmost being.

20 : 27

When justice is done, it brings joy to the righteous but terror to evildoers.

21 : 15

The mouth of an adulteress is a deep pit; he who is under the Lord's wrath will fall into it.

22 : 14

for the Lord will take up their case and will plunder those who plunder them.

22 : 23

for their Defender is strong; he will take up their case against you.

23 : 11

If you say, "But we knew nothing about this," does not he who weighs the heart perceive it? Does not he who guards your life know it? Will he not repay each person according to what he has done?

24 : 12

or the Lord will see and disapprove and turn his wrath away from him.

24 : 18

for those two will send sudden destruction upon them, and who knows what calamities they can bring?

24 : 22

I went past the field of the sluggard, past the vineyard of the man who lacks judgment;

24 : 30

His malice may be concealed by deception, but his wickedness will be exposed in the assembly.

26 : 26

A tyrannical ruler lacks judgment, but he who hates ill-gotten gain will enjoy a long life.

28 : 16

A man who remains stiff-necked after many rebukes will suddenly be destroyed -- without remedy.

29 : 1

judgment of God
I in turn will laugh at your disaster; I will mock when calamity overtakes you

1 : 26

judicial
A wicked man accepts a bribe in secret to pervert the course of justice.

17 : 23

judicial system
A truthful witness does not deceive, but a false witness pours out lies.

14 : 5

A truthful witness saves lives, but a false witness is deceitful.

14 : 25

248

Acquitting the guilty and condemning the innocent -- the Lord detests them both.

17 : 15

The first to present his case seems right, till another comes forward and questions him.

18 : 17

But it will go well with those who convict the guilty, and rich blessing will come upon them.

24 : 25

just

for acquiring a disciplined and prudent life, doing what is right and just and fair;

1 : 3

for he guards the course of the just and protects the way of his faithful ones.

2 : 8

Then you will understand what is right and just and fair -- every good path.

2 : 9

All the words of my mouth are just; none of them is crooked or perverse.

8 : 8

By me kings reign and rulers make laws that are just;

8 : 15

The plans of the righteous are just, but the advice of the wicked is deceitful.

12 : 5

Fools mock at making amends for sin, but goodwill is found among the upright.

14 : 9

To do what is right and just is more acceptable to the Lord than sacrifice.

21 : 3

If you find honey, just eat enough -- too much of it, and you will vomit.

25 : 16

just do it

for acquiring a disciplined and prudent life, doing what is right and just and fair;

1 : 3

then do this, my son, to free yourself, since you have fallen into your neighbor's hands: Go and humble yourself; press your plea with your neighbor!

6 : 3

just reward

A wise king winnows out the wicked; he drives the threshing wheel over them.

20 : 26

justice

I walk in the way of righteousness, along the paths of justice,

8 : 20

A poor man's field may produce abundant food, but injustice sweeps it away.

13 : 23

A greedy man brings trouble to his family, but he who hates bribes will live.

15 : 27

The lips of the king speak as an oracle, and his mouth should not betray justice.

16 : 10

A wicked man accepts a bribe in secret to pervert the course of justice.

17 : 23

It is not good to be partial to the wicked or to deprive the innocent of justice.

18 : 5

A corrupt witness mocks at justice, and the mouth of the wicked gulps down evil.

19 : 28

Penalties are prepared for mockers, and beatings for the backs of fools.

19 : 29

When justice is done, it brings joy to the righteous but terror to evildoers.

21 : 15

His malice may be concealed by deception, but his wickedness will be exposed in the assembly.

26 : 26

Evil men do not understand justice, but those who seek the Lord understand it fully.

28 : 5

By justice a king gives a country stability, but one who is greedy for bribes tears it down.

29 : 4

The righteous care about justice for the poor, but the wicked have no such concern.

29 : 7

If a king judges the poor with fairness, his throne will always be secure.

29 : 14

Many seek an audience with a ruler, but it is from the Lord that man gets justice.

29 : 26

K

keep

Thus you will walk in the ways of good men and keep to the paths of the righteous.

2 : 20

My son, do not forget my teaching, but keep my commands in your heart,

3 : 1

for the Lord will be your confidence and will keep your foot from being snared.

3 : 26

he taught me and said, "Lay hold of my words with all your heart; keep my commands and you will live.

4 : 4

Do not let them out of your sight, keep them within your heart;

4 : 21

Put away perversity from your mouth; keep corrupt talk far from your lips.

4 : 24

Do not swerve to the right or the left; keep your foot from evil.

4 : 27

Keep to a path far from her, do not go near the door of her house,

5 : 8

My son, keep your father's commands and do not forsake your mother's teaching.

6 : 20

My son, keep my words and store up my commands within you.

7 : 1

Keep my commands and you will live; guard my teachings as the apple of your eye.

7 : 2

they will keep you from the adulteress, from the wayward wife with her seductive words.

7 : 5

Now then, my sons, listen to me; blessed are those who keep my ways.

8 : 32

The path of life leads upward for the wise to keep him from going down to the grave.

15 : 24

A discerning man keeps wisdom in view, but a fool's eyes wander to the ends of the earth.

17 : 24

Love and faithfulness keep a king safe; through love his throne is made secure.

20 : 28

A prudent man sees danger and takes refuge, but the simple keep going and suffer for it.

22 : 3

for it is pleasing when you keep them in your heart and have all of them ready on your lips.

22 : 18

Listen, my son, and be wise, and keep your heart on the right path.

23 : 19

My son, give me your heart and let your eyes keep to my ways,

23 : 26

251

The prudent see danger and take refuge, but the simple keep going and suffer for it.

27 : 12

Those who forsake the law praise the wicked, but those who keep the law resist them.

28 : 4

Keep falsehood and lies far from me; give me neither poverty nor riches, but give me only my daily bread.

30 : 8

keep a secret
If you argue your case with a neighbor, do not betray another man's confidence,

25 : 9

keep away
Stay away from a foolish man, for you will not find knowledge on his lips.

14 : 7

keep going
The prudent see danger and take refuge, but the simple keep going and suffer for it.

27 : 12

keep the law
Those who forsake the law praise the wicked, but those who keep the law resist them.

28 : 4

keep watch
The eyes of the Lord keep watch over knowledge, but he frustrates the words of the unfaithful.

22 : 12

keeping
keeping you from the immoral woman, from the smooth tongue of the wayward wife.

6 : 24

keeping warm
When it snows, she has no fear for her household; for all of them are clothed in scarlet.

31 · 21

keeping watch
The eyes of the Lord are everywhere, keeping watch on the wicked and the good.

15 : 3

keeping your cool
A patient man has great understanding, but a quick-tempered man displays folly.

14 : 29

keeps
A gossip betrays a confidence, but a trustworthy man keeps a secret.

11 : 13

A prudent man keeps his knowledge to himself, but the heart of fools blurts out folly.

12 : 23

Folly delights a man who lacks judgment, but a man of understanding keeps a straight course.

15 : 21

The Lord tears down the proud man's house, but he keeps the widow's boundaries intact.

15 : 25

Even a fool is thought wise if he keeps silent, and discerning if he holds his tongue.

17 : 28

Casting the lot settles disputes and keeps strong opponents apart.

18 : 18

He who guards his mouth and his tongue keeps himself from calamity.

21 : 23

Where there is no revelation, the people cast off restraint; but blessed is he who keeps the law.

29 : 18

keeps a secret
A gossip betrays a confidence, but a trustworthy man keeps a secret.

11 : 13

keeps the law
He who keeps the law is a discerning son, but a companion of gluttons disgraces his father.

28 : 7

Where there is no revelation, the people cast off restraint; but blessed is he who keeps the law.

29 : 18

kept
Who can say, "I have kept my heart pure; I am clean and without sin"?

20 : 9

kept safe
He whose walk is blameless is kept safe, but he whose ways are perverse will suddenly fall.

28 : 18

He who trusts in himself is a fool, but he who walks in wisdom is kept safe.

28 : 26

Fear of man will prove to be a snare, but whoever trusts in the Lord is kept safe.

29 : 25

kill
Bloodthirsty men hate a man of integrity and seek to kill the upright.

29 : 10

kind
A kind man benefits himself, but a cruel man brings trouble on himself.

11 : 17

An anxious heart weighs a man down, but a kind word cheers him up.

12 : 25

He who despises his neighbor sins, but blessed is he who is kind to the needy.

14 : 21

He who oppresses the poor shows contempt for their Maker, but whoever is kind to the needy honors God.

14 : 31

He who is kind to the poor lends to the Lord, and he will reward him for what he has done.

19 : 17

for he is the kind of man who is always thinking about the cost. "Eat and drink," he says to you, but his heart is not with you.

23 : 7

He who increases his wealth by exorbitant interest amasses it for another, who will be kind to the poor.

28 : 8

kind word
An anxious heart weighs a man down, but a kind word cheers him up.

12 : 25

kind words
A gentle answer turns away wrath, but a harsh word stirs up anger.

15 : 1

Pleasant words are a honeycomb, sweet to the soul and healing to the bones.

16 : 24

He who loves a pure heart and whose speech is gracious will have the king for his friend.

22 : 11

Like cold water to a weary soul is good news from a distant land.

25 : 25

kindest

A righteous man cares for the needs of his animal, but the kindest acts of the wicked are cruel.

12 . 10

kindhearted

A kindhearted woman gains respect, but ruthless men gain only wealth.

11 : 16

kindness

Do not withhold good from those who deserve it, when it is in your power to act.

3 : 27

A man's wisdom gives him patience; it is to his glory to overlook an offense.

19 : 11

If your enemy is hungry, give him food to eat; if he is thirsty, give him water to drink.

25 : 21

In doing this, you will heap burning coals on his head, and the Lord will reward you.

25 : 22

He who increases his wealth by exorbitant interest amasses it for another, who will be kind to the poor.

28 : 8

king

The proverbs of Solomon son of David, king of Israel:

1 : 1

A large population is a king's glory, but without subjects a prince is ruined.

14 : 28

A king delights in a wise servant, but a shameful servant incurs his wrath.

14 : 35

The lips of the king speak as an oracle, and his mouth should not betray justice.

16 : 10

A king's wrath is a messenger of death, but a wise man will appease it.

16 : 14

When a king sits on his throne to judge, he winnows out all evil with his eyes.

20 : 8

A wise king winnows out the wicked; he drives the threshing wheel over them.

20 : 26

Love and faithfulness keep a king safe; through love his throne is made secure.

20 : 28

He who loves a pure heart and whose speech is gracious will have the king for his friend.

22 : 11

Fear the Lord and the king, my son, and do not join with the rebellious,

24 : 21

These are more proverbs of Solomon, copied by the men of Hezekiah king of Judah:

25 : 1

remove the wicked from the king's presence, and his throne will be established through righteousness.

25 : 5

Through patience a ruler can be persuaded, and a gentle tongue can break a bone.

25 : 15

By justice a king gives a country stability, but one who is greedy for bribes tears it down.

29 : 4

If a ruler listens to lies, all his officials become wicked.

29 : 12

If a king judges the poor with fairness, his throne will always be secure.

29 : 14

Many seek an audience with a ruler, but it is from the Lord that man gets justice.

29 : 26

Do not slander a servant to his master, or he will curse you, and you will pay for it.

30 : 10

a servant who becomes a king, a fool who is full of food,

30 : 22

locusts have no king, yet they advance together in ranks;

30 : 27

a strutting rooster, a he-goat, and a king with his army around him.

30 : 31

The sayings of King Lemuel -- an oracle his mother taught him:

31 : 1

king of Israel
The proverbs of Solomon son of David, king of Israel:

1 : 1

king of Judah
These are more proverbs of Solomon, copied by the men of Hezekiah king of Judah:

25 : 1

kings
By me kings reign and rulers make laws that are just;

8 : 15

Kings detest wrongdoing, for a throne is established through righteousness.

16 : 12

Kings take pleasure in honest lips; they value a man who speaks the truth.

16 : 13

Do you see a man skilled in his work? He will serve before kings, he will not serve before obscure men.

22 : 29

As the heavens are high and the earth is deep, so the hearts of kings are unsearchable.

25 : 3

do not spend your strength on women, your vigor on those who ruin kings.

31 : 3

"It is not for kings, O Lemuel -- not for kings to drink wine, not for rulers to crave beer,

31 : 4

king's
When a king's face brightens, it means life; his favor is like a rain cloud in spring.

16 : 15

king's face
When a king's face brightens, it means life; his favor is like a rain cloud in spring.

16 : 15

king's glory
A large population is a king's glory, but without subjects a prince is ruined.

14 : 28

king's heart
The king's heart is in the hand of the Lord; he directs it like a watercourse wherever he pleases.

21 : 1

kings' palaces

a lizard can be caught with the hand, yet it is found in kings' palaces.

30 : 28

king's presence

remove the wicked from the king's presence, and his throne will be established through righteousness.

25 : 5

Do not exalt yourself in the king's presence, and do not claim a place among great men;

25 : 6

king's rage

A king's rage is like the roar of a lion, but his favor is like dew on the grass.

19 : 12

king's wrath

A king's wrath is a messenger of death, but a wise man will appease it.

16 : 14

A king's wrath is like the roar of a lion; he who angers him forfeits his life.

20 : 2

kinsman

Say to wisdom, "You are my sister," and call understanding your kinsman;

7 : 4

kiss

An honest answer is like a kiss on the lips.

24 : 26

kissed

She took hold of him and kissed him and with a brazen face she said:

7 : 13

kisses

Wounds from a friend can be trusted, but an enemy multiplies kisses.

27 : 6

knew

If you say, "But we knew nothing about this," does not he who weighs the heart perceive it? Does not he who guards your life know it? Will he not repay each person according to what he has done?

24 : 12

knife

and put a knife to your throat if you are given to gluttony.

23 : 2

knives

those whose teeth are swords and whose jaws are set with knives to devour the poor from the earth, the needy from among mankind.

30 : 14

know

But the way of the wicked is like deep darkness; they do not know what makes them stumble.

4 : 19

But little do they know that the dead are there, that her guests are in the depths of the grave.

9 : 18

The lips of the righteous know what is fitting, but the mouth of the wicked only what is perverse.

10 : 32

Know also that wisdom is sweet to your soul; if you find it, there is a future hope for you, and your hope will not be cut off.

24 : 14

Do not boast about tomorrow, for you do not know what a day may bring forth.

27 : 1

Be sure you know the condition of your flocks, give careful attention to your herds;

27 : 23

knowledge
for giving prudence to the simple, knowledge and discretion to the young --

1 : 4

The fear of the Lord is the beginning of knowledge, but fools despise wisdom and discipline.

1 : 7

"How long will you simple ones love your simple ways? How long will mockers delight in mockery and fools hate knowledge?

1 : 22

Since they hated knowledge and did not choose to fear the Lord,

1 : 29

then you will understand the fear of the Lord and find the knowledge of God.

2 : 5

For the Lord gives wisdom, and from his mouth come knowledge and understanding.

2 : 6

For wisdom will enter your heart, and knowledge will be pleasant to your soul.

2 : 10

by his knowledge the deeps were divided, and the clouds let drop the dew.

3 : 20

that you may maintain discretion and your lips may preserve knowledge.

5 : 2

To the discerning all of them are right; they are faultless to those who have knowledge.

8 : 9

Choose my instruction instead of silver, knowledge rather than choice gold,

8 : 10

I, wisdom, dwell together with prudence; I possess knowledge and discretion.

8 : 12

"The fear of the Lord is the beginning of wisdom, and knowledge of the Holy One is understanding.

9 : 10

The woman Folly is loud; she is undisciplined and without knowledge.

9 : 13

Wise men store up knowledge, but the mouth of a fool invites ruin.

10 : 14

With his mouth the godless destroys his neighbor, but through knowledge the righteous escape.

11 : 9

Whoever loves discipline loves knowledge, but he who hates correction is stupid.

12 : 1

A prudent man keeps his knowledge to himself, but the heart of fools blurts out folly.

12 : 23

Every prudent man acts out of knowledge, but a fool exposes his folly.

13 : 16

The mocker seeks wisdom and finds none, but knowledge comes easily to the discerning.

14 : 6

Stay away from a foolish man, for you will not find knowledge on his lips.

14 : 7

The simple inherit folly, but the prudent are crowned with knowledge.

14 : 18

The tongue of the wise commends knowledge, but the mouth of the fool gushes folly.

15 : 2

The lips of the wise spread knowledge; not so the hearts of fools.

15 : 7

The discerning heart seeks knowledge, but the mouth of a fool feeds on folly.

15 : 14

A man of knowledge uses words with restraint, and a man of understanding is even-tempered.

17 : 27

The heart of the discerning acquires knowledge; the ears of the wise seek it out.

18 : 15

It is not good to have zeal without knowledge, nor to be hasty and miss the way.

19 : 2

Flog a mocker, and the simple will learn prudence; rebuke a discerning man, and he will gain knowledge.

19 : 25

Stop listening to instruction, my son, and you will stray from the words of knowledge.

19 : 27

Gold there is, and rubies in abundance, but lips that speak knowledge are a rare jewel.

20 : 15

When a mocker is punished, the simple gain wisdom; when a wise man is instructed, he gets knowledge.

21 : 11

The eyes of the Lord keep watch over knowledge, but he frustrates the words of the unfaithful.

22 : 12

Have I not written thirty sayings for you, sayings of counsel and knowledge,

22 : 20

Apply your heart to instruction and your ears to words of knowledge.

23 : 12

through knowledge its rooms are filled with rare and beautiful treasures.

24 : 4

A wise man has great power, and a man of knowledge increases strength;

24 : 5

When a country is rebellious, it has many rulers, but a man of understanding and knowledge maintains order.

28 : 2

I have not learned the wisdom, nor have I knowledge of the Holy One.

30 : 3

knowledge of God
then you will understand the fear of the Lord and find the knowledge of God.

2 : 5

known
If you had responded to my rebuke, I would have poured out my heart to you and made my thoughts known to you.

1 : 23

Wisdom reposes in the heart of the discerning and even among fools she lets herself be known.

14 : 33

Even a child is known by his actions, by whether his conduct is pure and right.

20 : 11

He who plots evil will be known as a schemer,

24 : 8

L

labor
Diligent hands will rule, but laziness ends in slave labor.

12 : 24

laborer
The laborer's appetite works for him; his hunger drives him on.

16 : 26

lack
He will die for lack of discipline, led astray by his own great folly.

5 : 23

"Let all who are simple come in here!" she says to those who lack judgment.

9 : 4

"Let all who are simple come in here!" she says to those who lack judgment.

9 : 16

The lips of the righteous nourish many, but fools die for lack of judgment.

10 : 21

For lack of guidance a nation falls, but many advisers make victory sure.

11 : 14

Plans fail for lack of counsel, but with many advisers they succeed.

15 : 22

if you lack the means to pay, your very bed will be snatched from under you.

22 : 27

He who gives to the poor will lack nothing, but he who closes his eyes to them receives many curses.

28 : 27

If a wise man goes to court with a fool, the fool rages and scoffs, and there is no peace.

29 : 9

lack judgment
"Let all who are simple come in here!" she says to those who lack judgment.

9 : 16

lack nothing
He who gives to the poor will lack nothing, but he who closes his eyes to them receives many curses.

28 : 27

lack of counsel
Plans fail for lack of counsel, but with many advisers they succeed.

15 : 22

lack of diligence
and poverty will come on you like a bandit and scarcity like an armed man.

24 : 34

lack of guidance
For lack of guidance a nation falls, but many advisers make victory sure.

11 : 14

lack of judgment
The lips of the righteous nourish many, but fools die for lack of judgment.

10 : 21

Do not answer a fool according to his folly, or you will be like him yourself.

26 : 4

lack of peace
If a wise man goes to court with a fool, the fool rages and scoffs, and there is no peace.

29 : 9

lack of purity
But a man who commits adultery lacks judgment; whoever does so destroys himself.

6 : 32

lack of wisdom
I saw among the simple, I noticed among the young men, a youth who lacked judgment.

7 : 7

For lack of guidance a nation falls, but many advisers make victory sure.

11 : 14

lacked judgment
I saw among the simple, I noticed among the young men, a youth who lacked judgment.

7 : 7

lacking
A man lacking in judgment strikes hands in pledge and puts up security for his neighbor.

17 : 18

lacking understanding
I am the most ignorant of men; I do not have a man's understanding.

30 : 2

lacks
But a man who commits adultery lacks judgment; whoever does so destroys himself.

6 : 32

Wisdom is found on the lips of the discerning, but a rod is for the back of him who lacks judgment.

10 : 13

A man who lacks judgment derides his neighbor, but a man of understanding holds his tongue.

11 : 12

He who works his land will have abundant food, but he who chases fantasies lacks judgment.

12 : 11

I went past the field of the sluggard, past the vineyard of the man who lacks judgment;

24 : 30

Like a city whose walls are broken down is a man who lacks self-control.

25 : 28

Her husband has full confidence in her and lacks nothing of value.

31 : 11

lacks judgment
But a man who commits adultery lacks judgment; whoever does so destroys himself.

6 : 32

A man who lacks judgment derides his neighbor, but a man of understanding holds his tongue.

11 : 12

He who works his land will have abundant food, but he who chases fantasies lacks judgment.

12 : 11

Folly delights a man who lacks judgment, but a man of understanding keeps a straight course.

15 : 21

I went past the field of the sluggard, past the vineyard of the man who lacks judgment;

24 : 30

A tyrannical ruler lacks judgment, but he who hates ill-gotten gain will enjoy a long life.

28 : 16

lacks nothing
Her husband has full confidence in her and lacks nothing of value.

31 : 11

lacks self-control
Like a city whose walls are broken down is a man who lacks self-control.

25 : 28

lacks wisdom
A man who lacks judgment derides his neighbor, but a man of understanding holds his tongue.

11 : 12

laid
By wisdom the Lord laid the earth's foundations, by understanding he set the heavens in place;

3 : 19

laid bare
The man of integrity walks securely, but he who takes crooked paths will be found out.

10 : 9

lambs
the lambs will provide you with clothing, and the goats with the price of a field.

27 : 26

lame foot
Like a bad tooth or a lame foot is reliance on the unfaithful in times of trouble.

25 : 19

lame man's legs
Like a lame man's legs that hang limp is a proverb in the mouth of a fool.

26 : 7

lamp
For these commands are a lamp, this teaching is a light, and the corrections of discipline are the way to life,

6 : 23

The light of the righteous shines brightly, but the lamp of the wicked is snuffed out.

13 : 9

If a man curses his father or mother, his lamp will be snuffed out in pitch darkness.

20 : 20

The lamp of the Lord searches the spirit of a man; it searches out his inmost being.

20 : 27

Haughty eyes and a proud heart, the lamp of the wicked, are sin!

21 : 4

She sees that her trading is profitable, and her lamp does not go out at night.

31 : 18

lamp of the wicked
The light of the righteous shines brightly, but the lamp of the wicked is snuffed out.

13 : 9

Haughty eyes and a proud heart, the lamp of the wicked, are sin!

21 : 4

land
For the upright will live in the land, and the blameless will remain in it;

2 : 21

but the wicked will be cut off from the land, and the unfaithful will be torn from it.

2 : 22

The righteous will never be uprooted, but the wicked will not remain in the land.

10 : 30

He who works his land will have abundant food, but he who chases fantasies lacks judgment.

12 : 11

Like cold water to a weary soul is good news from a distant land.

25 : 25

He who works his land will have abundant food, but the one who chases fantasies will have his fill of poverty.

28 : 19

the grave, the barren womb, land, which is never satisfied with water, and fire, which never says, 'Enough!'

30 : 16

She considers a field and buys it; out of her earnings she plants a vineyard.

31 : 16

Her husband is respected at the city gate, where he takes his seat among the elders of the land.

31 : 23

language

A scoundrel and villain, who goes about with a corrupt mouth,

6 : 12

A word aptly spoken is like apples of gold in settings of silver.

25 : 11

Though his speech is charming, do not believe him, for seven abominations fill his heart.

26 : 25

lap

Can a man scoop fire into his lap without his clothes being burned?

6 : 27

The lot is cast into the lap, but its every decision is from the Lord.

16 : 33

large population

A large population is a king's glory, but without subjects a prince is ruined.

14 : 28

lashes

A rebuke impresses a man of discernment more than a hundred lashes a fool.

17 : 10

later

Do not say to your neighbor, "Come back later; I'll give it tomorrow" -- when you now have it with you.

3 : 28

It is a trap for a man to dedicate something rashly and only later to consider his vows.

20 : 25

lattice

At the window of my house I looked out through the lattice.

7 : 6

laugh

I in turn will laugh at your disaster; I will mock when calamity overtakes you

1 : 26

She is clothed with strength and dignity; she can laugh at the days to come.

31 : 25

laughing

A happy heart makes the face cheerful, but heartache crushes the spirit.

15 : 13

laughter

Even in laughter the heart may ache, and joy may end in grief.

14 : 13

law

Whoever says to the guilty, "You are innocent" -- peoples will curse him and nations denounce him.

24 : 24

Like a club or a sword or a sharp arrow is the man who gives false testimony against his neighbor.

25 : 18

Those who forsake the law praise the wicked, but those who keep the law resist them.

28 : 4

He who keeps the law is a discerning son, but a companion of gluttons disgraces his father.

28 : 7

If anyone turns a deaf ear to the law, even his prayers are detestable.

28 : 9

Where there is no revelation, the people cast off restraint; but blessed is he who keeps the law.

29 : 18

lest they drink and forget what the law decrees, and deprive all the oppressed of the rights.

31 : 5

laws

By me kings reign and rulers make laws that are just;

8 : 15

A false witness will not go unpunished, and he who pours out lies will perish.

19 : 9

lawyer

for their Defender is strong; he will take up their case against you.

23 : 11

do not bring hastily to court, for what will you do in the end if your neighbor puts you to shame?

25 : 8

If you argue your case with a neighbor, do not betray another man's confidence,

25 : 9

If a wise man goes to court with a fool, the fool rages and scoffs, and there is no peace.

29 : 9

lawyers

But it will go well with those who convict the guilty, and rich blessing will come upon them.

24 : 25

lay hold

She is a tree of life to those who embrace her; those who lay hold of her will be blessed.

3 : 18

he taught me and said, "Lay hold of my words with all your heart; keep my commands and you will live.

4 : 4

laziness

Go to the ant, you sluggard; consider its ways and be wise!

6 : 6

How long will you lie there, you sluggard? When will you get up from your sleep?

6 : 9

Lazy hands make a man poor, but diligent hands bring wealth.

10 : 4

He who gathers crops in summer is a wise son, but he who sleeps during harvest is a disgraceful son.

10 : 5

264

As vinegar to the teeth and smoke to the eyes, so is a sluggard to those who send him.

10 : 26

Diligent hands will rule, but laziness ends in slave labor.

12 : 24

The sluggard craves and gets nothing, but the desires of the diligent are fully satisfied.

13 : 4

The way of the sluggard is blocked with thorns, but the path of the upright is a highway.

15 : 19

Laziness brings on deep sleep, and the shiftless man goes hungry.

19 : 15

The sluggard buries his hand in the dish; he will not even bring it back to his mouth!

19 : 24

Do not love sleep or you will grow poor; stay awake and you will have food to spare.

20 : 13

The sluggard's craving will be the death of him, because his hands refuse to work.

21 : 25

for drunkards and gluttons become poor, and drowsiness clothes them in rags.

23 : 21

I went past the field of the sluggard, past the vineyard of the man who lacks judgment;

24 : 30

and poverty will come on you like a bandit and scarcity like an armed man.

24 : 34

The sluggard says, "There is a lion in the road, a fierce lion roaming the streets!"

26 : 13

As a door turns on its hinges, so a sluggard turns on his bed.

26 : 14

The sluggard buries his hand in the dish; he is too lazy to bring it back to his mouth.

26 : 15

lazy

How long will you lie there, you sluggard? When will you get up from your sleep?

6 : 9

Lazy hands make a man poor, but diligent hands bring wealth.

10 : 4

The lazy man does not roast his game, but the diligent man prizes his possessions.

12 : 27

One who is slack in his work is brother to one who destroys.

18 : 9

The sluggard says, "There is a lion outside!" or "I will be murdered in the streets!"

22 : 13

The sluggard buries his hand in the dish; he is too lazy to bring it back to his mouth.

26 : 15

lazy man

The lazy man does not roast his game, but the diligent man prizes his possessions.

12 : 27

lead

I guide you in the way of wisdom and lead you along straight paths.

4 : 11

Her feet go down to death; her steps lead straight to the grave.

5 : 5

The plans of the diligent lead to profit as surely as haste leads to poverty.

21 : 5

lead astray

For they cannot sleep till they do evil; they are robbed of slumber till they make someone fall.

4 : 16

leader

A wise servant will rule over a disgraceful son, and will share the inheritance as one of the brothers.

17 : 2

leaders

By me kings reign and rulers make laws that are just;

8 : 15

by me princes govern, and all nobles who rule on earth.

8 : 16

leadership

Through the blessing of the upright a city is exalted, but by the mouth of the wicked it is destroyed.

11 : 11

For lack of guidance a nation falls, but many advisers make victory sure.

11 : 14

The light of the righteous shines brightly, but the lamp of the wicked is snuffed out.

13 : 9

He who walks with the wise grows wise, but a companion of fools suffers harm.

13 : 20

All hard work brings a profit, but mere talk leads only to poverty.

14 : 23

Plans fail for lack of counsel, but with many advisers they succeed.

15 : 22

The lips of the king speak as an oracle, and his mouth should not betray justice.

16 : 10

Kings detest wrongdoing, for a throne is established through righteousness.

16 : 12

A violent man entices his neighbor and leads him down a path that is not good.

16 : 29

Better a patient man than a warrior, a man who controls his temper than one who takes a city.

16 : 32

Better is open rebuke than hidden love.

27 : 5

As iron sharpens iron, so one man sharpens another.

27 : 17

As water reflects a face, so a man's heart reflects the man.

27 : 19

Like a roaring lion or a charging bear is a wicked man ruling over a helpless people.

28 : 15

A tyrannical ruler lacks judgment, but he who hates ill-gotten gain will enjoy a long life.

28 : 16

When the righteous thrive, the people rejoice; when the wicked rule, the people groan.

29 . 2

By justice a king gives a country stability, but one who is greedy for bribes tears it down.

29 : 4

Bloodthirsty men hate a man of integrity and seek to kill the upright.

29 : 10

If a ruler listens to lies, all his officials become wicked.

29 : 12

If a king judges the poor with fairness, his throne will always be secure.

29 : 14

Ants are creatures of little strength, yet they store up their food in the summer;

30 : 25

leading

Her house is a highway to the grave, leading down to the chambers of death.

7 : 27

beside the gates leading into the city, at the entrances, she cries aloud:

8 : 3

The lips of the king speak as an oracle, and his mouth should not betray justice.

16 : 10

leads

For her house leads down to death and her paths to the spirits of the dead.

2 : 18

He who heeds discipline shows the way to life, but whoever ignores correction leads others astray.

10 : 17

A righteous man is cautious in friendship, but the way of the wicked leads them astray

12 : 26

There is a way that seems right to a man, but in the end it leads to death.

14 : 12

All hard work brings a profit, but mere talk leads only to poverty.

14 : 23

The path of life leads upward for the wise to keep him from going down to the grave.

15 : 24

There is a way that seems right to a man, but in the end it leads to death.

16 : 25

A violent man entices his neighbor and leads him down a path that is not good.

16 : 29

The fear of the Lord leads to life: Then one rests content, untouched by trouble.

19 : 23

The righteous man leads a blameless life; blessed are his children after him.

20 : 7

The king's heart is in the hand of the Lord; he directs it like a watercourse wherever he pleases.

21 : 1

The plans of the diligent lead to profit as surely as haste leads to poverty.

21 : 5

He who leads the upright along an evil path will fall into his own trap, but the blameless will receive a good inheritance.

28 : 10

leads astray

A righteous man is cautious in friendship, but the way of the wicked leads them astray.

12 : 26

leads to death

There is a way that seems right to a man, but in the end it leads to death.

14 : 12

leads to life

The fear of the Lord leads to life: Then one rests content, untouched by trouble.

19 : 23

lean not

Trust in the Lord with all your heart and lean not on your own understanding;

3 : 5

learn

Flog a mocker, and the simple will learn prudence; rebuke a discerning man, and he will gain knowledge.

19 : 25

Pay attention and listen to the sayings of the wise; apply your heart to what I teach,

22 : 17

for it is pleasing when you keep them in your heart and have all of them ready on your lips.

22 : 18

learned

I applied my heart to what I observed and learned a lesson from what I saw:

24 : 32

I have not learned the wisdom, nor have I knowledge of the Holy One.

30 : 3

learning

let the wise listen and add to their learning, and let the discerning get guidance --

1 : 5

I give you sound learning, so do not forsake my teaching.

4 : 2

Instruct a wise man and he will be wiser still; teach a righteous man and he will add to his learning.

9 : 9

He who heeds discipline shows the way to life, but whoever ignores correction leads others astray.

10 : 17

Whoever loves discipline loves knowledge, but he who hates correction is stupid.

12 : 1

Pride only breeds quarrels, but wisdom is found in those who take advice.

13 : 10

The teaching of the wise is a fountain of life, turning a man from the snares of death.

13 : 14

The heart of the discerning acquires knowledge; the ears of the wise seek it out.

18 : 15

Ears that hear and eyes that see -- the Lord has made them both.

20 : 12

Pay attention and listen to the sayings of the wise; apply your heart to what I teach,

22 : 17

So that your trust may be in the Lord, I teach you today, even you.

22 : 19

Have I not written thirty sayings for you, sayings of counsel and knowledge,

22 : 20

Apply your heart to instruction and your ears to words of knowledge.

23 : 12

As iron sharpens iron, so one man sharpens another.

27 : 17

leave

who leave the straight paths to walk in dark ways,

2 : 13

Let love and faithfulness never leave you; bind them around your neck, write them on the tablet of your heart.

3 : 3

Leave your simple ways and you will live; walk in the way of understanding.

9 : 6

If a man pays back evil for good, evil will never leave his house.

17 : 13

leaving a legacy

The memory of the righteous will be a blessing, but the name of the wicked will rot.

10 : 7

leaving an inheritance

A good man leaves an inheritance for his children's children, but a sinner's wealth is stored up for the righteous.

13 : 22

led

He will die for lack of discipline, led astray by his own great folly.

5 : 23

led astray

She gives no thought to the way of life; her paths are crooked, but she knows it not.

5 : 6

He will die for lack of discipline, led astray by his own great folly.

5 : 23

Wine is a mocker and beer a brawler; whoever is led astray by them is not wise.

20 : 1

led away

Rescue those being led away to death; hold back those staggering toward slaughter.

24 : 11

leech

"The leech has two daughters. 'Give! Give!' they cry. "There are three things that are never satisfied, four that never say, 'Enough!':

30 : 15

left

who has left the partner of her youth and ignored the covenant she made before God.

2 : 17

Long life is in her right hand; in her left hand are riches and honor.

3 : 16

Do not swerve to the right or the left; keep your foot from evil.

4 : 27

The rod of correction imparts wisdom, but a child left to himself disgraces his mother.

29 : 15

left hand

Long life is in her right hand; in her left hand are riches and honor.

3 : 16

left to himself

The rod of correction imparts wisdom, but a child left to himself disgraces his mother.

29 : 15

legacy

The memory of the righteous will be a blessing, but the name of the wicked will rot.

10 : 7

legs

Like a lame man's legs that hang limp is a proverb in the mouth of a fool.

26 : 7

lend

He who is kind to the poor lends to the Lord, and he will reward him for what he has done.

19 : 17

lender

The rich rule over the poor, and the borrower is servant to the lender.

22 : 7

length

The fear of the Lord adds length to life, but the years of the wicked are cut short.

10 : 27

lesson

But whoever fails to find me harms himself; all who hate me love death.

8 : 36

I applied my heart to what I observed and learned a lesson from what I saw:

24 : 32

lesson of a life time

He who heeds discipline shows the way to life, but whoever ignores correction leads others astray.

10 : 17

lest

lest you give your best strength to others and your years to one who is cruel,

5 : 9

let

let the wise listen and add to their learning, and let the discerning get guidance --

1 : 5

Let love and faithfulness never leave you; bind them around your neck, write them on the tablet of your heart.

3 : 3

by his knowledge the deeps were divided, and the clouds let drop the dew.

3 : 20

My son, preserve sound judgment and discernment, do not let them out of your sight;

3 : 21

Hold on to instruction, do not let it go; guard it well, for it is your life.

4 : 13

Do not let them out of your sight, keep them within your heart;

4 : 21

Let your eyes look straight ahead, fix your gaze directly before you.

4 : 25

Let them be yours alone, never to be shared with strangers.

5 : 17

Do not lust in your heart after her beauty or let her captivate you with her eyes,

6 : 25

Do not let your heart turn to her ways or stray into her paths.

7 : 25

"Let all who are simple come in here!" she says to those who lack judgment.

9 : 4

"Let all who are simple come in here!" she says to those who lack judgment.

9 : 16

The Lord does not let the righteous go hungry but he thwarts the craving of the wicked.

10 : 3

Do not let your heart envy sinners, but always be zealous for the fear of the Lord.

23 : 17

Do not gloat when your enemy falls; when he stumbles, do not let your heart rejoice,

24 : 17

Let another praise you, and not your own mouth; someone else, and not your own lips.

27 : 2

A man tomented by the guilt of murder will be a fugitive till death; let no one support him.

28 : 17

let them drink and forget their poverty and remember their misery no more.

31 : 7

Give her the reward she has earned, and let her works bring her praise at the city gate.

31 : 31

let your yes be yes
The Lord detests lying lips, but he delights in men who are truthful.

12 : 22

level
Make level paths for your feet and take only ways that are firm.

4 : 26

liar
A scoundrel and villain, who goes about with a corrupt mouth,

6 : 12

haughty eyes, a lying tongue, hands that shed innocent blood,

6 : 17

A wicked man listens to evil lips; a liar pays attention to a malicious tongue.

17 : 4

A false witness will not go unpunished, and he who pours out lies will perish.

19 : 9

What a man desires is unfailing love; better to be poor than a liar.

19 : 22

A corrupt witness mocks at justice, and the mouth of the wicked gulps down evil.

19 : 28

A false witness will perish, and whoever listens to him will be destroyed forever.

21 : 28

Do not add to his words, or he will rebuke you and prove you a liar.

30 : 6

lie
If they say, "Come along with us; let's lie in wait for someone's blood, let's waylay some harmless soul;

1 : 11

These men lie in wait for their own blood; they waylay only themselves!

1 : 18

when you lie down, you will not be afraid; when you lie down, your sleep will be sweet.

3 : 24

if you have been trapped by what you said, ensnared by the words of your mouth,

6 : 2

How long will you lie there, you sluggard? When will you get up from your sleep?

6 : 9

Death and Destruction lie open before the Lord -- how much more the hearts of men!

15 : 11

In the paths of the wicked lie thorns and snares, but he who guards his soul stays far from them.

22 : 5

Do not testify against your neighbor without cause, or use your lips to deceive.

24 : 28

lie down
when you lie down, you will not be afraid; when you lie down, your sleep will be sweet.

3 : 24

lie in wait
If they say, "Come along with us; let's lie in wait for someone's blood, let's waylay some harmless soul;

1 : 11

These men lie in wait for their own blood; they waylay only themselves!

1 : 18

The words of the wicked lie in wait for blood, but the speech of the upright rescues them.

12 : 6

Do not lie in wait like an outlaw against a righteous man's house, do not raid his dwelling place;

24 : 15

lies
if you have been trapped by what you said, ensnared by the words of your mouth,

6 : 2

a false witness who pours out lies and a man who stirs up dissension among brothers.

6 : 19

An evil man is trapped by his sinful talk, but a righteous man escapes trouble.

12 : 13

A truthful witness gives honest testimony, but a false witness tells lies.

12 : 17

There is deceit in the hearts of those who plot evil, but joy for those who promote peace.

12 : 20

A truthful witness does not deceive, but a false witness pours out lies.

14 : 5

A false witness will not go unpunished, and he who pours out lies will not go free.

19 : 5

A false witness will not go unpunished, and he who pours out lies will perish.

19 : 9

The sluggard says, "There is a lion outside!" or "I will be murdered in the streets!"

22 : 13

If a ruler listens to lies, all his officials become wicked.

29 : 12

Keep falsehood and lies far from me; give me neither poverty nor riches, but give me only my daily bread.

30 : 8

lies in wait

Like a bandit she lies in wait, and multiplies the unfaithful among men.

23 : 28

life

for acquiring a disciplined and prudent life, doing what is right and just and fair;

1 : 3

Such is the end of all who go after ill-gotten gain; it takes away the life of those who get it.

1 : 19

None who go to her return or attain the paths of life.

2 : 19

for they will prolong your life many years and bring you prosperity.

3 : 2

Long life is in her right hand; in her left hand are riches and honor.

3 : 16

they will be life for you, an ornament to grace your neck.

3 : 22

Listen, my son, accept what I say, and the years of your life will be many.

4 : 10

Hold on to instruction, do not let it go; guard it well, for it is your life.

4 : 13

for they are life to those who find them and health to a man's whole body.

4 : 22

Above all else, guard your heart, for it is the wellspring of life.

4 : 23

She gives no thought to the way of life; her paths are crooked, but she knows it not.

5 : 6

At the end of your life you will groan, when your flesh and body are spent.

5 : 11

For these commands are a lamp, this teaching is a light, and the corrections of discipline are the way to life,

6 : 23

for the prostitute reduces you to a loaf of bread, and the adulteress preys upon your very life.

6 : 26

till an arrow pierces his liver, like a bird darting into a snare, little knowing it will cost him his life.

7 : 23

For whoever finds me finds life and receives favor from the Lord.

8 : 35

Leave your simple ways and you will live; walk in the way of understanding.

9 : 6

For through me your days will be many, and years will be added to your life.

9 : 11

The mouth of the righteous is a fountain of life, but violence overwhelms the mouth of the wicked.

10 : 11

The wages of the righteous bring them life, but the income of the wicked brings them punishment.

10 : 16

He who heeds discipline shows the way to life, but whoever ignores correction leads others astray.

10 : 17

The fear of the Lord adds length to life, but the years of the wicked are cut short.

10 : 27

The truly righteous man attains life, but he who pursues evil goes to his death.

11 : 19

The fruit of the righteous is a tree of life, and he who wins souls is wise.

11 : 30

A man cannot be established through wickedness, but the righteous cannot be uprooted.

12 : 3

In the way of righteousness there is life; along that path is immortality.

12 : 28

He who guards his lips guards his life, but he who speaks rashly will come to ruin.

13 : 3

A man's riches may ransom his life, but a poor man hears no threat.

13 : 8

Hope deferred makes the heart sick, but a longing fulfilled is a tree of life.

13 : 12

The teaching of the wise is a fountain of life, turning a man from the snares of death.

13 : 14

The fear of the Lord is a fountain of life, turning a man from the snares of death.

14 : 27

A heart at peace gives life to the body, but envy rots the bones.

14 : 30

The tongue that brings healing is a tree of life, but a deceitful tongue crushes the spirit.

15 : 4

The path of life leads upward for the wise to keep him from going down to the grave.

15 : 24

He who listens to a life-giving rebuke will be at home among the wise.

15 : 31

When a king's face brightens, it means life; his favor is like a rain cloud in spring.

16 : 15

The highway of the upright avoids evil; he who guards his way guards his life.

16 : 17

Understanding is a fountain of life to those who have it, but folly brings punishment to fools.

16 : 22

Gray hair is a crown of splendor; it is attained by a righteous life.

16 : 31

The words of a man's mouth are deep waters, but the fountain of wisdom is a bubbling brook.

18 : 4

The tongue has the power of life and death, and those who love it will eat its fruit.

18 : 21

Better a poor man whose walk is blameless than a fool whose lips are perverse.

19 : 1

A man's own folly ruins his life, yet his heart rages against the Lord.

19 : 3

He who obeys instructions guards his life, but he who is contemptuous of his ways will die.

19 : 16

The fear of the Lord leads to life: Then one rests content, untouched by trouble.

19 : 23

A king's wrath is like the roar of a lion; he who angers him forfeits his life.

20 : 2

The righteous man leads a blameless life; blessed are his children after him.

20 : 7

He who pursues righteousness and love finds life, prosperity and honor.

21 : 21

Humility and the fear of the Lord bring wealth and honor and life.

22 : 4

Listen to your father, who gave you life, and do not despise your mother when she is old.

23 : 22

If you say, "But we knew nothing about this," does not he who weighs the heart perceive it? Does not he who guards your life know it? Will he not repay each person according to what he has done?

24 : 12

A tyrannical ruler lacks judgment, but he who hates ill-gotten gain will enjoy a long life.

28 : 16

She brings him good, not harm, all the days of her life.

31 : 12

lifeless
How long will you lie there, you sluggard? When will you get up from your sleep?

6 : 9

lifestyle
Thus you will walk in the ways of good men and keep to the paths of the righteous.

2 : 20

Let love and faithfulness never leave you; bind them around your neck, write them on the tablet of your heart.

3 : 3

No harm befalls the righteous, but the wicked have their fill of trouble.

12 : 21

When a man's ways are pleasing to the Lord, he makes even his enemies live at peace with him.

16 : 7

light
The path of the righteous is like the first gleam of dawn, shining ever brighter till the full light of day.

4 : 18

For these commands are a lamp, this teaching is a light, and the corrections of discipline are the way to life,

6 : 23

The light of the righteous shines brightly, but the lamp of the wicked is snuffed out.

13 : 9

light of day
The path of the righteous is like the first gleam of dawn, shining ever brighter till the full light of day.

4 : 18

linen
She makes coverings for her bed; she is clothed in fine linen and purple.

31 : 22

She makes linen garments and sells them, and supplies the merchants with sashes.

31 : 24

linens
I have covered my bed with colored linens from Egypt.

7 : 16

linger
Those who linger over wine, who go to sample bowls of mixed wine,

23 : 30

lion
A king's rage is like the roar of a lion, but his favor is like dew on the grass.

19 : 12

A king's wrath is like the roar of a lion; he who angers him forfeits his life.

20 : 2

The sluggard says, "There is a lion outside!" or "I will be murdered in the streets!"

22 : 13

The sluggard says, "There is a lion in the road, a fierce lion roaming the streets!"

26 : 13

The wicked man flees though no one pursues, but the righteous are as bold as a lion.

28 : 1

Like a roaring lion or a charging bear is a wicked man ruling over a helpless people.

28 : 15

a lion, mighty among beasts, who retreats before nothing;

30 : 30

lips
Put away perversity from your mouth; keep corrupt talk far from your lips.

4 : 24

that you may maintain discretion and your lips may preserve knowledge.

5 : 2

For the lips of an adulteress drip honey, and her speech is smoother than oil;

5 : 3

Listen, for I have worthy things to say; I open my lips to speak what is right.

8 : 6

My mouth speaks what is true, for my lips detest wickedness.

8 : 7

Wisdom is found on the lips of the discerning, but a rod is for the back of him who lacks judgment.

10 : 13

He who conceals his hatred has lying lips, and whoever spreads slander is a fool.

10 : 18

The lips of the righteous nourish many, but fools die for lack of judgment.

10 : 21

The lips of the righteous know what is fitting, but the mouth of the wicked only what is perverse.

10 : 32

From the fruit of his lips a man is filled with good things as surely as the work of his hands rewards him.

12 : 14

Truthful lips endure forever, but a lying tongue lasts only a moment.

12 : 19

The Lord detests lying lips, but he delights in men who are truthful.

12 : 22

From the fruit of his lips a man enjoys good things, but the unfaithful have a craving for violence.

13 : 2

He who guards his lips guards his life, but he who speaks rashly will come to ruin.

13 : 3

A fool's talk brings a rod to his back, but the lips of the wise protect them.

14 : 3

Stay away from a foolish man, for you will not find knowledge on his lips.

14 : 7

The tongue of the wise commends knowledge, but the mouth of the fool gushes folly.

15 : 2

The lips of the wise spread knowledge; not so the hearts of fools.

15 : 7

The lips of the king speak as an oracle, and his mouth should not betray justice.

16 : 10

Kings take pleasure in honest lips; they value a man who speaks the truth.

16 : 13

A wise man's heart guides his mouth, and his lips promote instruction.

16 : 23

A scoundrel plots evil, and his speech is like a scorching fire.

16 : 27

He who winks with his eye is plotting perversity; he who purses his lips is bent on evil.

16 : 30

A wicked man listens to evil lips; a liar pays attention to a malicious tongue.

17 : 4

Arrogant lips are unsuited to a fool -- how much worse lying lips to a ruler!

17 : 7

Even a fool is thought wise if he keeps silent, and discerning if he holds his tongue.

17 : 28

A fool's lips bring him strife, and his mouth invites a beating.

18 : 6

A fool's mouth is his undoing, and his lips are a snare to his soul.

18 : 7

From the fruit of his mouth a man's stomach is filled; with the harvest from his lips he is satisfied.

18 : 20

Better a poor man whose walk is blameless than a fool whose lips are perverse.

19 : 1

Gold there is, and rubies in abundance, but lips that speak knowledge are a rare jewel.

20 : 15

A gossip betrays a confidence; so avoid a man who talks too much

20 : 19

for it is pleasing when you keep them in your heart and have all of them ready on your lips.

22 : 18

my inmost being will rejoice when your lips speak what is right.

23 : 16

for their hearts plot violence, and their lips talk about making trouble.

24 : 2

An honest answer is like a kiss on the lips.

24 : 26

Do not testify against your neighbor without cause, or use your lips to deceive.

24 : 28

Like a coating of glaze over earthenware are fervent lips with an evil heart.

26 : 23

A malicious man disguises himself with his lips, but in his heart he harbors deceit.

26 : 24

Let another praise you, and not your own mouth; someone else, and not your own lips.

27 : 2

listen

let the wise listen and add to their learning, and let the discerning get guidance --

1 : 5

Listen, my son, to your father's instruction and do not forsake your mother's teaching.

1 : 8

Listen, my sons, to a father's instruction; pay attention and gain understanding.

4 : 1

Listen, my son, accept what I say, and the years of your life will be many.

4 : 10

My son, pay attention to what I say; listen closely to my words.

4 : 20

My son, pay attention to my wisdom, listen well to my words of insight,

5 : 1

Now then, my sons, listen to me; do not turn aside from what I say.

5 : 7

I would not obey my teachers or listen to my instructors.

5 : 13

Now then, my sons, listen to me; pay attention to what I say.

7 : 24

Listen, for I have worthy things to say; I open my lips to speak what is right.

8 : 6

Now then, my sons, listen to me; blessed are those who keep my ways.

8 : 32

Listen to my instruction and be wise; do not ignore it.

8 : 33

A wise son heeds his father's instruction, but a mocker does not listen to rebuke.

13 : 1

Listen to advice and accept instruction, and in the end you will be wise.

19 : 20

Pay attention and listen to the sayings of the wise; apply your heart to what I teach,

22 : 17

Listen, my son, and be wise, and keep your heart on the right path.

23 : 19

Listen to your father, who gave you life, and do not despise your mother when she is old.

23 : 22

listening
let the wise listen and add to their learning, and let the discerning get guidance --

1 : 5

Listen, my son, to your father's instruction and do not forsake your mother's teaching.

1 : 8

The wise in heart accept commands, but a chattering fool comes to ruin.

10 : 8

Pride only breeds quarrels, but wisdom is found in those who take advice.

13 : 10

A mocker resents correction; he will not consult the wise.

15 : 12

Whoever gives heed to instruction prospers, and blessed is he who trusts in the Lord.

16 : 20

He who answers before listening -- that is his folly and his shame.

18 : 13

Stop listening to instruction, my son, and you will stray from the words of knowledge.

19 : 27

Apply your heart to instruction and your ears to words of knowledge.

23 : 12

Like an earring of gold or an ornament of fine gold is a wise man's rebuke to a listening ear.

25 : 12

listening ear
Like an earring of gold or an ornament of fine gold is a wise man's rebuke to a listening ear.

25 : 12

listens
but whoever listens to me will live in safety and be at ease, without fear of harm."

1 : 33

Blessed is the man who listens to me, watching daily at my doors, waiting at my doorway.

8 : 34

The way of a fool seems right to him, but a wise man listens to advice.

12 : 15

He who listens to a life-giving rebuke will be at home among the wise.

15 : 31

A wicked man listens to evil lips; a liar pays attention to a malicious tongue.

17 : 4

A false witness will perish, and whoever listens to him will be destroyed forever.

21 : 28

If a ruler listens to lies, all his officials become wicked.

29 : 12

little
A little sleep, a little slumber, a little folding of the hands to rest--

6 : 10

279

till an arrow pierces his liver, like a bird darting into a snare, little knowing it will cost him his life.

7 : 23

But little do they know that the dead are there, that her guests are in the depths of the grave.

9 : 18

The tongue of the righteous is choice silver, but the heart of the wicked is of little value.

10 : 20

Dishonest money dwindles away, but he who gathers money little by little makes it grow.

13 : 11

Better a little with the fear of the Lord than great wealth with turmoil.

15 : 16

Better a little with righteousness than much gain with injustice.

16 : 8

You will vomit up the little you have eaten and will have wasted your compliments.

23 : 8

A little sleep, a little slumber, a little folding of the hands to rest --

24 : 33

"Four things on earth are small, yet they are extremely wise:

30 : 24

Ants are creatures of little strength, yet they store up their food in the summer;

30 : 25

coneys are creatures of little power, yet they make their home in the crags;

30 : 26

little by little
Dishonest money dwindles away, but he who gathers money little by little makes it grow.

13 : 11

live
but whoever listens to me will live in safety and be at ease, without fear of harm."

1 : 33

For the upright will live in the land, and the blameless will remain in it;

2 : 21

he taught me and said, "Lay hold of my words with all your heart; keep my commands and you will live.

4 : 4

Keep my commands and you will live; guard my teachings as the apple of your eye.

7 : 2

Leave your simple ways and you will live; walk in the way of understanding.

9 : 6

A greedy man brings trouble to his family, but he who hates bribes will live.

15 : 27

When a man's ways are pleasing to the Lord, he makes even his enemies live at peace with him.

16 : 7

It is not fitting for a fool to live in luxury -- how much worse for a slave to rule over princes!

19 : 10

Better to live on a corner of the roof than share a house with a quarrelsome wife.

21 : 9

Better to live in a desert than with a quarrelsome and ill-tempered wife.

21 : 19

Do not withhold discipline from a child; if you punish him with the rod, he will not die.

23 : 13

Better to live on a corner of the roof than share a house with a quarrelsome wife.

25 : 24

live in safety
but whoever listens to me will live in safety and be at ease, without fear of harm."

1 : 33

liver
till an arrow pierces his liver, like a bird darting into a snare, little knowing it will cost him his life.

7 : 23

living
Thus you will walk in the ways of good men and keep to the paths of the righteous.

2 : 20

A greedy man brings trouble to his family, but he who hates bribes will live.

15 : 27

living for God
In the way of righteousness there is life; along that path is immortality.

12 : 28

living for the Lord
Better a poor man whose walk is blameless than a rich man whose ways are perverse.

28 : 6

living like Christ
The Lord detests the way of the wicked but he loves those who pursue righteousness.

15 : 9

lizard
a lizard can be caught with the hand, yet it is found in kings' palaces.

30 : 28

loaf of bread
for the prostitute reduces you to a loaf of bread, and the adulteress preys upon your very life.

6 : 26

loathes
He who is full loathes honey, but to the hungry even what is bitter tastes sweet.

27 : 7

locusts
locusts have no king, yet they advance together in ranks;

30 : 27

loneliness
Wealth brings many friends, but a poor man's friend deserts him.

19 : 4

long
"How long will you simple ones love your simple ways? How long will mockers delight in mockery and fools hate knowledge?

1 : 22

Long life is in her right hand; in her left hand are riches and honor.

3 : 16

How long will you lie there, you sluggard? When will you get up from your sleep?

6 : 9

My husband is not at home; he has gone on a long journey.

7 : 19

All day long he craves for more, but the righteous give without sparing.

21 : 26

A tyrannical ruler lacks judgment, but he who hates ill-gotten gain will enjoy a long life.

28 : 16

long journey
My husband is not at home; he has gone on a long journey.

7 : 19

long life
for they will prolong your life many years and bring you prosperity.

3 : 2

This will bring health to your body and nourishment to your bones.

3 : 8

Long life is in her right hand; in her left hand are riches and honor.

3 : 16

Listen, my son, accept what I say, and the years of your life will be many.

4 : 10

for they are life to those who find them and health to a man's whole body.

4 : 22

For through me your days will be many, and years will be added to your life.

9 : 11

A tyrannical ruler lacks judgment, but he who hates ill-gotten gain will enjoy a long life.

28 : 16

longevity
for they will prolong your life many years and bring you prosperity.

3 : 2

longing
Hope deferred makes the heart sick, but a longing fulfilled is a tree of life.

13 : 12

A longing fulfilled is sweet to the soul, but fools detest turning from evil.

13 : 19

Do not crave his delicacies, for that food is deceptive.

23 : 3

Do not eat the food of a stingy man, do not crave his delicacies.

23 : 6

Death and Destruction are never satisfied, and neither are the eyes of man.

27 : 20

look
"Then they will call to me but I will not answer; they will look for me but will not find me.

1 : 28

and if you look for it as for silver and search for it as for hidden treasure,

2 : 4

Let your eyes look straight ahead, fix your gaze directly before you.

4 : 25

A cheerful look brings joy to the heart, and good news gives health to the bones.

15 : 30

look to the ant
Go to the ant, you sluggard; consider its ways and be wise!

6 : 6

looked
So I came out to meet you; I looked for
you and have found you!
7 : 15

looked out
At the window of my house I looked
out through the lattice.
7 : 6

Lord
The fear of the Lord is the beginning of
knowledge, but fools despise wisdom
and discipline.
1 : 7

Since they hated knowledge and did not
choose to fear the Lord,
1 : 29

then you will understand the fear of the
Lord and find the knowledge of God.
2 : 5

For the Lord gives wisdom, and from
his mouth come knowledge and
understanding.
2 : 6

Trust in the Lord with all your heart and
lean not on your own understanding;
3 : 5

Do not be wise in your own eyes; fear
the Lord and shun evil.
3 : 7

Honor the Lord with your wealth, with
the firstfruits of all your crops;
3 : 9

because the Lord disciplines those he
loves, as a father the son he delights in.
3 : 12

By wisdom the Lord laid the earth's
foundations, by understanding he set the
heavens in place;
3 : 19

for the Lord will be your confidence
and will keep your foot from being
snared
3 : 26

for the Lord detests a perverse man but
takes the upright into his confidence.
3 : 32

For a man's ways are in full view of the
Lord, and he examines all his paths.
5 : 21

There are six things the Lord hates,
seven that are detestable to him:
6 : 16

To fear the Lord is to hate evil; I hate
pride and arrogance, evil behavior and
perverse speech.
8 : 13

"The Lord brought me forth as the first
of his works, before his deeds of old;
8 : 22

For whoever finds me finds life and
receives favor from the Lord.
8 : 35

"The fear of the Lord is the beginning
of wisdom, and knowledge of the Holy
One is understanding.
9 : 10

The Lord does not let the righteous go
hungry but he thwarts the craving of the
wicked.
10 : 3

The blessing of the Lord brings wealth,
and he adds no trouble to it.
10 : 22

The fear of the Lord adds length to life,
but the years of the wicked are cut
short.
10 : 27

The way of the Lord is a refuge for the righteous, but it is the ruin of those who do evil.

10 : 29

The Lord abhors dishonest scales, but accurate weights are his delight.

11 : 1

The Lord detests men of perverse heart but he delights in those whose ways are blameless.

11 : 20

A good man obtains favor from the Lord, but the Lord condemns a crafty man.

12 : 2

The Lord detests lying lips, but he delights in men who are truthful.

12 : 22

He whose walk is upright fears the Lord, but he whose ways are devious despises him.

14 : 2

A wise man fears the Lord and shuns evil, but a fool is hotheaded and reckless.

14 : 16

He who fears the Lord has a secure fortress, and for his children it will be a refuge.

14 : 26

The fear of the Lord is a fountain of life, turning a man from the snares of death.

14 : 27

The eyes of the Lord are everywhere, keeping watch on the wicked and the good.

15 : 3

The Lord detests the sacrifice of the wicked, but the prayer of the upright pleases him.

15 : 8

The Lord detests the way of the wicked but he loves those who pursue righteousness.

15 : 9

Death and Destruction lie open before the Lord -- how much more the hearts of men!

15 : 11

Better a little with the fear of the Lord than great wealth with turmoil.

15 : 16

The Lord tears down the proud man's house, but he keeps the widow's boundaries intact.

15 : 25

The Lord detests the thoughts of the wicked, but those of the pure are pleasing to him.

15 : 26

The Lord is far from the wicked but he hears the prayer of the righteous.

15 : 29

The fear of the Lord teaches a man wisdom, and humility comes before honor.

15 : 33

To man belong the plans of the heart, but from the Lord comes the reply of the tongue.

16 : 1

All a man's ways seem innocent to him, but motives are weighed by the Lord.

16 : 2

Commit to the Lord whatever you do, and your plans will succeed.

16 : 3

The Lord works out everything for his own ends -- even the wicked for a day of disaster.

16 : 4

The Lord detests all the proud of heart. Be sure of this: They will not go unpunished.

16 : 5

Through love and faithfulness sin is atoned for; through the fear of the Lord a man avoids evil.

16 : 6

When a man's ways are pleasing to the Lord, he makes even his enemies live at peace with him.

16 : 7

In his heart a man plans his course, but the Lord determines his steps.

16 : 9

Honest scales and balances are from the Lord; all the weights in the bag are of his making.

16 : 11

Whoever gives heed to instruction prospers, and blessed is he who trusts in the Lord.

16 : 20

The lot is cast into the lap, but its every decision is from the Lord.

16 : 33

The crucible for silver and the furnace for gold, but the Lord tests the heart.

17 : 3

Acquitting the guilty and condemning the innocent -- the Lord detests them both.

17 : 15

The name of the Lord is a strong tower; the righteous run to it and are safe.

18 : 10

He who finds a wife finds what is good and receives favor from the Lord.

18 : 22

A man's own folly ruins his life, yet his heart rages against the Lord.

19 : 3

Houses and wealth are inherited from parents, but a prudent wife is from the Lord.

19 : 14

He who is kind to the poor lends to the Lord, and he will reward him for what he has done.

19 : 17

The fear of the Lord leads to life: Then one rests content, untouched by trouble.

19 : 23

Differing weights and differing measures -- the Lord detests them both.

20 : 10

Ears that hear and eyes that see -- the Lord has made them both.

20 : 12

Do not say, "I'll pay you back for this wrong!" Wait for the Lord, and he will deliver you.

20 : 22

The Lord detests differing weights, and dishonest scales do not please him.

20 : 23

A man's steps are directed by the Lord. How then can anyone understand his own way?

20 : 24

The lamp of the Lord searches the spirit of a man; it searches out his inmost being.

20 : 27

The king's heart is in the hand of the Lord; he directs it like a watercourse wherever he pleases.

21 : 1

All a man's ways seem right to him, but the Lord weighs the heart.

21 : 2

To do what is right and just is more acceptable to the Lord than sacrifice.

21 : 3

There is no wisdom, no insight, no plan that can succeed against the Lord.

21 : 30

The horse is made ready for the day of battle, but victory rests with the Lord.

21 : 31

Rich and poor have this in common: The Lord is the Maker of them all.

22 : 2

Humility and the fear of the Lord bring wealth and honor and life.

22 : 4

The eyes of the Lord keep watch over knowledge, but he frustrates the words of the unfaithful.

22 : 12

So that your trust may be in the Lord, I teach you today, even you.

22 : 19

for the Lord will take up their case and will plunder those who plunder them.

22 : 23

Do not let your heart envy sinners, but always be zealous for the fear of the Lord.

23 : 17

or the Lord will see and disapprove and turn his wrath away from him.

24 : 18

Fear the Lord and the king, my son, and do not join with the rebellious,

24 : 21

In doing this, you will heap burning coals on his head, and the Lord will reward you.

25 : 22

He who tends a fig tree will eat its fruit, and he who looks after his master will be honored.

27 : 18

Evil men do not understand justice, but those who seek the Lord understand it fully.

28 : 5

Blessed is the man who always fears the Lord, but he who hardens his heart falls into trouble.

28 : 14

A greedy man stirs up dissension, but he who trusts in the Lord will prosper.

28 : 25

The poor man and the oppressor have this in common: The Lord gives sight to the eyes of both.

29 : 13

Fear of man will prove to be a snare, but whoever trusts in the Lord is kept safe.

29 : 25

Many seek an audience with a ruler, but it is from the Lord that man gets justice.

29 : 26

I have not learned the wisdom, nor have I knowledge of the Holy One.

30 : 3

Do not add to his words, or he will rebuke you and prove you a liar.

30 : 6

"Two things I ask of you, O Lord; do not refuse me before I die:

30 ; 7

Otherwise, I may have too much and disown you and say, 'Who is the Lord?' Or I may become poor and steal, and so dishonor the name of my God.

30 : 9

Charm is deceptive, and beauty is fleeting; but a woman who fears the Lord is to be praised.

31 : 30

Lord abhors
The Lord abhors dishonest scales, but accurate weights are his delight.

11 : 1

Lord's
The Lord's curse is on the house of the wicked, but he blesses the home of the righteous.

3 : 33

Lord's discipline
My son, do not despise the Lord's discipline and do not resent his rebuke,

3 : 11

Lord's purpose
Many are the plans in the man's heart, but it is the Lord's purpose that prevails.

19 : 21

Lord's wrath
The mouth of an adulteress is a deep pit; he who is under the Lord's wrath will fall into it.

22 : 14

lose
or he who hears it may shame you and you will never lose your bad reputation.

25 : 10

losing your cool
Do not make friends with a hot-tempered man, do not associate with one easily angered,

22 : 24

losing your temper
A patient man has great understanding, but a quick-tempered man displays folly.

14 : 29

An angry man stirs up dissension, and a hot-tempered one commits many sins.

29 : 22

lot
throw in your lot with us, and we will share a common purse" --

1 : 14

Blows and disgrace are his lot, and his shame will never be wiped away;

6 : 33

The lot is cast into the lap, but its every decision is from the Lord.

16 : 33

lottery
Ill-gotten treasures are of no value, but righteousness delivers from death.

10 : 2

loud
at the head of the noisy streets she cries out, in the gateways of the city she makes her speech:

1 : 21

She is loud and defiant, her feet never stay at home;

7 : 11

The woman Folly is loud; she is undisciplined and without knowledge.

9 : 13

loudly

If a man loudly blesses his neighbor
early in the morning, it will be taken as
a curse.

27 : 14

love

"How long will you simple ones love
your simple ways? How long will
mockers delight in mockery and fools
hate knowledge?

1 : 22

Let love and faithfulness never leave
you; bind them around your neck, write
them on the tablet of your heart.

3 : 3

Do not forsake wisdom, and she will
protect you; love her, and she will
watch over you.

4 : 6

May your fountain be blessed, and may
you rejoice in the wife of your youth.

5 : 18

A loving doe, a graceful deer -- may her
breasts satisfy you always, may you
ever be captivated by her love.

5 : 19

Come, let's drink deep of love till
morning; let's enjoy ourselves with
love!

7 : 18

I love those who love me, and those
who seek me find me.

8 : 17

bestowing wealth on those who love me
and making their treasuries full.

8 : 21

But whoever fails to find me harms
himself; all who hate me love death.

8 : 36

Do not rebuke a mocker or he will hate
you; rebuke a wise man and he will love
you.

9 : 8

Hatred stirs up dissension, but love
covers over all wrongs.

10 : 12

Do not those who plot evil go astray?
But those who plan what is good find
love and faithfulness.

14 : 22

Better a meal of vegetables where there
is love than a fattened calf with hatred.

15 : 17

Through love and faithfulness sin is
atoned for; through the fear of the Lord
a man avoids evil.

16 : 6

Children's children are a crown to the
aged, and parents are the pride of their
children.

17 : 6

He who covers over an offense
promotes love, but whoever repeats the
matter separates close friends.

17 : 9

The tongue has the power of life and
death, and those who love it will eat its
fruit.

18 : 21

What a man desires is unfailing love;
better to be poor than a liar.

19 : 22

Many a man claims to have unfailing
love, but a faithful man who can find?

20 : 6

Do not love sleep or you will grow
poor; stay awake and you will have
food to spare.

20 : 13

Love and faithfulness keep a king safe;
through love his throne is made secure.

20 : 28

He who pursues righteousness and love
finds life, prosperity and honor.

21 : 21

My son, if your heart is wise, then my
heart will be glad;

23 : 15

Without wood a fire goes out; without
gossip a quarrel dies down.

26 : 20

Better is open rebuke than hidden love.

27 : 5

Wounds from a friend can be trusted,
but an enemy multiplies kisses.

27 : 6

love of money
A greedy man brings trouble to his
family, but he who hates bribes will
live.

15 : 27

loves
because the Lord disciplines those he
loves, as a father the son he delights in.

3 : 12

Whoever loves discipline loves
knowledge, but he who hates correction
is stupid.

12 : 1

He who spares the rod hates his son, but
he who loves him is careful to
discipline him.

13 : 24

The Lord detests the way of the wicked
but he loves those who pursue
righteousness.

15 : 9

A friend loves at all times, and a brother
is born for adversity.

17 : 17

He who loves a quarrel loves sin; he
who builds a high gate invites
destruction.

17 : 19

He who gets wisdom loves his own
soul; he who cherishes understanding
prospers.

19 : 8

He who loves pleasure will become
poor; whoever loves wine and oil will
never be rich.

21 : 17

He who loves a pure heart and whose
speech is gracious will have the king for
his friend.

22 : 11

A man who loves wisdom brings joy to
his father, but a companion of
prostitutes squanders his wealth.

29 : 3

loving doe
A loving doe, a graceful deer -- may her
breasts satisfy you always, may you
ever be captivated by her love.

5 : 19

low
A man's pride brings him low, but a
man of lowly spirit gains honor.

29 : 23

lowly
Better to be lowly in spirit and among
the oppressed than to share plunder with
the proud.

16 : 19

A man's pride brings him low, but a
man of lowly spirit gains honor.

29 : 23

lowly spirit
A man's pride brings him low, but a man of lowly spirit gains honor.

29 : 23

lurks
now in the street, now in the squares, at every corner she lurks.

7 : 12

lust
For the lips of an adulteress drip honey, and her speech is smoother than oil;

5 : 3

Her feet go down to death; her steps lead straight to the grave.

5 : 5

She gives no thought to the way of life; her paths are crooked, but she knows it not.

5 : 6

Keep to a path far from her, do not go near the door of her house,

5 : 8

Why be captivated, my son, by an adulteress? Why embrace the bosom of another man's wife?

5 : 20

keeping you from the immoral woman, from the smooth tongue of the wayward wife.

6 : 24

Do not lust in your heart after her beauty or let her captivate you with her eyes,

6 : 25

Like a bandit she lies in wait, and multiplies the unfaithful among men.

23 : 28

Death and Destruction are never satisfied, and neither are the eyes of man.

27 : 20

luxury
It is not fitting for a fool to live in luxury -- how much worse for a slave to rule over princes!

19 : 10

lying
haughty eyes, a lying tongue, hands that shed innocent blood,

6 : 17

He who conceals his hatred has lying lips, and whoever spreads slander is a fool.

10 : 18

The Lord detests lying lips, but he delights in men who are truthful.

12 : 22

A truthful witness does not deceive, but a false witness pours out lies.

14 : 5

A truthful witness saves lives, but a false witness is deceitful.

14 : 25

Arrogant lips are unsuited to a fool -- how much worse lying lips to a ruler!

17 : 7

A man of perverse heart does not prosper; he whose tongue is deceitful falls into trouble.

17 : 20

Food gained by fraud tastes sweet to a man, but he ends up with a mouth full of gravel.

20 : 17

A fortune made by a lying tongue is a fleeting vapor and a deadly snare.

21 : 6

my inmost being will rejoice when your lips speak what is right.

23 : 16

290

You will be like one sleeping on the high seas, lying on top of the rigging.

23 : 34

Like a club or a sword or a sharp arrow is the man who gives false testimony against his neighbor.

25 : 18

A lying tongue hates those it hurts, and a flattering mouth works ruin.

26 : 28

lying lips
The Lord detests lying lips, but he delights in men who are truthful.

12 : 22

Arrogant lips are unsuited to a fool -- how much worse lying lips to a ruler!

17 : 7

lying tongue
haughty eyes, a lying tongue, hands that shed innocent blood,

6 : 17

Truthful lips endure forever, but a lying tongue lasts only a moment.

12 : 19

A fortune made by a lying tongue is a fleeting vapor and a deadly snare.

21 : 6

M

madman
Like a madman shooting firebrands or deadly arrows

26 : 18

maiden
the way of an eagle in the sky, the way of a snake on a rock, the way of a ship on the high seas, and the way of a man with a maiden.

30 : 19

maids
She has sent out her maids, and she calls from the highest point of the city.

9 : 3

maidservant
an unloved woman who is married, and a maidservant who displaces her mistress.

30 : 23

maintain
that you may maintain discretion and your lips may preserve knowledge.

5 : 2

maintains order
When a country is rebellious, it has many rulers, but a man of understanding and knowledge maintains order.

28 : 2

make
in all your ways acknowledge him, and he will make your paths straight.

3 : 6

For they cannot sleep till they do evil; they are robbed of slumber till they make someone fall.

4 : 16

Make level paths for your feet and take only ways that are firm.

4 : 26

By me kings reign and rulers make laws that are just;

8 : 15

Lazy hands make a man poor, but diligent hands bring wealth.

10 : 4

For lack of guidance a nation falls, but many advisers make victory sure.

11 : 14

Make plans by seeking advice; if you wage war, obtain guidance.

20 : 18

Do not make friends with a hot-tempered man, do not associate with one easily angered,

22 : 24

coneys are creatures of little power, yet they make their home in the crags;

30 : 26

Maker
He who oppresses the poor shows contempt for their Maker, but whoever is kind to the needy honors God.

14 : 31

He who mocks the poor shows contempt for their Maker; whoever gloats over disaster will not go unpunished.

17 : 5

Rich and poor have this in common: The Lord is the Maker of them all.

22 : 2

making peace
Without wood a fire goes out; without gossip a quarrel dies down.

26 : 20

malice
His malice may be concealed by deception, but his wickedness will be exposed in the assembly.

26 : 26

malicious
A wicked man listens to evil lips; a liar pays attention to a malicious tongue.

17 : 4

A malicious man disguises himself with his lips, but in his heart he harbors deceit.

26 : 24

malicious man
A malicious man disguises himself with his lips, but in his heart he harbors deceit.

26 : 24

maliciously
He who walks maliciously causes grief, and a chattering fool comes to ruin.

10 : 10

man
Then you will win favor and a good name in the sight of God and man.

3 : 4

Blessed is the man who finds wisdom, the man who gains understanding,

3 : 13

Do not accuse a man for no reason -- when he has done you no harm.

3 : 30

Do not envy a violent man or choose any of his ways,

3 : 31

for the Lord detests a perverse man but takes the upright into his confidence.

3 : 32

For a man's ways are in full view of the Lord, and he examines all his paths.

5 : 21

The evil deeds of a wicked man ensnare him; the cords of his sin hold him fast.

5 : 22

and poverty will come on you like a bandit and scarcity like an armed man.

6 : 11

a false witness who pours out lies and a man who stirs up dissension among brothers.

6 : 19

Can a man scoop fire into his lap without his clothes being burned?

6 : 27

Can a man walk on hot coals without his feet being scorched?

6 : 28

But a man who commits adultery lacks judgment; whoever does so destroys himself.

6 : 32

Blessed is the man who listens to me, watching daily at my doors, waiting at my doorway.

8 : 34

Whoever corrects a mocker invites insult; whoever rebukes a wicked man incurs abuse.

9 : 7

Do not rebuke a mocker or he will hate you; rebuke a wise man and he will love you.

9 : 8

Instruct a wise man and he will be wiser still; teach a righteous man and he will add to his learning.

9 : 9

Lazy hands make a man poor, but diligent hands bring wealth.

10 : 4

The man of integrity walks securely, but he who takes crooked paths will be found out.

10 : 9

A fool finds pleasure in evil conduct, but a man of understanding delights in wisdom.

10 : 23

When a wicked man dies, his hope perishes; all he expected from his power comes to nothing.

11 : 7

The righteous man is rescued from trouble, and it comes on the wicked instead.

11 : 8

A man who lacks judgment derides his neighbor, but a man of understanding holds his tongue.

11 : 12

A gossip betrays a confidence, but a trustworthy man keeps a secret.

11 : 13

A kind man benefits himself, but a cruel man brings trouble on himself.

11 : 17

The wicked man earns deceptive wages, but he who sows righteousness reaps a sure reward.

11 : 18

The truly righteous man attains life, but he who pursues evil goes to his death.

11 : 19

One man gives freely, yet gains even more; another withholds unduly, but comes to poverty.

11 : 24

People curse the man who hoards grain, but blessing crowns him who is willing to sell.

11 : 26

A good man obtains favor from the Lord, but the Lord condemns a crafty man.

12 : 2

A man cannot be established through wickedness, but the righteous cannot be uprooted.

12 : 3

A man is praised according to his wisdom, but men with warped minds are despised.

12 : 8

A righteous man cares for the needs of his animal, but the kindest acts of the wicked are cruel.

12 : 10

An evil man is trapped by his sinful talk, but a righteous man escapes trouble.

12 : 13

From the fruit of his lips a man is filled with good things as surely as the work of his hands rewards him.

12 : 14

The way of a fool seems right to him, but a wise man listens to advice.

12 : 15

A fool shows his annoyance at once, but a prudent man overlooks an insult.

12 : 16

A prudent man keeps his knowledge to himself, but the heart of fools blurts out folly.

12 : 23

An anxious heart weighs a man down, but a kind word cheers him up.

12 : 25

A righteous man is cautious in friendship, but the way of the wicked leads them astray.

12 : 26

The lazy man does not roast his game, but the diligent man prizes his possessions.

12 : 27

From the fruit of his lips a man enjoys good things, but the unfaithful have a craving for violence.

13 : 2

Righteousness guards the man of integrity, but wickedness overthrows the sinner.

13 : 6

One man pretends to be rich, yet has nothing; another pretends to be poor, yet has great wealth.

13 : 7

The teaching of the wise is a fountain of life, turning a man from the snares of death.

13 : 14

Every prudent man acts out of knowledge, but a fool exposes his folly.

13 : 16

A good man leaves an inheritance for his children's children, but a sinner's wealth is stored up for the righteous.

13 : 22

He whose walk is upright fears the Lord, but he whose ways are devious despises him.

14 : 2

Stay away from a foolish man, for you will not find knowledge on his lips.

14 : 7

There is a way that seems right to a man, but in the end it leads to death.

14 : 12

The faithless will be fully repaid for their ways, and the good man rewarded for his.

14 : 14

A simple man believes anything, but a prudent man gives thought to his steps.

14 : 15

A wise man fears the Lord and shuns evil, but a fool is hotheaded and reckless.

14 : 16

A quick-tempered man does foolish things, and a crafty man is hated.

14 : 17

The fear of the Lord is a fountain of life, turning a man from the snares of death.

14 : 27

A patient man has great understanding, but a quick-tempered man displays folly.

14 : 29

A hot-tempered man stirs up dissension, but a patient man calms a quarrel.

15 : 18

A wise son brings joy to his father, but a foolish man despises his mother.

15 : 20

Folly delights a man who lacks judgment, but a man of understanding keeps a straight course.

15 : 21

A man finds joy in giving an apt reply-- and how good is a timely word!

15 : 23

A greedy man brings trouble to his family, but he who hates bribes will live.

15 : 27

The fear of the Lord teaches a man wisdom, and humility comes before honor.

15 : 33

To man belong the plans of the heart, but from the Lord comes the reply of the tongue.

16 : 1

All a man's ways seem innocent to him, but motives are weighed by the Lord.

16 : 2

Through love and faithfulness sin is atoned for; through the fear of the Lord a man avoids evil.

16 : 6

In his heart a man plans his course, but the Lord determines his steps.

16 : 9

Kings take pleasure in honest lips; they value a man who speaks the truth.

16 : 13

A king's wrath is a messenger of death, but a wise man will appease it.

16 : 14

There is a way that seems right to a man, but in the end it leads to death.

16 : 25

A perverse man stirs up dissension, and a gossip separates close friends.

16 : 28

A violent man entices his neighbor and leads him down a path that is not good.

16 : 29

Better a patient man than a warrior, a man who controls his temper than one who takes a city.

16 : 32

A wicked man listens to evil lips; a liar pays attention to a malicious tongue.

17 : 4

A rebuke impresses a man of discernment more than a hundred lashes a fool.

17 : 10

An evil man is bent only on rebellion; a merciless official will be sent against him.

17 : 11

If a man pays back evil for good, evil will never leave his house.

17 : 13

A man lacking in judgment strikes hands in pledge and puts up security for his neighbor.

17 : 18

A man of perverse heart does not prosper; he whose tongue is deceitful falls into trouble.

17 : 20

A wicked man accepts a bribe in secret to pervert the course of justice.

17 : 23

A discerning man keeps wisdom in view, but a fool's eyes wander to the ends of the earth.

17 : 24

It is not good to punish an innocent man, or to flog officials for their integrity.

17 : 26

A man of knowledge uses words with restraint, and a man of understanding is even-tempered.

17 : 27

An unfriendly man pursues selfish ends; he defies all sound judgment.

18 : 1

A poor man pleads for mercy, but a rich man answers harshly.

18 : 23

A man of many companions may come to ruin, but there is a friend who sticks closer than a brother.

18 : 24

Better a poor man whose walk is blameless than a fool whose lips are perverse.

19 : 1

Many curry favor with a ruler, and everyone is the friend of a man who gives gifts.

19 : 6

A poor man is shunned by all his relatives -- how much more do his friends avoid him! Though he pursues them with pleading, they are nowhere to be found.

19 : 7

Laziness brings on deep sleep, and the shiftless man goes hungry.

19 : 15

A hot-tempered man must pay the penalty; if you rescue him, you will have to do it again.

19 : 19

What a man desires is unfailing love; better to be poor than a liar.

19 : 22

Flog a mocker, and the simple will learn prudence; rebuke a discerning man, and he will gain knowledge.

19 : 25

Many a man claims to have unfailing love, but a faithful man who can find?

20 : 6

Food gained by fraud tastes sweet to a man, but he ends up with a mouth full of gravel.

20 : 17

A gossip betrays a confidence; so avoid a man who talks too much.

20 : 19

If a man curses his father or mother, his lamp will be snuffed out in pitch darkness.

20 : 20

It is a trap for a man to dedicate something rashly and only later to consider his vows.

20 : 25

The lamp of the Lord searches the spirit of a man; it searches out his inmost being.

20 : 27

The wicked man craves evil; his neighbor gets no mercy from him.

21 : 10

When a mocker is punished, the simple gain wisdom; when a wise man is instructed, he gets knowledge.

21 : 11

If a man shuts his ears to the cry of the poor, he too will cry out and not be answered.

21 : 13

A man who strays from the path of understanding comes to rest in the company of the dead.

21 : 16

In the house of the wise are stores of choice food and oil, but a foolish man devours all he has.

21 : 20

A wise man attacks the city of the mighty and pulls down the stronghold in which they trust.

21 : 22

The proud and arrogant man -- "Mocker" is his name; he behaves with overweening pride.

21 : 24

A wicked man puts up a bold front, but an upright man gives thought to his ways.

21 : 29

A prudent man sees danger and takes refuge, but the simple keep going and suffer for it.

22 : 3

A generous man will himself be blessed, for he shares his food with the poor.

22 : 9

Do not make friends with a hot-tempered man, do not associate with one easily angered,

22 : 24

Do not be a man who strikes hands in pledge or puts up security for debts;

22 : 26

Do you see a man skilled in his work? He will serve before kings, he will not serve before obscure men.

22 : 29

Do not eat the food of a stingy man, do not crave his delicacies.

23 : 6

for he is the kind of man who is always thinking about the cost. "Eat and drink," he says to you, but his heart is not with you.

23 : 7

The father of a righteous man has great joy; he who has a wise son delights in him.

23 : 24

A wise man has great power, and a man of knowledge increases strength;

24 : 5

for though a righteous man falls seven times, he rises again, but the wicked are brought down by calamity.

24 : 16

for the evil man has no future hope, and the lamp of the wicked will be snuffed out.

24 : 20

Do not say, "I'll do to him as he has done to me; I'll pay that man back for what he did."

24 : 29

I went past the field of the sluggard, past the vineyard of the man who lacks judgment;

24 : 30

and poverty will come on you like a bandit and scarcity like an armed man.

24 : 34

Like a club or a sword or a sharp arrow is the man who gives false testimony against his neighbor.

25 : 18

Like a city whose walls are broken down is a man who lacks self-control.

25 : 28

Do you see a man wise in his own eyes? There is more hope for a fool than for him.

26 : 12

is a man who deceives his neighbor and says, "I was only joking!"

26 : 19

As charcoal to embers and as wood to fire, so is a quarrelsome man for kindling strife.

26 : 21

A malicious man disguises himself with his lips, but in his heart he harbors deceit.

26 : 24

If a man digs a pit, he will fall into it; if a man rolls a stone, it will roll back on him.

26 : 27

Like a bird that strays from its nest is a man who strays from his home.

27 : 8

If a man loudly blesses his neighbor early in the morning, it will be taken as a curse.

27 : 14

As iron sharpens iron, so one man sharpens another.

27 : 17

Death and Destruction are never satisfied, and neither are the eyes of man.

27 : 20

The crucible for silver and the furnace for gold, but man is tested by the praise he receives.

27 : 21

The wicked man flees though no one pursues, but the righteous are as bold as a lion.

28 : 1

When a country is rebellious, it has many rulers, but a man of understanding and knowledge maintains order.

28 : 2

Better a poor man whose walk is blameless than a rich man whose ways are perverse.

28 : 6

A rich man may be wise in his own eyes, but a poor man who has discernment sees through him.

28 : 11

Blessed is the man who always fears the Lord, but he who hardens his heart falls into trouble.

28 : 14

Like a roaring lion or a charging bear is a wicked man ruling over a helpless people.

28 : 15

A man tomented by the guilt of murder will be a fugitive till death; let no one support him.

28 : 17

A faithful man will be richly blessed, but one eager to get rich will not go unpunished.

28 : 20

To show partiality is not good -- yet a man will do wrong for a piece of bread.

28 : 21

A stingy man is eager to get rich and is unaware that poverty awaits him.

28 : 22

He who rebukes a man will in the end gain more favor than he who has a flattering tongue.

28 : 23

A greedy man stirs up dissension, but he who trusts in the Lord will prosper.

28 : 25

A man who remains stiff-necked after many rebukes will suddenly be destroyed -- without remedy.

29 : 1

A man who loves wisdom brings joy to his father, but a companion of prostitutes squanders his wealth.

29 : 3

An evil man is snared by his own sin, but a righteous one can sing and be glad.

29 : 6

If a wise man goes to court with a fool, the fool rages and scoffs, and there is no peace.

29 : 9

Bloodthirsty men hate a man of integrity and seek to kill the upright.

29 : 10

A fool gives full vent to his anger, but a wise man keeps himself under control.

29 : 11

The poor man and the oppressor have this in common: The Lord gives sight to the eyes of both.

29 : 13

Do you see a man who speaks in haste? There is more hope for a fool than for him.

29 : 20

An angry man stirs up dissension, and a hot-tempered one commits many sins.

29 : 22

A man's pride brings him low, but a man of lowly spirit gains honor.

29 : 23

Fear of man will prove to be a snare, but whoever trusts in the Lord is kept safe.

29 : 25

Many seek an audience with a ruler, but it is from the Lord that man gets justice.

29 : 26

The sayings of Agur son of Jakeh -- an oracle: This man declared to Ithiel, to Ithiel and to Ucal;

30 : 1

the way of an eagle in the sky, the way of a snake on a rock, the way of a ship on the high seas, and the way of a man with a maiden.

30 : 19

man of discernment

A rebuke impresses a man of discernment more than a hundred lashes a fool.

17 : 10

man of integrity

The man of integrity walks securely, but he who takes crooked paths will be found out.

10 : 9

Bloodthirsty men hate a man of integrity and seek to kill the upright.

29 : 10

man of knowledge

A man of knowledge uses words with restraint, and a man of understanding is even-tempered.

17 : 27

A wise man has great power, and a man of knowledge increases strength;

24 : 5

When a country is rebellious, it has many rulers, but a man of understanding and knowledge maintains order.

28 : 2

man of lowly spirit

A man's pride brings him low, but a man of lowly spirit gains honor.

29 : 23

man of understanding

A fool finds pleasure in evil conduct, but a man of understanding delights in wisdom.

10 : 23

A man who lacks judgment derides his neighbor, but a man of understanding holds his tongue.

11 : 12

A man of knowledge uses words with restraint, and a man of understanding is even-tempered.

17 : 27

When a country is rebellious, it has many rulers, but a man of understanding and knowledge maintains order.

28 : 2

management

A fool gives full vent to his anger, but a wise man keeps himself under control.

29 : 11

manger

Where there are no oxen, the manger is empty, but from the strength of an ox comes an abundant harvest.

14 : 4

mankind

"To you, O men, I call out; I raise my voice to all mankind.

8 : 4

rejoicing in his whole world and delighting in mankind.

8 : 31

those whose teeth are swords and whose jaws are set with knives to devour the poor from the earth, the needy from among mankind.

30 : 14

man's

for they are life to those who find them and health to a man's whole body.

4 : 22

For a man's ways are in full view of the Lord, and he examines all his paths.

5 : 21

A man's riches may ransom his life, but a poor man hears no threat.

13 : 8

All a man's ways seem innocent to him, but motives are weighed by the Lord.

16 : 2

A man's own folly ruins his life, yet his heart rages against the Lord.

19 : 3

A man's wisdom gives him patience; it is to his glory to overlook an offense.

19 : 11

Do not lie in wait like an outlaw against a righteous man's house, do not raid his dwelling place;

24 : 15

Like an earring of gold or an ornament of fine gold is a wise man's rebuke to a listening ear.

25 : 12

As water reflects a face, so a man's heart reflects the man.

27 : 19

man's folly
A man's own folly ruins his life, yet his heart rages against the Lord.
19 : 3

man's heart
Before his downfall a man's heart is proud, but humility comes before honor.
18 : 12

Many are the plans in the man's heart, but it is the Lord's purpose that prevails.
19 : 21

The purposes of a man's heart are deep waters, but a man of understanding draws them out.
20 : 5

As water reflects a face, so a man's heart reflects the man.
27 : 19

man's honor
It is to a man's honor to avoid strife, but every fool is quick to quarrel.
20 : 3

man's pride
A man's pride brings him low, but a man of lowly spirit gains honor.
29 : 23

man's rebuke
Like an earring of gold or an ornament of fine gold is a wise man's rebuke to a listening ear.
25 : 12

man's riches
A man's riches may ransom his life, but a poor man hears no threat.
13 : 8

man's spirit
A man's spirit sustains him in sickness, but a crushed spirit who can bear?
18 : 14

man's steps
A man's steps are directed by the Lord. How then can anyone understand his own way?
20 : 24

man's stomach
From the fruit of his mouth a man's stomach is filled; with the harvest from his lips he is satisfied.
18 : 20

man's understanding
I am the most ignorant of men; I do not have a man's understanding.
30 : 2

man's ways
For a man's ways are in full view of the Lord, and he examines all his paths.
5 : 21

All a man's ways seem innocent to him, but motives are weighed by the Lord.
16 : 2

All a man's ways seem right to him, but the Lord weighs the heart.
21 : 2

man's wisdom
A man's wisdom gives him patience; it is to his glory to overlook an offense.
19 : 11

many
for they will prolong your life many years and bring you prosperity.
3 : 2

Listen, my son, accept what I say, and the years of your life will be many.
4 : 10

For through me your days will be many, and years will be added to your life.
9 : 11

When words are many, sin is not absent, but he who holds his tongue is wise.

10 : 19

The lips of the righteous nourish many, but fools die for lack of judgment.

10 : 21

For lack of guidance a nation falls, but many advisers make victory sure.

11 : 14

The poor are shunned even by their neighbors, but the rich have many friends.

14 : 20

Plans fail for lack of counsel, but with many advisers they succeed.

15 : 22

A man of many companions may come to ruin, but there is a friend who sticks closer than a brother.

18 : 24

Wealth brings many friends, but a poor man's friend deserts him.

19 : 4

Many curry favor with a ruler, and everyone is the friend of a man who gives gifts.

19 : 6

Many are the plans in the man's heart, but it is the Lord's purpose that prevails.

19 : 21

Many a man claims to have unfailing love, but a faithful man who can find?

20 : 6

for waging war you need guidance, and for victory many advisers.

24 : 6

When a country is rebellious, it has many rulers, but a man of understanding and knowledge maintains order.

28 : 2

He who gives to the poor will lack nothing, but he who closes his eyes to them receives many curses.

28 : 27

A man who remains stiff-necked after many rebukes will suddenly be destroyed -- without remedy.

29 : 1

An angry man stirs up dissension, and a hot-tempered one commits many sins.

29 : 22

Many seek an audience with a ruler, but it is from the Lord that man gets justice.

29 : 26

Many women do noble things, but you surpass them all."

31 : 29

many advisers
Plans fail for lack of counsel, but with many advisers they succeed.

15 : 22

many companions
A man of many companions may come to ruin, but there is a friend who sticks closer than a brother.

18 : 24

many friends
The poor are shunned even by their neighbors, but the rich have many friends.

14 : 20

Wealth brings many friends, but a poor man's friend deserts him.

19 : 4

many rebukes
A man who remains stiff-necked after many rebukes will suddenly be destroyed -- without remedy.

29 : 1

many rulers
When a country is rebellious, it has many rulers, but a man of understanding and knowledge maintains order.

28 : 2

marked
I was there when he set the heavens in place, when he marked out the horizon on the face of the deep,

8 : 27

when he gave the sea its boundary so the waters would not overstep his command, and when he marked out the foundations of the earth.

8 : 29

marker
Do not move an ancient boundary stone set up by your forefathers.

22 : 28

marriage
Drink water from your own cistern, running water from your own well.

5 : 15

May your fountain be blessed, and may you rejoice in the wife of your youth.

5 : 18

A loving doe, a graceful deer -- may her breasts satisfy you always, may you ever be captivated by her love.

5 : 19

A wife of noble character is her husband's crown, but a disgraceful wife is like decay in his bones.

12 : 4

He who finds a wife finds what is good and receives favor from the Lord.

18 : 22

A foolish son is his father's ruin, and a quarrelsome wife is like a constant dripping.

19 : 13

Houses and wealth are inherited from parents, but a prudent wife is from the Lord.

19 : 14

Many a man claims to have unfailing love, but a faithful man who can find?

20 : 6

It is a trap for a man to dedicate something rashly and only later to consider his vows.

20 : 25

Better to live on a corner of the roof than share a house with a quarrelsome wife.

21 : 9

Better to live in a desert than with a quarrelsome and ill-tempered wife.

21 : 19

for a prostitute is a deep pit and a wayward wife is a narrow well.

23 : 27

Like a bandit she lies in wait, and multiplies the unfaithful among men.

23 : 28

Better to live on a corner of the roof than share a house with a quarrelsome wife.

25 : 24

Like a bird that strays from its nest is a man who strays from his home.

27 : 8

A quarrelsome wife is like a constant dripping on a rainy day;

27 : 15

restraining her is like restraining the wind or grasping oil with the hand.

27 : 16

the way of an eagle in the sky, the way of a snake on a rock, the way of a ship on the high seas, and the way of a man with a maiden.

30 : 19

"This is the way of an adulteress: She eats and wipes her mouth and says, 'I've done nothing wrong.'

30 : 20

an unloved woman who is married, and a maidservant who displaces her mistress.

30 : 23

Her husband is respected at the city gate, where he takes his seat among the elders of the land.

31 : 23

married
an unloved woman who is married, and a maidservant who displaces her mistress.

30 : 23

master
The rich rule over the poor, and the borrower is servant to the lender.

22 : 7

He who tends a fig tree will eat its fruit, and he who looks after his master will be honored.

27 : 18

Do not slander a servant to his master, or he will curse you, and you will pay for it.

30 : 10

masters
Like the coolness of snow at harvest time is a trustworthy messenger to those who send him; he refreshes the spirit of his masters.

25 : 13

material
Remove the dross from the silver, and out comes material for the silversmith;

25 : 4

material blessings
He who gets wisdom loves his own soul; he who cherishes understanding prospers.

19 : 8

He who increases his wealth by exorbitant interest amasses it for another, who will be kind to the poor.

28 : 8

material possessions
Better a little with righteousness than much gain with injustice.

16 : 8

Houses and wealth are inherited from parents, but a prudent wife is from the Lord.

19 : 14

"It's no good, it's no good!" says the buyer; then off he goes and boasts about his purchase.

20 : 14

for drunkards and gluttons become poor, and drowsiness clothes them in rags.

23 : 21

for riches do not endure forever, and a crown is not secure for all generations.

27 . 24

Otherwise, I may have too much and disown you and say, 'Who is the Lord?' Or I may become poor and steal, and so dishonor the name of my God.

30 : 9

materialism
Whoever trusts in his riches will fall, but the righteous will thrive like a green leaf.

11 : 28

One man pretends to be rich, yet has nothing; another pretends to be poor, yet has great wealth.

13 : 7

matter
He who covers over an offense promotes love, but whoever repeats the matter separates close friends.

17 : 9

Starting a quarrel is like breaching a dam; so drop the matter before a dispute breaks out.

17 : 14

It is the glory of God to conceal a matter; to search out a matter is the glory of kings.

25 : 2

maturity
Gray hair is a crown of splendor; it is attained by a righteous life.

16 : 31

The words of a man's mouth are deep waters, but the fountain of wisdom is a bubbling brook.

18 : 4

meal
Better a meal of vegetables where there is love than a fattened calf with hatred.

15 : 17

mean
He who walks maliciously causes grief, and a chattering fool comes to ruin.

10 : 10

A poor man pleads for mercy, but a rich man answers harshly.

18 : 23

means
if you lack the means to pay, your very bed will be snatched from under you.

22 : 27

measured
when he gave the sea its boundary so the waters would not overstep his command, and when he marked out the foundations of the earth.

8 : 29

measurement
Differing weights and differing measures -- the Lord detests them both.

20 : 10

measuring
Honest scales and balances are from the Lord; all the weights in the bag are of his making.

16 : 11

meat
She has prepared her meat and mixed her wine; she has also set her table.

9 : 2

Do not join those who drink too much wine or gorge themselves on meat,

23 : 20

meddles
Like one who seizes a dog by the ears is a passer-by who meddles in a quarrel not his own.

26 : 17

medicine

Pleasant words are a honeycomb, sweet
to the soul and healing to the bones.
16 : 24

A cheerful heart is good medicine, but a
crushed spirit dries up the bones.
17 : 22

meekness

Do not exalt yourself in the king's
presence, and do not claim a place
among great men;
25 : 6

A man's pride brings him low, but a
man of lowly spirit gains honor.
29 : 23

meet

Then out came a woman to meet him,
dressed like a prostitute and with crafty
intent.
7 : 10

So I came out to meet you; I looked for
you and have found you!
7 : 15

On the heights along the way, where the
paths meet, she takes her stand;
8 : 2

Better to meet a bear robbed of her cubs
than a fool in his folly.
17 : 12

meet a bear

Better to meet a bear robbed of her cubs
than a fool in his folly.
17 : 12

meeting needs

He who despises his neighbor sins, but
blessed is he who is kind to the needy.
14 : 21

A generous man will himself be
blessed, for he shares his food with the
poor.
22 : 9

memorize

for it is pleasing when you keep them in
your heart and have all of them ready
on your lips.
22 : 18

memory

The memory of the righteous will be a
blessing, but the name of the wicked
will rot.
10 : 7

men

These men lie in wait for their own
blood; they waylay only themselves!
1 : 18

Wisdom will save you from the ways of
wicked men, from men whose words
are perverse,
2 : 12

Thus you will walk in the ways of good
men and keep to the paths of the
righteous.
2 : 20

Do not set foot on the path of the
wicked or walk in the way of evil men.
4 : 14

Men do not despise a thief if he steals to
satisfy his hunger when he is starving.
6 : 30

I saw among the simple, I noticed
among the young men, a youth who
lacked judgment.
7 : 7

"To you, O men, I call out; I raise my
voice to all mankind.
8 : 4

Wise men store up knowledge, but the
mouth of a fool invites ruin.
10 : 14

A kindhearted woman gains respect, but
ruthless men gain only wealth.
11 : 16

307

The Lord detests men of perverse heart but he delights in those whose ways are blameless.

11 : 20

Wicked men are overthrown and are no more, but the house of the righteous stands firm.

12 : 7

A man is praised according to his wisdom, but men with warped minds are despised.

12 : 8

The wicked desire the plunder of evil men, but the root of the righteous flourishes.

12 : 12

The Lord detests lying lips, but he delights in men who are truthful.

12 : 22

Evil men will bow down in the presence of the good, and the wicked at the gates of the righteous.

14 : 19

Death and Destruction lie open before the Lord -- how much more the hearts of men!

15 : 11

The glory of young men is their strength, gray hair the splendor of the old.

20 : 29

Do you see a man skilled in his work? He will serve before kings, he will not serve before obscure men.

22 : 29

Like a bandit she lies in wait, and multiplies the unfaithful among men.

23 : 28

Do not envy wicked men, do not desire their company;

24 : 1

Do not fret because of evil men or be envious of the wicked,

24 : 19

These are more proverbs of Solomon, copied by the men of Hezekiah king of Judah:

25 : 1

Do not exalt yourself in the king's presence, and do not claim a place among great men;

25 : 6

The sluggard is wiser in his own eyes than seven men who answer discreetly.

26 : 16

Evil men do not understand justice, but those who seek the Lord understand it fully.

28 : 5

When the righteous triumph, there is great elation; but when the wicked rise to power, men go into hiding.

28 : 12

Mockers stir up a city, but wise men turn away anger.

29 : 8

Bloodthirsty men hate a man of integrity and seek to kill the upright.

29 : 10

I am the most ignorant of men; I do not have a man's understanding.

30 : 2

mentoring
So that your trust may be in the Lord, I teach you today, even you.

22 : 19

Have I not written thirty sayings for you, sayings of counsel and knowledge,

22 : 20

Apply your heart to instruction and your ears to words of knowledge.

23 : 12

My son, if your heart is wise, then my heart will be glad;

23 : 15

Listen, my son, and be wise, and keep your heart on the right path.

23 : 19

for waging war you need guidance, and for victory many advisers.

24 : 6

merchant
She is like the merchant ships, bringing her food from afar.

31 : 14

merchants
She makes linen garments and sells them, and supplies the merchants with sashes.

31 : 24

merciful
He who is kind to the poor lends to the Lord, and he will reward him for what he has done.

19 : 17

merciless
An evil man is bent only on rebellion; a merciless official will be sent against him.

17 : 11

mercy
for jealousy arouses a husband's fury, and he will show no mercy when he takes revenge.

6 : 34

A righteous man cares for the needs of his animal, but the kindest acts of the wicked are cruel.

12 : 10

When a king's face brightens, it means life; his favor is like a rain cloud in spring.

16 : 15

A poor man pleads for mercy, but a rich man answers harshly.

18 : 23

A man's wisdom gives him patience; it is to his glory to overlook an offense.

19 : 11

The wicked man craves evil; his neighbor gets no mercy from him.

21 : 10

If a man shuts his ears to the cry of the poor, he too will cry out and not be answered.

21 : 13

If your enemy is hungry, give him food to eat; if he is thirsty, give him water to drink.

25 : 21

In doing this, you will heap burning coals on his head, and the Lord will reward you.

25 : 22

He who conceals his sins does not prosper, but whoever confesses and renounces them finds mercy.

28 : 13

The righteous care about justice for the poor, but the wicked have no such concern.

29 : 7

message
Like cutting off one's feet or drinking violence is the sending of a message by the hand of a fool.

26 : 6

messenger
A wicked messenger falls into trouble,
but a trustworthy envoy brings healing.
13 : 17

A king's wrath is a messenger of death,
but a wise man will appease it.
16 : 14

Like the coolness of snow at harvest
time is a trustworthy messenger to those
who send him; he refreshes the spirit of
his masters.
25 : 13

midst
I have come to the brink of utter ruin in
the midst of the whole assembly.
5 : 14

mighty
Many are the victims she has brought
down; her slain are a mighty throng.
7 : 26

A gift opens the way for the giver and
ushers him into the presence of the
great.
18 : 16

A wise man attacks the city of the
mighty and pulls down the stronghold
in which they trust.
21 : 22

a lion, mighty among beasts, who
retreats before nothing;
30 : 30

mighty throng
Many are the victims she has brought
down; her slain are a mighty throng.
7 : 26

milk
You will have plenty of goat's milk to
feed you and your family and to nourish
your servant girls.
27 : 27

For as churning the milk produces
butter, and as twisting the nose
produces blood, so stirring up anger
produces strife."
30 : 33

mind
Your eyes will see strange sights and
your mind imagine confusing things.
23 : 33

minds
A man is praised according to his
wisdom, but men with warped minds
are despised.
12 : 8

mirror
As water reflects a face, so a man's
heart reflects the man.
27 : 19

misconceptions
The wealth of the rich is their fortified
city, but poverty is the ruin of the poor.
10 : 15

misery
let them drink and forget their poverty
and remember their misery no more.
31 : 7

misfortune
Misfortune pursues the sinner, but
prosperity is the reward of the
righteous.
13 : 21

misled
Wine is a mocker and beer a brawler;
whoever is led astray by them is not
wise.
20 : 1

miss the way
It is not good to have zeal without
knowledge, nor to be hasty and miss the
way.
19 : 2

mistake
A man lacking in judgment strikes hands in pledge and puts up security for his neighbor.

17 : 18

A hot-tempered man must pay the penalty; if you rescue him, you will have to do it again.

19 : 19

Do not answer a fool according to his folly, or you will be like him yourself.

26 : 4

mistaken
The way of a fool seems right to him, but a wise man listens to advice.

12 : 15

mistress
an unloved woman who is married, and a maidservant who displaces her mistress.

30 : 23

mixed
She has prepared her meat and mixed her wine; she has also set her table.

9 : 2

"Come, eat my food and drink the wine I have mixed.

9 : 5

mixed wine
Those who linger over wine, who go to sample bowls of mixed wine,

23 : 30

mock
I in turn will laugh at your disaster; I will mock when calamity overtakes you

1 : 26

Fools mock at making amends for sin, but goodwill is found among the upright.

14 : 9

or he who hears it may shame you and you will never lose your bad reputation.

25 : 10

mocker
Whoever corrects a mocker invites insult; whoever rebukes a wicked man incurs abuse.

9 : 7

Do not rebuke a mocker or he will hate you; rebuke a wise man and he will love you.

9 : 8

If you are wise, your wisdom will reward you; if you are a mocker, you alone will suffer."

9 : 12

A wise son heeds his father's instruction, but a mocker does not listen to rebuke.

13 : 1

The mocker seeks wisdom and finds none, but knowledge comes easily to the discerning.

14 : 6

A mocker resents correction; he will not consult the wise.

15 : 12

Flog a mocker, and the simple will learn prudence; rebuke a discerning man, and he will gain knowledge.

19 : 25

Wine is a mocker and beer a brawler; whoever is led astray by them is not wise.

20 : 1

When a mocker is punished, the simple gain wisdom; when a wise man is instructed, he gets knowledge.

21 : 11

The proud and arrogant man --
"Mocker" is his name; he behaves with
overweening pride.

21 : 24

Drive out the mocker, and out goes
strife; quarrels and insults are ended.

22 : 10

The schemes of folly are sin, and men
detest a mocker.

24 : 9

mockers

"How long will you simple ones love
your simple ways? How long will
mockers delight in mockery and fools
hate knowledge?

1 : 22

He mocks proud mockers but gives
grace to the humble.

3 : 34

Fools mock at making amends for sin,
but goodwill is found among the
upright.

14 : 9

Penalties are prepared for mockers, and
beatings for the backs of fools.

19 : 29

Mockers stir up a city, but wise men
turn away anger.

29 : 8

mockery

"How long will you simple ones love
your simple ways? How long will
mockers delight in mockery and fools
hate knowledge?

1 : 22

mocking

If a wise man goes to court with a fool,
the fool rages and scoffs, and there is no
peace.

29 : 9

mocks

He mocks proud mockers but gives
grace to the humble.

3 : 34

He who mocks the poor shows
contempt for their Maker; whoever
gloats over disaster will not go
unpunished.

17 : 5

A corrupt witness mocks at justice, and
the mouth of the wicked gulps down
evil.

19 : 28

The eye that mocks a father, that scorns
obedience to a mother, will be pecked
out by the ravens of the valley, will be
eaten by the vultures.

30 : 17

moderation

If you find honey, just eat enough -- too
much of it, and you will vomit.

25 : 16

Seldom set foot in your neighbor's
house -- too much of you, and he will
hate you.

25 : 17

It is not good to eat too much honey,
not is it honorable to seek one's own
honor.

25 : 27

moment

Truthful lips endure forever, but a lying
tongue lasts only a moment.

12 : 19

money

Such is the end of all who go after ill-
gotten gain; it takes away the life of
those who get it.

1 : 19

for they will prolong your life many years and bring you prosperity.

3 : 2

Honor the Lord with your wealth, with the firstfruits of all your crops;

3 : 9

and poverty will come on you like a bandit and scarcity like an armed man.

6 : 11

He took his purse filled with money and will not be home till full moon."

7 : 20

Ill-gotten treasures are of no value, but righteousness delivers from death.

10 : 2

Lazy hands make a man poor, but diligent hands bring wealth.

10 : 4

The wealth of the rich is their fortified city, but poverty is the ruin of the poor.

10 : 15

The wages of the righteous bring them life, but the income of the wicked brings them punishment.

10 : 16

The blessing of the Lord brings wealth, and he adds no trouble to it.

10 : 22

Wealth is worthless in the day of wrath, but righteousness delivers from death.

11 : 4

A kindhearted woman gains respect, but ruthless men gain only wealth.

11 : 16

The wicked man earns deceptive wages, but he who sows righteousness reaps a sure reward

11 : 18

One man gives freely, yet gains even more; another withholds unduly, but comes to poverty.

11 : 24

A generous man will prosper; he who refreshes others will himself be refreshed.

11 : 25

One man pretends to be rich, yet has nothing; another pretends to be poor, yet has great wealth.

13 : 7

A man's riches may ransom his life, but a poor man hears no threat.

13 : 8

Dishonest money dwindles away, but he who gathers money little by little makes it grow.

13 : 11

A good man leaves an inheritance for his children's children, but a sinner's wealth is stored up for the righteous.

13 : 22

The poor are shunned even by their neighbors, but the rich have many friends.

14 : 20

All hard work brings a profit, but mere talk leads only to poverty.

14 : 23

The wealth of the wise is their crown, but the folly of fools yields folly.

14 : 24

The house of the righteous contains great treasure, but the income of the wicked brings them trouble.

15 : 6

Better a little with the fear of the Lord than great wealth with turmoil.

15 : 16

A greedy man brings trouble to his family, but he who hates bribes will live.

15 : 27

Better a little with righteousness than much gain with injustice.

16 : 8

How much better to get wisdom than gold, to choose understanding rather than silver!

16 : 16

Of what use is money in the hand of a fool, since he has no desire to get wisdom?

17 : 16

The wealth of the rich is their fortified city; they imagine it an unscalable wall.

18 : 11

A gift opens the way for the giver and ushers him into the presence of the great.

18 : 16

Wealth brings many friends, but a poor man's friend deserts him.

19 : 4

What a man desires is unfailing love; better to be poor than a liar.

19 : 22

An inheritance quickly gained at the beginning will not be blessed at the end.

20 : 21

A fortune made by a lying tongue is a fleeting vapor and a deadly snare.

21 : 6

Rich and poor have this in common: The Lord is the Maker of them all.

22 : 2

Humility and the fear of the Lord bring wealth and honor and life.

22 : 4

The rich rule over the poor, and the borrower is servant to the lender.

22 : 7

Do not be a man who strikes hands in pledge or puts up security for debts;

22 : 26

if you lack the means to pay, your very bed will be snatched from under you.

22 : 27

Do not wear yourself out to get rich; have the wisdom to show restraint.

23 : 4

Cast but a glance at riches, and they are gone, for they will surely sprout wings and fly off to the sky like an eagle.

23 : 5

Like clouds and wind without rain is a man who boasts of gifts he does not give.

25 : 14

for riches do not endure forever, and a crown is not secure for all generations.

27 : 24

He who increases his wealth by exorbitant interest amasses it for another, who will be kind to the poor.

28 : 8

A tyrannical ruler lacks judgment, but he who hates ill-gotten gain will enjoy a long life.

28 : 16

A stingy man is eager to get rich and is unaware that poverty awaits him.

28 : 22

Otherwise, I may have too much and disown you and say, 'Who is the Lord?' Or I may become poor and steal, and so dishonor the name of my God.

30 : 9

moon
He took his purse filled with money and will not be home till full moon."
7 : 20

morality
The integrity of the upright guides them, but the unfaithful are destroyed by their duplicity.
11 : 3

He who seeks good finds goodwill, but evil comes to him who searches for it.
11 : 27

A man cannot be established through wickedness, but the righteous cannot be uprooted.
12 : 3

morals
A gossip betrays a confidence, but a trustworthy man keeps a secret.
11 : 13

more
for she is more profitable than silver and yields better returns than gold.
3 : 14

She is more precious than rubies; nothing you desire can compare with her.
3 : 15

for wisdom is more precious than rubies, and nothing you desire can compare with her.
8 : 11

One man gives freely, yet gains even more; another withholds unduly, but comes to poverty.
11 : 24

If the righteous receive their due on earth, how much more the ungodly and the sinner!
11 : 31

Wicked men are overthrown and are no more, but the house of the righteous stands firm.
12 : 7

Death and Destruction lie open before the Lord -- how much more the hearts of men!
15 : 11

A rebuke impresses a man of discernment more than a hundred lashes a fool.
17 : 10

An offended brother is more unyielding than a fortified city, and disputes are like the barred gates of a citadel.
18 : 19

A poor man is shunned by all his relatives -- how much more do his friends avoid him! Though he pursues them with pleading, they are nowhere to be found.
19 : 7

To do what is right and just is more acceptable to the Lord than sacrifice.
21 : 3

All day long he craves for more, but the righteous give without sparing.
21 : 26

The sacrifice of the wicked is detestable -- how much more so when brought with evil intent!
21 : 27

A good name is more desirable than great riches; to be esteemed is better than silver or gold.
22 : 1

These are more proverbs of Solomon, copied by the men of Hezekiah king of Judah:
25 : 1

315

Do you see a man wise in his own eyes?
There is more hope for a fool than for
him.

26 : 12

He who rebukes a man will in the end
gain more favor than he who has a
flattering tongue.

28 : 23

Do you see a man who speaks in haste?
There is more hope for a fool than for
him.

29 : 20

let them drink and forget their poverty
and remember their misery no more.

31 : 7

A wife of noble character who can find?
She is worth far more than rubies.

31 : 10

morning

Come, let's drink deep of love till
morning; let's enjoy ourselves with
love!

7 : 18

If a man loudly blesses his neighbor
early in the morning, it will be taken as
a curse.

27 : 14

morsels

The words of gossip are like choice
morsels; they go down to a man's
inmost parts.

18 : 8

The words of a gossip are like choice
morsels; they go down to a man's
inmost parts.

26 : 22

mortar

Though you grind a fool in a mortar,
grinding him like grain with a pestle,
you will not remove his folly from him.

27 : 22

mother

Listen, my son, to your father's
instruction and do not forsake your
mother's teaching.

1 : 8

When I was a boy in my father's house,
still tender, and an only child of my
mother,

4 : 3

The proverbs of Solomon: A wise son
brings joy to his father, but a foolish
son grief to his mother.

10 : 1

The wise woman builds her house, but
with her own hands the foolish one
tears hers down.

14 : 1

A wise son brings joy to his father, but
a foolish man despises his mother.

15 : 20

A foolish son brings grief to his father
and bitterness to the one who bore him.

17 : 25

He who robs his father and drives out
his mother is a son who brings shame
and disgrace.

19 : 26

If a man curses his father or mother, his
lamp will be snuffed out in pitch
darkness.

20 : 20

Train a child in the way he should go,
and when he is old he will not turn from
it.

22 : 6

Listen to your father, who gave you life,
and do not despise your mother when
she is old.

23 : 22

May your father and mother be glad;
may she who gave you birth rejoice!

23 : 25

He who robs his father or mother and
says, "It's not wrong" -- he is partner to
him who destroys.

28 : 24

The rod of correction imparts wisdom,
but a child left to himself disgraces his
mother.

29 : 15

The eye that mocks a father, that scorns
obedience to a mother, will be pecked
out by the ravens of the valley, will be
eaten by the vultures.

30 : 17

The sayings of King Lemuel -- an
oracle his mother taught him:

31 : 1

Mother Teresa
He who is kind to the poor lends to the
Lord, and he will reward him for what
he has done.

19 : 17

mothers
"There are those who curse their fathers
and do not bless their mothers;

30 : 11

mother's teaching
Listen, my son, to your father's
instruction and do not forsake your
mother's teaching.

1 : 8

My son, keep your father's commands
and do not forsake your mother's
teaching.

6 : 20

motions
who winks with his eye, signals with
his feet and motions with his fingers,

6 : 13

motivated
It has no commander, no overseer or
ruler,

6 : 7

motivating force
The laborer's appetite works for him;
his hunger drives him on.

16 : 26

motivation
The laborer's appetite works for him;
his hunger drives him on.

16 : 26

motive
All a man's ways seem right to him, but
the Lord weighs the heart.

21 : 2

The sacrifice of the wicked is detestable
-- how much more so when brought
with evil intent!

21 : 27

for he is the kind of man who is always
thinking about the cost. "Eat and
drink," he says to you, but his heart is
not with you.

23 : 7

motives
All a man's ways seem innocent to him,
but motives are weighed by the Lord.

16 : 2

mountains
before the mountains were settled in
place, before the hills, I was given birth,

8 : 25

mouth
For the Lord gives wisdom, and from
his mouth come knowledge and
understanding.

2 : 6

Put away perversity from your mouth;
keep corrupt talk far from your lips.

4 : 24

if you have been trapped by what you said, ensnared by the words of your mouth,

6 : 2

A scoundrel and villain, who goes about with a corrupt mouth,

6 : 12

My mouth speaks what is true, for my lips detest wickedness.

8 : 7

All the words of my mouth are just; none of them is crooked or perverse.

8 : 8

Blessings crown the head of the righteous, but violence overwhelms the mouth of the wicked.

10 : 6

The mouth of the righteous is a fountain of life, but violence overwhelms the mouth of the wicked.

10 : 11

Wise men store up knowledge, but the mouth of a fool invites ruin.

10 : 14

The mouth of the righteous brings forth wisdom, but a perverse tongue will be cut out.

10 : 31

The lips of the righteous know what is fitting, but the mouth of the wicked only what is perverse.

10 : 32

With his mouth the godless destroys his neighbor, but through knowledge the righteous escape.

11 : 9

Through the blessing of the upright a city is exalted, but by the mouth of the wicked it is destroyed.

11 : 11

The tongue of the wise commends knowledge, but the mouth of the fool gushes folly.

15 : 2

The discerning heart seeks knowledge, but the mouth of a fool feeds on folly.

15 : 14

The heart of the righteous weighs its answers, but the mouth of the wicked gushes evil.

15 : 28

The lips of the king speak as an oracle, and his mouth should not betray justice.

16 : 10

Kings take pleasure in honest lips; they value a man who speaks the truth.

16 : 13

A wise man's heart guides his mouth, and his lips promote instruction.

16 : 23

A scoundrel plots evil, and his speech is like a scorching fire.

16 : 27

A wicked man listens to evil lips; a liar pays attention to a malicious tongue.

17 : 4

Even a fool is thought wise if he keeps silent, and discerning if he holds his tongue.

17 : 28

The words of a man's mouth are deep waters, but the fountain of wisdom is a bubbling brook.

18 : 4

A fool's lips bring him strife, and his mouth invites a beating.

18 : 6

A fool's mouth is his undoing, and his lips are a snare to his soul.

18 : 7

From the fruit of his mouth a man's stomach is filled; with the harvest from his lips he is satisfied.

18 : 20

Better a poor man whose walk is blameless than a fool whose lips are perverse.

19 : 1

The sluggard buries his hand in the dish; he will not even bring it back to his mouth!

19 : 24

A corrupt witness mocks at justice, and the mouth of the wicked gulps down evil.

19 : 28

Food gained by fraud tastes sweet to a man, but he ends up with a mouth full of gravel.

20 : 17

A gossip betrays a confidence; so avoid a man who talks too much.

20 : 19

He who guards his mouth and his tongue keeps himself from calamity.

21 : 23

The mouth of an adulteress is a deep pit; he who is under the Lord's wrath will fall into it.

22 : 14

for it is pleasing when you keep them in your heart and have all of them ready on your lips.

22 : 18

Like a lame man's legs that hang limp is a proverb in the mouth of a fool.

26 : 7

Like a thornbush in a drunkard's hand is a proverb in the mouth of a fool.

26 : 9

The sluggard buries his hand in the dish; he is too lazy to bring it back to his mouth.

26 : 15

A lying tongue hates those it hurts, and a flattering mouth works ruin.

26 : 28

Let another praise you, and not your own mouth; someone else, and not your own lips.

27 : 2

"This is the way of an adulteress: She eats and wipes her mouth and says, 'I've done nothing wrong.'

30 : 20

"If you have played the fool and exalted yourself, or if you have planned evil, clap your hand over your mouth!

30 : 32

mouth of the wicked
A corrupt witness mocks at justice, and the mouth of the wicked gulps down evil.

19 : 28

move
Do not move an ancient boundary stone set up by your forefathers.

22 : 28

Do not move an ancient boundary stone or encroach on the fields of the fatherless,

23 : 10

"There are three things that are stately in their stride, four that move with stately bearing:

30 : 29

much
How much better to get wisdom than gold, to choose understanding rather than silver!

16 : 16

Do not join those who drink too much wine or gorge themselves on meat,

23 : 20

much worse

Arrogant lips are unsuited to a fool -- how much worse lying lips to a ruler!

17 : 7

muddied spring

Like a muddied spring or a polluted well is a righteous man who gives way to the wicked.

25 : 26

multiplies

Like a bandit she lies in wait, and multiplies the unfaithful among men.

23 : 28

Wounds from a friend can be trusted, but an enemy multiplies kisses.

27 : 6

murder

for their feet rush into sin, they are swift to shed blood.

1 : 16

haughty eyes, a lying tongue, hands that shed innocent blood,

6 : 17

A man tomented by the guilt of murder will be a fugitive till death; let no one support him.

28 : 17

murdered

The sluggard says, "There is a lion outside!" or "I will be murdered in the streets!"

22 : 13

music

Like one who takes away a garment on a cold day, or like vinegar poured on soda, is one who sings songs to a heavy heart.

25 : 20

my son

Listen, my son, to your father's instruction and do not forsake your mother's teaching.

1 : 8

My son, if sinners entice you, do not give in to them.

1 : 10

my son, do not go along with them, do not set foot on their paths;

1 : 15

My son, if you accept my words and store up my commands within you,

2 : 1

My son, do not forget my teaching, but keep my commands in your heart,

3 : 1

My son, do not despise the Lord's discipline and do not resent his rebuke,

3 : 11

My son, preserve sound judgment and discernment, do not let them out of your sight;

3 : 21

Listen, my son, accept what I say, and the years of your life will be many.

4 : 10

My son, pay attention to what I say; listen closely to my words.

4 : 20

My son, pay attention to my wisdom, listen well to my words of insight,

5 : 1

Why be captivated, my son, by an adulteress? Why embrace the bosom of another man's wife?

5 : 20

My son, if you have put up security for your neighbor, if you have struck hands in pledge for another,

6 : 1

then do this, my son, to free yourself, since you have fallen into your neighbor's hands: Go and humble yourself; press your plea with your neighbor!

6 : 3

My son, keep your father's commands and do not forsake your mother's teaching.

6 : 20

My son, keep my words and store up my commands within you.

7 : 1

Stop listening to instruction, my son, and you will stray from the words of knowledge.

19 : 27

My son, if your heart is wise, then my heart will be glad;

23 : 15

Listen, my son, and be wise, and keep your heart on the right path.

23 : 19

My son, give me your heart and let your eyes keep to my ways,

23 : 26

Eat honey, my son, for it is good; honey from the comb is sweet to your taste.

24 : 13

Fear the Lord and the king, my son, and do not join with the rebellious,

24 : 21

Be wise, my son, and bring joy to my heart; then I can answer anyone who treats me with contempt

27 : 11

"O my son, O son of my womb, O son of my vows,

31 : 2

my sons
Listen, my sons, to a father's instruction; pay attention and gain understanding.

4 : 1

Now then, my sons, listen to me; do not turn aside from what I say.

5 : 7

Now then, my sons, listen to me; pay attention to what I say.

7 : 24

Now then, my sons, listen to me; blessed are those who keep my ways.

8 : 32

myrrh
I have perfumed my bed with myrrh, aloes and cinnamon.

7 : 17

N

nagging
A quarrelsome wife is like a constant
dripping on a rainy day;

27 : 15

restraining her is like restraining the
wind or grasping oil with the hand.

27 : 16

name
Then you will win favor and a good
name in the sight of God and man.

3 : 4

The memory of the righteous will be a
blessing, but the name of the wicked
will rot.

10 : 7

The name of the Lord is a strong tower;
the righteous run to it and are safe.

18 : 10

The proud and arrogant man --
"Mocker" is his name; he behaves with
overweening pride.

21 : 24

A good name is more desirable than
great riches; to be esteemed is better
than silver or gold.

22 : 1

Who has gone up to heaven and come
down? Who has gathered up the wind
in the hollow of his hands? Who has
wrapped up the waters in his cloak?
Who has established all the ends of the
earth? What is his name, and the name
of his son? Tell me if you know!

30 : 4

Otherwise, I may have too much and
disown you and say, 'Who is the Lord?'
Or I may become poor and steal, and so
dishonor the name of my God.

30 : 9

name of my God
Otherwise, I may have too much and
disown you and say, 'Who is the Lord?'
Or I may become poor and steal, and so
dishonor the name of my God.

30 : 9

name of the Lord
The name of the Lord is a strong tower;
the righteous run to it and are safe.

18 : 10

nap
A little sleep, a little slumber, a little
folding of the hands to rest --

24 : 33

narrow well
for a prostitute is a deep pit and a
wayward wife is a narrow well.

23 : 27

nation
For lack of guidance a nation falls, but
many advisers make victory sure.

11 : 14

Righteousness exalts a nation, but sin is
a disgrace to any people.

14 : 34

By justice a king gives a country
stability, but one who is greedy for
bribes tears it down.

29 : 4

nations
Whoever says to the guilty, "You are
innocent" -- peoples will curse him and
nations denounce him.

24 : 24

nature
the way of an eagle in the sky, the way
of a snake on a rock, the way of a ship
on the high seas, and the way of a man
with a maiden.

30 : 19

nature of God
The Lord does not let the righteous go
hungry but he thwarts the craving of the
wicked.

10 : 3

near
Do not plot harm against your neighbor,
who lives trustfully near you.

3 : 29

Keep to a path far from her, do not go
near the door of her house,

5 : 8

He was going down the street near her
corner, walking along in the direction of
her house

7 : 8

neck
They will be a garland to grace your
head and a chain to adorn your neck.

1 : 9

Let love and faithfulness never leave
you; bind them around your neck, write
them on the tablet of your heart.

3 : 3

they will be life for you, an ornament to
grace your neck.

3 : 22

Bind them upon your heart forever;
fasten them around your neck.

6 : 21

needs
A righteous man cares for the needs of
his animal, but the kindest acts of the
wicked are cruel.

12 : 10

the lambs will provide you with
clothing, and the goats with the price of
a field.

27 : 26

needs met
The righteous eat to their hearts'
content, but the stomach of the wicked
goes hungry.

13 : 25

the lambs will provide you with
clothing, and the goats with the price of
a field.

27 : 26

Keep falsehood and lies far from me;
give me neither poverty nor riches, but
give me only my daily bread.

30 : 8

She opens her arms to the poor and
extends her hands to the needy.

31 : 20

needy
He who despises his neighbor sins, but
blessed is he who is kind to the needy.

14 : 21

He who oppresses the poor shows
contempt for their Maker, but whoever
is kind to the needy honors God.

14 : 31

Do not exploit the poor because they
are poor and do not crush the needy in
court,

22 : 22

those whose teeth are swords and whose jaws are set with knives to devour the poor from the earth, the needy from among mankind.

30 : 14

Speak up and judge fairly; defend the rights of the poor and needy."

31 : 9

She opens her arms to the poor and extends her hands to the needy.

31 : 20

negotiating

"It's no good, it's no good!" says the buyer; then off he goes and boasts about his purchase.

20 : 14

neighbor

Do not say to your neighbor, "Come back later; I'll give it tomorrow" -- when you now have it with you.

3 : 28

Do not plot harm against your neighbor, who lives trustfully near you.

3 : 29

My son, if you have put up security for your neighbor, if you have struck hands in pledge for another,

6 : 1

then do this, my son, to free yourself, since you have fallen into your neighbor's hands: Go and humble yourself; press your plea with your neighbor!

6 : 3

With his mouth the godless destroys his neighbor, but through knowledge the righteous escape.

11 : 9

A man who lacks judgment derides his neighbor, but a man of understanding holds his tongue.

11 : 12

He who despises his neighbor sins, but blessed is he who is kind to the needy.

14 : 21

A violent man entices his neighbor and leads him down a path that is not good.

16 : 29

A man lacking in judgment strikes hands in pledge and puts up security for his neighbor.

17 : 18

The wicked man craves evil; his neighbor gets no mercy from him.

21 : 10

Do not testify against your neighbor without cause, or use your lips to deceive.

24 : 28

do not bring hastily to court, for what will you do in the end if your neighbor puts you to shame?

25 : 8

If you argue your case with a neighbor, do not betray another man's confidence,

25 : 9

Like a club or a sword or a sharp arrow is the man who gives false testimony against his neighbor.

25 : 18

is a man who deceives his neighbor and says, "I was only joking!"

26 : 19

Do not forsake your friend and the friend of your father, and do not go to your brother's house when disaster strikes you -- better a neighbor nearby than a brother far away.

27 : 10

neighbors

If a man loudly blesses his neighbor early in the morning, it will be taken as a curse.

27 : 14

Whoever flatters his neighbor is spreading a net for his feet.

29 : 5

neighbors
The poor are shunned even by their neighbors, but the rich have many friends.

14 : 20

neighbor's
then do this, my son, to free yourself, since you have fallen into your neighbor's hands: Go and humble yourself; press your plea with your neighbor!

6 : 3

Seldom set foot in your neighbor's house -- too much of you, and he will hate you.

25 : 17

nest
Like a bird that strays from its nest is a man who strays from his home.

27 : 8

net
How useless to spread a net in full view of all the birds!

1 : 17

Whoever flatters his neighbor is spreading a net for his feet.

29 : 5

never
Let love and faithfulness never leave you; bind them around your neck, write them on the tablet of your heart.

3 : 3

Let them be yours alone, never to be shared with strangers.

5 : 17

Blows and disgrace are his lot, and his shame will never be wiped away;

6 : 33

She is loud and defiant, her feet never stay at home;

7 : 11

The righteous will never be uprooted, but the wicked will not remain in the land.

10 : 30

If a man pays back evil for good, evil will never leave his house.

17 : 13

He who loves pleasure will become poor; whoever loves wine and oil will never be rich.

21 : 17

or he who hears it may shame you and you will never lose your bad reputation.

25 : 10

Death and Destruction are never satisfied, and neither are the eyes of man.

27 : 20

"The leech has two daughters. 'Give! Give!' they cry. "There are three things that are never satisfied, four that never say, 'Enough!':

30 : 15

the grave, the barren womb, land, which is never satisfied with water, and fire, which never says, 'Enough!'

30 : 16

never satisfied
"The leech has two daughters. 'Give! Give!' they cry. "There are three things that are never satisfied, four that never say, 'Enough!':

30 : 15

the grave, the barren womb, land, which is never satisfied with water, and fire, which never says, 'Enough!'

30 : 16

new
then your barns will be filled to overflowing, and your vats will brim over with new wine.

3 : 10

When the hay is removed and new growth appears and the grass from the hills is gathered in,

27 : 25

new beginning
for though a righteous man falls seven times, he rises again, but the wicked are brought down by calamity.

24 : 16

new growth
When the hay is removed and new growth appears and the grass from the hills is gathered in,

27 : 25

new wine
then your barns will be filled to overflowing, and your vats will brim over with new wine.

3 : 10

news
Like cold water to a weary soul is good news from a distant land.

25 : 25

night
at twilight, as the day was fading, as the dark of night set in.

7 : 9

She sees that her trading is profitable, and her lamp does not go out at night.

31 : 18

no
But since you rejected me when I called and no one gave heed when I stretched out my hand,

1 : 24

Have no fear of sudden disaster or of the ruin that overtakes the wicked,

3 : 25

Do not accuse a man for no reason -- when he has done you no harm.

3 : 30

She gives no thought to the way of life; her paths are crooked, but she knows it not.

5 : 6

Allow no sleep to your eyes, no slumber to your eyelids.

6 : 4

It has no commander, no overseer or ruler,

6 : 7

So is he who sleeps with another man's wife; no one who touches her will go unpunished.

6 : 29

for jealousy arouses a husband's fury, and he will show no mercy when he takes revenge.

6 : 34

When there were no oceans, I was given birth, when there were no springs abounding with water;

8 : 24

Ill-gotten treasures are of no value, but righteousness delivers from death.

10 : 2

The blessing of the Lord brings wealth, and he adds no trouble to it.

10 : 22

Like a gold ring in a pig's snout is a beautiful woman who shows no discretion.

11 : 22

Wicked men are overthrown and are no more, but the house of the righteous stands firm.

12 : 7

Better to be a nobody and yet have a servant than pretend to be somebody and have no food.

12 : 9

No harm befalls the righteous, but the wicked have their fill of trouble.

12 : 21

A man's riches may ransom his life, but a poor man hears no threat.

13 : 8

Where there are no oxen, the manger is empty, but from the strength of an ox comes an abundant harvest.

14 : 4

Each heart knows its own bitterness, and no one else can share its joy.

14 : 10

Of what use is money in the hand of a fool, since he has no desire to get wisdom?

17 : 16

To have a fool for a son brings grief; there is no joy for the father of a fool.

17 : 21

A fool finds no pleasure in understanding but delights in airing his own opinions.

18 : 2

The wicked man craves evil; his neighbor gets no mercy from him.

21 : 10

There is no wisdom, no insight, no plan that can succeed against the Lord.

21 : 30

for the evil man has no future hope, and the lamp of the wicked will be snuffed out.

24 : 20

The wicked man flees though no one pursues, but the righteous are as bold as a lion.

28 : 1

A ruler who oppresses the poor is like a driving rain that leaves no crops.

28 : 3

A man tomented by the guilt of murder will be a fugitive till death; let no one support him.

28 : 17

The righteous care about justice for the poor, but the wicked have no such concern.

29 : 7

If a wise man goes to court with a fool, the fool rages and scoffs, and there is no peace.

29 : 9

Where there is no revelation, the people cast off restraint; but blessed is he who keeps the law.

29 : 18

locusts have no king, yet they advance together in ranks;

30 : 27

let them drink and forget their poverty and remember their misery no more.

31 : 7

When it snows, she has no fear for her household; for all of them are clothed in scarlet.

31 : 21

no commander

It has no commander, no overseer or ruler,

6 : 7

no discretion

Like a gold ring in a pig's snout is a beautiful woman who shows no discretion.

11 : 22

no fear

when you lie down, you will not be afraid; when you lie down, your sleep will be sweet.

3 : 24

Have no fear of sudden disaster or of the ruin that overtakes the wicked,

3 : 25

When it snows, she has no fear for her household; for all of them are clothed in scarlet.

31 : 21

no good

"It's no good, it's no good!" says the buyer; then off he goes and boasts about his purchase.

20 : 14

no hope

When a wicked man dies, his hope perishes; all he expected from his power comes to nothing.

11 : 7

no mercy

for jealousy arouses a husband's fury, and he will show no mercy when he takes revenge.

6 : 34

The wicked man craves evil; his neighbor gets no mercy from him.

21 : 10

no money

and poverty will come on you like a bandit and scarcity like an armed man.

6 : 11

no more

let them drink and forget their poverty and remember their misery no more.

31 : 7

no one

But since you rejected me when I called and no one gave heed when I stretched out my hand,

1 : 24

So is he who sleeps with another man's wife; no one who touches her will go unpunished.

6 : 29

Each heart knows its own bitterness, and no one else can share its joy.

14 : 10

A man tomented by the guilt of murder will be a fugitive till death; let no one support him.

28 : 17

no overseer

It has no commander, no overseer or ruler,

6 : 7

no peace

If a wise man goes to court with a fool, the fool rages and scoffs, and there is no peace.

29 : 9

no sleep

Allow no sleep to your eyes, no slumber to your eyelids.

6 : 4

no slumber
Allow no sleep to your eyes, no slumber
to your eyelids.

6 : 4

no value
Ill-gotten treasures are of no value, but
righteousness delivers from death.

10 : 2

noble
A wife of noble character is her
husband's crown, but a disgraceful wife
is like decay in his bones.

12 : 4

A wife of noble character who can find?
She is worth far more than rubies.

31 : 10

Many women do noble things, but you
surpass them all."

31 : 29

nobleman
it is better for him to say to you, "Come
up here," than for him to humiliate you
before a nobleman. What you have seen
with your eyes

25 : 7

nobles
by me princes govern, and all nobles
who rule on earth.

8 : 16

nobody
Better to be a nobody and yet have a
servant than pretend to be somebody
and have no food.

12 : 9

noise
If a man loudly blesses his neighbor
early in the morning, it will be taken as
a curse.

27 : 14

none
None who go to her return or attain the
paths of life.

2 : 19

The mocker seeks wisdom and finds
none, but knowledge comes easily to
the discerning.

14 : 6

noose
All at once he followed her like an ox
going to the slaughter, like a deer
stepping into a noose

7 : 22

north wind
As a north wind brings rain, so a sly
tongue brings angry looks.

25 : 23

nose
Like a gold ring in a pig's snout is a
beautiful woman who shows no
discretion.

11 : 22

For as churning the milk produces
butter, and as twisting the nose
produces blood, so stirring up anger
produces strife."

30 : 33

not
The sluggard buries his hand in the
dish; he will not even bring it back to
his mouth!

19 : 24

A servant cannot be corrected by mere
words; though he understands, he will
not respond.

29 : 19

not accept
since you ignored all my advice and
would not accept my rebuke,

1 : 25

not fitting

It is not fitting for a fool to live in luxury -- how much worse for a slave to rule over princes!

19 : 10

not go

A false witness will not go unpunished, and he who pours out lies will not go free.

19 : 5

A false witness will not go unpunished, and he who pours out lies will perish.

19 : 9

not good

A violent man entices his neighbor and leads him down a path that is not good.

16 : 29

It is not good to punish an innocent man, or to flog officials for their integrity.

17 : 26

It is not good to be partial to the wicked or to deprive the innocent of justice.

18 : 5

It is not good to have zeal without knowledge, nor to be hasty and miss the way.

19 : 2

These also are sayings to the wise: To show partiality in judging is not good:

24 : 23

It is not good to eat too much honey, not is it honorable to seek one's own honor.

25 : 27

To show partiality is not good -- yet a man will do wrong for a piece of bread.

28 : 21

not guilty

It is not good to punish an innocent man, or to flog officials for their integrity.

17 : 26

nothing

She is more precious than rubies; nothing you desire can compare with her.

3 : 15

for wisdom is more precious than rubies, and nothing you desire can compare with her.

8 : 11

The prospect of the righteous is joy, but the hopes of the wicked come to nothing.

10 : 28

When a wicked man dies, his hope perishes; all he expected from his power comes to nothing.

11 : 7

The sluggard craves and gets nothing, but the desires of the diligent are fully satisfied.

13 : 4

One man pretends to be rich, yet has nothing; another pretends to be poor, yet has great wealth.

13 : 7

A sluggard does not plow in season; so at harvest time he looks but finds nothing.

20 : 4

Wisdom is too high for a fool; in the assembly at the gate he has nothing to say.

24 : 7

If you say, "But we knew nothing about this," does not he who weighs the heart perceive it? Does not he who guards your life know it? Will he not repay each person according to what he has done?

24 : 12

He who gives to the poor will lack nothing, but he who closes his eyes to them receives many curses.

28 : 27

"This is the way of an adulteress: She eats and wipes her mouth and says, 'I've done nothing wrong.'

30 : 20

a lion, mighty among beasts, who retreats before nothing;

30 : 30

Her husband has full confidence in her and lacks nothing of value.

31 : 11

nothing hidden
For a man's ways are in full view of the Lord, and he examines all his paths.

5 : 21

nothing to say
Wisdom is too high for a fool; in the assembly at the gate he has nothing to say.

24 : 7

nourish
The lips of the righteous nourish many, but fools die for lack of judgment.

10 : 21

You will have plenty of goat's milk to feed you and your family and to nourish your servant girls.

27 : 27

nourishment
This will bring health to your body and nourishment to your bones.

3 : 8

now
Do not say to your neighbor, "Come back later; I'll give it tomorrow" -- when you now have it with you.

3 : 28

now in the street, now in the squares, at every corner she lurks.

7 : 12

Now then, my sons, listen to me; blessed are those who keep my ways.

8 : 32

nowhere to be found
A poor man is shunned by all his relatives -- how much more do his friends avoid him! Though he pursues them with pleading, they are nowhere to be found.

19 : 7

numbers
There are six things the Lord hates, seven that are detestable to him:

6 : 16

Yet if he is caught, he must pay sevenfold, though it costs him all the wealth of his house.

6 : 31

A rebuke impresses a man of discernment more than a hundred lashes a fool.

17 : 10

for though a righteous man falls seven times, he rises again, but the wicked are brought down by calamity.

24 : 16

The sluggard is wiser in his own eyes than seven men who answer discreetly.

26 : 16

Though his speech is charming, do not believe him, for seven abominations fill his heart.

26 : 25

"Two things I ask of you, O Lord; do not refuse me before I die:

30 : 7

"The leech has two daughters. 'Give! Give!' they cry. "There are three things that are never satisfied, four that never say, 'Enough!':

30 : 15

There are three things that are too amazing for me, four that I do not understand:

30 : 18

"Under three things the earth trembles, under four it cannot bear up:

30 : 21

"Four things on earth are small, yet they are extremely wise:

30 : 24

"There are three things that are stately in their stride, four that move with stately bearing:

30 : 29

nutrition
Eat honey, my son, for it is good; honey from the comb is sweet to your taste.

24 : 13

O

oath

The accomplice of a thief is his own enemy; he is put under oath and dare not testify.

29 : 24

obedience

She is a tree of life to those who embrace her; those who lay hold of her will be blessed.

3 : 18

I give you sound learning, so do not forsake my teaching.

4 : 2

Listen, my son, accept what I say, and the years of your life will be many.

4 : 10

The path of the righteous is like the first gleam of dawn, shining ever brighter till the full light of day.

4 : 18

Do not swerve to the right or the left; keep your foot from evil.

4 : 27

My son, keep your father's commands and do not forsake your mother's teaching.

6 : 20

Bind them upon your heart forever; fasten them around your neck.

6 : 21

Now then, my sons, listen to me; blessed are those who keep my ways.

8 : 32

The proverbs of Solomon: A wise son brings joy to his father, but a foolish son grief to his mother.

10 : 1

He who scorns instruction will pay for it, but he who respects a command is rewarded.

13 : 13

He who ignores discipline comes to poverty and shame, but whoever heeds correction is honored.

13 : 18

A king delights in a wise servant, but a shameful servant incurs his wrath.

14 : 35

A fool spurns the father's discipline, but whoever heeds correction shows prudence.

15 : 5

Stern discipline awaits him who leaves the path; he who hates correction will die.

15 : 10

A wise son brings joy to his father, but a foolish man despises his mother.

15 : 20

He who ignores discipline despises himself, but whoever heeds correction gains understanding.

15 : 32

He who obeys instructions guards his life, but he who is contemptuous of his ways will die.

19 : 16

Stop listening to instruction, my son, and you will stray from the words of knowledge.

19 : 27

To do what is right and just is more acceptable to the Lord than sacrifice.

21 : 3

Be wise, my son, and bring joy to my heart; then I can answer anyone who treats me with contempt.

27 : 11

Where there is no revelation, the people cast off restraint; but blessed is he who keeps the law.

29 : 18

The eye that mocks a father, that scorns obedience to a mother, will be pecked out by the ravens of the valley, will be eaten by the vultures.

30 : 17

obedient
The Lord's curse is on the house of the wicked, but he blesses the home of the righteous.

3 : 33

obey
Get wisdom, get understanding; do not forget my words or swerve from them.

4 : 5

I would not obey my teachers or listen to my instructors.

5 : 13

My son, keep your father's commands and do not forsake your mother's teaching.

6 : 20

Leave your simple ways and you will live; walk in the way of understanding.

9 : 6

obeying
Whoever gives heed to instruction prospers, and blessed is he who trusts in the Lord.

16 : 20

obeying the Lord
The way of the Lord is a refuge for the righteous, but it is the ruin of those who do evil.

10 : 29

obnoxious
She is loud and defiant, her feet never stay at home;

7 : 11

The woman Folly is loud; she is undisciplined and without knowledge.

9 : 13

The proud and arrogant man -- "Mocker" is his name; he behaves with overweening pride.

21 : 24

obscure men
Do you see a man skilled in his work? He will serve before kings, he will not serve before obscure men.

22 : 29

observed
I applied my heart to what I observed and learned a lesson from what I saw:

24 : 32

obtain
Make plans by seeking advice; if you wage war, obtain guidance.

20 : 18

obvious
at the head of the noisy streets she cries out, in the gateways of the city she makes her speech:

1 : 21

A rich man may be wise in his own eyes, but a poor man who has discernment sees through him.

28 : 11

ocean
when he established the clouds above
and fixed securely the fountains of the
deep,

8 : 28

when he gave the sea its boundary so
the waters would not overstep his
command, and when he marked out the
foundations of the earth.

8 : 29

the way of an eagle in the sky, the way
of a snake on a rock, the way of a ship
on the high seas, and the way of a man
with a maiden.

30 : 19

oceans
When there were no oceans, I was given
birth, when there were no springs
abounding with water;

8 : 24

when he established the clouds above
and fixed securely the fountains of the
deep,

8 : 28

off
but the wicked will be cut off from the
land, and the unfaithful will be torn
from it.

2 : 22

"It's no good, it's no good!" says the
buyer; then off he goes and boasts about
his purchase.

20 : 14

Cast but a glance at riches, and they are
gone, for they will surely sprout wings
and fly off to the sky like an eagle.

23 : 5

There is surely a future hope for you,
and your hope will not be cut off.

23 : 18

Know also that wisdom is sweet to your
soul; if you find it, there is a future hope
for you, and your hope will not be cut
off.

24 : 14

Like cutting off one's feet or drinking
violence is the sending of a message by
the hand of a fool.

26 : 6

Where there is no revelation, the people
cast off restraint; but blessed is he who
keeps the law.

29 : 18

offended
An offended brother is more unyielding
than a fortified city, and disputes are
like the barred gates of a citadel.

18 : 19

offense
He who covers over an offense
promotes love, but whoever repeats the
matter separates close friends.

17 : 9

A man's wisdom gives him patience; it
is to his glory to overlook an offense.

19 : 11

offerings
"I have fellowship offerings at home;
today I fulfilled my vows.

7 : 14

official
An evil man is bent only on rebellion; a
merciless official will be sent against
him.

17 : 11

officials
It is not good to punish an innocent
man, or to flog officials for their
integrity.

17 : 26

If a ruler listens to lies, all his officials become wicked.

29 : 12

oil

For the lips of an adulteress drip honey, and her speech is smoother than oil;

5 : 3

He who loves pleasure will become poor; whoever loves wine and oil will never be rich.

21 : 17

In the house of the wise are stores of choice food and oil, but a foolish man devours all he has.

21 : 20

restraining her is like restraining the wind or grasping oil with the hand.

27 : 16

old

"The Lord brought me forth as the first of his works, before his deeds of old;

8 : 22

The glory of young men is their strength, gray hair the splendor of the old.

20 : 29

Train a child in the way he should go, and when he is old he will not turn from it.

22 : 6

Listen to your father, who gave you life, and do not despise your mother when she is old.

23 : 22

old age

Gray hair is a crown of splendor; it is attained by a righteous life.

16 : 31

The glory of young men is their strength, gray hair the splendor of the old.

20 : 29

omnipotent

The Lord tears down the proud man's house, but he keeps the widow's boundaries intact.

15 : 25

The Lord works out everything for his own ends -- even the wicked for a day of disaster.

16 : 4

Rich and poor have this in common: The Lord is the Maker of them all.

22 : 2

Who has gone up to heaven and come down? Who has gathered up the wind in the hollow of his hands? Who has wrapped up the waters in his cloak? Who has established all the ends of the earth? What is his name, and the name of his son? Tell me if you know!

30 : 4

omnipresent

The eyes of the Lord are everywhere, keeping watch on the wicked and the good.

15 : 3

The eyes of the Lord keep watch over knowledge, but he frustrates the words of the unfaithful.

22 : 12

omniscient

For a man's ways are in full view of the Lord, and he examines all his paths.

5 : 21

The Lord detests men of perverse heart but he delights in those whose ways are blameless.

11 : 20

The eyes of the Lord are everywhere, keeping watch on the wicked and the good.

15 : 3

All a man's ways seem innocent to him, but motives are weighed by the Lord.

16 : 2

The Lord works out everything for his own ends -- even the wicked for a day of disaster.

16 : 4

The lot is cast into the lap, but its every decision is from the Lord.

16 : 33

The lamp of the Lord searches the spirit of a man; it searches out his inmost being.

20 : 27

All a man's ways seem right to him, but the Lord weighs the heart.

21 : 2

It is the glory of God to conceal a matter; to search out a matter is the glory of kings.

25 : 2

Do not add to his words, or he will rebuke you and prove you a liar.

30 : 6

on
The laborer's appetite works for him; his hunger drives him on.

16 : 26

one
One who is slack in his work is brother to one who destroys.

18 : 9

The fear of the Lord leads to life: Then one rests content, untouched by trouble.

19 : 23

The Righteous One takes note of the house of the wicked and brings the wicked to ruin.

21 : 12

I have not learned the wisdom, nor have I knowledge of the Holy One.

30 : 3

one hundred
A rebuke impresses a man of discernment more than a hundred lashes a fool.

17 : 10

open
For a man's ways are in full view of the Lord, and he examines all his paths.

5 : 21

Listen, for I have worthy things to say; I open my lips to speak what is right.

8 : 6

Death and Destruction lie open before the Lord -- how much more the hearts of men!

15 : 11

Better is open rebuke than hidden love.

27 : 5

opens
A gift opens the way for the giver and ushers him into the presence of the great.

18 : 16

She opens her arms to the poor and extends her hands to the needy.

31 : 20

opinions
A fool finds no pleasure in understanding but delights in airing his own opinions.

18 : 2

opponents
Casting the lot settles disputes and keeps strong opponents apart.

18 : 18

opportunity
It is not good to have zeal without knowledge, nor to be hasty and miss the way.

19 : 2

oppressed
All the days of the oppressed are wretched, but the cheerful heart has a continual feast.

15 : 15

Better to be lowly in spirit and among the oppressed than to share plunder with the proud.

16 : 19

lest they drink and forget what the law decrees, and deprive all the oppressed of the rights.

31 : 5

oppresses
He who oppresses the poor shows contempt for their Maker, but whoever is kind to the needy honors God.

14 : 31

He who oppresses the poor to increase his wealth and he who gives gifts to the rich -- both come to poverty.

22 : 16

A ruler who oppresses the poor is like a driving rain that leaves no crops.

28 : 3

oppresses the poor
He who oppresses the poor shows contempt for their Maker, but whoever is kind to the needy honors God.

14 : 31

A ruler who oppresses the poor is like a driving rain that leaves no crops.

28 : 3

oppressor
The poor man and the oppressor have this in common: The Lord gives sight to the eyes of both.

29 : 13

oracle
The lips of the king speak as an oracle, and his mouth should not betray justice.

16 : 10

The sayings of Agur son of Jakeh -- an oracle: This man declared to Ithiel, to Ithiel and to Ucal;

30 : 1

The sayings of King Lemuel -- an oracle his mother taught him:

31 : 1

order
When a country is rebellious, it has many rulers, but a man of understanding and knowledge maintains order.

28 : 2

orderly
Finish your outdoor work and get your fields ready; after that, build your house.

24 : 27

organization
Finish your outdoor work and get your fields ready; after that, build your house.

24 : 27

ornament
they will be life for you, an ornament to grace your neck.

3 : 22

Like an earring of gold or an ornament of fine gold is a wise man's rebuke to a listening ear.

25 : 12

orphan

Do not move an ancient boundary stone or encroach on the fields of the fatherless,

23 : 10

others

lest you give your best strength to others and your years to one who is cruel,

5 : 9

He who heeds discipline shows the way to life, but whoever ignores correction leads others astray.

10 : 17

A generous man will prosper; he who refreshes others will himself be refreshed.

11 : 25

otherwise

Otherwise, I may have too much and disown you and say, 'Who is the Lord?' Or I may become poor and steal, and so dishonor the name of my God.

30 : 9

out

My son, preserve sound judgment and discernment, do not let them out of your sight;

3 : 21

Do not let them out of your sight, keep them within your heart;

4 : 21

At the window of my house I looked out through the lattice.

7 : 6

So I came out to meet you; I looked for you and have found you!

7 : 15

"To you, O men, I call out; I raise my voice to all mankind.

8 : 4

The man of integrity walks securely, but he who takes crooked paths will be found out.

10 : 9

The mouth of the righteous brings forth wisdom, but a perverse tongue will be cut out.

10 : 31

A false witness will not go unpunished, and he who pours out lies will not go free.

19 : 5

Drive out the mocker, and out goes strife; quarrels and insults are ended.

22 : 10

Do not wear yourself out to get rich; have the wisdom to show restraint.

23 : 4

out of control

Like a city whose walls are broken down is a man who lacks self-control.

25 : 28

outdoor

Finish your outdoor work and get your fields ready; after that, build your house.

24 : 27

outlaw

Do not lie in wait like an outlaw against a righteous man's house, do not raid his dwelling place;

24 : 15

outside
The sluggard says, "There is a lion outside!" or "I will be murdered in the streets!"

22 : 13

over
when calamity overtakes you like a storm, when disaster sweeps over you like a whirlwind, when distress and trouble overwhelm you.

1 : 27

then your barns will be filled to overflowing, and your vats will brim over with new wine.

3 : 10

Do not forsake wisdom, and she will protect you; love her, and she will watch over you.

4 : 6

When you walk, they will guide you; when you sleep, they will watch over you; when you awake, they will speak to you.

6 : 22

Hatred stirs up dissension, but love covers over all wrongs.

10 : 12

A wise servant will rule over a disgraceful son, and will share the inheritance as one of the brothers.

17 : 2

He who mocks the poor shows contempt for their Maker; whoever gloats over disaster will not go unpunished.

17 : 5

He who covers over an offense promotes love, but whoever repeats the matter separates close friends.

17 : 9

It is not fitting for a fool to live in luxury -- how much worse for a slave to rule over princes!

19 : 10

A wise king winnows out the wicked; he drives the threshing wheel over them.

20 : 26

The rich rule over the poor, and the borrower is servant to the lender.

22 : 7

The eyes of the Lord keep watch over knowledge, but he frustrates the words of the unfaithful.

22 : 12

Those who linger over wine, who go to sample bowls of mixed wine,

23 : 30

Like a coating of glaze over earthenware are fervent lips with an evil heart.

26 : 23

Like a roaring lion or a charging bear is a wicked man ruling over a helpless people.

28 : 15

"If you have played the fool and exalted yourself, or if you have planned evil, clap your hand over your mouth!

30 : 32

She watches over the affairs of her household and does not eat the bread of idleness.

31 : 27

overbearing
The proud and arrogant man -- "Mocker" is his name; he behaves with overweening pride.

21 : 24

overflow
Should your springs overflow in the streets, your streams of water in the public squares?

5 : 16

overflowing
then your barns will be filled to overflowing, and your vats will brim over with new wine.

3 : 10

overlook
She sits at the door of her house, on a seat at the highest point of the city,

9 : 14

A man's wisdom gives him patience; it is to his glory to overlook an offense.

19 : 11

overlooks
A fool shows his annoyance at once, but a prudent man overlooks an insult.

12 : 16

overseer
It has no commander, no overseer or ruler,

6 : 7

overstep
when he gave the sea its boundary so the waters would not overstep his command, and when he marked out the foundations of the earth.

8 : 29

overtake
Therefore disaster will overtake him in an instant; he will suddenly be destroyed -- without remedy.

6 : 15

What the wicked dreads will overtake him; what the righteous desire will be granted.

10 : 24

overtakes
I in turn will laugh at your disaster; I will mock when calamity overtakes you

1 : 26

when calamity overtakes you like a storm, when disaster sweeps over you like a whirlwind, when distress and trouble overwhelm you.

1 : 27

Have no fear of sudden disaster or of the ruin that overtakes the wicked,

3 : 25

overthrown
Wicked men are overthrown and are no more, but the house of the righteous stands firm.

12 : 7

overthrows
Righteousness guards the man of integrity, but wickedness overthrows the sinner.

13 : 6

overweening
The proud and arrogant man -- "Mocker" is his name; he behaves with overweening pride.

21 : 24

overwhelm
when calamity overtakes you like a storm, when disaster sweeps over you like a whirlwind, when distress and trouble overwhelm you.

1 : 27

overwhelming
Anger is cruel and fury overwhelming, but who can stand before jealousy?

27 : 4

overwhelms
Blessings crown the head of the righteous, but violence overwhelms the mouth of the wicked.

10 : 6

The mouth of the righteous is a fountain of life, but violence overwhelms the mouth of the wicked.

10 : 11

own

These men lie in wait for their own blood; they waylay only themselves!

1 : 18

Trust in the Lord with all your heart and lean not on your own understanding;

3 : 5

Do not be wise in your own eyes; fear the Lord and shun evil.

3 : 7

Drink water from your own cistern, running water from your own well.

5 : 15

The righteousness of the blameless makes a straight way for them, but the wicked are brought down by their own wickedness.

11 : 5

The wise woman builds her house, but with her own hands the foolish one tears hers down.

14 : 1

Each heart knows its own bitterness, and no one else can share its joy.

14 : 10

A fool finds no pleasure in understanding but delights in airing his own opinions.

18 : 2

A man's own folly ruins his life, yet his heart rages against the Lord.

19 : 3

He who gets wisdom loves his own soul; he who cherishes understanding prospers.

19 : 8

A man's steps are directed by the Lord. How then can anyone understand his own way?

20 : 24

It is not good to eat too much honey, not is it honorable to seek one's own honor.

25 : 27

Do you see a man wise in his own eyes? There is more hope for a fool than for him.

26 : 12

The sluggard is wiser in his own eyes than seven men who answer discreetly.

26 : 16

Like one who seizes a dog by the ears is a passer-by who meddles in a quarrel not his own.

26 : 17

Let another praise you, and not your own mouth; someone else, and not your own lips.

27 : 2

He who leads the upright along an evil path will fall into his own trap, but the blameless will receive a good inheritance.

28 : 10

A rich man may be wise in his own eyes, but a poor man who has discernment sees through him.

28 : 11

The accomplice of a thief is his own enemy; he is put under oath and dare not testify.

29 : 24

those who are pure in their own eyes and yet are not cleansed of their filth;

30 : 12

own eyes

Do not be wise in your own eyes; fear
the Lord and shun evil

3 : 7

own understanding

Trust in the Lord with all your heart and
lean not on your own understanding;

3 : 5

own way

A man's steps are directed by the Lord.
How then can anyone understand his
own way?

20 : 24

ox

All at once he followed her like an ox
going to the slaughter, like a deer
stepping into a noose

7 : 22

Where there are no oxen, the manger is
empty, but from the strength of an ox
comes an abundant harvest.

14 : 4

oxen

Where there are no oxen, the manger is
empty, but from the strength of an ox
comes an abundant harvest.

14 : 4

P

pacifies
A gift given in secret soothes anger, and
a bribe concealed in the cloak pacifies
great wrath.

21 : 14

pain
Even in laughter the heart may ache,
and joy may end in grief.

14 : 13

A man's spirit sustains him in sickness,
but a crushed spirit who can bear?

18 : 14

Who has woe? Who has sorrow? Who
has strife? Who has complaints? Who
has needless bruises? Who has
bloodshot eyes?

23 : 29

Wounds from a friend can be trusted,
but an enemy multiplies kisses.

27 : 6

The prudent see danger and take refuge,
but the simple keep going and suffer for
it.

27 : 12

painful
As vinegar to the teeth and smoke to the
eyes, so is a sluggard to those who send
him.

10 : 26

palaces
a lizard can be caught with the hand, yet
it is found in kings' palaces.

30 : 28

pampers
If a man pampers his servant from
youth, he will bring grief in the end.

29 : 21

parables
for understanding proverbs and
parables, the sayings and riddles of the
wise.

1 : 6

paradox
a lizard can be caught with the hand, yet
it is found in kings' palaces.

30 : 28

parental advice
my son, do not go along with them, do
not set foot on their paths;

1 : 15

Listen to your father, who gave you life,
and do not despise your mother when
she is old.

23 : 22

parenting
My son, do not forget my teaching, but
keep my commands in your heart,

3 : 1

because the Lord disciplines those he
loves, as a father the son he delights in.

3 : 12

Listen, my sons, to a father's
instruction; pay attention and gain
understanding.

4 : 1

When I was a boy in my father's house,
still tender, and an only child of my
mother,

4 : 3

he taught me and said, "Lay hold of my words with all your heart; keep my commands and you will live.

4 : 4

I guide you in the way of wisdom and lead you along straight paths.

4 : 11

My son, pay attention to what I say; listen closely to my words.

4 : 20

My son, pay attention to my wisdom, listen well to my words of insight,

5 : 1

My son, keep your father's commands and do not forsake your mother's teaching.

6 : 20

The proverbs of Solomon: A wise son brings joy to his father, but a foolish son grief to his mother.

10 : 1

A wise son heeds his father's instruction, but a mocker does not listen to rebuke.

13 : 1

He who fears the Lord has a secure fortress, and for his children it will be a refuge.

14 : 26

A fool spurns the father's discipline, but whoever heeds correction shows prudence.

15 : 5

Stern discipline awaits him who leaves the path; he who hates correction will die.

15 : 10

To have a fool for a son brings grief; there is no joy for the father of a fool.

17 : 21

A foolish son brings grief to his father and bitterness to the one who bore him.

17 : 25

Discipline your son, for in that there is hope; do not be a willing party to his death.

19 : 18

Train a child in the way he should go, and when he is old he will not turn from it.

22 : 6

Folly is bound up in the heart of a child, but the rod of discipline will drive it far from him.

22 : 15

Do not withhold discipline from a child; if you punish him with the rod, he will not die.

23 : 13

Punish him with the rod and save his soul from death.

23 : 14

My son, if your heart is wise, then my heart will be glad;

23 : 15

Listen, my son, and be wise, and keep your heart on the right path.

23 : 19

The father of a righteous man has great joy; he who has a wise son delights in him.

23 : 24

May your father and mother be glad; may she who gave you birth rejoice!

23 : 25

Better is open rebuke than hidden love.

27 : 5

Be wise, my son, and bring joy to my heart; then I can answer anyone who treats me with contempt.

27 : 11

He who keeps the law is a discerning son, but a companion of gluttons disgraces his father.

28 : 7

The rod of correction imparts wisdom, but a child left to himself disgraces his mother.

29 : 15

Discipline your son, and he will give you peace; he will bring delight to your soul.

29 : 17

parents

Children's children are a crown to the aged, and parents are the pride of their children.

17 : 6

Houses and wealth are inherited from parents, but a prudent wife is from the Lord.

19 : 14

If a man curses his father or mother, his lamp will be snuffed out in pitch darkness.

20 : 20

By wisdom a house is built, and through understanding it is established;

24 : 3

He who robs his father or mother and says, "It's not wrong" -- he is partner to him who destroys.

28 : 24

"There are those who curse their fathers and do not bless their mothers;

30 : 11

The sayings of King Lemuel -- an oracle his mother taught him:

31 : 1

partake

"Come, eat my food and drink the wine I have mixed.

9 : 5

partial

It is not good to be partial to the wicked or to deprive the innocent of justice.

18 : 5

partiality

These also are sayings to the wise: To show partiality in judging is not good:

24 : 23

To show partiality is not good -- yet a man will do wrong for a piece of bread.

28 : 21

participant

Discipline your son, for in that there is hope; do not be a willing party to his death.

19 : 18

partner

who has left the partner of her youth and ignored the covenant she made before God.

2 : 17

He who robs his father or mother and says, "It's not wrong" -- he is partner to him who destroys.

28 : 24

parts

The words of gossip are like choice morsels; they go down to a man's inmost parts.

18 : 8

The words of a gossip are like choice morsels; they go down to a man's inmost parts.

26 : 22

pass
calling out to those who pass by, who
go straight on their way.

9 : 15

past
I went past the field of the sluggard,
past the vineyard of the man who lacks
judgment;

24 : 30

path
Then you will understand what is right
and just and fair -- every good path.

2 : 9

Then you will go on your way in safety,
and your foot will not stumble;

3 : 23

Do not set foot on the path of the
wicked or walk in the way of evil men.

4 : 14

The path of the righteous is like the first
gleam of dawn, shining ever brighter till
the full light of day.

4 : 18

Do not swerve to the right or the left;
keep your foot from evil.

4 : 27

Keep to a path far from her, do not go
near the door of her house,

5 : 8

In the way of righteousness there is life;
along that path is immortality.

12 : 28

Stern discipline awaits him who leaves
the path; he who hates correction will
die.

15 : 10

The way of the sluggard is blocked with
thorns, but the path of the upright is a
highway.

15 : 19

Folly delights a man who lacks
judgment, but a man of understanding
keeps a straight course.

15 : 21

The path of life leads upward for the
wise to keep him from going down to
the grave.

15 : 24

The highway of the upright avoids evil;
he who guards his way guards his life.

16 : 17

A violent man entices his neighbor and
leads him down a path that is not good.

16 : 29

A man's steps are directed by the Lord.
How then can anyone understand his
own way?

20 : 24

A man who strays from the path of
understanding comes to rest in the
company of the dead.

21 : 16

Listen, my son, and be wise, and keep
your heart on the right path.

23 : 19

He who leads the upright along an evil
path will fall into his own trap, but the
blameless will receive a good
inheritance.

28 : 10

path of life
The path of life leads upward for the
wise to keep him from going down to
the grave.

15 : 24

paths
my son, do not go along with them, do
not set foot on their paths;

1 : 15

who leave the straight paths to walk in dark ways,

2 : 13

whose paths are crooked and who are devious in their ways.

2 : 15

For her house leads down to death and her paths to the spirits of the dead.

2 : 18

None who go to her return or attain the paths of life.

2 : 19

Thus you will walk in the ways of good men and keep to the paths of the righteous.

2 : 20

in all your ways acknowledge him, and he will make your paths straight.

3 : 6

Her ways are pleasant ways, and all her paths are peace.

3 : 17

I guide you in the way of wisdom and lead you along straight paths.

4 : 11

Make level paths for your feet and take only ways that are firm.

4 : 26

She gives no thought to the way of life; her paths are crooked, but she knows it not.

5 : 6

For a man's ways are in full view of the Lord, and he examines all his paths.

5 : 21

Do not let your heart turn to her ways or stray into her paths.

7 : 25

On the heights along the way, where the paths meet, she takes her stand;

8 : 2

The man of integrity walks securely, but he who takes crooked paths will be found out.

10 : 9

In the paths of the wicked lie thorns and snares, but he who guards his soul stays far from them.

22 : 5

paths of life
None who go to her return or attain the paths of life.

2 : 19

paths of righteousness
The righteousness of the blameless makes a straight way for them, but the wicked are brought down by their own wickedness.

11 : 5

paths of the righteous
Thus you will walk in the ways of good men and keep to the paths of the righteous.

2 : 20

patience
A fool shows his annoyance at once, but a prudent man overlooks an insult.

12 : 16

A patient man has great understanding, but a quick-tempered man displays folly.

14 : 29

The heart of the righteous weighs its answers, but the mouth of the wicked gushes evil.

15 : 28

A king's wrath is a messenger of death, but a wise man will appease it.

16 : 14

A man's wisdom gives him patience; it is to his glory to overlook an offense.

19 : 11

The plans of the diligent lead to profit as surely as haste leads to poverty.

21 : 5

Through patience a ruler can be persuaded, and a gentle tongue can break a bone.

25 : 15

patient

A patient man has great understanding, but a quick-tempered man displays folly.

14 : 29

A hot-tempered man stirs up dissension, but a patient man calms a quarrel.

15 : 18

patient man

A patient man has great understanding, but a quick-tempered man displays folly.

14 : 29

A hot-tempered man stirs up dissension, but a patient man calms a quarrel.

15 : 18

Better a patient man than a warrior, a man who controls his temper than one who takes a city.

16 : 32

pay

My son, pay attention to what I say; listen closely to my words.

4 : 20

Yet if he is caught, he must pay sevenfold, though it costs him all the wealth of his house.

6 : 31

He who scorns instruction will pay for it, but he who respects a command is rewarded.

13 : 13

A hot-tempered man must pay the penalty; if you rescue him, you will have to do it again.

19 : 19

if you lack the means to pay, your very bed will be snatched from under you.

22 : 27

Do not say, "I'll do to him as he has done to me; I'll pay that man back for what he did."

24 : 29

Do not slander a servant to his master, or he will curse you, and you will pay for it.

30 : 10

pay attention

Listen, my sons, to a father's instruction; pay attention and gain understanding.

4 : 1

My son, pay attention to what I say; listen closely to my words.

4 : 20

My son, pay attention to my wisdom, listen well to my words of insight,

5 : 1

Now then, my sons, listen to me; pay attention to what I say.

7 : 24

A wicked man listens to evil lips; a liar pays attention to a malicious tongue.

17 : 4

Pay attention and listen to the sayings of the wise; apply your heart to what I teach,

22 : 17

pay back
Do not say, "I'll pay you back for this wrong!" Wait for the Lord, and he will deliver you.

20 : 22

Do not say, "I'll do to him as he has done to me; I'll pay that man back for what he did."

24 : 29

pay off
But little do they know that the dead are there, that her guests are in the depths of the grave.

9 : 18

payment
When justice is done, it brings joy to the righteous but terror to evildoers.

21 : 15

The wicked become a ransom for the righteous, and the unfaithful for the upright.

21 : 18

pays back
If a man pays back evil for good, evil will never leave his house.

17 : 13

peace
Her ways are pleasant ways, and all her paths are peace.

3 : 17

when you lie down, you will not be afraid; when you lie down, your sleep will be sweet.

3 : 24

For whoever finds me finds life and receives favor from the Lord.

8 : 35

There is deceit in the hearts of those who plot evil, but joy for those who promote peace.

12 : 20

A man's riches may ransom his life, but a poor man hears no threat.

13 : 8

A heart at peace gives life to the body, but envy rots the bones.

14 : 30

When a man's ways are pleasing to the Lord, he makes even his enemies live at peace with him.

16 : 7

Better a dry crust with peace and quiet than a house full of feasting with strife.

17 : 1

The fear of the Lord leads to life: Then one rests content, untouched by trouble.

19 : 23

Like a fluttering sparrow or a darting swallow, an undeserved curse does not come to rest.

26 : 2

Without wood a fire goes out; without gossip a quarrel dies down.

26 : 20

An evil man is snared by his own sin, but a righteous one can sing and be glad.

29 : 6

Mockers stir up a city, but wise men turn away anger.

29 : 8

If a wise man goes to court with a fool, the fool rages and scoffs, and there is no peace.

29 : 9

Discipline your son, and he will give you peace; he will bring delight to your soul.

29 : 17

peacemaker

There is deceit in the hearts of those who plot evil, but joy for those who promote peace.

12 : 20

A hot-tempered man stirs up dissension, but a patient man calms a quarrel.

15 : 18

It is to a man's honor to avoid strife, but every fool is quick to quarrel.

20 : 3

peer pressure

Do not set foot on the path of the wicked or walk in the way of evil men.

4 : 14

Fear the Lord and the king, my son, and do not join with the rebellious,

24 : 21

peers

Do not envy wicked men, do not desire their company;

24 : 1

Fear the Lord and the king, my son, and do not join with the rebellious,

24 : 21

penalties

Penalties are prepared for mockers, and beatings for the backs of fools.

19 : 29

penalty

There is a way that seems right to a man, but in the end it leads to death.

14 : 12

A hot-tempered man must pay the penalty; if you rescue him, you will have to do it again.

19 : 19

Do not slander a servant to his master, or he will curse you, and you will pay for it.

30 : 10

penned

Have I not written thirty sayings for you, sayings of counsel and knowledge,

22 : 20

people

People curse the man who hoards grain, but blessing crowns him who is willing to sell.

11 : 26

Righteousness exalts a nation, but sin is a disgrace to any people.

14 : 34

Like a roaring lion or a charging bear is a wicked man ruling over a helpless people.

28 : 15

When the wicked rise to power, people go into hiding; but when the wicked perish, the righteous thrive.

28 : 28

When the righteous thrive, the people rejoice; when the wicked rule, the people groan.

29 : 2

Where there is no revelation, the people cast off restraint; but blessed is he who keeps the law.

29 : 18

peoples

Whoever says to the guilty, "You are innocent" -- peoples will curse him and nations denounce him.

24 : 24

perfect

Who can say, "I have kept my heart pure; I am clean and without sin"?

20 : 9

Every word of God is flawless; he is a shield to those who take refuge in him.

30 : 5

perfume

Perfume and incense bring joy to the heart, and the pleasantness of one's friend springs from his earnest counsel.

27 : 9

perfumed

I have perfumed my bed with myrrh, aloes and cinnamon.

7 : 17

perish

When the righteous prosper, the city rejoices; when the wicked perish, there are shouts of joy.

11 : 10

A false witness will not go unpunished, and he who pours out lies will perish.

19 : 9

A false witness will perish, and whoever listens to him will be destroyed forever.

21 : 28

When the wicked rise to power, people go into hiding; but when the wicked perish, the righteous thrive.

28 : 28

perishes

When a wicked man dies, his hope perishes; all he expected from his power comes to nothing.

11 : 7

perishing

Give beer to those who are perishing, wine to those who are in anguish;

31 : 6

perseverance

My son, if sinners entice you, do not give in to them.

1 : 10

The crucible for silver and the furnace for gold, but the Lord tests the heart.

17 : 3

persevere

A man's spirit sustains him in sickness, but a crushed spirit who can bear?

18 : 14

persistent

Allow no sleep to your eyes, no slumber to your eyelids.

6 : 4

The sluggard craves and gets nothing, but the desires of the diligent are fully satisfied.

13 : 4

persuaded

Through patience a ruler can be persuaded, and a gentle tongue can break a bone.

25 : 15

persuasive

With persuasive words she led him astray; she seduced him with her smooth talk.

7 : 21

perverse

Wisdom will save you from the ways of wicked men, from men whose words are perverse,

2 : 12

who delight in doing wrong and rejoice in the perverseness of evil,

2 : 14

for the Lord detests a perverse man but takes the upright into his confidence.

3 : 32

All the words of my mouth are just; none of them is crooked or perverse.

8 : 8

To fear the Lord is to hate evil; I hate pride and arrogance, evil behavior and perverse speech.

8 : 13

The mouth of the righteous brings forth wisdom, but a perverse tongue will be cut out.

10 : 31

The lips of the righteous know what is fitting, but the mouth of the wicked only what is perverse.

10 : 32

The Lord detests men of perverse heart but he delights in those whose ways are blameless.

11 : 20

A perverse man stirs up dissension, and a gossip separates close friends.

16 : 28

A man of perverse heart does not prosper; he whose tongue is deceitful falls into trouble.

17 : 20

Better a poor man whose walk is blameless than a fool whose lips are perverse.

19 : 1

Better a poor man whose walk is blameless than a rich man whose ways are perverse.

28 : 6

He whose walk is blameless is kept safe, but he whose ways are perverse will suddenly fall.

28 : 18

perverse heart
A man of perverse heart does not prosper; he whose tongue is deceitful falls into trouble.

17 : 20

perverse man
A man is praised according to his wisdom, but men with warped minds are despised.

12 : 8

A perverse man stirs up dissension, and a gossip separates close friends.

16 : 28

perverseness
who delight in doing wrong and rejoice in the perverseness of evil,

2 : 14

perversity
Put away perversity from your mouth; keep corrupt talk far from your lips.

4 : 24

He who winks with his eye is plotting perversity; he who purses his lips is bent on evil.

16 : 30

pervert
A wicked man accepts a bribe in secret to pervert the course of justice.

17 : 23

pestle
Though you grind a fool in a mortar, grinding him like grain with a pestle, you will not remove his folly from him.

27 : 22

phony
Better to be a nobody and yet have a servant than pretend to be somebody and have no food.

12 : 9

Like clouds and wind without rain is a man who boasts of gifts he does not give.

25 : 14

piece of bread
To show partiality is not good -- yet a man will do wrong for a piece of bread.

28 : 21

pierce
Reckless words pierce like a sword, but the tongue of the wise brings healing.

12 : 18

Like a club or a sword or a sharp arrow
is the man who gives false testimony
against his neighbor.

25 : 18

pig's snout

Like a gold ring in a pig's snout is a
beautiful woman who shows no
discretion.

11 : 22

pillage

The wicked desire the plunder of evil
men, but the root of the righteous
flourishes.

12 : 12

pillars

Wisdom has built her house; she has
hewn out its seven pillars.

9 : 1

pit

let's swallow them alive, like the grave,
and whole, like those who go down to
the pit;

1 : 12

The mouth of an adulteress is a deep
pit; he who is under the Lord's wrath
will fall into it.

22 : 14

for a prostitute is a deep pit and a
wayward wife is a narrow well.

23 : 27

If a man digs a pit, he will fall into it; if
a man rolls a stone, it will roll back on
him.

26 : 27

pitch

If a man curses his father or mother, his
lamp will be snuffed out in pitch
darkness.

20 : 20

pitch darkness

If a man curses his father or mother, his
lamp will be snuffed out in pitch
darkness.

20 · 20

place

By wisdom the Lord laid the earth's
foundations, by understanding he set the
heavens in place;

3 : 19

before the mountains were settled in
place, before the hills, I was given birth,

8 : 25

I was there when he set the heavens in
place, when he marked out the horizon
on the face of the deep,

8 : 27

Do not lie in wait like an outlaw against
a righteous man's house, do not raid his
dwelling place;

24 : 15

Do not exalt yourself in the king's
presence, and do not claim a place
among great men;

25 : 6

plan

Do not those who plot evil go astray?
But those who plan what is good find
love and faithfulness.

14 : 22

There is no wisdom, no insight, no plan
that can succeed against the Lord.

21 : 30

planned evil

Then out came a woman to meet him,
dressed like a prostitute and with crafty
intent.

7 : 10

"If you have played the fool and exalted yourself, or if you have planned evil, clap your hand over your mouth!

30 : 32

planning

Plans fail for lack of counsel, but with many advisers they succeed.

15 : 22

In his heart a man plans his course, but the Lord determines his steps.

16 : 9

A scoundrel plots evil, and his speech is like a scorching fire.

16 : 27

Finish your outdoor work and get your fields ready; after that, build your house.

24 : 27

Ants are creatures of little strength, yet they store up their food in the summer;

30 : 25

plans

The plans of the righteous are just, but the advice of the wicked is deceitful.

12 : 5

Plans fail for lack of counsel, but with many advisers they succeed.

15 : 22

To man belong the plans of the heart, but from the Lord comes the reply of the tongue.

16 : 1

Commit to the Lord whatever you do, and your plans will succeed.

16 : 3

Many are the plans in the man's heart, but it is the Lord's purpose that prevails.

19 : 21

Make plans by seeking advice; if you wage war, obtain guidance.

20 . 18

The plans of the diligent lead to profit as surely as haste leads to poverty.

21 : 5

plans ahead

yet it stores its provisions in summer and gathers its food at harvest.

6 : 8

plans of the heart

To man belong the plans of the heart, but from the Lord comes the reply of the tongue.

16 : 1

planted

The righteous will never be uprooted, but the wicked will not remain in the land.

10 : 30

planting

The wicked man earns deceptive wages, but he who sows righteousness reaps a sure reward.

11 : 18

plants

She considers a field and buys it; out of her earnings she plants a vineyard.

31 : 16

playing with fire

He was going down the street near her corner, walking along in the direction of her house

7 : 8

plea

then do this, my son, to free yourself, since you have fallen into your neighbor's hands: Go and humble yourself; press your plea with your neighbor!

6 : 3

"Come, eat my food and drink the wine I have mixed.

9 : 5

pleading
A poor man is shunned by all his relatives -- how much more do his friends avoid him! Though he pursues them with pleading, they are nowhere to be found.

19 : 7

pleads
A poor man pleads for mercy, but a rich man answers harshly.

18 : 23

pleasant
For wisdom will enter your heart, and knowledge will be pleasant to your soul.

2 : 10

Her ways are pleasant ways, and all her paths are peace.

3 : 17

The wise in heart are called discerning, and pleasant words promote instruction.

16 : 21

Pleasant words are a honeycomb, sweet to the soul and healing to the bones.

16 : 24

pleasant words
The wise in heart are called discerning, and pleasant words promote instruction.

16 : 21

please
The Lord detests differing weights, and dishonest scales do not please him.

20 : 23

pleases
The Lord detests the sacrifice of the wicked, but the prayer of the upright pleases him.

15 : 8

The king's heart is in the hand of the Lord; he directs it like a watercourse wherever he pleases.

21 : 1

pleasing
A longing fulfilled is sweet to the soul, but fools detest turning from evil.

13 : 19

The Lord detests the thoughts of the wicked, but those of the pure are pleasing to him.

15 : 26

When a man's ways are pleasing to the Lord, he makes even his enemies live at peace with him.

16 : 7

for it is pleasing when you keep them in your heart and have all of them ready on your lips.

22 : 18

pleasing God
The Lord detests the sacrifice of the wicked, but the prayer of the upright pleases him.

15 : 8

pleasure
A fool finds pleasure in evil conduct, but a man of understanding delights in wisdom.

10 : 23

Kings take pleasure in honest lips; they value a man who speaks the truth.

16 : 13

A fool finds no pleasure in understanding but delights in airing his own opinions.

18 : 2

He who loves pleasure will become poor; whoever loves wine and oil will never be rich.

21 : 17

pledge

My son, if you have put up security for your neighbor, if you have struck hands in pledge for another,

6 : 1

He who puts up security for another will surely suffer, but whoever refuses to strike hands in pledge is safe.

11 : 15

A man lacking in judgment strikes hands in pledge and puts up security for his neighbor.

17 : 18

Take the garment of one who puts up security for a stranger; hold it in pledge if he does it for a wayward woman.

20 : 16

Do not be a man who strikes hands in pledge or puts up security for debts;

22 : 26

if you lack the means to pay, your very bed will be snatched from under you.

22 : 27

Take a garment of one who puts up security for a stranger; hold it in pledge if he does it for a wayward woman.

27 : 13

plenty

He who is full loathes honey, but to the hungry even what is bitter tastes sweet.

27 : 7

You will have plenty of goat's milk to feed you and your family and to nourish your servant girls.

27 : 27

plot

Do not plot harm against your neighbor, who lives trustfully near you.

3 : 29

A scoundrel plots evil, and his speech is like a scorching fire.

16 : 27

He who winks with his eye is plotting perversity; he who purses his lips is bent on evil.

16 : 30

plot evil

Do not those who plot evil go astray? But those who plan what is good find love and faithfulness.

14 : 22

plots evil

who plots evil with deceit in his heart -- he always stirs up dissension.

6 : 14

A scoundrel plots evil, and his speech is like a scorching fire.

16 : 27

He who plots evil will be known as a schemer,

24 : 8

plow

A sluggard does not plow in season; so at harvest time he looks but finds nothing.

20 : 4

plunder

we will get all sorts of valuable things and fill our houses with plunder;

1 : 13

The wicked desire the plunder of evil men, but the root of the righteous flourishes.

12 : 12

Better to be lowly in spirit and among the oppressed than to share plunder with the proud.

16 : 19

for the Lord will take up their case and will plunder those who plunder them.

22 : 23

point
She has sent out her maids, and she calls from the highest point of the city.

9 : 3

She sits at the door of her house, on a seat at the highest point of the city,

9 : 14

poisons
In the end it bites like a snake and poisons like a viper.

23 : 32

politics
By me kings reign and rulers make laws that are just;

8 : 15

polluted well
Like a muddied spring or a polluted well is a righteous man who gives way to the wicked.

25 : 26

poor
and poverty will come on you like a bandit and scarcity like an armed man.

6 : 11

Lazy hands make a man poor, but diligent hands bring wealth.

10 : 4

The wealth of the rich is their fortified city, but poverty is the ruin of the poor.

10 : 15

One man pretends to be rich, yet has nothing; another pretends to be poor, yet has great wealth.

13 : 7

A man's riches may ransom his life, but a poor man hears no threat.

13 : 8

A poor man's field may produce abundant food, but injustice sweeps it away.

13 : 23

The poor are shunned even by their neighbors, but the rich have many friends.

14 : 20

He who despises his neighbor sins, but blessed is he who is kind to the needy.

14 : 21

He who oppresses the poor shows contempt for their Maker, but whoever is kind to the needy honors God.

14 : 31

He who mocks the poor shows contempt for their Maker; whoever gloats over disaster will not go unpunished.

17 : 5

A poor man pleads for mercy, but a rich man answers harshly.

18 : 23

Better a poor man whose walk is blameless than a fool whose lips are perverse.

19 : 1

Wealth brings many friends, but a poor man's friend deserts him.

19 : 4

A poor man is shunned by all his relatives -- how much more do his friends avoid him! Though he pursues them with pleading, they are nowhere to be found.

19 : 7

He who is kind to the poor lends to the Lord, and he will reward him for what he has done.

19 : 17

What a man desires is unfailing love; better to be poor than a liar.

19 · 22

Do not love sleep or you will grow poor; stay awake and you will have food to spare.

20 : 13

If a man shuts his ears to the cry of the poor, he too will cry out and not be answered.

21 : 13

He who loves pleasure will become poor; whoever loves wine and oil will never be rich.

21 : 17

Rich and poor have this in common: The Lord is the Maker of them all.

22 : 2

The rich rule over the poor, and the borrower is servant to the lender.

22 : 7

A generous man will himself be blessed, for he shares his food with the poor.

22 : 9

He who oppresses the poor to increase his wealth and he who gives gifts to the rich -- both come to poverty.

22 : 16

Do not exploit the poor because they are poor and do not crush the needy in court,

22 : 22

for the Lord will take up their case and will plunder those who plunder them.

22 : 23

for drunkards and gluttons become poor, and drowsiness clothes them in rags.

23 : 21

A ruler who oppresses the poor is like a driving rain that leaves no crops.

28 . 3

Better a poor man whose walk is blameless than a rich man whose ways are perverse.

28 : 6

He who increases his wealth by exorbitant interest amasses it for another, who will be kind to the poor.

28 : 8

A rich man may be wise in his own eyes, but a poor man who has discernment sees through him.

28 : 11

A stingy man is eager to get rich and is unaware that poverty awaits him.

28 : 22

He who gives to the poor will lack nothing, but he who closes his eyes to them receives many curses.

28 : 27

The righteous care about justice for the poor, but the wicked have no such concern.

29 : 7

The poor man and the oppressor have this in common: The Lord gives sight to the eyes of both.

29 : 13

If a king judges the poor with fairness, his throne will always be secure.

29 : 14

Otherwise, I may have too much and disown you and say, 'Who is the Lord?' Or I may become poor and steal, and so dishonor the name of my God.

30 : 9

those whose teeth are swords and whose jaws are set with knives to devour the poor from the earth, the needy from among mankind.

30 : 14

Speak up and judge fairly; defend the rights of the poor and needy."

31 : 9

She opens her arms to the poor and extends her hands to the needy.

31 : 20

poor decisions
The man of integrity walks securely, but he who takes crooked paths will be found out.

10 : 9

poor health
A man's spirit sustains him in sickness, but a crushed spirit who can bear?

18 : 14

poor judgment
The lips of the righteous nourish many, but fools die for lack of judgment.

10 : 21

An unfriendly man pursues selfish ends; he defies all sound judgment.

18 : 1

poor man
A poor man's field may produce abundant food, but injustice sweeps it away.

13 : 23

A poor man pleads for mercy, but a rich man answers harshly.

18 : 23

Better a poor man whose walk is blameless than a fool whose lips are perverse.

19 : 1

Wealth brings many friends, but a poor man's friend deserts him.

19 : 4

A poor man is shunned by all his relatives -- how much more do his friends avoid him! Though he pursues them with pleading, they are nowhere to be found.

19 : 7

Better a poor man whose walk is blameless than a rich man whose ways are perverse.

28 : 6

A rich man may be wise in his own eyes, but a poor man who has discernment sees through him.

28 : 11

The poor man and the oppressor have this in common: The Lord gives sight to the eyes of both.

29 : 13

popularity
Many curry favor with a ruler, and everyone is the friend of a man who gives gifts.

19 : 6

population
A large population is a king's glory, but without subjects a prince is ruined.

14 : 28

portfolio
The wealth of the rich is their fortified city, but poverty is the ruin of the poor.

10 : 15

portions
She gets up while it is still dark; she provides food for her family and portions for her servant girls.

31 : 15

possess

I, wisdom, dwell together with prudence; I possess knowledge and discretion.

8 : 12

possessions

The lazy man does not roast his game, but the diligent man prizes his possessions.

12 : 27

if you lack the means to pay, your very bed will be snatched from under you.

22 : 27

poured

If you had responded to my rebuke, I would have poured out my heart to you and made my thoughts known to you.

1 : 23

Like one who takes away a garment on a cold day, or like vinegar poured on soda, is one who sings songs to a heavy heart.

25 : 20

poured out

If you had responded to my rebuke, I would have poured out my heart to you and made my thoughts known to you.

1 : 23

pours

a false witness who pours out lies and a man who stirs up dissension among brothers.

6 : 19

A truthful witness does not deceive, but a false witness pours out lies.

14 : 5

A false witness will not go unpunished, and he who pours out lies will not go free.

19 : 5

A false witness will not go unpunished, and he who pours out lies will perish.

19 : 9

poverty

and poverty will come on you like a bandit and scarcity like an armed man.

6 : 11

Men do not despise a thief if he steals to satisfy his hunger when he is starving.

6 : 30

The wealth of the rich is their fortified city, but poverty is the ruin of the poor.

10 : 15

One man gives freely, yet gains even more; another withholds unduly, but comes to poverty.

11 : 24

He who ignores discipline comes to poverty and shame, but whoever heeds correction is honored.

13 : 18

The poor are shunned even by their neighbors, but the rich have many friends.

14 : 20

All hard work brings a profit, but mere talk leads only to poverty.

14 : 23

He who oppresses the poor shows contempt for their Maker, but whoever is kind to the needy honors God.

14 : 31

A poor man pleads for mercy, but a rich man answers harshly.

18 : 23

What a man desires is unfailing love; better to be poor than a liar.

19 : 22

Do not love sleep or you will grow poor; stay awake and you will have food to spare.

20 : 13

The plans of the diligent lead to profit as surely as haste leads to poverty.

21 : 5

If a man shuts his ears to the cry of the poor, he too will cry out and not be answered.

21 : 13

He who loves pleasure will become poor; whoever loves wine and oil will never be rich.

21 : 17

He who oppresses the poor to increase his wealth and he who gives gifts to the rich -- both come to poverty.

22 : 16

Do not exploit the poor because they are poor and do not crush the needy in court,

22 : 22

for drunkards and gluttons become poor, and drowsiness clothes them in rags.

23 : 21

and poverty will come on you like a bandit and scarcity like an armed man.

24 : 34

He who works his land will have abundant food, but the one who chases fantasies will have his fill of poverty.

28 : 19

To show partiality is not good -- yet a man will do wrong for a piece of bread.

28 : 21

A stingy man is eager to get rich and is unaware that poverty awaits him.

28 : 22

Keep falsehood and lies far from me; give me neither poverty nor riches, but give me only my daily bread.

30 : 8

let them drink and forget their poverty and remember their misery no more.

31 : 7

power

Do not withhold good from those who deserve it, when it is in your power to act.

3 : 27

Counsel and sound judgment are mine; I have understanding and power.

8 : 14

When a wicked man dies, his hope perishes; all he expected from his power comes to nothing.

11 : 7

A large population is a king's glory, but without subjects a prince is ruined.

14 : 28

The wealth of the rich is their fortified city; they imagine it an unscalable wall.

18 : 11

The tongue has the power of life and death, and those who love it will eat its fruit.

18 : 21

A king's wrath is like the roar of a lion; he who angers him forfeits his life.

20 : 2

A wise man has great power, and a man of knowledge increases strength;

24 : 5

for those two will send sudden destruction upon them, and who knows what calamities they can bring?

24 : 22

Through patience a ruler can be persuaded, and a gentle tongue can break a bone.

25 : 15

When the righteous triumph, there is great elation; but when the wicked rise to power, men go into hiding.

28 : 12

When the wicked rise to power, people go into hiding; but when the wicked perish, the righteous thrive.

28 : 28

coneys are creatures of little power, yet they make their home in the crags;

30 : 26

locusts have no king, yet they advance together in ranks;

30 : 27

power of life
The tongue has the power of life and death, and those who love it will eat its fruit.

18 : 21

power of persuasion
Through patience a ruler can be persuaded, and a gentle tongue can break a bone.

25 : 15

praise
Let another praise you, and not your own mouth; someone else, and not your own lips.

27 : 2

The crucible for silver and the furnace for gold, but man is tested by the praise he receives.

27 : 21

Those who forsake the law praise the wicked, but those who keep the law resist them.

28 : 4

Give her the reward she has earned, and let her works bring her praise at the city gate

31 : 31

praised
A man is praised according to his wisdom, but men with warped minds are despised.

12 : 8

Charm is deceptive, and beauty is fleeting; but a woman who fears the Lord is to be praised.

31 : 30

praises
Her children arise and call her blessed; her husband also, and he praises her:

31 : 28

prayer
The Lord detests the sacrifice of the wicked, but the prayer of the upright pleases him.

15 : 8

The Lord is far from the wicked but he hears the prayer of the righteous.

15 : 29

"Two things I ask of you, O Lord; do not refuse me before I die:

30 : 7

prayers
If anyone turns a deaf ear to the law, even his prayers are detestable.

28 : 9

preacher
A wicked messenger falls into trouble, but a trustworthy envoy brings healing.

13 : 17

precious
She is more precious than rubies; nothing you desire can compare with her.

3 : 15

Choose my instruction instead of silver, knowledge rather than choice gold,

8 : 10

for wisdom is more precious than rubies, and nothing you desire can compare with her.

8 : 11

Gold there is, and rubies in abundance, but lips that speak knowledge are a rare jewel.

20 : 15

prejudice

These also are sayings to the wise: To show partiality in judging is not good:

24 : 23

preparation

She has prepared her meat and mixed her wine; she has also set her table.

9 : 2

To man belong the plans of the heart, but from the Lord comes the reply of the tongue.

16 : 1

In the house of the wise are stores of choice food and oil, but a foolish man devours all he has.

21 : 20

The horse is made ready for the day of battle, but victory rests with the Lord.

21 : 31

Finish your outdoor work and get your fields ready; after that, build your house.

24 : 27

Ants are creatures of little strength, yet they store up their food in the summer;

30 : 25

prepare

yet it stores its provisions in summer and gathers its food at harvest.

6 : 8

prepared

Penalties are prepared for mockers, and beatings for the backs of fools.

19 : 29

prerequisites

My son, if you accept my words and store up my commands within you,

2 : 1

presence

Then I was the craftsman at his side. I was filled with delight day after day, rejoicing always in his presence,

8 : 30

Evil men will bow down in the presence of the good, and the wicked at the gates of the righteous.

14 : 19

A gift opens the way for the giver and ushers him into the presence of the great.

18 : 16

remove the wicked from the king's presence, and his throne will be established through righteousness.

25 : 5

Do not exalt yourself in the king's presence, and do not claim a place among great men;

25 : 6

present

She will set a garland of grace on your head and present you with a crown of splendor.

4 : 9

The first to present his case seems right, till another comes forward and questions him.

18 : 17

presents

Many curry favor with a ruler, and everyone is the friend of a man who gives gifts.

19 : 6

preserve

My son, preserve sound judgment and discernment, do not let them out of your sight;

3 : 21

that you may maintain discretion and your lips may preserve knowledge.

5 : 2

press

then do this, my son, to free yourself, since you have fallen into your neighbor's hands: Go and humble yourself; press your plea with your neighbor!

6 : 3

pretend

Better to be a nobody and yet have a servant than pretend to be somebody and have no food.

12 : 9

pretends

One man pretends to be rich, yet has nothing; another pretends to be poor, yet has great wealth.

13 : 7

pretentiousness

One man pretends to be rich, yet has nothing; another pretends to be poor, yet has great wealth.

13 : 7

prevails

Many are the plans in the man's heart, but it is the Lord's purpose that prevails.

19 : 21

prey

Many are the victims she has brought down; her slain are a mighty throng.

7 : 26

preys

for the prostitute reduces you to a loaf of bread, and the adulteress preys upon your very life.

6 : 26

price

the lambs will provide you with clothing, and the goats with the price of a field.

27 : 26

pride

Do not be wise in your own eyes; fear the Lord and shun evil.

3 : 7

haughty eyes, a lying tongue, hands that shed innocent blood,

6 : 17

To fear the Lord is to hate evil; I hate pride and arrogance, evil behavior and perverse speech.

8 : 13

When pride comes, then comes disgrace, but with humility comes wisdom.

11 : 2

One man pretends to be rich, yet has nothing; another pretends to be poor, yet has great wealth.

13 : 7

Pride only breeds quarrels, but wisdom is found in those who take advice.

13 : 10

The Lord tears down the proud man's house, but he keeps the widow's boundaries intact.

15 : 25

The fear of the Lord teaches a man wisdom, and humility comes before honor.

15 : 33

The Lord detests all the proud of heart. Be sure of this: They will not go unpunished.

16 : 5

Pride goes before destruction, a haughty spirit before a fall.

16 : 18

Better to be lowly in spirit and among the oppressed than to share plunder with the proud.

16 : 19

He who mocks the poor shows contempt for their Maker; whoever gloats over disaster will not go unpunished.

17 : 5

Children's children are a crown to the aged, and parents are the pride of their children.

17 : 6

The wealth of the rich is their fortified city; they imagine it an unscalable wall.

18 : 11

Before his downfall a man's heart is proud, but humility comes before honor.

18 : 12

He who answers before listening -- that is his folly and his shame.

18 : 13

"It's no good, it's no good!" says the buyer; then off he goes and boasts about his purchase.

20 : 14

Haughty eyes and a proud heart, the lamp of the wicked, are sin!

21 : 4

The proud and arrogant man -- "Mocker" is his name; he behaves with overweening pride.

21 : 24

Do not gloat when your enemy falls; when he stumbles, do not let your heart rejoice,

24 : 17

Do not exalt yourself in the king's presence, and do not claim a place among great men;

25 : 6

it is better for him to say to you, "Come up here," than for him to humiliate you before a nobleman. What you have seen with your eyes

25 : 7

Do not boast about tomorrow, for you do not know what a day may bring forth.

27 : 1

Let another praise you, and not your own mouth; someone else, and not your own lips.

27 : 2

Anger is cruel and fury overwhelming, but who can stand before jealousy?

27 : 4

A rich man may be wise in his own eyes, but a poor man who has discernment sees through him.

28 : 11

He who trusts in himself is a fool, but he who walks in wisdom is kept safe.

28 : 26

A man who remains stiff-necked after many rebukes will suddenly be destroyed -- without remedy.

29 : 1

A man's pride brings him low, but a man of lowly spirit gains honor.

29 : 23

those whose eyes are ever so haughty, whose glances are so disdainful;

30 : 13

prideful
When pride comes, then comes disgrace, but with humility comes wisdom.

11 : 2

Do you see a man wise in his own eyes? There is more hope for a fool than for him.

26 : 12

Otherwise, I may have too much and disown you and say, 'Who is the Lord?' Or I may become poor and steal, and so dishonor the name of my God.

30 : 9

prince
A large population is a king's glory, but without subjects a prince is ruined.

14 : 28

princes
by me princes govern, and all nobles who rule on earth.

8 : 16

It is not fitting for a fool to live in luxury -- how much worse for a slave to rule over princes!

19 : 10

principle
What a man desires is unfailing love; better to be poor than a liar.

19 : 22

priorities
Choose my instruction instead of silver, knowledge rather than choice gold,

8 : 10

for wisdom is more precious than rubies, and nothing you desire can compare with her.

8 : 11

A fool finds pleasure in evil conduct, but a man of understanding delights in wisdom.

10 : 23

Better a meal of vegetables where there is love than a fattened calf with hatred.

15 : 17

How much better to get wisdom than gold, to choose understanding rather than silver!

16 : 16

Better a dry crust with peace and quiet than a house full of feasting with strife.

17 : 1

Of what use is money in the hand of a fool, since he has no desire to get wisdom?

17 : 16

To do what is right and just is more acceptable to the Lord than sacrifice.

21 : 3

Do not wear yourself out to get rich; have the wisdom to show restraint.

23 : 4

Cast but a glance at riches, and they are gone, for they will surely sprout wings and fly off to the sky like an eagle.

23 : 5

Do not let your heart envy sinners, but always be zealous for the fear of the Lord.

23 : 17

A faithful man will be richly blessed, but one eager to get rich will not go unpunished.

28 : 20

priority
Wisdom calls aloud in the street, she
raises her voice in the public squares;

1 : 20

Wisdom is supreme; therefore get
wisdom. Though it cost all you have,
get understanding.

4 : 7

Above all else, guard your heart, for it
is the wellspring of life.

4 : 23

Keep my commands and you will live;
guard my teachings as the apple of your
eye.

7 : 2

Wealth is worthless in the day of wrath,
but righteousness delivers from death.

11 : 4

A good name is more desirable than
great riches; to be esteemed is better
than silver or gold.

22 : 1

Buy the truth and do not sell it; get
wisdom, discipline and understanding.

23 : 23

private
Should your springs overflow in the
streets, your streams of water in the
public squares?

5 : 16

prizes
The lazy man does not roast his game,
but the diligent man prizes his
possessions.

12 : 27

problems
when calamity overtakes you like a
storm, when disaster sweeps over you
like a whirlwind, when distress and
trouble overwhelm you.

1 : 27

Have no fear of sudden disaster or of
the ruin that overtakes the wicked,

3 : 25

The blessing of the Lord brings wealth,
and he adds no trouble to it.

10 : 22

The righteous man is rescued from
trouble, and it comes on the wicked
instead.

11 : 8

A kind man benefits himself, but a cruel
man brings trouble on himself.

11 : 17

He who brings trouble on his family
will inherit only wind, and the fool will
be servant to the wise.

11 : 29

An evil man is trapped by his sinful
talk, but a righteous man escapes
trouble.

12 : 13

No harm befalls the righteous, but the
wicked have their fill of trouble.

12 : 21

One man pretends to be rich, yet has
nothing; another pretends to be poor,
yet has great wealth.

13 : 7

When calamity comes, the wicked are
brought down, but even in death the
righteous have a refuge.

14 : 32

The house of the righteous contains
great treasure, but the income of the
wicked brings them trouble.

15 : 6

A greedy man brings trouble to his
family, but he who hates bribes will
live.

15 : 27

A friend loves at all times, and a brother is born for adversity.

17 : 17

A man of perverse heart does not prosper; he whose tongue is deceitful falls into trouble.

17 : 20

The fear of the Lord leads to life: Then one rests content, untouched by trouble.

19 : 23

He who guards his mouth and his tongue keeps himself from calamity.

21 : 23

He who sows wickedness reaps trouble, and the rod of his fury will be destroyed.

22 : 8

If you falter in times of trouble, how small is your strength!

24 : 10

Like a bad tooth or a lame foot is reliance on the unfaithful in times of trouble.

25 : 19

Like one who takes away a garment on a cold day, or like vinegar poured on soda, is one who sings songs to a heavy heart.

25 : 20

Blessed is the man who always fears the Lord, but he who hardens his heart falls into trouble.

28 : 14

She sees that her trading is profitable, and her lamp does not go out at night.

31 : 18

produces

For as churning the milk produces butter, and as twisting the nose produces blood, so stirring up anger produces strife."

30 : 33

profit

All hard work brings a profit, but mere talk leads only to poverty.

14 : 23

The plans of the diligent lead to profit as surely as haste leads to poverty.

21 : 5

profitable

for she is more profitable than silver and yields better returns than gold.

3 : 14

She sees that her trading is profitable, and her lamp does not go out at night.

31 : 18

prolong

for they will prolong your life many years and bring you prosperity.

3 : 2

promise

Do not be a man who strikes hands in pledge or puts up security for debts;

22 : 26

An honest answer is like a kiss on the lips.

24 : 26

promise keepers

Bloodthirsty men hate a man of integrity and seek to kill the upright.

29 : 10

promises

for the Lord will be your confidence and will keep your foot from being snared.

3 : 26

It is a trap for a man to dedicate something rashly and only later to consider his vows.

20 : 25

Do not boast about tomorrow, for you do not know what a day may bring forth.

27 : 1

promote
A wise man's heart guides his mouth, and his lips promote instruction.

16 : 23

promote instruction
The wise in heart are called discerning, and pleasant words promote instruction.

16 : 21

promote peace
There is deceit in the hearts of those who plot evil, but joy for those who promote peace.

12 : 20

promotes
He who covers over an offense promotes love, but whoever repeats the matter separates close friends.

17 : 9

proper
If you find honey, just eat enough -- too much of it, and you will vomit.

25 : 16

Like snow in summer or rain in harvest, honor is not fitting for a fool.

26 : 1

property
Do not move an ancient boundary stone or encroach on the fields of the fatherless,

23 : 10

prospect
The prospect of the righteous is joy, but the hopes of the wicked come to nothing.

10 : 28

prosper
When the righteous prosper, the city rejoices; when the wicked perish, there are shouts of joy.

11 : 10

A generous man will prosper; he who refreshes others will himself be refreshed.

11 : 25

Whoever trusts in his riches will fall, but the righteous will thrive like a green leaf.

11 : 28

A man of perverse heart does not prosper; he whose tongue is deceitful falls into trouble.

17 : 20

He who conceals his sins does not prosper, but whoever confesses and renounces them finds mercy.

28 : 13

A greedy man stirs up dissension, but he who trusts in the Lord will prosper.

28 : 25

prosperity
for they will prolong your life many years and bring you prosperity.

3 : 2

With me are the riches and honor, enduring wealth and prosperity.

8 : 18

The blessing of the Lord brings wealth, and he adds no trouble to it.

10 : 22

A generous man will prosper; he who refreshes others will himself be refreshed.

11 : 25

Misfortune pursues the sinner, but prosperity is the reward of the righteous.

13 : 21

He who pursues righteousness and love finds life, prosperity and honor.

21 : 21

prospers
Whoever gives heed to instruction prospers, and blessed is he who trusts in the Lord.

16 : 20

He who gets wisdom loves his own soul; he who cherishes understanding prospers.

19 : 8

prostitute
For her house leads down to death and her paths to the spirits of the dead.

2 : 18

She gives no thought to the way of life; her paths are crooked, but she knows it not.

5 : 6

Keep to a path far from her, do not go near the door of her house,

5 : 8

for the prostitute reduces you to a loaf of bread, and the adulteress preys upon your very life.

6 : 26

Then out came a woman to meet him, dressed like a prostitute and with crafty intent.

7 : 10

She is loud and defiant, her feet never stay at home;

7 : 11

now in the street, now in the squares, at every corner she lurks.

7 : 12

I have perfumed my bed with myrrh, aloes and cinnamon.

7 : 17

He took his purse filled with money and will not be home till full moon."

7 : 20

Many are the victims she has brought down; her slain are a mighty throng.

7 : 26

Her house is a highway to the grave, leading down to the chambers of death.

7 : 27

for a prostitute is a deep pit and a wayward wife is a narrow well.

23 : 27

Like a bandit she lies in wait, and multiplies the unfaithful among men.

23 : 28

A man who loves wisdom brings joy to his father, but a companion of prostitutes squanders his wealth.

29 : 3

"This is the way of an adulteress: She eats and wipes her mouth and says, 'I've done nothing wrong.'

30 : 20

protect
Discretion will protect you, and understanding will guard you.

2 : 11

Do not forsake wisdom, and she will protect you; love her, and she will watch over you.

4 : 6

371

Hold on to instruction, do not let it go;
guard it well, for it is your life.

4 : 13

Above all else, guard your heart, for it
is the wellspring of life.

4 : 23

Keep my commands and you will live;
guard my teachings as the apple of your
eye.

7 : 2

A fool's talk brings a rod to his back,
but the lips of the wise protect them.

14 : 3

protection

He holds victory in store for the upright,
he is a shield to those whose walk is
blameless,

2 : 7

for he guards the course of the just and
protects the way of his faithful ones.

2 : 8

Discretion will protect you, and
understanding will guard you.

2 : 11

Wisdom will save you from the ways of
wicked men, from men whose words
are perverse,

2 : 12

It will save you also from the
adulteress, from the wayward wife with
her seductive words,

2 : 16

Then you will go on your way in safety,
and your foot will not stumble;

3 : 23

for the Lord will be your confidence
and will keep your foot from being
snared.

3 : 26

Do not forsake wisdom, and she will
protect you; love her, and she will
watch over you.

4 : 6

they will keep you from the adulteress,
from the wayward wife with her
seductive words.

7 : 5

Ill-gotten treasures are of no value, but
righteousness delivers from death.

10 : 2

The way of the Lord is a refuge for the
righteous, but it is the ruin of those who
do evil.

10 : 29

Righteousness guards the man of
integrity, but wickedness overthrows
the sinner.

13 : 6

The highway of the upright avoids evil;
he who guards his way guards his life.

16 : 17

A wise man's heart guides his mouth,
and his lips promote instruction.

16 : 23

The name of the Lord is a strong tower;
the righteous run to it and are safe.

18 : 10

He who obeys instructions guards his
life, but he who is contemptuous of his
ways will die.

19 : 16

Love and faithfulness keep a king safe;
through love his throne is made secure.

20 : 28

Every word of God is flawless; he is a
shield to those who take refuge in him.

30 : 5

protects
for he guards the course of the just and
protects the way of his faithful ones.
2 : 8

proud
He mocks proud mockers but gives
grace to the humble.
3 : 34

The Lord tears down the proud man's
house, but he keeps the widow's
boundaries intact.
15 : 25

The Lord detests all the proud of heart.
Be sure of this: They will not go
unpunished.
16 : 5

Better to be lowly in spirit and among
the oppressed than to share plunder with
the proud.
16 : 19

Before his downfall a man's heart is
proud, but humility comes before
honor.
18 : 12

Haughty eyes and a proud heart, the
lamp of the wicked, are sin!
21 : 4

The proud and arrogant man --
"Mocker" is his name; he behaves with
overweening pride.
21 : 24

proud heart
Haughty eyes and a proud heart, the
lamp of the wicked, are sin!
21 : 4

proud man
The proud and arrogant man --
"Mocker" is his name; he behaves with
overweening pride.
21 : 24

prove
Fear of man will prove to be a snare,
but whoever trusts in the Lord is kept
safe.
29 : 25

Do not add to his words, or he will
rebuke you and prove you a liar.
30 : 6

proverb
Like a lame man's legs that hang limp is
a proverb in the mouth of a fool.
26 : 7

Like a thornbush in a drunkard's hand is
a proverb in the mouth of a fool.
26 : 9

proverbs
The proverbs of Solomon son of David,
king of Israel:
1 : 1

for understanding proverbs and
parables, the sayings and riddles of the
wise.
1 : 6

The proverbs of Solomon: A wise son
brings joy to his father, but a foolish
son grief to his mother.
10 : 1

These are more proverbs of Solomon,
copied by the men of Hezekiah king of
Judah:
25 : 1

proverbs of Solomon
The proverbs of Solomon son of David,
king of Israel:
1 : 1

provide
the lambs will provide you with
clothing, and the goats with the price of
a field.
27 : 26

When it snows, she has no fear for her household; for all of them are clothed in scarlet.

31 : 21

provides

She gets up while it is still dark; she provides food for her family and portions for her servant girls.

31 : 15

providing

The sluggard's craving will be the death of him, because his hands refuse to work.

21 : 25

provision

When the hay is removed and new growth appears and the grass from the hills is gathered in,

27 : 25

the lambs will provide you with clothing, and the goats with the price of a field.

27 : 26

You will have plenty of goat's milk to feed you and your family and to nourish your servant girls.

27 : 27

He who works his land will have abundant food, but the one who chases fantasies will have his fill of poverty.

28 : 19

Keep falsehood and lies far from me; give me neither poverty nor riches, but give me only my daily bread.

30 : 8

provisions

yet it stores its provisions in summer and gathers its food at harvest.

6 : 8

provocation

Stone is heavy and sand a burden, but provocation by a fool is heavier than both.

27 : 3

provoked

Stone is heavy and sand a burden, but provocation by a fool is heavier than both.

27 : 3

prudence

for giving prudence to the simple, knowledge and discretion to the young --

1 : 4

You who are simple, gain prudence; you who are foolish, gain understanding.

8 : 5

I, wisdom, dwell together with prudence; I possess knowledge and discretion.

8 : 12

A fool spurns the father's discipline, but whoever heeds correction shows prudence.

15 : 5

Flog a mocker, and the simple will learn prudence; rebuke a discerning man, and he will gain knowledge.

19 : 25

prudent

for acquiring a disciplined and prudent life, doing what is right and just and fair;

1 : 3

A fool shows his annoyance at once, but a prudent man overlooks an insult.

12 : 16

A prudent man keeps his knowledge to himself, but the heart of fools blurts out folly.

12 : 23

Dishonest money dwindles away, but he who gathers money little by little makes it grow.

13 : 11

Every prudent man acts out of knowledge, but a fool exposes his folly.

13 : 16

The wisdom of the prudent is to give thought to their ways, but the folly of fools is deception.

14 : 8

A simple man believes anything, but a prudent man gives thought to his steps.

14 : 15

The simple inherit folly, but the prudent are crowned with knowledge.

14 : 18

Houses and wealth are inherited from parents, but a prudent wife is from the Lord.

19 : 14

In the house of the wise are stores of choice food and oil, but a foolish man devours all he has.

21 : 20

A prudent man sees danger and takes refuge, but the simple keep going and suffer for it.

22 : 3

The prudent see danger and take refuge, but the simple keep going and suffer for it.

27 : 12

prudent life
for acquiring a disciplined and prudent life, doing what is right and just and fair;

1 : 3

prudent man
A fool shows his annoyance at once, but a prudent man overlooks an insult.

12 : 16

A prudent man keeps his knowledge to himself, but the heart of fools blurts out folly.

12 : 23

Every prudent man acts out of knowledge, but a fool exposes his folly.

13 : 16

A simple man believes anything, but a prudent man gives thought to his steps.

14 : 15

A prudent man sees danger and takes refuge, but the simple keep going and suffer for it.

22 : 3

prudent wife
Houses and wealth are inherited from parents, but a prudent wife is from the Lord.

19 : 14

public
Wisdom calls aloud in the street, she raises her voice in the public squares;

1 : 20

at the head of the noisy streets she cries out, in the gateways of the city she makes her speech:

1 : 21

Should your springs overflow in the streets, your streams of water in the public squares?

5 : 16

375

public squares
Should your springs overflow in the streets, your streams of water in the public squares?

5 : 16

pulls down
A wise man attacks the city of the mighty and pulls down the stronghold in which they trust.

21 : 22

punish
It is not good to punish an innocent man, or to flog officials for their integrity.

17 : 26

Flog a mocker, and the simple will learn prudence; rebuke a discerning man, and he will gain knowledge.

19 : 25

Do not withhold discipline from a child; if you punish him with the rod, he will not die.

23 : 13

Punish him with the rod and save his soul from death.

23 : 14

punished
Be sure of this: The wicked will not go unpunished, but those who are righteous will go free.

11 : 21

punishment
Yet if he is caught, he must pay sevenfold, though it costs him all the wealth of his house.

6 : 31

Wisdom is found on the lips of the discerning, but a rod is for the back of him who lacks judgment.

10 : 13

The wages of the righteous bring them life, but the income of the wicked brings them punishment.

10 : 16

A good man obtains favor from the Lord, but the Lord condemns a crafty man.

12 : 2

A fool's talk brings a rod to his back, but the lips of the wise protect them.

14 : 3

The house of the wicked will be destroyed, but the tent of the upright will flourish.

14 : 11

The Lord detests all the proud of heart. Be sure of this: They will not go unpunished.

16 : 5

Understanding is a fountain of life to those who have it, but folly brings punishment to fools.

16 : 22

A false witness will not go unpunished, and he who pours out lies will not go free.

19 : 5

A false witness will not go unpunished, and he who pours out lies will perish.

19 : 9

When a mocker is punished, the simple gain wisdom; when a wise man is instructed, he gets knowledge.

21 : 11

When justice is done, it brings joy to the righteous but terror to evildoers.

21 : 15

A false witness will perish, and whoever listens to him will be destroyed forever.

21 : 28

for though a righteous man falls seven times, he rises again, but the wicked are brought down by calamity.

24 : 16

Whoever says to the guilty, "You are innocent" -- peoples will curse him and nations denounce him.

24 : 24

A whip for the horse, a halter for the donkey, and a rod for the backs of fools!

26 : 3

A ruler who oppresses the poor is like a driving rain that leaves no crops.

28 : 3

Do not slander a servant to his master, or he will curse you, and you will pay for it.

30 : 10

purchase
"It's no good, it's no good!" says the buyer; then off he goes and boasts about his purchase.

20 : 14

She considers a field and buys it; out of her earnings she plants a vineyard.

31 : 16

pure
The Lord detests the thoughts of the wicked, but those of the pure are pleasing to him.

15 : 26

It is not good to be partial to the wicked or to deprive the innocent of justice.

18 : 5

Better a poor man whose walk is blameless than a fool whose lips are perverse.

19 : 1

The righteous man leads a blameless life; blessed are his children after him.

20 : 7

Who can say, "I have kept my heart pure; I am clean and without sin"?

20 : 9

Even a child is known by his actions, by whether his conduct is pure and right.

20 : 11

He who loves a pure heart and whose speech is gracious will have the king for his friend.

22 : 11

those who are pure in their own eyes and yet are not cleansed of their filth;

30 : 12

pure heart
All day long he craves for more, but the righteous give without sparing.

21 : 26

He who loves a pure heart and whose speech is gracious will have the king for his friend.

22 : 11

pure speech
The mouth of the righteous brings forth wisdom, but a perverse tongue will be cut out.

10 : 31

purge
Blows and wounds cleanse away evil, and beatings purge the inmost being.

20 : 30

purify
Remove the dross from the silver, and out comes material for the silversmith;

25 : 4

remove the wicked from the king's presence, and his throne will be established through righteousness.

25 : 5

purity

Now then, my sons, listen to me; do not turn aside from what I say.

5 : 7

Keep to a path far from her, do not go near the door of her house,

5 : 8

they will keep you from the adulteress, from the wayward wife with her seductive words.

7 : 5

In the paths of the wicked lie thorns and snares, but he who guards his soul stays far from them.

22 : 5

purple

She makes coverings for her bed; she is clothed in fine linen and purple.

31 : 22

purpose

Many are the plans in the man's heart, but it is the Lord's purpose that prevails.

19 : 21

The purposes of a man's heart are deep waters, but a man of understanding draws them out.

20 : 5

purse

throw in your lot with us, and we will share a common purse" --

1 : 14

He took his purse filled with money and will not be home till full moon."

7 : 20

purses

He who winks with his eye is plotting perversity; he who purses his lips is bent on evil.

16 : 30

pursue

The Lord detests the way of the wicked but he loves those who pursue righteousness.

15 : 9

pursues

The truly righteous man attains life, but he who pursues evil goes to his death.

11 : 19

Misfortune pursues the sinner, but prosperity is the reward of the righteous.

13 : 21

An unfriendly man pursues selfish ends; he defies all sound judgment.

18 : 1

A poor man is shunned by all his relatives -- how much more do his friends avoid him! Though he pursues them with pleading, they are nowhere to be found.

19 : 7

He who pursues righteousness and love finds life, prosperity and honor.

21 : 21

The wicked man flees though no one pursues, but the righteous are as bold as a lion.

28 : 1

pursues evil

The truly righteous man attains life, but he who pursues evil goes to his death.

11 : 19

put

Put away perversity from your mouth; keep corrupt talk far from your lips.

4 : 24

My son, if you have put up security for your neighbor, if you have struck hands in pledge for another,

6 : 1

and put a knife to your throat if you are given to gluttony.

23 : 2

The accomplice of a thief is his own enemy; he is put under oath and dare not testify.

29 : 24

put away

Put away perversity from your mouth; keep corrupt talk far from your lips.

4 : 24

put up

My son, if you have put up security for your neighbor, if you have struck hands in pledge for another,

6 : 1

puts

do not bring hastily to court, for what will you do in the end if your neighbor puts you to shame?

25 : 8

puts up

He who puts up security for another will surely suffer, but whoever refuses to strike hands in pledge is safe.

11 : 15

A man lacking in judgment strikes hands in pledge and puts up security for his neighbor.

17 : 18

Take the garment of one who puts up security for a stranger; hold it in pledge if he does it for a wayward woman.

20 : 16

A wicked man puts up a bold front, but an upright man gives thought to his ways.

21 : 29

Do not be a man who strikes hands in pledge or puts up security for debts;

22 : 26

Take a garment of one who puts up security for a stranger; hold it in pledge if he does it for a wayward woman.

27 : 13

379

Q

quarrel

A hot-tempered man stirs up dissension, but a patient man calms a quarrel.

15 : 18

Starting a quarrel is like breaching a dam; so drop the matter before a dispute breaks out.

17 : 14

He who loves a quarrel loves sin; he who builds a high gate invites destruction.

17 : 19

It is to a man's honor to avoid strife, but every fool is quick to quarrel.

20 : 3

Like one who seizes a dog by the ears is a passer-by who meddles in a quarrel not his own.

26 : 17

Without wood a fire goes out; without gossip a quarrel dies down.

26 : 20

quarrels

Pride only breeds quarrels, but wisdom is found in those who take advice.

13 : 10

Casting the lot settles disputes and keeps strong opponents apart.

18 : 18

Drive out the mocker, and out goes strife; quarrels and insults are ended.

22 : 10

quarrelsome

A foolish son is his father's ruin, and a quarrelsome wife is like a constant dripping.

19 : 13

Better to live on a corner of the roof than share a house with a quarrelsome wife.

21 : 9

Better to live in a desert than with a quarrelsome and ill-tempered wife.

21 : 19

Better to live on a corner of the roof than share a house with a quarrelsome wife.

25 : 24

As charcoal to embers and as wood to fire, so is a quarrelsome man for kindling strife.

26 : 21

A quarrelsome wife is like a constant dripping on a rainy day;

27 : 15

quarrelsome man

As charcoal to embers and as wood to fire, so is a quarrelsome man for kindling strife.

26 : 21

quarrelsome wife

A quarrelsome wife is like a constant dripping on a rainy day;

27 : 15

quest

He who seeks good finds goodwill, but evil comes to him who searches for it.

11 : 27

question

Who can say, "I have kept my heart
pure; I am clean and without sin"?

20 : 9

do not bring hastily to court, for what
will you do in the end if your neighbor
puts you to shame?

25 : 8

questions

Does not wisdom call out? Does not
understanding raise her voice?

8 : 1

The first to present his case seems right,
till another comes forward and
questions him.

18 : 17

quick

a heart that devises wicked schemes,
feet that are quick to rush into evil,

6 : 18

It is to a man's honor to avoid strife, but
every fool is quick to quarrel.

20 : 3

quickly

He who answers before listening -- that
is his folly and his shame.

18 : 13

An inheritance quickly gained at the
beginning will not be blessed at the end.

20 : 21

quick-tempered

A quick-tempered man does foolish
things, and a crafty man is hated.

14 : 17

A patient man has great understanding,
but a quick-tempered man displays
folly.

14 : 29

quiet

Better a dry crust with peace and quiet
than a house full of feasting with strife.

17 : 1

Wisdom is too high for a fool; in the
assembly at the gate he has nothing to
say.

24 : 7

R

rabble rouser
a false witness who pours out lies and a man who stirs up dissension among brothers.

6 : 19

radiates
The light of the righteous shines brightly, but the lamp of the wicked is snuffed out.

13 : 9

rage
A king's rage is like the roar of a lion, but his favor is like dew on the grass.

19 : 12

Anger is cruel and fury overwhelming, but who can stand before jealousy?

27 : 4

rages
A man's own folly ruins his life, yet his heart rages against the Lord.

19 : 3

If a wise man goes to court with a fool, the fool rages and scoffs, and there is no peace.

29 : 9

rags
for drunkards and gluttons become poor, and drowsiness clothes them in rags.

23 : 21

raises
Wisdom calls aloud in the street, she raises her voice in the public squares;

1 : 20

raid
Do not lie in wait like an outlaw against a righteous man's house, do not raid his dwelling place;

24 : 15

rain
When a king's face brightens, it means life; his favor is like a rain cloud in spring.

16 : 15

Like clouds and wind without rain is a man who boasts of gifts he does not give.

25 : 14

As a north wind brings rain, so a sly tongue brings angry looks.

25 : 23

Like snow in summer or rain in harvest, honor is not fitting for a fool.

26 : 1

A ruler who oppresses the poor is like a driving rain that leaves no crops.

28 : 3

rain cloud
When a king's face brightens, it means life; his favor is like a rain cloud in spring.

16 : 15

rainy day
A quarrelsome wife is like a constant dripping on a rainy day;

27 : 15

raise
"To you, O men, I call out; I raise my voice to all mankind.

8 : 4

raising a child
Folly is bound up in the heart of a child, but the rod of discipline will drive it far from him.

22 : 15

Do not withhold discipline from a child; if you punish him with the rod, he will not die.

23 : 13

Punish him with the rod and save his soul from death.

23 : 14

The father of a righteous man has great joy; he who has a wise son delights in him.

23 : 24

raising children

He who spares the rod hates his son, but he who loves him is careful to discipline him.

13 : 24

He who fears the Lord has a secure fortress, and for his children it will be a refuge.

14 : 26

A fool spurns the father's discipline, but whoever heeds correction shows prudence.

15 : 5

Train a child in the way he should go, and when he is old he will not turn from it.

22 : 6

The rod of correction imparts wisdom, but a child left to himself disgraces his mother.

29 : 15

Discipline your son, and he will give you peace; he will bring delight to your soul.

29 : 17

random

Like an archer who wounds at random is he who hires a fool or any passer-by.

26 : 10

ranks

locusts have no king, yet they advance together in ranks;

30 : 27

ransom

A man's riches may ransom his life, but a poor man hears no threat.

13 : 8

The wicked become a ransom for the righteous, and the unfaithful for the upright.

21 : 18

Take a garment of one who puts up security for a stranger; hold it in pledge if he does it for a wayward woman.

27 : 13

rare

through knowledge its rooms are filled with rare and beautiful treasures.

24 : 4

rare jewel

Gold there is, and rubies in abundance, but lips that speak knowledge are a rare jewel.

20 : 15

rashly

He who guards his lips guards his life, but he who speaks rashly will come to ruin.

13 : 3

It is a trap for a man to dedicate something rashly and only later to consider his vows.

20 : 25

rather

Choose my instruction instead of silver, knowledge rather than choice gold,

8 : 10

How much better to get wisdom than gold, to choose understanding rather than silver!

16 : 16

ravens
The eye that mocks a father, that scorns obedience to a mother, will be pecked out by the ravens of the valley, will be eaten by the vultures.

30 : 17

reaching the lost
The fruit of the righteous is a tree of life, and he who wins souls is wise.

11 : 30

ready
She has prepared her meat and mixed her wine; she has also set her table.

9 : 2

The horse is made ready for the day of battle, but victory rests with the Lord.

21 : 31

for it is pleasing when you keep them in your heart and have all of them ready on your lips.

22 : 18

Finish your outdoor work and get your fields ready; after that, build your house.

24 : 27

reap
A sluggard does not plow in season; so at harvest time he looks but finds nothing.

20 : 4

reaping what you sow
they will eat the fruit of their ways and be filled with the fruit of their schemes.

1 : 31

If you are wise, your wisdom will reward you; if you are a mocker, you alone will suffer."

9 : 12

The wages of the righteous bring them life, but the income of the wicked brings them punishment.

10 : 16

The righteousness of the blameless makes a straight way for them, but the wicked are brought down by their own wickedness.

11 : 5

The righteous man is rescued from trouble, and it comes on the wicked instead.

11 : 8

A kind man benefits himself, but a cruel man brings trouble on himself.

11 : 17

The wicked man earns deceptive wages, but he who sows righteousness reaps a sure reward.

11 : 18

One man gives freely, yet gains even more; another withholds unduly, but comes to poverty.

11 : 24

A generous man will prosper; he who refreshes others will himself be refreshed.

11 : 25

He who seeks good finds goodwill, but evil comes to him who searches for it.

11 : 27

If the righteous receive their due on earth, how much more the ungodly and the sinner!

11 : 31

From the fruit of his lips a man is filled with good things as surely as the work of his hands rewards him.

12 : 14

The faithless will be fully repaid for their ways, and the good man rewarded for his.

14 : 14

Do not those who plot evil go astray? But those who plan what is good find love and faithfulness.

14 : 22

The house of the righteous contains great treasure, but the income of the wicked brings them trouble.

15 : 6

A greedy man brings trouble to his family, but he who hates bribes will live.

15 : 27

If a man pays back evil for good, evil will never leave his house.

17 : 13

He who sows wickedness reaps trouble, and the rod of his fury will be destroyed.

22 : 8

A generous man will himself be blessed, for he shares his food with the poor.

22 : 9

for the Lord will take up their case and will plunder those who plunder them.

22 : 23

If a man digs a pit, he will fall into it; if a man rolls a stone, it will roll back on him.

26 : 27

He who conceals his sins does not prosper, but whoever confesses and renounces them finds mercy.

28 : 13

He who gives to the poor will lack nothing, but he who closes his eyes to them receives many curses.

28 : 27

An evil man is snared by his own sin, but a righteous one can sing and be glad.

29 : 6

reason
Do not accuse a man for no reason -- when he has done you no harm.

3 : 30

There are three things that are too amazing for me, four that I do not understand:

30 : 18

rebellion
A fool spurns the father's discipline, but whoever heeds correction shows prudence.

15 : 5

Stern discipline awaits him who leaves the path; he who hates correction will die.

15 : 10

A mocker resents correction; he will not consult the wise.

15 : 12

He who ignores discipline despises himself, but whoever heeds correction gains understanding.

15 : 32

An evil man is bent only on rebellion; a merciless official will be sent against him.

17 : 11

Stop listening to instruction, my son, and you will stray from the words of knowledge.

19 : 27

The violence of the wicked will drag them away, for they refuse to do what is right.

21 : 7

rebellious

Fear the Lord and the king, my son, and do not join with the rebellious,

24 : 21

When a country is rebellious, it has many rulers, but a man of understanding and knowledge maintains order.

28 : 2

rebuke

If you had responded to my rebuke, I would have poured out my heart to you and made my thoughts known to you.

1 : 23

since you ignored all my advice and would not accept my rebuke,

1 : 25

since they would not accept my advice and spurned my rebuke,

1 : 30

My son, do not despise the Lord's discipline and do not resent his rebuke,

3 : 11

Do not rebuke a mocker or he will hate you; rebuke a wise man and he will love you.

9 : 8

A wise son heeds his father's instruction, but a mocker does not listen to rebuke.

13 : 1

He who listens to a life-giving rebuke will be at home among the wise.

15 : 31

A rebuke impresses a man of discernment more than a hundred lashes a fool.

17 : 10

Flog a mocker, and the simple will learn prudence; rebuke a discerning man, and he will gain knowledge.

19 : 25

Like an earring of gold or an ornament of fine gold is a wise man's rebuke to a listening ear.

25 : 12

Better is open rebuke than hidden love.

27 : 5

Do not add to his words, or he will rebuke you and prove you a liar.

30 : 6

rebukes

Whoever corrects a mocker invites insult; whoever rebukes a wicked man incurs abuse.

9 : 7

He who rebukes a man will in the end gain more favor than he who has a flattering tongue.

28 : 23

A man who remains stiff-necked after many rebukes will suddenly be destroyed -- without remedy.

29 : 1

rebukes a man

He who rebukes a man will in the end gain more favor than he who has a flattering tongue.

28 : 23

receive
If the righteous receive their due on earth, how much more the ungodly and the sinner!
11 : 31

He who leads the upright along an evil path will fall into his own trap, but the blameless will receive a good inheritance.
28 : 10

receives
For whoever finds me finds life and receives favor from the Lord.
8 : 35

Whoever corrects a mocker invites insult; whoever rebukes a wicked man incurs abuse.
9 : 7

He who finds a wife finds what is good and receives favor from the Lord.
18 : 22

The crucible for silver and the furnace for gold, but man is tested by the praise he receives.
27 : 21

He who gives to the poor will lack nothing, but he who closes his eyes to them receives many curses.
28 : 27

receives many curses
He who gives to the poor will lack nothing, but he who closes his eyes to them receives many curses.
28 : 27

reciprocal
I love those who love me, and those who seek me find me.
8 : 17

reckless
Reckless words pierce like a sword, but the tongue of the wise brings healing
12 : 18

A wise man fears the Lord and shuns evil, but a fool is hotheaded and reckless.
14 : 16

red
Do not gaze at wine when it is red, when it sparkles in the cup, when it goes down smoothly!
23 : 31

When it snows, she has no fear for her household; for all of them are clothed in scarlet.
31 : 21

reduces
for the prostitute reduces you to a loaf of bread, and the adulteress preys upon your very life.
6 : 26

reflects
As water reflects a face, so a man's heart reflects the man.
27 : 19

refreshed
A generous man will prosper; he who refreshes others will himself be refreshed.
11 : 25

refreshes
A generous man will prosper; he who refreshes others will himself be refreshed.
11 : 25

Like the coolness of snow at harvest time is a trustworthy messenger to those who send him; he refreshes the spirit of his masters.
25 : 13

refuge

The way of the Lord is a refuge for the righteous, but it is the ruin of those who do evil.

10 : 29

He who fears the Lord has a secure fortress, and for his children it will be a refuge.

14 : 26

When calamity comes, the wicked are brought down, but even in death the righteous have a refuge.

14 : 32

A prudent man sees danger and takes refuge, but the simple keep going and suffer for it.

22 : 3

The prudent see danger and take refuge, but the simple keep going and suffer for it.

27 : 12

Every word of God is flawless; he is a shield to those who take refuge in him.

30 : 5

refuse

He will not accept any compensation; he will refuse the bribe, however great it is.

6 : 35

The violence of the wicked will drag them away, for they refuse to do what is right.

21 : 7

The sluggard's craving will be the death of him, because his hands refuse to work.

21 : 25

"Two things I ask of you, O Lord; do not refuse me before I die:

30 : 7

refuse to work

The sluggard's craving will be the death of him, because his hands refuse to work.

21 : 25

refuses

He who puts up security for another will surely suffer, but whoever refuses to strike hands in pledge is safe.

11 : 15

reign

By me kings reign and rulers make laws that are just;

8 : 15

reject

He whose walk is upright fears the Lord, but he whose ways are devious despises him.

14 : 2

rejected

But since you rejected me when I called and no one gave heed when I stretched out my hand,

1 : 24

rejection

But since you rejected me when I called and no one gave heed when I stretched out my hand,

1 : 24

rejoice

who delight in doing wrong and rejoice in the perverseness of evil,

2 : 14

May your fountain be blessed, and may you rejoice in the wife of your youth.

5 : 18

my inmost being will rejoice when your lips speak what is right.

23 : 16

May your father and mother be glad;
may she who gave you birth rejoice!

23 : 25

Do not gloat when your enemy falls;
when he stumbles, do not let your heart
rejoice,

24 : 17

When the righteous thrive, the people
rejoice; when the wicked rule, the
people groan.

29 : 2

rejoices
When the righteous prosper, the city
rejoices; when the wicked perish, there
are shouts of joy.

11 : 10

rejoicing
Then I was the craftsman at his side. I
was filled with delight day after day,
rejoicing always in his presence,

8 : 30

rejoicing in his whole world and
delighting in mankind.

8 : 31

related
One who is slack in his work is brother
to one who destroys.

18 : 9

relationships
Wounds from a friend can be trusted,
but an enemy multiplies kisses.

27 : 6

Perfume and incense bring joy to the
heart, and the pleasantness of one's
friend springs from his earnest counsel.

27 : 9

A quarrelsome wife is like a constant
dripping on a rainy day;

27 : 15

relatives
A poor man is shunned by all his
relatives -- how much more do his
friends avoid him! Though he pursues
them with pleading, they are nowhere to
be found.

19 : 7

relentless
For they cannot sleep till they do evil;
they are robbed of slumber till they
make someone fall.

4 : 16

reliable
teaching you true and reliable words, so
that you can give sound answers to him
who sent you?

22 : 21

reliable words
teaching you true and reliable words, so
that you can give sound answers to him
who sent you?

22 : 21

reliance
Like a bad tooth or a lame foot is
reliance on the unfaithful in times of
trouble.

25 : 19

remain
For the upright will live in the land, and
the blameless will remain in it;

2 : 21

The righteous will never be uprooted,
but the wicked will not remain in the
land.

10 : 30

remains
A man who remains stiff-necked after
many rebukes will suddenly be
destroyed -- without remedy.

29 : 1

remedy
Therefore disaster will overtake him in an instant; he will suddenly be destroyed -- without remedy.

6 : 15

A man who remains stiff-necked after many rebukes will suddenly be destroyed -- without remedy.

29 : 1

remember
Bind them on your fingers; write them on the tablet of your heart.

7 : 3

let them drink and forget their poverty and remember their misery no more.

31 : 7

removal
Blows and wounds cleanse away evil, and beatings purge the inmost being.

20 : 30

remove
Remove the dross from the silver, and out comes material for the silversmith;

25 : 4

remove the wicked from the king's presence, and his throne will be established through righteousness.

25 : 5

Though you grind a fool in a mortar, grinding him like grain with a pestle, you will not remove his folly from him.

27 : 22

removed
When the hay is removed and new growth appears and the grass from the hills is gathered in,

27 : 25

renounce
He who conceals his sins does not prosper, but whoever confesses and renounces them finds mercy.

28 : 13

repaid
The faithless will be fully repaid for their ways, and the good man rewarded for his.

14 : 14

repay
If you say, "But we knew nothing about this," does not he who weighs the heart perceive it? Does not he who guards your life know it? Will he not repay each person according to what he has done?

24 : 12

repeats
He who covers over an offense promotes love, but whoever repeats the matter separates close friends.

17 : 9

repentance
Fools mock at making amends for sin, but goodwill is found among the upright.

14 : 9

He who conceals his sins does not prosper, but whoever confesses and renounces them finds mercy.

28 : 13

those who are pure in their own eyes and yet are not cleansed of their filth;

30 : 12

reply
A man finds joy in giving an apt reply-- and how good is a timely word!

15 : 23

To man belong the plans of the heart, but from the Lord comes the reply of the tongue.

16 : 1

reposes

Wisdom reposes in the heart of the discerning and even among fools she lets herself be known.

14 : 33

reputation

A good name is more desirable than great riches; to be esteemed is better than silver or gold.

22 : 1

He who plots evil will be known as a schemer,

24 : 8

do not bring hastily to court, for what will you do in the end if your neighbor puts you to shame?

25 : 8

or he who hears it may shame you and you will never lose your bad reputation.

25 : 10

request

"Two things I ask of you, O Lord; do not refuse me before I die:

30 : 7

rescue

A hot-tempered man must pay the penalty; if you rescue him, you will have to do it again.

19 : 19

Rescue those being led away to death; hold back those staggering toward slaughter.

24 : 11

rescued

The righteous man is rescued from trouble, and it comes on the wicked instead.

11 : 8

rescues

The words of the wicked lie in wait for blood, but the speech of the upright rescues them.

12 : 6

research

She considers a field and buys it; out of her earnings she plants a vineyard.

31 : 16

resent

My son, do not despise the Lord's discipline and do not resent his rebuke,

3 : 11

resentful

Do not rebuke a mocker or he will hate you; rebuke a wise man and he will love you.

9 : 8

A mocker resents correction; he will not consult the wise.

15 : 12

resents

A mocker resents correction; he will not consult the wise.

15 : 12

resist

Those who forsake the law praise the wicked, but those who keep the law resist them.

28 : 4

respect

Esteem her, and she will exalt you; embrace her, and she will honor you.

4 : 8

A kindhearted woman gains respect, but ruthless men gain only wealth.

11 : 16

He who ignores discipline comes to poverty and shame, but whoever heeds correction is honored.

13 : 18

He whose walk is upright fears the Lord, but he whose ways are devious despises him.

14 : 2

Better a little with the fear of the Lord than great wealth with turmoil.

15 : 16

A wise son brings joy to his father, but a foolish man despises his mother.

15 : 20

A foolish son brings grief to his father and bitterness to the one who bore him.

17 : 25

Before his downfall a man's heart is proud, but humility comes before honor.

18 : 12

He who pursues righteousness and love finds life, prosperity and honor.

21 : 21

Humility and the fear of the Lord bring wealth and honor and life.

22 : 4

He who loves a pure heart and whose speech is gracious will have the king for his friend.

22 : 11

Do not move an ancient boundary stone or encroach on the fields of the fatherless,

23 : 10

Do not let your heart envy sinners, but always be zealous for the fear of the Lord.

23 : 17

Listen to your father, who gave you life, and do not despise your mother when she is old.

23 : 22

Fear the Lord and the king, my son, and do not join with the rebellious,

24 : 21

Like snow in summer or rain in harvest, honor is not fitting for a fool.

26 : 1

Like tying a stone in a sling is the giving of honor to a fool.

26 : 8

He who tends a fig tree will eat its fruit, and he who looks after his master will be honored.

27 : 18

Fear of man will prove to be a snare, but whoever trusts in the Lord is kept safe.

29 : 25

"There are those who curse their fathers and do not bless their mothers;

30 : 11

The eye that mocks a father, that scorns obedience to a mother, will be pecked out by the ravens of the valley, will be eaten by the vultures.

30 : 17

respected

Her husband is respected at the city gate, where he takes his seat among the elders of the land.

31 : 23

respects

He who scorns instruction will pay for it, but he who respects a command is rewarded.

13 : 13

respond

A servant cannot be corrected by mere words; though he understands, he will not respond.

29 : 19

responded

If you had responded to my rebuke, I would have poured out my heart to you and made my thoughts known to you.

1 : 23

response

He who answers before listening -- that is his folly and his shame.

18 : 13

A poor man pleads for mercy, but a rich man answers harshly.

18 : 23

rest

when you lie down, you will not be afraid; when you lie down, your sleep will be sweet.

3 : 24

A little sleep, a little slumber, a little folding of the hands to rest--

6 : 10

A man who strays from the path of understanding comes to rest in the company of the dead.

21 : 16

A little sleep, a little slumber, a little folding of the hands to rest --

24 : 33

Like a fluttering sparrow or a darting swallow, an undeserved curse does not come to rest.

26 : 2

restoration

Reckless words pierce like a sword, but the tongue of the wise brings healing,

12 : 18

When a man's ways are pleasing to the Lord, he makes even his enemies live at peace with him.

16 : 7

He who covers over an offense promotes love, but whoever repeats the matter separates close friends.

17 : 9

restraining

restraining her is like restraining the wind or grasping oil with the hand.

27 : 16

restraint

A man of knowledge uses words with restraint, and a man of understanding is even-tempered.

17 : 27

Do not wear yourself out to get rich; have the wisdom to show restraint.

23 : 4

A fool gives full vent to his anger, but a wise man keeps himself under control.

29 : 11

Where there is no revelation, the people cast off restraint; but blessed is he who keeps the law.

29 : 18

rests

The fear of the Lord leads to life: Then one rests content, untouched by trouble.

19 : 23

The horse is made ready for the day of battle, but victory rests with the Lord.

21 : 31

393

result
The fruit of the righteous is a tree of life, and he who wins souls is wise.
11 : 30

From the fruit of his lips a man is filled with good things as surely as the work of his hands rewards him.
12 : 14

From the fruit of his mouth a man's stomach is filled; with the harvest from his lips he is satisfied.
18 : 20

Listen to advice and accept instruction, and in the end you will be wise.
19 : 20

result of sin
I have come to the brink of utter ruin in the midst of the whole assembly.
5 : 14

results
since you ignored all my advice and would not accept my rebuke,
1 : 25

He holds victory in store for the upright, he is a shield to those whose walk is blameless,
2 : 7

for he guards the course of the just and protects the way of his faithful ones.
2 : 8

Then you will understand what is right and just and fair -- every good path.
2 : 9

Then you will win favor and a good name in the sight of God and man.
3 : 4

Then you will go on your way in safety, and your foot will not stumble;
3 : 23

She will set a garland of grace on your head and present you with a crown of splendor.
4 : 9

Listen, my son, accept what I say, and the years of your life will be many.
4 : 10

that you may maintain discretion and your lips may preserve knowledge.
5 : 2

but in the end she is bitter as gall, sharp as a double-edged sword.
5 : 4

Her feet go down to death; her steps lead straight to the grave.
5 : 5

lest you give your best strength to others and your years to one who is cruel,
5 : 9

lest strangers feast on your wealth and your toil enrich another man's house.
5 : 10

You will say, "How I hated discipline! How my heart spurned correction!
5 : 12

The evil deeds of a wicked man ensnare him; the cords of his sin hold him fast.
5 : 22

Therefore disaster will overtake him in an instant; he will suddenly be destroyed -- without remedy.
6 : 15

for the prostitute reduces you to a loaf of bread, and the adulteress preys upon your very life.
6 : 26

Blows and disgrace are his lot, and his shame will never be wiped away;
6 : 33

Keep my commands and you will live;
guard my teachings as the apple of your
eye.

7 : 2

My fruit is better than fine gold; what I
yield surpasses choice silver.

8 : 19

If you are wise, your wisdom will
reward you; if you are a mocker, you
alone will suffer."

9 : 12

But little do they know that the dead are
there, that her guests are in the depths
of the grave.

9 : 18

Lazy hands make a man poor, but
diligent hands bring wealth.

10 : 4

The mouth of the righteous is a fountain
of life, but violence overwhelms the
mouth of the wicked.

10 : 11

The wages of the righteous bring them
life, but the income of the wicked
brings them punishment.

10 : 16

The blessing of the Lord brings wealth,
and he adds no trouble to it.

10 : 22

When pride comes, then comes
disgrace, but with humility comes
wisdom.

11 : 2

No harm befalls the righteous, but the
wicked have their fill of trouble.

12 : 21

In the way of righteousness there is life;
along that path is immortality.

12 : 28

The light of the righteous shines
brightly, but the lamp of the wicked is
snuffed out.

13 : 9

The highway of the upright avoids evil;
he who guards his way guards his life.

16 : 17

As a north wind brings rain, so a sly
tongue brings angry looks.

25 : 23

results of sin

At the end of your life you will groan,
when your flesh and body are spent.

5 : 11

Can a man walk on hot coals without
his feet being scorched?

6 : 28

So is he who sleeps with another man's
wife; no one who touches her will go
unpunished.

6 : 29

Yet if he is caught, he must pay
sevenfold, though it costs him all the
wealth of his house.

6 : 31

All at once he followed her like an ox
going to the slaughter, like a deer
stepping into a noose

7 : 22

till an arrow pierces his liver, like a bird
darting into a snare, little knowing it
will cost him his life.

7 : 23

retreats

a lion, mighty among beasts, who
retreats before nothing;

30 : 30

retribution

If you say, "But we knew nothing about this," does not he who weighs the heart perceive it? Does not he who guards your life know it? Will he not repay each person according to what he has done?

24 : 12

Do not say, "I'll do to him as he has done to me; I'll pay that man back for what he did."

24 : 29

return

None who go to her return or attain the paths of life.

2 : 19

returns

for she is more profitable than silver and yields better returns than gold.

3 : 14

As a dog returns to its vomit, so a fool repeats his folly.

26 : 11

revealing

Wisdom reposes in the heart of the discerning and even among fools she lets herself be known.

14 : 33

All a man's ways seem innocent to him, but motives are weighed by the Lord.

16 : 2

revelation

Where there is no revelation, the people cast off restraint; but blessed is he who keeps the law.

29 : 18

revenge

for jealousy arouses a husband's fury, and he will show no mercy when he takes revenge.

6 : 34

Do not say, "I'll pay you back for this wrong!" Wait for the Lord, and he will deliver you.

20 : 22

Do not say, "I'll do to him as he has done to me; I'll pay that man back for what he did."

24 : 29

revered

He who tends a fig tree will eat its fruit, and he who looks after his master will be honored.

27 : 18

reverence

He whose walk is upright fears the Lord, but he whose ways are devious despises him.

14 : 2

The fear of the Lord is a fountain of life, turning a man from the snares of death.

14 : 27

Better a little with the fear of the Lord than great wealth with turmoil.

15 : 16

The fear of the Lord teaches a man wisdom, and humility comes before honor.

15 : 33

Blessed is the man who always fears the Lord, but he who hardens his heart falls into trouble.

28 : 14

revival

Through the blessing of the upright a city is exalted, but by the mouth of the wicked it is destroyed.

11 : 11

reward

For whoever finds me finds life and receives favor from the Lord.

8 : 35

If you are wise, your wisdom will reward you; if you are a mocker, you alone will suffer."

9 : 12

The wicked man earns deceptive wages, but he who sows righteousness reaps a sure reward.

11 : 18

Misfortune pursues the sinner, but prosperity is the reward of the righteous.

13 : 21

Where there are no oxen, the manger is empty, but from the strength of an ox comes an abundant harvest.

14 : 4

The wealth of the wise is their crown, but the folly of fools yields folly.

14 : 24

When calamity comes, the wicked are brought down, but even in death the righteous have a refuge.

14 : 32

All the days of the oppressed are wretched, but the cheerful heart has a continual feast.

15 : 15

A wise servant will rule over a disgraceful son, and will share the inheritance as one of the brothers.

17 : 2

Children's children are a crown to the aged, and parents are the pride of their children.

17 : 6

The tongue has the power of life and death, and those who love it will eat its fruit.

18 : 21

He who is kind to the poor lends to the Lord, and he will reward him for what he has done.

19 : 17

Do not love sleep or you will grow poor; stay awake and you will have food to spare.

20 : 13

The glory of young men is their strength, gray hair the splendor of the old.

20 : 29

There is surely a future hope for you, and your hope will not be cut off.

23 : 18

If you say, "But we knew nothing about this," does not he who weighs the heart perceive it? Does not he who guards your life know it? Will he not repay each person according to what he has done?

24 : 12

In doing this, you will heap burning coals on his head, and the Lord will reward you.

25 : 22

He who tends a fig tree will eat its fruit, and he who looks after his master will be honored.

27 : 18

He who leads the upright along an evil path will fall into his own trap, but the blameless will receive a good inheritance.

28 : 10

He who works his land will have abundant food, but the one who chases fantasies will have his fill of poverty.

28 : 19

A greedy man stirs up dissension, but he who trusts in the Lord will prosper.

28 : 25

He who trusts in himself is a fool, but he who walks in wisdom is kept safe.

28 : 26

When the wicked thrive, so does sin, but the righteous will see their downfall.

29 : 16

Discipline your son, and he will give you peace; he will bring delight to your soul.

29 : 17

Give her the reward she has earned, and let her works bring her praise at the city gate.

31 : 31

rewarded

He who scorns instruction will pay for it, but he who respects a command is rewarded.

13 : 13

The faithless will be fully repaid for their ways, and the good man rewarded for his.

14 : 14

rewards

If you had responded to my rebuke, I would have poured out my heart to you and made my thoughts known to you.

1 : 23

This will bring health to your body and nourishment to your bones.

3 : 8

then your barns will be filled to overflowing, and your vats will brim over with new wine.

3 : 10

Then you will go on your way in safety, and your foot will not stumble;

3 : 23

The Lord's curse is on the house of the wicked, but he blesses the home of the righteous.

3 : 33

He mocks proud mockers but gives grace to the humble.

3 : 34

The wise inherit honor, but fools he holds up to shame.

3 : 35

that you may maintain discretion and your lips may preserve knowledge.

5 : 2

bestowing wealth on those who love me and making their treasuries full.

8 : 21

Blessed is the man who listens to me, watching daily at my doors, waiting at my doorway.

8 : 34

For through me your days will be many, and years will be added to your life.

9 : 11

The wages of the righteous bring them life, but the income of the wicked brings them punishment.

10 : 16

When the righteous prosper, the city rejoices; when the wicked perish, there are shouts of joy.

11 : 10

A kind man benefits himself, but a cruel man brings trouble on himself.

11 . 17

The truly righteous man attains life, but he who pursues evil goes to his death.

11 : 19

Be sure of this: The wicked will not go unpunished, but those who are righteous will go free.

11 : 21

People curse the man who hoards grain, but blessing crowns him who is willing to sell.

11 : 26

If the righteous receive their due on earth, how much more the ungodly and the sinner!

11 : 31

From the fruit of his lips a man is filled with good things as surely as the work of his hands rewards him.

12 : 14

A longing fulfilled is sweet to the soul, but fools detest turning from evil.

13 : 19

He whose walk is blameless is kept safe, but he whose ways are perverse will suddenly fall.

28 : 18

rich

The wealth of the rich is their fortified city, but poverty is the ruin of the poor.

10 : 15

One man pretends to be rich, yet has nothing; another pretends to be poor, yet has great wealth.

13 : 7

The poor are shunned even by their neighbors, but the rich have many friends.

14 : 20

The wealth of the rich is their fortified city; they imagine it an unscalable wall.

18 : 11

A poor man pleads for mercy, but a rich man answers harshly.

18 : 23

He who loves pleasure will become poor; whoever loves wine and oil will never be rich.

21 : 17

Rich and poor have this in common: The Lord is the Maker of them all.

22 : 2

The rich rule over the poor, and the borrower is servant to the lender.

22 : 7

He who oppresses the poor to increase his wealth and he who gives gifts to the rich -- both come to poverty.

22 : 16

Do not wear yourself out to get rich; have the wisdom to show restraint.

23 : 4

But it will go well with those who convict the guilty, and rich blessing will come upon them.

24 : 25

Better a poor man whose walk is blameless than a rich man whose ways are perverse.

28 : 6

A rich man may be wise in his own eyes, but a poor man who has discernment sees through him.

28 : 11

A faithful man will be richly blessed, but one eager to get rich will not go unpunished.

28 : 20

A stingy man is eager to get rich and is unaware that poverty awaits him.

28 : 22

rich and poor
Rich and poor have this in common: The Lord is the Maker of them all.

22 : 2

rich blessing
But it will go well with those who convict the guilty, and rich blessing will come upon them.

24 : 25

rich man
A poor man pleads for mercy, but a rich man answers harshly.

18 : 23

Better a poor man whose walk is blameless than a rich man whose ways are perverse.

28 : 6

A rich man may be wise in his own eyes, but a poor man who has discernment sees through him.

28 : 11

rich vs. poor
A rich man may be wise in his own eyes, but a poor man who has discernment sees through him.

28 : 11

riches
Long life is in her right hand; in her left hand are riches and honor.

3 : 16

With me are the riches and honor, enduring wealth and prosperity.

8 : 18

bestowing wealth on those who love me and making their treasuries full.

8 : 21

One man gives freely, yet gains even more; another withholds unduly, but comes to poverty.

11 : 24

A generous man will prosper; he who refreshes others will himself be refreshed.

11 : 25

Whoever trusts in his riches will fall, but the righteous will thrive like a green leaf.

11 : 28

A man's riches may ransom his life, but a poor man hears no threat.

13 : 8

A poor man's field may produce abundant food, but injustice sweeps it away.

13 : 23

Better a little with the fear of the Lord than great wealth with turmoil.

15 : 16

Whoever gives heed to instruction prospers, and blessed is he who trusts in the Lord.

16 : 20

The crucible for silver and the furnace for gold, but the Lord tests the heart.

17 : 3

Of what use is money in the hand of a fool, since he has no desire to get wisdom?

17 : 16

It is not fitting for a fool to live in luxury -- how much worse for a slave to rule over princes!

19 : 10

Houses and wealth are inherited from parents, but a prudent wife is from the Lord.

19 : 14

Do not love sleep or you will grow poor; stay awake and you will have food to spare.

20 : 13

Gold there is, and rubies in abundance, but lips that speak knowledge arc a rare jewel.

20 : 15

The plans of the diligent lead to profit as surely as haste leads to poverty.

21 : 5

He who pursues righteousness and love finds life, prosperity and honor.

21 : 21

A good name is more desirable than great riches; to be esteemed is better than silver or gold.

22 : 1

Humility and the fear of the Lord bring wealth and honor and life.

22 : 4

A generous man will himself be blessed, for he shares his food with the poor.

22 : 9

He who oppresses the poor to increase his wealth and he who gives gifts to the rich -- both come to poverty.

22 : 16

Cast but a glance at riches, and they are gone, for they will surely sprout wings and fly off to the sky like an eagle.

23 : 5

for riches do not endure forever, and a crown is not secure for all generations.

27 : 24

A faithful man will be richly blessed, but one eager to get rich will not go unpunished.

28 : 20

A man who loves wisdom brings joy to his father, but a companion of prostitutes squanders his wealth.

29 : 3

Keep falsehood and lies far from me; give me neither poverty nor riches, but give me only my daily bread.

30 : 8

richly blessed
A faithful man will be richly blessed, but one eager to get rich will not go unpunished.

28 : 20

riddles
for understanding proverbs and parables, the sayings and riddles of the wise.

1 : 6

riddles of the wise
for understanding proverbs and parables, the sayings and riddles of the wise.

1 : 6

rigging
You will be like one sleeping on the high seas, lying on top of the rigging.

23 : 34

right
for acquiring a disciplined and prudent life, doing what is right and just and fair;

1 : 3

Then you will understand what is right and just and fair -- every good path.

2 : 9

Long life is in her right hand; in her left hand are riches and honor.

3 : 16

Do not swerve to the right or the left; keep your foot from evil.

4 : 27

Listen, for I have worthy things to say; I open my lips to speak what is right.

8 : 6

All the words of my mouth are just; none of them is crooked or perverse.

8 : 8

To the discerning all of them are right; they are faultless to those who have knowledge.

8 : 9

The way of a fool seems right to him, but a wise man listens to advice.

12 : 15

There is a way that seems right to a man, but in the end it leads to death.

14 : 12

There is a way that seems right to a man, but in the end it leads to death.

16 : 25

The first to present his case seems right, till another comes forward and questions him.

18 : 17

Even a child is known by his actions, by whether his conduct is pure and right.

20 : 11

All a man's ways seem right to him, but the Lord weighs the heart.

21 : 2

To do what is right and just is more acceptable to the Lord than sacrifice.

21 : 3

The violence of the wicked will drag them away, for they refuse to do what is right.

21 : 7

my inmost being will rejoice when your lips speak what is right.

23 : 16

right hand

Long life is in her right hand; in her left hand are riches and honor.

3 : 16

right path

Listen, my son, and be wise, and keep your heart on the right path.

23 : 19

righteous

Thus you will walk in the ways of good men and keep to the paths of the righteous.

2 : 20

The Lord's curse is on the house of the wicked, but he blesses the home of the righteous.

3 : 33

The path of the righteous is like the first gleam of dawn, shining ever brighter till the full light of day.

4 : 18

Instruct a wise man and he will be wiser still; teach a righteous man and he will add to his learning.

9 : 9

The Lord does not let the righteous go hungry but he thwarts the craving of the wicked.

10 : 3

Blessings crown the head of the righteous, but violence overwhelms the mouth of the wicked.

10 : 6

The memory of the righteous will be a blessing, but the name of the wicked will rot.

10 : 7

The mouth of the righteous is a fountain of life, but violence overwhelms the mouth of the wicked.

10 : 11

The wages of the righteous bring them life, but the income of the wicked brings them punishment.

10 : 16

The tongue of the righteous is choice silver, but the heart of the wicked is of little value.

10 : 20

The lips of the righteous nourish many, but fools die for lack of judgment.

10 : 21

What the wicked dreads will overtake him; what the righteous desire will be granted.

10 : 24

When the storm has swept by, the wicked are gone, but the righteous stand firm forever.

10 : 25

The prospect of the righteous is joy, but the hopes of the wicked come to nothing.

10 : 28

The way of the Lord is a refuge for the righteous, but it is the ruin of those who do evil.

10 : 29

The righteous will never be uprooted, but the wicked will not remain in the land.

10 : 30

The mouth of the righteous brings forth wisdom, but a perverse tongue will be cut out.

10 : 31

The lips of the righteous know what is fitting, but the mouth of the wicked only what is perverse.

10 : 32

The righteous man is rescued from trouble, and it comes on the wicked instead.

11 : 8

With his mouth the godless destroys his neighbor, but through knowledge the righteous escape.

11 : 9

When the righteous prosper, the city rejoices; when the wicked perish, there are shouts of joy.

11 : 10

The truly righteous man attains life, but he who pursues evil goes to his death.

11 : 19

Be sure of this: The wicked will not go unpunished, but those who are righteous will go free.

11 : 21

The desire of the righteous ends only in good, but the hope of the wicked only in wrath.

11 : 23

Whoever trusts in his riches will fall, but the righteous will thrive like a green leaf.

11 : 28

The fruit of the righteous is a tree of life, and he who wins souls is wise.

11 : 30

If the righteous receive their due on earth, how much more the ungodly and the sinner!

11 : 31

A man cannot be established through wickedness, but the righteous cannot be uprooted.

12 : 3

The plans of the righteous are just, but the advice of the wicked is deceitful.

12 : 5

The words of the wicked lie in wait for blood, but the speech of the upright rescues them.

12 : 6

Wicked men are overthrown and are no more, but the house of the righteous stands firm.

12 : 7

A righteous man cares for the needs of his animal, but the kindest acts of the wicked are cruel.

12 : 10

The wicked desire the plunder of evil men, but the root of the righteous flourishes.

12 : 12

No harm befalls the righteous, but the wicked have their fill of trouble.

12 : 21

A righteous man is cautious in friendship, but the way of the wicked leads them astray.

12 : 26

The righteous hate what is false, but the wicked bring shame and disgrace.

13 : 5

The light of the righteous shines brightly, but the lamp of the wicked is snuffed out.

13 : 9

Misfortune pursues the sinner, but prosperity is the reward of the righteous.

13 : 21

A good man leaves an inheritance for his children's children, but a sinner's wealth is stored up for the righteous.

13 : 22

The righteous eat to their hearts' content, but the stomach of the wicked goes hungry.

13 : 25

Fools mock at making amends for sin, but goodwill is found among the upright.

14 : 9

The house of the wicked will be destroyed, but the tent of the upright will flourish.

14 : 11

The faithless will be fully repaid for their ways, and the good man rewarded for his.

14 : 14

Evil men will bow down in the presence of the good, and the wicked at the gates of the righteous.

14 : 19

When calamity comes, the wicked are brought down, but even in death the righteous have a refuge.

14 : 32

The eyes of the Lord are everywhere, keeping watch on the wicked and the good.

15 : 3

The house of the righteous contains great treasure, but the income of the wicked brings them trouble.

15 : 6

The Lord detests the sacrifice of the wicked, but the prayer of the upright pleases him.

15 : 8

The way of the sluggard is blocked with thorns, but the path of the upright is a highway.

15 : 19

The heart of the righteous weighs its answers, but the mouth of the wicked gushes evil.

15 : 28

The Lord is far from the wicked but he hears the prayer of the righteous.

15 : 29

Gray hair is a crown of splendor; it is attained by a righteous life.

16 : 31

The name of the Lord is a strong tower; the righteous run to it and are safe.

18 : 10

The righteous man leads a blameless life; blessed are his children after him.

20 : 7

The way of the guilty is devious, but the conduct of the innocent is upright.

21 : 8

When justice is done, it brings joy to the righteous but terror to evildoers.

21 : 15

The wicked become a ransom for the righteous, and the unfaithful for the upright.

21 : 18

All day long he craves for more, but the righteous give without sparing.

21 : 26

A wicked man puts up a bold front, but an upright man gives thought to his ways.

21 : 29

The father of a righteous man has great joy; he who has a wise son delights in him.

23 : 24

Do not lie in wait like an outlaw against a righteous man's house, do not raid his dwelling place;

24 : 15

for though a righteous man falls seven times, he rises again, but the wicked are brought down by calamity.

24 : 16

Like a muddied spring or a polluted well is a righteous man who gives way to the wicked.

25 : 26

The wicked man flees though no one pursues, but the righteous are as bold as a lion.

28 : 1

He who leads the upright along an evil path will fall into his own trap, but the blameless will receive a good inheritance.

28 : 10

When the righteous triumph, there is great elation; but when the wicked rise to power, men go into hiding.

28 : 12

When the wicked rise to power, people go into hiding; but when the wicked perish, the righteous thrive.

28 : 28

When the righteous thrive, the people rejoice; when the wicked rule, the people groan.

29 : 2

An evil man is snared by his own sin, but a righteous one can sing and be glad.

29 : 6

The righteous care about justice for the poor, but the wicked have no such concern.

29 : 7

Bloodthirsty men hate a man of integrity and seek to kill the upright.

29 : 10

When the wicked thrive, so does sin, but the righteous will see their downfall.

29 : 16

The righteous detest the dishonest; the wicked detest the upright.

29 : 27

righteous man

Instruct a wise man and he will be wiser still; teach a righteous man and he will add to his learning.

9 : 9

The righteous man is rescued from trouble, and it comes on the wicked instead.

11 : 8

The truly righteous man attains life, but he who pursues evil goes to his death.

11 : 19

A righteous man cares for the needs of his animal, but the kindest acts of the wicked are cruel.

12 : 10

An evil man is trapped by his sinful talk, but a righteous man escapes trouble.

12 : 13

A righteous man is cautious in friendship, but the way of the wicked leads them astray.

12 : 26

The father of a righteous man has great joy; he who has a wise son delights in him.

23 : 24

Do not lie in wait like an outlaw against a righteous man's house, do not raid his dwelling place;

24 : 15

for though a righteous man falls seven times, he rises again, but the wicked are brought down by calamity.

24 : 16

Like a muddied spring or a polluted well is a righteous man who gives way to the wicked.

25 : 26

Righteous One

The Righteous One takes note of the house of the wicked and brings the wicked to ruin.

21 : 12

righteousness

for the Lord detests a perverse man but takes the upright into his confidence.

3 : 32

I walk in the way of righteousness, along the paths of justice,

8 : 20

Ill-gotten treasures are of no value, but righteousness delivers from death.

10 : 2

Wealth is worthless in the day of wrath, but righteousness delivers from death.

11 : 4

The righteousness of the blameless makes a straight way for them, but the wicked are brought down by their own wickedness.

11 : 5

The righteousness of the upright delivers them, but the unfaithful are trapped by evil desires.

11 : 6

The wicked man earns deceptive wages, but he who sows righteousness reaps a sure reward.

11 : 18

In the way of righteousness there is life; along that path is immortality.

12 : 28

Righteousness guards the man of integrity, but wickedness overthrows the sinner.

13 : 6

Righteousness exalts a nation, but sin is a disgrace to any people.

14 : 34

The Lord detests the way of the wicked but he loves those who pursue righteousness.

15 : 9

Better a little with righteousness than much gain with injustice.

16 : 8

Kings detest wrongdoing, for a throne is established through righteousness.

16 : 12

The highway of the upright avoids evil; he who guards his way guards his life.

16 : 17

Even a child is known by his actions, by whether his conduct is pure and right.

20 : 11

He who pursues righteousness and love finds life, prosperity and honor.

21 : 21

remove the wicked from the king's presence, and his throne will be established through righteousness.

25 : 5

Better a poor man whose walk is blameless than a rich man whose ways are perverse.

28 : 6

He whose walk is blameless is kept safe, but he whose ways are perverse will suddenly fall.

28 : 18

rights

lest they drink and forget what the law decrees, and deprive all the oppressed of the rights.

31 : 5

"Speak up for those who cannot speak for themselves, for the rights of all who are destitute.

31 : 8

Speak up and judge fairly; defend the rights of the poor and needy."

31 : 9

ring

Like a gold ring in a pig's snout is a beautiful woman who shows no discretion.

11 : 22

rise

When the righteous triumph, there is great elation; but when the wicked rise to power, men go into hiding.

28 : 12

When the wicked rise to power, people go into hiding; but when the wicked perish, the righteous thrive.

28 : 28

rise to power

When the wicked rise to power, people go into hiding; but when the wicked perish, the righteous thrive.

28 : 28

rises
for though a righteous man falls seven times, he rises again, but the wicked are brought down by calamity.

24 : 16

rising and falling
When a country is rebellious, it has many rulers, but a man of understanding and knowledge maintains order.

28 : 2

rising to the top
Diligent hands will rule, but laziness ends in slave labor.

12 : 24

river
The king's heart is in the hand of the Lord; he directs it like a watercourse wherever he pleases.

21 : 1

road
The sluggard says, "There is a lion in the road, a fierce lion roaming the streets!"

26 : 13

roaming
The sluggard says, "There is a lion in the road, a fierce lion roaming the streets!"

26 : 13

roar of a lion
A king's rage is like the roar of a lion, but his favor is like dew on the grass.

19 : 12

A king's wrath is like the roar of a lion; he who angers him forfeits his life.

20 : 2

roaring lion
Like a roaring lion or a charging bear is a wicked man ruling over a helpless people.

28 : 15

roast
The lazy man does not roast his game, but the diligent man prizes his possessions.

12 . 27

rob
He who robs his father and drives out his mother is a son who brings shame and disgrace.

19 : 26

robbed
For they cannot sleep till they do evil; they are robbed of slumber till they make someone fall.

4 : 16

Better to meet a bear robbed of her cubs than a fool in his folly.

17 : 12

robs
He who robs his father or mother and says, "It's not wrong" -- he is partner to him who destroys.

28 : 24

rock
the way of an eagle in the sky, the way of a snake on a rock, the way of a ship on the high seas, and the way of a man with a maiden.

30 : 19

rocks
coneys are creatures of little power, yet they make their home in the crags;

30 : 26

rod
Wisdom is found on the lips of the discerning, but a rod is for the back of him who lacks judgment.

10 : 13

He who spares the rod hates his son, but he who loves him is careful to discipline him.

13 : 24

A fool's talk brings a rod to his back,
but the lips of the wise protect them.

14 : 3

He who sows wickedness reaps trouble,
and the rod of his fury will be
destroyed.

22 : 8

Folly is bound up in the heart of a child,
but the rod of discipline will drive it far
from him.

22 : 15

Do not withhold discipline from a child;
if you punish him with the rod, he will
not die.

23 : 13

Punish him with the rod and save his
soul from death.

23 : 14

A whip for the horse, a halter for the
donkey, and a rod for the backs of
fools!

26 : 3

The rod of correction imparts wisdom,
but a child left to himself disgraces his
mother.

29 : 15

rod of correction
The rod of correction imparts wisdom,
but a child left to himself disgraces his
mother.

29 : 15

roll
If a man digs a pit, he will fall into it; if
a man rolls a stone, it will roll back on
him.

26 : 27

roof
Better to live on a corner of the roof
than share a house with a quarrelsome
wife.

21 : 9

Better to live on a corner of the roof
than share a house with a quarrelsome
wife.

25 : 24

rooms
through knowledge its rooms are filled
with rare and beautiful treasures.

24 : 4

rooster
a strutting rooster, a he-goat, and a king
with his army around him.

30 : 31

root
The wicked desire the plunder of evil
men, but the root of the righteous
flourishes.

12 : 12

root of the problem
There is deceit in the hearts of those
who plot evil, but joy for those who
promote peace.

12 : 20

roots
The righteous will never be uprooted,
but the wicked will not remain in the
land.

10 : 30

A man cannot be established through
wickedness, but the righteous cannot be
uprooted.

12 : 3

rot
The memory of the righteous will be a
blessing, but the name of the wicked
will rot.

10 : 7

rots
A heart at peace gives life to the body,
but envy rots the bones.

14 : 30

rubies

She is more precious than rubies;
nothing you desire can compare with
her.

3 : 15

for wisdom is more precious than
rubies, and nothing you desire can
compare with her.

8 : 11

Gold there is, and rubies in abundance,
but lips that speak knowledge are a rare
jewel.

20 : 15

A wife of noble character who can find?
She is worth far more than rubies.

31 : 10

rude

The woman Folly is loud; she is
undisciplined and without knowledge.

9 : 13

As a north wind brings rain, so a sly
tongue brings angry looks.

25 : 23

If a man loudly blesses his neighbor
early in the morning, it will be taken as
a curse.

27 : 14

ruin

Have no fear of sudden disaster or of
the ruin that overtakes the wicked,

3 : 25

I have come to the brink of utter ruin in
the midst of the whole assembly.

5 : 14

The wise in heart accept commands, but
a chattering fool comes to ruin.

10 : 8

He who walks maliciously causes grief,
and a chattering fool comes to ruin.

10 : 10

Wise men store up knowledge, but the
mouth of a fool invites ruin.

10 : 14

The wealth of the rich is their fortified
city, but poverty is the ruin of the poor.

10 : 15

The way of the Lord is a refuge for the
righteous, but it is the ruin of those who
do evil.

10 : 29

He who guards his lips guards his life,
but he who speaks rashly will come to
ruin.

13 : 3

A man of many companions may come
to ruin, but there is a friend who sticks
closer than a brother.

18 : 24

A foolish son is his father's ruin, and a
quarrelsome wife is like a constant
dripping.

19 : 13

An inheritance quickly gained at the
beginning will not be blessed at the end.

20 : 21

The Righteous One takes note of the
house of the wicked and brings the
wicked to ruin.

21 : 12

The mouth of an adulteress is a deep
pit; he who is under the Lord's wrath
will fall into it.

22 : 14

and poverty will come on you like a
bandit and scarcity like an armed man.

24 : 34

A lying tongue hates those it hurts, and
a flattering mouth works ruin.

26 : 28

do not spend your strength on women,
your vigor on those who ruin kings.

31 : 3

ruin your witness
or he who hears it may shame you and
you will never lose your bad reputation.

25 : 10

ruined
A large population is a king's glory, but
without subjects a prince is ruined.

14 : 28

Like a muddied spring or a polluted
well is a righteous man who gives way
to the wicked.

25 : 26

ruins
One who is slack in his work is brother
to one who destroys.

18 : 9

A man's own folly ruins his life, yet his
heart rages against the Lord.

19 : 3

thorns had come up everywhere, the
ground was covered with weeds, and
the stone wall was in ruins.

24 : 31

rule
by me princes govern, and all nobles
who rule on earth.

8 : 16

Diligent hands will rule, but laziness
ends in slave labor.

12 : 24

A wise servant will rule over a
disgraceful son, and will share the
inheritance as one of the brothers.

17 : 2

It is not fitting for a fool to live in
luxury -- how much worse for a slave to
rule over princes!

19 : 10

The rich rule over the poor, and the
borrower is servant to the lender.

22 : 7

When the righteous thrive, the people
rejoice; when the wicked rule, the
people groan.

29 : 2

rule over
It is not fitting for a fool to live in
luxury -- how much worse for a slave to
rule over princes!

19 : 10

The rich rule over the poor, and the
borrower is servant to the lender.

22 : 7

ruler
It has no commander, no overseer or
ruler,

6 : 7

Kings detest wrongdoing, for a throne is
established through righteousness.

16 : 12

Better a patient man than a warrior, a
man who controls his temper than one
who takes a city.

16 : 32

Arrogant lips are unsuited to a fool --
how much worse lying lips to a ruler!

17 : 7

Many curry favor with a ruler, and
everyone is the friend of a man who
gives gifts.

19 : 6

When a king sits on his throne to judge,
he winnows out all evil with his eyes.

20 : 8

When you sit to dine with a ruler, note
well what is before you,

23 : 1

remove the wicked from the king's presence, and his throne will be established through righteousness.

25 : 5

Do not exalt yourself in the king's presence, and do not claim a place among great men;

25 : 6

Through patience a ruler can be persuaded, and a gentle tongue can break a bone.

25 : 15

A ruler who oppresses the poor is like a driving rain that leaves no crops.

28 : 3

A tyrannical ruler lacks judgment, but he who hates ill-gotten gain will enjoy a long life.

28 : 16

By justice a king gives a country stability, but one who is greedy for bribes tears it down.

29 : 4

If a ruler listens to lies, all his officials become wicked.

29 : 12

If a king judges the poor with fairness, his throne will always be secure.

29 : 14

Many seek an audience with a ruler, but it is from the Lord that man gets justice.

29 : 26

a servant who becomes a king, a fool who is full of food,

30 : 22

rulers
By me kings reign and rulers make laws that are just;

8 : 15

When a country is rebellious, it has many rulers, but a man of understanding and knowledge maintains order.

28 : 2

"It is not for kings, O Lemuel -- not for kings to drink wine, not for rulers to crave beer,

31 : 4

ruling
Like a roaring lion or a charging bear is a wicked man ruling over a helpless people.

28 : 15

ruling over
Like a roaring lion or a charging bear is a wicked man ruling over a helpless people.

28 : 15

rumors
The words of gossip are like choice morsels; they go down to a man's inmost parts.

18 : 8

run
When you walk, your steps will not be hampered; when you run, you will not stumble.

4 : 12

The name of the Lord is a strong tower; the righteous run to it and are safe.

18 : 10

run from evil
Keep to a path far from her, do not go near the door of her house,

5 : 8

Do not let your heart turn to her ways or stray into her paths.

7 : 25

running
Drink water from your own cistern,
running water from your own well.
5 : 15

A man tomented by the guilt of murder
will be a fugitive till death; let no one
support him.
28 : 17

running water
Drink water from your own cistern,
running water from your own well.
5 : 15

running with the wrong crowd
He who keeps the law is a discerning
son, but a companion of gluttons
disgraces his father.
28 : 7

rush
for their feet rush into sin, they are swift
to shed blood.
1 : 16

a heart that devises wicked schemes,
feet that are quick to rush into evil,
6 : 18

rush into evil
a heart that devises wicked schemes,
feet that are quick to rush into evil,
6 : 18

rush into sin
for their feet rush into sin, they are swift
to shed blood.
1 : 16

ruthless
A kindhearted woman gains respect, but
ruthless men gain only wealth.
11 : 16

A kind man benefits himself, but a cruel
man brings trouble on himself.
11 : 17

ruthless men
A kindhearted woman gains respect, but
ruthless men gain only wealth.
11 : 16

S

sacrifice

Wisdom is supreme; therefore get wisdom. Though it cost all you have, get understanding.

4 : 7

The Lord detests the sacrifice of the wicked, but the prayer of the upright pleases him.

15 : 8

To do what is right and just is more acceptable to the Lord than sacrifice.

21 : 3

The sacrifice of the wicked is detestable -- how much more so when brought with evil intent!

21 : 27

safe

He who puts up security for another will surely suffer, but whoever refuses to strike hands in pledge is safe.

11 : 15

The name of the Lord is a strong tower; the righteous run to it and are safe.

18 : 10

Love and faithfulness keep a king safe; through love his throne is made secure.

20 : 28

He whose walk is blameless is kept safe, but he whose ways are perverse will suddenly fall.

28 : 18

Fear of man will prove to be a snare, but whoever trusts in the Lord is kept safe.

29 : 25

safety

but whoever listens to me will live in safety and be at ease, without fear of harm."

1 : 33

Wisdom will save you from the ways of wicked men, from men whose words are perverse,

2 : 12

Then you will go on your way in safety, and your foot will not stumble;

3 : 23

The wicked man flees though no one pursues, but the righteous are as bold as a lion.

28 : 1

He who trusts in himself is a fool, but he who walks in wisdom is kept safe.

28 : 26

Every word of God is flawless; he is a shield to those who take refuge in him.

30 : 5

said

he taught me and said, "Lay hold of my words with all your heart; keep my commands and you will live.

4 : 4

if you have been trapped by what you said, ensnared by the words of your mouth,

6 : 2

She took hold of him and kissed him and with a brazen face she said:

7 : 13

salary

The house of the righteous contains great treasure, but the income of the wicked brings them trouble.

15 : 6

salvation

The fruit of the righteous is a tree of life, and he who wins souls is wise.

11 : 30

The fear of the Lord is a fountain of life, turning a man from the snares of death.

14 : 27

The name of the Lord is a strong tower; the righteous run to it and are safe.

18 : 10

Punish him with the rod and save his soul from death.

23 : 14

same mistake

Do not answer a fool according to his folly, or you will be like him yourself.

26 : 4

sample

Those who linger over wine, who go to sample bowls of mixed wine,

23 : 30

sand

Stone is heavy and sand a burden, but provocation by a fool is heavier than both.

27 : 3

sashes

She makes linen garments and sells them, and supplies the merchants with sashes.

31 : 24

satisfaction

From the fruit of his lips a man is filled with good things as surely as the work of his hands rewards him.

12 : 14

The sluggard craves and gets nothing, but the desires of the diligent are fully satisfied.

13 : 4

He who loves pleasure will become poor; whoever loves wine and oil will never be rich.

21 : 17

satisfied

The sluggard craves and gets nothing, but the desires of the diligent are fully satisfied.

13 : 4

From the fruit of his mouth a man's stomach is filled; with the harvest from his lips he is satisfied.

18 : 20

Death and Destruction are never satisfied, and neither are the eyes of man.

27 : 20

"The leech has two daughters. 'Give! Give!' they cry. "There are three things that are never satisfied, four that never say, 'Enough!':

30 : 15

the grave, the barren womb, land, which is never satisfied with water, and fire, which never says, 'Enough!'

30 : 16

satisfy

A loving doe, a graceful deer -- may her breasts satisfy you always, may you ever be captivated by her love.

5 : 19

Men do not despise a thief if he steals to
satisfy his hunger when he is starving.

6 : 30

satisfy his hunger
Men do not despise a thief if he steals to
satisfy his hunger when he is starving.

6 : 30

save
Wisdom will save you from the ways of
wicked men, from men whose words
are perverse,

2 : 12

It will save you also from the
adulteress, from the wayward wife with
her seductive words,

2 : 16

Punish him with the rod and save his
soul from death.

23 : 14

saved
The name of the Lord is a strong tower;
the righteous run to it and are safe.

18 : 10

saves
The words of the wicked lie in wait for
blood, but the speech of the upright
rescues them.

12 : 6

A truthful witness saves lives, but a
false witness is deceitful.

14 : 25

saves lives
A truthful witness saves lives, but a
false witness is deceitful.

14 : 25

savings
He who gathers crops in summer is a
wise son, but he who sleeps during
harvest is a disgraceful son.

10 : 5

Dishonest money dwindles away, but he
who gathers money little by little makes
it grow.

13 : 11

A good man leaves an inheritance for
his children's children, but a sinner's
wealth is stored up for the righteous.

13 : 22

In the house of the wise are stores of
choice food and oil, but a foolish man
devours all he has.

21 : 20

saw
I saw among the simple, I noticed
among the young men, a youth who
lacked judgment.

7 : 7

I applied my heart to what I observed
and learned a lesson from what I saw:

24 : 32

say
If they say, "Come along with us; let's
lie in wait for someone's blood, let's
waylay some harmless soul;

1 : 11

Do not say to your neighbor, "Come
back later; I'll give it tomorrow" --
when you now have it with you.

3 : 28

Listen, my son, accept what I say, and
the years of your life will be many.

4 : 10

My son, pay attention to what I say;
listen closely to my words.

4 : 20

Now then, my sons, listen to me; do not
turn aside from what I say.

5 : 7

You will say, "How I hated discipline!
How my heart spurned correction!

5 : 12

Say to wisdom, "You are my sister,"
and call understanding your kinsman;

7 : 4

Now then, my sons, listen to me; pay
attention to what I say.

7 : 24

Listen, for I have worthy things to say; I
open my lips to speak what is right.

8 : 6

Who can say, "I have kept my heart
pure; I am clean and without sin"?

20 : 9

Do not say, "I'll pay you back for this
wrong!" Wait for the Lord, and he will
deliver you.

20 : 22

"They hit me," you will say, "but I'm
not hurt! They beat me, but I don't feel
it! When will I wake up so I can find
another drink?"

23 : 35

Wisdom is too high for a fool; in the
assembly at the gate he has nothing to
say.

24 : 7

If you say, "But we knew nothing about
this," does not he who weighs the heart
perceive it? Does not he who guards
your life know it? Will he not repay
each person according to what he has
done?

24 : 12

Do not say, "I'll do to him as he has
done to me; I'll pay that man back for
what he did."

24 : 29

it is better for him to say to you, "Come
up here," than for him to humiliate you
before a nobleman. What you have seen
with your eyes

25 : 7

Otherwise, I may have too much and
disown you and say, 'Who is the Lord?'
Or I may become poor and steal, and so
dishonor the name of my God.

30 : 9

sayings

for understanding proverbs and
parables, the sayings and riddles of the
wise.

1 : 6

Pay attention and listen to the sayings
of the wise; apply your heart to what I
teach,

22 : 17

Have I not written thirty sayings for
you, sayings of counsel and knowledge,

22 : 20

These also are sayings to the wise: To
show partiality in judging is not good:

24 : 23

The sayings of Agur son of Jakeh -- an
oracle: This man declared to Ithiel, to
Ithiel and to Ucal;

30 : 1

The sayings of King Lemuel -- an
oracle his mother taught him:

31 : 1

sayings of the wise

Pay attention and listen to the sayings
of the wise; apply your heart to what I
teach,

22 : 17

scales

The Lord abhors dishonest scales, but
accurate weights are his delight.

11 : 1

Honest scales and balances are from the
Lord; all the weights in the bag are of
his making.

16 : 11

417

The Lord detests differing weights, and dishonest scales do not please him.

20 : 23

Stone is heavy and sand a burden, but provocation by a fool is heavier than both.

27 : 3

scarcity

and poverty will come on you like a bandit and scarcity like an armed man.

6 : 11

and poverty will come on you like a bandit and scarcity like an armed man.

24 : 34

scarlet

When it snows, she has no fear for her household; for all of them are clothed in scarlet.

31 : 21

scarred conscience

"This is the way of an adulteress: She eats and wipes her mouth and says, 'I've done nothing wrong.'

30 : 20

scents

Perfume and incense bring joy to the heart, and the pleasantness of one's friend springs from his earnest counsel.

27 : 9

scheme

He who plots evil will be known as a schemer,

24 : 8

schemer

He who plots evil will be known as a schemer,

24 : 8

schemes

they will eat the fruit of their ways and be filled with the fruit of their schemes.

1 : 31

a heart that devises wicked schemes, feet that are quick to rush into evil,

6 : 18

The schemes of folly are sin, and men detest a mocker.

24 : 9

school

The teaching of the wise is a fountain of life, turning a man from the snares of death.

13 : 14

scoffs

If a wise man goes to court with a fool, the fool rages and scoffs, and there is no peace.

29 : 9

scoop fire

Can a man scoop fire into his lap without his clothes being burned?

6 : 27

scorched

Can a man walk on hot coals without his feet being scorched?

6 : 28

scorching

A scoundrel plots evil, and his speech is like a scorching fire.

16 : 27

scorn

Do not speak to a fool, for he will scorn the wisdom of your words.

23 : 9

scorns

He who scorns instruction will pay for it, but he who respects a command is rewarded.

13 : 13

The eye that mocks a father, that scorns obedience to a mother, will be pecked out by the ravens of the valley, will be eaten by the vultures.

30 : 17

scoundrel

A scoundrel and villain, who goes about with a corrupt mouth,

6 : 12

A scoundrel plots evil, and his speech is like a scorching fire.

16 : 27

Scripture

Every word of God is flawless; he is a shield to those who take refuge in him.

30 : 5

Do not add to his words, or he will rebuke you and prove you a liar.

30 : 6

sea

by his knowledge the deeps were divided, and the clouds let drop the dew.

3 : 20

when he established the clouds above and fixed securely the fountains of the deep,

8 : 28

when he gave the sea its boundary so the waters would not overstep his command, and when he marked out the foundations of the earth.

8 : 29

seamstress

She makes linen garments and sells them, and supplies the merchants with sashes.

31 : 24

search

and if you look for it as for silver and search for it as for hidden treasure,

2 : 4

The heart of the discerning acquires knowledge; the ears of the wise seek it out.

18 : 15

A sluggard does not plow in season; so at harvest time he looks but finds nothing.

20 : 4

It is the glory of God to conceal a matter; to search out a matter is the glory of kings.

25 : 2

search out

It is the glory of God to conceal a matter; to search out a matter is the glory of kings.

25 : 2

searches

He who seeks good finds goodwill, but evil comes to him who searches for it.

11 : 27

The lamp of the Lord searches the spirit of a man; it searches out his inmost being.

20 : 27

searches out

The lamp of the Lord searches the spirit of a man; it searches out his inmost being.

20 : 27

seas

You will be like one sleeping on the high seas, lying on top of the rigging.

23 : 34

the way of an eagle in the sky, the way of a snake on a rock, the way of a ship on the high seas, and the way of a man with a maiden.

30 : 19

seasick

You will be like one sleeping on the high seas, lying on top of the rigging.

23 : 34

season

A sluggard does not plow in season; so at harvest time he looks but finds nothing.

20 : 4

seat

She sits at the door of her house, on a seat at the highest point of the city,

9 : 14

Her husband is respected at the city gate, where he takes his seat among the elders of the land.

31 : 23

second chance

for though a righteous man falls seven times, he rises again, but the wicked are brought down by calamity.

24 : 16

secrecy

One man pretends to be rich, yet has nothing; another pretends to be poor, yet has great wealth.

13 : 7

secret

Stolen water is sweet; food eaten in secret is delicious!"

9 : 17

A gossip betrays a confidence, but a trustworthy man keeps a secret.

11 : 13

A wicked man accepts a bribe in secret to pervert the course of justice.

17 : 23

A gossip betrays a confidence; so avoid a man who talks too much.

20 : 19

A gift given in secret soothes anger, and a bribe concealed in the cloak pacifies great wrath.

21 : 14

secret to prosperity

A generous man will prosper; he who refreshes others will himself be refreshed.

11 : 25

secure

He who fears the Lord has a secure fortress, and for his children it will be a refuge.

14 : 26

Love and faithfulness keep a king safe; through love his throne is made secure.

20 : 28

for riches do not endure forever, and a crown is not secure for all generations.

27 : 24

If a king judges the poor with fairness, his throne will always be secure.

29 : 14

securely

when he established the clouds above and fixed securely the fountains of the deep,

8 : 28

The man of integrity walks securely, but he who takes crooked paths will be found out.

10 : 9

security
My son, if you have put up security for
your neighbor, if you have struck hands
in pledge for another,

6 : 1

He who puts up security for another
will surely suffer, but whoever refuses
to strike hands in pledge is safe.

11 : 15

A man lacking in judgment strikes
hands in pledge and puts up security for
his neighbor.

17 : 18

Take the garment of one who puts up
security for a stranger; hold it in pledge
if he does it for a wayward woman.

20 : 16

Do not be a man who strikes hands in
pledge or puts up security for debts;

22 : 26

Like a bird that strays from its nest is a
man who strays from his home.

27 : 8

Take a garment of one who puts up
security for a stranger; hold it in pledge
if he does it for a wayward woman.

27 : 13

seduced
With persuasive words she led him
astray; she seduced him with her
smooth talk.

7 : 21

seductive
It will save you also from the
adulteress, from the wayward wife with
her seductive words,

2 : 16

they will keep you from the adulteress,
from the wayward wife with her
seductive words.

7 : 5

seductive words
they will keep you from the adulteress,
from the wayward wife with her
seductive words.

7 : 5

seductress
now in the street, now in the squares, at
every corner she lurks.

7 : 12

I have perfumed my bed with myrrh,
aloes and cinnamon.

7 : 17

Come, let's drink deep of love till
morning; let's enjoy ourselves with
love!

7 : 18

My husband is not at home; he has gone
on a long journey.

7 : 19

see
Ears that hear and eyes that see -- the
Lord has made them both.

20 : 12

A prudent man sees danger and takes
refuge, but the simple keep going and
suffer for it.

22 : 3

Do you see a man skilled in his work?
He will serve before kings, he will not
serve before obscure men.

22 : 29

Your eyes will see strange sights and
your mind imagine confusing things.

23 : 33

or the Lord will see and disapprove and
turn his wrath away from him.

24 : 18

Do you see a man wise in his own eyes?
There is more hope for a fool than for
him.

26 : 12

The prudent see danger and take refuge, but the simple keep going and suffer for it.

27 : 12

When the wicked thrive, so does sin, but the righteous will see their downfall.

29 : 16

Do you see a man who speaks in haste? There is more hope for a fool than for him.

29 : 20

seeing

it is better for him to say to you, "Come up here," than for him to humiliate you before a nobleman. What you have seen with your eyes

25 : 7

seek

Blessed is the man who finds wisdom, the man who gains understanding,

3 : 13

I love those who love me, and those who seek me find me.

8 : 17

The mocker seeks wisdom and finds none, but knowledge comes easily to the discerning.

14 : 6

The heart of the discerning acquires knowledge; the ears of the wise seek it out.

18 : 15

It is not good to eat too much honey, not is it honorable to seek one's own honor.

25 : 27

Evil men do not understand justice, but those who seek the Lord understand it fully.

28 : 5

Bloodthirsty men hate a man of integrity and seek to kill the upright.

29 : 10

Many seek an audience with a ruler, but it is from the Lord that man gets justice.

29 : 26

seek the Lord

Evil men do not understand justice, but those who seek the Lord understand it fully.

28 : 5

seeking

Make plans by seeking advice; if you wage war, obtain guidance.

20 : 18

seeking advice

Make plans by seeking advice; if you wage war, obtain guidance.

20 : 18

seeking after evil

The truly righteous man attains life, but he who pursues evil goes to his death.

11 : 19

seeking counsel

A mocker resents correction; he will not consult the wise.

15 : 12

Plans fail for lack of counsel, but with many advisers they succeed.

15 : 22

Make plans by seeking advice; if you wage war, obtain guidance.

20 : 18

seeking favor

then do this, my son, to free yourself, since you have fallen into your neighbor's hands: Go and humble yourself; press your plea with your neighbor!

6 : 3

seeking wisdom
The mocker seeks wisdom and finds none, but knowledge comes easily to the discerning.

14 : 6

Of what use is money in the hand of a fool, since he has no desire to get wisdom?

17 : 16

seeks
He who seeks good finds goodwill, but evil comes to him who searches for it.

11 : 27

The discerning heart seeks knowledge, but the mouth of a fool feeds on folly.

15 : 14

seem
All a man's ways seem innocent to him, but motives are weighed by the Lord.

16 : 2

All a man's ways seem right to him, but the Lord weighs the heart.

21 : 2

seems
The way of a fool seems right to him, but a wise man listens to advice.

12 : 15

There is a way that seems right to a man, but in the end it leads to death.

14 : 12

The first to present his case seems right, till another comes forward and questions him.

18 : 17

seems right
There is a way that seems right to a man, but in the end it leads to death.

14 : 12

There is a way that seems right to a man, but in the end it leads to death.

16 : 25

seen
it is better for him to say to you, "Come up here," than for him to humiliate you before a nobleman. What you have seen with your eyes

25 : 7

sees
A prudent man sees danger and takes refuge, but the simple keep going and suffer for it.

22 : 3

A rich man may be wise in his own eyes, but a poor man who has discernment sees through him.

28 : 11

She sees that her trading is profitable, and her lamp does not go out at night.

31 : 18

seizes
Like one who seizes a dog by the ears is a passer-by who meddles in a quarrel not his own.

26 : 17

seldom
Seldom set foot in your neighbor's house -- too much of you, and he will hate you.

25 : 17

selects
She selects wool and flax and works with eager hands.

31 : 13

self-centeredness
One man pretends to be rich, yet has nothing; another pretends to be poor, yet has great wealth.

13 : 7

self-control
He who guards his lips guards his life, but he who speaks rashly will come to ruin.

13 : 3

A gentle answer turns away wrath, but a harsh word stirs up anger.

15 : 1

Like a city whose walls are broken down is a man who lacks self-control.

25 : 28

A fool gives full vent to his anger, but a wise man keeps himself under control.

29 : 11

self-destruct
Pride goes before destruction, a haughty spirit before a fall.

16 : 18

Like a city whose walls are broken down is a man who lacks self-control.

25 : 28

self-destruction
These men lie in wait for their own blood; they waylay only themselves!

1 : 18

self-discipline
He who guards his mouth and his tongue keeps himself from calamity.

21 : 23

selfish
Do not say to your neighbor, "Come back later; I'll give it tomorrow" -- when you now have it with you.

3 : 28

An unfriendly man pursues selfish ends; he defies all sound judgment.

18 : 1

selfish gains
An unfriendly man pursues selfish ends; he defies all sound judgment.

18 : 1

selfishness
People curse the man who hoards grain, but blessing crowns him who is willing to sell.

11 : 26

An unfriendly man pursues selfish ends; he defies all sound judgment.

18 : 1

selflessness
Do not say to your neighbor, "Come back later; I'll give it tomorrow" -- when you now have it with you.

3 : 28

self-motivator
It has no commander, no overseer or ruler,

6 : 7

self-reliance
He who trusts in himself is a fool, but he who walks in wisdom is kept safe.

28 : 26

self-respect
Avoid it, do not travel on it; turn from it and go on your way.

4 : 15

self-starter
It has no commander, no overseer or ruler,

6 : 7

sell
Buy the truth and do not sell it; get wisdom, discipline and understanding.

23 : 23

selling
People curse the man who hoards grain, but blessing crowns him who is willing to sell.

11 : 26

sells
She makes linen garments and sells them, and supplies the merchants with sashes.

31 : 24

send

As vinegar to the teeth and smoke to the eyes, so is a sluggard to those who send him.

10 : 26

for those two will send sudden destruction upon them, and who knows what calamities they can bring?

24 : 22

Like the coolness of snow at harvest time is a trustworthy messenger to those who send him; he refreshes the spirit of his masters.

25 : 13

sending

Like cutting off one's feet or drinking violence is the sending of a message by the hand of a fool.

26 : 6

sent

She has sent out her maids, and she calls from the highest point of the city.

9 : 3

An evil man is bent only on rebellion; a merciless official will be sent against him.

17 : 11

teaching you true and reliable words, so that you can give sound answers to him who sent you?

22 : 21

separates

A perverse man stirs up dissension, and a gossip separates close friends.

16 : 28

He who covers over an offense promotes love, but whoever repeats the matter separates close friends.

17 : 9

servant

He who brings trouble on his family will inherit only wind, and the fool will be servant to the wise.

11 : 29

Better to be a nobody and yet have a servant than pretend to be somebody and have no food.

12 : 9

A king delights in a wise servant, but a shameful servant incurs his wrath.

14 : 35

A wise servant will rule over a disgraceful son, and will share the inheritance as one of the brothers.

17 : 2

The rich rule over the poor, and the borrower is servant to the lender.

22 : 7

You will have plenty of goat's milk to feed you and your family and to nourish your servant girls.

27 : 27

A servant cannot be corrected by mere words; though he understands, he will not respond.

29 : 19

If a man pampers his servant from youth, he will bring grief in the end.

29 : 21

Do not slander a servant to his master, or he will curse you, and you will pay for it.

30 : 10

a servant who becomes a king, a fool who is full of food,

30 : 22

She gets up while it is still dark; she provides food for her family and portions for her servant girls.

31 : 15

servant girls
She gets up while it is still dark; she
provides food for her family and
portions for her servant girls
31 : 15

servants
A large population is a king's glory, but
without subjects a prince is ruined.
14 : 28

serve
Do you see a man skilled in his work?
He will serve before kings, he will not
serve before obscure men.
22 : 29

She opens her arms to the poor and
extends her hands to the needy.
31 : 20

serving the Lord
The way of the Lord is a refuge for the
righteous, but it is the ruin of those who
do evil.
10 : 29

Better a poor man whose walk is
blameless than a rich man whose ways
are perverse.
28 : 6

set
I was there when he set the heavens in
place, when he marked out the horizon
on the face of the deep,
8 : 27

She has prepared her meat and mixed
her wine; she has also set her table.
9 : 2

those whose teeth are swords and whose
jaws are set with knives to devour the
poor from the earth, the needy from
among mankind.
30 : 14

set aside
yet it stores its provisions in summer
and gathers its food at harvest.
6 : 8

set foot
my son, do not go along with them, do
not set foot on their paths;
1 : 15

Do not set foot on the path of the
wicked or walk in the way of evil men.
4 : 14

Seldom set foot in your neighbor's
house -- too much of you, and he will
hate you.
25 : 17

set in
at twilight, as the day was fading, as the
dark of night set in.
7 : 9

set the heavens
By wisdom the Lord laid the earth's
foundations, by understanding he set the
heavens in place;
3 : 19

set up
Do not move an ancient boundary stone
set up by your forefathers.
22 : 28

sets
She sets about her work vigorously; her
arms are strong for her tasks.
31 : 17

settings
A word aptly spoken is like apples of
gold in settings of silver.
25 : 11

settings of silver
A word aptly spoken is like apples of
gold in settings of silver.
25 : 11

settled

before the mountains were settled in place, before the hills, I was given birth,

8 : 25

settles

Casting the lot settles disputes and keeps strong opponents apart.

18 : 18

seven

There are six things the Lord hates, seven that are detestable to him:

6 : 16

Wisdom has built her house; she has hewn out its seven pillars.

9 : 1

for though a righteous man falls seven times, he rises again, but the wicked are brought down by calamity.

24 : 16

The sluggard is wiser in his own eyes than seven men who answer discreetly.

26 : 16

Though his speech is charming, do not believe him, for seven abominations fill his heart.

26 : 25

seven deadly sins

There are six things the Lord hates, seven that are detestable to him:

6 : 16

sevenfold

Yet if he is caught, he must pay sevenfold, though it costs him all the wealth of his house.

6 : 31

sewing

She makes linen garments and sells them, and supplies the merchants with sashes.

31 : 24

sexual immorality

My husband is not at home; he has gone on a long journey.

7 : 19

"This is the way of an adulteress: She eats and wipes her mouth and says, 'I've done nothing wrong.'

30 : 20

sexual temptation

Keep to a path far from her, do not go near the door of her house,

5 : 8

shakes

"Under three things the earth trembles, under four it cannot bear up:

30 : 21

shame

The wise inherit honor, but fools he holds up to shame.

3 : 35

Blows and disgrace are his lot, and his shame will never be wiped away;

6 : 33

The righteous hate what is false, but the wicked bring shame and disgrace.

13 : 5

He who ignores discipline comes to poverty and shame, but whoever heeds correction is honored.

13 : 18

When wickedness comes, so does contempt, and with shame comes disgrace.

18 : 3

He who answers before listening -- that is his folly and his shame.

18 : 13

He who robs his father and drives out his mother is a son who brings shame and disgrace.

19 : 26

do not bring hastily to court, for what will you do in the end if your neighbor puts you to shame?

25 : 8

or he who hears it may shame you and you will never lose your bad reputation.

25 : 10

shameful
A king delights in a wise servant, but a shameful servant incurs his wrath.

14 : 35

shaping
For these commands are a lamp, this teaching is a light, and the corrections of discipline are the way to life,

6 : 23

share
throw in your lot with us, and we will share a common purse" --

1 : 14

Do not say to your neighbor, "Come back later; I'll give it tomorrow" -- when you now have it with you.

3 : 28

Each heart knows its own bitterness, and no one else can share its joy.

14 : 10

Better to be lowly in spirit and among the oppressed than to share plunder with the proud.

16 : 19

A wise servant will rule over a disgraceful son, and will share the inheritance as one of the brothers.

17 : 2

Better to live on a corner of the roof than share a house with a quarrelsome wife.

21 : 9

teaching you true and reliable words, so that you can give sound answers to him who sent you?

22 : 21

Better to live on a corner of the roof than share a house with a quarrelsome wife.

25 : 24

shared
Let them be yours alone, never to be shared with strangers.

5 : 17

shares
A generous man will himself be blessed, for he shares his food with the poor.

22 : 9

sharing
All day long he craves for more, but the righteous give without sparing.

21 : 26

sharing knowledge
The lips of the wise spread knowledge; not so the hearts of fools.

15 : 7

sharp
but in the end she is bitter as gall, sharp as a double-edged sword.

5 : 4

Like a club or a sword or a sharp arrow is the man who gives false testimony against his neighbor.

25 : 18

sharp arrow
Like a club or a sword or a sharp arrow is the man who gives false testimony against his neighbor.

25 : 18

sharpens
As iron sharpens iron, so one man sharpens another.

27 : 17

she
for she is more profitable than silver and yields better returns than gold.

3 : 14

She is more precious than rubies; nothing you desire can compare with her.

3 : 15

Do not forsake wisdom, and she will protect you; love her, and she will watch over you.

4 : 6

Esteem her, and she will exalt you; embrace her, and she will honor you.

4 : 8

She will set a garland of grace on your head and present you with a crown of splendor.

4 : 9

She is loud and defiant, her feet never stay at home;

7 : 11

now in the street, now in the squares, at every corner she lurks.

7 : 12

She took hold of him and kissed him and with a brazen face she said:

7 : 13

With persuasive words she led him astray; she seduced him with her smooth talk.

7 : 21

She sits at the door of her house, on a seat at the highest point of the city,

9 : 14

shed
for their feet rush into sin, they are swift to shed blood.

1 : 16

haughty eyes, a lying tongue, hands that shed innocent blood,

6 : 17

shed blood
for their feet rush into sin, they are swift to shed blood.

1 : 16

shelter
The prudent see danger and take refuge, but the simple keep going and suffer for it.

27 : 12

shield
He holds victory in store for the upright, he is a shield to those whose walk is blameless,

2 : 7

Every word of God is flawless; he is a shield to those who take refuge in him.

30 : 5

shiftless man
Laziness brings on deep sleep, and the shiftless man goes hungry.

19 : 15

shines
The light of the righteous shines brightly, but the lamp of the wicked is snuffed out.

13 : 9

shining
The path of the righteous is like the first gleam of dawn, shining ever brighter till the full light of day.

4 : 18

ship
the way of an eagle in the sky, the way
of a snake on a rock, the way of a ship
on the high seas, and the way of a man
with a maiden.

30 : 19

ships
She is like the merchant ships, bringing
her food from afar.

31 : 14

shooting
Like a madman shooting firebrands or
deadly arrows

26 : 18

short
The fear of the Lord adds length to life,
but the years of the wicked are cut
short.

10 : 27

should
Should your springs overflow in the
streets, your streams of water in the
public squares?

5 : 16

The lips of the king speak as an oracle,
and his mouth should not betray justice.

16 : 10

Train a child in the way he should go,
and when he is old he will not turn from
it.

22 : 6

shout
beside the gates leading into the city, at
the entrances, she cries aloud:

8 : 3

"To you, O men, I call out; I raise my
voice to all mankind.

8 : 4

shouts
She has sent out her maids, and she
calls from the highest point of the city.

9 : 3

When the righteous prosper, the city
rejoices; when the wicked perish, there
are shouts of joy.

11 : 10

shouts of joy
When the righteous prosper, the city
rejoices; when the wicked perish, there
are shouts of joy.

11 : 10

show
for jealousy arouses a husband's fury,
and he will show no mercy when he
takes revenge.

6 : 34

Do not wear yourself out to get rich;
have the wisdom to show restraint.

23 : 4

These also are sayings to the wise: To
show partiality in judging is not good:

24 : 23

show partiality
To show partiality is not good -- yet a
man will do wrong for a piece of bread.

28 : 21

show restraint
Do not wear yourself out to get rich;
have the wisdom to show restraint.

23 : 4

showing compassion
He who despises his neighbor sins, but
blessed is he who is kind to the needy.

14 : 21

showing kindness
In doing this, you will heap burning
coals on his head, and the Lord will
reward you.

25 : 22

showing mercy

He who increases his wealth by
exorbitant interest amasses it for
another, who will be kind to the poor.

28 : 8

showing off

The lazy man does not roast his game,
but the diligent man prizes his
possessions.

12 : 27

shows

He who heeds discipline shows the way
to life, but whoever ignores correction
leads others astray.

10 : 17

Like a gold ring in a pig's snout is a
beautiful woman who shows no
discretion.

11 : 22

He who oppresses the poor shows
contempt for their Maker, but whoever
is kind to the needy honors God.

14 : 31

A fool spurns the father's discipline, but
whoever heeds correction shows
prudence.

15 : 5

He who mocks the poor shows
contempt for their Maker; whoever
gloats over disaster will not go
unpunished.

17 : 5

shows contempt

He who oppresses the poor shows
contempt for their Maker, but whoever
is kind to the needy honors God.

14 : 31

He who mocks the poor shows
contempt for their Maker; whoever
gloats over disaster will not go
unpunished.

17 : 5

shows prudence

A fool spurns the father's discipline, but
whoever heeds correction shows
prudence.

15 : 5

shows the way

He who heeds discipline shows the way
to life, but whoever ignores correction
leads others astray.

10 : 17

shun

Do not be wise in your own eyes; fear
the Lord and shun evil.

3 : 7

shun evil

Do not be wise in your own eyes; fear
the Lord and shun evil.

3 : 7

A wise man fears the Lord and shuns
evil, but a fool is hotheaded and
reckless.

14 : 16

shunned

The poor are shunned even by their
neighbors, but the rich have many
friends.

14 : 20

A poor man is shunned by all his
relatives -- how much more do his
friends avoid him! Though he pursues
them with pleading, they are nowhere to
be found.

19 : 7

shuns

A wise man fears the Lord and shuns
evil, but a fool is hotheaded and
reckless.

14 : 16

shuts
If a man shuts his ears to the cry of the poor, he too will cry out and not be answered.

21 : 13

sick
Hope deferred makes the heart sick, but a longing fulfilled is a tree of life.

13 : 12

You will vomit up the little you have eaten and will have wasted your compliments.

23 : 8

If you find honey, just eat enough -- too much of it, and you will vomit.

25 : 16

sickness
A man's spirit sustains him in sickness, but a crushed spirit who can bear?

18 : 14

side
Then I was the craftsman at his side. I was filled with delight day after day, rejoicing always in his presence,

8 : 30

sight
Then you will win favor and a good name in the sight of God and man.

3 : 4

My son, preserve sound judgment and discernment, do not let them out of your sight;

3 : 21

Do not let them out of your sight, keep them within your heart;

4 : 21

The poor man and the oppressor have this in common: The Lord gives sight to the eyes of both.

29 : 13

signals
who winks with his eye, signals with his feet and motions with his fingers,

6 : 13

significant
"Four things on earth are small, yet they are extremely wise:

30 : 24

locusts have no king, yet they advance together in ranks;

30 : 27

a lizard can be caught with the hand, yet it is found in kings' palaces.

30 : 28

silent
Even a fool is thought wise if he keeps silent, and discerning if he holds his tongue.

17 : 28

silliness
Like a gold ring in a pig's snout is a beautiful woman who shows no discretion.

11 : 22

silver
and if you look for it as for silver and search for it as for hidden treasure,

2 : 4

for she is more profitable than silver and yields better returns than gold.

3 : 14

Choose my instruction instead of silver, knowledge rather than choice gold,

8 : 10

My fruit is better than fine gold; what I yield surpasses choice silver.

8 : 19

The tongue of the righteous is choice silver, but the heart of the wicked is of little value.

10 : 20

How much better to get wisdom than gold, to choose understanding rather than silver!

16 : 16

The crucible for silver and the furnace for gold, but the Lord tests the heart.

17 : 3

A good name is more desirable than great riches; to be esteemed is better than silver or gold.

22 : 1

Remove the dross from the silver, and out comes material for the silversmith;

25 : 4

A word aptly spoken is like apples of gold in settings of silver.

25 : 11

The crucible for silver and the furnace for gold, but man is tested by the praise he receives.

27 : 21

silver or gold
The crucible for silver and the furnace for gold, but the Lord tests the heart.

17 : 3

A good name is more desirable than great riches; to be esteemed is better than silver or gold.

22 : 1

silversmith
Remove the dross from the silver, and out comes material for the silversmith;

25 : 4

simple
for giving prudence to the simple, knowledge and discretion to the young -

1 : 4

"How long will you simple ones love your simple ways? How long will mockers delight in mockery and fools hate knowledge?

1 : 22

For the waywardness of the simple will kill them, and the complacency of fools will destroy them;

1 : 32

I saw among the simple, I noticed among the young men, a youth who lacked judgment.

7 : 7

You who are simple, gain prudence; you who are foolish, gain understanding.

8 : 5

"Let all who are simple come in here!" she says to those who lack judgment.

9 : 4

Leave your simple ways and you will live; walk in the way of understanding.

9 : 6

"Let all who are simple come in here!" she says to those who lack judgment.

9 : 16

The simple inherit folly, but the prudent are crowned with knowledge.

14 : 18

Flog a mocker, and the simple will learn prudence; rebuke a discerning man, and he will gain knowledge.

19 : 25

When a mocker is punished, the simple gain wisdom; when a wise man is instructed, he gets knowledge.

21 : 11

A prudent man sees danger and takes refuge, but the simple keep going and suffer for it.

22 : 3

433

The prudent see danger and take refuge, but the simple keep going and suffer for it.

27 : 12

simple man

A simple man believes anything, but a prudent man gives thought to his steps.

14 : 15

simple ones

"How long will you simple ones love your simple ways? How long will mockers delight in mockery and fools hate knowledge?

1 : 22

simple ways

"How long will you simple ones love your simple ways? How long will mockers delight in mockery and fools hate knowledge?

1 : 22

Leave your simple ways and you will live; walk in the way of understanding.

9 : 6

sin

for their feet rush into sin, they are swift to shed blood.

1 : 16

The evil deeds of a wicked man ensnare him; the cords of his sin hold him fast.

5 : 22

There are six things the Lord hates, seven that are detestable to him:

6 : 16

a heart that devises wicked schemes, feet that are quick to rush into evil,

6 : 18

for the prostitute reduces you to a loaf of bread, and the adulteress preys upon your very life.

6 : 26

Can a man scoop fire into his lap without his clothes being burned?

6 : 27

He was going down the street near her corner, walking along in the direction of her house

7 : 8

When words are many, sin is not absent, but he who holds his tongue is wise.

10 : 19

The righteousness of the blameless makes a straight way for them, but the wicked are brought down by their own wickedness.

11 : 5

The righteousness of the upright delivers them, but the unfaithful are trapped by evil desires.

11 : 6

Fools mock at making amends for sin, but goodwill is found among the upright.

14 : 9

Righteousness exalts a nation, but sin is a disgrace to any people.

14 : 34

The Lord is far from the wicked but he hears the prayer of the righteous.

15 : 29

Through love and faithfulness sin is atoned for; through the fear of the Lord a man avoids evil.

16 : 6

He who loves a quarrel loves sin; he who builds a high gate invites destruction.

17 : 19

Who can say, "I have kept my heart pure; I am clean and without sin"?

20 : 9

Haughty eyes and a proud heart, the lamp of the wicked, are sin!

21 : 4

for a prostitute is a deep pit and a wayward wife is a narrow well.

23 : 27

The schemes of folly are sin, and men detest a mocker.

24 : 9

Death and Destruction are never satisfied, and neither are the eyes of man.

27 : 20

When a country is rebellious, it has many rulers, but a man of understanding and knowledge maintains order.

28 : 2

Better a poor man whose walk is blameless than a rich man whose ways are perverse.

28 : 6

Blessed is the man who always fears the Lord, but he who hardens his heart falls into trouble.

28 : 14

A man tomented by the guilt of murder will be a fugitive till death; let no one support him.

28 : 17

A man who loves wisdom brings joy to his father, but a companion of prostitutes squanders his wealth.

29 : 3

An evil man is snared by his own sin, but a righteous one can sing and be glad.

29 : 6

When the wicked thrive, so does sin, but the righteous will see their downfall.

29 : 16

those who are pure in their own eyes and yet are not cleansed of their filth;

30 : 12

those whose eyes are ever so haughty, whose glances are so disdainful;

30 : 13

"This is the way of an adulteress: She eats and wipes her mouth and says, 'I've done nothing wrong.'

30 : 20

sin destroys one's body

lest you give your best strength to others and your years to one who is cruel,

5 : 9

At the end of your life you will groan, when your flesh and body are spent.

5 : 11

since

But since you rejected me when I called and no one gave heed when I stretched out my hand,

1 : 24

since you ignored all my advice and would not accept my rebuke,

1 : 25

Since they hated knowledge and did not choose to fear the Lord,

1 : 29

Of what use is money in the hand of a fool, since he has no desire to get wisdom?

17 : 16

sincere

There is a way that seems right to a man, but in the end it leads to death.

16 : 25

sincerity

There is a way that seems right to a man, but in the end it leads to death.

14 : 12

All a man's ways seem right to him, but the Lord weighs the heart.

21 : 2

sinful

He whose walk is blameless is kept safe, but he whose ways are perverse will suddenly fall.

28 : 18

sing

An evil man is snared by his own sin, but a righteous one can sing and be glad.

29 : 6

sings

Like one who takes away a garment on a cold day, or like vinegar poured on soda, is one who sings songs to a heavy heart.

25 : 20

sinner

If the righteous receive their due on earth, how much more the ungodly and the sinner!

11 : 31

Righteousness guards the man of integrity, but wickedness overthrows the sinner.

13 : 6

Misfortune pursues the sinner, but prosperity is the reward of the righteous.

13 : 21

sinners

My son, if sinners entice you, do not give in to them.

1 : 10

Do not let your heart envy sinners, but always be zealous for the fear of the Lord.

23 : 17

The wicked man flees though no one pursues, but the righteous are as bold as a lion.

28 : 1

The accomplice of a thief is his own enemy; he is put under oath and dare not testify.

29 : 24

sins

He who despises his neighbor sins, but blessed is he who is kind to the needy.

14 : 21

He who conceals his sins does not prosper, but whoever confesses and renounces them finds mercy.

28 : 13

An angry man stirs up dissension, and a hot-tempered one commits many sins.

29 : 22

sister

Say to wisdom, "You are my sister," and call understanding your kinsman;

7 : 4

sit

When you sit to dine with a ruler, note well what is before you,

23 : 1

sits

She sits at the door of her house, on a seat at the highest point of the city,

9 : 14

When a king sits on his throne to judge, he winnows out all evil with his eyes.

20 : 8

six things
There are six things the Lord hates,
seven that are detestable to him:

6 : 16

skilled
Do you see a man skilled in his work?
He will serve before kings, he will not
serve before obscure men.

22 : 29

sky
Cast but a glance at riches, and they are
gone, for they will surely sprout wings
and fly off to the sky like an eagle.

23 : 5

the way of an eagle in the sky, the way
of a snake on a rock, the way of a ship
on the high seas, and the way of a man
with a maiden.

30 : 19

slack
One who is slack in his work is brother
to one who destroys.

18 : 9

slain
Many are the victims she has brought
down; her slain are a mighty throng.

7 : 26

slander
He who conceals his hatred has lying
lips, and whoever spreads slander is a
fool.

10 : 18

With his mouth the godless destroys his
neighbor, but through knowledge the
righteous escape.

11 : 9

The words of a gossip are like choice
morsels; they go down to a man's
inmost parts.

26 : 22

A lying tongue hates those it hurts, and
a flattering mouth works ruin.

26 : 28

Do not slander a servant to his master,
or he will curse you, and you will pay
for it.

30 : 10

slaughter
All at once he followed her like an ox
going to the slaughter, like a deer
stepping into a noose

7 : 22

Rescue those being led away to death;
hold back those staggering toward
slaughter.

24 : 11

slave
He who brings trouble on his family
will inherit only wind, and the fool will
be servant to the wise.

11 : 29

Diligent hands will rule, but laziness
ends in slave labor.

12 : 24

It is not fitting for a fool to live in
luxury -- how much worse for a slave to
rule over princes!

19 : 10

The rich rule over the poor, and the
borrower is servant to the lender.

22 : 7

Do not slander a servant to his master,
or he will curse you, and you will pay
for it.

30 : 10

slave labor
Diligent hands will rule, but laziness
ends in slave labor.

12 : 24

sleep

when you lie down, you will not be afraid; when you lie down, your sleep will be sweet.

3 : 24

For they cannot sleep till they do evil; they are robbed of slumber till they make someone fall.

4 : 16

Allow no sleep to your eyes, no slumber to your eyelids.

6 : 4

How long will you lie there, you sluggard? When will you get up from your sleep?

6 : 9

A little sleep, a little slumber, a little folding of the hands to rest--

6 : 10

When you walk, they will guide you; when you sleep, they will watch over you; when you awake, they will speak to you.

6 : 22

Laziness brings on deep sleep, and the shiftless man goes hungry.

19 : 15

Do not love sleep or you will grow poor; stay awake and you will have food to spare.

20 : 13

for drunkards and gluttons become poor, and drowsiness clothes them in rags.

23 : 21

A little sleep, a little slumber, a little folding of the hands to rest --

24 : 33

sleeping

You will be like one sleeping on the high seas, lying on top of the rigging.

23 : 34

sleeps

So is he who sleeps with another man's wife; no one who touches her will go unpunished.

6 : 29

He who gathers crops in summer is a wise son, but he who sleeps during harvest is a disgraceful son.

10 : 5

sling

Like tying a stone in a sling is the giving of honor to a fool.

26 : 8

sluggard

Go to the ant, you sluggard; consider its ways and be wise!

6 : 6

How long will you lie there, you sluggard? When will you get up from your sleep?

6 : 9

As vinegar to the teeth and smoke to the eyes, so is a sluggard to those who send him.

10 : 26

The sluggard craves and gets nothing, but the desires of the diligent are fully satisfied.

13 : 4

The way of the sluggard is blocked with thorns, but the path of the upright is a highway.

15 : 19

Laziness brings on deep sleep, and the shiftless man goes hungry.

19 : 15

The sluggard buries his hand in the dish; he will not even bring it back to his mouth!

19 : 24

A sluggard does not plow in season; so at harvest time he looks but finds nothing.

20 : 4

The sluggard says, "There is a lion outside!" or "I will be murdered in the streets!"

22 : 13

I went past the field of the sluggard, past the vineyard of the man who lacks judgment;

24 : 30

and poverty will come on you like a bandit and scarcity like an armed man.

24 : 34

The sluggard says, "There is a lion in the road, a fierce lion roaming the streets!"

26 : 13

As a door turns on its hinges, so a sluggard turns on his bed.

26 : 14

The sluggard buries his hand in the dish; he is too lazy to bring it back to his mouth.

26 : 15

The sluggard is wiser in his own eyes than seven men who answer discreetly.

26 : 16

sluggard's
The sluggard's craving will be the death of him, because his hands refuse to work.

21 : 25

slumber
For they cannot sleep till they do evil; they are robbed of slumber till they make someone fall.

4 : 16

Allow no sleep to your eyes, no slumber to your eyelids.

6 : 4

A little sleep, a little slumber, a little folding of the hands to rest--

6 : 10

A little sleep, a little slumber, a little folding of the hands to rest --

24 : 33

sly
As a north wind brings rain, so a sly tongue brings angry looks.

25 : 23

small
If you falter in times of trouble, how small is your strength!

24 : 10

"Four things on earth are small, yet they are extremely wise:

30 : 24

smile
A happy heart makes the face cheerful, but heartache crushes the spirit.

15 : 13

When a king's face brightens, it means life; his favor is like a rain cloud in spring.

16 : 15

smiles upon
The Lord detests men of perverse heart but he delights in those whose ways are blameless.

11 : 20

smoke

As vinegar to the teeth and smoke to the eyes, so is a sluggard to those who send him.

10 : 26

smooth

keeping you from the immoral woman, from the smooth tongue of the wayward wife.

6 : 24

With persuasive words she led him astray; she seduced him with her smooth talk.

7 : 21

smooth talk

With persuasive words she led him astray; she seduced him with her smooth talk.

7 : 21

smooth tongue

keeping you from the immoral woman, from the smooth tongue of the wayward wife.

6 : 24

smoother

For the lips of an adulteress drip honey, and her speech is smoother than oil;

5 : 3

smoothly

Do not gaze at wine when it is red, when it sparkles in the cup, when it goes down smoothly!

23 : 31

snake

In the end it bites like a snake and poisons like a viper.

23 : 32

the way of an eagle in the sky, the way of a snake on a rock, the way of a ship on the high seas, and the way of a man with a maiden.

30 : 19

snare

Free yourself, like a gazelle from the hand of the hunter, like a bird from the snare of the fowler.

6 : 5

till an arrow pierces his liver, like a bird darting into a snare, little knowing it will cost him his life.

7 : 23

A fool's mouth is his undoing, and his lips are a snare to his soul.

18 : 7

It is a trap for a man to dedicate something rashly and only later to consider his vows.

20 : 25

A fortune made by a lying tongue is a fleeting vapor and a deadly snare.

21 : 6

Fear of man will prove to be a snare, but whoever trusts in the Lord is kept safe.

29 : 25

snared

for the Lord will be your confidence and will keep your foot from being snared.

3 : 26

An evil man is snared by his own sin, but a righteous one can sing and be glad.

29 : 6

snares

The teaching of the wise is a fountain of life, turning a man from the snares of death.

13 : 14

The fear of the Lord is a fountain of life, turning a man from the snares of death.

14 : 27

In the paths of the wicked lie thorns and snares, but he who guards his soul stays far from them.

22 : 5

snarl

The mouth of an adulteress is a deep pit; he who is under the Lord's wrath will fall into it.

22 : 14

snatched

if you lack the means to pay, your very bed will be snatched from under you.

22 : 27

snout

Like a gold ring in a pig's snout is a beautiful woman who shows no discretion.

11 : 22

snow

Like the coolness of snow at harvest time is a trustworthy messenger to those who send him; he refreshes the spirit of his masters.

25 : 13

Like snow in summer or rain in harvest, honor is not fitting for a fool.

26 : 1

snows

When it snows, she has no fear for her household; for all of them are clothed in scarlet.

31 : 21

snuffed out

The light of the righteous shines brightly, but the lamp of the wicked is snuffed out.

13 : 9

If a man curses his father or mother, his lamp will be snuffed out in pitch darkness.

20 : 20

for the evil man has no future hope, and the lamp of the wicked will be snuffed out.

24 : 20

so

So I came out to meet you; I looked for you and have found you!

7 : 15

soda

Like one who takes away a garment on a cold day, or like vinegar poured on soda, is one who sings songs to a heavy heart.

25 : 20

Solomon

The proverbs of Solomon son of David, king of Israel:

1 : 1

When I was a boy in my father's house, still tender, and an only child of my mother,

4 : 3

Listen, my son, accept what I say, and the years of your life will be many.

4 : 10

The proverbs of Solomon: A wise son brings joy to his father, but a foolish son grief to his mother.

10 : 1

These are more proverbs of Solomon, copied by the men of Hezekiah king of Judah:

25 : 1

some

If they say, "Come along with us; let's lie in wait for someone's blood, let's waylay some harmless soul;

1 : 11

somebody

Better to be a nobody and yet have a servant than pretend to be somebody and have no food.

12 : 9

someone

For they cannot sleep till they do evil; they are robbed of slumber till they make someone fall.

4 : 16

Let another praise you, and not your own mouth; someone else, and not your own lips.

27 : 2

someone's

If they say, "Come along with us; let's lie in wait for someone's blood, let's waylay some harmless soul;

1 : 11

something

It is a trap for a man to dedicate something rashly and only later to consider his vows.

20 : 25

son

The proverbs of Solomon son of David, king of Israel:

1 : 1

Listen, my son, to your father's instruction and do not forsake your mother's teaching.

1 : 8

My son, if sinners entice you, do not give in to them.

1 : 10

my son, do not go along with them, do not set foot on their paths;

1 : 15

My son, if you accept my words and store up my commands within you,

2 : 1

My son, do not forget my teaching, but keep my commands in your heart,

3 : 1

My son, do not despise the Lord's discipline and do not resent his rebuke,

3 : 11

because the Lord disciplines those he loves, as a father the son he delights in.

3 : 12

My son, preserve sound judgment and discernment, do not let them out of your sight;

3 : 21

Listen, my son, accept what I say, and the years of your life will be many.

4 : 10

My son, pay attention to what I say; listen closely to my words.

4 : 20

My son, pay attention to my wisdom, listen well to my words of insight,

5 : 1

Why be captivated, my son, by an adulteress? Why embrace the bosom of another man's wife?

5 : 20

My son, if you have put up security for your neighbor, if you have struck hands in pledge for another,

6 : 1

then do this, my son, to free yourself, since you have fallen into your neighbor's hands: Go and humble yourself; press your plea with your neighbor!

6 : 3

My son, keep your father's commands and do not forsake your mother's teaching.

6 : 20

My son, keep my words and store up my commands within you.

7 : 1

The proverbs of Solomon: A wise son brings joy to his father, but a foolish son grief to his mother.

10 : 1

He who gathers crops in summer is a wise son, but he who sleeps during harvest is a disgraceful son.

10 : 5

A wise son heeds his father's instruction, but a mocker does not listen to rebuke.

13 : 1

He who spares the rod hates his son, but he who loves him is careful to discipline him.

13 : 24

A wise son brings joy to his father, but a foolish man despises his mother.

15 : 20

A wise servant will rule over a disgraceful son, and will share the inheritance as one of the brothers.

17 : 2

To have a fool for a son brings grief; there is no joy for the father of a fool.

17 : 21

A foolish son brings grief to his father and bitterness to the one who bore him.

17 : 25

A foolish son is his father's ruin, and a quarrelsome wife is like a constant dripping.

19 : 13

Discipline your son, for in that there is hope; do not be a willing party to his death.

19 : 18

He who robs his father and drives out his mother is a son who brings shame and disgrace.

19 : 26

Stop listening to instruction, my son, and you will stray from the words of knowledge.

19 : 27

My son, if your heart is wise, then my heart will be glad;

23 : 15

Listen, my son, and be wise, and keep your heart on the right path.

23 : 19

The father of a righteous man has great joy; he who has a wise son delights in him.

23 : 24

My son, give me your heart and let your eyes keep to my ways,

23 : 26

Eat honey, my son, for it is good; honey from the comb is sweet to your taste.

24 : 13

Fear the Lord and the king, my son, and do not join with the rebellious,

24 : 21

Be wise, my son, and bring joy to my heart; then I can answer anyone who treats me with contempt.

27 : 11

He who keeps the law is a discerning son, but a companion of gluttons disgraces his father.

28 : 7

Discipline your son, and he will give you peace; he will bring delight to your soul.

29 : 17

The sayings of Agur son of Jakeh -- an oracle: This man declared to Ithiel, to Ithiel and to Ucal;

30 : 1

"O my son, O son of my womb, O son of my vows,

31 : 2

son of David

The proverbs of Solomon son of David, king of Israel:

1 : 1

songs

Like one who takes away a garment on a cold day, or like vinegar poured on soda, is one who sings songs to a heavy heart.

25 : 20

sons

Listen, my sons, to a father's instruction; pay attention and gain understanding.

4 : 1

Now then, my sons, listen to me; do not turn aside from what I say.

5 : 7

Now then, my sons, listen to me; pay attention to what I say.

7 : 24

Now then, my sons, listen to me; blessed are those who keep my ways.

8 : 32

soothes

A gift given in secret soothes anger, and a bribe concealed in the cloak pacifies great wrath.

21 : 14

sorrow

Who has woe? Who has sorrow? Who has strife? Who has complaints? Who has needless bruises? Who has bloodshot eyes?

23 : 29

for the evil man has no future hope, and the lamp of the wicked will be snuffed out.

24 : 20

sorts

we will get all sorts of valuable things and fill our houses with plunder;

1 : 13

soul

If they say, "Come along with us; let's lie in wait for someone's blood, let's waylay some harmless soul;

1 : 11

For wisdom will enter your heart, and knowledge will be pleasant to your soul.

2 : 10

A longing fulfilled is sweet to the soul, but fools detest turning from evil.

13 : 19

Pleasant words are a honeycomb, sweet to the soul and healing to the bones.

16 : 24

A fool's mouth is his undoing, and his lips are a snare to his soul.

18 : 7

The words of gossip are like choice morsels; they go down to a man's inmost parts.

18 : 8

He who gets wisdom loves his own soul; he who cherishes understanding prospers.

19 : 8

The lamp of the Lord searches the spirit of a man; it searches out his inmost being.

20 : 27

In the paths of the wicked lie thorns and snares, but he who guards his soul stays far from them.

22 : 5

Punish him with the rod and save his soul from death.

23 : 14

Know also that wisdom is sweet to your soul; if you find it, there is a future hope for you, and your hope will not be cut off.

24 : 14

Like cold water to a weary soul is good news from a distant land.

25 : 25

Discipline your son, and he will give you peace; he will bring delight to your soul.

29 : 17

soul winning
The fruit of the righteous is a tree of life, and he who wins souls is wise.

11 : 30

sound advice
If a ruler listens to lies, all his officials become wicked.

29 : 12

sound answers
teaching you true and reliable words, so that you can give sound answers to him who sent you?

22 : 21

sound instruction
Hold on to instruction, do not let it go; guard it well, for it is your life.

4 : 13

sound judgment
My son, preserve sound judgment and discernment, do not let them out of your sight;

3 : 21

Counsel and sound judgment are mine; I have understanding and power.

8 : 14

An unfriendly man pursues selfish ends; he defies all sound judgment.

18 : 1

sound learning
I give you sound learning, so do not forsake my teaching.

4 : 2

sovereign
The Lord works out everything for his own ends -- even the wicked for a day of disaster.

16 : 4

Many seek an audience with a ruler, but it is from the Lord that man gets justice.

29 : 26

Do not add to his words, or he will rebuke you and prove you a liar.

30 : 6

sovereignty
By me kings reign and rulers make laws that are just;

8 : 15

I walk in the way of righteousness, along the paths of justice,

8 : 20

In his heart a man plans his course, but the Lord determines his steps.

16 : 9

The lot is cast into the lap, but its every decision is from the Lord.

16 : 33

Many are the plans in the man's heart,
but it is the Lord's purpose that prevails.

19 : 21

A man's steps are directed by the Lord.
How then can anyone understand his
own way?

20 : 24

The king's heart is in the hand of the
Lord; he directs it like a watercourse
wherever he pleases.

21 : 1

There is no wisdom, no insight, no plan
that can succeed against the Lord.

21 : 30

The horse is made ready for the day of
battle, but victory rests with the Lord.

21 : 31

Rich and poor have this in common:
The Lord is the Maker of them all.

22 : 2

The eyes of the Lord keep watch over
knowledge, but he frustrates the words
of the unfaithful.

22 : 12

Who has gone up to heaven and come
down? Who has gathered up the wind
in the hollow of his hands? Who has
wrapped up the waters in his cloak?
Who has established all the ends of the
earth? What is his name, and the name
of his son? Tell me if you know!

30 : 4

Keep falsehood and lies far from me;
give me neither poverty nor riches, but
give me only my daily bread.

30 : 8

sowing

A sluggard does not plow in season; so
at harvest time he looks but finds
nothing.

20 : 4

sowing and reaping

then your barns will be filled to
overflowing, and your vats will brim
over with new wine.

3 : 10

The righteousness of the blameless
makes a straight way for them, but the
wicked are brought down by their own
wickedness.

11 : 5

The righteous man is rescued from
trouble, and it comes on the wicked
instead.

11 : 8

A kind man benefits himself, but a cruel
man brings trouble on himself.

11 : 17

The wicked man earns deceptive wages,
but he who sows righteousness reaps a
sure reward.

11 : 18

One man gives freely, yet gains even
more; another withholds unduly, but
comes to poverty.

11 : 24

A generous man will prosper; he who
refreshes others will himself be
refreshed.

11 : 25

He who seeks good finds goodwill, but
evil comes to him who searches for it.

11 : 27

If the righteous receive their due on
earth, how much more the ungodly and
the sinner!

11 : 31

From the fruit of his lips a man is filled
with good things as surely as the work
of his hands rewards him.

12 : 14

The faithless will be fully repaid for their ways, and the good man rewarded for his.

14 : 14

The wealth of the wise is their crown, but the folly of fools yields folly.

14 : 24

A greedy man brings trouble to his family, but he who hates bribes will live.

15 : 27

If a man pays back evil for good, evil will never leave his house.

17 : 13

He who sows wickedness reaps trouble, and the rod of his fury will be destroyed.

22 : 8

A generous man will himself be blessed, for he shares his food with the poor.

22 : 9

for the Lord will take up their case and will plunder those who plunder them.

22 : 23

If a man digs a pit, he will fall into it; if a man rolls a stone, it will roll back on him.

26 : 27

He who conceals his sins does not prosper, but whoever confesses and renounces them finds mercy.

28 : 13

He who works his land will have abundant food, but the one who chases fantasies will have his fill of poverty.

28 : 19

He who gives to the poor will lack nothing, but he who closes his eyes to them receives many curses.

28 : 27

An evil man is snared by his own sin, but a righteous one can sing and be glad.

29 : 6

sows

The wicked man earns deceptive wages, but he who sows righteousness reaps a sure reward.

11 : 18

He who sows wickedness reaps trouble, and the rod of his fury will be destroyed.

22 : 8

sows wickedness

He who sows wickedness reaps trouble, and the rod of his fury will be destroyed.

22 : 8

spanking

He who spares the rod hates his son, but he who loves him is careful to discipline him.

13 : 24

Folly is bound up in the heart of a child, but the rod of discipline will drive it far from him.

22 : 15

Do not withhold discipline from a child; if you punish him with the rod, he will not die.

23 : 13

Punish him with the rod and save his soul from death.

23 : 14

A whip for the horse, a halter for the donkey, and a rod for the backs of fools!

26 : 3

The rod of correction imparts wisdom, but a child left to himself disgraces his mother.

29 : 15

spare
Do not love sleep or you will grow poor; stay awake and you will have food to spare.

20 : 13

spares
He who spares the rod hates his son, but he who loves him is careful to discipline him.

13 : 24

sparing
All day long he craves for more, but the righteous give without sparing.

21 : 26

sparrow
Like a fluttering sparrow or a darting swallow, an undeserved curse does not come to rest.

26 : 2

speak
When you walk, they will guide you; when you sleep, they will watch over you; when you awake, they will speak to you.

6 : 22

Listen, for I have worthy things to say; I open my lips to speak what is right.

8 : 6

The lips of the king speak as an oracle, and his mouth should not betray justice.

16 : 10

Gold there is, and rubies in abundance, but lips that speak knowledge are a rare jewel.

20 : 15

Do not speak to a fool, for he will scorn the wisdom of your words.

23 : 9

my inmost being will rejoice when your lips speak what is right.

23 : 16

"Speak up for those who cannot speak for themselves, for the rights of all who are destitute.

31 : 8

Speak up and judge fairly; defend the rights of the poor and needy."

31 : 9

speak up
"Speak up for those who cannot speak for themselves, for the rights of all who are destitute.

31 : 8

Speak up and judge fairly; defend the rights of the poor and needy."

31 : 9

speaking
The wise in heart accept commands, but a chattering fool comes to ruin.

10 : 8

The lips of the righteous know what is fitting, but the mouth of the wicked only what is perverse.

10 : 32

speaks
My mouth speaks what is true, for my lips detest wickedness.

8 : 7

He who guards his lips guards his life, but he who speaks rashly will come to ruin.

13 : 3

Do you see a man who speaks in haste? There is more hope for a fool than for him.

29 : 20

She speaks with wisdom, and faithful instruction is on her tongue.

31 : 26

speaks the truth

Kings take pleasure in honest lips; they value a man who speaks the truth.

16 : 13

speech

at the head of the noisy streets she cries out, in the gateways of the city she makes her speech:

1 : 21

For the lips of an adulteress drip honey, and her speech is smoother than oil;

5 : 3

if you have been trapped by what you said, ensnared by the words of your mouth,

6 : 2

haughty eyes, a lying tongue, hands that shed innocent blood,

6 : 17

To fear the Lord is to hate evil; I hate pride and arrogance, evil behavior and perverse speech.

8 : 13

The mouth of the righteous is a fountain of life, but violence overwhelms the mouth of the wicked.

10 : 11

Wise men store up knowledge, but the mouth of a fool invites ruin.

10 : 14

When words are many, sin is not absent, but he who holds his tongue is wise.

10 : 19

The tongue of the righteous is choice silver, but the heart of the wicked is of little value.

10 : 20

The lips of the righteous know what is fitting, but the mouth of the wicked only what is perverse.

10 : 32

The words of the wicked lie in wait for blood, but the speech of the upright rescues them.

12 : 6

An evil man is trapped by his sinful talk, but a righteous man escapes trouble.

12 : 13

From the fruit of his lips a man is filled with good things as surely as the work of his hands rewards him.

12 : 14

Reckless words pierce like a sword, but the tongue of the wise brings healing.

12 : 18

Truthful lips endure forever, but a lying tongue lasts only a moment.

12 : 19

An anxious heart weighs a man down, but a kind word cheers him up.

12 : 25

He who guards his lips guards his life, but he who speaks rashly will come to ruin.

13 : 3

A fool's talk brings a rod to his back, but the lips of the wise protect them.

14 : 3

Stay away from a foolish man, for you will not find knowledge on his lips.

14 : 7

A gentle answer turns away wrath, but a harsh word stirs up anger.

15 : 1

The tongue of the wise commends knowledge, but the mouth of the fool gushes folly.

15 : 2

Kings take pleasure in honest lips; they value a man who speaks the truth.

16 : 13

A wise man's heart guides his mouth, and his lips promote instruction.

16 : 23

A scoundrel plots evil, and his speech is like a scorching fire.

16 : 27

A wicked man listens to evil lips; a liar pays attention to a malicious tongue.

17 : 4

A man of perverse heart does not prosper; he whose tongue is deceitful falls into trouble.

17 : 20

A fool finds no pleasure in understanding but delights in airing his own opinions.

18 : 2

A fool's lips bring him strife, and his mouth invites a beating.

18 : 6

A fool's mouth is his undoing, and his lips are a snare to his soul.

18 : 7

From the fruit of his mouth a man's stomach is filled; with the harvest from his lips he is satisfied.

18 : 20

Better a poor man whose walk is blameless than a fool whose lips are perverse.

19 : 1

A gossip betrays a confidence; so avoid a man who talks too much.

20 : 19

He who guards his mouth and his tongue keeps himself from calamity.

21 : 23

He who loves a pure heart and whose speech is gracious will have the king for his friend.

22 : 11

Do not speak to a fool, for he will scorn the wisdom of your words.

23 : 9

my inmost being will rejoice when your lips speak what is right.

23 : 16

Wisdom is too high for a fool; in the assembly at the gate he has nothing to say.

24 : 7

An honest answer is like a kiss on the lips.

24 : 26

Do not testify against your neighbor without cause, or use your lips to deceive.

24 : 28

A word aptly spoken is like apples of gold in settings of silver.

25 : 11

Though his speech is charming, do not believe him, for seven abominations fill his heart.

26 : 25

speechless
Wisdom is too high for a fool; in the assembly at the gate he has nothing to say.

24 : 7

spend
do not spend your strength on women,
your vigor on those who ruin kings.

31 : 3

spent
At the end of your life you will groan,
when your flesh and body are spent.

5 : 11

spindle
In her hand she holds the distaff and
grasps the spindle with her fingers.

31 : 19

spirit
The tongue that brings healing is a tree
of life, but a deceitful tongue crushes
the spirit.

15 : 4

A happy heart makes the face cheerful,
but heartache crushes the spirit.

15 : 13

Pride goes before destruction, a haughty
spirit before a fall.

16 : 18

Better to be lowly in spirit and among
the oppressed than to share plunder with
the proud.

16 : 19

A cheerful heart is good medicine, but a
crushed spirit dries up the bones.

17 : 22

A man's spirit sustains him in sickness,
but a crushed spirit who can bear?

18 : 14

The lamp of the Lord searches the spirit
of a man; it searches out his inmost
being.

20 : 27

Like the coolness of snow at harvest
time is a trustworthy messenger to those
who send him; he refreshes the spirit of
his masters.

25 : 13

A man's pride brings him low, but a
man of lowly spirit gains honor.

29 : 23

spirit of a man
The lamp of the Lord searches the spirit
of a man; it searches out his inmost
being.

20 : 27

spirits of the dead
For her house leads down to death and
her paths to the spirits of the dead.

2 : 18

spiritual warfare
Righteousness guards the man of
integrity, but wickedness overthrows
the sinner.

13 : 6

splendor
She will set a garland of grace on your
head and present you with a crown of
splendor.

4 : 9

Gray hair is a crown of splendor; it is
attained by a righteous life.

16 : 31

The glory of young men is their
strength, gray hair the splendor of the
old.

20 : 29

spoils
If a man pampers his servant from
youth, he will bring grief in the end.

29 : 21

451

spoken
A word aptly spoken is like apples of
gold in settings of silver.
25 : 11

spouse
May your fountain be blessed, and may
you rejoice in the wife of your youth.
5 : 18

Better to live on a corner of the roof
than share a house with a quarrelsome
wife.
25 : 24

Her husband has full confidence in her
and lacks nothing of value.
31 : 11

Her children arise and call her blessed;
her husband also, and he praises her:
31 : 28

spread
How useless to spread a net in full view
of all the birds!
1 : 17

The lips of the wise spread knowledge;
not so the hearts of fools.
15 : 7

spreading a net
Whoever flatters his neighbor is
spreading a net for his feet.
29 : 5

spreads
He who conceals his hatred has lying
lips, and whoever spreads slander is a
fool.
10 : 18

spring
When a king's face brightens, it means
life; his favor is like a rain cloud in
spring.
16 : 15

Like a muddied spring or a polluted
well is a righteous man who gives way
to the wicked.
25 : 26

springs
Should your springs overflow in the
streets, your streams of water in the
public squares?
5 : 16

When there were no oceans, I was given
birth, when there were no springs
abounding with water;
8 : 24

Perfume and incense bring joy to the
heart, and the pleasantness of one's
friend springs from his earnest counsel.
27 : 9

sprout
Cast but a glance at riches, and they are
gone, for they will surely sprout wings
and fly off to the sky like an eagle.
23 : 5

spurned
since they would not accept my advice
and spurned my rebuke,
1 : 30

You will say, "How I hated discipline!
How my heart spurned correction!
5 : 12

spurning the Lord's rebuke
since they would not accept my advice
and spurned my rebuke,
1 : 30

spurns
A fool spurns the father's discipline, but
whoever heeds correction shows
prudence.
15 : 5

squandering wealth
A man who loves wisdom brings joy to his father, but a companion of prostitutes squanders his wealth.
29 : 3

squanders
A man who loves wisdom brings joy to his father, but a companion of prostitutes squanders his wealth.
29 : 3

square
Should your springs overflow in the streets, your streams of water in the public squares?
5 : 16

now in the street, now in the squares, at every corner she lurks.
7 : 12

squares
Wisdom calls aloud in the street, she raises her voice in the public squares;
1 : 20

stability
The righteous will never be uprooted, but the wicked will not remain in the land.
10 : 30

By justice a king gives a country stability, but one who is greedy for bribes tears it down.
29 : 4

staggering
Rescue those being led away to death; hold back those staggering toward slaughter.
24 : 11

stand
On the heights along the way, where the paths meet, she takes her stand;
8 : 2

When the storm has swept by, the wicked are gone, but the righteous stand firm forever.
10 : 25

Anger is cruel and fury overwhelming, but who can stand before jealousy?
27 : 4

stand firm
When the storm has swept by, the wicked are gone, but the righteous stand firm forever.
10 : 25

stands firm
Wicked men are overthrown and are no more, but the house of the righteous stands firm.
12 : 7

starting
Starting a quarrel is like breaching a dam; so drop the matter before a dispute breaks out.
17 : 14

starvation
Better to be a nobody and yet have a servant than pretend to be somebody and have no food.
12 : 9

starving
Men do not despise a thief if he steals to satisfy his hunger when he is starving.
6 : 30

He who is full loathes honey, but to the hungry even what is bitter tastes sweet.
27 : 7

stately
"There are three things that are stately in their stride, four that move with stately bearing:
30 : 29

stay
She is loud and defiant, her feet never
stay at home;

7 : 11

Stay away from a foolish man, for you
will not find knowledge on his lips.

14 : 7

Do not love sleep or you will grow
poor; stay awake and you will have
food to spare.

20 : 13

stay awake
Allow no sleep to your eyes, no slumber
to your eyelids.

6 : 4

stay away
Stay away from a foolish man, for you
will not find knowledge on his lips.

14 : 7

stay away from temptation
Keep to a path far from her, do not go
near the door of her house,

5 : 8

stay home
Drink water from your own cistern,
running water from your own well.

5 : 15

stay pure
She gives no thought to the way of life;
her paths are crooked, but she knows it
not.

5 : 6

staying focused
A discerning man keeps wisdom in
view, but a fool's eyes wander to the
ends of the earth.

17 : 24

steal
we will get all sorts of valuable things
and fill our houses with plunder;

1 : 13

Otherwise, I may have too much and
disown you and say, 'Who is the Lord?'
Or I may become poor and steal, and so
dishonor the name of my God.

30 : 9

stealing
Ill-gotten treasures are of no value, but
righteousness delivers from death.

10 : 2

steals
Men do not despise a thief if he steals to
satisfy his hunger when he is starving.

6 : 30

stepping
All at once he followed her like an ox
going to the slaughter, like a deer
stepping into a noose

7 : 22

steps
When you walk, your steps will not be
hampered; when you run, you will not
stumble.

4 : 12

Her feet go down to death; her steps
lead straight to the grave.

5 : 5

A simple man believes anything, but a
prudent man gives thought to his steps.

14 : 15

In his heart a man plans his course, but
the Lord determines his steps.

16 : 9

A man's steps are directed by the Lord.
How then can anyone understand his
own way?

20 : 24

stern discipline
Stern discipline awaits him who leaves
the path; he who hates correction will
die.

15 : 10

stewardship
Honor the Lord with your wealth, with the firstfruits of all your crops;
3 : 9

One man gives freely, yet gains even more; another withholds unduly, but comes to poverty.
11 : 24

A generous man will prosper; he who refreshes others will himself be refreshed.
11 : 25

An inheritance quickly gained at the beginning will not be blessed at the end.
20 : 21

sticks closer than a brother
A man of many companions may come to ruin, but there is a friend who sticks closer than a brother.
18 : 24

stick-to-itiveness
Allow no sleep to your eyes, no slumber to your eyelids.
6 : 4

stiff-necked
A man who remains stiff-necked after many rebukes will suddenly be destroyed -- without remedy.
29 : 1

still
When I was a boy in my father's house, still tender, and an only child of my mother,
4 : 3

She gets up while it is still dark; she provides food for her family and portions for her servant girls.
31 : 15

stingy
Do not eat the food of a stingy man, do not crave his delicacies.
23 : 6

A stingy man is eager to get rich and is unaware that poverty awaits him.
28 : 22

stingy man
Do not eat the food of a stingy man, do not crave his delicacies.
23 : 6

A stingy man is eager to get rich and is unaware that poverty awaits him.
28 : 22

stir up
Mockers stir up a city, but wise men turn away anger.
29 : 8

stirring up
For as churning the milk produces butter, and as twisting the nose produces blood, so stirring up anger produces strife."
30 : 33

stirs up
who plots evil with deceit in his heart -- he always stirs up dissension.
6 : 14

a false witness who pours out lies and a man who stirs up dissension among brothers.
6 : 19

Hatred stirs up dissension, but love covers over all wrongs.
10 : 12

A gentle answer turns away wrath, but a harsh word stirs up anger.
15 : 1

A hot-tempered man stirs up dissension, but a patient man calms a quarrel.
15 : 18

A perverse man stirs up dissension, and a gossip separates close friends.

16 : 28

A greedy man stirs up dissension, but he who trusts in the Lord will prosper.

28 : 25

An angry man stirs up dissension, and a hot-tempered one commits many sins.

29 : 22

stirs up anger
A gentle answer turns away wrath, but a harsh word stirs up anger.

15 : 1

stolen
we will get all sorts of valuable things and fill our houses with plunder;

1 : 13

Stolen water is sweet; food eaten in secret is delicious!"

9 : 17

stomach
The righteous eat to their hearts' content, but the stomach of the wicked goes hungry.

13 : 25

From the fruit of his mouth a man's stomach is filled; with the harvest from his lips he is satisfied.

18 : 20

You will vomit up the little you have eaten and will have wasted your compliments.

23 : 8

stone
Do not move an ancient boundary stone set up by your forefathers.

22 : 28

Do not move an ancient boundary stone or encroach on the fields of the fatherless,

23 : 10

thorns had come up everywhere, the ground was covered with weeds, and the stone wall was in ruins.

24 : 31

Like tying a stone in a sling is the giving of honor to a fool.

26 : 8

If a man digs a pit, he will fall into it; if a man rolls a stone, it will roll back on him.

26 : 27

Stone is heavy and sand a burden, but provocation by a fool is heavier than both.

27 : 3

stone wall
thorns had come up everywhere, the ground was covered with weeds, and the stone wall was in ruins.

24 : 31

stop
Stop listening to instruction, my son, and you will stray from the words of knowledge.

19 : 27

store
My son, if you accept my words and store up my commands within you,

2 : 1

He holds victory in store for the upright, he is a shield to those whose walk is blameless,

2 : 7

My son, keep my words and store up my commands within you.

7 : 1

Wise men store up knowledge, but the mouth of a fool invites ruin.

10 : 14

store up
My son, if you accept my words and store up my commands within you,
2 : 1

My son, keep my words and store up my commands within you.
7 : 1

Wise men store up knowledge, but the mouth of a fool invites ruin.
10 : 14

Ants arc creatures of little strength, yet they store up their food in the summer;
30 : 25

stored
A good man leaves an inheritance for his children's children, but a sinner's wealth is stored up for the righteous.
13 : 22

stored up
A good man leaves an inheritance for his children's children, but a sinner's wealth is stored up for the righteous.
13 : 22

stores
yet it stores its provisions in summer and gathers its food at harvest.
6 : 8

In the house of the wise are stores of choice food and oil, but a foolish man devours all he has.
21 : 20

storm
when calamity overtakes you like a storm, when disaster sweeps over you like a whirlwind, when distress and trouble overwhelm you.
1 : 27

When the storm has swept by, the wicked are gone, but the righteous stand firm forever.
10 : 25

straight
who leave the straight paths to walk in dark ways,
2 : 13

in all your ways acknowledge him, and he will make your paths straight.
3 : 6

I guide you in the way of wisdom and lead you along straight paths.
4 : 11

Let your eyes look straight ahead, fix your gaze directly before you.
4 : 25

Her feet go down to death; her steps lead straight to the grave.
5 : 5

calling out to those who pass by, who go straight on their way.
9 : 15

Folly delights a man who lacks judgment, but a man of understanding keeps a straight course.
15 : 21

straight paths
who leave the straight paths to walk in dark ways,
2 : 13

I guide you in the way of wisdom and lead you along straight paths.
4 : 11

straight way
The righteousness of the blameless makes a straight way for them, but the wicked are brought down by their own wickedness.
11 : 5

strange
Your eyes will see strange sights and your mind imagine confusing things.
23 : 33

stranger

Take the garment of one who puts up security for a stranger; hold it in pledge if he does it for a wayward woman.

20 : 16

Take a garment of one who puts up security for a stranger; hold it in pledge if he does it for a wayward woman.

27 : 13

strangers

lest strangers feast on your wealth and your toil enrich another man's house.

5 : 10

Let them be yours alone, never to be shared with strangers.

5 : 17

strategy

The plans of the diligent lead to profit as surely as haste leads to poverty.

21 : 5

stray

Do not let your heart turn to her ways or stray into her paths.

7 : 25

Stop listening to instruction, my son, and you will stray from the words of knowledge.

19 : 27

A man who strays from the path of understanding comes to rest in the company of the dead.

21 : 16

stream

The words of a man's mouth are deep waters, but the fountain of wisdom is a bubbling brook.

18 : 4

streams

Should your springs overflow in the streets, your streams of water in the public squares?

5 : 16

street

Wisdom calls aloud in the street, she raises her voice in the public squares;

1 : 20

He was going down the street near her corner, walking along in the direction of her house

7 : 8

now in the street, now in the squares, at every corner she lurks.

7 : 12

The sluggard says, "There is a lion outside!" or "I will be murdered in the streets!"

22 : 13

streets

at the head of the noisy streets she cries out, in the gateways of the city she makes her speech:

1 : 21

Should your springs overflow in the streets, your streams of water in the public squares?

5 : 16

The sluggard says, "There is a lion in the road, a fierce lion roaming the streets!"

26 : 13

strength

lest you give your best strength to others and your years to one who is cruel,

5 : 9

Where there are no oxen, the manger is empty, but from the strength of an ox comes an abundant harvest.

14 : 4

The name of the Lord is a strong tower; the righteous run to it and are safe.

18 : 10

Love and faithfulness keep a king safe; through love his throne is made secure.

20 : 28

The glory of young men is their strength, gray hair the splendor of the old.

20 : 29

A wise man attacks the city of the mighty and pulls down the stronghold in which they trust.

21 : 22

A wise man has great power, and a man of knowledge increases strength;

24 : 5

If you falter in times of trouble, how small is your strength!

24 : 10

Ants are creatures of little strength, yet they store up their food in the summer;

30 : 25

do not spend your strength on women, your vigor on those who ruin kings.

31 : 3

She is clothed with strength and dignity; she can laugh at the days to come.

31 : 25

strength and dignity

She is clothed with strength and dignity; she can laugh at the days to come.

31 : 25

stretched

But since you rejected me when I called and no one gave heed when I stretched out my hand,

1 : 24

stride

"There are three things that are stately in their stride, four that move with stately bearing:

30 : 29

strife

Better a dry crust with peace and quiet than a house full of feasting with strife.

17 : 1

A fool's lips bring him strife, and his mouth invites a beating.

18 : 6

It is to a man's honor to avoid strife, but every fool is quick to quarrel.

20 : 3

Drive out the mocker, and out goes strife; quarrels and insults are ended.

22 : 10

Who has woe? Who has sorrow? Who has strife? Who has complaints? Who has needless bruises? Who has bloodshot eyes?

23 : 29

As charcoal to embers and as wood to fire, so is a quarrelsome man for kindling strife.

26 : 21

For as churning the milk produces butter, and as twisting the nose produces blood, so stirring up anger produces strife."

30 : 33

strike hands
He who puts up security for another
will surely suffer, but whoever refuses
to strike hands in pledge is safe.

11 : 15

strikes
A man lacking in judgment strikes
hands in pledge and puts up security for
his neighbor.

17 : 18

Do not forsake your friend and the
friend of your father, and do not go to
your brother's house when disaster
strikes you -- better a neighbor nearby
than a brother far away.

27 : 10

strikes hands
A man lacking in judgment strikes
hands in pledge and puts up security for
his neighbor.

17 : 18

Do not be a man who strikes hands in
pledge or puts up security for debts;

22 : 26

strong
The name of the Lord is a strong tower;
the righteous run to it and are safe.

18 : 10

Casting the lot settles disputes and
keeps strong opponents apart.

18 : 18

for their Defender is strong; he will take
up their case against you.

23 : 11

A wise man has great power, and a man
of knowledge increases strength;

24 : 5

She sets about her work vigorously; her
arms are strong for her tasks.

31 : 17

strong tower
The name of the Lord is a strong tower;
the righteous run to it and are safe.

18 : 10

stronghold
A wise man attacks the city of the
mighty and pulls down the stronghold
in which they trust.

21 : 22

struck
My son, if you have put up security for
your neighbor, if you have struck hands
in pledge for another,

6 : 1

strutting
a strutting rooster, a he-goat, and a king
with his army around him.

30 : 31

strutting rooster
a strutting rooster, a he-goat, and a king
with his army around him.

30 : 31

student
Apply your heart to instruction and your
ears to words of knowledge.

23 : 12

stumble
Then you will go on your way in safety,
and your foot will not stumble;

3 : 23

When you walk, your steps will not be
hampered; when you run, you will not
stumble.

4 : 12

But the way of the wicked is like deep
darkness; they do not know what makes
them stumble.

4 : 19

stumbles
Do not gloat when your enemy falls;
when he stumbles, do not let your heart
rejoice,

24 : 17

stupid
How useless to spread a net in full view
of all the birds!

1 : 17

Whoever loves discipline loves
knowledge, but he who hates correction
is stupid.

12 : 1

Like one who seizes a dog by the ears is
a passer-by who meddles in a quarrel
not his own.

26 : 17

subjects
A large population is a king's glory, but
without subjects a prince is ruined.

14 : 28

succeed
Plans fail for lack of counsel, but with
many advisers they succeed.

15 : 22

Commit to the Lord whatever you do,
and your plans will succeed.

16 : 3

There is no wisdom, no insight, no plan
that can succeed against the Lord.

21 : 30

succeeds
A bribe is a charm to the one who gives
it; wherever he turns, he succeeds.

17 : 8

success
With me are the riches and honor,
enduring wealth and prosperity.

8 : 18

Commit to the Lord whatever you do,
and your plans will succeed.

16 : 3

A bribe is a charm to the one who gives
it; wherever he turns, he succeeds.

17 : 8

He who gets wisdom loves his own
soul; he who cherishes understanding
prospers.

19 : 8

such
Such is the end of all who go after ill-
gotten gain; it takes away the life of
those who get it.

1 : 19

The righteous care about justice for the
poor, but the wicked have no such
concern.

29 : 7

sudden
Have no fear of sudden disaster or of
the ruin that overtakes the wicked,

3 : 25

for those two will send sudden
destruction upon them, and who knows
what calamities they can bring?

24 : 22

sudden destruction
for those two will send sudden
destruction upon them, and who knows
what calamities they can bring?

24 : 22

sudden disaster
Have no fear of sudden disaster or of
the ruin that overtakes the wicked,

3 : 25

suddenly
Therefore disaster will overtake him in
an instant; he will suddenly be
destroyed -- without remedy.

6 : 15

461

He whose walk is blameless is kept safe, but he whose ways are perverse will suddenly fall.

28 . 18

A man who remains stiff-necked after many rebukes will suddenly be destroyed -- without remedy.

29 : 1

sue

do not bring hastily to court, for what will you do in the end if your neighbor puts you to shame?

25 : 8

suffer

If you are wise, your wisdom will reward you; if you are a mocker, you alone will suffer."

9 : 12

He who puts up security for another will surely suffer, but whoever refuses to strike hands in pledge is safe.

11 : 15

A prudent man sees danger and takes refuge, but the simple keep going and suffer for it.

22 : 3

Wounds from a friend can be trusted, but an enemy multiplies kisses.

27 : 6

The prudent see danger and take refuge, but the simple keep going and suffer for it.

27 : 12

suffering

Even in laughter the heart may ache, and joy may end in grief.

14 : 13

suffers

He who walks with the wise grows wise, but a companion of fools suffers harm.

13 : 20

suing

Do not exploit the poor because they are poor and do not crush the needy in court,

22 : 22

sultry

Do not lust in your heart after her beauty or let her captivate you with her eyes,

6 : 25

summer

yet it stores its provisions in summer and gathers its food at harvest.

6 : 8

He who gathers crops in summer is a wise son, but he who sleeps during harvest is a disgraceful son.

10 : 5

Like snow in summer or rain in harvest, honor is not fitting for a fool.

26 : 1

Ants are creatures of little strength, yet they store up their food in the summer;

30 : 25

summon

"To you, O men, I call out; I raise my voice to all mankind.

8 : 4

sunset

at twilight, as the day was fading, as the dark of night set in.

7 : 9

supplies
She makes linen garments and sells
them, and supplies the merchants with
sashes.

31 : 24

supply
the lambs will provide you with
clothing, and the goats with the price of
a field.

27 : 26

You will have plenty of goat's milk to
feed you and your family and to nourish
your servant girls.

27 : 27

support
Do not forsake your friend and the
friend of your father, and do not go to
your brother's house when disaster
strikes you -- better a neighbor nearby
than a brother far away.

27 : 10

A man tomented by the guilt of murder
will be a fugitive till death; let no one
support him.

28 : 17

"Speak up for those who cannot speak
for themselves, for the rights of all who
are destitute.

31 : 8

suppress
lest they drink and forget what the law
decrees, and deprive all the oppressed
of the rights.

31 : 5

supreme
Wisdom is supreme; therefore get
wisdom. Though it cost all you have,
get understanding.

4 : 7

sure
For lack of guidance a nation falls, but
many advisers make victory sure.

11 : 14

The wicked man earns deceptive wages,
but he who sows righteousness reaps a
sure reward.

11 : 18

Be sure of this: The wicked will not go
unpunished, but those who are righteous
will go free.

11 : 21

The Lord detests all the proud of heart.
Be sure of this: They will not go
unpunished.

16 : 5

Be sure you know the condition of your
flocks, give careful attention to your
herds;

27 : 23

surely
He who puts up security for another
will surely suffer, but whoever refuses
to strike hands in pledge is safe.

11 : 15

From the fruit of his lips a man is filled
with good things as surely as the work
of his hands rewards him.

12 : 14

The plans of the diligent lead to profit
as surely as haste leads to poverty.

21 : 5

Cast but a glance at riches, and they are
gone, for they will surely sprout wings
and fly off to the sky like an eagle.

23 : 5

There is surely a future hope for you,
and your hope will not be cut off.

23 : 18

surpass

Many women do noble things, but you surpass them all."

31 : 29

surpasses

My fruit is better than fine gold; what I yield surpasses choice silver.

8 : 19

surrender

Trust in the Lord with all your heart and lean not on your own understanding;

3 : 5

survey

At the window of my house I looked out through the lattice.

7 : 6

sustains

A man's spirit sustains him in sickness, but a crushed spirit who can bear?

18 : 14

swallow

let's swallow them alive, like the grave, and whole, like those who go down to the pit;

1 : 12

Like a fluttering sparrow or a darting swallow, an undeserved curse does not come to rest.

26 : 2

swallow alive

let's swallow them alive, like the grave, and whole, like those who go down to the pit;

1 : 12

swearing

Put away perversity from your mouth; keep corrupt talk far from your lips.

4 : 24

The mouth of the righteous brings forth wisdom, but a perverse tongue will be cut out.

10 : 31

If a man curses his father or mother, his lamp will be snuffed out in pitch darkness.

20 : 20

sweeps

when calamity overtakes you like a storm, when disaster sweeps over you like a whirlwind, when distress and trouble overwhelm you.

1 : 27

A poor man's field may produce abundant food, but injustice sweeps it away.

13 : 23

sweet

when you lie down, you will not be afraid; when you lie down, your sleep will be sweet.

3 : 24

Stolen water is sweet; food eaten in secret is delicious!"

9 : 17

A longing fulfilled is sweet to the soul, but fools detest turning from evil.

13 : 19

Pleasant words are a honeycomb, sweet to the soul and healing to the bones.

16 : 24

Food gained by fraud tastes sweet to a man, but he ends up with a mouth full of gravel.

20 : 17

Eat honey, my son, for it is good; honey from the comb is sweet to your taste.

24 : 13

Know also that wisdom is sweet to your soul; If you find it, there is a future hope for you, and your hope will not be cut off.

24 : 14

He who is full loathes honey, but to the hungry even what is bitter tastes sweet.

27 : 7

swept
When the storm has swept by, the wicked are gone, but the righteous stand firm forever.

10 : 25

swerve
Get wisdom, get understanding; do not forget my words or swerve from them.

4 : 5

Do not swerve to the right or the left; keep your foot from evil.

4 : 27

swift
for their feet rush into sin, they are swift to shed blood.

1 : 16

sword
but in the end she is bitter as gall, sharp as a double-edged sword.

5 : 4

Reckless words pierce like a sword, but the tongue of the wise brings healing.

12 : 18

Like a club or a sword or a sharp arrow is the man who gives false testimony against his neighbor.

25 : 18

swords
those whose teeth are swords and whose jaws are set with knives to devour the poor from the earth, the needy from among mankind.

30 : 14

T

table
She has prepared her meat and mixed her wine; she has also set her table.

9 : 2

tablet
Let love and faithfulness never leave you; bind them around your neck, write them on the tablet of your heart.

3 : 3

tablet of your heart
Bind them on your fingers; write them on the tablet of your heart.

7 : 3

tact
Wisdom is too high for a fool; in the assembly at the gate he has nothing to say.

24 : 7

A word aptly spoken is like apples of gold in settings of silver.

25 : 11

Through patience a ruler can be persuaded, and a gentle tongue can break a bone.

25 : 15

If a man loudly blesses his neighbor early in the morning, it will be taken as a curse.

27 : 14

take
Make level paths for your feet and take only ways that are firm.

4 : 26

Pride only breeds quarrels, but wisdom is found in those who take advice.

13 : 10

Kings take pleasure in honest lips; they value a man who speaks the truth.

16 : 13

Take the garment of one who puts up security for a stranger; hold it in pledge if he does it for a wayward woman.

20 : 16

for the Lord will take up their case and will plunder those who plunder them.

22 : 23

for their Defender is strong; he will take up their case against you.

23 : 11

Take a garment of one who puts up security for a stranger; hold it in pledge if he does it for a wayward woman.

27 : 13

Every word of God is flawless; he is a shield to those who take refuge in him.

30 : 5

take advice
Pride only breeds quarrels, but wisdom is found in those who take advice.

13 : 10

take pleasure
Kings take pleasure in honest lips; they value a man who speaks the truth.

16 : 13

take refuge
Every word of God is flawless; he is a shield to those who take refuge in him.

30 : 5

take up

for the Lord will take up their case and
will plunder those who plunder them.

22 : 23

taken

If a man loudly blesses his neighbor
early in the morning, it will be taken as
a curse.

27 : 14

takes

Such is the end of all who go after ill-
gotten gain; it takes away the life of
those who get it.

1 : 19

for the Lord detests a perverse man but
takes the upright into his confidence.

3 : 32

for jealousy arouses a husband's fury,
and he will show no mercy when he
takes revenge.

6 : 34

On the heights along the way, where the
paths meet, she takes her stand;

8 : 2

The man of integrity walks securely,
but he who takes crooked paths will be
found out.

10 : 9

Better a patient man than a warrior, a
man who controls his temper than one
who takes a city.

16 : 32

A prudent man sees danger and takes
refuge, but the simple keep going and
suffer for it.

22 : 3

Her husband is respected at the city
gate, where he takes his seat among the
elders of the land.

31 : 23

takes away

Such is the end of all who go after ill-
gotten gain; it takes away the life of
those who get it.

1 : 19

Like one who takes away a garment on
a cold day, or like vinegar poured on
soda, is one who sings songs to a heavy
heart.

25 : 20

takes note

The Righteous One takes note of the
house of the wicked and brings the
wicked to ruin.

21 : 12

taking advantage

He who oppresses the poor to increase
his wealth and he who gives gifts to the
rich -- both come to poverty.

22 : 16

talent

Do you see a man skilled in his work?
He will serve before kings, he will not
serve before obscure men.

22 : 29

talk

Put away perversity from your mouth;
keep corrupt talk far from your lips.

4 : 24

With persuasive words she led him
astray; she seduced him with her
smooth talk.

7 : 21

An evil man is trapped by his sinful
talk, but a righteous man escapes
trouble.

12 : 13

A fool's talk brings a rod to his back,
but the lips of the wise protect them.

14 : 3

All hard work brings a profit, but mere talk leads only to poverty.

14 : 23

Do not speak to a fool, for he will scorn the wisdom of your words.

23 : 9

for their hearts plot violence, and their lips talk about making trouble.

24 : 2

talker

A fool finds no pleasure in understanding but delights in airing his own opinions.

18 : 2

talking a mile a minute

The wise in heart accept commands, but a chattering fool comes to ruin.

10 : 8

talking to God

The Lord detests the sacrifice of the wicked, but the prayer of the upright pleases him.

15 : 8

talking too much

When words are many, sin is not absent, but he who holds his tongue is wise.

10 : 19

talks

A gossip betrays a confidence; so avoid a man who talks too much.

20 : 19

talks too much

A gossip betrays a confidence; so avoid a man who talks too much.

20 : 19

taming the tongue

Wise men store up knowledge, but the mouth of a fool invites ruin.

10 : 14

tasks

She sets about her work vigorously; her arms are strong for her tasks.

31 : 17

taste

Food gained by fraud tastes sweet to a man, but he ends up with a mouth full of gravel.

20 : 17

Do not crave his delicacies, for that food is deceptive.

23 : 3

Eat honey, my son, for it is good; honey from the comb is sweet to your taste.

24 : 13

tastes

He who is full loathes honey, but to the hungry even what is bitter tastes sweet.

27 : 7

taught

he taught me and said, "Lay hold of my words with all your heart; keep my commands and you will live.

4 : 4

When a mocker is punished, the simple gain wisdom; when a wise man is instructed, he gets knowledge.

21 : 11

The sayings of King Lemuel -- an oracle his mother taught him:

31 : 1

teach

he taught me and said, "Lay hold of my words with all your heart; keep my commands and you will live.

4 : 4

I guide you in the way of wisdom and lead you along straight paths.

4 : 11

468

Instruct a wise man and he will be wiser still; teach a righteous man and he will add to his learning.

9 : 9

Pay attention and listen to the sayings of the wise; apply your heart to what I teach,

22 : 17

So that your trust may be in the Lord, I teach you today, even you.

22 : 19

The sayings of King Lemuel -- an oracle his mother taught him:

31 : 1

teachable

Instruct a wise man and he will be wiser still; teach a righteous man and he will add to his learning.

9 : 9

A wise son heeds his father's instruction, but a mocker does not listen to rebuke.

13 : 1

Listen to advice and accept instruction, and in the end you will be wise.

19 : 20

teacher

I guide you in the way of wisdom and lead you along straight paths.

4 : 11

teachers

I would not obey my teachers or listen to my instructors.

5 : 13

teaches

The fear of the Lord teaches a man wisdom, and humility comes before honor.

15 : 33

teaching

Listen, my son, to your father's instruction and do not forsake your mother's teaching.

1 : 8

My son, if sinners entice you, do not give in to them.

1 : 10

My son, do not forget my teaching, but keep my commands in your heart,

3 : 1

I give you sound learning, so do not forsake my teaching.

4 : 2

My son, keep your father's commands and do not forsake your mother's teaching.

6 : 20

For these commands are a lamp, this teaching is a light, and the corrections of discipline are the way to life,

6 : 23

The teaching of the wise is a fountain of life, turning a man from the snares of death.

13 : 14

When a mocker is punished, the simple gain wisdom; when a wise man is instructed, he gets knowledge.

21 : 11

Have I not written thirty sayings for you, sayings of counsel and knowledge,

22 : 20

teaching you true and reliable words, so that you can give sound answers to him who sent you?

22 : 21

Apply your heart to instruction and your ears to words of knowledge.

23 : 12

As iron sharpens iron, so one man sharpens another.

27 : 17

teachings
Keep my commands and you will live; guard my teachings as the apple of your eye.

7 : 2

Bind them on your fingers; write them on the tablet of your heart.

7 : 3

teamwork
locusts have no king, yet they advance together in ranks;

30 : 27

tears down
The wise woman builds her house, but with her own hands the foolish one tears hers down.

14 : 1

The Lord tears down the proud man's house, but he keeps the widow's boundaries intact.

15 : 25

By justice a king gives a country stability, but one who is greedy for bribes tears it down.

29 : 4

teeth
As vinegar to the teeth and smoke to the eyes, so is a sluggard to those who send him.

10 : 26

those whose teeth are swords and whose jaws are set with knives to devour the poor from the earth, the needy from among mankind.

30 : 14

tell me
Who has gone up to heaven and come down? Who has gathered up the wind in the hollow of his hands? Who has wrapped up the waters in his cloak? Who has established all the ends of the earth? What is his name, and the name of his son? Tell me if you know!

30 : 4

telling a lie
Truthful lips endure forever, but a lying tongue lasts only a moment.

12 : 19

The Lord detests lying lips, but he delights in men who are truthful.

12 : 22

telling the truth
A truthful witness gives honest testimony, but a false witness tells lies.

12 : 17

Truthful lips endure forever, but a lying tongue lasts only a moment.

12 : 19

The Lord detests lying lips, but he delights in men who are truthful.

12 : 22

A truthful witness does not deceive, but a false witness pours out lies.

14 : 5

tells lies
A truthful witness gives honest testimony, but a false witness tells lies.

12 : 17

temper
A wise man fears the Lord and shuns evil, but a fool is hotheaded and reckless.

14 : 16

A quick-tempered man does foolish things, and a crafty man is hated.

14 : 17

A gentle answer turns away wrath, but a harsh word stirs up anger.

15 : 1

A hot-tempered man stirs up dissension, but a patient man calms a quarrel.

15 : 18

Better a patient man than a warrior, a man who controls his temper than one who takes a city.

16 : 32

A man of knowledge uses words with restraint, and a man of understanding is even-tempered.

17 : 27

Even a fool is thought wise if he keeps silent, and discerning if he holds his tongue.

17 : 28

A hot-tempered man must pay the penalty; if you rescue him, you will have to do it again.

19 : 19

Better to live in a desert than with a quarrelsome and ill-tempered wife.

21 : 19

Do not make friends with a hot-tempered man, do not associate with one easily angered,

22 : 24

or you may learn his ways and get yourself ensnared.

22 : 25

temporary

a servant who becomes a king, a fool who is full of food,

30 : 22

temptation

My son, if sinners entice you, do not give in to them.

1 : 10

It will save you also from the adulteress, from the wayward wife with her seductive words,

2 : 16

Avoid it, do not travel on it; turn from it and go on your way.

4 : 15

For the lips of an adulteress drip honey, and her speech is smoother than oil;

5 : 3

Her feet go down to death; her steps lead straight to the grave.

5 : 5

She gives no thought to the way of life; her paths are crooked, but she knows it not.

5 : 6

Keep to a path far from her, do not go near the door of her house,

5 : 8

At the end of your life you will groan, when your flesh and body are spent.

5 : 11

Why be captivated, my son, by an adulteress? Why embrace the bosom of another man's wife?

5 : 20

keeping you from the immoral woman, from the smooth tongue of the wayward wife.

6 : 24

Can a man scoop fire into his lap without his clothes being burned?

6 : 27

But a man who commits adultery lacks judgment; whoever does so destroys himself.

6 : 32

they will keep you from the adulteress, from the wayward wife with her seductive words.

7 : 5

He was going down the street near her corner, walking along in the direction of her house

7 : 8

She is loud and defiant, her feet never stay at home;

7 : 11

now in the street, now in the squares, at every corner she lurks.

7 : 12

I have covered my bed with colored linens from Egypt.

7 : 16

I have perfumed my bed with myrrh, aloes and cinnamon.

7 : 17

Come, let's drink deep of love till morning; let's enjoy ourselves with love!

7 : 18

My husband is not at home; he has gone on a long journey.

7 : 19

With persuasive words she led him astray; she seduced him with her smooth talk.

7 : 21

All at once he followed her like an ox going to the slaughter, like a deer stepping into a noose

7 : 22

calling out to those who pass by, who go straight on their way.

9 : 15

Stolen water is sweet; food eaten in secret is delicious!"

9 . 17

Righteousness guards the man of integrity, but wickedness overthrows the sinner.

13 : 6

In the paths of the wicked lie thorns and snares, but he who guards his soul stays far from them.

22 : 5

The mouth of an adulteress is a deep pit; he who is under the Lord's wrath will fall into it.

22 : 14

My son, give me your heart and let your eyes keep to my ways,

23 : 26

for a prostitute is a deep pit and a wayward wife is a narrow well.

23 : 27

Like a bandit she lies in wait, and multiplies the unfaithful among men.

23 : 28

Do not gaze at wine when it is red, when it sparkles in the cup, when it goes down smoothly!

23 : 31

"They hit me," you will say, "but I'm not hurt! They beat me, but I don't feel it! When will I wake up so I can find another drink?"

23 : 35

temptress

Do not lust in your heart after her beauty or let her captivate you with her eyes,

6 : 25

Come, let's drink deep of love till morning; let's enjoy ourselves with love!

7 : 18

My husband is not at home; he has gone on a long journey.

7 : 19

tender

When I was a boy in my father's house, still tender, and an only child of my mother,

4 : 3

tent

The house of the wicked will be destroyed, but the tent of the upright will flourish.

14 : 11

terror

When justice is done, it brings joy to the righteous but terror to evildoers.

21 : 15

tested

The crucible for silver and the furnace for gold, but man is tested by the praise he receives.

27 : 21

testify

Do not testify against your neighbor without cause, or use your lips to deceive.

24 : 28

The accomplice of a thief is his own enemy; he is put under oath and dare not testify.

29 : 24

testimony

A truthful witness gives honest testimony, but a false witness tells lies.

12 : 17

A truthful witness does not deceive, but a false witness pours out lies.

14 . 5

A truthful witness saves lives, but a false witness is deceitful.

14 : 25

Like a club or a sword or a sharp arrow is the man who gives false testimony against his neighbor.

25 : 18

tests

The crucible for silver and the furnace for gold, but the Lord tests the heart.

17 : 3

therefore

Wisdom is supreme; therefore get wisdom. Though it cost all you have, get understanding.

4 : 7

Therefore disaster will overtake him in an instant; he will suddenly be destroyed -- without remedy.

6 : 15

thief

Men do not despise a thief if he steals to satisfy his hunger when he is starving.

6 : 30

and poverty will come on you like a bandit and scarcity like an armed man.

24 : 34

The accomplice of a thief is his own enemy; he is put under oath and dare not testify.

29 : 24

thieves

throw in your lot with us, and we will share a common purse" --

1 : 14

things
we will get all sorts of valuable things and fill our houses with plunder;

1 : 13

There are six things the Lord hates, seven that are detestable to him:

6 : 16

Listen, for I have worthy things to say; I open my lips to speak what is right.

8 : 6

From the fruit of his lips a man is filled with good things as surely as the work of his hands rewards him.

12 : 14

From the fruit of his lips a man enjoys good things, but the unfaithful have a craving for violence.

13 : 2

A quick-tempered man does foolish things, and a crafty man is hated.

14 : 17

Your eyes will see strange sights and your mind imagine confusing things.

23 : 33

"Two things I ask of you, O Lord; do not refuse me before I die:

30 : 7

There are three things that are too amazing for me, four that I do not understand:

30 : 18

"There are three things that are stately in their stride, four that move with stately bearing:

30 : 29

Many women do noble things, but you surpass them all."

31 : 29

thinking
for he is the kind of man who is always thinking about the cost. "Eat and drink," he says to you, but his heart is not with you.

23 : 7

thirsting
They eat the bread of wickedness and drink the wine of violence.

4 : 17

thirsty
If your enemy is hungry, give him food to eat; if he is thirsty, give him water to drink.

25 : 21

thirty
Have I not written thirty sayings for you, sayings of counsel and knowledge,

22 : 20

thornbush
Like a thornbush in a drunkard's hand is a proverb in the mouth of a fool.

26 : 9

thorns
The way of the sluggard is blocked with thorns, but the path of the upright is a highway.

15 : 19

In the paths of the wicked lie thorns and snares, but he who guards his soul stays far from them.

22 : 5

thorns had come up everywhere, the ground was covered with weeds, and the stone wall was in ruins.

24 : 31

those who do not fear the Lord
Since they hated knowledge and did not choose to fear the Lord,

1 : 29

those who lack judgment

"Let all who are simple come in here!"
she says to those who lack judgment.

9 : 4

though

Wisdom is supreme; therefore get
wisdom. Though it cost all you have,
get understanding.

4 : 7

Yet if he is caught, he must pay
sevenfold, though it costs him all the
wealth of his house.

6 : 31

A poor man is shunned by all his
relatives -- how much more do his
friends avoid him! Though he pursues
them with pleading, they are nowhere to
be found.

19 : 7

for though a righteous man falls seven
times, he rises again, but the wicked are
brought down by calamity.

24 : 16

Though his speech is charming, do not
believe him, for seven abominations fill
his heart.

26 : 25

Though you grind a fool in a mortar,
grinding him like grain with a pestle,
you will not remove his folly from him.

27 : 22

The wicked man flees though no one
pursues, but the righteous are as bold as
a lion.

28 : 1

A servant cannot be corrected by mere
words; though he understands, he will
not respond.

29 : 19

thought

She gives no thought to the way of life;
her paths are crooked, but she knows it
not.

5 : 6

The wisdom of the prudent is to give
thought to their ways, but the folly of
fools is deception.

14 : 8

A simple man believes anything, but a
prudent man gives thought to his steps.

14 : 15

Even a fool is thought wise if he keeps
silent, and discerning if he holds his
tongue.

17 : 28

A wicked man puts up a bold front, but
an upright man gives thought to his
ways.

21 : 29

thoughts

If you had responded to my rebuke, I
would have poured out my heart to you
and made my thoughts known to you.

1 : 23

The Lord detests the thoughts of the
wicked, but those of the pure are
pleasing to him.

15 : 26

threat

A man's riches may ransom his life, but
a poor man hears no threat.

13 : 8

three

"The leech has two daughters. 'Give!
Give!' they cry. "There are three things
that are never satisfied, four that never
say, 'Enough!':

30 : 15

There are three things that are too amazing for me, four that I do not understand:

30 : 18

"Under three things the earth trembles, under four it cannot bear up:

30 : 21

"There are three things that are stately in their stride, four that move with stately bearing:

30 : 29

threshing wheel
A wise king winnows out the wicked; he drives the threshing wheel over them.

20 : 26

thrive
Whoever trusts in his riches will fall, but the righteous will thrive like a green leaf.

11 : 28

When the wicked rise to power, people go into hiding; but when the wicked perish, the righteous thrive.

28 : 28

When the righteous thrive, the people rejoice; when the wicked rule, the people groan.

29 : 2

When the wicked thrive, so does sin, but the righteous will see their downfall.

29 : 16

throat
and put a knife to your throat if you are given to gluttony.

23 : 2

throne
Kings detest wrongdoing, for a throne is established through righteousness.

16 : 12

When a king sits on his throne to judge, he winnows out all evil with his eyes.

20 : 8

Love and faithfulness keep a king safe; through love his throne is made secure.

20 : 28

remove the wicked from the king's presence, and his throne will be established through righteousness.

25 : 5

If a king judges the poor with fairness, his throne will always be secure.

29 : 14

throng
Many are the victims she has brought down; her slain are a mighty throng.

7 : 26

through
At the window of my house I looked out through the lattice.

7 : 6

For through me your days will be many, and years will be added to your life.

9 : 11

With his mouth the godless destroys his neighbor, but through knowledge the righteous escape.

11 : 9

Through the blessing of the upright a city is exalted, but by the mouth of the wicked it is destroyed.

11 : 11

A man cannot be established through wickedness, but the righteous cannot be uprooted.

12 : 3

Through love and faithfulness sin is atoned for; through the fear of the Lord a man avoids evil.

16 : 6

Kings detest wrongdoing, for a throne is established through righteousness.

16 : 12

Love and faithfulness keep a king safe; through love his throne is made secure.

20 : 28

By wisdom a house is built, and through understanding it is established;

24 : 3

through knowledge its rooms are filled with rare and beautiful treasures.

24 : 4

remove the wicked from the king's presence, and his throne will be established through righteousness.

25 : 5

Through patience a ruler can be persuaded, and a gentle tongue can break a bone.

25 : 15

A rich man may be wise in his own eyes, but a poor man who has discernment sees through him.

28 : 11

throw
throw in your lot with us, and we will share a common purse" --

1 : 14

throw up
If you find honey, just eat enough -- too much of it, and you will vomit.

25 : 16

thwarts
The Lord does not let the righteous go hungry but he thwarts the craving of the wicked.

10 : 3

till
For they cannot sleep till they do evil; they are robbed of slumber till they make someone fall.

4 : 16

The path of the righteous is like the first gleam of dawn, shining ever brighter till the full light of day.

4 : 18

Come, let's drink deep of love till morning; let's enjoy ourselves with love!

7 : 18

He took his purse filled with money and will not be home till full moon."

7 : 20

till an arrow pierces his liver, like a bird darting into a snare, little knowing it will cost him his life.

7 : 23

The first to present his case seems right, till another comes forward and questions him.

18 : 17

A man tomented by the guilt of murder will be a fugitive till death; let no one support him.

28 : 17

tills the land
He who works his land will have abundant food, but he who chases fantasies lacks judgment.

12 : 11

time
A sluggard does not plow in season; so at harvest time he looks but finds nothing.

20 : 4

Like the coolness of snow at harvest time is a trustworthy messenger to those who send him; he refreshes the spirit of his masters.

25 : 13

timely
A man finds joy in giving an apt reply-- and how good is a timely word!

15 : 23

timely word
A man finds joy in giving an apt reply-- and how good is a timely word!

15 : 23

times
A friend loves at all times, and a brother is born for adversity.

17 : 17

for though a righteous man falls seven times, he rises again, but the wicked are brought down by calamity.

24 : 16

Like a bad tooth or a lame foot is reliance on the unfaithful in times of trouble.

25 : 19

times of trouble
If you falter in times of trouble, how small is your strength!

24 : 10

Like a bad tooth or a lame foot is reliance on the unfaithful in times of trouble.

25 : 19

tiny
"Four things on earth are small, yet they are extremely wise:

30 : 24

tired
A little sleep, a little slumber, a little folding of the hands to rest --

24 : 33

tithing
Honor the Lord with your wealth, with the firstfruits of all your crops;

3 : 9

today
Do not say to your neighbor, "Come back later; I'll give it tomorrow" -- when you now have it with you.

3 : 28

"I have fellowship offerings at home; today I fulfilled my vows.

7 : 14

So that your trust may be in the Lord, I teach you today, even you.

22 : 19

Do not boast about tomorrow, for you do not know what a day may bring forth.

27 : 1

together
I, wisdom, dwell together with prudence; I possess knowledge and discretion.

8 : 12

locusts have no king, yet they advance together in ranks;

30 : 27

toil
lest strangers feast on your wealth and your toil enrich another man's house.

5 : 10

tomorrow
Do not say to your neighbor, "Come back later; I'll give it tomorrow" -- when you now have it with you.

3 : 28

Do not boast about tomorrow, for you do not know what a day may bring forth.

27 : 1

tongue

haughty eyes, a lying tongue, hands that shed innocent blood,

6 : 17

keeping you from the immoral woman, from the smooth tongue of the wayward wife.

6 : 24

He who walks maliciously causes grief, and a chattering fool comes to ruin.

10 : 10

When words are many, sin is not absent, but he who holds his tongue is wise.

10 : 19

The tongue of the righteous is choice silver, but the heart of the wicked is of little value.

10 : 20

The mouth of the righteous brings forth wisdom, but a perverse tongue will be cut out.

10 : 31

A man who lacks judgment derides his neighbor, but a man of understanding holds his tongue.

11 : 12

A truthful witness gives honest testimony, but a false witness tells lies.

12 : 17

Reckless words pierce like a sword, but the tongue of the wise brings healing.

12 : 18

Truthful lips endure forever, but a lying tongue lasts only a moment.

12 : 19

He who guards his lips guards his life, but he who speaks rashly will come to ruin.

13 : 3

Stay away from a foolish man, for you will not find knowledge on his lips.

14 : 7

A quick-tempered man does foolish things, and a crafty man is hated.

14 : 17

The tongue of the wise commends knowledge, but the mouth of the fool gushes folly.

15 : 2

The tongue that brings healing is a tree of life, but a deceitful tongue crushes the spirit.

15 : 4

To man belong the plans of the heart, but from the Lord comes the reply of the tongue.

16 : 1

A wicked man listens to evil lips; a liar pays attention to a malicious tongue.

17 : 4

A man of perverse heart does not prosper; he whose tongue is deceitful falls into trouble.

17 : 20

Even a fool is thought wise if he keeps silent, and discerning if he holds his tongue.

17 : 28

The tongue has the power of life and death, and those who love it will eat its fruit.

18 : 21

A fortune made by a lying tongue is a fleeting vapor and a deadly snare.

21 : 6

He who guards his mouth and his tongue keeps himself from calamity.

21 : 23

He who loves a pure heart and whose speech is gracious will have the king for his friend.

22 : 11

Through patience a ruler can be persuaded, and a gentle tongue can break a bone.

25 : 15

As a north wind brings rain, so a sly tongue brings angry looks.

25 : 23

A lying tongue hates those it hurts, and a flattering mouth works ruin.

26 : 28

He who rebukes a man will in the end gain more favor than he who has a flattering tongue.

28 : 23

She speaks with wisdom, and faithful instruction is on her tongue.

31 : 26

too much
If you find honey, just eat enough -- too much of it, and you will vomit.

25 : 16

Seldom set foot in your neighbor's house -- too much of you, and he will hate you.

25 : 17

took
She took hold of him and kissed him and with a brazen face she said:

7 : 13

He took his purse filled with money and will not be home till full moon."

7 : 20

tooth
Like a bad tooth or a lame foot is reliance on the unfaithful in times of trouble.

25 : 19

top
You will be like one sleeping on the high seas, lying on top of the rigging.

23 : 34

tormented
A man tomented by the guilt of murder will be a fugitive till death; let no one support him.

28 : 17

torn
but the wicked will be cut off from the land, and the unfaithful will be torn from it.

2 : 22

torture
A man tomented by the guilt of murder will be a fugitive till death; let no one support him.

28 : 17

touches
So is he who sleeps with another man's wife; no one who touches her will go unpunished.

6 : 29

toward
Rescue those being led away to death; hold back those staggering toward slaughter.

24 : 11

tower
The name of the Lord is a strong tower; the righteous run to it and are safe.

18 : 10

An offended brother is more unyielding than a fortified city, and disputes are like the barred gates of a citadel.

18 : 19

town squares
now in the street, now in the squares, at every corner she lurks.

7 : 12

trading
She sees that her trading is profitable,
and her lamp does not go out at night.
31 : 18

tragedy
Have no fear of sudden disaster or of
the ruin that overtakes the wicked,
3 : 25

train
Train a child in the way he should go,
and when he is old he will not turn from
it.
22 : 6

transparency
Each heart knows its own bitterness,
and no one else can share its joy.
14 : 10

Death and Destruction lie open before
the Lord -- how much more the hearts
of men!
15 : 11

Who can say, "I have kept my heart
pure; I am clean and without sin"?
20 : 9

trap
till an arrow pierces his liver, like a bird
darting into a snare, little knowing it
will cost him his life.
7 : 23

The teaching of the wise is a fountain of
life, turning a man from the snares of
death.
13 : 14

A fool's mouth is his undoing, and his
lips are a snare to his soul.
18 : 7

It is a trap for a man to dedicate
something rashly and only later to
consider his vows.
20 : 25

The mouth of an adulteress is a deep
pit; he who is under the Lord's wrath
will fall into it.
22 : 14

He who leads the upright along an evil
path will fall into his own trap, but the
blameless will receive a good
inheritance.
28 : 10

A faithful man will be richly blessed,
but one eager to get rich will not go
unpunished.
28 : 20

A stingy man is eager to get rich and is
unaware that poverty awaits him.
28 : 22

Whoever flatters his neighbor is
spreading a net for his feet.
29 : 5

An evil man is snared by his own sin,
but a righteous one can sing and be
glad.
29 : 6

Fear of man will prove to be a snare,
but whoever trusts in the Lord is kept
safe.
29 : 25

trapped
if you have been trapped by what you
said, ensnared by the words of your
mouth,
6 : 2

The righteousness of the upright
delivers them, but the unfaithful are
trapped by evil desires.
11 : 6

An evil man is trapped by his sinful
talk, but a righteous man escapes
trouble.
12 : 13

or you may learn his ways and get
yourself ensnared.

22 : 25

travel
Avoid it, do not travel on it; turn from it
and go on your way.

4 : 15

treasure
and if you look for it as for silver and
search for it as for hidden treasure,

2 : 4

The house of the righteous contains
great treasure, but the income of the
wicked brings them trouble.

15 : 6

treasures
Ill-gotten treasures are of no value, but
righteousness delivers from death.

10 : 2

through knowledge its rooms are filled
with rare and beautiful treasures.

24 : 4

treasuries
bestowing wealth on those who love me
and making their treasuries full.

8 : 21

tree
She is a tree of life to those who
embrace her; those who lay hold of her
will be blessed.

3 : 18

Hope deferred makes the heart sick, but
a longing fulfilled is a tree of life.

13 : 12

The tongue that brings healing is a tree
of life, but a deceitful tongue crushes
the spirit.

15 : 4

He who tends a fig tree will eat its fruit,
and he who looks after his master will
be honored.

27 : 18

tree of life
She is a tree of life to those who
embrace her; those who lay hold of her
will be blessed.

3 : 18

The fruit of the righteous is a tree of
life, and he who wins souls is wise.

11 : 30

Hope deferred makes the heart sick, but
a longing fulfilled is a tree of life.

13 : 12

The tongue that brings healing is a tree
of life, but a deceitful tongue crushes
the spirit.

15 : 4

trembles
"Under three things the earth trembles,
under four it cannot bear up:

30 : 21

trial
A fool's lips bring him strife, and his
mouth invites a beating.

18 : 6

The first to present his case seems right,
till another comes forward and
questions him.

18 : 17

Like a bad tooth or a lame foot is
reliance on the unfaithful in times of
trouble.

25 : 19

trials
When the storm has swept by, the
wicked are gone, but the righteous stand
firm forever.

10 : 25

The righteous man is rescued from trouble, and it comes on the wicked instead.

11 : 8

When calamity comes, the wicked are brought down, but even in death the righteous have a refuge.

14 : 32

The crucible for silver and the furnace for gold, but the Lord tests the heart.

17 : 3

A friend loves at all times, and a brother is born for adversity.

17 : 17

thorns had come up everywhere, the ground was covered with weeds, and the stone wall was in ruins.

24 : 31

The crucible for silver and the furnace for gold, but man is tested by the praise he receives.

27 : 21

Blessed is the man who always fears the Lord, but he who hardens his heart falls into trouble.

28 : 14

tribulation
When the storm has swept by, the wicked are gone, but the righteous stand firm forever.

10 : 25

trickery
Like a coating of glaze over earthenware are fervent lips with an evil heart.

26 : 23

triumph
Evil men will bow down in the presence of the good, and the wicked at the gates of the righteous.

14 : 19

When the righteous triumph, there is great elation; but when the wicked rise to power, men go into hiding.

28 : 12

trouble
when calamity overtakes you like a storm, when disaster sweeps over you like a whirlwind, when distress and trouble overwhelm you.

1 : 27

Hatred stirs up dissension, but love covers over all wrongs.

10 : 12

The blessing of the Lord brings wealth, and he adds no trouble to it.

10 : 22

The righteous man is rescued from trouble, and it comes on the wicked instead.

11 : 8

A kind man benefits himself, but a cruel man brings trouble on himself.

11 : 17

He who brings trouble on his family will inherit only wind, and the fool will be servant to the wise.

11 : 29

An evil man is trapped by his sinful talk, but a righteous man escapes trouble.

12 : 13

No harm befalls the righteous, but the wicked have their fill of trouble.

12 : 21

A wicked messenger falls into trouble, but a trustworthy envoy brings healing.

13 : 17

A quick-tempered man does foolish things, and a crafty man is hated.

14 : 17

The simple inherit folly, but the prudent are crowned with knowledge.

14 : 18

The house of the righteous contains great treasure, but the income of the wicked brings them trouble.

15 : 6

Better a little with the fear of the Lord than great wealth with turmoil.

15 : 16

A hot-tempered man stirs up dissension, but a patient man calms a quarrel.

15 : 18

A greedy man brings trouble to his family, but he who hates bribes will live.

15 : 27

A man of perverse heart does not prosper; he whose tongue is deceitful falls into trouble.

17 : 20

The fear of the Lord leads to life: Then one rests content, untouched by trouble.

19 : 23

In the paths of the wicked lie thorns and snares, but he who guards his soul stays far from them.

22 : 5

He who sows wickedness reaps trouble, and the rod of his fury will be destroyed.

22 : 8

Drive out the mocker, and out goes strife; quarrels and insults are ended.

22 : 10

for their hearts plot violence, and their lips talk about making trouble.

24 : 2

If you falter in times of trouble, how small is your strength!

24 : 10

Like a bad tooth or a lame foot is reliance on the unfaithful in times of trouble.

25 : 19

Blessed is the man who always fears the Lord, but he who hardens his heart falls into trouble.

28 : 14

Mockers stir up a city, but wise men turn away anger.

29 : 8

An angry man stirs up dissension, and a hot-tempered one commits many sins.

29 : 22

The accomplice of a thief is his own enemy; he is put under oath and dare not testify.

29 : 24

troublemaker
who plots evil with deceit in his heart -- he always stirs up dissension.

6 : 14

a false witness who pours out lies and a man who stirs up dissension among brothers.

6 : 19

A perverse man stirs up dissension, and a gossip separates close friends.

16 : 28

troubles
A fool's lips bring him strife, and his mouth invites a beating.

18 : 6

true
My mouth speaks what is true, for my lips detest wickedness.

8 : 7

All the words of my mouth are just;
none of them is crooked or perverse.

8 : 8

teaching you true and reliable words, so
that you can give sound answers to him
who sent you?

22 : 21

true leader

A wise servant will rule over a
disgraceful son, and will share the
inheritance as one of the brothers.

17 : 2

true love

Many a man claims to have unfailing
love, but a faithful man who can find?

20 : 6

true riches

Misfortune pursues the sinner, but
prosperity is the reward of the
righteous.

13 : 21

true understanding

"The fear of the Lord is the beginning
of wisdom, and knowledge of the Holy
One is understanding.

9 : 10

true wealth

Better a meal of vegetables where there
is love than a fattened calf with hatred.

15 : 17

Whoever gives heed to instruction
prospers, and blessed is he who trusts in
the Lord.

16 : 20

true wisdom

The fear of the Lord is the beginning of
knowledge, but fools despise wisdom
and discipline.

1 : 7

"The fear of the Lord is the beginning
of wisdom, and knowledge of the Holy
One is understanding.

9 : 10

true words

teaching you true and reliable words, so
that you can give sound answers to him
who sent you?

22 : 21

truly

The truly righteous man attains life, but
he who pursues evil goes to his death.

11 : 19

trust

Trust in the Lord with all your heart and
lean not on your own understanding;

3 : 5

A man's steps are directed by the Lord.
How then can anyone understand his
own way?

20 : 24

A wise man attacks the city of the
mighty and pulls down the stronghold
in which they trust.

21 : 22

So that your trust may be in the Lord, I
teach you today, even you.

22 : 19

If you argue your case with a neighbor,
do not betray another man's confidence,

25 : 9

Otherwise, I may have too much and
disown you and say, 'Who is the Lord?'
Or I may become poor and steal, and so
dishonor the name of my God.

30 : 9

trust in the Lord

Trust in the Lord with all your heart and
lean not on your own understanding;

3 : 5

485

So that your trust may be in the Lord, I teach you today, even you.

22 : 19

A greedy man stirs up dissension, but he who trusts in the Lord will prosper.

28 : 25

trusted

Wounds from a friend can be trusted, but an enemy multiplies kisses.

27 : 6

trustfully

Do not plot harm against your neighbor, who lives trustfully near you.

3 : 29

trusts

Whoever trusts in his riches will fall, but the righteous will thrive like a green leaf.

11 : 28

The horse is made ready for the day of battle, but victory rests with the Lord.

21 : 31

A greedy man stirs up dissension, but he who trusts in the Lord will prosper.

28 : 25

He who trusts in himself is a fool, but he who walks in wisdom is kept safe.

28 : 26

Fear of man will prove to be a snare, but whoever trusts in the Lord is kept safe.

29 : 25

trusts in the Lord

Whoever gives heed to instruction prospers, and blessed is he who trusts in the Lord.

16 : 20

Fear of man will prove to be a snare, but whoever trusts in the Lord is kept safe.

29 : 25

trustworthy

A gossip betrays a confidence, but a trustworthy man keeps a secret.

11 : 13

A wicked messenger falls into trouble, but a trustworthy envoy brings healing.

13 : 17

Like the coolness of snow at harvest time is a trustworthy messenger to those who send him; he refreshes the spirit of his masters.

25 : 13

Like a bad tooth or a lame foot is reliance on the unfaithful in times of trouble.

25 : 19

truth

Listen, for I have worthy things to say; I open my lips to speak what is right.

8 : 6

All the words of my mouth are just; none of them is crooked or perverse.

8 : 8

The light of the righteous shines brightly, but the lamp of the wicked is snuffed out.

13 : 9

A truthful witness saves lives, but a false witness is deceitful.

14 : 25

The lips of the king speak as an oracle, and his mouth should not betray justice.

16 : 10

Kings take pleasure in honest lips; they value a man who speaks the truth.

16 : 13

my inmost being will rejoice when your lips speak what is right.

23 : 16

Buy the truth and do not sell it; get
wisdom, discipline and understanding.

23 : 23

Do not testify against your neighbor
without cause, or use your lips to
deceive.

24 : 28

Do not add to his words, or he will
rebuke you and prove you a liar.

30 : 6

truthful

A truthful witness gives honest
testimony, but a false witness tells lies.

12 : 17

Truthful lips endure forever, but a lying
tongue lasts only a moment.

12 : 19

The Lord detests lying lips, but he
delights in men who are truthful.

12 : 22

A truthful witness does not deceive, but
a false witness pours out lies.

14 : 5

A truthful witness saves lives, but a
false witness is deceitful.

14 : 25

truthfulness

He who conceals his hatred has lying
lips, and whoever spreads slander is a
fool.

10 : 18

An evil man is trapped by his sinful
talk, but a righteous man escapes
trouble.

12 : 13

The righteous hate what is false, but the
wicked bring shame and disgrace.

13 : 5

Kings take pleasure in honest lips; they
value a man who speaks the truth.

16 : 13

Arrogant lips are unsuited to a fool --
how much worse lying lips to a ruler!

17 : 7

A corrupt witness mocks at justice, and
the mouth of the wicked gulps down
evil.

19 : 28

A fortune made by a lying tongue is a
fleeting vapor and a deadly snare.

21 : 6

An honest answer is like a kiss on the
lips.

24 : 26

Like a club or a sword or a sharp arrow
is the man who gives false testimony
against his neighbor.

25 : 18

turmoil

Better a little with the fear of the Lord
than great wealth with turmoil.

15 : 16

turn

I in turn will laugh at your disaster; I
will mock when calamity overtakes you

1 : 26

Avoid it, do not travel on it; turn from it
and go on your way.

4 : 15

Do not let your heart turn to her ways or
stray into her paths.

7 : 25

Train a child in the way he should go,
and when he is old he will not turn from
it.

22 : 6

or the Lord will see and disapprove and turn his wrath away from him.

24 : 18

turn aside

Now then, my sons, listen to me; do not turn aside from what I say.

5 : 7

turn away

Mockers stir up a city, but wise men turn away anger.

29 : 8

turning

turning your ear to wisdom and applying your heart to understanding,

2 : 2

The teaching of the wise is a fountain of life, turning a man from the snares of death.

13 : 14

A longing fulfilled is sweet to the soul, but fools detest turning from evil.

13 : 19

The fear of the Lord is a fountain of life, turning a man from the snares of death.

14 : 27

turns

A bribe is a charm to the one who gives it; wherever he turns, he succeeds.

17 : 8

As a door turns on its hinges, so a sluggard turns on his bed.

26 : 14

If anyone turns a deaf ear to the law, even his prayers are detestable.

28 : 9

turns away

A gentle answer turns away wrath, but a harsh word stirs up anger.

15 : 1

twilight

at twilight, as the day was fading, as the dark of night set in.

7 : 9

twisting

For as churning the milk produces butter, and as twisting the nose produces blood, so stirring up anger produces strife."

30 : 33

two

for those two will send sudden destruction upon them, and who knows what calamities they can bring?

24 : 22

"Two things I ask of you, O Lord; do not refuse me before I die:

30 : 7

"The leech has two daughters. 'Give! Give!' they cry. "There are three things that are never satisfied, four that never say, 'Enough!':

30 : 15

tyrannical

A tyrannical ruler lacks judgment, but he who hates ill-gotten gain will enjoy a long life.

28 : 16

tyrannical ruler

A tyrannical ruler lacks judgment, but he who hates ill-gotten gain will enjoy a long life.

28 : 16

u

unanswered prayer
"Then they will call to me but I will not answer; they will look for me but will not find me.

1 : 28

unaware
A stingy man is eager to get rich and is unaware that poverty awaits him.

28 : 22

unbecoming
Like snow in summer or rain in harvest, honor is not fitting for a fool.

26 : 1

unbelievable
There are three things that are too amazing for me, four that I do not understand:

30 : 18

unbelievers
Since they hated knowledge and did not choose to fear the Lord,

1 : 29

under
The mouth of an adulteress is a deep pit; he who is under the Lord's wrath will fall into it.

22 : 14

if you lack the means to pay, your very bed will be snatched from under you.

22 : 27

The accomplice of a thief is his own enemy; he is put under oath and dare not testify.

29 : 24

"Under three things the earth trembles, under four it cannot bear up:

30 . 21

under control
A fool gives full vent to his anger, but a wise man keeps himself under control.

29 : 11

under oath
The accomplice of a thief is his own enemy; he is put under oath and dare not testify.

29 : 24

understand
then you will understand the fear of the Lord and find the knowledge of God.

2 : 5

Then you will understand what is right and just and fair -- every good path.

2 : 9

Discretion will protect you, and understanding will guard you.

2 : 11

A man's steps are directed by the Lord. How then can anyone understand his own way?

20 : 24

Evil men do not understand justice, but those who seek the Lord understand it fully.

28 : 5

There are three things that are too amazing for me, four that I do not understand:

30 : 18

understanding

for attaining wisdom and discipline; for understanding words of insight;

1 : 2

for understanding proverbs and parables, the sayings and riddles of the wise.

1 : 6

turning your ear to wisdom and applying your heart to understanding,

2 : 2

and if you call out for insight and cry aloud for understanding,

2 : 3

For the Lord gives wisdom, and from his mouth come knowledge and understanding.

2 : 6

Discretion will protect you, and understanding will guard you.

2 : 11

Trust in the Lord with all your heart and lean not on your own understanding;

3 : 5

Blessed is the man who finds wisdom, the man who gains understanding,

3 : 13

By wisdom the Lord laid the earth's foundations, by understanding he set the heavens in place;

3 : 19

Listen, my sons, to a father's instruction; pay attention and gain understanding.

4 : 1

Get wisdom, get understanding; do not forget my words or swerve from them.

4 : 5

Wisdom is supreme; therefore get wisdom. Though it cost all you have, get understanding.

4 : 7

Men do not despise a thief if he steals to satisfy his hunger when he is starving.

6 : 30

Say to wisdom, "You are my sister," and call understanding your kinsman;

7 : 4

Does not wisdom call out? Does not understanding raise her voice?

8 : 1

You who are simple, gain prudence; you who are foolish, gain understanding.

8 : 5

Counsel and sound judgment are mine; I have understanding and power.

8 : 14

Leave your simple ways and you will live; walk in the way of understanding.

9 : 6

"The fear of the Lord is the beginning of wisdom, and knowledge of the Holy One is understanding.

9 : 10

A fool finds pleasure in evil conduct, but a man of understanding delights in wisdom.

10 : 23

A man who lacks judgment derides his neighbor, but a man of understanding holds his tongue.

11 : 12

Good understanding wins favor, but the way of the unfaithful is hard.

13 : 15

understanding parables

A patient man has great understanding, but a quick-tempered man displays folly.

14 : 29

Folly delights a man who lacks judgment, but a man of understanding keeps a straight course.

15 : 21

He who ignores discipline despises himself, but whoever heeds correction gains understanding.

15 : 32

How much better to get wisdom than gold, to choose understanding rather than silver!

16 : 16

Understanding is a fountain of life to those who have it, but folly brings punishment to fools.

16 : 22

A man of knowledge uses words with restraint, and a man of understanding is even-tempered.

17 : 27

A fool finds no pleasure in understanding but delights in airing his own opinions.

18 : 2

He who gets wisdom loves his own soul; he who cherishes understanding prospers.

19 : 8

The purposes of a man's heart are deep waters, but a man of understanding draws them out.

20 : 5

Ears that hear and eyes that see -- the Lord has made them both.

20 : 12

A man who strays from the path of understanding comes to rest in the company of the dead.

21 : 16

Buy the truth and do not sell it; get wisdom, discipline and understanding.

23 : 23

By wisdom a house is built, and through understanding it is established;

24 : 3

When a country is rebellious, it has many rulers, but a man of understanding and knowledge maintains order.

28 : 2

I am the most ignorant of men; I do not have a man's understanding.

30 : 2

understanding parables
for understanding proverbs and parables, the sayings and riddles of the wise.

1 : 6

understanding proverbs
for understanding proverbs and parables, the sayings and riddles of the wise.

1 : 6

understanding riddles
for understanding proverbs and parables, the sayings and riddles of the wise.

1 : 6

understands
A servant cannot be corrected by mere words; though he understands, he will not respond.

29 : 19

undeserved
Like a fluttering sparrow or a darting swallow, an undeserved curse does not come to rest.

26 : 2

undisciplined
He will die for lack of discipline, led astray by his own great folly.

5 : 23

The woman Folly is loud; she is undisciplined and without knowledge.

9 : 13

undoing
A fool's mouth is his undoing, and his lips are a snare to his soul.

18 : 7

uneducated
"Let all who are simple come in here!" she says to those who lack judgment.

9 : 16

unethical
whose paths are crooked and who are devious in their ways.

2 : 15

unfailing love
What a man desires is unfailing love; better to be poor than a liar.

19 : 22

Many a man claims to have unfailing love, but a faithful man who can find?

20 : 6

unfair
The Lord abhors dishonest scales, but accurate weights are his delight.

11 : 1

A poor man's field may produce abundant food, but injustice sweeps it away.

13 : 23

unfaithful
but the wicked will be cut off from the land, and the unfaithful will be torn from it.

2 : 22

The integrity of the upright guides them, but the unfaithful are destroyed by their duplicity.

11 : 3

The righteousness of the upright delivers them, but the unfaithful are trapped by evil desires.

11 : 6

From the fruit of his lips a man enjoys good things, but the unfaithful have a craving for violence.

13 : 2

Good understanding wins favor, but the way of the unfaithful is hard.

13 : 15

The wicked become a ransom for the righteous, and the unfaithful for the upright.

21 : 18

The eyes of the Lord keep watch over knowledge, but he frustrates the words of the unfaithful.

22 : 12

Like a bandit she lies in wait, and multiplies the unfaithful among men.

23 : 28

Like a bad tooth or a lame foot is reliance on the unfaithful in times of trouble.

25 : 19

unfaithfulness
It will save you also from the adulteress, from the wayward wife with her seductive words,

2 : 16

492

who has left the partner of her youth
and ignored the covenant she made
before God.

2 : 17

For the lips of an adulteress drip honey,
and her speech is smoother than oil;

5 : 3

Why be captivated, my son, by an
adulteress? Why embrace the bosom of
another man's wife?

5 : 20

So is he who sleeps with another man's
wife; no one who touches her will go
unpunished.

6 : 29

Come, let's drink deep of love till
morning; let's enjoy ourselves with
love!

7 : 18

My husband is not at home; he has gone
on a long journey.

7 : 19

A man who strays from the path of
understanding comes to rest in the
company of the dead.

21 : 16

unfit

Like snow in summer or rain in harvest,
honor is not fitting for a fool.

26 : 1

unfriendliness

Do not plot harm against your neighbor,
who lives trustfully near you.

3 : 29

unfriendly man

An unfriendly man pursues selfish ends;
he defies all sound judgment.

18 : 1

unfulfilled

the grave, the barren womb, land, which
is never satisfied with water, and fire,
which never says, 'Enough!'

30 : 16

ungodliness

The wicked man earns deceptive wages,
but he who sows righteousness reaps a
sure reward.

11 : 18

The Lord detests men of perverse heart
but he delights in those whose ways are
blameless.

11 : 20

ungodly

If the righteous receive their due on
earth, how much more the ungodly and
the sinner!

11 : 31

unholy

those who are pure in their own eyes
and yet are not cleansed of their filth;

30 : 12

uniqueness

Each heart knows its own bitterness,
and no one else can share its joy.

14 : 10

unity

throw in your lot with us, and we will
share a common purse" --

1 : 14

Hatred stirs up dissension, but love
covers over all wrongs.

10 : 12

When a man's ways are pleasing to the
Lord, he makes even his enemies live at
peace with him.

16 : 7

Starting a quarrel is like breaching a dam; so drop the matter before a dispute breaks out.

17 : 14

It is to a man's honor to avoid strife, but every fool is quick to quarrel.

20 : 3

Better to live on a corner of the roof than share a house with a quarrelsome wife.

21 : 9

Better to live in a desert than with a quarrelsome and ill-tempered wife.

21 : 19

unknown
I have not learned the wisdom, nor have I knowledge of the Holy One.

30 : 3

unloved
an unloved woman who is married, and a maidservant who displaces her mistress.

30 : 23

unloved woman
an unloved woman who is married, and a maidservant who displaces her mistress.

30 : 23

unmet needs
Laziness brings on deep sleep, and the shiftless man goes hungry.

19 : 15

unpunished
So is he who sleeps with another man's wife; no one who touches her will go unpunished.

6 : 29

Be sure of this: The wicked will not go unpunished, but those who are righteous will go free.

11 : 21

The Lord detests all the proud of heart. Be sure of this: They will not go unpunished.

16 : 5

He who mocks the poor shows contempt for their Maker; whoever gloats over disaster will not go unpunished.

17 : 5

A false witness will not go unpunished, and he who pours out lies will not go free.

19 : 5

A false witness will not go unpunished, and he who pours out lies will perish.

19 : 9

A faithful man will be richly blessed, but one eager to get rich will not go unpunished.

28 : 20

unraveling
A fool's mouth is his undoing, and his lips are a snare to his soul.

18 : 7

unrighteousness
those who are pure in their own eyes and yet are not cleansed of their filth;

30 : 12

unsatisfied
an unloved woman who is married, and a maidservant who displaces her mistress.

30 : 23

unscalable wall
The wealth of the rich is their fortified city; they imagine it an unscalable wall.

18 : 11

unsearchable
As the heavens are high and the earth is deep, so the hearts of kings are unsearchable.

25 : 3

unsophisticated
"Let all who are simple come in here!" she says to those who lack judgment.

9 : 4

unsuited
Arrogant lips are unsuited to a fool -- how much worse lying lips to a ruler!

17 : 7

untouched by trouble
The fear of the Lord leads to life: Then one rests content, untouched by trouble.

19 : 23

unwise
He will die for lack of discipline, led astray by his own great folly.

5 : 23

"Let all who are simple come in here!" she says to those who lack judgment.

9 : 16

Stolen water is sweet; food eaten in secret is delicious!"

9 : 17

Better to meet a bear robbed of her cubs than a fool in his folly.

17 : 12

He who answers before listening -- that is his folly and his shame.

18 : 13

Wine is a mocker and beer a brawler; whoever is led astray by them is not wise.

20 : 1

I went past the field of the sluggard, past the vineyard of the man who lacks judgment;

24 : 30

Like tying a stone in a sling is the giving of honor to a fool.

26 . 8

As a dog returns to its vomit, so a fool repeats his folly.

26 : 11

is a man who deceives his neighbor and says, "I was only joking!"

26 : 19

unyielding
An offended brother is more unyielding than a fortified city, and disputes are like the barred gates of a citadel.

18 : 19

up
My son, if you accept my words and store up my commands within you,

2 : 1

The wise inherit honor, but fools he holds up to shame.

3 : 35

My son, if you have put up security for your neighbor, if you have struck hands in pledge for another,

6 : 1

How long will you lie there, you sluggard? When will you get up from your sleep?

6 : 9

who plots evil with deceit in his heart -- he always stirs up dissension.

6 : 14

a false witness who pours out lies and a man who stirs up dissension among brothers.

6 : 19

My son, keep my words and store up my commands within you.

7 : 1

Hatred stirs up dissension, but love covers over all wrongs.

10 : 12

Wise men store up knowledge, but the mouth of a fool invites ruin.

10 : 14

He who puts up security for another will surely suffer, but whoever refuses to strike hands in pledge is safe.

11 : 15

An anxious heart weighs a man down, but a kind word cheers him up.

12 : 25

A good man leaves an inheritance for his children's children, but a sinner's wealth is stored up for the righteous.

13 : 22

A gentle answer turns away wrath, but a harsh word stirs up anger.

15 : 1

A hot-tempered man stirs up dissension, but a patient man calms a quarrel.

15 : 18

A perverse man stirs up dissension, and a gossip separates close friends.

16 : 28

A man lacking in judgment strikes hands in pledge and puts up security for his neighbor.

17 : 18

A cheerful heart is good medicine, but a crushed spirit dries up the bones.

17 : 22

Take the garment of one who puts up security for a stranger; hold it in pledge if he does it for a wayward woman.

20 : 16

Food gained by fraud tastes sweet to a man, but he ends up with a mouth full of gravel.

20 : 17

A wicked man puts up a bold front, but an upright man gives thought to his ways.

21 : 29

Folly is bound up in the heart of a child, but the rod of discipline will drive it far from him.

22 : 15

for the Lord will take up their case and will plunder those who plunder them.

22 : 23

Do not be a man who strikes hands in pledge or puts up security for debts;

22 : 26

Do not move an ancient boundary stone set up by your forefathers.

22 : 28

You will vomit up the little you have eaten and will have wasted your compliments.

23 : 8

thorns had come up everywhere, the ground was covered with weeds, and the stone wall was in ruins.

24 : 31

it is better for him to say to you, "Come up here," than for him to humiliate you before a nobleman. What you have seen with your eyes

25 : 7

Take a garment of one who puts up security for a stranger; hold it in pledge if he does it for a wayward woman.

27 : 13

A greedy man stirs up dissension, but he who trusts in the Lord will prosper.

28 : 25

Mockers stir up a city, but wise men turn away anger.

29 : 8

Who has gone up to heaven and come down? Who has gathered up the wind in the hollow of his hands? Who has wrapped up the waters in his cloak? Who has established all the ends of the earth? What is his name, and the name of his son? Tell me if you know!

30 : 4

uplift
The lips of the righteous nourish many, but fools die for lack of judgment.

10 : 21

upright
He holds victory in store for the upright, he is a shield to those whose walk is blameless,

2 : 7

For the upright will live in the land, and the blameless will remain in it;

2 : 21

for the Lord detests a perverse man but takes the upright into his confidence.

3 : 32

The integrity of the upright guides them, but the unfaithful are destroyed by their duplicity.

11 : 3

The righteousness of the upright delivers them, but the unfaithful are trapped by evil desires.

11 : 6

Through the blessing of the upright a city is exalted, but by the mouth of the wicked it is destroyed.

11 : 11

The words of the wicked lie in wait for blood, but the speech of the upright rescues them.

12 : 6

He whose walk is upright fears the Lord, but he whose ways are devious despises him.

14 : 2

Fools mock at making amends for sin, but goodwill is found among the upright.

14 : 9

The house of the wicked will be destroyed, but the tent of the upright will flourish.

14 : 11

The Lord detests the sacrifice of the wicked, but the prayer of the upright pleases him.

15 : 8

The way of the sluggard is blocked with thorns, but the path of the upright is a highway.

15 : 19

The Lord is far from the wicked but he hears the prayer of the righteous.

15 : 29

The highway of the upright avoids evil; he who guards his way guards his life.

16 : 17

The way of the guilty is devious, but the conduct of the innocent is upright.

21 : 8

The wicked become a ransom for the righteous, and the unfaithful for the upright.

21 : 18

A wicked man puts up a bold front, but an upright man gives thought to his ways.

21 : 29

He who leads the upright along an evil path will fall into his own trap, but the blameless will receive a good inheritance.

28 : 10

Bloodthirsty men hate a man of integrity and seek to kill the upright.

29 : 10

The righteous detest the dishonest; the wicked detest the upright.

29 : 27

upright man

A wicked man puts up a bold front, but an upright man gives thought to his ways.

21 : 29

uprooted

The righteous will never be uprooted, but the wicked will not remain in the land.

10 : 30

A man cannot be established through wickedness, but the righteous cannot be uprooted.

12 : 3

upward

The path of life leads upward for the wise to keep him from going down to the grave.

15 : 24

use

Of what use is money in the hand of a fool, since he has no desire to get wisdom?

17 : 16

Do not testify against your neighbor without cause, or use your lips to deceive.

24 : 28

useless

How useless to spread a net in full view of all the birds!

1 : 17

Like a lame man's legs that hang limp is a proverb in the mouth of a fool.

26 : 7

uses

A man of knowledge uses words with restraint, and a man of understanding is even-tempered.

17 : 27

ushers

A gift opens the way for the giver and ushers him into the presence of the great.

18 : 16

utter ruin

I have come to the brink of utter ruin in the midst of the whole assembly.

5 : 14

V

vain

When a wicked man dies, his hope
perishes; all he expected from his power
comes to nothing.

11 : 7

valley

The eye that mocks a father, that scorns
obedience to a mother, will be pecked
out by the ravens of the valley, will be
eaten by the vultures.

30 : 17

valuable

we will get all sorts of valuable things
and fill our houses with plunder;

1 : 13

Choose my instruction instead of silver,
knowledge rather than choice gold,

8 : 10

for wisdom is more precious than
rubies, and nothing you desire can
compare with her.

8 : 11

My fruit is better than fine gold; what I
yield surpasses choice silver.

8 : 19

The tongue of the righteous is choice
silver, but the heart of the wicked is of
little value.

10 : 20

valuable things

we will get all sorts of valuable things
and fill our houses with plunder;

1 : 13

value

She is more precious than rubies;
nothing you desire can compare with
her.

3 : 15

Ill-gotten treasures are of no value, but
righteousness delivers from death.

10 : 2

The tongue of the righteous is choice
silver, but the heart of the wicked is of
little value.

10 : 20

A man's riches may ransom his life, but
a poor man hears no threat.

13 : 8

Kings take pleasure in honest lips; they
value a man who speaks the truth.

16 : 13

How much better to get wisdom than
gold, to choose understanding rather
than silver!

16 : 16

Take the garment of one who puts up
security for a stranger; hold it in pledge
if he does it for a wayward woman.

20 : 16

Remove the dross from the silver, and
out comes material for the silversmith;

25 : 4

A word aptly spoken is like apples of
gold in settings of silver.

25 : 11

A wife of noble character who can find?
She is worth far more than rubies.

31 : 10

Her husband has full confidence in her
and lacks nothing of value.

31 : 11

vanity
He who brings trouble on his family
will inherit only wind, and the fool will
be servant to the wise.

11 : 29

Better to be a nobody and yet have a
servant than pretend to be somebody
and have no food.

12 : 9

vapor
A fortune made by a lying tongue is a
fleeting vapor and a deadly snare.

21 : 6

vats
then your barns will be filled to
overflowing, and your vats will brim
over with new wine.

3 : 10

vegetables
Better a meal of vegetables where there
is love than a fattened calf with hatred.

15 : 17

vent
A fool gives full vent to his anger, but a
wise man keeps himself under control.

29 : 11

victims
Many are the victims she has brought
down; her slain are a mighty throng.

7 : 26

victorious
Evil men will bow down in the presence
of the good, and the wicked at the gates
of the righteous.

14 : 19

victory
He holds victory in store for the upright,
he is a shield to those whose walk is
blameless,

2 : 7

When the storm has swept by, the
wicked are gone, but the righteous stand
firm forever.

10 : 25

For lack of guidance a nation falls, but
many advisers make victory sure.

11 : 14

Wicked men are overthrown and are no
more, but the house of the righteous
stands firm.

12 : 7

Evil men will bow down in the presence
of the good, and the wicked at the gates
of the righteous.

14 : 19

The highway of the upright avoids evil;
he who guards his way guards his life.

16 : 17

The horse is made ready for the day of
battle, but victory rests with the Lord.

21 : 31

for waging war you need guidance, and
for victory many advisers.

24 : 6

for though a righteous man falls seven
times, he rises again, but the wicked are
brought down by calamity.

24 : 16

When the righteous triumph, there is
great elation; but when the wicked rise
to power, men go into hiding.

28 : 12

view
How useless to spread a net in full view
of all the birds!

1 : 17

For a man's ways are in full view of the Lord, and he examines all his paths.

5 : 21

She sits at the door of her house, on a seat at the highest point of the city,

9 : 14

A discerning man keeps wisdom in view, but a fool's eyes wander to the ends of the earth.

17 : 24

vigor

do not spend your strength on women, your vigor on those who ruin kings.

31 : 3

vigorously

She sets about her work vigorously; her arms are strong for her tasks.

31 : 17

villain

A scoundrel and villain, who goes about with a corrupt mouth,

6 : 12

who plots evil with deceit in his heart -- he always stirs up dissension.

6 : 14

vinegar

As vinegar to the teeth and smoke to the eyes, so is a sluggard to those who send him.

10 : 26

Like one who takes away a garment on a cold day, or like vinegar poured on soda, is one who sings songs to a heavy heart.

25 : 20

vineyard

I went past the field of the sluggard, past the vineyard of the man who lacks judgment;

24 : 30

She considers a field and buys it; out of her earnings she plants a vineyard.

31 . 16

violence

If they say, "Come along with us; let's lie in wait for someone's blood, let's waylay some harmless soul;

1 : 11

for their feet rush into sin, they are swift to shed blood.

1 : 16

Do not envy a violent man or choose any of his ways,

3 : 31

They eat the bread of wickedness and drink the wine of violence.

4 : 17

Blessings crown the head of the righteous, but violence overwhelms the mouth of the wicked.

10 : 6

The mouth of the righteous is a fountain of life, but violence overwhelms the mouth of the wicked.

10 : 11

The words of the wicked lie in wait for blood, but the speech of the upright rescues them.

12 : 6

From the fruit of his lips a man enjoys good things, but the unfaithful have a craving for violence.

13 : 2

A violent man entices his neighbor and leads him down a path that is not good.

16 : 29

A fool's lips bring him strife, and his mouth invites a beating.

18 : 6

The violence of the wicked will drag them away, for they refuse to do what is right.

21 : 7

for their hearts plot violence, and their lips talk about making trouble.

24 : 2

Like cutting off one's feet or drinking violence is the sending of a message by the hand of a fool.

26 : 6

violent

Do not envy a violent man or choose any of his ways,

3 : 31

violent man

Do not envy a violent man or choose any of his ways,

3 : 31

A violent man entices his neighbor and leads him down a path that is not good.

16 : 29

viper

In the end it bites like a snake and poisons like a viper.

23 : 32

virtue

He who seeks good finds goodwill, but evil comes to him who searches for it.

11 : 27

A wife of noble character is her husband's crown, but a disgraceful wife is like decay in his bones.

12 : 4

vision

My son, preserve sound judgment and discernment, do not let them out of your sight;

3 : 21

Let your eyes look straight ahead, fix your gaze directly before you.

4 : 25

it is better for him to say to you, "Come up here," than for him to humiliate you before a nobleman. What you have seen with your eyes

25 : 7

visit

Seldom set foot in your neighbor's house -- too much of you, and he will hate you.

25 : 17

voice

Wisdom calls aloud in the street, she raises her voice in the public squares;

1 : 20

Does not wisdom call out? Does not understanding raise her voice?

8 : 1

"To you, O men, I call out; I raise my voice to all mankind.

8 : 4

void

But the way of the wicked is like deep darkness; they do not know what makes them stumble.

4 : 19

The prospect of the righteous is joy, but the hopes of the wicked come to nothing.

10 : 28

for the evil man has no future hope, and the lamp of the wicked will be snuffed out.

24 : 20

vomit

You will vomit up the little you have eaten and will have wasted your compliments.

23 : 8

If you find honey, just eat enough -- too much of it, and you will vomit.

25 : 16

As a dog returns to its vomit, so a fool repeats his folly.

26 : 11

voting
The lot is cast into the lap, but its every decision is from the Lord.

16 : 33

Casting the lot settles disputes and keeps strong opponents apart.

18 : 18

vows
"I have fellowship offerings at home; today I fulfilled my vows.

7 : 14

It is a trap for a man to dedicate something rashly and only later to consider his vows.

20 : 25

"This is the way of an adulteress: She eats and wipes her mouth and says, 'I've done nothing wrong.'

30 : 20

"O my son, O son of my womb, O son of my vows,

31 : 2

vulnerable
a lizard can be caught with the hand, yet it is found in kings' palaces.

30 : 28

vultures
The eye that mocks a father, that scorns obedience to a mother, will be pecked out by the ravens of the valley, will be eaten by the vultures.

30 : 17

wage
Make plans by seeking advice; if you wage war, obtain guidance.
20 : 18

wage war
Make plans by seeking advice; if you wage war, obtain guidance.
20 : 18

wages
The wages of the righteous bring them life, but the income of the wicked brings them punishment.
10 : 16

The wicked man earns deceptive wages, but he who sows righteousness reaps a sure reward.
11 : 18

wages of sin
The evil deeds of a wicked man ensnare him; the cords of his sin hold him fast.
5 : 22

waging war
for waging war you need guidance, and for victory many advisers.
24 : 6

wait
If they say, "Come along with us; let's lie in wait for someone's blood, let's waylay some harmless soul;
1 : 11

These men lie in wait for their own blood; they waylay only themselves!
1 : 18

The words of the wicked lie in wait for blood, but the speech of the upright rescues them.
12 : 6

Do not say, "I'll pay you back for this wrong!" Wait for the Lord, and he will deliver you.
20 : 22

Like a bandit she lies in wait, and multiplies the unfaithful among men.
23 : 28

Do not lie in wait like an outlaw against a righteous man's house, do not raid his dwelling place;
24 : 15

wait for the Lord
Do not say, "I'll pay you back for this wrong!" Wait for the Lord, and he will deliver you.
20 : 22

waiting
Blessed is the man who listens to me, watching daily at my doors, waiting at my doorway.
8 : 34

wake up
How long will you lie there, you sluggard? When will you get up from your sleep?
6 : 9

"They hit me," you will say, "but I'm not hurt! They beat me, but I don't feel it! When will I wake up so I can find another drink?"
23 : 35

walk
He holds victory in store for the upright, he is a shield to those whose walk is blameless,

2 : 7

who leave the straight paths to walk in dark ways,

2 : 13

Thus you will walk in the ways of good men and keep to the paths of the righteous.

2 : 20

When you walk, your steps will not be hampered; when you run, you will not stumble.

4 : 12

Do not set foot on the path of the wicked or walk in the way of evil men.

4 : 14

Make level paths for your feet and take only ways that are firm.

4 : 26

When you walk, they will guide you; when you sleep, they will watch over you; when you awake, they will speak to you.

6 : 22

Can a man walk on hot coals without his feet being scorched?

6 : 28

I walk in the way of righteousness, along the paths of justice,

8 : 20

Leave your simple ways and you will live; walk in the way of understanding.

9 : 6

He whose walk is upright fears the Lord, but he whose ways are devious despises him.

14 : 2

A simple man believes anything, but a prudent man gives thought to his steps.

14 . 15

Better a poor man whose walk is blameless than a fool whose lips are perverse.

19 : 1

Better a poor man whose walk is blameless than a rich man whose ways are perverse.

28 : 6

He whose walk is blameless is kept safe, but he whose ways are perverse will suddenly fall.

28 : 18

walking
He was going down the street near her corner, walking along in the direction of her house

7 : 8

walking uprightly
Folly delights a man who lacks judgment, but a man of understanding keeps a straight course.

15 : 21

walks
The man of integrity walks securely, but he who takes crooked paths will be found out.

10 : 9

He who walks maliciously causes grief, and a chattering fool comes to ruin.

10 : 10

He who walks with the wise grows wise, but a companion of fools suffers harm.

13 : 20

He who trusts in himself is a fool, but he who walks in wisdom is kept safe.

28 : 26

wall
The wealth of the rich is their fortified
city; they imagine it an unscalable wall.
18 : 11

thorns had come up everywhere, the
ground was covered with weeds, and
the stone wall was in ruins.
24 : 31

walls
Like a city whose walls are broken
down is a man who lacks self-control.
25 : 28

wander
She is loud and defiant, her feet never
stay at home;
7 : 11

A discerning man keeps wisdom in
view, but a fool's eyes wander to the
ends of the earth.
17 : 24

war
Make plans by seeking advice; if you
wage war, obtain guidance.
20 : 18

for waging war you need guidance, and
for victory many advisers.
24 : 6

As charcoal to embers and as wood to
fire, so is a quarrelsome man for
kindling strife.
26 : 21

warning
Avoid it, do not travel on it; turn from it
and go on your way.
4 : 15

warning against adultery
For the lips of an adulteress drip honey,
and her speech is smoother than oil;
5 : 3

but in the end she is bitter as gall, sharp
as a double-edged sword.
5 : 4

Her feet go down to death; her steps
lead straight to the grave.
5 : 5

lest you give your best strength to
others and your years to one who is
cruel,
5 : 9

Drink water from your own cistern,
running water from your own well.
5 : 15

Why be captivated, my son, by an
adulteress? Why embrace the bosom of
another man's wife?
5 : 20

warped minds
A man is praised according to his
wisdom, but men with warped minds
are despised.
12 : 8

warrior
Better a patient man than a warrior, a
man who controls his temper than one
who takes a city.
16 : 32

waste
Like a lame man's legs that hang limp is
a proverb in the mouth of a fool.
26 : 7

wasted
You will vomit up the little you have
eaten and will have wasted your
compliments.
23 : 8

wasted honor
Like tying a stone in a sling is the
giving of honor to a fool.
26 : 8

wasted words
Do not speak to a fool, for he will scorn
the wisdom of your words.

23 : 9

wasting one's life
lest strangers feast on your wealth and
your toil enrich another man's house.

5 : 10

At the end of your life you will groan,
when your flesh and body are spent.

5 : 11

watch
Do not forsake wisdom, and she will
protect you; love her, and she will
watch over you.

4 : 6

When you walk, they will guide you;
when you sleep, they will watch over
you; when you awake, they will speak
to you.

6 : 22

The eyes of the Lord are everywhere,
keeping watch on the wicked and the
good.

15 : 3

The eyes of the Lord keep watch over
knowledge, but he frustrates the words
of the unfaithful.

22 : 12

watch over
Do not forsake wisdom, and she will
protect you; love her, and she will
watch over you.

4 : 6

When you walk, they will guide you;
when you sleep, they will watch over
you; when you awake, they will speak
to you.

6 : 22

The eyes of the Lord keep watch over
knowledge, but he frustrates the words
of the unfaithful.

22 : 12

watched
I applied my heart to what I observed
and learned a lesson from what I saw:

24 : 32

watches
She watches over the affairs of her
household and does not eat the bread of
idleness.

31 : 27

watches over
She watches over the affairs of her
household and does not eat the bread of
idleness.

31 : 27

watching
Blessed is the man who listens to me,
watching daily at my doors, waiting at
my doorway.

8 : 34

water
Drink water from your own cistern,
running water from your own well.

5 : 15

Should your springs overflow in the
streets, your streams of water in the
public squares?

5 : 16

When there were no oceans, I was given
birth, when there were no springs
abounding with water;

8 : 24

Stolen water is sweet; food eaten in
secret is delicious!"

9 : 17

If your enemy is hungry, give him food to eat; if he is thirsty, give him water to drink.

25 : 21

Like cold water to a weary soul is good news from a distant land.

25 : 25

As water reflects a face, so a man's heart reflects the man.

27 : 19

the grave, the barren womb, land, which is never satisfied with water, and fire, which never says, 'Enough!'

30 : 16

watercourse
The king's heart is in the hand of the Lord; he directs it like a watercourse wherever he pleases.

21 : 1

waters
when he gave the sea its boundary so the waters would not overstep his command, and when he marked out the foundations of the earth.

8 : 29

The words of a man's mouth are deep waters, but the fountain of wisdom is a bubbling brook.

18 : 4

The purposes of a man's heart are deep waters, but a man of understanding draws them out.

20 : 5

Who has gone up to heaven and come down? Who has gathered up the wind in the hollow of his hands? Who has wrapped up the waters in his cloak? Who has established all the ends of the earth? What is his name, and the name of his son? Tell me if you know!

30 : 4

way
for he guards the course of the just and protects the way of his faithful ones.

2 : 8

Then you will go on your way in safety, and your foot will not stumble;

3 : 23

I guide you in the way of wisdom and lead you along straight paths.

4 : 11

Do not set foot on the path of the wicked or walk in the way of evil men.

4 : 14

Avoid it, do not travel on it; turn from it and go on your way.

4 : 15

She gives no thought to the way of life; her paths are crooked, but she knows it not.

5 : 6

For these commands are a lamp, this teaching is a light, and the corrections of discipline are the way to life,

6 : 23

On the heights along the way, where the paths meet, she takes her stand;

8 : 2

I walk in the way of righteousness, along the paths of justice,

8 : 20

Leave your simple ways and you will live; walk in the way of understanding.

9 : 6

calling out to those who pass by, who go straight on their way.

9 : 15

He who heeds discipline shows the way to life, but whoever ignores correction leads others astray.

10 : 17

The way of the Lord is a refuge for the righteous, but it is the ruin of those who do evil.

10 : 29

The righteousness of the blameless makes a straight way for them, but the wicked are brought down by their own wickedness.

11 : 5

The way of a fool seems right to him, but a wise man listens to advice.

12 : 15

A righteous man is cautious in friendship, but the way of the wicked leads them astray.

12 : 26

In the way of righteousness there is life; along that path is immortality.

12 : 28

Good understanding wins favor, but the way of the unfaithful is hard.

13 : 15

There is a way that seems right to a man, but in the end it leads to death.

14 : 12

The Lord detests the way of the wicked but he loves those who pursue righteousness.

15 : 9

The way of the sluggard is blocked with thorns, but the path of the upright is a highway.

15 : 19

The highway of the upright avoids evil; he who guards his way guards his life.

16 : 17

There is a way that seems right to a man, but in the end it leads to death.

16 : 25

A violent man entices his neighbor and leads him down a path that is not good.

16 . 29

A gift opens the way for the giver and ushers him into the presence of the great.

18 : 16

It is not good to have zeal without knowledge, nor to be hasty and miss the way.

19 : 2

He who obeys instructions guards his life, but he who is contemptuous of his ways will die.

19 : 16

A man's steps are directed by the Lord. How then can anyone understand his own way?

20 : 24

All a man's ways seem right to him, but the Lord weighs the heart.

21 : 2

The way of the guilty is devious, but the conduct of the innocent is upright.

21 : 8

Train a child in the way he should go, and when he is old he will not turn from it.

22 : 6

Listen, my son, and be wise, and keep your heart on the right path.

23 : 19

Like a muddied spring or a polluted well is a righteous man who gives way to the wicked.

25 : 26

the way of an eagle in the sky, the way of a snake on a rock, the way of a ship on the high seas, and the way of a man with a maiden.

30 : 19

way of a fool
The way of a fool seems right to him, but a wise man listens to advice.

12 : 15

way of a man
the way of an eagle in the sky, the way of a snake on a rock, the way of a ship on the high seas, and the way of a man with a maiden.

30 : 19

way of a ship
the way of an eagle in the sky, the way of a snake on a rock, the way of a ship on the high seas, and the way of a man with a maiden.

30 : 19

way of a snake
the way of an eagle in the sky, the way of a snake on a rock, the way of a ship on the high seas, and the way of a man with a maiden.

30 : 19

way of an eagle
the way of an eagle in the sky, the way of a snake on a rock, the way of a ship on the high seas, and the way of a man with a maiden.

30 : 19

way of death
Stolen water is sweet; food eaten in secret is delicious!"

9 : 17

way of life
She gives no thought to the way of life; her paths are crooked, but she knows it not.

5 : 6

way of righteousness
In the way of righteousness there is life; along that path is immortality.

12 : 28

way of the guilty
The way of the guilty is devious, but the conduct of the innocent is upright.

21 : 8

way of the Lord
The way of the Lord is a refuge for the righteous, but it is the ruin of those who do evil.

10 : 29

way of the sluggard
The way of the sluggard is blocked with thorns, but the path of the upright is a highway.

15 : 19

way of the unfaithful
Good understanding wins favor, but the way of the unfaithful is hard.

13 : 15

way of the wicked
A righteous man is cautious in friendship, but the way of the wicked leads them astray.

12 : 26

The Lord detests the way of the wicked but he loves those who pursue righteousness.

15 : 9

way of understanding
Leave your simple ways and you will live; walk in the way of understanding.

9 : 6

way of wisdom
I guide you in the way of wisdom and lead you along straight paths.

4 : 11

way that seems right
There is a way that seems right to a man, but in the end it leads to death.

14 : 12

way to life

For these commands are a lamp, this teaching is a light, and the corrections of discipline are the way to life,

6 : 23

He who heeds discipline shows the way to life, but whoever ignores correction leads others astray.

10 : 17

ways

"How long will you simple ones love your simple ways? How long will mockers delight in mockery and fools hate knowledge?

1 : 22

they will eat the fruit of their ways and be filled with the fruit of their schemes.

1 : 31

Wisdom will save you from the ways of wicked men, from men whose words are perverse,

2 : 12

who leave the straight paths to walk in dark ways,

2 : 13

whose paths are crooked and who are devious in their ways.

2 : 15

Thus you will walk in the ways of good men and keep to the paths of the righteous.

2 : 20

in all your ways acknowledge him, and he will make your paths straight.

3 : 6

Her ways are pleasant ways, and all her paths are peace.

3 : 17

Do not envy a violent man or choose any of his ways,

3 : 31

Make level paths for your feet and take only ways that are firm.

4 . 26

For a man's ways are in full view of the Lord, and he examines all his paths.

5 : 21

Go to the ant, you sluggard; consider its ways and be wise!

6 : 6

Do not let your heart turn to her ways or stray into her paths.

7 : 25

Now then, my sons, listen to me; blessed are those who keep my ways.

8 : 32

Leave your simple ways and you will live; walk in the way of understanding.

9 : 6

The Lord detests men of perverse heart but he delights in those whose ways are blameless.

11 : 20

He whose walk is upright fears the Lord, but he whose ways are devious despises him.

14 : 2

The wisdom of the prudent is to give thought to their ways, but the folly of fools is deception.

14 : 8

The faithless will be fully repaid for their ways, and the good man rewarded for his.

14 : 14

All a man's ways seem innocent to him, but motives are weighed by the Lord.

16 : 2

When a man's ways are pleasing to the Lord, he makes even his enemies live at peace with him.

16 : 7

In his heart a man plans his course, but the Lord determines his steps.

16 : 9

A wicked man puts up a bold front, but an upright man gives thought to his ways.

21 : 29

My son, give me your heart and let your eyes keep to my ways,

23 : 26

wayward wife
It will save you also from the adulteress, from the wayward wife with her seductive words,

2 : 16

keeping you from the immoral woman, from the smooth tongue of the wayward wife.

6 : 24

they will keep you from the adulteress, from the wayward wife with her seductive words.

7 : 5

for a prostitute is a deep pit and a wayward wife is a narrow well.

23 : 27

wayward woman
Take the garment of one who puts up security for a stranger; hold it in pledge if he does it for a wayward woman.

20 : 16

Take a garment of one who puts up security for a stranger; hold it in pledge if he does it for a wayward woman.

27 : 13

waywardness
For the waywardness of the simple will kill them, and the complacency of fools will destroy them;

1 : 32

weakness
If you falter in times of trouble, how small is your strength!

24 : 10

If a man pampers his servant from youth, he will bring grief in the end.

29 : 21

wealth
Honor the Lord with your wealth, with the firstfruits of all your crops;

3 : 9

With me are the riches and honor, enduring wealth and prosperity.

8 : 18

Lazy hands make a man poor, but diligent hands bring wealth.

10 : 4

The blessing of the Lord brings wealth, and he adds no trouble to it.

10 : 22

Wealth is worthless in the day of wrath, but righteousness delivers from death.

11 : 4

A kindhearted woman gains respect, but ruthless men gain only wealth.

11 : 16

One man pretends to be rich, yet has nothing; another pretends to be poor, yet has great wealth.

13 : 7

The wealth of the wise is their crown, but the folly of fools yields folly.

14 : 24

He who increases his wealth by
exorbitant interest amasses it for
another, who will be kind to the poor.

28 : 8

wealthy
He who loves pleasure will become
poor; whoever loves wine and oil will
never be rich.

21 : 17

weapon
Like a club or a sword or a sharp arrow
is the man who gives false testimony
against his neighbor.

25 : 18

Like tying a stone in a sling is the
giving of honor to a fool.

26 : 8

weapons
Like a madman shooting firebrands or
deadly arrows

26 : 18

wear
Do not wear yourself out to get rich;
have the wisdom to show restraint.

23 : 4

wear down your body
lest you give your best strength to
others and your years to one who is
cruel,

5 : 9

weary
Like cold water to a weary soul is good
news from a distant land.

25 : 25

weary soul
Like cold water to a weary soul is good
news from a distant land.

25 : 25

weather
by his knowledge the deeps were
divided, and the clouds let drop the
dew.

3 : 20

Like clouds and wind without rain is a
man who boasts of gifts he does not
give.

25 : 14

As a north wind brings rain, so a sly
tongue brings angry looks.

25 : 23

Like snow in summer or rain in harvest,
honor is not fitting for a fool.

26 : 1

A quarrelsome wife is like a constant
dripping on a rainy day;

27 : 15

restraining her is like restraining the
wind or grasping oil with the hand.

27 : 16

weaving
In her hand she holds the distaff and
grasps the spindle with her fingers.

31 : 19

weeds
thorns had come up everywhere, the
ground was covered with weeds, and
the stone wall was in ruins.

24 : 31

weighed
All a man's ways seem innocent to him,
but motives are weighed by the Lord.

16 : 2

weighs
An anxious heart weighs a man down,
but a kind word cheers him up.

12 : 25

The heart of the righteous weighs its answers, but the mouth of the wicked gushes evil.

15 : 28

If you say, "But we knew nothing about this," does not he who weighs the heart perceive it? Does not he who guards your life know it? Will he not repay each person according to what he has done?

24 : 12

weighs the heart
All a man's ways seem right to him, but the Lord weighs the heart.

21 : 2

weights
The Lord abhors dishonest scales, but accurate weights are his delight.

11 : 1

Honest scales and balances are from the Lord; all the weights in the bag are of his making.

16 : 11

Differing weights and differing measures -- the Lord detests them both.

20 : 10

The Lord detests differing weights, and dishonest scales do not please him.

20 : 23

welcome
"Let all who are simple come in here!" she says to those who lack judgment.

9 : 4

well
Hold on to instruction, do not let it go; guard it well, for it is your life.

4 : 13

My son, pay attention to my wisdom, listen well to my words of insight,

5 : 1

Drink water from your own cistern, running water from your own well.

5 : 15

for a prostitute is a deep pit and a wayward wife is a narrow well.

23 : 27

But it will go well with those who convict the guilty, and rich blessing will come upon them.

24 : 25

wellspring
Above all else, guard your heart, for it is the wellspring of life.

4 : 23

went
I went past the field of the sluggard, past the vineyard of the man who lacks judgment;

24 : 30

what use
Of what use is money in the hand of a fool, since he has no desire to get wisdom?

17 : 16

whatever you do
Commit to the Lord whatever you do, and your plans will succeed.

16 : 3

wheel
A wise king winnows out the wicked; he drives the threshing wheel over them.

20 : 26

wherever
A bribe is a charm to the one who gives it; wherever he turns, he succeeds.

17 : 8

whip
Flog a mocker, and the simple will learn prudence; rebuke a discerning man, and he will gain knowledge.

19 : 25

Penalties are prepared for mockers, and beatings for the backs of fools.

19 : 29

A whip for the horse, a halter for the donkey, and a rod for the backs of fools!

26 : 3

whirlwind
when calamity overtakes you like a storm, when disaster sweeps over you like a whirlwind, when distress and trouble overwhelm you.

1 : 27

whoever
but whoever listens to me will live in safety and be at ease, without fear of harm."

1 : 33

But a man who commits adultery lacks judgment; whoever does so destroys himself.

6 : 32

For whoever finds me finds life and receives favor from the Lord.

8 : 35

But whoever fails to find me harms himself; all who hate me love death.

8 : 36

Whoever corrects a mocker invites insult; whoever rebukes a wicked man incurs abuse.

9 : 7

He who heeds discipline shows the way to life, but whoever ignores correction leads others astray.

10 : 17

He who conceals his hatred has lying lips, and whoever spreads slander is a fool.

10 : 18

He who puts up security for another will surely suffer, but whoever refuses to strike hands in pledge is safe.

11 : 15

Whoever trusts in his riches will fall, but the righteous will thrive like a green leaf.

11 : 28

Whoever loves discipline loves knowledge, but he who hates correction is stupid.

12 : 1

He who ignores discipline comes to poverty and shame, but whoever heeds correction is honored.

13 : 18

He who oppresses the poor shows contempt for their Maker, but whoever is kind to the needy honors God.

14 : 31

A fool spurns the father's discipline, but whoever heeds correction shows prudence.

15 : 5

He who ignores discipline despises himself, but whoever heeds correction gains understanding.

15 : 32

Whoever gives heed to instruction prospers, and blessed is he who trusts in the Lord.

16 : 20

He who mocks the poor shows contempt for their Maker; whoever gloats over disaster will not go unpunished.

17 : 5

He who covers over an offense promotes love, but whoever repeats the matter separates close friends.

17 : 9

Wine is a mocker and beer a brawler; whoever is led astray by them is not wise.

20 : 1

He who loves pleasure will become poor; whoever loves wine and oil will never be rich.

21 : 17

Whoever says to the guilty, "You are innocent" -- peoples will curse him and nations denounce him.

24 : 24

He who conceals his sins does not prosper, but whoever confesses and renounces them finds mercy.

28 : 13

Whoever flatters his neighbor is spreading a net for his feet.

29 : 5

Fear of man will prove to be a snare, but whoever trusts in the Lord is kept safe.

29 : 25

whole
let's swallow them alive, like the grave, and whole, like those who go down to the pit;

1 : 12

for they are life to those who find them and health to a man's whole body.

4 : 22

I have come to the brink of utter ruin in the midst of the whole assembly.

5 : 14

rejoicing in his whole world and delighting in mankind.

8 : 31

why
Why be captivated, my son, by an adulteress? Why embrace the bosom of another man's wife?

5 : 20

why doesn't God answer?
"Then they will call to me but I will not answer; they will look for me but will not find me.

1 : 28

why me?
"Then they will call to me but I will not answer; they will look for me but will not find me.

1 : 28

wicked
Wisdom will save you from the ways of wicked men, from men whose words are perverse,

2 : 12

who delight in doing wrong and rejoice in the perverseness of evil,

2 : 14

but the wicked will be cut off from the land, and the unfaithful will be torn from it.

2 : 22

Have no fear of sudden disaster or of the ruin that overtakes the wicked,

3 : 25

for the Lord detests a perverse man but takes the upright into his confidence.

3 : 32

The Lord's curse is on the house of the wicked, but he blesses the home of the righteous.

3 : 33

Do not set foot on the path of the wicked or walk in the way of evil men.

4 : 14

But the way of the wicked is like deep darkness; they do not know what makes them stumble.

4 : 19

The evil deeds of a wicked man ensnare him; the cords of his sin hold him fast.

5 : 22

Whoever corrects a mocker invites insult; whoever rebukes a wicked man incurs abuse.

9 : 7

The Lord does not let the righteous go hungry but he thwarts the craving of the wicked.

10 : 3

Blessings crown the head of the righteous, but violence overwhelms the mouth of the wicked.

10 : 6

The memory of the righteous will be a blessing, but the name of the wicked will rot.

10 : 7

The mouth of the righteous is a fountain of life, but violence overwhelms the mouth of the wicked.

10 : 11

The wages of the righteous bring them life, but the income of the wicked brings them punishment.

10 : 16

The tongue of the righteous is choice silver, but the heart of the wicked is of little value.

10 : 20

What the wicked dreads will overtake him; what the righteous desire will be granted.

10 : 24

When the storm has swept by, the wicked are gone, but the righteous stand firm forever.

10 : 25

The fear of the Lord adds length to life, but the years of the wicked are cut short.

10 : 27

The prospect of the righteous is joy, but the hopes of the wicked come to nothing.

10 : 28

The righteous will never be uprooted, but the wicked will not remain in the land.

10 : 30

The lips of the righteous know what is fitting, but the mouth of the wicked only what is perverse.

10 : 32

The righteousness of the blameless makes a straight way for them, but the wicked are brought down by their own wickedness.

11 : 5

When a wicked man dies, his hope perishes; all he expected from his power comes to nothing.

11 : 7

The righteous man is rescued from trouble, and it comes on the wicked instead.

11 : 8

When the righteous prosper, the city rejoices; when the wicked perish, there are shouts of joy.

11 : 10

Through the blessing of the upright a city is exalted, but by the mouth of the wicked it is destroyed.

11 : 11

The wicked man earns deceptive wages, but he who sows righteousness reaps a sure reward.

11 : 18

Be sure of this: The wicked will not go unpunished, but those who are righteous will go free.

11 : 21

The desire of the righteous ends only in good, but the hope of the wicked only in wrath.

11 : 23

If the righteous receive their due on earth, how much more the ungodly and the sinner!

11 : 31

The plans of the righteous are just, but the advice of the wicked is deceitful.

12 : 5

The words of the wicked lie in wait for blood, but the speech of the upright rescues them.

12 : 6

Wicked men are overthrown and are no more, but the house of the righteous stands firm.

12 : 7

A righteous man cares for the needs of his animal, but the kindest acts of the wicked are cruel.

12 : 10

The wicked desire the plunder of evil men, but the root of the righteous flourishes.

12 : 12

No harm befalls the righteous, but the wicked have their fill of trouble.

12 : 21

A righteous man is cautious in friendship, but the way of the wicked leads them astray.

12 : 26

The righteous hate what is false, but the wicked bring shame and disgrace.

13 : 5

The light of the righteous shines brightly, but the lamp of the wicked is snuffed out.

13 : 9

A wicked messenger falls into trouble, but a trustworthy envoy brings healing.

13 : 17

The righteous eat to their hearts' content, but the stomach of the wicked goes hungry.

13 : 25

He whose walk is upright fears the Lord, but he whose ways are devious despises him.

14 : 2

The house of the wicked will be destroyed, but the tent of the upright will flourish.

14 : 11

Evil men will bow down in the presence of the good, and the wicked at the gates of the righteous.

14 : 19

When calamity comes, the wicked are brought down, but even in death the righteous have a refuge.

14 : 32

The eyes of the Lord are everywhere, keeping watch on the wicked and the good.

15 : 3

The house of the righteous contains great treasure, but the income of the wicked brings them trouble.

15 : 6

The Lord detests the sacrifice of the wicked, but the prayer of the upright pleases him.

15 : 8

The Lord detests the way of the wicked but he loves those who pursue righteousness.

15 : 9

The Lord detests the thoughts of the wicked, but those of the pure are pleasing to him.

15 : 26

The heart of the righteous weighs its answers, but the mouth of the wicked gushes evil.

15 : 28

The Lord is far from the wicked but he hears the prayer of the righteous.

15 : 29

The Lord works out everything for his own ends -- even the wicked for a day of disaster.

16 : 4

He who winks with his eye is plotting perversity; he who purses his lips is bent on evil.

16 : 30

A wicked man listens to evil lips; a liar pays attention to a malicious tongue.

17 : 4

If a man pays back evil for good, evil will never leave his house.

17 : 13

A man of perverse heart does not prosper; he whose tongue is deceitful falls into trouble.

17 : 20

A wicked man accepts a bribe in secret to pervert the course of justice.

17 : 23

It is not good to be partial to the wicked or to deprive the innocent of justice.

18 : 5

Better a poor man whose walk is blameless than a fool whose lips are perverse.

19 : 1

A corrupt witness mocks at justice, and the mouth of the wicked gulps down evil.

19 : 28

A wise king winnows out the wicked; he drives the threshing wheel over them.

20 : 26

Haughty eyes and a proud heart, the lamp of the wicked, are sin!

21 : 4

The violence of the wicked will drag them away, for they refuse to do what is right.

21 : 7

The wicked man craves evil; his neighbor gets no mercy from him.

21 : 10

The Righteous One takes note of the house of the wicked and brings the wicked to ruin.

21 : 12

The wicked become a ransom for the righteous, and the unfaithful for the upright.

21 : 18

The sacrifice of the wicked is detestable -- how much more so when brought with evil intent!

21 : 27

A wicked man puts up a bold front, but an upright man gives thought to his ways.

21 : 29

In the paths of the wicked lie thorns and snares, but he who guards his soul stays far from them.

22 : 5

Do not envy wicked men, do not desire their company;

24 : 1

for their hearts plot violence, and their lips talk about making trouble.

24 : 2

He who plots evil will be known as a schemer,

24 : 8

for though a righteous man falls seven times, he rises again, but the wicked are brought down by calamity.

24 : 16

Do not fret because of evil men or be envious of the wicked,

24 : 19

for the evil man has no future hope, and the lamp of the wicked will be snuffed out.

24 : 20

remove the wicked from the king's presence, and his throne will be established through righteousness.

25 : 5

Like a muddied spring or a polluted well is a righteous man who gives way to the wicked.

25 : 26

The wicked man flees though no one pursues, but the righteous are as bold as a lion.

28 : 1

Those who forsake the law praise the wicked, but those who keep the law resist them.

28 : 4

When the righteous triumph, there is great elation; but when the wicked rise to power, men go into hiding.

28 : 12

When the wicked rise to power, people go into hiding; but when the wicked perish, the righteous thrive.

28 : 28

When the righteous thrive, the people rejoice; when the wicked rule, the people groan.

29 : 2

The righteous care about justice for the poor, but the wicked have no such concern.

29 : 7

If a ruler listens to lies, all his officials become wicked.

29 : 12

When the wicked thrive, so does sin, but the righteous will see their downfall.

29 : 16

The righteous detest the dishonest; the wicked detest the upright.

29 : 27

wicked heart
a heart that devises wicked schemes, feet that are quick to rush into evil,

6 : 18

wicked man
Whoever corrects a mocker invites insult; whoever rebukes a wicked man incurs abuse.

9 : 7

The wicked man earns deceptive wages, but he who sows righteousness reaps a sure reward.

11 : 18

A wicked man listens to evil lips; a liar pays attention to a malicious tongue.

17 : 4

An evil man is bent only on rebellion; a merciless official will be sent against him.

17 : 11

A wicked man accepts a bribe in secret to pervert the course of justice.

17 : 23

The wicked man craves evil; his neighbor gets no mercy from him.

21 : 10

A wicked man puts up a bold front, but an upright man gives thought to his ways.

21 : 29

He who plots evil will be known as a schemer,

24 : 8

The wicked man flees though no one pursues, but the righteous are as bold as a lion.

28 : 1

Like a roaring lion or a charging bear is a wicked man ruling over a helpless people.

28 : 15

wicked men

Wicked men are overthrown and are no more, but the house of the righteous stands firm.

12 : 7

Do not envy wicked men, do not desire their company;

24 : 1

for their hearts plot violence, and their lips talk about making trouble.

24 . 2

wicked person

who plots evil with deceit in his heart -- he always stirs up dissension.

6 : 14

wicked schemes

a heart that devises wicked schemes, feet that are quick to rush into evil,

6 : 18

wickedness

For they cannot sleep till they do evil; they are robbed of slumber till they make someone fall.

4 : 16

They eat the bread of wickedness and drink the wine of violence.

4 : 17

My mouth speaks what is true, for my lips detest wickedness.

8 : 7

The righteousness of the blameless makes a straight way for them, but the wicked are brought down by their own wickedness.

11 : 5

A man cannot be established through wickedness, but the righteous cannot be uprooted.

12 : 3

Righteousness guards the man of integrity, but wickedness overthrows the sinner.

13 : 6

A longing fulfilled is sweet to the soul, but fools detest turning from evil.

13 : 19

When wickedness comes, so does contempt, and with shame comes disgrace.

18 : 3

A corrupt witness mocks at justice, and the mouth of the wicked gulps down evil.

19 : 28

When a king sits on his throne to judge, he winnows out all evil with his eyes.

20 : 8

Blows and wounds cleanse away evil, and beatings purge the inmost being.

20 : 30

He who sows wickedness reaps trouble, and the rod of his fury will be destroyed.

22 : 8

His malice may be concealed by deception, but his wickedness will be exposed in the assembly.

26 : 26

widow's
The Lord tears down the proud man's house, but he keeps the widow's boundaries intact.

15 : 25

wife
It will save you also from the adulteress, from the wayward wife with her seductive words,

2 : 16

who has left the partner of her youth and ignored the covenant she made before God.

2 : 17

May your fountain be blessed, and may you rejoice in the wife of your youth.

5 : 18

A loving doe, a graceful deer -- may her breasts satisfy you always, may you ever be captivated by her love.

5 : 19

Why be captivated, my son, by an adulteress? Why embrace the bosom of another man's wife?

5 : 20

keeping you from the immoral woman, from the smooth tongue of the wayward wife.

6 : 24

So is he who sleeps with another man's wife; no one who touches her will go unpunished.

6 : 29

they will keep you from the adulteress, from the wayward wife with her seductive words.

7 : 5

A wife of noble character is her husband's crown, but a disgraceful wife is like decay in his bones.

12 : 4

He who finds a wife finds what is good and receives favor from the Lord.

18 : 22

A foolish son is his father's ruin, and a quarrelsome wife is like a constant dripping.

19 : 13

Houses and wealth are inherited from parents, but a prudent wife is from the Lord.

19 : 14

Better to live on a corner of the roof than share a house with a quarrelsome wife.

21 : 9

Better to live in a desert than with a quarrelsome and ill-tempered wife.

21 : 19

for a prostitute is a deep pit and a wayward wife is a narrow well.

23 : 27

Better to live on a corner of the roof than share a house with a quarrelsome wife.

25 : 24

A quarrelsome wife is like a constant dripping on a rainy day;

27 : 15

restraining her is like restraining the wind or grasping oil with the hand.

27 : 16

A wife of noble character who can find? She is worth far more than rubies.

31 : 10

She considers a field and buys it; out of her earnings she plants a vineyard.

31 : 16

She sets about her work vigorously; her arms are strong for her tasks.

31 : 17

In her hand she holds the distaff and grasps the spindle with her fingers.

31 : 19

She opens her arms to the poor and extends her hands to the needy.

31 : 20

Her husband is respected at the city gate, where he takes his seat among the elders of the land.

31 : 23

wife of noble character
A wife of noble character who can find? She is worth far more than rubies.

31 : 10

wife of your youth
May your fountain be blessed, and may you rejoice in the wife of your youth.

5 : 18

wild
Like an archer who wounds at random is he who hires a fool or any passer-by.

26 : 10

will
Houses and wealth are inherited from parents, but a prudent wife is from the Lord.

19 : 14

will be
for the Lord will be your confidence and will keep your foot from being snared.

3 : 26

will not
He will not accept any compensation; he will refuse the bribe, however great it is.

6 : 35

Be sure of this: The wicked will not go unpunished, but those who are righteous will go free.

11 : 21

An inheritance quickly gained at the beginning will not be blessed at the end.

20 : 21

will of God
The Lord works out everything for his own ends -- even the wicked for a day of disaster.

16 : 4

In his heart a man plans his course, but the Lord determines his steps.

16 : 9

The lot is cast into the lap, but its every decision is from the Lord.

16 : 33

Many are the plans in the man's heart,
but it is the Lord's purpose that prevails.

19 : 21

A man's steps are directed by the Lord.
How then can anyone understand his
own way?

20 : 24

There is no wisdom, no insight, no plan
that can succeed against the Lord.

21 : 30

The horse is made ready for the day of
battle, but victory rests with the Lord.

21 : 31

Rich and poor have this in common:
The Lord is the Maker of them all.

22 : 2

willing

People curse the man who hoards grain,
but blessing crowns him who is willing
to sell.

11 : 26

Discipline your son, for in that there is
hope; do not be a willing party to his
death.

19 : 18

win

Then you will win favor and a good
name in the sight of God and man.

3 : 4

wind

He who brings trouble on his family
will inherit only wind, and the fool will
be servant to the wise.

11 : 29

Like clouds and wind without rain is a
man who boasts of gifts he does not
give.

25 : 14

As a north wind brings rain, so a sly
tongue brings angry looks.

25 : 23

restraining her is like restraining the
wind or grasping oil with the hand.

27 : 16

Who has gone up to heaven and come
down? Who has gathered up the wind
in the hollow of his hands? Who has
wrapped up the waters in his cloak?
Who has established all the ends of the
earth? What is his name, and the name
of his son? Tell me if you know!

30 : 4

window

At the window of my house I looked
out through the lattice.

7 : 6

wine

then your barns will be filled to
overflowing, and your vats will brim
over with new wine.

3 : 10

They eat the bread of wickedness and
drink the wine of violence.

4 : 17

She has prepared her meat and mixed
her wine; she has also set her table.

9 : 2

"Come, eat my food and drink the wine
I have mixed.

9 : 5

Wine is a mocker and beer a brawler;
whoever is led astray by them is not
wise.

20 : 1

He who loves pleasure will become
poor; whoever loves wine and oil will
never be rich.

21 : 17

Do not join those who drink too much
wine or gorge themselves on meat,

23 : 20

for drunkards and gluttons become poor, and drowsiness clothes them in rags.

23 : 21

Who has woe? Who has sorrow? Who has strife? Who has complaints? Who has needless bruises? Who has bloodshot eyes?

23 : 29

Those who linger over wine, who go to sample bowls of mixed wine,

23 : 30

Do not gaze at wine when it is red, when it sparkles in the cup, when it goes down smoothly!

23 : 31

In the end it bites like a snake and poisons like a viper.

23 : 32

Your eyes will see strange sights and your mind imagine confusing things.

23 : 33

You will be like one sleeping on the high seas, lying on top of the rigging.

23 : 34

"They hit me," you will say, "but I'm not hurt! They beat me, but I don't feel it! When will I wake up so I can find another drink?"

23 : 35

"It is not for kings, O Lemuel -- not for kings to drink wine, not for rulers to crave beer,

31 : 4

Give beer to those who are perishing, wine to those who are in anguish;

31 : 6

wings
Cast but a glance at riches, and they are gone, for they will surely sprout wings and fly off to the sky like an eagle.

23 : 5

wining and dining
for he is the kind of man who is always thinking about the cost. "Eat and drink," he says to you, but his heart is not with you.

23 : 7

winks
who winks with his eye, signals with his feet and motions with his fingers,

6 : 13

He who winks with his eye is plotting perversity; he who purses his lips is bent on evil.

16 : 30

winning souls
The fruit of the righteous is a tree of life, and he who wins souls is wise.

11 : 30

winnows
When a king sits on his throne to judge, he winnows out all evil with his eyes.

20 : 8

A wise king winnows out the wicked; he drives the threshing wheel over them.

20 : 26

wins
The fruit of the righteous is a tree of life, and he who wins souls is wise.

11 : 30

Good understanding wins favor, but the way of the unfaithful is hard.

13 : 15

winter clothes
When it snows, she has no fear for her household; for all of them are clothed in scarlet.

31 : 21

wiped away
Blows and disgrace are his lot, and his shame will never be wiped away;

6 : 33

wipes
"This is the way of an adulteress: She eats and wipes her mouth and says, 'I've done nothing wrong.'

30 : 20

wisdom
for attaining wisdom and discipline; for understanding words of insight;

1 : 2

The fear of the Lord is the beginning of knowledge, but fools despise wisdom and discipline.

1 : 7

Wisdom calls aloud in the street, she raises her voice in the public squares;

1 : 20

at the head of the noisy streets she cries out, in the gateways of the city she makes her speech:

1 : 21

turning your ear to wisdom and applying your heart to understanding,

2 : 2

and if you look for it as for silver and search for it as for hidden treasure,

2 : 4

For the Lord gives wisdom, and from his mouth come knowledge and understanding.

2 : 6

For wisdom will enter your heart, and knowledge will be pleasant to your soul.

2 : 10

Wisdom will save you from the ways of wicked men, from men whose words are perverse,

2 : 12

Blessed is the man who finds wisdom, the man who gains understanding,

3 : 13

for she is more profitable than silver and yields better returns than gold.

3 : 14

She is more precious than rubies; nothing you desire can compare with her.

3 : 15

Long life is in her right hand; in her left hand are riches and honor.

3 : 16

Her ways are pleasant ways, and all her paths are peace.

3 : 17

She is a tree of life to those who embrace her; those who lay hold of her will be blessed.

3 : 18

By wisdom the Lord laid the earth's foundations, by understanding he set the heavens in place;

3 : 19

My son, preserve sound judgment and discernment, do not let them out of your sight;

3 : 21

they will be life for you, an ornament to grace your neck.

3 : 22

Listen, my sons, to a father's instruction; pay attention and gain understanding.

4 : 1

he taught me and said, "Lay hold of my words with all your heart; keep my commands and you will live.

4 : 4

Get wisdom, get understanding; do not forget my words or swerve from them.

4 : 5

Do not forsake wisdom, and she will protect you; love her, and she will watch over you.

4 : 6

Wisdom is supreme; therefore get wisdom. Though it cost all you have, get understanding.

4 : 7

Esteem her, and she will exalt you; embrace her, and she will honor you.

4 : 8

She will set a garland of grace on your head and present you with a crown of splendor.

4 : 9

I guide you in the way of wisdom and lead you along straight paths.

4 : 11

Do not let them out of your sight, keep them within your heart;

4 : 21

My son, pay attention to my wisdom, listen well to my words of insight,

5 : 1

Go to the ant, you sluggard; consider its ways and be wise!

6 : 6

Say to wisdom, "You are my sister," and call understanding your kinsman;

7 : 4

Now then, my sons, listen to me; pay attention to what I say.

7 : 24

Does not wisdom call out? Does not understanding raise her voice?

8 : 1

beside the gates leading into the city, at the entrances, she cries aloud:

8 : 3

"To you, O men, I call out; I raise my voice to all mankind.

8 : 4

Listen, for I have worthy things to say; I open my lips to speak what is right.

8 : 6

My mouth speaks what is true, for my lips detest wickedness.

8 : 7

Choose my instruction instead of silver, knowledge rather than choice gold,

8 : 10

for wisdom is more precious than rubies, and nothing you desire can compare with her.

8 : 11

I, wisdom, dwell together with prudence; I possess knowledge and discretion.

8 : 12

Counsel and sound judgment are mine; I have understanding and power.

8 : 14

By me kings reign and rulers make laws that are just;

8 : 15

by me princes govern, and all nobles
who rule on earth.

8 : 16

I love those who love me, and those
who seek me find me.

8 : 17

With me are the riches and honor,
enduring wealth and prosperity.

8 : 18

My fruit is better than fine gold; what I
yield surpasses choice silver.

8 : 19

bestowing wealth on those who love me
and making their treasuries full.

8 : 21

I was appointed from eternity, from the
beginning, before the world began,

8 : 23

When there were no oceans, I was given
birth, when there were no springs
abounding with water;

8 : 24

before the mountains were settled in
place, before the hills, I was given birth,

8 : 25

I was there when he set the heavens in
place, when he marked out the horizon
on the face of the deep,

8 : 27

Then I was the craftsman at his side. I
was filled with delight day after day,
rejoicing always in his presence,

8 : 30

Wisdom has built her house; she has
hewn out its seven pillars.

9 : 1

"The fear of the Lord is the beginning
of wisdom, and knowledge of the Holy
One is understanding.

9 : 10

If you are wise, your wisdom will
reward you; if you are a mocker, you
alone will suffer."

9 : 12

Wisdom is found on the lips of the
discerning, but a rod is for the back of
him who lacks judgment.

10 : 13

When words are many, sin is not
absent, but he who holds his tongue is
wise.

10 : 19

A fool finds pleasure in evil conduct,
but a man of understanding delights in
wisdom.

10 : 23

The mouth of the righteous brings forth
wisdom, but a perverse tongue will be
cut out.

10 : 31

When pride comes, then comes
disgrace, but with humility comes
wisdom.

11 : 2

A man who lacks judgment derides his
neighbor, but a man of understanding
holds his tongue.

11 : 12

The fruit of the righteous is a tree of
life, and he who wins souls is wise.

11 : 30

Whoever loves discipline loves
knowledge, but he who hates correction
is stupid.

12 : 1

A man is praised according to his
wisdom, but men with warped minds
are despised.

12 : 8

The way of a fool seems right to him, but a wise man listens to advice.

12 : 15

Pride only breeds quarrels, but wisdom is found in those who take advice.

13 : 10

The wise woman builds her house, but with her own hands the foolish one tears hers down.

14 : 1

The mocker seeks wisdom and finds none, but knowledge comes easily to the discerning.

14 : 6

Stay away from a foolish man, for you will not find knowledge on his lips.

14 : 7

The wisdom of the prudent is to give thought to their ways, but the folly of fools is deception.

14 : 8

A simple man believes anything, but a prudent man gives thought to his steps.

14 : 15

A wise man fears the Lord and shuns evil, but a fool is hotheaded and reckless.

14 : 16

Wisdom reposes in the heart of the discerning and even among fools she lets herself be known.

14 : 33

The heart of the righteous weighs its answers, but the mouth of the wicked gushes evil.

15 : 28

He who ignores discipline despises himself, but whoever heeds correction gains understanding.

15 : 32

The fear of the Lord teaches a man wisdom, and humility comes before honor.

15 : 33

How much better to get wisdom than gold, to choose understanding rather than silver!

16 : 16

Gray hair is a crown of splendor; it is attained by a righteous life.

16 : 31

Of what use is money in the hand of a fool, since he has no desire to get wisdom?

17 : 16

A discerning man keeps wisdom in view, but a fool's eyes wander to the ends of the earth.

17 : 24

The words of a man's mouth are deep waters, but the fountain of wisdom is a bubbling brook.

18 : 4

He who gets wisdom loves his own soul; he who cherishes understanding prospers.

19 : 8

A man's wisdom gives him patience; it is to his glory to overlook an offense.

19 : 11

Flog a mocker, and the simple will learn prudence; rebuke a discerning man, and he will gain knowledge.

19 : 25

Ears that hear and eyes that see -- the Lord has made them both.

20 : 12

The glory of young men is their strength, gray hair the splendor of the old.

20 : 29

When a mocker is punished, the simple gain wisdom; when a wise man is instructed, he gets knowledge.

21 : 11

A wicked man puts up a bold front, but an upright man gives thought to his ways.

21 : 29

There is no wisdom, no insight, no plan that can succeed against the Lord.

21 : 30

teaching you true and reliable words, so that you can give sound answers to him who sent you?

22 : 21

Do not wear yourself out to get rich; have the wisdom to show restraint.

23 : 4

Do not speak to a fool, for he will scorn the wisdom of your words.

23 : 9

Buy the truth and do not sell it; get wisdom, discipline and understanding.

23 : 23

By wisdom a house is built, and through understanding it is established;

24 : 3

A wise man has great power, and a man of knowledge increases strength;

24 : 5

Wisdom is too high for a fool; in the assembly at the gate he has nothing to say.

24 : 7

Know also that wisdom is sweet to your soul; if you find it, there is a future hope for you, and your hope will not be cut off.

24 : 14

Like an earring of gold or an ornament of fine gold is a wise man's rebuke to a listening ear.

25 : 12

He who trusts in himself is a fool, but he who walks in wisdom is kept safe.

28 : 26

A man who loves wisdom brings joy to his father, but a companion of prostitutes squanders his wealth.

29 : 3

The rod of correction imparts wisdom, but a child left to himself disgraces his mother.

29 : 15

I have not learned the wisdom, nor have I knowledge of the Holy One.

30 : 3

Ants are creatures of little strength, yet they store up their food in the summer;

30 : 25

She speaks with wisdom, and faithful instruction is on her tongue.

31 : 26

wise

let the wise listen and add to their learning, and let the discerning get guidance --

1 : 5

for understanding proverbs and parables, the sayings and riddles of the wise.

1 : 6

Do not be wise in your own eyes; fear the Lord and shun evil.

3 : 7

The wise inherit honor, but fools he holds up to shame.

3 : 35

Go to the ant, you sluggard; consider its ways and be wise!

6 : 6

Listen to my instruction and be wise; do not ignore it.

8 : 33

Do not rebuke a mocker or he will hate you; rebuke a wise man and he will love you.

9 : 8

Instruct a wise man and he will be wiser still; teach a righteous man and he will add to his learning.

9 : 9

If you are wise, your wisdom will reward you; if you are a mocker, you alone will suffer."

9 : 12

The proverbs of Solomon: A wise son brings joy to his father, but a foolish son grief to his mother.

10 : 1

He who gathers crops in summer is a wise son, but he who sleeps during harvest is a disgraceful son.

10 : 5

The wise in heart accept commands, but a chattering fool comes to ruin.

10 : 8

Wise men store up knowledge, but the mouth of a fool invites ruin.

10 : 14

When words are many, sin is not absent, but he who holds his tongue is wise.

10 : 19

He who brings trouble on his family will inherit only wind, and the fool will be servant to the wise.

11 : 29

The fruit of the righteous is a tree of life, and he who wins souls is wise.

11 : 30

The way of a fool seems right to him, but a wise man listens to advice.

12 : 15

Reckless words pierce like a sword, but the tongue of the wise brings healing.

12 : 18

A wise son heeds his father's instruction, but a mocker does not listen to rebuke.

13 : 1

The teaching of the wise is a fountain of life, turning a man from the snares of death.

13 : 14

He who walks with the wise grows wise, but a companion of fools suffers harm.

13 : 20

The wise woman builds her house, but with her own hands the foolish one tears hers down.

14 : 1

A fool's talk brings a rod to his back, but the lips of the wise protect them.

14 : 3

A wise man fears the Lord and shuns evil, but a fool is hotheaded and reckless.

14 : 16

The wealth of the wise is their crown, but the folly of fools yields folly.

14 : 24

A king delights in a wise servant, but a shameful servant incurs his wrath.

14 : 35

The tongue of the wise commends knowledge, but the mouth of the fool gushes folly.

15 : 2

The lips of the wise spread knowledge; not so the hearts of fools.

15 : 7

A mocker resents correction; he will not consult the wise.

15 : 12

The path of life leads upward for the wise to keep him from going down to the grave.

15 : 24

He who listens to a life-giving rebuke will be at home among the wise.

15 : 31

A king's wrath is a messenger of death, but a wise man will appease it.

16 : 14

The wise in heart are called discerning, and pleasant words promote instruction.

16 : 21

A wise man's heart guides his mouth, and his lips promote instruction.

16 : 23

A wise servant will rule over a disgraceful son, and will share the inheritance as one of the brothers.

17 : 2

Even a fool is thought wise if he keeps silent, and discerning if he holds his tongue.

17 : 28

The heart of the discerning acquires knowledge; the ears of the wise seek it out.

18 : 15

Listen to advice and accept instruction, and in the end you will be wise.

19 : 20

Wine is a mocker and beer a brawler; whoever is led astray by them is not wise.

20 : 1

When a king sits on his throne to judge, he winnows out all evil with his eyes.

20 : 8

A wise king winnows out the wicked; he drives the threshing wheel over them.

20 : 26

When a mocker is punished, the simple gain wisdom; when a wise man is instructed, he gets knowledge.

21 : 11

In the house of the wise are stores of choice food and oil, but a foolish man devours all he has.

21 : 20

A wise man attacks the city of the mighty and pulls down the stronghold in which they trust.

21 : 22

Pay attention and listen to the sayings of the wise; apply your heart to what I teach,

22 : 17

My son, if your heart is wise, then my heart will be glad;

23 : 15

Listen, my son, and be wise, and keep your heart on the right path.

23 : 19

The father of a righteous man has great joy; he who has a wise son delights in him.

23 : 24

A wise man has great power, and a man of knowledge increases strength;

24 : 5

These also are sayings to the wise: To show partiality in judging is not good:

24 : 23

I applied my heart to what I observed and learned a lesson from what I saw:

24 : 32

Like an earring of gold or an ornament of fine gold is a wise man's rebuke to a listening ear.

25 : 12

Answer a fool according to his folly, or he will be wise in his own eyes.

26 : 5

Do you see a man wise in his own eyes? There is more hope for a fool than for him.

26 : 12

Be wise, my son, and bring joy to my heart; then I can answer anyone who treats me with contempt.

27 : 11

A rich man may be wise in his own eyes, but a poor man who has discernment sees through him.

28 : 11

"Four things on earth are small, yet they are extremely wise:

30 : 24

wise king
A wise king winnows out the wicked; he drives the threshing wheel over them.

20 : 26

wise man
Do not rebuke a mocker or he will hate you; rebuke a wise man and he will love you.

9 : 8

Instruct a wise man and he will be wiser still, teach a righteous man and he will add to his learning.

9 : 9

The way of a fool seems right to him, but a wise man listens to advice.

12 : 15

A prudent man keeps his knowledge to himself, but the heart of fools blurts out folly.

12 : 23

A wise man fears the Lord and shuns evil, but a fool is hotheaded and reckless.

14 : 16

A king's wrath is a messenger of death, but a wise man will appease it.

16 : 14

The wise in heart are called discerning, and pleasant words promote instruction.

16 : 21

A wise man's heart guides his mouth, and his lips promote instruction.

16 : 23

When a mocker is punished, the simple gain wisdom; when a wise man is instructed, he gets knowledge.

21 : 11

A wise man attacks the city of the mighty and pulls down the stronghold in which they trust.

21 : 22

A wise man has great power, and a man of knowledge increases strength;

24 : 5

If a wise man goes to court with a fool, the fool rages and scoffs, and there is no peace.

29 : 9

533

A fool gives full vent to his anger, but a wise man keeps himself under control.

29 : 11

wise men

Wise men store up knowledge, but the mouth of a fool invites ruin.

10 : 14

Mockers stir up a city, but wise men turn away anger.

29 : 8

wise servant

A wise servant will rule over a disgraceful son, and will share the inheritance as one of the brothers.

17 : 2

wise son

A wise son heeds his father's instruction, but a mocker does not listen to rebuke.

13 : 1

A wise son brings joy to his father, but a foolish man despises his mother.

15 : 20

wise woman

The wise woman builds her house, but with her own hands the foolish one tears hers down.

14 : 1

wise words

The lips of the righteous know what is fitting, but the mouth of the wicked only what is perverse.

10 : 32

wiser

The sluggard is wiser in his own eyes than seven men who answer discreetly.

26 : 16

wiser still

Instruct a wise man and he will be wiser still; teach a righteous man and he will add to his learning.

9 : 9

withhold

Do not withhold good from those who deserve it, when it is in your power to act.

3 : 27

He who spares the rod hates his son, but he who loves him is careful to discipline him.

13 : 24

Do not withhold discipline from a child; if you punish him with the rod, he will not die.

23 : 13

withholds

One man gives freely, yet gains even more; another withholds unduly, but comes to poverty.

11 : 24

within

My son, if you accept my words and store up my commands within you,

2 : 1

Do not let them out of your sight, keep them within your heart;

4 : 21

My son, keep my words and store up my commands within you.

7 : 1

within you

My son, keep my words and store up my commands within you.

7 : 1

without
but whoever listens to me will live in
safety and be at ease, without fear of
harm."

1 : 33

Can a man scoop fire into his lap
without his clothes being burned?

6 : 27

Can a man walk on hot coals without
his feet being scorched?

6 : 28

The woman Folly is loud; she is
undisciplined and without knowledge.

9 : 13

A large population is a king's glory, but
without subjects a prince is ruined.

14 : 28

It is not good to have zeal without
knowledge, nor to be hasty and miss the
way.

19 : 2

All day long he craves for more, but the
righteous give without sparing.

21 : 26

Like clouds and wind without rain is a
man who boasts of gifts he does not
give.

25 : 14

Without wood a fire goes out; without
gossip a quarrel dies down.

26 : 20

without cause
Do not testify against your neighbor
without cause, or use your lips to
deceive.

24 : 28

without remedy
Therefore disaster will overtake him in
an instant; he will suddenly be
destroyed -- without remedy.

6 : 15

A man who remains stiff-necked after
many rebukes will suddenly be
destroyed -- without remedy.

29 : 1

without sin
Who can say, "I have kept my heart
pure; I am clean and without sin"?

20 : 9

withstand
"Under three things the earth trembles,
under four it cannot bear up:

30 : 21

witness
a false witness who pours out lies and a
man who stirs up dissension among
brothers.

6 : 19

A truthful witness gives honest
testimony, but a false witness tells lies.

12 : 17

A truthful witness does not deceive, but
a false witness pours out lies.

14 : 5

A truthful witness saves lives, but a
false witness is deceitful.

14 : 25

A false witness will not go unpunished,
and he who pours out lies will not go
free.

19 : 5

A false witness will not go unpunished,
and he who pours out lies will perish.

19 : 9

A corrupt witness mocks at justice, and
the mouth of the wicked gulps down
evil.

19 : 28

A false witness will perish, and
whoever listens to him will be
destroyed forever.

21 : 28

Do not testify against your neighbor without cause, or use your lips to deceive.

24 : 28

The accomplice of a thief is his own enemy; he is put under oath and dare not testify.

29 : 24

witnessed

it is better for him to say to you, "Come up here," than for him to humiliate you before a nobleman. What you have seen with your eyes

25 : 7

woe

Who has woe? Who has sorrow? Who has strife? Who has complaints? Who has needless bruises? Who has bloodshot eyes?

23 : 29

woman

keeping you from the immoral woman, from the smooth tongue of the wayward wife.

6 : 24

Then out came a woman to meet him, dressed like a prostitute and with crafty intent.

7 : 10

The woman Folly is loud; she is undisciplined and without knowledge.

9 : 13

A kindhearted woman gains respect, but ruthless men gain only wealth.

11 : 16

Like a gold ring in a pig's snout is a beautiful woman who shows no discretion.

11 : 22

The wise woman builds her house, but with her own hands the foolish one tears hers down.

14 : 1

Take the garment of one who puts up security for a stranger; hold it in pledge if he does it for a wayward woman.

20 : 16

Take a garment of one who puts up security for a stranger; hold it in pledge if he does it for a wayward woman.

27 : 13

an unloved woman who is married, and a maidservant who displaces her mistress.

30 : 23

She is like the merchant ships, bringing her food from afar.

31 : 14

She considers a field and buys it; out of her earnings she plants a vineyard.

31 : 16

She sets about her work vigorously; her arms are strong for her tasks.

31 : 17

Charm is deceptive, and beauty is fleeting; but a woman who fears the Lord is to be praised.

31 : 30

womb

the grave, the barren womb, land, which is never satisfied with water, and fire, which never says, 'Enough!'

30 : 16

"O my son, O son of my womb, O son of my vows,

31 : 2

women

He who finds a wife finds what is good and receives favor from the Lord.

18 : 22

do not spend your strength on women,
your vigor on those who ruin kings.

31 : 3

Many women do noble things, but you
surpass them all."

31 : 29

wood
Without wood a fire goes out; without
gossip a quarrel dies down.

26 : 20

As charcoal to embers and as wood to
fire, so is a quarrelsome man for
kindling strife.

26 : 21

wool
She selects wool and flax and works
with eager hands.

31 : 13

word
Bind them on your fingers; write them
on the tablet of your heart.

7 : 3

A gentle answer turns away wrath, but a
harsh word stirs up anger.

15 : 1

A man finds joy in giving an apt reply--
and how good is a timely word!

15 : 23

A word aptly spoken is like apples of
gold in settings of silver.

25 : 11

Every word of God is flawless; he is a
shield to those who take refuge in him.

30 : 5

word of God
Every word of God is flawless; he is a
shield to those who take refuge in him.

30 : 5

word to the wise
With his mouth the godless destroys his
neighbor, but through knowledge the
righteous escape.

11 : 9

words
for attaining wisdom and discipline; for
understanding words of insight;

1 : 2

My son, if you accept my words and
store up my commands within you,

2 : 1

Wisdom will save you from the ways of
wicked men, from men whose words
are perverse,

2 : 12

It will save you also from the
adulteress, from the wayward wife with
her seductive words,

2 : 16

he taught me and said, "Lay hold of my
words with all your heart; keep my
commands and you will live.

4 : 4

Get wisdom, get understanding; do not
forget my words or swerve from them.

4 : 5

My son, pay attention to what I say;
listen closely to my words.

4 : 20

My son, pay attention to my wisdom,
listen well to my words of insight,

5 : 1

if you have been trapped by what you
said, ensnared by the words of your
mouth,

6 : 2

My son, keep my words and store up
my commands within you.

7 : 1

they will keep you from the adulteress, from the wayward wife with her seductive words.

7 : 5

With persuasive words she led him astray; she seduced him with her smooth talk.

7 : 21

All the words of my mouth are just; none of them is crooked or perverse.

8 : 8

The mouth of the righteous is a fountain of life, but violence overwhelms the mouth of the wicked.

10 : 11

When words are many, sin is not absent, but he who holds his tongue is wise.

10 : 19

The tongue of the righteous is choice silver, but the heart of the wicked is of little value.

10 : 20

The mouth of the righteous brings forth wisdom, but a perverse tongue will be cut out.

10 : 31

The words of the wicked lie in wait for blood, but the speech of the upright rescues them.

12 : 6

A truthful witness gives honest testimony, but a false witness tells lies.

12 : 17

Reckless words pierce like a sword, but the tongue of the wise brings healing.

12 : 18

Truthful lips endure forever, but a lying tongue lasts only a moment.

12 : 19

An anxious heart weighs a man down, but a kind word cheers him up.

12 : 25

A fool's talk brings a rod to his back, but the lips of the wise protect them.

14 : 3

Stay away from a foolish man, for you will not find knowledge on his lips.

14 : 7

A gentle answer turns away wrath, but a harsh word stirs up anger.

15 : 1

The tongue of the wise commends knowledge, but the mouth of the fool gushes folly.

15 : 2

The tongue that brings healing is a tree of life, but a deceitful tongue crushes the spirit.

15 : 4

The wise in heart are called discerning, and pleasant words promote instruction.

16 : 21

Pleasant words are a honeycomb, sweet to the soul and healing to the bones.

16 : 24

A scoundrel plots evil, and his speech is like a scorching fire.

16 : 27

A man of knowledge uses words with restraint, and a man of understanding is even-tempered.

17 : 27

The words of a man's mouth are deep waters, but the fountain of wisdom is a bubbling brook.

18 : 4

A fool's lips bring him strife, and his mouth invites a beating.

18 : 6

A fool's mouth is his undoing, and his lips are a snare to his soul.

18 : 7

The words of gossip are like choice morsels; they go down to a man's inmost parts.

18 : 8

Stop listening to instruction, my son, and you will stray from the words of knowledge.

19 : 27

He who loves a pure heart and whose speech is gracious will have the king for his friend.

22 : 11

The eyes of the Lord keep watch over knowledge, but he frustrates the words of the unfaithful.

22 : 12

teaching you true and reliable words, so that you can give sound answers to him who sent you?

22 : 21

Do not speak to a fool, for he will scorn the wisdom of your words.

23 : 9

Apply your heart to instruction and your ears to words of knowledge.

23 : 12

my inmost being will rejoice when your lips speak what is right.

23 : 16

An honest answer is like a kiss on the lips.

24 : 26

As a north wind brings rain, so a sly tongue brings angry looks.

25 : 23

The words of a gossip are like choice morsels; they go down to a man's inmost parts.

26 : 22

Though his speech is charming, do not believe him, for seven abominations fill his heart.

26 : 25

A servant cannot be corrected by mere words; though he understands, he will not respond.

29 : 19

Do you see a man who speaks in haste? There is more hope for a fool than for him.

29 : 20

Do not add to his words, or he will rebuke you and prove you a liar.

30 : 6

words of insight
for attaining wisdom and discipline; for understanding words of insight;

1 : 2

words of knowledge
Stop listening to instruction, my son, and you will stray from the words of knowledge.

19 : 27

words of wisdom
Pay attention and listen to the sayings of the wise; apply your heart to what I teach,

22 : 17

for it is pleasing when you keep them in your heart and have all of them ready on your lips.

22 : 18

work
yet it stores its provisions in summer and gathers its food at harvest.

6 : 8

Lazy hands make a man poor, but diligent hands bring wealth.

10 : 4

He who gathers crops in summer is a wise son, but he who sleeps during harvest is a disgraceful son.

10 : 5

He who works his land will have abundant food, but he who chases fantasies lacks judgment.

12 : 11

From the fruit of his lips a man is filled with good things as surely as the work of his hands rewards him.

12 : 14

Dishonest money dwindles away, but he who gathers money little by little makes it grow.

13 : 11

All hard work brings a profit, but mere talk leads only to poverty.

14 : 23

The house of the righteous contains great treasure, but the income of the wicked brings them trouble.

15 : 6

One who is slack in his work is brother to one who destroys.

18 : 9

The sluggard's craving will be the death of him, because his hands refuse to work.

21 : 25

Do you see a man skilled in his work? He will serve before kings, he will not serve before obscure men.

22 : 29

Finish your outdoor work and get your fields ready; after that, build your house.

24 : 27

Like an archer who wounds at random is he who hires a fool or any passer-by.

26 : 10

As a door turns on its hinges, so a sluggard turns on his bed.

26 : 14

He who tends a fig tree will eat its fruit, and he who looks after his master will be honored.

27 : 18

She sets about her work vigorously; her arms are strong for her tasks.

31 : 17

work hard
Go to the ant, you sluggard; consider its ways and be wise!

6 : 6

work of his hands
From the fruit of his lips a man is filled with good things as surely as the work of his hands rewards him.

12 : 14

work the land
He who works his land will have abundant food, but he who chases fantasies lacks judgment.

12 : 11

worker
yet it stores its provisions in summer and gathers its food at harvest.

6 : 8

The laborer's appetite works for him; his hunger drives him on.

16 : 26

working hard
Diligent hands will rule, but laziness ends in slave labor.

12 : 24

workIng up the ladder
Diligent hands will rule, but laziness
ends in slave labor.

12 : 24

works
yet it stores its provisions in summer
and gathers its food at harvest.

6 : 8

"The Lord brought me forth as the first
of his works, before his deeds of old;

8 : 22

He who works his land will have
abundant food, but the one who chases
fantasies will have his fill of poverty.

28 : 19

She selects wool and flax and works
with eager hands.

31 : 13

Give her the reward she has earned, and
let her works bring her praise at the city
gate.

31 : 31

works his land
He who works his land will have
abundant food, but the one who chases
fantasies will have his fill of poverty.

28 : 19

works ruin
A lying tongue hates those it hurts, and
a flattering mouth works ruin.

26 : 28

works with eager hands
She selects wool and flax and works
with eager hands.

31 : 13

world
I was appointed from eternity, from the
beginning, before the world began,

8 : 23

before he made the earth or its fields or
any of the dust of the world.

8 : 26

rejoicing in his whole world and
delighting in mankind.

8 : 31

worldly
Do not let your heart envy sinners, but
always be zealous for the fear of the
Lord.

23 : 17

worn out
A little sleep, a little slumber, a little
folding of the hands to rest --

24 : 33

Like cold water to a weary soul is good
news from a distant land.

25 : 25

worry
An anxious heart weighs a man down,
but a kind word cheers him up.

12 : 25

worse
Arrogant lips are unsuited to a fool --
how much worse lying lips to a ruler!

17 : 7

It is not fitting for a fool to live in
luxury -- how much worse for a slave to
rule over princes!

19 : 10

worth
She is more precious than rubies;
nothing you desire can compare with
her.

3 : 15

Choose my instruction instead of silver,
knowledge rather than choice gold,

8 . 10

541

for wisdom is more precious than rubies, and nothing you desire can compare with her.

8 : 11

Ill-gotten treasures are of no value, but righteousness delivers from death.

10 : 2

The tongue of the righteous is choice silver, but the heart of the wicked is of little value.

10 : 20

Kings take pleasure in honest lips; they value a man who speaks the truth.

16 : 13

How much better to get wisdom than gold, to choose understanding rather than silver!

16 : 16

Remove the dross from the silver, and out comes material for the silversmith;

25 : 4

A word aptly spoken is like apples of gold in settings of silver.

25 : 11

A wife of noble character who can find? She is worth far more than rubies.

31 : 10

worthless
Wealth is worthless in the day of wrath, but righteousness delivers from death.

11 : 4

worthy
Listen, for I have worthy things to say; I open my lips to speak what is right.

8 : 6

would
If you had responded to my rebuke, I would have poured out my heart to you and made my thoughts known to you.

1 : 23

since you ignored all my advice and would not accept my rebuke,

1 : 25

would not
since they would not accept my advice and spurned my rebuke,

1 : 30

I would not obey my teachers or listen to my instructors.

5 : 13

wounds
Blows and wounds cleanse away evil, and beatings purge the inmost being.

20 : 30

Like an archer who wounds at random is he who hires a fool or any passer-by.

26 : 10

Wounds from a friend can be trusted, but an enemy multiplies kisses.

27 : 6

wrapped
Who has gone up to heaven and come down? Who has gathered up the wind in the hollow of his hands? Who has wrapped up the waters in his cloak? Who has established all the ends of the earth? What is his name, and the name of his son? Tell me if you know!

30 : 4

wrapped up
Who has gone up to heaven and come down? Who has gathered up the wind in the hollow of his hands? Who has wrapped up the waters in his cloak? Who has established all the ends of the earth? What is his name, and the name of his son? Tell me if you know!

30 : 4

wrath
Wealth is worthless in the day of wrath, but righteousness delivers from death.

11 : 4

The desire of the righteous ends only in good, but the hope of the wicked only in wrath.

11 : 23

A king delights in a wise servant, but a shameful servant incurs his wrath.

14 : 35

A gentle answer turns away wrath, but a harsh word stirs up anger.

15 : 1

A king's wrath is a messenger of death, but a wise man will appease it.

16 : 14

A king's wrath is like the roar of a lion; he who angers him forfeits his life.

20 : 2

A gift given in secret soothes anger, and a bribe concealed in the cloak pacifies great wrath.

21 : 14

The mouth of an adulteress is a deep pit; he who is under the Lord's wrath will fall into it.

22 : 14

or the Lord will see and disapprove and turn his wrath away from him.

24 : 18

wretched
All the days of the oppressed are wretched, but the cheerful heart has a continual feast.

15 : 15

write
Let love and faithfulness never leave you; bind them around your neck, write them on the tablet of your heart.

3 : 3

Bind them on your fingers; write them on the tablet of your heart.

7 : 3

written
Have I not written thirty sayings for you, sayings of counsel and knowledge,

22 : 20

wrong
who delight in doing wrong and rejoice in the perverseness of evil,

2 : 14

Do not say, "I'll pay you back for this wrong!" Wait for the Lord, and he will deliver you.

20 : 22

To show partiality is not good -- yet a man will do wrong for a piece of bread.

28 : 21

He who robs his father or mother and says, "It's not wrong" -- he is partner to him who destroys.

28 : 24

"This is the way of an adulteress: She eats and wipes her mouth and says, 'I've done nothing wrong.'

30 : 20

wrongdoing
Kings detest wrongdoing, for a throne is established through righteousness.

16 : 12

He who winks with his eye is plotting perversity; he who purses his lips is bent on evil.

16 : 30

wrongs
Hatred stirs up dissension, but love covers over all wrongs.

10 : 12

Y

years
for they will prolong your life many years and bring you prosperity.

3 : 2

Listen, my son, accept what I say, and the years of your life will be many.

4 : 10

lest you give your best strength to others and your years to one who is cruel,

5 : 9

For through me your days will be many, and years will be added to your life.

9 : 11

The fear of the Lord adds length to life, but the years of the wicked are cut short.

10 : 27

yet
yet it stores its provisions in summer and gathers its food at harvest.

6 : 8

Yet if he is caught, he must pay sevenfold, though it costs him all the wealth of his house.

6 : 31

One man gives freely, yet gains even more; another withholds unduly, but comes to poverty.

11 : 24

Better to be a nobody and yet have a servant than pretend to be somebody and have no food.

12 : 9

One man pretends to be rich, yet has nothing; another pretends to be poor, yet has great wealth.

13 : 7

A man's own folly ruins his life, yet his heart rages against the Lord.

19 : 3

To show partiality is not good -- yet a man will do wrong for a piece of bread.

28 : 21

those who are pure in their own eyes and yet are not cleansed of their filth;

30 : 12

"Four things on earth are small, yet they are extremely wise:

30 : 24

Ants are creatures of little strength, yet they store up their food in the summer;

30 : 25

coneys are creatures of little power, yet they make their home in the crags;

30 : 26

locusts have no king, yet they advance together in ranks;

30 : 27

a lizard can be caught with the hand, yet it is found in kings' palaces.

30 : 28

yield
My fruit is better than fine gold; what I yield surpasses choice silver.

8 : 19

yielding to temptation
Her feet go down to death; her steps lead straight to the grave.

5 : 5

At the end of your life you will groan, when your flesh and body are spent.

5 : 11

All at once he followed her like an ox going to the slaughter, like a deer stepping into a noose

7 : 22

Do not let your heart turn to her ways or stray into her paths.

7 : 25

yields
for she is more profitable than silver and yields better returns than gold.

3 : 14

The wealth of the wise is their crown, but the folly of fools yields folly.

14 : 24

you will not be afraid
when you lie down, you will not be afraid; when you lie down, your sleep will be sweet.

3 : 24

young
for giving prudence to the simple, knowledge and discretion to the young --

1 : 4

I saw among the simple, I noticed among the young men, a youth who lacked judgment.

7 : 7

The glory of young men is their strength, gray hair the splendor of the old.

20 : 29

young men
I saw among the simple, I noticed among the young men, a youth who lacked judgment.

7 : 7

The glory of young men is their strength, gray hair the splendor of the old.

20 : 29

your sight
My son, preserve sound judgment and discernment, do not let them out of your sight;

3 : 21

youth
who has left the partner of her youth and ignored the covenant she made before God.

2 : 17

May your fountain be blessed, and may you rejoice in the wife of your youth.

5 : 18

I saw among the simple, I noticed among the young men, a youth who lacked judgment.

7 : 7

The glory of young men is their strength, gray hair the splendor of the old.

20 : 29

If a man pampers his servant from youth, he will bring grief in the end.

29 : 21

Z

zeal

It is not good to have zeal without knowledge, nor to be hasty and miss the way.

19 : 2

zealous

Do not let your heart envy sinners, but always be zealous for the fear of the Lord.

23 : 17

INDEX

551

E

552

555

565

568